Encyclopedia of
AGING

EDITORIAL BOARD

Encyclopedia of
AGING

David J. Ekerdt, Editor in Chief

VOLUME 2

Ear – Kin

**MACMILLAN
REFERENCE
USA™**

THOMSON

GALE

New York • Detroit • San Diego • San Francisco • Cleveland • New Haven, Conn. • Waterville, Maine • London • Munich

Encyclopedia of Aging

David J. Ekerdt, Editor in Chief

For permission to use material from this product, submit your request via Web at http://www.gale-edit.com/permissions, or you may download our Permissions Request form and submit your request by fax or mail to:

Permissions Department
The Gale Group, Inc.
27500 Drake Rd.
Farmington Hills, MI 48331-3535
Permissions hotline:
248-699-8006 or 800-877-4253, ext. 8006
Fax: 248-699-8074 or 800-762-4058

LIBRARY OF CONGRESS CATALOG-IN-PUBLICATION DATA

Encyclopedia of aging / David J. Ekerdt, editor.— 1st ed.
    p. cm.
        Includes bibliographical references and index.
        ISBN 0-02-865472-2 (set : hardcover : alk. paper)
        1. Gerontology—Encyclopedias. 2. Aged—Encyclopedias. 3.
    Aging—Encyclopedias. I. Ekerdt, David J. (David Joseph), 1949-

    HQ1061 .E534 2002
    305.26'03—dc21
        2002002596

ISBNs
Volume 1: 0-02-865468-4
Volume 2: 0-02-865469-2
Volume 3: 0-02-865470-6
Volume 4: 0-02-865471-4

Printed in the United States of America
10 9 8 7 6 5 4 3 2 1

E

EAR

See BRAIN; HEARING

EAST EUROPE AND FORMER USSR

At the start of the twenty-first century, over four hundred million people lived in eastern Europe and the former Soviet Union, more than in all of North America. Spanning twenty-seven independent countries, these populations represented every imaginable situation in which people grow old. Predominant religions in these countries included Islamic (central Asia and Albania), Orthodox (most European former Soviet republics, Bulgaria, Romania, and Serbia), and Roman Catholic (Poland, Czech and Slovak Republics, Croatia, and Slovenia) with important and substantial religious minorities throughout the region. Low per capita real incomes, with annual purchasing power equivalent to one or two thousand U.S. dollars, characterized central Asia and parts of the Balkans. Countries in central Europe (Poland, the Czech Republic, and Hungary) and the Baltic republics (Estonia, Latvia, and Lithuania) were much more highly educated, urbanized, and industrialized, but real annual incomes again lagged behind other features of development, with purchasing power equivalent to five to seven thousand U.S. dollars per capita.

Aspects of family organization, variations in centralization of government, and other important variations also distinguished these countries. Finally, the rate and level of population aging also varied tremendously across eastern Europe and the former Soviet Union. The youngest countries (Turkmenistan and Tajikistan in central Asia, on the northern borders of Iran and Afghanistan) counted less than 4 percent of their people at ages sixty-five or older. More than 40 percent were children below age fifteen, so for each person sixty-five or older these countries had ten children under fifteen.

By contrast, the oldest countries in the region, Bulgaria and Hungary, counted about 16 percent of their people at ages sixty-five or older. A matching 16 percent had not yet reached age fifteen, so for each person sixty-five or older there was only one child under fifteen. The percentage of people aged sixty-five or older was four times higher in the two old eastern European countries than in the two young central Asian countries. These examples were among the youngest and oldest populations found anywhere in the world at the turn of the century.

Population aging and the birth rate

Despite this cultural and economic diversity, only one fact is needed to explain such age contrasts. Low birth rates produce old populations. High birth rates produce young populations. Mortality and migration can affect age structure, but fertility dominates the picture. In this sense, the story of population aging is a simple one.

Figure 1 shows this graphically for eastern Europe and the former Soviet Union. The vertical axis measures children that a woman in each country could expect in her lifetime, given birth rates at the end of the century. The horizontal axis shows a ratio of people at age sixty-five or over to people under age fifteen. Bulgaria and Hungary, as described above, appear in the

Bosnian Muslim Ajka Civic prays at the grave of her son at a Tuzla, Bosnia, cemetery on the second day of the Eid al-Fitr festival in January 2000. Bosnian Muslims traditionally visit cemeteries on the festival's second day to pray for those who lost their lives during the three-year Bosnian War, which ended in 1995. (AP photo by Amel Emric.)

lower right corner of this figure. Turkmenistan and Tajikistan occupy the top left corner. All the other countries of the region array themselves along a line between these extremes, except for one country (Bosnia-Herzegovina) in the bottom left part of the figure that falls below this imaginary line.

Bosnia-Herzegovina had a higher birth rate during the twentieth century than most countries in eastern Europe. As a result, at the end of the century its youthful age structure still resembled Moldova or Armenia. However, Bosnia's birth rate fell drastically in the 1990s in the context of tragic political events. By the end of the century the birth rate looked "too low" for such a young country. Neighboring Albania, by comparison, had an even younger population. However, this even more Islamic country still had a high birth rate at the end of the century, so it conformed to the pattern in Figure 1. The apparent inconsistency of a young Bosnia with a low birth rate was only a transitional phase. With

continued low fertility, population aging would bring Bosnia back into the pattern of other countries.

Sex ratio contrasts in old age

Like the rule that low birth rates make old populations, the sex difference in survival forms another worldwide demographic constant. At younger ages, low absolute death rates keep this difference from having much demographic effect. The sex ratio in all countries hovers near one man per woman until about age fifty. As people grow older and death rates increase, however, the survival difference begins to matter. Each generation becomes more "female" in old age. The ratio of men to women declines from about one man per woman at age fifty, to less than half a man per woman (or more than two women per man) by about age eighty. At the turn of the century, this rule was equally true in very young central Asian republics and in much older eastern European populations. However, the larger share of people at old ages in the European populations meant that the weight of the social problems created there was greater. The clearest such consequence concerns marital status at advanced ages.

Marital status contrasts at old ages

While widowhood is the normal marital status for women at advanced ages, most of the fewer surviving men spend most of their later years married. This standard pattern appeared throughout eastern Europe and the former Soviet republics.

For example, in Hungary at the end of the century, three-fourths of all men in their seventies remained married. A majority (52 percent) of men were married even after age eighty. In the oldest country in the region (Bulgaria) and in the young Asian republics of Tajikistan and Turkmenistan, the proportions of men married at these ages were about the same as in Hungary.

By contrast, in Hungary only one-fourth of women in their seventies remained married. Less than one woman out of ten remained married after age eighty. Just as for men, the percentage of women married at old age were about the same in the young Asian republics as in old eastern Europe.

Even though the shares of women married or widowed by age were about the same across all

Figure 1

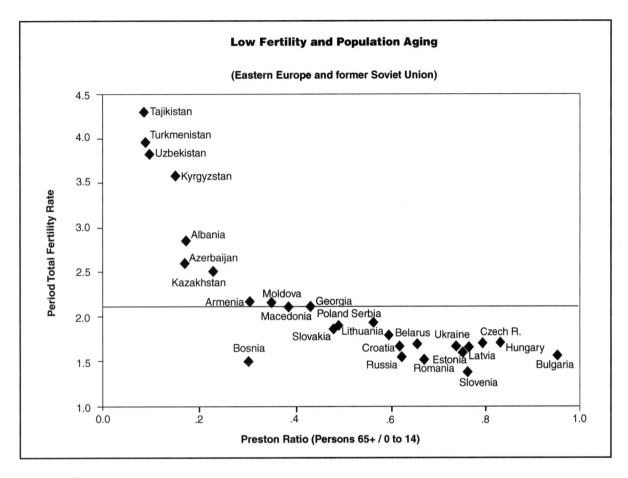

SOURCE: Author

of these very diverse countries, population aging magnified the "widow problem" in older countries. For example, in younger Kazakhstan, percentages unmarried translated into slightly more than half a million unmarried women over age sixty-five, or about one out of every fourteen women in the total female population. In older Poland, similar percentages of unmarried women translated into almost two million unmarried women over age sixty-five, or about one out of every ten women in the total female population.

Availability of children

Because most women at old ages have no husbands, children become an important alternative source of social contact and support. However, the same low birth rates responsible for population aging also guarantee fewer children

in aging populations. Figure 1 showed this parallel for entire populations, though Total Fertility Rates are only temporary annual measures of childbearing. Their volatility overstates long-term changes in completed family sizes. For individual women in populations, the change is less dramatic but still noticeable for different generations. Lifetime completed fertility of women also declined throughout the region. The long-term decline began earlier in the twentieth century in eastern Europe, and extended into the twenty-first century in the central Asian republics. Children as sources of support became more scarce at precisely the time that older widows increased as a share of the population.

This demographic paradox was accented in several eastern European and former Soviet countries at the turn of the century by the legacy of very severe losses of young men during the Second World War. Particularly for Russia, Germany, and other central combatants, an unusual share of women growing old as the twentieth century came to an end had either lost husbands early in life or never married at all. They were particularly unlikely to be married or to have any children or other immediate family. As their generation gradually passed from the stage in the twenty-first century, this intense shortage of family ties in a few countries was relaxed for younger generations.

Government support of aging populations

Not only do low birth rates directly cause population aging in a purely arithmetic way, by reducing the relative number of young people, but the economic and political context of these trends further reinforces the relationship. Traditional family-based intergenerational networks become unworkable when challenged by more people (mostly women who no longer have husbands) surviving longer, with fewer children. Many countries in the world faced this problem, and raised taxes on working-age households to pay for new programs for the growing older population. Demographic aging coincided with the appearance of the "welfare state" in many countries. In the national budgets of several prosperous but demographically old western European countries at the turn of the century, it was common for government revenues to account for nearly half of the total gross domestic product of the economy. Heavy taxes reduced disposable income of younger families, further discouraging births. Fewer births then reinforced population aging, in a spiral that generated growing concern among policy makers and scholars of population worldwide.

This strategy was no longer available to governments in eastern Europe and the former Soviet Union entering the twenty-first century. They were saddled with a legacy of centralization, mismanagement, and oppression that thoroughly discredited the previous political system, and for many people, destroyed trust in government itself. Alienation and cynicism, pervasive throughout the region, produced massive evasion of taxes. The state sectors of these economies shriveled throughout the region, from the Baltic to the Caspian Seas. At the turn of the century, available figures showed government revenues as a far smaller share of gross domestic product in these countries than in western Europe (even assuming that it was possible to measure gross domestic product in these disrupted economies).

Governments faced with revenue collapse had to decide where to allocate meager remaining funds. One victim of the shortage of government money was the health care system, since in all these countries the health professions had been largely absorbed into government employment. To the extent that this remained the case, health care was starved of resources. To the extent that health care was privatized, it immediately became inflated out of the reach of many ordinary citizens of these countries. As a result, economic prosperity was linked to enjoyment of healthy old age, both within and between countries in eastern Europe and the former Soviet Union. Figure 2 shows that in more prosperous countries (particularly central Europe and the Baltic republics) the share of life spent by women in a disabled state was much smaller than in poorer countries of the region (particularly the central Asian republics). For example, the relative prosperity of the Czech Republic explains why health in old age was better in that country (see Fig. 2). Of course, the link between money and health is not unique to this region. It appears wherever market forces dominate life.

Hardest-hit of all sectors of the population were the growing numbers of old-age pensioners, a crisis made even worse by the peculiar retirement ages adopted in the state socialist epoch: men generally retired at sixty, and women in many of these countries retired at fifty-five even though they consistently outlived men by many years. Actuarial pressures raised these ages in several countries after the collapse of state socialist governments, but even so, older citizens of the countries in eastern Europe and the former Soviet Union found their monthly benefits shrank to the vanishing point in real purchasing power. Although largely invisible because it involved people too old and frail to take to the streets and too dependent to go on strike, the resulting poverty and desperation formed a very real human tragedy.

In terms of care of the oldest members of the population, the initial transition out of communism is judged by history as a discouraging failure. However, precisely because the societies of eastern Europe and the former Soviet Union could not turn to old answers of the twentieth century in responding to population aging, they entered the new century with a stronger incentive than any other part of the world to develop

Figure 2

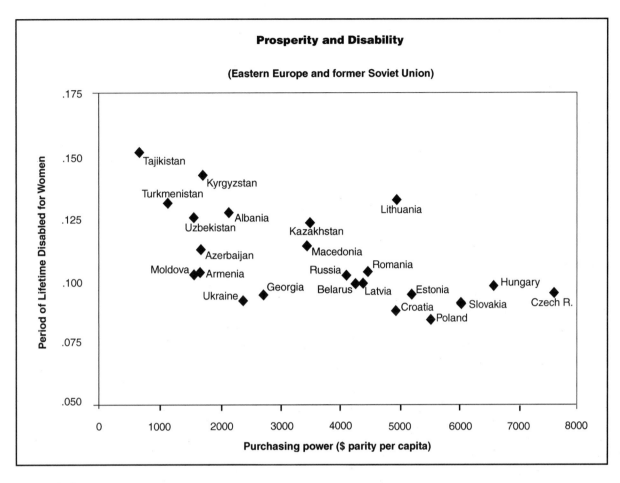

Prosperity and Disability

(Eastern Europe and former Soviet Union)

new and innovative ways to deal with this demographic challenge.

For further details about the situation in eastern Europe and the former Soviet Union, and for sources of many figures used here, consult the U.S. Census Bureau publication *Aging in Eastern Europe and the Soviet Union*, by Velkoff and Kinsella and see the Internet web sites of the World Health Organization and the World Bank.

ELWOOD CARLSON

See also POPULATION AGING; WEST EUROPE.

BIBLIOGRAPHY

CARLSON, E. "European Contrasts in Sex Ratios: Implications for Living Arrangements in Old Age." *European Journal of Population* 6, no. 2 (1990): 117–141.

COALE, A. "How a Population Ages or Grows Younger." In *Population: The Vital Revolution.* Edited by Ronald Freedman. Garden City, N.Y.: Doubleday-Anchor, 1964. Pages 47–58.

United States Census Bureau. *Aging in Eastern Europe and the Soviet Union.* Washington, D.C.

VELKOFF, V., and KINSELLA, K. *Aging in Eastern Europe and the Former Soviet Union.* Washington, D.C.: U.S. Government Printing Office, 1993.

World Bank. "World Development Indicators." Available on the World Wide Web at www. worldbank.org

World Health Organization. "World Health Report 2000." Available on the Internet at www.who.org

ECONOMIC WELL-BEING

This entry provides information on the economic circumstances of older Americans by looking at differences in both the economic well-being among older adults and differences in economic well-being between older adults and others. Traditionally, policymakers have been interested in the economic well-being of groups that are particularly vulnerable—those individuals in society that theoretically cannot improve their own economic well-being. In addition to children and the disabled, elderly adults usually fall into this category, mainly because it is assumed that they have little access to labor markets. Older adults are defined as those past the traditional retirement age of sixty-five, although there is an emerging body of work looking at the economic status of the "oldest old," usually defined as those over eighty-five.

Consumption as a measure of economic well-being

The most common way to measure economic well-being is to determine the market value of goods that are consumed by an economic "agent" over a period of time. This raises a host of questions. First, what determines an agent? In general, there is a problem with determining individual well-being from household data. Second, what is the appropriate length of time to measure well-being? Economic well-being can be examined in the short term ("what is my economic well-being right now?") or a longer time horizon ("will my grandchild be able to afford college?"). Third, goods and services are not all that make up economic well-being. Leisure, or free time is a good example of a resource that presumably generates economic well-being on its own. Although it should not be assumed that households do not derive economic well-being from commodities besides goods and services, this discussion will focus on access to goods and services, which will be measured in monetary terms. This is because the proverbial slope could become quite slippery if we attempt to measure all nonpecuniary aspects of economic well-being. Nevertheless, our imperfect measure of well-being should be duly noted. Fourth, availability of resources can generate well-being even if they are not consumed. Having an abundance of savings that one never plans to consume, or that one gives to one's heirs, will no doubt provide economic well-being even though no consumption

is observed. This fourth point suggests that instead of looking at consumption, we should measure well-being in terms of access to consumption. Fifth, measuring only flows of goods and services ignores our ability to increase that flow. Assuming that leisure time is a choice, the amount of goods you purchase is determined to a certain extent by your preferences. This means if we measure goods and services flows, we will underestimate the well-being of people who choose to purchase more free time. Furthermore, if people who consume more tend to work less (consume more leisure) we will underestimate inequality of economic well-being, but if people who consume more also tend to work harder for it, we will end up overestimating inequality.

Access to resources as a measure of economic well-being

Perhaps the most popular measures of economic well-being are household income and household net worth. Income measures the amount of money that enters a household over a period of time (usually measured over a one-year period), and net worth measures the amount of resources a household owns at a particular point in time, less any debts the household owes. These measures are useful for several reasons. First, they are both relative and absolute measures. You can make comparisons between households (although you still have to account for family size and structure) and the absolute values—they are usually measured in currency—also have meaning. Also, these measures reflect access to goods and services (dollars), regardless of whether or not funds are actually spent.

Although economists are usually careful not to attempt to make comparisons of economic satisfaction or "utility" between households, there is an implicit assumption, when using monetary measures of well-being, that we are doing exactly that. Before we go on, we must spend some time considering the relative pros and cons of different measures. It should be noted that for this entry, we will not consider measures that attempt to determine whether individuals have enough to meet the most basic necessities.

Measurement problems

One problem with comparing well-being is that it is difficult to define the unit of analysis. Although our goal might be to define the economic

Table 1

Living Arrangements of the Over-65 Population

	Alone %	With Spouse %	With Relatives %	With Other %
Men				
1960	12	69	14	4
1980	14	75	8	3
1998	17	73	7	3
Women				
1960	24	36	34	4
1980	40	37	20	2
1998	27	50	22	1

SOURCE: *U.S. Census Current Population Survey* (2000)

well-being of individuals, most individuals live in families or households, and most of our measures of economic well-being are either conceptualized or measured at the household level. Household measures of well-being make it impossible, for example, to compare the economic well-being of wives with that of their husbands. Very little has been done to examine differences in individual well-being within households, and it is usually assumed that resources within the household are shared. Therefore, when comparing differences in economic well-being among the aged, one must account for relationships that exist between economic well-being and the size and structure of households in which older householders exist. Furthermore, we will have to account for the fact that older households live in different "types" of households that the non-aged, making comparisons between the economic well-being of the aged and the non-aged difficult.

Table 1 shows the changes that have taken place with respect to the living arrangements of the aged over the last forty years. The fact that more of the aged live as heads of households than forty years ago (i.e., fewer of them living with relatives that are not their spouse or non-relatives) indicates an improvement in the economic well-being of the aged. This is because moving in with relatives is often a signal, for an individual of any age, that one's economic well-being is not sufficient to maintain a household of one's -own. When comparing the well-being of the aged to the nonaged with household data, the aged will seem better off than they really are,

because such an analysis fails to account for older Americans who choose not to be household heads. These older Americans, whose economic well-being has driven them to live with relatives, for example, are not picked up in the data. However, the data from Table 1 also suggest that this sort of bias decreased over time, so that any comparison of the aged and nonaged over time will underestimate any relative advances the aged make and underestimate any relative declines.

Individual versus household differences aside, one could argue that measuring household consumption, and using that as a measure of economic well-being, addresses both the limitations of the two more common measures while at the same time preserving their benefits. Aside from the problem of accounting for family size and structure, how much a household spends, one could argue, is a good measure of both how they are doing now, and how they expect to be doing in the future, which captures the essence of economic well-being. The problem is that households may have different measures of necessities. The health care example is relevant here—is John better off than Jeff if he spends twice as much on health care, but the same as Jeff on all other goods? Answering "no" to this question condemns consumption as a measure of economic well-being, and is obviously relevant when examining the economic well-being of the aged.

Looking at average measures of well-being does not account for the fact that there is inequality in economic well-being, that is, wide dispersion in the incomes of households, both for the aged and the nonaged. In general, inequality can be measured by comparing the values of certain households in a population. For example, one measure of inequality would be to compare the income level at which 20 percent of American households have less income and 80 percent have greater income (the lower quintile) with that of the income at which 80 percent of households have less income and 20 percent have more (the upper quintile). A distribution where the difference between those two numbers is greater, then, would be the one where income is distributed less equally. Another measure of inequality, where these comparisons are taken to their most extreme, is the *Gini Coefficient*, which compares not just two households, but all households in describing inequality. The Gini coefficient is calculated by taking the differences between the incomes of every household (this would be n times (n-1) differences for a sample of n households), averaging them, and dividing by two times the average household income. Again, a larger Gini coefficient means that inequality is larger. One of the benefits of the Gini coefficient is that it standardizes inequality to the absolute amount of the variable in question (in the case of the example, income).

Another way to measure the economic well-being of the aged is to compare any measures to those of the nonaged. There are a number of reasons why it is difficult to compare the well-being of older individuals and those who are not old. Economic vulnerability aside, issues of economic necessity need to be considered. In particular, the propensity of older Americans to consume health care services must be considered. Also problematic is the fact that most of our measures are monetary, that is, the ability of the household to purchase goods. Differences in leisure time between the aged and the nonaged are ignored in the tables below.

When thinking about comparing the economic well-being of people at different ages, both income and net worth are incomplete measures. Income underestimates the well-being of older Americans relative to younger Americans, since older Americans tend to have larger asset values to protect them from periods of low income. On the other hand, net worth overestimates the well-being of older Americans relative to younger Americans, because older households must draw a larger portion of their income from net worth.

Income is probably the measure of economic well-being that treats the old and the young "fairest." Ideally, both the old and young will have income—resources flowing into their households over a period of time. For the old, this will be made up mostly of return on investment capital—interest, capital gains, Social Security (which can be viewed as return on past savings, even though it does not really work that way in practice)—while the young are generating income from human capital—earnings. In this way, the life course can be seen as transforming your wealth from human capital into investment capital. For this reason, net worth seems to underestimate the economic well-being of the young—their wealth is still in the form of human capital. Nevertheless, both income and net worth can be used to show inequality within the two groups, and we will also use net worth to show how differences in well-being between the young and old have changed over time.

Table 2
Household Income

Mean Household Income in 1999 Dollars

YEAR	Household Head is over 65	All Households	Ratio
1975	27,077	44,460	0.61
1987	29,855	47,198	0.63
1999	34,671	54,842	0.63

SOURCE: *U.S. Census Current Population Survey* (2000)

Changes in economic well-being over time

Table 2 shows the Census Bureau estimates of income in 1975, 1987, and 1999 for households headed by someone over sixty-five versus all households, adjusted for changes in the prices of goods and services between those years (they are comparable to 1999 prices). According to the Census, mean income for households headed by someone age sixty-five and over in 1999 was $34,671. This was 63 percent of the mean for all U.S. households ($54,842). This percentage is up from thirty years ago, when it was 54 percent, but it has remained stable since its peak of 65 percent in 1985. It is also important to note that there are some older individuals that live in households where the head is not over sixty-five (i.e., the older individual is not the head). Since these individuals are more likely to have fewer resources, the ratios in Table 2 probably underestimate the actual differences in income between older adults and the young. On the other hand, any improvement in economic well-being by the older relative to the young is probably underestimated by this Table, since more older Americans are living independently now relative to thirty years ago.

Table 3 gives the changes that have occurred over time in the sources of income of the aged. In general, Social Security is the most important source of income for the aged, and is of greater importance for individuals with low incomes. The proportions have remained relatively stable over time, except that in recent years, a declining proportion of total income has come from earnings, while more has come from assets and pensions. This trend exists even in the face of more opportunities in the labor market for older workers and more strict regulations in employment

Table 3
Where Do Older Americans Get Their Income?

Percent of Income

YEAR	Social Security	Pensions	Assets	Earnings	Other
1967	34	15	15	29	7
1976	39	16	18	23	4
1984	38	15	28	16	3
1990	36	26	16	17	5
1998	38	20	19	21	2

SOURCE: *U.S. Census Current Population Survey* (2000)

procedures. What is no doubt offsetting these opportunities are more incentives provided by employers in the form of pension benefits, and the tendency for increases in economic well-being to cause earlier retirement for many older Americans.

One statement that is commonly used to implicitly compare the economic well-being of older adults to that of the young—that older people are more vulnerable to inflation—is largely mythical. For low-income households, the majority of retirement income comes from Social Security retirement benefits, which, since 1975, are automatically indexed to the Consumer Price Index to account for price changes over time. For high-income households, most income comes from savings, where rates of return are generally correlated with inflation. Defined Benefit Pensions are not necessarily indexed to inflation. Nevertheless, it is a misrepresentation to talk about the aged as a group of citizens that generally have "fixed" incomes.

According to the U.S. Census, the distribution of income of older Americans is more equal than the distribution of nonaged, although the distribution has become more dispersed for both groups. While the Gini coefficient for the distribution of younger Americans' income went from .44 to .47 from 1973-1999, it went from .36 to .42 for the over-sixty-five population. Social Security and defined benefits, and entitlement programs such as Supplementary Security Income and the Social Security Earnings Test work to make the distribution of income more equal for both groups. This seems to be true, even though one might expect differences in financial planning and financial preparation for retirement, earnings inequality, and varying investment performance between households to skew the incomes of older Americans more than those of the young.

Table 4 shows the wealth differences between older households and all households in 1995 and 1998 (not included in the wealth measures are pension and social security wealth). It is not surprising that the net worth of the average older American is greater than that of the population in general. In 1998, households headed by someone sixty-five and over had a mean net worth of $392,187, compared to $282,979 for the entire U.S. population. Older households own more of just about every type of asset—monetary (highly liquid assets such as savings accounts, checking accounts, and money market accounts), investment assets (stocks, bonds, mutual funds, etc.) housing assets, and nonhousing real property. Furthermore, older households have much less debt. This latter fact should not surprise, given that older households have less earnings with which to guarantee future payment, and their higher asset levels make credit less necessary. Recall that we would expect older households to have more wealth *ceteris paribus*, since more of a younger household's economic well-being is made up of earnings ability. It should also be expected that the distribution of wealth among households over sixty-five is more equal than that of the population in general. For example, while the net worth of the household at the 25th percentile is only 4.7 percent of the wealth of the 75th percentile household for the population in general, the comparable statistic for over-sixty-five households is 16.9 percent, suggesting that the distribution of wealth is "tighter" for

Table 4
Net Worth

	1995		1998	
	Over 65	All House-holds	Over 65	All House-holds
Monetary Assets	57,509	29,529	64,064	37,655
Investment Assets	79,190	56,217	132,636	96,615
Housing Assets	80,793	74,426	104,926	92,052
Other Assets	91,434	56,277	106,365	104,208
Total Assets	308,927	243,699	407,992	330,531
Mortgage Debt	7,421	29,594	11,851	37,267
Other Debt	2,368	7,022	3,954	9,926
Total Debt				
Mean Net Worth	299,317	207,083	392,187	282,979
25th Percentile	28,800	9,530	53,000	9,860
75th Percentile	226,080	158,500	313,600	208,770

SOURCE: *Federal Reserve Board of Governors' Survey of Consumer Finances*

older households. Nevertheless, 10 percent of households over sixty-five have net worth of $4200 or less, not enough to generate significant levels of income.

Examining the changes that have occurred in the wealth characteristics of older households over the last few years reveals some cause for concern. From 1995 to 1998, the net worth of over-sixty-five households increased 31 percent, from $299,317 to $ 392,187 in 1998. The comparable increase for all U.S. households was 36 percent. This is surprising since the strong performance of investment markets implies that households with many assets would be the most fortunate. It seems that for some reason, older households were not able to take as much advantage of the unparalleled prosperity in the American economy as their younger counterparts, even when using an aged-biased criterion like net worth. This could be because of an inability to take advantage of labor markets the way younger individuals can. It might also suggest that the conservative investment habits of older Americans might prevent them from taking advantage of opportunities in capital markets.

Explaining differences in economic well-being

Among older Americans, health status and access to health care have a substantial effect on economic well-being. According to the Federal Reserve's *Survey of Consumer Finances,* health status definitely impacts economic well-being in old age, and inequality among the aged. For example, households where the head is aged seventy to seventy-nine and self-reports poor or fair health have a mean net worth of $225,462. This compares to $554,909 for heads aged seventy to seventy-nine that report good or excellent health, more than double their poor-health counterparts. The differences arise from two phenomena. One, health status has a significant impact on the number of hours worked during one's lifetime, which therefore affects past income, savings, and eventually net worth. Two, older households face higher out-of-pocket health costs, which deplete assets and, therefore, income from assets.

Aside from health status, often the same personal characteristics that are associated with low economic well-being in "young" households also contribute to low levels of economic well-being in old age. According to Census estimates, for both the older Americans and the young, the poor are overrepresented by female-headed households, households where the head did not attend any college, and households that are not white. The largest difference is the overrepresentation of minorities among the aged poor. While households headed by a non-white make up only 12.8 percent of older households, they make up nearly 29 percent of poor older households.

How could the economic well-being of older people be further improved? In the short run, such policies would involve either direct transfers, such as increased Social Security benefits, or policies that raise real interest rates, since the aged generate more of their income from returns on assets. These short-run policies would tend to come at the expense of the economic well-being of younger generations. In the long run, policies that insure stable incomes for older adults will serve to make their incomes more equal. The trend toward defined contribution pension plans and away from defined benefit plans (even Social Security may become a defined contribution plan) will likely add to inequality of outcomes, due to varying performances by households in investment markets, even if their effect on the overall well-being of older Americans as a group is unclear. Policies and programs that improve the physical health of the older adults would also lead to an improvement in financial health. Since so much of an individual's economic well-being in old age is determined by their financial preparation, policies that help promote sound financial planning for retirement, including policies encouraging workers to save, should increase overall well-being. It is unclear whether these types of policies increase inequality, however, since it is the members of society at the top of the distribution more likely to take advantage of such policies.

CHARLES B. HATCHER

See also ASSETS AND WEALTH; BEQUESTS AND INHERITANCES; ESTATE PLANNING; PENSIONS, PLAN TYPES AND POLICY APPROACHES; POVERTY; SOCIAL SECURITY.

BIBLIOGRAPHY

Federal Reserve Board. *Survey of Consumer Finances.* Washington, D.C.: Federal Reserve Board, 2000.
HURD, M. D. "Research on the Elderly: Economic Status, Retirement, and Consumption." *Journal of Economic Literature* 28, no. 2 (1990): 566–637.
SCHULZ, J. H. *The Economics of Aging*, 6th ed. Westport, Conn.: Auburn House, 1995.
United States Census Bureau. *Current Population Survey.* Washington, D.C.: U.S. Census Bureau, 1999.

EDUCATION

When people think about education, they gradually think about the traditional school, and about their own personal experience. Education functions in all settings of modern society, however, and educational forms have changed over the years. During the industrial revolution, the advent of formal education undermined the authority of older people because older people's knowledge of farming, rural life, and crafts did not prove useful to young people working in factories in growing cities. During the mid-twentieth century, the first gerontologists saw lifelong learning as a rare experimental program

and worried about the loss of the educational function of grandparents. Parents worried about entrusting their children's education to their own parents, fearing they would be out of touch with the rapid pace of social change. As retirement became commonplace and longevity provided more healthy years of leisure, many older persons looked for educational opportunities through special programs and at institutions of higher education. The advent of the information age brought many older persons into learning again with computer technology, though this time it was often grandchildren helping grandparents learn the new technologies.

Trends in years of schooling

The education gap between younger and older adults in the United States is closing. For example, the gap in median years of education for those age twenty-five to thirty-four and those fifty-five and over shrank from 4.4 years in 1947 to 0.2 years in 1991 (see Figure 1). The improvement for older adults came rapidly during the 1960s and 1970s, reflecting the growth of public education in the first decades of the twentieth century. More than half of the young adults in the United States had completed twelve years of education by 1952, while it was 1979 before half of the older adults had achieved this level. The gap between men and women in median years of education has nearly disappeared for all age groups, especially for young adults.

Until the 1930s, a typical childhood pattern of education involved completing the sixth grade and then going to work. Many Americans never attended high school. Since 1940, rates of finishing school before high school graduation have decreased while rates of graduating high school (or higher levels of education) have increased. Until the late 1950s it was uncommon for middle-aged people to have completed high school. Since 1990, rising college enrollment has led to a drop in the percentage of adults who only graduate from high school. The percentage of young adults who finished their schooling with high school declined from 44 percent in 1973 to about 31 percent in 2000, but has remained steady in the 1990s for older adults. At the turn of the twenty-first century similar proportions of young adults had completed their schooling with some college (28 percent) or had completed a college degree (29 percent). Older adults will reflect this trend of increasing educational attainment by the middle of the twenty-first century.

A 70-year-old woman celebrates with her son (left) and grandson as she becomes the oldest graduate at Austin College in 1997. (Photo by Delia DeWald. Used with permission of Janet Huber Lowry.)

The statistic of median years of schooling hides a lot of variation in educational attainment among racial and ethnic groups. Wide differences remain, and gender differences linger among older persons in various racial and ethnic groups. The gap is closing for high school completion rates, and gender differences barely exist at this level. High school graduation rates for whites remained above 80 percent in the 1990s, while rates for blacks stayed above 70 percent after 1993. Although 1980 census figures showed two-thirds of Hispanics completing high school, from 1990 to 2000 the rates remained below 60 percent, reflecting the recent immigrant status of many Hispanics. Asian and Pacific Islander men have the highest levels—up to 88 percent completed high school in the 1990s—and women in this category hovered around 80 percent.

Similar trends in college degree completion show differences between the genders in racial and ethnic groups. The gender gap is most extreme for older adults (see Figure 2). Asian and Pacific Islanders have the highest level of college degree completion among U.S. groups, with men around 32 percent and women above 15 percent. For other older men, whites have a college degree completion rate of 23.2 percent,

while Hispanics are at 9.3 percent and blacks are at 7.5 percent. For other older women, the frequency of college completion is: whites, 12 percent; blacks, 8.3 percent; and Hispanics, 5.3 percent.

Although 30 percent of older adults (compared to 10 percent of younger adults) in the United States still lack a high school degree, the education gap is shrinking rapidly. A gap persists at the higher-education level due to an expansion of opportunities since the mid-twentieth century, and minor regional differences persist. High school completion levels for those age twenty-five and over were highest for the Midwest (87 percent) and lowest for the South (82 percent). When baby boomers reach retirement, the education gap will begin to close. Older people in Europe and Japan are generally not as educated as their counterparts in the United States.

Differences remain for members of minority groups in the United States, but these are not uniform. Non-Hispanic blacks have a lower level of educational attainment by all measures, though the rate for black women exceeds that of black men. Asians have the highest education rates, while Hispanics are often the least educated at all ages, despite both these groups having

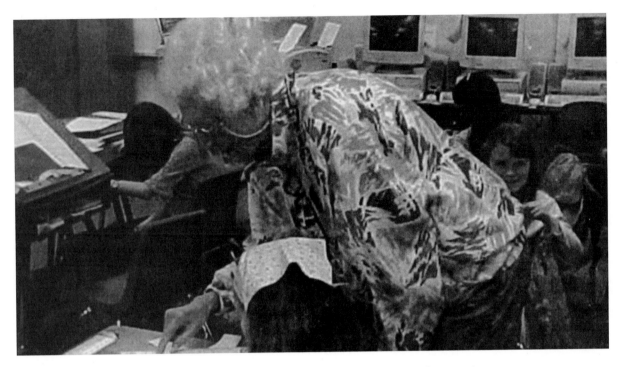

A foster grandparent volunteers at an elementary school. (Photo by Teresa Wegener.)

recent immigrant status. These cultures are more patriarchal and strongly favor the education of men. Elizabeth Vierck reports that, in the United States, one in ten people over age sixty-five speaks a foreign language at home. Gender differences for older adults persist in Asian and non-Hispanic whites, although they appear to be fading. In the developing world, however, education levels among older women are generally low or nonexistent.

The impact of education

Education is a significant factor in aging. It is modestly related to income and strongly related to occupational prestige, both of which lead to better health care throughout life, a key to the enjoyment of later years. Ronald Manheimer reports that "education is associated with increased participation in politics and the electoral process, more aggressive health-seeking behavior, different styles of consumerism, and the desire for life-long learning" (p. 45). Further, "education must prepare the individual not only for the tasks of early and middle age, but for those of old age as well" (Erikson, Erikson, and Kivnick, p. 336). Arguing from a developmental perspective, Erikson, Erikson, and Kivnick advocate more practical courses in public schools, and they stress knowledge of the aging human body as an aid in maintenance and long-range survival.

Education has been linked to maintaining self-esteem, developing leadership abilities for volunteer roles, and empowering older people as health care consumers. Helena Lopata, famous for her studies of widows, reminds us that education helps people cope with loss. By providing the skills to develop friendships and commitments to voluntary associations, education links people to sources of support during periods of adjustment.

Health and economic dependency vary significantly with educational attainment. Comfort in interacting with doctors and adherence to treatment regimens come from greater learning. Obtaining work that supplies health benefits is usually contingent on completing high school or college. Having greater income for proper nutrition and regular preventive health care is also associated with higher education. These factors set up differences in longevity related to education. Because racial, ethnic, and cultural heritage are linked to differences in education and economic resources, longevity varies by these categories as well.

Figure 1
Median Years of Education by Age

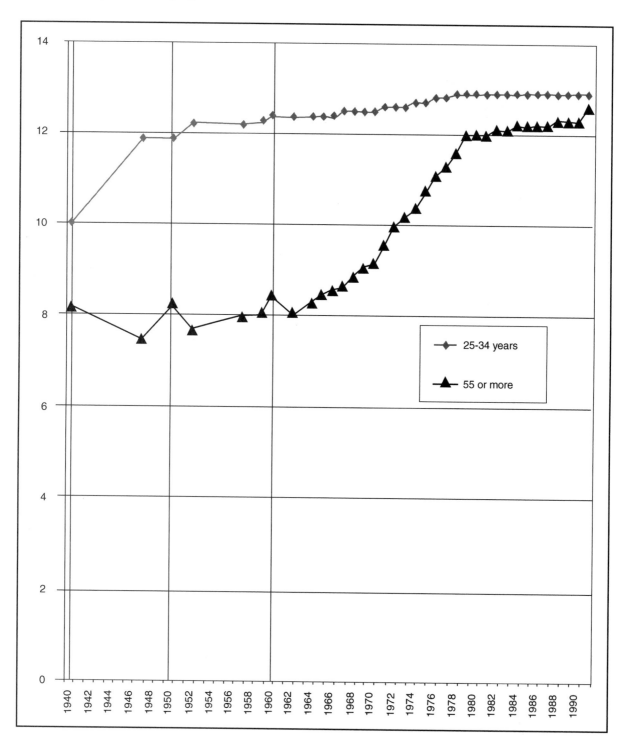

SOURCE: 1947, 1952 to 1998 *March Current Population Survey,* (noninstitutional population, excluding members of the Armed Forces living in barracks); 1960, 1950, and 1940 Census of Population (resident population).

Figure 2
Percent 65 Years and Over with Bachelor's Degree or Higher Educational Attainment, by Racial-Ethnic and Sex Status—March 2000

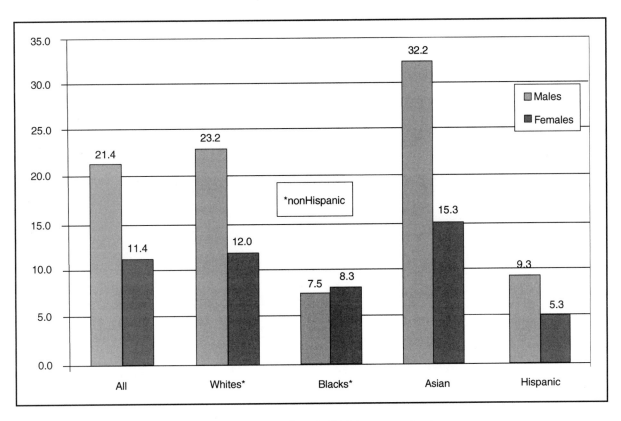

SOURCE: U.S. Census Bureau, Internet Release data, December 19, 2000 (www.census/gov/)

Lifelong learning

Interestingly, while years of education and life have increased more than 150 percent since 1900, the percentage of life that Americans spend in an educational setting has remained at around 17 percent. People now participate in education in more mixed patterns, however, with cyclical or blended variations occurring throughout the life course. As the baby boomers aged during the 1980s, there was a drop in the number of young people entering college, and many community colleges began to open their doors to older adults. The bulk of adults over sixty-five are enrolled in community colleges, primarily studying part-time in public institutions. Computer technology and corporate downsizing also sent many older adults back to school for retraining in the 1980s. Older women significantly outnumbered older men in college and graduate school at the end of the twentieth century.

The increase in leisure time in later life and the explosion of higher education after 1950 fueled the growth in life-long learning. Elderhostel emerged in the 1970s to provide short-term (typically weeklong) educational opportunities for people age fifty-five and older. It began with five campuses and 220 participants in 1975, and in 2000 there were over 270,000 hostellers participating in over 10,000 Elderhostel programs in over seventy countries. In 1988, twenty-four established Institutes for Learning in Retirement (ILRs) collaborated with Elderhostel to form the Elderhostel Institute Network, a series of permanent programs at sponsoring college and university campuses involving noncredit courses and activities staffed by older volunteers. In 2000 there were over 225 such ILRs in the network, providing over 3,000 courses a term to 52,000 network members. In 1992 a service program began with opportunities such as teaching English, archaeological digs, and building affordable housing throughout the world. In conjunction with the Institute Network, the typical college campus offers three or four courses of considerable variety and takes advantage of local attractions with extracurricular activities during the week of Elderhostel. A typical Elderhostel week includes three different classes taught by college professors and various field trips in the evening to local interest sites. For example, "Music in the Big Band Era," "The Many Cultures of Texas," and "Feminist Theology," tours at a local dairy farm, a lake outing, and a visit to a historic house might constitute a week's offerings.

SeniorNet is an organization that began in the 1980s to help older persons take advantage of the information age. It focuses on computer technology instruction and establishing learning communities online. Through small lab sites, often donated by businesses, volunteers teach about computer software and the Internet. According to Mary Russell and Laura Ginsburg's report for the National Center on Adult Literacy, SeniorNet's success comes from characteristics of good online learning communities: its learning environment uses nonformal (and informal) models of learning; it embraces a vision of adult learning and development attuned to social, psychological, and political dimensions; its instructional model is interactive and generative, acknowledging the experience older learners bring to classes; and its social construct supports collective and participatory communication. Diversity and outreach remain special challenges.

Countless local programs are emerging in response to the interest in involving older people in formal education. Grants from the Funds for the Improvement of Post-Secondary Education (FIPSE) have helped traditional liberal arts colleges develop programs to stimulate young people by involving retired professionals in regular classes. Foster Grandparents programs and Retired and Senior Volunteer programs place volunteers in elementary schools for tutoring. Many volunteer associations consider education a significant part of their mission. AARP sponsors driver education courses that assist older persons with insurance deductions and improve road safety.

Public policy has supported education for older citizens through a variety of statutes enacted since passage of the Older Americans Act of 1965. In addition to statutes addressing adult, technical, vocational, and bilingual education, various laws have supported older veterans, displaced homemakers, and women. These enactments stress the importance of education for productive life and service.

The benefits of education are many. Older adults know this and are pioneers in the new era of lifelong learning. The education gaps between young and old are becoming a thing of the past, and a traditional age for learning is fading with them.

JANET HUBER LOWRY

See also LEISURE; LIFE COURSE; VOLUNTEER ACTIVITIES AND PROGRAMS.

BIBLIOGRAPHY

ERIKSON, J. M.; ERIKSON, E. H.; and KIVNICK, H. *Vital Involvement in Old Age.* New York: W. W. Norton & Company, 1986.

KAPLAN, M. "Adult Education as Part of a Leisure Program." In *Handbook of Social Gerontology: Societal Aspects of Aging.* Edited by C. Tibbitts. Chicago: University of Chicago Press, 1960.

KOFF, T. H., and PARK, RICHARD W. *Aging Public Policy: Bonding the Generations,* 2d ed. Amityville, N.Y.: Baywood Publishing Company, 1999.

LOPATA, H. Z. *Women as Widows: Support Systems.* New York: Elsevier, 1979.

MANHEIMER, R. J., ed., with North Carolina Center for Creative Retirement, University of North Carolina at Asheville. *Older Americans Almanac—A Reference Work for Seniors in the United States.* Detroit, Mich.: Gale Research Inc., 1994.

SMITH, M. C., and POURCHOT, T., eds. *Adult Learning and Development: Perspectives from Educational Psychology.* Mahwah, N.J.: Lawrence Erlbaum, 1998.

VIERCK, E. *Fact Book on Aging.* Santa Barbara, Calif.: ABC-CLIO, Inc., 1990.

YNTEMA, S., ed. *Americans 55 & Older—A Changing Market.* Ithaca, N.Y.: New Strategists Publications, Inc., 1997.

INTERNET RESOURCES

Elderhostel, Incorporated. *www.elderhostel.org.*

National Center for Health Statistics. "Life Expectancy." Available at *www.cdc.gov/*

RUSSELL, M., and GINSBURG, L. "Learning Online: Extending the Meaning of Community: A Review of Three Programs from the Southeastern United States." National Council on

Adult Literacy (NCAL) Technical Report TR99–01. Graduate School of Education, University of Pennsylvania for the Southeast, and Islands Regional Technology in Education Consortium, 1999. Available at *http://literacyonline.org/products/*
SeniorNet Organization. *www.seniornet.org*

ELDER ABUSE AND NEGLECT

The American family has historically been viewed as a sacrosanct institution for care of the individual—the inviolate haven of love, safety, and protection. Growing awareness of family violence, however, has shown this view to be faulty, first with the "discovery" of child neglect and abuse in the 1960s, followed by spouse abuse in the early 1970s, and elder neglect and abuse in the mid-1970s. Yet, Peter Stearns and Shulamit Reinharz believe that family violence, in general, and elder mistreatment, specifically, have existed since the beginning of human history. Early examples of elder neglect and abuse include adult sons killing their aged parents in Teutonic societies and Native American tribes abandoning their elders when they can no longer travel (Sumner).

Acceptance of these historical facts as evidence depends on one's definitions of elder abuse and neglect. The likelihood of disagreement is considerable, since these concepts are value-laden and typically trigger emotional responses before logical thought. In addition, the perception of violence varies from society to society, and culture to culture. William Sumner argues that either honor or destruction underpin societies. When it is the former, older adults are respected and honored, while with the latter they are viewed as societal burdens which sap the strength of the society. This negative view of older adults sets the stage for ageism and mistreatment.

Although mistreatment of older adults is probably not a new phenomenon, awareness that some elders are mistreated and interest in examining the problem are relatively new. Initial professional recognition occurred almost simultaneously in Great Britain and America. In 1975, G. R. Burston wrote of "granny bashing" and Robert Butler described the "battered old person syndrome." In 1978 Suzanne Steinmetz shared her "discovery" of battered elders. Over the succeeding years as more cases were uncovered, initial disbelief and denial have given way to acknowledgment of the societal problems of elder neglect and abuse. In the early 1980s, researchers began to investigate elder mistreatment, and the House Select Committee on Aging began a series of public hearings around the country.

Most of the early research, which viewed elder neglect as a more benign subtype of elder abuse, examined the extent and nature of elder mistreatment among older adults living alone or with family members, friends, or other relatives and caretakers in the community. The prevailing view was that elder mistreatment was a domestic issue; it occurred within the family.

The early studies documented the existence of elder abuse and neglect, but did not provide clear or consistent information on the antecedents, causes, or consequences, or on the characteristics of the perpetrators or victims. For example, many of the early researchers identified functional disability, impairment, or dependence of the older adult as common correlates of both elder abuse and neglect (Douglass, Hickey, and Noel; O'Malley et al.; Steuer and Austin). More recent studies, which employed comparison of elder abuse and elder neglect cases, have found these characteristics are correlated with elder neglect but not with abuse (Phillips; Pillemer; Wolf). Some experts in the field believe that elder neglect is not a subtype of elder abuse (Fulmer and Gould; Hudson, 1986, 1991; Pedrick-Cornell and Gelles). Yet most of the research has included elder neglect as a subtype of abuse, confounding the findings for these two main forms of elder mistreatment. A few researchers have addressed both in the same study but have analyzed the results separately, providing evidence that elder abuse and neglect are distinct phenomena with differing risk factors and perpetrators.

Definitions and types of abuse and neglect

Since the definitions used by researchers and in state statutes vary, one instance of agreement is presented. In 1988, a three-round Delphi study was conducted with a nationwide panel of elder mistreatment experts to reach agreement on the types of elder abuse and neglect and on the definition of each type (Hudson, 1991). These researchers, clinicians, educators, and policy makers produced a taxonomy of elder mistreatment (Figure 1) and theoretical definitions of the eleven categories identified (Figure 2).

Figure 1

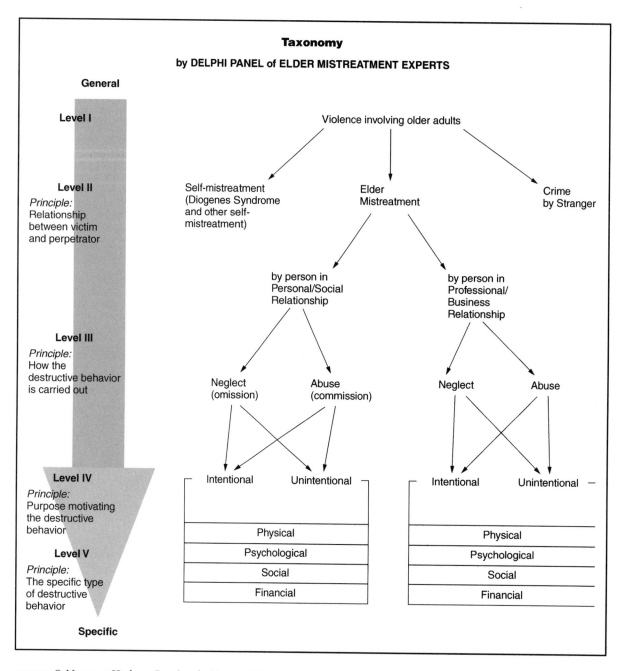

Further, the panel made decisions about four previously debated issues. First, that elder mistreatment is not limited to domestic violence, but also includes mistreatment of older adults by persons in professional and business roles that connote trust, such as lawyers, doctors, nurses, and nurses' aides. Second, elder neglect and abuse are distinct forms of elder mistreatment that would be most effectively studied separately. Third, intentional and unintentional forms of both elder abuse and neglect exist, and thus, intentionality is not an essential characteristics of either but, rather, an intervention issue. Last, dependence of the elder on the abuser or neglector is not an essential characteristic of either form, although it is commonly

Figure 2
Theoretical Definitions

Level II	Elder Mis-treatment	Destructive behavior that is directed toward an older adult, occurs within the context of a relationship connoting trust and is of sufficient intensity and/or frequency to produce harmful physical, psychological, social and/or financial effects of unnecessary suffering, injury, pain, loss and/or violation of human rights and poorer quality of life for the older adult.
	Personal/ Social Re-lationship	Persons in close personal relationships with an older adult connoting trust and some socially established behavioral norms, e.g., relatives by blood or marriage, friends, neighbors, any "significant other."
	Professional/ Business Re-lationship	Persons in a formal relationship with an older adult that denotes trust and expected services, e.g., physicians, nurses, social workers, nursing aides, bankers, lawyers, nursing home staff, home health personnel, landlords, etc.
Level III	Elder Abuse	Aggressive or invasive behavior/action(s), or threats of same, inflicted on an older adult and resulting in harmful effects for the older adult.
	Elder Neglect	The failure of a responsible party(ies) to act so as to provide, or to provide what is prudently deemed adequate and reasonable assistance that is available and warranted to ensure that the older adult's basic physical, psychological, social, and financial needs are met, resulting in harmful effects for the older adult.
Level IV	Intentional	Abusive or neglectful behavior or acts that are carried out for the purpose of harming, deceiving, coercing or controlling the older adult so as to produce gain for the perpetrator (often labeled "active" abuse/neglect in the literature).
	Unintentional	Abusive or neglectful behavior or acts that are carried out, but NOT for the purpose of harming, deceiving, coercing or controlling the older adult, so as to produce gain for the perpetrator (often labeled "passive" abuse/neglect in the literature).
Level V	Physical	Behavior(s)/action(s) in which physical force(s) is used to inflict the abuse; or available and warranted physical assistance is not provided, resulting in neglect.
	Psychological	Behavior(s)/action(s) in which verbal force is used to inflict the abuse; or available and warranted psychological/emotional assistance/support is not provided, resulting in neglect.
	Social	Behavior(s)/action(s) that prevents the basic social needs of an older adult from being met; or failure to provide available and warranted means by which an older adult's basic social needs can be met.
	Financial	Theft or misuse of an older adult's funds or property; or failure to provide available and warranted means by which an older adult's basic material needs can be met.

SOURCE: © Margaret Hudson. Reprinted with permission.

seen among victims of elder neglect (Hudson, 1991).

The five-level taxonomy produced was based on perpetrator behaviors. Level I, violence involving older adults, fits elder mistreatment into the scheme of violence phenomena while distinguishing it from violence involving persons of other ages. Level II, which is based on the relationship between perpetrator and victim, differentiates elder mistreatment from two closely related phenomena that involve harm to older adults—self-mistreatment and crime against elders by strangers. Level II also broadens the concept of elder mistreatment beyond domestic mistreatment to include professional mistreatment of elders. Level III is based on the manner

in which the harmful behavior is carried out, that is, by commission (abuse) or omission (neglect). Level IV, based on the purpose of the destructive behavior, promotes awareness that elder abuse and neglect occur intentionally and unintentionally, and conveys the experts' belief that detection can occur without the determination of intent or placement of blame. Level V focuses on the specific type of harmful behaviors involved in elder neglect and abuse. Categories include theoretically distinct behaviors that often are not mutually exclusive in actuality, so that a case may fit into more than one category. For example, the adult son who threatens and beats his mother while stealing her money fits into the categories of physical, psychological, and financial abuse; an adult daughter who has the needed resources but allows her frail mother to unsafely live alone in an unmaintained home and to become isolated, malnourished, and injured from falling fits into the categories of physical, social, psychological, and financial neglect (Hudson, 1991). As the taxonomy levels proceed from general to specific, definitions of the more specific forms of neglect and abuse build from the general ones.

Elder neglect is the careless, indifferent, or malicious lack of attention by a designated or implied caregiver that results in harm from an elder's basic human needs not being met. This lack of action, or omission, makes neglect less tangible and more amorphous than elder abuse, because abuse is typically seen as an act of commission, or the misuse of power and/or the use of force, such as beating, shoving, confining, threatening, or belittling an elder. Because neglect is a lack of action, it is often not recognized until its cumulative effects are seen on the elder. Acts of neglect range in severity from intermittent inattention to an elder's daily fluid intake to total abandonment of an incapacitated elder. While the dynamics of elder neglect are different from those of abuse, the effects on the elder can be equally dire—premature death that is due to malnutrition, dehydration, untreated medical conditions, hypothermia, imposed immobility, and so on—rather than death from injuries due to assault. Although neglect is the most common form of elder mistreatment, surprisingly, it is also the form that has been given the least attention by researchers. Therefore, we know far less about elder neglect per se than we do about elder abuse. While both healthy and frail elders of various ages are abused, it is frail elders of advanced age—eighty years and older and dependent on others for their basic care—who are most at risk for neglect.

Incidence and prevalence

Determining the incidence and prevalence of elder abuse and neglect is very difficult, mainly because most cases are not known to anyone outside of the situation. Also, differing definitions of abuse and neglect, reporting agencies not keeping adequate information, and important differences in study methods have made reliable data elusive. While the actual incidence and prevalence of elder mistreatment in domestic and institutional settings is unknown and can only be estimated, all of the studies clearly indicate that most cases are unreported in spite of mandatory

reporting laws in all fifty states. Nevertheless, estimates from five studies provide some indications of the extent of elder neglect and abuse.

From interviews with community-dwelling elders in Boston, Pillemer and Finkelhor estimated that yearly in Massachusetts some 3.2 percent of older adults are physically or psychologically abused or neglected by their caregivers (financial and social abuse and self-neglect were not included). Yet only one in every fourteen of these cases came to professional attention in spite of the state's mandatory reporting law. In their survey of nurses and nurses' aides from area nursing homes, Pillemer and Moore found that 36 percent of the staff had seen at least one incident of a resident being physically abused in the previous year, while 81 percent had seen psychological abuse. Most of this mistreatment did not get reported to authorities. Another study, in which older adults were interviewed, found that 7.5 percent of the respondents reported that they had been physically, psychologically, socially, or financially abused since turning sixty-five years of age (Hudson and Carlson, 1998, 1999). If neglect or self-neglect were added, the prevalence rate would be higher.

Tatara conducted a survey to estimate the national incidence of domestic elder mistreatment. Based on data from only twenty-nine states, he estimated that 735,000 elders were victims of abuse or neglect during 1991, while another 842,000 were victims of self-neglect. He also found that only 14.4 percent of these cases of mistreatment were reported to protective services agencies. The National Elder Abuse Incidence Study (Takamura and Golden) included reported and unreported cases of abuse, neglect, and self-neglect. The findings suggested that some 551,011 adults over the age of sixty living in domestic settings (institutional mistreatment was not included) were abused or neglected during 1996, and for every reported case of mistreatment, approximately five went unreported. Neglect was the most common form of mistreatment found, followed by psychological abuse, financial abuse, and physical abuse. As compared to their composition in the older adult population, women were disproportionately represented in all the abuse categories, and men were disproportionately found in the abandoned group. The neglect cases showed a more proportional distribution between men (40 percent) and women (60 percent).

ELDER ABUSE AND NEGLECT 409

Victim and perpetrator characteristics

Some studies have addressed specific types of elder abuse and/or neglect to identify the characteristics associated with each. The findings from these studies produced three distinct patterns of victim and perpetrator characteristics. Victims of both physical and psychological elder abuse were found to be both men and women who were young-old (sixty-five to seventy-four years), married, more independent in activities of daily living but in poor emotional health with low morale, in troubled marriages, living with others, lacking confidants, and socially isolated. Their perpetrators were often spouses who had histories of mental illness or problems, had abused alcohol, had a recent decline in mental and/or physical health, were dependent on and lived with the victim, and had experienced recent stress. The perpetrators' characteristics and the quality of the abuser-victim relationship were more related to the abuse than the victims' characteristics, which left victims with few resources for dealing with the abuse.

Participants in material abuse, or exploitation, had a different set of characteristics. Victims tended to be unmarried (widowed, divorced, or never married), older women or men who lived alone and had problems with money management and transportation. They lacked adequate social supports or confidants. Health problems, poor morale, and/or depression limited their activities. Their perpetrators tended to be younger, distant relatives or nonrelatives who abused alcohol and had physical or emotional problems. They did not live with the victims but were financially dependent on them. In material abuse, the victims' characteristics seemed to make them vulnerable to perpetrators who could not function independently (Anetzberger, Korbin, and Austin; Pillemer; Podnieks; Wolf, Godkin, and Pillemer).

In contrast to elder abuse, in which perpetrator characteristics seem to be most relevant, the victims' characteristics seem to be most relevant to elder neglect. Based on studies that compared abuse with neglect, neglect victims were more often old-old (eighty years and older), widowed, disabled women who were dependent on caregivers due to poor health and physical and/or mental impairment. Often they lived with the person who neglected them and had few other people in their social networks. The male and female perpetrators were family members and un-

related caregivers who had experienced losses in their own support system, and viewed the elder as the source of stress (Podnieks; Wolf, Godkin, and Pillemer).

Prevention and intervention

Research has yet to adequately address these aspects of elder mistreatment. One of the most established programs serving mistreated elders is the Elder Abuse Project sponsored by the Victim Services Agency at Mt. Sinai Hospital in New York directed by Risa Breckman (Breckman and Adelman). Breckman is also the codirector of the Elder Abuse Training and Resources Center, which provides training, technical assistance, and case consultation services to organizations through out the country. Rosalie Wolf and Karl Pillemer present four of the best practice models—a multidisciplinary case conference team from San Francisco, a volunteer advocacy program from Madison, Wisconsin, a victim support group from New York City, and a master's degree adult protective services track in social work in Hawaii. They also address some of the common problems faced by community agencies that deal with elder mistreatment cases—the fragmented human services system, the resistance and reluctance of victims to accept services, and the shortage of trained personnel.

Effective intervention in elder mistreatment cases is often difficult to accomplish. First and foremost, since many mistreated elders are competent adults they have the right to refuse assistance even when it is obviously needed. Many of them deny that abuse or neglect is occurring or refuse any assistance offered, often due to embarrassment or fear of retaliation. Only when an older adult is ruled mentally incompetent by a court and a guardian is appointed can intervention be instigated without the elder's consent. Second, in many communities the resources needed for intervention are nonexistent or very limited. Sometimes the only option available is to remove the elder from his or her home. Yet both abuse and neglect also occur in rest and nursing homes. So for some elders the treatment is worse than the original problem. Third, the care of mistreated elders typically requires a multidisciplinary team of health care and human services providers who are well trained regarding the needs of older adults and the needs of abused or neglected elders, and who can address their medical, social, psychological, housing, and legal needs. Fourth, since very little research has been done on elder mistreatment intervention, including which strategies produce the most effective and efficient outcomes, practitioners have little evidence-based information to guide them in caring for these elders. Last, funding has been very limited for instituting or maintaining new initiatives for managing mistreatment cases.

Theoretically speaking, the prevention of elder abuse and neglect will require that ageism be eliminated in our society, and that we restore respect for and honor to our older adults. In addition, it will require that we educate everyone about aging, instill the value of people over material objects, and establish the resources needed to provide quality care for our aged members. Empirically speaking we do not yet know how to effectively prevent or intervene in elder abuse or neglect cases. Very little research has been done on these aspects of elder mistreatment, and there is very little outcome or programmatic evaluation data. Therefore, clinical judgment typically guides prevention and intervention. Until sound research addresses these important aspects of elder mistreatment, this will continue to be the case.

MARGARET F. HUDSON

See also AGEISM; CRIMINAL VICTIMIZATION.

BIBLIOGRAPHY

ANETZBERGER, G. J.; KORBIN, J. E.; and AUSTIN, C. C. "Alcoholism and Elder Abuse." *Journal of Interpersonal Violence* 9 (1994): 184–193.

BRECKMAN, R. S., and ALDERMAN, R. D. *Strategies for Helping Victims of Elder Mistreatment*. Newbury Park, Calif.: Sage, 1988.

BURSTON, G. R. "Granny-Battering." *British Medical Journal* (6 September 1975): 592.

BUTLER, R. N. *Why Survive? Being Old in America*. New York: Harper & Row, 1975.

DOUGLASS, R. L., and NOEL, C. "A Study of Maltreatment of the Elderly and Other Vulnerable Adults." *Final Report to the U.S. Administration on Aging, Department of HEW and the Michigan Department of Social Services*. Ann Arbor, Mich.: Institute of Gerontology, University of Michigan, 1980.

FULMER, T. T., and GOULD, C. S. "Assessing Neglect." *Abuse, Neglect, and Exploitation of Older Persons*. Edited by L. A. Baumhover and S. C. Beal. Baltimore: Health Professionals Press, 1996. Pages 89–99.

HUDSON, M. F. "Elder Mistreatment: Current Research." *Elder Abuse: Conflict in the Family*. Edited by K. A. Pillemer and R. S. Wolf. Dover, Mass.: Auburn House, 1986. Pages 125–166.

HUDSON, M. F. "Elder Mistreatment: A Taxonomy with Definitions by Delphi." *Journal of Elder Abuse and Neglect* 3 (1991): 1–20.

HUDSON, M. F., and CARLSON, J. R. "Elder Abuse: Expert and Public Perspectives on it's Meaning." *Journal of Elder Abuse and Neglect* 9 (1998): 77–97.

HUDSON, M. F., and CARLSON, J. R. "Elder Abuse: Its Meaning to Caucasians, African-Americans, and Native Americans." *Understanding Elder Abuse in Minority Populations*. Edited by T. Tatara. Washington, D.C.: Taylor and Francis, 1999. Pages 187–204.

O'MALLEY, H.; SEGARS, H.; PEREZ, R.; MITCHELL, V.; and KNUEPFEL, G. M. *Elder Abuse in Massachusetts: A Survey of Professionals and Paraprofessionals*. Boston, Mass.: Legal Research and Services for the Elderly. 1979.

PEDRICK-CORNELL, C., and GELLES, R. "Elder Abuse: The Status of Current Knowledge." *Family Relations* 31 (1982): 457–465.

PHILLIPS, L. R. "Abuse and Neglect of the Frail Elderly at Home: An Explanation of Theoretical Relationships." *Journal of Advanced Nursing* 8 (1983): 379–392.

PILLEMER, K. A. "The Dangers of Dependency: New Findings on Domestic Violence Against the Elderly." *Social Problems* 33 (1985): 146–158.

PILLEMER, K. A., and FINKELHOR, D. "The Prevalence of Elder Abuse: A Random Sample Survey." *The Gerontologist* 28 (1988): 51–57.

PILLEMER, K. A., and MOORE, D. W. "Abuse Patients in Nursing Homes: Findings from a Survey of Staff." *The Gerontologist* 29 (1989): 314–320.

PODNIEKS, E. "National Survey on Abuse of the Elderly in Canada." *Journal of Elder Abuse and Neglect* 4 (1992): 5–57.

REINHARZ, S. "Loving and Hating One's Elders: Twin Themes in Legend and Literature." In *Elder Abuse: Conflict in the Family*. Edited by K. A. Pillemer and R. S. Wolf. Dover, Mass.: Auburn House, 1986. Pages 25–48.

STEARNS, P. J. "Old Age Family Conflict: The Perspective of the Past." In *Elder Abuse: Conflict in the Family*. Edited by K. A. Pillemer and R. S. Wolf. Dover, Mass.: Auburn House, 1986. Pages 3–24.

STEINMETZ, S. K. "The Politics of Aging, Battered Parents." *Society* (July/August 1978): 54–55.

STEUER, J., and AUSTIN, E. "Family Abuse of the Elderly." *Journal of the American Geriatrics Society* 28 (1980): 372–376.

SUMNER, W. G. *Folkways: A Study of the Sociological Importance of Usage, Manners, Customs, Mores, and Morals.* New York: The New American Library, 1960.

TATARA, T. "Understanding the Nature and Scope of Domestic Elder Abuse with the Use of State Aggregate Data: Summaries of Key Findings of a National Survey of State APS and Aging Agencies." *Journal of Elder Abuse and Neglect* 5 (1993): 35–37.

TAKAMURA, J. C., and GOLDEN, O. *The National Elder Abuse Incidence Study: Final Report.* Washington, D.C.: National Center on Elder Abuse, 1998.

WOLF, R. S. "Major Findings From the Three Model Projects on Elder Abuse." In *Elder Abuse: Conflict in the Family.* Edited by K. A. Pillemer and R. S. Wolf. Dover, Mass.: Auburn House, 1986. Pages 218–238.

WOLF, R. S.; GODKIN, M. A.; and PILLEMER, K. A. *Elder Abuse and Neglect: Final Report from Three Model Projects.* Worcester, Mass.: University Center on Aging, University of Massachusetts Medical Center, 1984.

WOLF, R. S., and PILLEMER, K. A. "What's New in Elder Abuse Programming? Four Bright Ideas." *The Gerontologist* 34 (1994): 126–129.

ELDER MISTREATMENT

See ELDER ABUSE AND NEGLECT

ELECTROCONVULSIVE THERAPY

Electroconvulsive therapy (ECT) involves the use of a brief electrical current to produce a seizure in the brain. Many studies have shown ECT to be an effective treatment for severe psychiatric disorders, particularly major depressive disorders. ECT is believed to work by regulating neurotransmitter systems in the brain, the same way other somatic (physical) psychiatric treatments (including medications) work.

Historical origins

ECT was discovered in Europe in the first part of the twentieth century. In 1934, a Hungarian psychiatrist, Ladislas von Meduna reported on the successful use of a chemical product, camphor, to induce epileptic seizures (convulsions) in a series of patients with schizophrenia. This form of convulsive therapy was found to be efficacious but extremely unpleasant. Four years later, the Italians Ugo Cerletti and Luigi Bini used electricity to induce seizures.

ECT was first used in the United States in 1940, and within a few years it became widely used. Following the development of effective psychiatric medications in the 1950s, the use of ECT and other somatic psychiatric treatments, such as psychosurgery, decreased markedly. However, a number of studies have shown that some patients who do not respond to medications can be treated successfully with ECT. As of 2000, it was estimated that about 100,000 American patients with severe psychiatric disorders were treated annually with ECT.

Indications

Over the years, ECT equipment and techniques have been perfected, and recent scientific studies have confirmed that ECT is an extremely safe and effective treatment. However, in large part due to its negative and sensational portrayal in the media, ECT remains a controversial treatment. As a result, it is usually used when pharmacotherapy (drug treatment) has been ineffective or poorly tolerated. Nevertheless, ECT can be used as a first-line treatment when a rapid response is needed—for instance to treat an actively suicidal patient; a depressed patient refusing fluids, food, or medications; a patient that presents with a recurrence of a disorder that has responded to ECT but not to medications in the past; or a patient that requests to be treated with ECT rather than medications.

ECT is mostly used to treat severe depressive episodes associated with recurrent depression, bipolar disorder (manic-depressive illness), or due to general medical conditions. ECT can also be used to treat other conditions when they have not responded to pharmacotherapy or when rapid treatment is needed; such conditions include manic episodes; schizophrenia and other psychotic disorders; catatonic states of any cause; or prominent depressive symptoms associated with Alzheimer's disease and other dementias. In rare instances, ECT has been used to treat other psychiatric disorders and some physical disorders (e.g., treatment-resistant Parkinson's disease). Older patients with severe depression often present with psychosis, suicidal thoughts, or refusal of food and fluid requiring rapid treat-

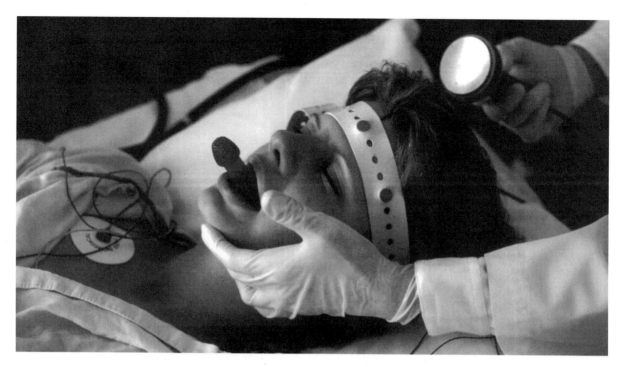

A woman undergoes electroconvulsive therapy at Duke University Medical Center. (Photo Researchers, Inc.)

ment. Thus, while age does not constitute an indication for, or a predictor of, favorable response to ECT, older patients are particularly likely to meet the current indications for ECT.

Risks

While there are no absolute contraindications to ECT, it should not be used when its associated risks outweigh its potential benefits. During the ECT procedure, intracranial pressure, heart rate, and blood pressure (and thus myocardial demand in oxygen) are increased. As a result, ECT should be avoided in patients with brain tumors, vascular aneurysms, recent myocardial or cerebral infarction, and severe pulmonary disease. Poor health status, rather than advancing age, increases the risk for the rare but potentially severe physical complications associated with general anesthesia and ECT, such as cardiac arrhythmias, aspiration pneumonia, spinal compression fractures, or mouth injury.

ECT does not appear to impair the ability to learn and retain new information and it is usually associated with subjective cognitive improvement. However, ECT may cause some objective cognitive impairment. This impairment typically consists of a transient inability to retrieve some memories, in particular for events occurring during the few months preceding or following the ECT course. In addition to these transient memory deficits, many patients also experience permanent memory loss for events occurring during the course of treatment, particularly events on treatment days. Cognitive impairment can be minimized with the use of the proper ECT techniques.

Elderly patients are at greater risks for prolonged confusion and even delirium, particularly when they suffer from a degenerative or vascular dementia. However, elderly patients presenting with a dementia syndrome associated with depression may experience a dramatic improvement in cognition when they are treated with ECT. Thus, cognitive impairment should not constitute by itself a contraindication to ECT.

Procedures

Typically, a course of ECT consists of a total of six to twelve treatments given over two to four weeks, with two or three treatments per week. All treatments are given under general anesthesia with patients being oxygenated and closely monitored. Once patients are asleep, they are given a paralyzing agent so that they can experience a seizure in their brain without motor convulsions. Two electrodes are then applied to the scalp and a brief controlled current is circulated from one electrode to the other through the patient's skull and brain. To minimize risks of confusion, treatment is usually initiated in older patients with unilateral ECT (i.e., with placement of both electrodes over the right-sided nondominant hemisphere). Regardless of electrode placement, a brief-pulse, square-wave current is now routinely used, since its efficacy is similar to a sine-wave current but it is less likely to induce significant adverse cognitive effects. Similarly, optimization of current intensity, based on a systematic determination of each patient's seizure threshold, has been shown to improve efficacy and to decrease cognitive impairment. ECT is typically discontinued once a patient's mood is back to baseline or when it reaches a plateau after two consecutive treatments. Once the acute course of ECT is completed, the majority of patients are given psychiatric medications to maintain their improvement and prevent relapses. In a small number of selected patients who exhibit a good response to ECT but relapse rapidly despite adequate continuation pharmacotherapy, the use of ECT can be continued. Typically, this consists of ECT given on an outpatient basis every two to four weeks for several months or years.

BENOIT H. MULSANT, M. D.

See also ANTIDEPRESSANTS; DEPRESSION.

BIBLIOGRAPHY

ABRAMS, R. *Electroconvulsive Therapy*, 3d. ed. New York: Oxford University Press, 1997.

American Psychiatric Association Committee on Electroconvulsive Therapy. *The Practice of Electroconvulsive Therapy: Recommendations for Treatment, Training, and Privileging*, 2d ed. Washington, D.C.: American Psychiatric Association, 2001.

OLFSON, M.; MARCUS, S.; SACKEIM, H. A.; THOMPSON, J.; and PINCUS, H. A. "Use of ECT for the Inpatient Treatment of Recurrent Major Depression." *American Journal of Psychiatry* 155 (1998): 22–29.

SACKEIM, H. A.; HASKETT, R. F.; MULSANT, B. H.; THASE, M. E.; MANN, J. J.; PETTINATI, H. M.; GREENBERG, R. M.; CROWE, R. R.; COOPER, T. B.; and PRUDIC, J. "Continuation Pharmacotherapy in the Prevention of Relapse Following Electroconvulsive Therapy." *Journal of the American Medical Association* 285, no. 10 (2001): 1299–1307.

SACKEIM, H. A.; PRUDIC, J.; DEVANAND, D. P.; NOBLER, M. S.; LISANSBY, S. H.; PEYSER, S.; FITZSIMMONS, L.; MOODY, B. J.; and CLARK, J. "A Prospective, Randomized, Double-Blind Comparison of Bilateral and Right Unilateral Electroconvulsive Therapy at Different Stimulus Intensities." *Archives of General Psychiatry* 57 (2000): 425–434.

TEW, J. D.; MULSANT, B. H.; HASKETT, R. F.; PRUDIC, J.; THASE, M. E.; CROWE, R.; DOLATA, D.; BEGLEY, A. E.; REYNOLDS, C. F.; and SACKEIM, H. A. "Acute Efficacy of ECT in the Treatment of Major Depression in the Old-Old." *American Journal of Psychiatry* 156 (1999): 1865–1870.

EMERGENCY ROOM

The hospital emergency department has become a very important access point for health care for elderly persons and this trend will likely continue. The emergency room serves as the site of hospital entry for many patients, with scheduled admissions largely restricted to elective surgical procedures. Elderly patients are more likely to enter the hospital via the emergency room than younger patients (Sanders). Typically, the overall hospital admission rate from an emergency room will be 10 to 30 percent, but admission rates in the population over sixty-five may exceed 40 percent.

Due to twenty-four-hour availability and the access to hospital-based technology, the emergency room has become an attractive site for patients with nonemergency medical problems. Call sharing by primary care physicians and their relative decline in numbers may result in increased emergency department use, although elderly persons are more likely to have a personal physician than are younger patients.

The emergency room has also become a safety net when a smooth transition from one health care facility or state of health is disrupted. With reductions in hospital length of stay, and the general patchwork of available home care, the emergency room has reluctantly assumed this role.

Numerous studies have confirmed the appropriateness of emergency room utilization by the elderly population (Gold and Bergman). Elderly adults tend to have multiple medical conditions, atypical presentation of common diseases, and significant issues in caregiver support, requiring complex assessment in the emergency room and high admission rates to hospital. Use of emergency medical services (ambulances) is also higher in the elderly population (Moir et al.). Although concerns have been raised about the appropriate use of ambulance services, often there are few alternatives for elderly adults because of limited transportation services, mobility problems, and the decline of the primary care physician house call.

The emergency room visit—what to expect

Due to high visit volumes, all emergency rooms utilize a triage system to sort patients by severity of illness or injury. This system inevitably results in waiting periods, especially for those with less acute problems. This can be frustrating for patients and family. Attempts should be made to make the emergency room environment more receptive to the needs of the elderly patient. A visit to the emergency room may be a key decision point in the health care of an elderly person. The decisions made during this visit may result in hospital admission, consideration of admission to a long-term care facility, or significant alterations in the home environment.

The medical history is a key component to the evaluation. This can be challenging and time consuming in a busy emergency environment. Obtaining a collateral history from family members, consulting with the primary care physician, and a review of all health records are critical. A precise review of current medication is important due to the high rate of polypharmacy in elderly persons and should include the use of over-the-counter medication.

Communication may be difficult due to cognitive deficits and reduction of hearing. A dignified approach to history taking cannot be overemphasized, since the Emergency Department is a confusing and frightening place for many patients. Use of a mental status screening tool such as the Mini-Mental Status Exam is a valuable tool to guide further evaluation (Moir et al.).

The physical examination needs to be thorough due to the often nonspecific symptoms of serious illness in elderly patients. Important features include a focused cardiovascular exam, ab-

dominal assessment, skin exam for evidence of cellulitis or skin ulcers, and an assessment of joint mobility (Wofford, Schwartz, and Byrum). Perhaps the most important part of the physical exam is observation of the ability to stand and walk independently. Many elderly patients live alone. If a patient cannot stand and walk, they cannot be safely discharged from the emergency room without significant additions of home care resources, usually beyond the scope of most current programs.

Due to the presence of many chronic medical conditions and high medication use, the use of laboratory and other tests such as x-rays is an important component of the emergency evaluation. Testing for low blood, blood sugar, and kidney function are routinely done. The high rate of osteoporosis means that x-rays should be requested liberally to detect fractures. Often a CT scan (brain x-ray) is necessary to determine head injury after a fall, or change in mental condition. The need for additional testing may prolong an emergency room visit but will help to make the correct disposition decision (Sinclair, Svendsen, and Marrie).

The disposition decision in the emergency room for an elderly patient is perhaps the most complex in emergency medicine. A functional approach must be made since often a definitive diagnosis cannot be made. Consideration of home support and social factors is paramount. The emergency room must act as a patient advocate due to the reduced availability of hospital beds, and fragmented home care resources. Patients and family need to be active participants in these decisions.

Many progressive emergency rooms have now added resources such as a discharge planning nurse and social workers to attempt to improve care for the elderly patient (Boyak and Bucknum). Traditional home care programs have limited use in the emergency department setting because of the length of time required for intake and limited resources available to individual patients. Home care programs specifically designed for the emergency department (often called Quick Response Programs or QRPs) include a rapid emergency department intake, and front-end loading of resources, including nursing, home support, rehabilitation services, and pharmacy support, to enable the safe discharge of patients who would have been admitted to hospital (Weir et al.).

Another recent innovation in emergency room care is the provision of a multidisciplinary geriatric assessment team for consultation (Gold and Bergman). This team may complete assessments in the emergency room or in the home environment and provide follow-up and admission to geriatric day hospitals or other programs. In conclusion, a visit to the emergency room is an often unavoidable event for an elderly person. Hopefully, a better understanding of its crucial role in health care decisions will assist patients and families during this stressful period.

DOUGLAS E, SINCLAIR, M.D.

See also ASSESSMENT; BALANCE AND MOBILITY; GERIATRIC ASSESSMENT UNIT; HOME VISITS.

BIBLIOGRAPHY

EAGLE, D. J.; RIDEOUT, E.; PRICE, P.; et al. "Misuse of the Emergency Department by the Elderly Population: Myth or Reality?" *Journal of Emergency Nursing* 19, no. 3 (1993): 212–218.
GERSON, L. W., and SKVARCH, L. "Emergency Medical Service Utilization by the Elderly." *Annals of Emergency Medicine* 11, no. 11 (1982): 610–612.
GOLD, S., and BERGMAN, H. "A Geriatric Consultation Team in the Emergency Department." *Journal of the American Geriatrics Society* 45 (1997): 764–767.
MOIR, V.; WILCOX, V.; RUKOWSKI, V.; and HIRIS, J. "Functional Transitions Among Elderly: Patterns, Predictors and Related Hospital Use." *American Journal of Public Health* 84, no. 8 (1994): 1274–1280.
SANDERS, A. B. "Care of the Elderly in Emergency Departments: Conclusions and Recommendations." *Annals of Emergency Medicine* 21, no. 7 (1992): 830–834.
SINCLAIR, D.; SVENDSEN, A.; and MARRIE, T. "Bacteremia in Nursing Home Patients: Prevalence Among Patients Presenting to an Emergency Department." *Canadian Family Physician* 44 (1998): 317–322.
WEIR, J.; BROWNE, G.; BYRNE, C.; et al. "The Efficacy and Efficiency of the Quick Response Program: A Randomized Controlled Trial." *Canadian Journal of Aging* 17, no. 3 (1998): 272–295.
WOFFORD, J. L.; SCHWARTZ, E.; and BYRUM, J. E. "The Role of Emergency Services in Health Care for the Elderly: A Review." *Journal of Emergency Medicine* 11 (1993): 317–326.

EMOTION

The term *emotion* or *affect* is used to refer to a broad class of behaviors that include facial and vocal expressions as well as neurological and physiological patterns. The term *feeling* refers to the subjective experience of emotion—which may last seconds or minutes—and the term *mood* involves feelings that last over a protracted period of time. The scientific study of emotional behavior, feelings, and moods has a relatively short history, and the study of emotion and aging has had even a more limited history. Fortunately, during the last two decades of the twentieth century, the field of psychology began to accumulate a great deal that is of importance to understanding emotion and the aging process.

Historical perspective

For most of recorded time, at least in the Western world, the vast majority of people, including scientists, regarded emotion as the antithesis of reason or rational thought. Emotion was also associated with being female—the other gender being ruled by logic. Furthermore, emotion was seen as a disruptive force in life, to be harnessed and controlled. Because of these implicit assumptions and stereotypes, emotion was not regarded as a fit topic for scientific research until Charles Darwin began to record the emotional expressions of animals and humans late in the nineteenth century and noted their evolutionary significance. His works introduced the idea that there were certain basic emotions and that emotions served adaptive functions—that is, that they were essential to survival rather than something that interfered with it. These basic emotions include anger, fear, sadness, disgust, shame, contempt, joy, interest, and surprise.

In the early part of the twentieth century, the behaviorist John Watson began using laboratory studies to examine the basic or fundamental emotions in human infants. Although he believed, along with Darwin, that certain emotions were innate, his studies showed that emotional behaviors were responses that could become "conditioned" and thus shape the personality of the child. However, his work did little to redeem the value of emotions in the mind of the public because he shared the view of most of his contemporaries that emotions caused pathological problems and needed to be constrained. In fact, in his popular childrearing guide of 1928, *Psychological Care of the Infant and Child,* he urged parents to strictly control their displays of affection toward their children and to engage in behaviors designed to ensure that children would dampen or suppress their emotions.

After a small flurry of research inspired by Watson's work, the field lay relatively dormant until the late 1970s. At this time, the theoretical contributions of Silvan Tomkins, Carroll Izard, Paul Ekman, and Robert Plutchik sparked a new wave of research on the emotions. These theories stressed the unique motivational, expressive, physiological, neurological, and feeling states of the basic emotions. They also repeated and amplified Darwin's notion that emotions are fundamentally adaptive, though of course certain conditions could lead to more problematic behaviors such as depression or anxiety disorder. The new surge of research inspired by these theories led to fresh insights on the role of emotion and moods on cognition, memory, personality, and interpersonal process; there was also a good deal of research on how emotional expressions of infants and children changed over time and how children learned to talk about their emotions.

Research on emotional development in adulthood and aging accumulated more slowly. In some of the early studies before the 1980s, the general impression of both the lay public and developmental psychologists was that aging was accompanied by a blunting of the emotions; people also thought that there was a drift toward negative affect over the adult years. However, this impression was based largely on studies of institutionalized persons and therefore hardly representative of the population at large, since, both then, as well as presently, only about 5 percent of the older population live in nursing homes.

Work on affect and aging that began in the 1980s took an entirely different approach. It started to examine emotion as a life course process, and the work on older adults at the upper end of the life span was based on persons living independent lives in their own communities. By the end of the twentieth century, there was a substantial corpus of theory as well as research mapping continuities and changes in emotion over the adult life course. The key figures in the field include Laura Carstensen, Caroll Izard, Gisela Labouvie-Vief, Powell Lawton, Carol Malatesta Magai, and Richard Schulz. The bulk of this literature has centered on issues of continuity and change in physiological patterns, expressive behavior, feeling states, emotion regulation, and emotion traits.

Emotions over the life course

Most of the research on continuities and change in emotional patterns during the adult years shows that the fundamental properties of the emotions remain relatively stable. However, there are also subtle changes.

Physiological patterns. The emotions are linked to certain anatomical sites in the brain such as the amgydala and to neurological and neurochemical processes that govern the autonomic nervous system. The chief way that psychologists have studied the physiological aspects of emotion involves monitoring the autonomic nervous system during states of emotional arousal. Although there has been a good deal of work on the physiological aspects of emotion during the latter decades of the twentieth century, research on adult development and aging is particularly meager. In one study that is relevant (Levenson, Carstensen, Friesen, and Ekman, 1991), participants were asked to participate in two emotion evoking conditions while their skin conductance, heart rate, and other physiological measures were monitored: to recollect and relive salient emotional events, and to make facial expressions of emotion. The researchers found that older people showed the same emotion-specific pattern of response as younger individuals, though the magnitude of the response was less pronounced in older subjects. That is, older people showed smaller increases in heart rate for anger, fear, and sadness. Nevertheless, the older participants reported the same degree of subjective emotional experience. In another relevant study (Levenson, Carstensen, and Gottman, 1994), where younger and older couples were asked to talk about neutral, problem, and pleasant situations with their spouses, the older couples had smaller heart rate increases and greater lengthening of pulse transmission time to ear, indicating less physiological reactivity.

A much larger body of literature has examined whether emotion inhibition—the deliberate attempt to suppress emotional feelings or expressions—alters physiological reactivity in adults. The literature indicates that emotionally inexpressive individuals are more physiologically reactive than expressive persons, though this does not necessarily mean that inexpressive persons deliberately inhibit their emotions. There is also literature indicating that the chronic inhibition of some emotions, particularly anger or hostility, is linked to essential hypertension and coronary heart disease. However, these correlational studies do not necessarily mean that emotion inhibition causes disease. Emotion-expressive or inhibitory patterns and health may both be influenced by a third factor such as genetic background. Experimental work helps clarify the pattern. Indeed, laboratory studies in which participants are asked to deliberately suppress their emotions while physiological measures are monitored, have shown that inhibition is associated with a number of changes in physiological measures and that the changes are emotion specific. For example, the inhibition of the visible expression of disgust causes an increase in parasympathetic arousal, as indexed by increased skin conductance and decreased finger pulse amplitude; in contrast, suppression of sadness expressions leads to cardiovascular activation. These findings have been obtained with college-age research participants. There are as yet no experimental investigations examining the effects of emotion inhibition in older respondents. Nor is it known what the consequence might be of a lifetime pattern of emotion inhibition, though it has been argued that if inhibition requires a form of "work," then prolonged or repeated efforts at inhibition may cause wear and tear on bodily systems and result in disease.

Expressive patterns. There is a more substantial body of literature concerning expressive behavior, almost all of it having to do with facial expressions of emotion; this literature goes beyond the study of the association between facial expressions and physiological reactions. For the most part, the literature on facial expressions has centered on changes in the expression of emotion with development as well as changes in sensitivity to the perception of emotion in others.

Changes in emotion expression. In early development, facial expressions of emotion, which are innate and gradually unfold during the opening months of life, become more modulated and take on the characteristics of family and culture. In general, expressive behavior becomes more conventionalized, and this includes a dampening of expressive behavior; these changes are well in place by adolescence. But there are also changes during the adult years. For example, one study showed that when emotional memories were prompted and subjects asked to relate their experiences, older adults were more facially expressive in terms of the frequency of emotional expressions than younger individuals across a range of emotions, as detected by an objective facial affect coding system (Malalesta-Magai, Jonas, Shephard, and Culver, 1992). In another study, researchers also found that the expressions of older adults (women in this case) were more telegraphic in the sense that their expressive behaviors tended to involve fewer regions of the face, and yet more complex in that they used more blended or mixed expressions when recounting emotional events (Malatesta and Izard, 1984). These changes, in part, account for why the facial expressions of older adults are more difficult to read.

One of the other changes that comes with age that make older faces more difficult to read involves the wrinkling of the facial skin and the sag of facial musculature. What is particularly interesting is that the pattern of wrinkling is so different across individuals. Of course, part of this is due to biologically based aspects of aging, but individual differences also appear linked to personality process. One study (Malatesta, Fiore, and Messina, 1987) was able to show that facial patterns were related to dominant personality characteristics. For example, persons who tended to experience contempt frequently, had facial expressions that looked contempt-like, even when they were attempting to pose other kinds of emotion—that is, the contempt that was dominant in their personalities tended to leak through and contaminate the clarity of the posed expressions.

Other studies have looked at expressive behaviors in late life and under conditions of dementia. These studies, using observational methods and objective coding of facial and bodily expressions, indicate that for the most part the expressive behavior of dementia patients resembles that of nondemented older adults (Magai, Cohen, Gomberg, Malatesta, and Culver, 1996). The entire range of basic emotion expressions can be detected, and recognizable facial expressions of emotion are observed across the spectrum of cognitive deterioration, including the most severely impaired, end-stage patients, although there are changes with advancing intellectual impairment. Of note, there is a lower frequency and duration of happiness or pleasure, especially in the later stages of the disease. These findings indicate that the ability to express affect, as observed in interpersonal contexts, remains intact during the course of one form of debilitating disease, dementia; in fact, sensitivity to affect encoded in nonverbal communication may be even more acute in dementia patients since the neuronal fallout associated with dementia releases cortical inhibitory control of the centers that control emotion.

Emotion expressions seen in dementia patients appear linked to precipitating events in the environment rather than constituting random muscle movement patterns. For example, one study showed that as patients—all of whom were moderately to severely impaired—were observed during a family visit, their faces expressed sadness when their relatives prepared to leave (Malatesta et al., 1996).

Changes in sensitivity to the expressive behavior of others. A few studies have looked at potential age-related changes in the ability to read the expressive behavior of social partners. In one study (Malatesta, Izard, Culver, and Nicolich, 1987), where older and younger individuals were asked to identify negative and neutral facial expressions, the older adults were significantly less accurate than the younger participants. Similarly, in another study, where young, middle-aged, and older untrained "judges" attempted to label the facial expressions of other young, middle-aged, and older women, the older women did most poorly, but their performance was best for older faces. This suggests that contact with like-aged peers assists the process of understanding the emotional messages of interactants. Moreover, older individuals may have a greater facility in discounting the "noise" of facial wrinkling so as to discern the essential emotional messages of older social partners.

A handful of other studies have examined sensitivity to other nonverbal channels of emotion expression. One study found an overall decline in the ability of older adults to identify specific emotions from vocal indicators (Allen and Brosgole, 1993). In another case, where researchers examined age-related differences in the ability of adults to read emotion signals through body movements and gestures, the study found that while both younger and older adults made accurate emotion identifications well above chance levels, older adults made more errors overall. They were especially inaccurate with negative emotions, and were especially likely to misidentify emotional displays as being neutral in content (Montepare, Koff, Zaitchik, and Albert, 1999). It must be noted, however, that the actors who depicted the emotions were all young adults, and if age congruence between sender and receiver makes a difference, as one study suggested, this research will bear replication.

In summary, the data on the expression and perception of emotion across the life span indicates that there are developmental trends indicating increased complexity of facial expressions in terms of greater idiosyncratic responses, increased use of blended affect, and changes in facial musculature and skin elasticity, all of which make it more difficult to read the emotional expressions of adults as they age. However, this is compensated by familiarity with social peers. Moreover, since expressive behavior does not occur in a vacuum, but is typically accompanied by verbal expressions of emotion, the above findings do not suggest that older adults are at risk for misinterpretation of their feelings. Indeed, there is a small but substantive body of literature indicating that older adults up through middle age become more adept at describing their experiences than younger adults, and that their descriptions are more complex and nuanced; very old persons, however, seem to show a decline in this ability, though this may be a cohort effect, that is, one related to the historical epoch in which they were reared, rather than an aging effect per se. Persons born earlier in the twentieth century were born during less child-centered and permissive times and their parents were exposed to the exortations of John Watson, who remonstrated against the open expression of emotion and physical affection. In terms of the perception of emotion in others, the slim literature that exists suggests that there may be declines in the accuracy with which nonverbal emotion signals are understood, though age congruence between social partners may compensate.

Feeling states. Research in this area has covered the frequency and intensity of emotion states, as well as the quality of emotional feelings; the latter have included the salience of emotional stimuli and their ability to elicit emotional reactions, hedonic tone (pleasure/unpleasure), discrete emotions (anger, fear, sadness, etc.), and emotional complexity (emotional/cognitive interaction).

Intensity. Although there are conflicting data on changes in affective intensity with age, in general, studies have indicated that there is no substantive decline in affective intensity or the intensity with which a person experiences emotions. This pattern holds true when adults of different ages are asked to gauge whether the intensity of their emotions has changed over the years, when they report the intensity of their emotional experiences as sampled randomly throughout the day, or when they recount emotional experiences in the laboratory.

Hedonic tone.   In terms of general hedonic tone, the bulk of the literature indicates that the frequency or level of positive affect either remains the same or increases over the adult years until very late in life, when there is a decline. In terms of negative affect, the most sophisticated studies seem to indicate that there is a gradual lessening of negative affect over the adult years up to approximately age sixty, after which there is a nonsignificant increase. The subtle changes in positive and negative affect during late life are likely linked to release from childrearing and work roles—in the case of gains in happiness—and chronic debilitating illnesses of old age as well as the deaths of important intimates such as spouses and friends—in the case of negative affect.

Discrete emotions.   Investigators have also looked at changes in discrete emotions—that is, the various emotions that comprise positive affect and negative affect. This is the area of greatest disparity in findings, largely due to the use of different methodologies for assessing change and stability in emotion, and in the range and kinds of emotions sampled. However, one fairly consistent finding stands out. Across a range of studies, both cross-sectional and longitudinal in nature, results indicate that there is a decrease in the level and frequency of anger across the adult years. The reason for this may relate to the functional role of anger, which is to overcome obstacles and barriers to goals. To the extent that age brings with it changes in a reduction of blocked goals, its prevalence should decline. Research has also suggested that older adults shift from an external to internal strategy to control feelings associated with success and failure of goals. Rather than acting on the environment—expressing anger openly—they may use more internally controlled responses such as positive reframing or repression. Finally, as social networks narrow and older adults depend on a fewer, more intimate partners for their socioemotional needs, the expression of anger may pose a threat to these relationships.

In terms of emotional complexity, in memory tasks, narrative analyses of recollected emotional experiences, and in experience-sampling methodologies, research indicates that emotional experience becomes more complex across the adult years. In the experience-sampling work, older adults report more mixed and bittersweet emotions and more poignancy within the same sampled moment. Older adults also orient to the emotional significance of events more so than younger adults. For example, when older and younger participants were asked to recall narrative material that they had read, older individuals recalled more of the emotional versus the neutral material. In recounting emotional experiences, young adults rarely refer to inner subjective feelings and are likely to describe their experiences in terms of normative proscriptions; middle-aged adults, in contrast, are able to acknowledge complex feelings, are less influenced by conventional standards, and can sustain feelings of ambivalence and tension without needing to resolve them immediately. Moreover, research indicates that emotional complexity—the interaction between emotion and cognition and their integration—appears to improve with age, although the data also suggest that this trend peaks during middle age, after which there is a decline.

In summary, emotions become more important to individuals as they mature, they are better at tolerating mixed feelings, and there is a deepening appreciation of the emotional complexity of the world both within and around the self. The fact that these trends do not continue into old age, at least on the basis of this research, may be related to cohort effects and/or to changes in emotional regulatory strategies, as discussed in the next section.

Emotion regulation.   Emotion regulation is the ability to modulate feeling states and emotional responses in reaction to emotional elicitors. People can moderate emotion by avoiding emotionally charged situations, by cognitive strategies such as denial and intellectualization, or by engaging in processes that permit the cognitive elaboration and integration of experience. The literature suggests that there is an age trend toward *affective optimization* or the tendency of persons to actively create environments that permit them to achieve a better mix of emotionally stimulating versus insulating features. Older adults also report greater abilities to control their emotions and to moderate affective responses. However, there are also distinct individual differences in terms of the tendency to dampen versus elaborate emotional experiences. One style, which is responsible for maintaining an affectively positive self core involves *equilibrium-regulating* strategy; negative affect is dampened, lessening the deviation from positive affect. In contrast, the other style, an *affect-elaborating* strategy, permits movement into a zone that is more chaotic or unstable; it tolerates and even seeks out a range of experience and is therefore more flexible and results in the ability to integrate positive and negative affect. There may be a preference for affect dampening strategies in old age, given greater physical frailty and reduced energy reserves. If so, this would explain why older persons seem oriented toward actively avoiding conflict. Another means by which older adults accomplish affective regulation involves the selective narrowing of social networks. Both cross-sectional and longitudinal studies show that adults shed more peripheral relationships in later life, while retaining those that are most intimate and emotionally gratifying.

In summary, the literature on emotion regulation indicates that there is increasing facility at emotion regulation with age. Some of this is achieved through an ability to tolerate and sustain ambiguity and mixedness of experience and to integrate positive and negative affect, while some is due to active avoidance of emotionally charged circumstance and the narrowing of social relationships.

Emotion in personality.   As people mature their personalities become more stable or crystallized. That is, a young woman who is extroverted is likely to be extroverted in later life as well; a man who shows neurotic behavior in his thirties, is likely to show these same features in his fifties and sixties.

One personality dimension, sensitization/repression, relates to the way in which persons habitually attend to or avoid emotionally disturbing or threatening stimuli. Repressors tend to avoid or disattend to threatening stimuli or to route them from consciousness, whereas sensitizers monitor the environment for the presence of such stimuli. The literature indicates that these tendencies are relatively stable over short periods of time; less is known about the stability of these traits over longer stretches of the adult life course, however, sensitization is related to trait anxiety and thus stability for this characteristic may be quite strong, as indicated in the literature on trait emotion.

Many dimensions of personality have an affective aspect to them. Some theorists have even argued that personalities are organized around distinctive affective patterns or emotional traits. Indeed, on an informal basis, it is widely observed that some individuals are more hostile than others, some more somber, some more ebullient, and so forth. The empirical research on emotion traits has generated substantial support for this observation. These affective organizations create emotionally biased ways of processing the world that affect attention, perception, memory, judgment, and other cognitive processes, and also affect behavior and interpersonal process. Emotion traits for the broad dimensions of positive and negative affect, as well as the specific mood states of anxiety, sadness, and anger, among others, have shown substantial stability over months and even years. Such data suggest that emotional moods may represent enduring dispositions. However, these stability figures mask individual differences in change. Sophisticated modeling procedures indicate that there are substantial inter-individual differences in longitudinal change over a number of years, at least when it comes to broad personality traits such as neuroticism and extroversion; some people's trajectory remains level, others show increases, and still others show decline. Inter-individual differences in the pattern of personality change may as well hold for more circumscribed emotion traits or aspects of emotional organization, as suggested by a slim but growing literature.

Given the evidence of both stability and change, some commentators have suggested that one of the more challenging jobs for today's personality researchers is to account for the processes underlying personality change. Examination of the factors that support personality change have only begun, but two factors have emerged. There is some preliminary evidence that severe illness can precipitate personality change. Another major precipitant appears to involve emotionally charged events that involve interpersonal process. Events associated with change include psychotherapy, and participation in groups, workshops, or retreats, where intense affiliative relationships are experienced. One study (Magai, 1999) tracked changes in adults' emotion traits and their perspectives, goals, personality, feelings, and ways of relating to others over an eight-year period, using personality scales, as well as self-reports and observer reports. There was evidence of both stability and change. Emotion traits tended to remain stable, although individual differences were also in evidence. An aggregate measure of personality change in terms of ratings on feelings, attitudes, and goals, indicated that change was associated with positive and negative interpersonal life events including marriage, divorce, and death of loved ones. Change was unassociated with other emotionally charged high and low points in people's lives such as job losses, career advances, changes in residence, and more distant social relationships.

In summary, there is substantial support for the stability of emotion traits in personality when mean level or aggregate data are examined. When individual trajectories are examined, we find more evidence of inter-individual variation, with some persons evidencing no change, other showing increments or decrements. It is now clear that structural change in personality, including aspects related to emotional organization, is possible under certain circumstances. Experiences with acute or chronic illness is one such precipitant, and emotionally charged interpersonal encounters is another. However, a full description of the causes, the process, and the types of affective change have yet to be charted.

Summary

This entry covered the issue of continuity and/or change in aspects of emotional development over the life course of adults, including physiology, expressive behavior, subjective experience, emotion regulation, and emotion traits. The substantial literature that accumulated over the last two decades of the twentieth century, during an upsurge of research on emotions in the adult years, indicates that emotional capacities remain functional across the life span. There are, however, some changes, refinements, and upper boundaries to emotional development. The literature indicates that physiological patterns remain relatively unmodified, though the amplitude of responses appear somewhat reduced. In terms of phenomenology, however, the subjective aspects remain relatively intact in terms of intensity, hedonic balance, and frequency of distinct affective experiences. Changes include a decrease in the level and frequency of anger, which is a robust finding across cross-sectional and longitudinal studies. The data also indicate a curvilinear function with respect to emotional complexity, with a peak in middle age,

although there are strong individual differences as well; complexity appears to undergo a change in later life, with a preference for positivity over complexity, though it is not yet clear that this is a true developmental change or an artifact of the fact that work on affective complexity has relied only on cross-sectional studies. Expressive behavior becomes more nuanced and complexly textured. In terms of the perception of affect, the ability to read emotional signals of a facial, vocal, or bodily nature may become less accurate with age, although it is difficult to ascertain with certainty since, again, the studies involved have been cross-sectional rather than longitudinal. The literature also suggests that people become more comfortable with their emotional selves as they age, that they are more likely to acknowledge their emotional states and to recognize and acknowledge the mixedness of affective life. Emotions apparently become more complex and experienced more keenly, even as emotion regulation capacities in general improve, in the sense that there is greater affective control in maintaining positive states and avoiding negative states. The organization of emotion in personality is a relatively enduring trait, although also responsive to environmental challenge, at which point both positive and negative transformations may evolve. All in all, the picture of emotional development across the adult years, based on empirical research rather than stereotype, is more positive than the earlier literature in the field indicated. Adults do not become more affectively blunted with age; neither is there a drift toward negative affect.

The above relatively sanguine picture of emotional aging is tempered by the recognition that at very advanced ages the picture may change. In any case, the literature thus far only begins to map the trajectory of emotional life in adults and there is clearly room for further research, especially longitudinal studies that will help clarify whether age differences observed in cross-sectional studies are really age changes or an artifact of cohort differences.

CAROL MAGAI

See also ANXIETY; DEPRESSION; PERSONALITY.

BIBLIOGRAPHY

CARSTENSEN, L. L. "Social and Emotional Patterns in Adulthood: Support for Socioemotional Selectivity Theory. *Psychology and Aging* 7 (1992): 331–338.

LABOUVIE-VIEF, G.; HAKIN-LARSON, J.; DEVOE, M.; and SCHOEBERLEIN, S. "Emotions and Self-regulation: A Lifespan View." *Human Development* 32 (1989): 279–299.

LAWTON, M. P. "Environmental Proactivity and Affect in Older People." In *The Social Psychology of Aging.* Edited by S. Spacapan and S. Oskamp. Newbury Park, Calif.: Sage, 1989. Pages 135–163.

LEVENSON, R. W.; CARSTENSEN, L.; FRIESEN, W. V.; and EKMAN, P. "Emotion, Physiology and Expression in Old Age." *Psychology and Aging* 6 (1991): 28–35.

LEVENSON, R. W.; CARSTENSEN, L. L.; and GOTTMAN, J. M. "The Influence of Age and Gender on Affect, Physiology, and their Interrelations: A Study of Long-term Marriages." *Journal of Social and Personality Psychology* 67 (1994): 56–68.

MAGAI, C., and MCFADDEN, S. H., eds. *The Role of Emotion in Social and Personality Development.* New York: Plenum, 1995.

MAGAI, C. "Emotion Over the Lifecourse." In *Handbook of the Psychology of Aging.* Edited by J. Birren and K. W. Schaie. San Diego: Academic Press. Forthcoming.

SCHULZ, R., and HECKHAUSEN., J. "Emotion and Control: A Life-Span Perspective." In *Annual Review of Gerontology and Geriatrics.* Series edited by P. Lawton. Vol. 17, *Focus on Emotion and Adult Development.* Volume edited by K. W. Schaie. New York: Springer, 1998. Pages 185–205.

EMPLOYEE HEALTH INSURANCE

Almost one out of every seven dollars spent in the United States is spent on health care, with average expenditures per person increasing with age. It is not surprising, then, that health care insurance is of primary importance not only for all Americans, but especially for aging Americans. While all individuals over the age of sixty-five are eligible for Medicare, the federal government program of health insurance for elderly persons, the predominant option for adults under the age of sixty-five is health insurance that is related to employment. With a focus on individuals nearing traditional retirement age, this article will discuss the history and economic theory behind employer-provided health insurance, the prevalence and types of coverage provided, the impacts on work and retirement decisions of having health insurance be tied to employment, and recent legislation of health insurance in the United States.

The history and economic theory of employer-provided health insurance

Prior to World War II, very few American companies provided health insurance for their employees, and less than half of the U.S. population was covered by health insurance. During the war, however, as soldiers went to serve overseas, there was a shortage of workers back home. The combination of a reduced supply of workers, a booming economy, and rationing of scarce consumer goods led the government to impose price and wage freezes to try to limit inflation. Since employers were not allowed to increase wages to attract new workers, they began offering fringe benefits such as health insurance as a way to attract and keep workers. Thus, having employer-provided health insurance became prevalent not because of economic justification for insurance being linked with employment, but as a way for employers to circumvent the wage freezes imposed by government.

A second factor that has contributed significantly to the prevalence of employer-provided health insurance is a special tax treatment such that while wages are subject to taxation, employees do not have to pay any income tax for health insurance benefits. This has provided a strong financial incentive for employees to get insurance from their employer rather than purchasing insurance privately, since these insurance policies are essentially purchased with pre-tax dollars. In the 1950s, when federal marginal tax rates reached over 90 percent (meaning that an individual must pay more than 90 cents in taxes for each additional dollar in income), the tax incentives were particularly intense, and thus the momentum begun by the labor shortages during the war continued long after the war. While marginal tax rates are much lower than they were in the 1950s, a study in 2000 by Anne Beeson Royalty found that the tax rate continues to have a significant effect on employer-provided health care—a one-point increase in the marginal tax rate increases the probability an employee will be offered employer-provided health insurance by almost 1 percent. The Congressional Budget Office estimated that having health insurance benefits be tax-free reduced government tax revenue by $120 billion in 2001.

Although it may seem that having employers provide insurance is a benefit to the employee and a cost to the employer, according to economic theory the employee pays the cost of insurance in the form of lower wages. The demand for workers depends on the total compensation that employers must pay, both wages and fringe benefits; if total compensation is higher, the firm is not willing to hire as many workers. The supply of workers is determined by how many workers are willing to work at various compensation levels. If an employer offers health insurance benefits at the current wage, the total compensation package increases and more people are willing to work. Thus, if employers offer health insurance while keeping wages the same, there will be a surplus of workers because employers want to hire a smaller number of workers at the same time that more workers are willing to be employed.

The result of a surplus of workers is a reduction in wages until wages reach the point where the number of workers a firm wants to hire equals the number of workers willing to work at that compensation level. Because the supply of workers is less sensitive to wage changes than the demand for workers, most of the cost of insurance gets passed on to the worker in the form of lower wages. The lower wages may not happen immediately, since employers are often hesitant to reduce employee wages, but more likely will happen over time in the form of smaller raises to compensate for the higher benefits package. The bottom line, from the economic theory, is clear; the cost of health insurance gets passed on to the employee in the form of lower wages. (For more discussion of this, see Mark Pauly's book *Health Benefits at Work*, which provides a thorough, nontechnical explanation of the economic theory of who pays for employer-provided health insurance. For a more technical treatment, see B. Mitchell and Charles Phelps's 1976 article in the *Journal of Political Economy*.)

Prevalence and types of health insurance coverage

Approximately 84 percent of the United States population has some type of health insurance coverage. This coverage comes from one of five sources: (1) health insurance provided by an employer, (2) individual insurance policies purchased in the private market, (3) Medicaid (the government program for low-income families), (4) Medicare (the government program for disabled persons and elderly persons), and (5) military or veterans insurance. Figure 1 shows the percentage of individuals with each type of insurance, by age, for individuals between 25 and 64 years of age. Individuals age 65 and older (not shown in the graph) are eligible for Medicare and thus have the highest rate of insurance, with 98.9 percent of this population covered by insurance. Less than 14 percent of individuals age 45 to 64 are uninsured, compared to over 16 percent of individuals age 35 to 44, and over 22 percent of individuals age 25 to 34. Thus the rate of insurance is quite high for the elderly and near-elderly, relative to younger adults.

The type of insurance coverage varies dramatically with age, with the youngest and oldest workers being least likely to receive coverage from employer-based insurance. Only 65 percent of individuals age 55 to 64 receive employer-provided health insurance, compared to 74 percent of individuals age 45 to 54. These older individuals (age 55 to 64) counter this lack of employer-provided insurance with a greater reliance on the individual insurance market. Over 8 percent of the near-elderly purchase individual insurance, almost twice as many as in other age groups. Finally, Medicare is an important provider of insurance for those age 55 to 64 as they begin to experience escalating health problems, with almost 6 percent qualifying for Medicare because of disability.

The average rate of insurance for individuals nearing retirement age masks some important differences experienced by subgroups of this population. Richard Johnson and Stephen Crystal (1997) did a detailed breakdown of insurance coverage for a sample of 12,000 individuals age 53 to 64 who were interviewed about their health and insurance in 1992, and again in 1994. In their sample, 75 percent of the individuals in this age group were covered by employment-based insurance, 9 percent had no insurance coverage, and the other 16 percent were covered by government insurance (including Medicare and Medicaid) or privately purchased insurance.

While Johnson and Crystal found no gender differences in the prevalence of coverage by employer-provided insurance, 11 percent of women in the sample had no insurance, compared to only 7 percent of men. However, this gender difference is primarily related to differences in marital status rather than gender itself. Women are less likely to be currently married, and married couples are significantly more likely to be covered by insurance than individuals who are not married (8 percent of married individuals have no insurance, compared to 16 percent of divorced, 17 percent of widowed, and 12 percent of never-married individuals). These differences in insurance coverage by marital status are directly related to employment-based insurance. Seventy-eight percent of married individuals are covered by employment-based insurance (either their own or their spouse's) compared to only 55 to 60 percent of those not currently married.

Race and education also play a role in whether an individual has employment-based insurance, other insurance, or no insurance at all. African Americans are more than twice as likely to have no insurance coverage than whites (14.2 percent compared to 7 percent), and Hispanics are almost four times as likely to have no insurance than whites (27.7 percent compared to 7 percent). Similar differences can be seen in coverage by employment-based insurance (78 percent of whites have employment-based insurance compared to 62.8 percent of African Americans and 48.8 percent of Hispanics). The more education an individual has, the less likely there will be no insurance coverage and the greater the likelihood of employment-based insurance. For example, 23.2 percent of individuals who have no high school education have no insurance and 43.8 percent of these individuals have employment-based insurance, while only 4.2 percent of those with a college degree have no insurance and 85.4 percent have employment-based insurance.

It is also informative to examine how employer-provided insurance varies by the type of employer. Just over half of all firms (52.4 percent) offer some form of major health insurance plan. Firms in the manufacturing industry are most likely to offer insurance (68.4 percent), while those in agriculture, forestry, and fishing are least likely to offer it (21.6 percent). Large firms are much more likely to offer insurance than small firms are, so while only 52.4 percent of firms offer insurance, those firms that do offer insurance employ 85.7 percent of the workers in America. For example, 98.2 percent of firms with more than one thousand employees offer insurance, compared to only 63.5 percent of firms with ten to twenty-four employees and 32.9 percent of firms with less than ten employees.

There are three primary types of insurance plans that are offered by employers: fee-for-service plans, health maintenance organizations (HMOs), and preferred provider organizations (PPOs). Under a fee-for-service plan, health care providers are reimbursed based on the care they provide, with the patient usually required to pay either a deductible or co-payment (a percentage of the total cost of care). Fee-for-service plans offer patients the greatest flexibility, as there is often no restriction on what doctor a patient can see. Under HMO insurance, the HMO receives a fixed amount of money per person enrolled, regardless of the actual care provided. This provides an incentive for HMOs to consider not only the health benefits of providing a test or procedure, but also the financial costs. Patients are required to see only doctors who are included in the plan (unless the patient is referred to a specialist by a doctor in the HMO) in order to have insurance pay for the visit. PPOs are similar to HMOs in that patients have a certain network of doctors that they can see; however, patients do have greater flexibility because if they choose to see a doctor who is not a part of the network their insurance will still pay a portion of the cost of the visit.

Johnson and Crystal found that workers age fifty-three to sixty-four who are receiving employer-provided insurance are fairly evenly split between the three types of plans (29 percent have an HMO, 28 percent have a PPO, and 40 percent have fee-for-service). Firms with fewer employees (particularly less than fifteen employees) who offer health insurance are more likely to offer fee-for-service than either a HMO or PPO. While some employers offered employees the choice of more than one type of plan, less than half of those covered by employer-provided insurance had such a choice (42 percent) and most of those who did have a choice were in large firms or were making high hourly wages. The amount that employees had to contribute towards premiums (cost-sharing) was very similar across all three types of plans.

The effects of employer-provided health insurance on work and retirement decisions

The near-elderly face important decisions about work and retirement. While almost three-quarters of individuals between the ages of fifty-five and sixty-one were employed in 1996, less than half of those age sixty-two to sixty-four were working, and many were only working part-time.

Some of this early retirement is by choice, but some of it is because of declining health status or employer cutbacks. Almost one-third of the near-elderly that were not working in 1996 reported illness or disability as the reason they were not working. (The breakdown of those not working was: 47.2 percent retirement, 30.4 percent ill or disabled, 18.9 percent caring for home or family, 1.5 percent could not find work, and 2 percent other factors.)

Since the majority of individuals receive health insurance from their employers, leaving the labor force before age sixty-five (the age at which an individual becomes eligible for Medicare) may result in a loss of health insurance coverage. Fewer than 40 percent of large employers offered health coverage for retirees in 1998, compared to 60 to 70 percent during the 1980s. In addition, retirees often have to share the cost of employer-provided insurance by paying a higher premium than workers; in 1995 a retired worker's contribution to employer-provided health insurance was, on average, $2,340—$655 more per year than the contribution of active workers. For individuals who do not receive employer-provided health care if they retire, purchasing insurance in the private market is often quite expensive. A General Accounting Office survey of selected health insurance companies found that a healthy sixty-four year old male can expect to pay between $100 and $300 per month more in premiums than a healthy twenty-five year old male, while an older male with high health risks may pay between $300 and $600 more per month than his younger, healthy counterpart—if the high-risk man can find an insurance company that will offer him any coverage at all. As a result, older workers who would like to retire may find that the loss of health insurance prevents them from being able to retire.

There have been some government regulations that attempt to ease the burden for those who lose their employer-provided insurance, either because they choose to retire early, have health conditions that necessitate their early retirement, or lose their job for other reasons. The Consolidated Omnibus Budget Reconciliation Act of 1985, often referred to as COBRA, allows workers and their families that have left jobs providing health insurance to continue to purchase the group policy for up to eighteen months. However, the employee must pay the entire premium amount plus a 2 percent administrative fee. Another major piece of legislation, the Health Insurance Portability and Accountability Act of 1996 (HIPAA), helps to ease the transition if an individual changes jobs or switches from employer-provided health care to individually purchased health care. HIPAA limits insurance company exclusions for pre-existing conditions, prohibits discrimination against employees based on health status, and guarantees that individuals who have been receiving health insurance are able to purchase individual insurance policies (although it does not limit the premiums the insurance company can charge for the policy).

Despite these government efforts to make it easier for workers to switch jobs or retire early by removing barriers related to health insurance, numerous studies find that having employer-provided health insurance has a large impact on the retirement and work decisions of the near-elderly. Bridgette Madrian and Nancy Dean Beaulieu (1998) reviewed nine economic studies that used different data sets and methodologies and found that having retiree health benefits or the option of purchasing continuing coverage (such as COBRA) significantly increases the likelihood than an individual will retire early. For example, one of these studies, by Jonathan Gruber and Madrian, found that the availability of continuing coverage (through COBRA and various state laws that applied prior to COBRA) could explain as much as 60 percent of the rise in retirement for males fifty-five to sixty-four years old during the 1980s. However, while legislation such as COBRA and HIPAA may give the near-elderly more choices for when to retire, having health insurance tied to employers may still provide a large barrier to job changes or early retirements. Jeannette Rogowski and Lynn Karoly (2000) found that older male workers (in their late fifties and early sixties) with health benefits that continue after retirement are 68 percent more likely to retire than those who have employer-based coverage that only covers current workers.

Major legislation affecting employer-provided health insurance

Both COBRA and HIPPA are amendments to a previous piece of legislation on retirement and pensions, the Employee Retirement Income Security Act of 1974 (ERISA). As was discussed above, one concern about having health insurance tied to employment is that workers may lose their insurance coverage if they change jobs, retire, or lose their job for any reason. In response to this, COBRA was enacted in 1986 to help workers and their families continue to receive group health care coverage even if they are no longer at the same job.

There are conditions for eligibility for both the employer and the worker. The employer must offer health insurance benefits as a part of the worker benefit package and employ more than twenty employees. The worker or family member must have lost coverage of employee-provided group health insurance for one of the following qualifying events: voluntary or involuntary termination of employment for any reason other than gross misconduct; a reduction of hours of work for the employee, the employee became eligible for Medicare but wants to continue coverage for a spouse or dependent, a divorce or legal separation from a covered employee, death of a covered employee, or an individual is no longer a dependent child of the employee.

Individuals who meet the employer and employee requirements above may choose to purchase the group health insurance the employer had provided for a period of eighteen months if the qualifying event is a change in employment, or thirty-six months if the qualifying event is a change in family structure. The individual may be required to pay the entire premium for coverage plus a 2 percent administrative fee (a total of 102 percent of the premium price) as well as paying whatever deductibles or co-insurance that are part of the insurance plan. Individuals who want to use COBRA must notify their employer within sixty days of becoming eligible for coverage.

COBRA provides an opportunity for workers to continue to receive health insurance as the bridge between jobs, or to retire prior to age sixty-five. Despite this, studies find that only a small proportion of the near-elderly use COBRA—only 21 percent of those who become eligible for COBRA enroll. However, the rate is higher for those who become eligible because a spouse became eligible for Medicare, with 60 percent electing to participate in COBRA. In addition, only 10 percent of the near-elderly who use COBRA use it for the entire eighteen (or thirty-six) month period, with the average length of use being only one year. Part of the reason for the low take-up rates may be the cost of coverage. While COBRA limits that the premiums for a

policy be at the same price as the employer pays, there is no longer an employer subsidy of premiums. The General Accounting Office reports that the average total annual premium for employer-provided health coverage is $3,820, a potentially large financial strain for a retiree or someone between jobs. (For more information on the regulations for COBRA, see the U.S. Department of Labor publication *Health Benefits Under the Consolidated Omnibus Budget Reconciliation Act*; for more information on the use of COBRA see chapter five of the General Accounting Office publication *Insurance Access for 55- to 64-Year Olds*.)

The Health Insurance Portability and Accountability Act of 1996 (HIPAA) is designed to make it easier for people to change jobs without losing health coverage. HIPAA limits exclusions for pre-existing conditions, prohibits discrimination in enrollment and in premiums charged to employees in group health plans (such as employer-provided health care) based on their health status, and guarantees renewability and availability of individual health insurance plans for people not covered by group plans—provided they have exhausted their other insurance options.

Many individuals may be hesitant to switch jobs or insurance plans for fear that current health problems will not be covered due to pre-existing conditions clauses in insurance policies. HIPAA seeks to reduce this constraint by limiting health insurance exclusions for pre-existing conditions. If an individual has had prior medical problems but has not received medical advice, diagnosis, care, or treatment for the condition during the six months prior to enrollment in a health insurance plan, the plan cannot exclude coverage for the condition. In addition, if there is a pre-existing condition during the six months prior to enrollment, the insurance company can only exclude coverage for the condition for a maximum of twelve months if an individual enrolled in a plan as soon as he or she was eligible for the plan, or for eighteen months if the individual enrolled in the plan at a date later than the eligibility date. The twelve (or eighteen) month period can be shortened if an individual is switching from one insurance plan to another insurance plan, since the length of time the individual received the earlier insurance coverage counts towards the twelve (or eighteen) month time limit, provided that there is not a break in insurance coverage of more than sixty-three days. (For example, if someone has been receiving employer-provided health insurance for the previous eight months and then decides to purchase a different insurance policy, as long as the new policy is purchased within sixty-three days of when the earlier policy ended, then the waiting period for preexisting conditions with the new policy will only be four months because the individual will receive eight months of credit toward the twelve-month limit.)

The nondiscrimination requirements in HIPAA prevent an individual from losing group health insurance coverage, being denied coverage, or having to pay higher premiums because of health-related factors. For example, a group health-insurance policy cannot require an individual to pass a physical before becoming eligible for coverage, as this would be considered discriminating on eligibility based on health-related factors. Nor can a group insurance policy require that individuals who have certain health conditions, such as diabetes or HIV, pay a higher premium. (However, insurance companies are able to determine what types of coverage they will provide for various health problems. For example, a health insurance company can have a policy that they will not provide coverage for heart transplants or experimental drugs, provided these benefit restrictions apply to all individuals covered by the insurance policy.)

The final primary area HIPAA seeks to address is the availability of individual health insurance policies for those who do not have access to group policies. If an individual has had coverage for at least eighteen months, has exhausted COBRA coverage or is not eligible for COBRA, has no other insurance coverage and is not eligible for any government health plan such as Medicare or Medicaid, and did not lose group coverage eligibility because of fraud or nonpayment of premiums, then the individual cannot be denied the purchase of an individual insurance policy. However, while HIPAA guarantees access to an individual policy, it does not limit the premium that insurance companies can charge. Some have considered this to be a drawback of the law, since individual policies may be offered at premiums that make them prohibitively costly. (For further information on HIPAA see the U.S. Department of Labor publications *Questions and Answers: Recent Changes in Health Care Law* and *Pension and Health Care Coverage. . .Questions and Answers for Dislocated Workers.* In addition, a good Internet source for government information on health-related questions and relevant issues is www.healthfinder.gov)

Summary

For many older Americans, health insurance and employment are very closely tied. The majority of the near-elderly receive health insurance coverage as a benefit from their employer, although economic theory indicates that the true cost of insurance is borne by the employee through lower wages. Having employers provide health insurance provides some tax benefits for employees, since health insurance benefits are not taxable, but it also introduces constraints on the work and retirement decisions of the near-elderly. With employer-provided benefits ending when an individual leaves a job, and a reduction in the percentage of employers who are offering health benefits to retirees, individuals under the age of sixty-five may find they lose their insurance coverage if they leave their job. Legislation such as COBRA and HIPAA has attempted to lessen this burden by allowing individuals to continue to purchase insurance from their former employers, reducing pre-existing condition limitations for insurance companies, and expanding the guarantee of access to group and individual insurance policies. However, until an individual reaches age sixty-five and is eligible for Medicare, health insurance coverage continues to be an important issue for aging Americans.

KATHRYN WILSON

See also ECONOMIC WELL-BEING; HEALTH INSURANCE, NATIONAL APPROACHES; MEDIGAP; MEDICARE; RETIREMENT, DECISION MAKING.

BIBLIOGRAPHY

Congressional Budget Office. *Budget Options, 2001.* Available online at http://www.cbo.gov.

General Accounting Office. "Private Health Insurance: Declining Employer Coverage May Affect Access for 55- to 64-Year-Olds." GAO/HEHS-98-133, 1998. Available on the World Wide Web at www.gao.gov

GRUBER, J., and MADRIAN, B. "Health-Insurance Availability and the Retirement Decision." *The American Economic Review* 85 (1995): 938–948.

JOHNSON, R. W., and CRYSTAL, S. "Health Insurance Coverage at Midlife: Characteristics, Costs, and Dynamics." *Health Care Financing Review* 18 (1997): 123–148.

MADRIAN, B. C., and BEAULIEU, N. D. "Does Medicare Eligibility Affect Retirement?" In *Inquiries in the Economics of Aging*. Edited by David A Wise. Chicago: The University of Chicago Press, 1998. Pages 109–132.

MITCHELL, J. M., and PHELPS, C. E. "National Health Insurance: Some Costs and Effects of Mandated Employee Coverage." *Journal of Political Economy* 84 (1976): 553–571.

PAULY, M. V. *Health Benefits at Work: An Economic and Political Analysis of Employer-Provided Health Insurance*. Ann Arbor: University of Michigan Press, 1997.

ROGOWSKI, J., and KAROLY, L. "Health Insurance and Retirement Behavior: Evidence from the Health and Retirement Survey." *Journal of Health Economics* 19 (2000): 529–539.

ROYALTY, A. B. "Tax Preferences for Fringe Benefits and Workers' Eligibility for Employer Health Insurance." *Journal of Public Economics* 75 (2000): 209–227.

SCHULZ, J. H. *The Economics of Aging*, 7th ed. Westport, Conn.: Auburn House, 2001.

U.S. Census Bureau. *Statistical Abstract of the United States*. Washington, D.C.: U.S. Census Bureau, 2000.

U.S. Department of Labor. *Health Benefits Under the Consolidated Omnibus Budget Reconciliation Act*. Washington, D.C.: DoL, 1999. Available online at www.dol.gov

U.S. Department of Labor. *Questions and Answers: Recent Changes in Health Care Law*. Washington, D.C.: DoL, 1999. Available on the World Wide Web at www.dol.gov

U.S. Department of Labor. *Pension and Health Care Coverage. . . Questions and Answers for Dislocated Workers*. Washington, D.C.: DoL, 2001. Available online at www.dol.gov

WISE, D. A., ed. *Inquiries in the Economics of Aging*. Chicago: The University of Chicago Press, 1998.

WISE, D. A., ed. *Frontiers in the Economics of Aging*. Chicago: The University of Chicago Press, 1998.

EMPLOYEE RETIREMENT INCOME SECURITY ACT

The Employee Retirement Income Security Act (ERISA) was signed into law by President Gerald Ford on Labor Day, 2 September 1974. This landmark law provides extensive rules governing private pension plans and other employee benefit plans. The primary function of ERISA has been to help ensure greater retirement security for those American workers who have pensions. ERISA has largely achieved this result by (1) requiring that private pension plans hold plan assets in trust for the benefit of the employees and their beneficiaries, (2) requiring that pension plans be funded on a timely basis, and (3) ensuring that most covered employees with more than five years of service have a vested (i.e., nonforfeitable) right to receive their pension benefits.

It is important to note that the United States has a *voluntary* pension system. Private employers are not required to have pensions, but if they do, ERISA is applicable. Since it was enacted, ERISA has been amended numerous times, and a whole regulatory system has grown up to enforce its provisions. The key agencies charged with the administration of ERISA are the U.S. Department of Labor, the Internal Revenue Service (IRS), and the Pension Benefit Guaranty Corporation (PBGC).

From 1975 until 1995, the total number of private tax-qualified retirement plans rose from 311,000 to 693,000, and the total number of plan participants (including workers, retirees, and survivors) rose from 45 million to 87 million. In 1995, these plans held more than $2.7 billion in assets.

Private pension-plan participation and coverage are by no means universal, however. In 1993, for example, only 44 percent of U.S. civilian workers participated in a private pension plan, and only about 38 percent were vested. The government has long been interested in expanding private retirement-plan coverage, and this concern has motivated many of the changes to ERISA.

History leading up to ERISA

Pensions are a relatively modern phenomenon. Prior to 1900, few employers provided pensions to their employees, and there was little legislation to govern the pension plans that did exist. Private pension-plan growth was slow until after World War II, and the pace of pension legislation has paralleled the growth of the private pension system.

Tax legislation was the earliest mechanism for regulating private pension plans. For example, the Revenue Acts of 1921 and 1926 allowed employers to deduct pension-plan contributions from corporate income; they allowed for pension-fund income to accumulate tax-free; and

Table 1
The Structure of ERISA

Title I   Protection of Employee Benefit Rights Definitions
          Part 1. Reporting and Disclosure
          Part 2. Participation and Vesting
          Part 3. Funding
          Part 4. Fiduciary Responsibility
          Part 5. Administration and Enforcement
          Part 6. Group Health Plans
          Part 7. Group Health Plan Portability, Access,
               and Renewability Requirements
Title II   Amendments to the Internal Revenue Code
Title III Miscellanea
Title IV   Plan Termination Insurance

SOURCE: Author

they provided that participants would not be taxed until pensions were distributed to them. To qualify for favorable tax treatment, however, pension plans had to meet certain minimum requirements pertaining to employee coverage and employer contributions. The Revenue Act of 1942 imposed stricter participation requirements and, for the first time, disclosure requirements.

During and after World War II, pension coverage expanded greatly, as did reports of mismanagement and abuse of pension funds. For example, Jimmy Hoffa, the leader of the International Brotherhood of Teamsters, was alleged to have abused his union's Central and Southern States Pension Fund. The need for government regulation of private pensions culminated in the passage of the Welfare and Pension Plans Disclosure Act (WPPDA) in 1959. The WPPDA required plan sponsors (e.g., employers and labor unions) to file plan descriptions and annual financial reports with the Department of Labor, and these materials were also made available to plan participants and beneficiaries. The WPPDA was amended in 1962 to give the Department of Labor additional enforcement, interpretive, and investigatory powers over employee benefit plans. The WPPDA had a very limited scope, and eventually it was replaced by ERISA's much more comprehensive system for pension regulation.

One of the seminal events leading up to the passage of ERISA was the December 1963 shutdown of the Studebaker automobile company in

South Bend, Indiana. Studebaker had promised its employees generous retirement benefits, but it had never adequately funded its plan. Consequently, the Studebaker plan was able to pay full retirement benefits only to its 3,600 retirees and to those active workers who had reached the permitted retirement age of sixty, while the company's remaining 7,000 workers were left with little or nothing to show for their years of work.

In the 1960s, Congress held numerous hearings on private pension plans, but reform came slowly. U.S. Senator Jacob K. Javits (R-New York) introduced the first broad-scale pension reform bill in 1967. This bill ultimately became the Employee Retirement Income Security Act of 1974 (ERISA), which was designed to secure the benefits of participants in private pension plans through participation, vesting, funding, reporting, and disclosure rules, and through the establishment of the Pension Benefit Guaranty Corporation.

The administration of ERISA is divided among the Department of Labor's Pension and Welfare Benefits Administration (PWBA), the Internal Revenue Service (IRS), and the Pension Benefit Guaranty Corporation (PBGC). Title I of ERISA, which contains rules for reporting and disclosure, vesting, participation, funding, fiduciary conduct, and civil enforcement, is administered primarily by the PWBA. Title II of ERISA, which amended the Internal Revenue Code to parallel many of the Title I rules, is administered by the IRS. Title III of ERISA is concerned with jurisdictional matters and with coordination of enforcement and regulatory activities by the PWBA and the IRS. Finally, Title IV covers the insurance of defined-benefit pension plans, and it is administered by the PBGC.

Subsequent amendments to ERISA

Since its enactment in 1974, ERISA has been amended many times to help meet the changing retirement and health care needs of employees and their families. The Retirement Equity Act of 1984 addressed a broad variety of women's issues. The act reduced the maximum age that an employer may require for participation in a pension plan from twenty-five to twenty-one; lengthened the period of time a participant could be absent from work without losing pension credits; and created spousal rights to pension benefits through a qualified domestic relations order (QDRO) in the event of divorce, and through preretirement survivor annuities.

The Tax Reform Act of 1986 established faster minimum vesting schedules and mandated broader coverage of rank-and-file workers. The Older Workers Benefit Protection Act of 1990 amended the Age Discrimination in Employment Act (ADEA) to apply to employee benefits.

With respect to health care plans, the Consolidated Omnibus Budget Reconciliation Act of 1985 (COBRA) added a new part 6 to Title I of ERISA that provides for the continuation of health care coverage for employees and their beneficiaries (for a limited period of time) if certain events would otherwise result in a reduction in benefits. More recently, the Health Insurance Portability and Accountability Act of 1996 (HIPAA) added a new Part 7 to Title I of ERISA aimed at making health care coverage more portable and secure for employees.

Types of ERISA-covered retirement plans

Most private retirement plans are governed by ERISA, and they typically qualify for favorable tax treatment. Basically, an employer's contributions to a tax-qualified retirement plan on behalf of an employee are not taxable to the employee. Nevertheless, the employer is allowed a current deduction for those contributions (within limits). Moreover, the pension fund's earnings on those contributions are tax-exempt. Workers pay tax only when they receive distributions of their pension benefits, and at that point the usual rules for taxing annuities apply.

Private retirement plans generally fall into two broad categories, based on the nature of the benefits provided: (1) defined benefit plans and (2) defined contribution plans. In a defined benefit plan, an employer promises employees a specific benefit at retirement. To provide this benefit, the employer makes payments into a trust fund and makes withdrawals from the trust fund. Employer contributions are based on actuarial valuations, and the employer bears all of the investment risks and responsibilities. Benefits are guaranteed by the Pension Benefit Guaranty Corporation.

Under a typical defined contribution plan, the employer simply contributes a specified percentage of the worker's compensation to an individual investment account for the worker. For example, contributions might be set at 10 percent of annual compensation. The benefit at retirement would be based on all such contributions plus investment earnings. There are a variety of different types of defined contribution plans, including money purchase pension plans, target benefit plans, profit-sharing plans, stock bonus plans, and employee stock ownership plans (ESOPs).

Profit-sharing and stock bonus plans may include a feature that allows workers to choose between receiving cash currently or deferring taxation by placing the money in a retirement account (401(k) plans or cash or deferred arrangements (CODAs)). The maximum annual amount of elective deferrals that can be made by an individual in the year 2001 is $11,000, and it is scheduled to rise to $15,000 in 2006.

Alternatively, many companies rely on *hybrid* retirement plans that mix the features of both defined benefit and defined contribution plans. Still another approach is for an employer to offer a combination of defined benefit and defined contribution plans. For example, many companies with traditional defined benefit plans have recently added supplemental 401(k) plans.

The major requirements of ERISA

ERISA does not require employers to provide benefits to their employess, but if an employer chooses to have a plan, ERISA regulates that plan. ERISA requires that an employee benefit plan be established and maintained by an employer. The plan must be in writing, and it must be communicated to employees. The plan must be operated for the exclusive benefit of employees or their beneficiaries, and ERISA generally requires that plan assets be held in a trust.

To protect the interests of plan participants, ERISA requires significant reporting and disclosure in the administration and operation of employee benefit plans. For example, a typical pension plan will have to file reports with the IRS and the Department of Labor, and it will have to provide a summary plan description and a summary annual report to each participant.

In addition, ERISA imposes significant participation, coverage, vesting, benefit accrual, and funding requirements on private retirement plans. For example, a retirement plan generally may not require, as a condition of participation, that an employee complete a period of service extending beyond either age twenty-one or one year of service. Also, a plan may not exclude employees from participation just because they have reached a certain age (e.g., age sixty-five). Employees can be excluded for other reasons, however. For example, a plan might be able to cover only those employees working at a particular location or in a particular job category. Under the minimum coverage rules, however, a retirement plan must usually cover a significant percentage of the employer's work force. Alternatively, a plan may be able to satisfy the minimum coverage rules if it benefits a certain class of employees, as long as it does not discriminate in favor of the employer's highly compensated employees.

Retirement plans must also meet certain minimum vesting requirements. A worker's retirement benefit is said to be *vested* when the worker has a nonforfeitable right to receive the benefit. For example, under the five-year cliff-vesting schedule, an employee who has completed at least five years of service must have a nonforfeitable right to 100 percent of his or her accrued benefit. Alternatively, under three-to-seven-year *graded* vesting, an employee must have a nonforfeitable right to 20 percent of her or his accrued benefit after three years of service, 40 percent after four years of service, and so on up to 100 percent after seven years of service. These are minimum vesting requirements, and a plan is free to use a faster vesting schedule, or even to provide for immediate vesting.

ERISA also imposes rules on how benefits accrue under retirement plans. These rules help ensure that retirement benefits accrue at certain minimum rates, and they keep employers from skewing ("backloading") benefits in favor of their long-service employees. For example, each plan must comply with at least one of three alternative minimum-benefit accrual rules. Under the so-called 3 percent rule, for example, a worker must accrue, for each year of participation (up to 33 and 1/3 years) at least 3 percent of the normal retirement benefit that would be received if she or he stayed with the employer until age sixty-five.

Retirement plans must also meet certain minimum funding standards. These rules help ensure that the money needed to pay the promised benefits is set aside in a trust fund where it can earn income until it is used to pay benefits when the employee retires. ERISA also imposes extensive fiduciary responsibilities on employers and administrators of employee benefit plans. These *parties in interest* must manage the plan for the exclusive benefit of workers and their beneficiaries, and they must act prudently, diversify

plan investments, and follow the plan provisions. Failure to meet these responsibilities is a breach of duty that can result in personal liability.

In addition, ERISA's prohibited-transaction rules prevent parties in interest from engaging in certain transactions with the plan. For example, an employer usually cannot sell, exchange, or lease any property to the plan. A person who participates in a prohibited transaction is subject to a 15 percent excise tax, which is increased to 100 percent unless the transaction is reversed.

Title IV of ERISA created the Pension Benefit Guaranty Corporation (PBGC) and a plan-termination insurance program. Defined benefit plans generally pay annual termination insurance premiums to the PBGC. In the event an underfunded plan terminates (e.g., because the employer went out of business), the PBGC will guarantee payment of pension benefits to the participants (up to a maximum limit, in the year 2001, of $40,705 per year, per participant).

ERISA also provides for various judicial remedies. For example, plan participants or beneficiaries can sue plans and plan administrators to recover benefits, enforce rights, or clarify future rights to plan benefits. ERISA also permits the secretary of labor to bring lawsuits to enforce ERISA's fiduciary responsibility rules.

One of the central objectives of ERISA was to federalize pension and employee-benefit law. In particular, Section 514 provides that the provisions of Titles I and IV of ERISA "shall supersede any and all State laws as they may now or hereafter relate to any employee benefit plan." The courts have generally interpreted this preemption language broadly; for example, to prevent states from requiring ERISA-covered health care plans to provide specific benefits (i.e., chiropractic or psychiatric benefits). Similarly, the courts have relied on this language to prevent plaintiffs from bringing state tort and tort-related causes of action against employee benefit plans.

Retirement savings not covered by ERISA

ERISA covers employment-based private retirement plans (and health care plans). It does not apply to government plans such as Social Security or a state teachers retirement system. State and local government plans are, however, subject to many of the usual tax qualification rules in the Internal Revenue Code, but these plans are not subject to the minimum funding rules, nor are they required to pay premiums to insure their plans with the BGC.

Favorable tax rules are also available for certain individual retirement accounts (IRAs). Almost any worker can set up an IRA account with a bank or other financial institution and contribute up to a specified maximum amount per year to that account. Workers who are not covered by another retirement plan usually can deduct their IRA contributions. If a worker is covered by another retirement plan however, the deduction may be reduced or eliminated if the worker's income exceeds $33,000 for a single taxpayer or $53,000 for married taxpayers (in the year 2001). Like private pensions, IRA earnings are tax-exempt, and distributions are taxable.

Since 1998, individuals have also been permitted to set up so-called Roth IRAs. Unlike regular IRAs, contributions to Roth IRAs are not tax-deductible. Instead, withdrawals are tax-free. Like regular IRAs, however, the earnings of these IRAs are tax-exempt.

Pension coverage

Even though Americans have a greater and greater need for additional retirement savings, pension coverage remains far from universal. Even among workers between forty and sixty years of age, only 60 percent are covered by a pension plan (as of 1999). While 71.6 percent of employees at medium- and large-size private firms (100 or more employees) participated in a pension plan in 1997, only 37.3 percent of workers at smaller firms participated in a plan that year. Also, there is a particularly large gender gap concerning private pension income. In 1995, 46.4 percent of men over age sixty-five received pension and/or annuity income (averaging $11,460 per year), but only 26.4 percent of women over age sixty-five that year received a pension or annuity, and these averaged just $6,684 per year.

The future of ERISA

Over the years, there have been a number of proposals to expand participation in employer-sponsored pensions. In particular, many analysts have suggested shortening the vesting period, promoting pension-plan portability, and increasing participation (e.g., by covering part-time workers). Another alternative would be to allow designated financial institutions to administer defined contribution *megaplans* for numerous small employers. Employers would contribute to these megaplans, each employee would have her or his own account, and the financial institution would take on all of the reporting, disclosure, and fiduciary responsibilities.

Another approach would be to mandate private pensions. Depending upon the size of the program, this approach could compel most workers to set aside a large enough share of their earnings over their careers to fund adequate retirement benefits. For example, in 1981, the President's Commission on Pension Policy recommended adoption of a Mandatory Universal Pension System (MUPS). Basically, the proposal would have required all employers to contribute at least 3 percent of wages to private pensions for their workers. The proposal drew little interest at the time. Recently, however, there has been renewed interest in mandated pensions.

One design for a mandatory pension system would be to piggyback a system of individual retirement savings accounts (IRSAs) onto the existing Social Security withholding system. For example, both employers and employees could each be required to contribute 1.5 percent of payroll to these IRSAs (and the self-employed would be required to contribute the entire 3 percent). These accounts could be held by the government, invested in secure equity funds, and annuitized on retirement. Alternatively, these individual accounts could be held by financial institutions and their investment could be directed by individual workers.

A different approach would be for the government to mandate that employers provide a suitable defined benefit plan for their employees. In that regard, the government might authorize employers to use a central clearinghouse where employers could send pension contributions on behalf of their employees. Over the course of a career, each worker would earn entitlement to a defined benefit that, at retirement, would supplement Social Security.

JONATHAN BARRY FORMAN

See also ECONOMIC WELL-BEING; EMPLOYEE HEALTH INSURANCE; FEDERAL AGENCIES AND AGING; PENSIONS: FINANCING AND REGULATION; PENSIONS: HISTORY; PENSIONS: PLAN TYPES AND POLICY APPROACHES; RETIREMENT PLANNING.

BIBLIOGRAPHY

BERNSTEIN, M. C. *The Future of Private Pensions.* New York: Free Press, 1964.

Committee for Economic Development. *New Opportunities for Older Workers: A Statement on National Policy by the Research and Policy Committee of the Committee for Economic Development.* New York: Committee for Economic Development, 1999.

CONISON, J. *Employee Benefit Plans in a Nutshell.* 2d ed. St. Paul, Minn.: West Publishing Co., 1998.

COSTA, D. L. *The Evolution of Retirement: An American Economic History, 1880–1990.* Chicago: University of Chicago Press, 1998.

Council of Economic Advisors. "Annual Report of the Council of Economic Advisors." In *Economic Report of the President.* Washington, D.C.: Government Printing Office, 1999. Pages 7–454.

EISENBERG, D. "The Big Pension Swap; Accounts That Yield Benefits Sooner Are Replacing Traditional Plans, but Older Workers Are Crying Foul." *Time* 19 April 1999, p. 36.

Employee Benefit Research Institute. *EBRI Databook on Employee Benefits,* 4th ed. Washington, D.C.: Employee Benefit Research Institute, 1997.

Employee Retirement Income Security Act of 1974, Public Law No. 93-406, 88 Statutes at Large 829 (1974) (codified as amended in scattered sections of Titles 26 and 29 of the United States Code).

FORMAN, J. B. "Universal Pensions." *Chapman Law Review* 2 (1999): 95–131.

President's Commission on Pension Policy. *Coming of Age: Toward a National Retirement Income Policy.* Washington, D.C.: President's Commission on Pension Policy, 1981.

SASS, S. A. *The Promise of Private Pensions: The First Hundred Years.* Cambridge, Mass.: Harvard University Press, 1997.

STEUERLE, C. E., and BAKIJA, J. M. *Retooling Social Security For The 21st Century: Right & Wrong Approaches To Reform.* Washington, D.C.: Urban Institute Press, 1994.

U.S. Congress, Joint Committee on Taxation. *Overview of Present-Law Tax Rules and Issues Relating to Employer-Sponsored Retirement Plans.* Report No. JCX-16-99. Washington, D.C.: Joint Committee on Taxation, 1999.

U.S. Congress, Staff of the House Committee on Ways and Means. *1998 Green Book: Background Material and Date on Programs within the Jurisdiction of the Committee on Ways and Means, 105th Congress, 2d Session.* Committee Print No. WMCP: 105–107. Washington, D.C.: U.S. Government Printing Office, 1998.

U.S. Department of Labor. *PWBA History and ERISA.* 2000. Available on the World Wide Web at http://www.dol.gov/dol/pwba/public/aboutpwba/history4.htm

U.S. General Accounting Office. *Implications of Demographic Trends for Social Security and Pension Reform.* Report No. GAO/HEHS-97-81. Washington, D.C.: U.S. Government Printing Office, 1997.

World Bank. *Averting the Old-Age Crisis.* Oxford: Oxford University Press, 1994.

YAKOBOSKI, P. "Overview of the U.S. Employment-Based Retirement Income System." In *The Future of Private Retirement Plans.* Edited by Dallas A. Salisbury. Washington, D.C.: Employee Benefits Research Institute, 2000. Pages 19–37.

ZELINSKY, E. A. "ERISA and the Emergence of the Defined Contribution Society." In *Proceedings of the Fifty-Seventh New York University Institute on Federal Taxation—Employee Benefits and Executive Compensation.* Edited by Alvin D. Lurie. New York: Matthew Bender, 1999. Pages 6-1 and 6-29.

EMPLOYMENT OF OLDER WORKERS

People are considered to be employed if they are working for pay in a job that provides them with a salary or a wage, or if they are working for profit, as in a family-owned business. For most people, employment forms a central activity for much of adulthood and not only provides access to income but also contributes to one's identity and sense of self. Yet embedded within the norms about work in the United States is the expectation that as people age, they will give up their paid employment activities. Indeed, many individuals in later life have achieved economic security through private pensions and other forms of wealth accumulated through employment in early and middle adulthood. These individuals often choose a mix of leisure and productive activities such as volunteer work as alternatives to continued employment. Relinquishing paid employment is not a universal experience, however. Some older individuals choose to continue working as a means of supplementing otherwise inadequate economic resources. Still others continue to work for intrinsic reasons, such as enjoyment of work, desire for meaningful activity, or to maintain social connec-

An elderly store clerk assists a young customer. Many senior citizens are finding jobs in the retail sector. (Corbis photo by David Turnley.)

tions. Although most older people do not work full-time or year-round, many do participate in employment well into later life.

The age profile of employment

Among both men and women of all racial and ethnic groups in the United States, employment levels reach a peak in midlife. As teenagers and young adults, work often competes with the pursuit of education and training. For many young adults, paid work also may compete with childbearing and child-rearing activities. However, the vast majority of individuals in their forties are employed.

Figure 1 presents the pattern of labor force participation for people age forty and over in 1998. Labor force participants include not only those who are employed but also those who are unemployed and looking for work. Because the unemployment rate is typically quite low among older individuals, the labor force patterns seen in Figure 1 largely reflect rates of employment. More than 90 percent of white men, 80 percent or more of black men and women, and nearly as large a share of white women in their early forties participate in the labor force. Adults fifty or older

are progressively less likely to be employed and, among those sixty to sixty-four years of age, fewer than 60 percent are working. However, some individuals are employed well beyond the normative retirement ages. Close to 30 percent of white men aged sixty-five to sixty-nine and nearly 20 percent of white men aged seventy to seventy-four were still in the labor force in 1998, and rates of participation were only slightly lower for the other groups. These individuals often obtain considerable benefits from their work, including economic resources, identity or status enhancement, or meaningful interpersonal relationships (Parnes and Sommers). Although the precise rates of activity fluctuate from year to year, this patterning across age groups characterized the 1990s and is expected to continue for some time.

Race, gender, and employment

As with younger individuals, the levels and types of labor force activity in later life are related to race and gender. Among the groups considered in Figure 1, white men have the highest rates of labor force participation. Black men have the next highest rate, although the gap between white and black men is as great as 10 percentage

Figure 1
Labor Force Participation Rates by Age Group, Gender, and Race: 1998

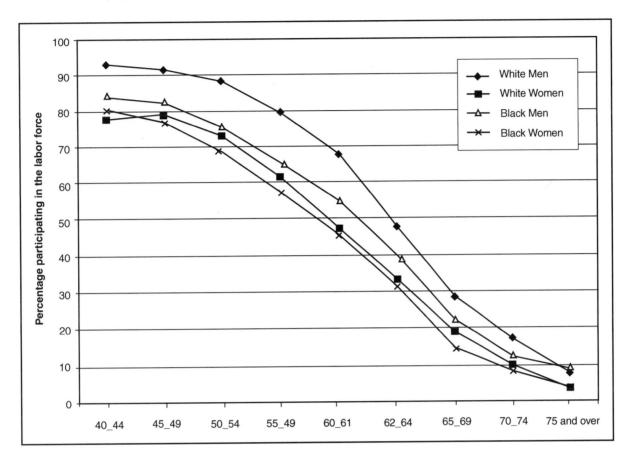

SOURCE: Author

points among those in their fifties and early sixties. This difference is thought to be a result of several factors, including most notably the higher levels of disability among black men (Bound, Schoenbaum, and Waidmann; Hayward, Friedman and Chen). Although not shown in Figure 1, Hispanic men have rates of labor force participation that are as high or higher than those of white men throughout later life (Hobbs and Damon).

White and black women are much more similar to one another in levels of employment than are their male counterparts, but Hispanic women report lower levels of participation than either group. Keeping in mind that standard assessments of employment take into account only work that is paid or generates profit in a business, the figures show that all groups of women are less likely to be employed than are men. An important factor underlying the gender differ-

ence in employment is the fact that many women over age fifty in 1998 were not employed outside of the home for significant periods of time when they were younger. Their later-life activity patterns are therefore shaped not only by ongoing family responsibilities but also by the gender role expectations and work experiences accumulated earlier in life (Pienta, Burr, and Mutchler).

Older individuals are also more likely to work part-time than are their younger counterparts. About 90 percent of workers in their forties work full-time, but this percentage is lower among older age groups; fewer than half of workers aged sixty-five and over work full-time (U.S. Bureau of the Census). Working part-time may be motivated by health limitations, the availability of nonwork income, the desire for leisure, or difficulty in finding full-time work. Nevertheless, more than 90 percent of part-time workers in their sixties report that they prefer part-time to full-time work. Thus, older individuals are less likely to work than are younger individuals, and they are more likely to substitute part-time for full-time work. Notably, this process of reducing participation and hours of employment is evident among people as young as fifty years old.

Historical changes in employment in later life

Prior to the start of the twentieth century, most people were engaged in gainful activity throughout later life. In the absence of the economic security provided by individual wealth or a public or private pension, individuals had no choice but to continue working, or to become dependent on family members or charity (Haber and Gratton). Indeed, retirement emerged as a "social institution" only within the last hundred years (Atchley).

Over the last half of the twentieth century, labor force participation rates among older men declined, while the rates for older women increased. Between 1950 and 1990, participation among men declined; for example, nearly nine out of ten men aged fifty-five to sixty-four participated in the paid workforce in 1950, but only seven out of ten similarly aged men did so in 1990. The most dramatic decline in participation among men sixty-five and over occurred in the 1950s, with more gradual declines occurring over the next three decades. During the 1990s, small increases in employment among older men were evident. Although it is too early to tell if the increases will continue, it appears that the substantial declines in work activity among men that occurred throughout the twentieth century has leveled off. Indeed, projections generated by the Bureau of Labor Statistics indicate that slight increases in activity are expected to continue into the first part of the twenty-first century.

A different pattern of change is observed for older women. Women aged fifty-five to sixty-four doubled their work participation since the 1950s. While about one-quarter of the women in this age group worked in 1950, by the end of the twentieth century half of the women in this age group were employed. In contrast to the sizable increase in employment among women fifty-five to sixty-four, labor force activity among women sixty-five and over has changed very little since 1950 and is expected to remain at 10 percent or less into the twenty-first century.

Several factors explain the trajectories of labor force activity over time among older men and women. During the last half of the twentieth century, participation in Social Security became more widespread, and coverage by private pensions became more common. These forms of nonwork income have resulted in more individuals having investments in public and private pension systems that provide an acceptable standard of living in the absence of work. The declines in employment among younger men—those aged fifty-five to sixty-four—are often linked to the availability of disability income, which serves as an alternative income source for those too disabled to work (Burr, Massagli, Mutchler, and Pienta). Also important for this age group is the reduction of the minimum age of eligibility for receiving Social Security benefits to age sixty-two in the early 1960s.

Working women have been affected by these shifts, but their dramatic increase in labor force activity is largely a reflection of *cohort replacement*. The women aged fifty-five to sixty-four in 1960, for example, had accumulated little paid work experience over their lifetimes. Often working sporadically, most had married and most had spent substantial periods of time at home raising their children (Moen). In contrast, contemporary cohorts have maintained stronger commitments to paid work throughout their lifetimes. As current cohorts of young women approach later life, we may expect the work activity levels of older women to resemble those of men even more closely.

Several sets of factors account for these changing employment profiles among women. Significant changes in gender roles and improved work opportunities for women have resulted in more women being employed for larger portions of their lives. Another contributing factor has been changes in family life, including more divorce and fewer children among women currently approaching later life. Additional influences on employment levels for both men and women over the last decades of the twentieth century were exerted by shifting economic conditions and associated policies that pushed older workers out of the workforce during recessionary periods, but facilitated their employment or reemployment during times of labor force shortages.

Diversity in late-life employment transitions

A great deal of diversity characterizes employment behavior in later life. Once considered a "crisp" transition between work and nonwork, the transition to retirement is now regarded as a process rather than an event, with many individuals spending years negotiating a "blurred" transition from worker to retiree (Mutchler, Burr, Pienta and Massagli). For many older individuals, the last years of employment are characterized by repeated moves in and out of the work force, along with job changes and fluctuation between full- and part-time work.

Many factors shape whether individuals continue working in later life. Some of the most important factors include the extent to which they can afford not to work, their physical ability to continue working, and their desire to engage in activities that compete with paid labor. In part because the decision to work or retire is so complex and depends on many factors, workers display a variety of pathways through the final years of their work lives. Some workers retire gradually, reducing their hours of work to accommodate their desire for leisure or their changing health or family circumstances, while retaining the financial and other benefits of working. Others change jobs relatively late in life, retiring from long-term employment once they are eligible for pension income and taking on new careers, or shifting to "bridge jobs" that may offer lower status and fewer hours. Some individuals who have retired in their fifties or earlier subsequently return to work either because additional income is required, or because the stimulation or social contact provided by work is desired. Still others never formally retire at all—experiencing in later life a series of short-term or part-time jobs that represent a continuation of work instability throughout the life course.

Gradual retirement from career jobs. Surveys suggest that many older people would like to retire gradually rather than leave the labor force abruptly. For many, the opportunity to remain employed at the same job on a part-time basis, while beginning to draw retirement income, is very appealing. And, because many of today's older people are relatively free from physical disability, gradual retirement provides an attractive alternative to leaving the labor force altogether. Yet gradual retirement is often difficult to negotiate. For example, Quinn, Burkhauser, and Myers estimate that only about one-quarter of those leaving career jobs shift to part-time employment on the same job. Although personal preference plays a part in shaping this low rate of gradual retirement,

organizational and institutional barriers are also important. Many employers and private pension plans are unwilling to facilitate gradual retirement. Moreover, until the policy was changed in 2000, many older individuals eligible for Social Security received reduced benefits if they received too much wage or salary income.

Bridge jobs. Rather than remain working at one's existing job or retiring completely, some older individuals change jobs late in their work lives. If an older individual wants to continue working, a job change may be required if his or her existing job is no longer acceptable (for example, if the work is too physically demanding, or if the employer cannot meet the individual's desire for part-time work). Moreover, although mandatory retirement is no longer legal for most workers, some older individuals experience pressures to retire before they would like. Regardless of the reason for job loss, many older individuals need or want to work. These individuals often seek "bridge employment" to span the time period between retirement from or loss of one's career job and permanent retirement (Ruhm).

The kinds of jobs chosen by individuals seeking bridge employment are typically part-time and offer a considerable amount of flexibility. However, they also often pay poorly and offer few benefits, and many of these jobs represent declines in occupational status from the career job. Self-employment is chosen by many as a type of bridge employment in the later years of work life (Quinn and Kozy).

Returning to employment. Some evidence suggests that it is not uncommon for retirees—especially those leaving employment in their fifties or earlier—to return to work following a period of full-time retirement. Although some of these returns may be motivated by a revised assessment of the appeal of nonwork, the evidence suggests that returns to employment commonly occur because retirees are seeking the income and noncash benefits associated with work. Individuals retiring in their fifties will not typically be eligible for Medicare for many years, and the desire for employer-provided or employer-subsidized health insurance coverage alone may be a motivating force for a return to work. Early retirees may also discover that their pension resources are inadequate to maintain the standard of living desired. Herz suggests that younger retirees may experience retirement with a lower accumulation or more rapid depletion of pension resources than they might have expected had they continued working. Beyond these factors, the low-unemployment environment of the late twentieth century may have generated a greater need for older workers and the emergence of more attractive work opportunities.

Jobs of older workers. The kinds of jobs held by older workers reflect the fact that fewer than half of the population over age sixty-two is employed. Those who are employed in later life are different from those who have retired in many ways, which has implications for the kinds of jobs they hold. Some of those who are working beyond this point are individuals who take great personal satisfaction from their jobs, such as some professionals and some people who are self-employed. Other older workers continue employment because they need the money, and their job opportunities may be less intrinsically satisfying. Some industrial shifts have reduced the employment prospects for older workers, such as the loss of manufacturing jobs; but emerging opportunities in the service and sales sectors have been beneficial, especially for those older workers desiring part-time, flexible, or less physically demanding work (Quadagno and Hardy). Overall, the kinds of jobs held by older workers are not dramatically different from those of their younger counterparts. Among the most common occupational categories for all age groups over age forty are executives, professionals, and administrative support positions such as clerical workers. Compared to middle-aged workers, a somewhat larger share of workers sixty-five and over are in sales, service, or farming occupations (U.S. Bureau of the Census).

Looking ahead

Because the population as a whole is aging, we can expect that the pool of employed or potentially employed people will also age during the first decades of the twenty-first century. Projections of the labor force suggest that the median age of the labor force in the year 2008 will be almost forty years—higher than any time since the early 1960s (Fullerton, 1999a). This does not necessarily mean that the labor force participation rate of men and women in their sixties or seventies will increase. Whether individuals in these age groups choose to participate in the labor force in the future will be determined by their individual characteristics that drive employment choices, as well as by the changing poli-

cy environment within which those choices are made.

Older individuals decide whether or not to work based on their need for continued income or other resources generated through work, their physical ability to continue working, and the attractiveness of their work opportunities as compared to other activities. We can expect that individual decisions will continue to be made on these bases, although each cohort will bring a somewhat different mix of resources and characteristics to the decision-making process. For example, people in their sixties at the start of the twenty-first century are in better health than were earlier cohorts, making continued employment a more realistic option for many. People who reach later life in good health, but with inadequate nonwork economic resources, will be attracted to continued work, or returns to work. Late-life employment will be especially likely if employers offer attractive and flexible job opportunities to older workers.

These individual decisions are made within a policy environment that shapes employment and retirement decisions. For example, the age at which full Social Security benefits may be received began to increase in the year 2000. In addition, in the spring of 2000, Congress lifted the earnings cap for retirees aged sixty-five to sixty-nine, meaning that individuals in this age range can earn as much income as they are able without having their Social Security benefits reduced. These actions may cause some older individuals to remain working for longer periods of time, especially those with few private nonwork resources. It seems likely, however, that employment will continue to occur among only those segments of the older population who find employment a particularly appealing alternative to unpaid activities, as well as those with ongoing needs for wage income.

JAN E. MUTCHLER

See also JOB PERFORMANCE; PENSIONS; RETIREMENT PLANNING; RETIREMENT TRANSITION; SOCIAL SECURITY ADMINISTRATION.

BIBLIOGRAPHY

ATCHLEY, R. C. "Retirement as a Social Institution." *Annual Review of Sociology* 8 (1982): 263–287.
BOUND, J.; SCHOENBAUM, M.; and WAIDMANN, T. "Race Differences in Labor Force Attachment

and Disability Status." *The Gerontologist* 36 (1996): 311–321.

BURR, J. A.; MASSAGLI, M. P.; MUTCHLER, J. E.; and PIENTA, A. M. "Labor Force Transitions among Older African Americans and Whites." *Social Forces* 74 (1996): 963–982.

FULLERTON, H. N., JR. "Labor Force Projections to 2008: Steady Growth and Changing Composition." *Monthly Labor Review* 11 (1999a): 19–32.

FULLERTON, H. N., JR. "Labor Force Participation: 75 Years of Change, 1950–98 and 1998–2025." *Monthly Labor Review* 12 (1999b): 3–12.

HABER, C., and GRATTON, B. *Old Age and the Search for Security.* Bloomington: Indiana University Press, 1994.

HAYWARD, M. D.; FRIEDMAN, S.; and CHEN, H. "Race Inequities in Men's Retirement." *Journal of Gerontology: Social Sciences* 51B (1996): S1–S10.

HERZ, D. E. "Work after Early Retirement: An Increasing Trend among Men." *Monthly Labor Review* 4 (1995): 13–20.

HOBBS, F., and DAMON, B. *65+ in the United States.* Washington, D.C.: U. S. Bureau of the Census, 1996.

MOEN, P. "Continuities and Discontinuities in Women's Labor Force Activity." In *Life Course Dynamics.* Edited by G. Elder. Ithaca, N.Y.: Cornell University Press, 1985. Pages 113–155.

MUTCHLER, J. E.; BURR, J. A.; PIENTA, A. M.; and MASSAGLI, M. P. "Pathways to Labor Force Exit: Work Transitions and Work Instability." *Journal of Gerontology: Social Sciences* 52B (1997): S4–S12.

PARNES, H. S., and SOMMERS, D. G. "Shunning Retirement: Work Experience of Men in Their Seventies and Early Eighties." *Journal of Gerontology: Social Sciences* 49 (1994): S117–S124.

PIENTA, A.; BURR, J. A.; and MUTCHLER, J. E. "Women's Labor Force Participation in Later Life: The Effects of Early Work and Family Experience." *Journal of Gerontology: Social Sciences* 49 (1994): S231–S239.

QUADAGNO, J., and HARDY, M. "Work and Retirement." In *Handbook of Aging and the Social Sciences,* 4th ed. Edited by R. Binstock and L. George. New York: Academic Press, 1996. Pages 325–345.

QUINN, J. F.; BURKHAUSER, R. V.; and MYERS, D. A. *Passing the Torch: The Influence of Economic Incentives on Work and Retirement.* Kalamazoo, Mich.: W. E. Upjohn Institute, 1990.

QUINN, J. F., and KOZY, M. "The Role of Bridge Jobs in the Retirement Transition: Gender, Race, and Ethnicity." *The Gerontologist* 36 (1996): 363–372.

RUHM, C. J. "Bridge Jobs and Partial Retirement." *Journal of Labor Economics* 8 (1990): 482–501.

U.S. Bureau of the Census. *Current Population Survey: Annual Demographic Survey, 1998.* Machine-readable data file obtained through FERRET (Federal Electronic Research and Review Extraction Tool). Available on the Internet at www.census.gov

ENDOCRINE SYSTEM

Among the most intellectually compelling theories of aging are those based on the notion that selection pressure favors those mechanisms which increase the probability of reproductive success (i.e., of producing a next generation of viable offspring). This relationship would be true even if, for example, the mechanisms utilized early in life to assure reproductive success ultimately contribute to senescence and reduce the longevity of postreproductive-age adults (Rose). The dual and apparently contradictory nature of this particular proposal is reflected in the term used to describe it, "antagonistic pleiotropy." Similar to antagonistic pleiotropy is another hypothesis called the "disposable soma." According to this view, the soma (body) is principally a vehicle for reproduction that becomes disposable once reproductive success has been achieved. In practice, this means that the resources of the body are targeted to assuring the perpetuation of the species instead of being distributed in a manner that may also help increase life span (Kirkwood).

Reproduction, including the antecedent development of reproductive organs and secondary sexual characteristics, is under strong hormonal control. If aging and life span are linked to the cessation of reproductive activity, as proposed above, then it follows that hormones likely play an important role in these events. In humans the most prominent sex hormones are the steroids estrogen (estradiol), progesterone, and testosterone. Of these, estrogen has probably received the greatest attention as a putative regulator of the aging process. Estrogen availability and levels determine the occurrence of two landmark events in the life cycle of women, menarche and menopause, and its virtual disappearance in postmenopausal women is associated with a variety of disorders and regressive tissue changes

Figure 1
An illustration showing the human endocrine system.

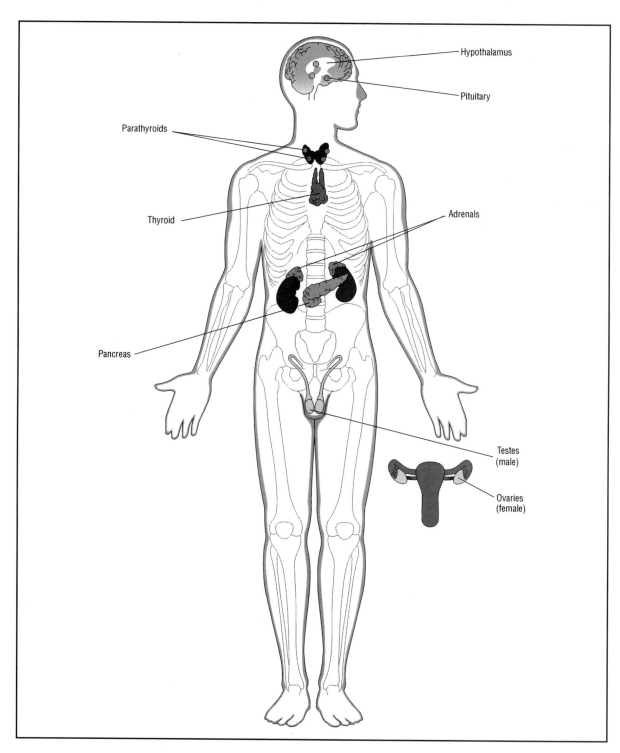

SOURCE: Argosy, Inc. for the Gale Group

commonly associated with aging (Perry). These associations include the loss of bone (osteoporosis) and changes in skin texture, and the increased risk of cataracts, cardiovascular disease, and dementia. In addition, because of the reciprocal relationship between hormone levels and, for example, bone loss, estrogen has been used extensively in hormone replacement therapy (HRT), the goal being to counteract the negative effects of postmenopausal estrogen deficiency, that is, those changes commonly associated with aging (Palacios). Thus, by this criterion, estrogen is an antiaging hormone.

While estrogen is almost certainly the most widely recognized sex hormone that likely plays a role in aging, it is not the only sex hormone that has this distinction. There are two others that also have gained significant attention. One of these is testosterone, which was recognized many years ago, albeit indirectly, as an agent (factor) important in maintaining the vigor and general vitality of older males. This association had its origins in nineteenth-century research involving testicular transplants in animals (the goal being to restore the sexual activity of valuable old, stud animals), and progressed to the use of both transplants and testicular extracts in middle-aged to elderly human males (Gosden). This early work gave results that were at best equivocal, but it did establish the basis for research on hormone isolation and characterization, and the rationale for the use of testosterone in HRT. Testosterone levels in men do decline with age (the phenomenon is called *andropause*), and low levels of the hormone have been equated with the loss of libido and cognitive skills, physical frailty, and bone loss. Testosterone HRT is an accepted form of therapy, particularly for men who are clearly hypogonadal (defined as bioavailable testosterone below the reference range for young men), but its widespread use remains controversial because of side effects (Bain).

The other sex steroid that has been widely implicated in the aging process is dehydroepiandrosterone (DHEA). DHEA is a weak androgen, produced by the adrenal gland, that can act directly on target tissues or indirectly as a precursor molecule for both estrogen and testosterone. DHEA, and its sulfated derivative DHEA-S, reach peak levels in young adults and decline steadily thereafter in most individuals. The blood levels at age eighty-five are, on average, about 10 percent of that in young adults. This diminution in DHEA/DHEA-S is called *adrenopause*. Lower levels of the hormone have been associated with age-related changes in body composition, the frequency of some forms of cancer, type II diabetes, atherosclerosis, and ischemic heart disease (Hinson and Raven). As is the case with estrogen and testosterone, DHEA has been and is being used in HRT, frequently in uncontrolled circumstances by the public at large in the United States. Although data from animal studies indicate that DHEA supplementation can counter some age-related changes (e.g., in immune function), the results on healthy, older humans leave the question of benefit in doubt (Svec and Porter). However, DHEA may be of help in some medical conditions, including serum lupus erythematosis and serious depression. No adverse effects have been reported.

No discussion of hormones and aging would be complete without consideration of human growth hormone (HGH) and insulin-like growth factor-1 (IGF-1). HGH is produced by the pituitary and affects target tissues principally through a mediating hormone/cytokine, IGF-1, that is synthesized in peripheral tissue. HGH and IGF-1 are potent anabolic agents capable of stimulating cell proliferation and protein synthesis, and recombinant HGH is the intervention of choice for treating individuals with short stature and adult HGH deficiency. HGH and IGF-1 levels decline with age (*somatopause*) (Vermeulen), and HGH and HGH secretagogue therapy have emerged as strategies for helping the frail elderly regain strength and muscle mass. However, as is the case with testosterone, it remains to be seen whether the benefits of such an approach outweigh the risks to the individuals, including peripheral edema and a decrease in insulin sensitivity (Cummings and Merriam). Ironically, recent data show that dwarf mice with growth hormone deficiency and, as a consequence, reduced body size live longer than their normal littermates.

ARNOLD KAHN

See also ANDROGEN; ANDROPAUSE; BIOMARKERS; DHEA; ESTROGEN; GROWTH HORMONE; INSULIN; LONGEVITY, REPRODUCTION; MENOPAUSE; NEUROENDOCRINE SYSTEM; THEORIES OF BIOLOGICAL AGING: DISPOSABLE SOMA.

BIBLIOGRAPHY

BAIN, J. "Andropause. Testosterone Replacement Therapy for Aging Men." *Canadian Family Physician* 47 (2001): 91–97.

CUMMINGS, D. E., and MERRIAM, G. R. "Age-Related Changes in Growth Hormone: Should the Somatopause Be Treated?" *Seminar in Reproductive Endocrinology* 17, no. 4 (1999): 311–325.

GOSDEN, R. *Cheating Time: Science, Sex and Aging.* New York: W. H. Freeman, 1996.

HINSON, J. P., and RAVEN, P. W. "DHEA Deficiency Syndrome: A New Term for Old Age?" *Journal of Endocrinology* 163 (1999): 1–5.

KIRKWOOD, B. L. "Evolution of Aging." *Nature* 270 (1977): 301–304.

PALACIOS, S. "Current Perspectives on the Benefits of HRT in Menopausal Women." *Maturitas* 33, supp. 1 (November 1999): S1–S13.

PERRY, H. M., III "The Endocrinology of Aging." *Clinical Chemistry* 45, no. 8 (pt 2) (1999): 1369–1376.

ROSE, M. R. *Evolutionary Biology of Aging.* New York: Oxford University Press, 1991.

SVEC, F., and PORTER, J. R. "The Actions of Exogenous Dehydroepiandrosterone in Experimental Animals and Humans." *Proceedings of the Society for Experimental Biology and Medicine* 218 (1997): 174–191.

VERMEULEN, A. "Andropause." *Maturitas* 34, no. 1 (2000): 5–15.

EPIDEMIOLOGY

Epidemiology has been defined as "the study of the distribution and determinants of disease frequency in human populations" (Hennekens and Buring). Based on the underlying tenet that disease does not occur at random, this definition provides a framework for the systematic investigation of health, disability, and illness in human populations. Thus, epidemiology has been identified as the science that forms the basis upon which public health decisions can be made.

In its relatively short history, the field of epidemiology has evolved to reflect the changing nature of the primary causes of morbidity (illness) and mortality (death). The term "epidemiology" was first used to refer to the study of the great "epidemics" of the nineteenth century, such as cholera and diphtheria, in an era when infectious diseases accounted for the overwhelming majority of deaths. Improvements in nutrition, sanitation, housing conditions, and water quality in the early twentieth century resulted in the eradication of many infectious diseases and an increase in life expectancy. Today chronic diseases are emerging as the leading causes of death and disability in developed nations, and there is

a shift in the demographic profile toward an increasingly aging population. In turn, the understanding of an epidemic has been broadened to reflect any disease that occurs at a greater frequency than would usually be expected in a specified population or geographic region. It has also been recognized that many chronic conditions have a consistent, endemic presence in a given population or geographic area, such as arthritis among older women. Other conditions are so widespread across a country, or even worldwide, that they are considered pandemic, such as obesity in the Western world.

Quantifying the occurrence of disease and its distribution in relation to the characteristics of person, place, and time falls within the domain of descriptive epidemiology. Measures of disease frequency rely on "count" information, the most basic of which is to add up individuals with a condition. However, for making direct comparisons among different groups it is necessary to determine the denominator, or the source population that the individuals come from. "Incidence" refers to the number of new cases of a condition that develop in a defined population within a specified time interval; it is a useful measure to study disease etiology. "Prevalence" refers to all occurrences of a condition in a defined population at a specific point in time; it is useful for health resource planning. Incidence and prevalence are interrelated in that prevalence is a function of both incidence and duration of a condition. For example, the prevalence of Alzheimer's disease exceeds the incidence of Alzheimer's disease because, once diagnosed, Alzheimer's patients live for many years with the disease. Prevalence is a "snapshot" that captures both newly diagnosed cases and previously diagnosed cases still alive. Institutionalized individuals are often excluded from the numerator (cases) and/or the denominator (persons at risk). Given that institutionalization rises dramatically with age, this poses a unique challenge for the reporting of morbidity rates among older age groups.

Analytic epidemiology

Studying the determinants of disease frequency falls within the domain of analytic epidemiology. The interest in causal relationships determines the type of study designs that epidemiologists employ. An experimental design is rarely appropriate to investigate disease etiology in humans: imagine the implications of randomly assigning individuals to smoke or not to smoke in order to study the effects on lung cancer. Therefore, epidemiologists must rely largely on observational study designs to determine association and to assess causation. The two most common observational study designs are the case-control study, in which individuals with and without the disease of interest are selected and prior exposure history is assessed, and the cohort study, in which individuals with and without the exposure of interest are selected and followed to determine the development of disease.

Relative and attributable risk

Measures of disease association include relative and attributable risk. Relative risk estimates the magnitude of an association between exposure and disease, based on the incidence of disease in the exposed group relative to the unexposed group. A relative risk of 1.0 indicates that there is no association between the exposure and outcome; a relative risk of greater than 1.0 indicates a positive association or increased risk; and a relative risk of less than 1.0 indicates an inverse association, or decreased risk (a protective effect). Incidence usually cannot be calculated in a case-control study, because participants are selected on the basis of disease. In this instance, the odds ratio (the ratio of odds of exposure among the cases to that of the controls) approximates the relative risk. Attributable risk, or risk difference, is the absolute difference in incidence between an exposed and unexposed group. It quantifies the risk of disease in the exposed group attributable to the exposure by removing the risk that would have occurred due to other causes. Expressed differently, attributable risk calculates the number of cases of disease among the exposed that could be eliminated if the exposure were eliminated. This is a useful measure of the public health impact of an exposure, assuming there is a cause-effect relationship. It is not possible to calculate attributable risk for most case-control studies, because incidence cannot be determined.

SUSAN A. KIRKLAND

See also HEALTH, SOCIAL FACTORS; SURVEYS.

BIBLIOGRAPHY

EBRAHIM, S., and KALACHE, A., eds. *Epidemiology in Old Age.* London: BMJ Publishing Group, 1996.
HENNEKENS, C. H., and BURING, J. E. *Epidemiology of Medicine.* Edited by Sherry L. Mayrent. Boston: Little, Brown, 1987.
ROTHMAN, K. J., and GREENLAND, S. *Modern Epidemiology*, 2d ed. Philadelphia, Pa.: Lippincott-Raven, 1998.

EPILEPSY

Contrary to what has been asserted in the past, recent literature has demonstrated that the incidence of provoked and unprovoked seizures and of epilepsy and the prevalence of epilepsy in older people is high. It is therefore regrettable that seizures in old age are still relatively under-researched. There are reasons for not relying on data obtained from the general adult population when deriving a picture of epilepsy in old age. The presentation, the etiology, the clinical pharmacology, the functional consequences, and the associated core morbidity are all different in old age.

Presentation and diagnosis

Since many older people live alone, there may be an inadequate history and older people may present with a history of recurrent unexplained falls or of being found on the floor. The vast majority of seizures in old age are either partial seizures with, for example, focal motor events such as recurrent jerking of an arm or leg, or secondary generalized seizure that may present either with disturbances of higher level function as in complex partial seizures or with convulsive movements. The list of conditions that may be confused with epilepsy is very long and includes: fainting; low blood sugar; transient ischaemic attacks; recurrent paroxysmal behavioral disturbances, such as clapping or calling out, secondary to dementia; drop attacks and other nonepileptic causes of falls; transient global amnesia; and nonepileptic attack disorder or psychogenic attacks. Conversely, there is an equally long list of conditions that are genuinely epileptic but may be thought to be nonepileptic; partial motor status epilepticus (e.g., persistent involuntary movement of an arm or leg) may be thought to be an extrapyramidal movement disorder such as Parkinson's disease; sensory epilepsy may be thought to be a transient ischaemic attack; complex partial seizures in which a patient may stare or call out can be confused with psychoses; atonic seizures can be confused with drop attacks or hysteria; and Todd's palsy (transient weakness) following a generalized seizure can be confused with a new stroke or a transient ischaemic attack.

The biggest challenge in elderly epileptology is determining whether or not the patient's events are seizures or fainting (syncope). Differentiating the two conditions may be extremely difficult in the absence of an eyewitness report. Moreover, the usual features that differentiate the two conditions may not apply to older people. For example, whereas syncope is not usually associated with either incontinence (loss of bladder and/or bowel control) or post-event confusion, an elderly person who is already incontinent or has background confusion may be incontinent or confused in association with a syncope attack. Even so, the history remains the most powerful diagnostic tool. Investigations will be guided by the history and the findings on examination. The EEG will rarely be useful in making a diagnosis of epilepsy and certainly should not be used to make up for the shortfalls in history taking. The indications for neuroimaging are not well defined and depend at least in part on the availability of radiological services. Strong indications for neuroimaging include unexplained focal neurological signs, progressive or new neurological symptoms, especially those of raised intracranial pressure, progressive or new neurological signs or poor control of fits not attributable to poor compliance, or continued exposure to precipitants such as alcohol.

The most common cause of seizures in old age is cerebrovascular disease: seizures may be a harbinger of future manifestations of cerebrovascular disease; late onset seizures are associated with a higher level of occult cerebral ischaemia; and overt strokes may trigger seizures either acutely or subsequently. Any patient who develops a seizure for the first time in old age when there was no obvious cause should be thoroughly investigated for cardiovascular risk factors and possibly placed on low dose aspirin, so long as there is no contraindication. Other cerebral causes of seizures include tumor, which may account for 10 to 15 percent of elderly onset cases. However, the proportion of these cases in which seizure is the only manifestation and the proportion in which any underlying tumor

found is benign and/or resectable is not known. Seizures may occur in nonvascular cerebral degenerative disease, such as Alzheimer's disease. Non-cerebral causes of seizures include those which are secondary to cerebral anoxia as in prolonged syncopal attacks due, for example, to cardiac arythmias. Seizures may also be triggered by a wide variety of drugs that have proconvulsant side effects, notably tricyclic antidepressants, phenothiazines, and aminophylline. The role of alcohol in triggering seizures in older people or in interfering with control must not be forgotten.

Management

Reassurance, education, and information are of paramount importance in the management of elderly patients with seizures as in any other age group. Guidance on driving regulations, reasonable risk-taking, and the avoidance of precipitants of seizures should be covered. The mainstay of treatment is drug therapy. This should not be undertaken lightly and a so-called therapeutic trial of antiepileptic drugs in patients whose episodes are of uncertain nature is usually undesirable, unless the events are occurring with such frequency that the response to drugs can be assessed very quickly. It must be remembered that the adverse impact of drugs may outweigh the episodic discomfort of an occasional seizure. Drug treatment is usually started in patients who have more than one unprovoked generalized seizure or a single major seizure where there is a continuing underlying cause as in the case of a patient who has had a cerebral infarct in the past. The evidence that early treatment prevents recurrent epilepsy from becoming chronic (the notion that "fits breed fits") is poor. Patients with minor seizures that are not in any way interfering with their life may, if the episodes are infrequent, reasonably elect not to have drug treatment.

Recent meta-analyses have made the choice of anticonvulsant a little easier. There is evidence that carbamazepine has some advantages over the other first-line drugs (phenytoin or sodium valproate) for the generality of elderly people who have partial or secondary generalized seizures. However, there may be a case for using other drugs for first-line treatment in patients with specific problems. Where compliance demands that patients receive medication once daily, there may be a case for phenytoin, although this may predispose to bone demineralization as well as having the neuropsychiatric effects shared with other anticonvulsants. Carbamazepine may predispose to hyponatraemia (low sodium in the blood or less than 130 mmol/l), particularly in patients on diuretics or who have recurrent chest infections. Sodium valproate may be the drug of choice for patients who cannot tolerate either phenytoin or carbamazepine or in the small number of patients who have primary generalized seizures. There is relatively little evidence about the newer generation of anticonvulsants but lamotragine appears to be at least as effective as carbamazepine and may have fewer side effects, although it is expensive; and gabapentin has the advantage of not interacting with other drugs as well as being relatively nontoxic, although it may also be relatively less effect in controlling seizures. There are no recommended doses of anticonvulsants for older people. Overall, the retrospective analysis of a Veterans Administration's study of the effect of age on epilepsy and its treatment showed that older patients' seizures were better controlled and they were on lower doses of anticonvulsants than were younger patients. However, there is enormous variation between older people. Anti-epileptic drug monitoring may be particularly useful in the case of phenytoin and carbamazepine. The prognosis for control is at least as good as, or possibly better than, in the general adult population. There is little evidence about the appropriateness of withdrawal of anticonvulsants as studies have not been done in older people. Presently, an elderly person who has been started appropriately on an anticonvulsant may have to remain on it for the rest of his or her life.

Services for elderly people with epilepsy are often poorly developed: such patients fall between geriatrics and neurology services. There is a case for developing specialized epilepsy services for older people that can address both management of seizures and other concurrent problems and associated disabilities. A key element of that service would be a specialist epilepsy nurse.

RAYMOND C. TALLIS

See also BALANCE AND MOBILITY; DEMENTIA; DISEASE PRESENTATION; DRUGS AND AGING; FAINTING; STROKE.

BIBLIOGRAPHY

KRÄMER, G. *Epilepsy in the Elderly—Clinical Aspects and Pharmacology.* Stuttgart: Georg Thieme Verlag, 1999.
ROWAN, J. A., and RAMSEY, R. E. *Seizures and Epilepsy in the Elderly.* Newton, Mass.: Butterworth-Heinemann, 1997.
TALLIS, R. C. *Epilepsy in Elderly People.* London: Martin Dunitz, 1995.

ERECTILE DYSFUNCTION

See ANDROPAUSE; MENOPAUSE; SEXUALITY

ESTATE PLANNING

The property and property rights a person owns are considered his or her *estate. Estate planning* can be defined as thinking about and developing a plan for the acquisition, conservation, use, and ultimately the disposition of one's estate. However, estate planning is even broader, in the sense that it involves people as well as property. Some of the most powerful motivations for estate planning arise out of concern for family members and other people who are important in a person's life.

Everyone, in fact, has an estate plan—whether or not it results from planning. People make decisions and take actions throughout their lives that affect what assets they will acquire, how much they will acquire, how many of those assets they will retain at the end of their lives, and how those remaining assets will transfer to their heirs upon their death. Estate planning seeks to bring order to what might otherwise be a haphazard process of managing one's estate.

Purpose of estate planning

Although many American households do not develop an estate plan, there are several practical reasons for making one. After a person dies, he or she usually wants his or her possessions to go to certain individuals and/or charities. People who are supporting someone, such as a spouse or children, want that financial support to continue. A parent of a minor child needs to indicate who the guardian will be for that child. People who own small businesses may hope to see the business continued by the next generation, and those with sufficient wealth to incur estate taxes want to minimize these taxes as much as possible.

The estate planning process

The first step in the estate planning process typically involves gathering data about the properties owned, how they are owned, and their value. Then the objectives of the estate owner need to be clarified, conflicts between competing objectives recognized, and priorities established. The various available techniques for accomplishing these specific objectives need to be considered, as oftentimes there will be more than one alternative technique available and the techniques that are most likely to accomplish the estate owner's objectives should be selected. Once a plan of action is selected, it needs to be implemented, and after implementation, it should be reviewed periodically and revised, if necessary. Whenever there is a major change in a family or a change in ownership of property, it is important to review the estate plan.

Property transfers and estate planning. Anyone who owns property may transfer it during their lifetime by either sale or gift. A gift is a transfer in exchange for nothing in return or for less than the full value of the gifted property. Any person can also declare their intent to give property to individuals or organizations upon their death by making a *will*. A will identifies who will receive the assets in an estate. It may also be used to accomplish other estate planning objectives, such as naming a guardian for minor children. A will must conform to legal formalities established by the law of the state in which it will be administered. Wills should be reviewed regularly and updated periodically.

Will substitutes. Certain types of property interests transfer at death by operation of law, by contractual arrangement, or by trust. A will is powerless to affect the transfer of these assets, and these forms of transfer take precedence over transfers by will. As a group, all property interests that have their own built-in transfer mechanism at death are called *will substitutes*. Examples of will substitutes are property owned in joint tenancy with the right of survivorship; individual retirement accounts (IRAs) that transfer property, by contractual agreement, to a named beneficiary other than the decedent's estate, and revocable living trusts. Federal law protects a surviving spouse's interests in a deceased spouse's qualified retirement benefits, except for IRAs, even when the surviving spouse is not the named beneficiary. Assets that are will substitutes bypass the formal estate administration processes established by state laws. As a result, will substitutes can be used to accomplish objectives such as reducing estate administration costs, increasing privacy, and making a quicker and easier transfer to intended heirs.

Intestacy. Property that is not transferred at death by either a will substitute or a valid will transfers according to state intestacy laws. A person is said to die *intestate* when they die without leaving a valid will. State intestacy laws set forth a plan for how assets transfer to heirs that are not transferred by will or will substitute. Typically, intestacy laws provide for distribution of a portion of estate assets, first to a surviving spouse, then to surviving children, and grandchildren, then to parents, then to other blood relatives, and finally to the state if there are no surviving blood relatives.

Probate. The property and intestacy laws of the state in which a decedent is domiciled or, if it is real estate, in the state in which the property is located control the estate administration process. A *domicile* is a person's permanent residence. *Probate* refers specifically to the process whereby a will is admitted to court (to prove the authenticity of the will) or a deceased person is determined to have died without a will. Probate is usually handled in the local county court system. The term *probate* is also widely used to refer to the entire estate administration process. The probate court appoints someone to handle the affairs of the deceased; to inventory the assets of the deceased person; to have the value of those assets appraised; to pay the debts of the decedent; to file any income, gift, or estate tax returns due from the estate; to pay any taxes owed by the estate; to distribute the remaining property according to the terms of the will or as state intestacy law dictates; and to file a final accounting with the probate court.

Community property. Nine U.S. states are *community property states*. The nine states are Arizona, California, Idaho, Louisiana, Nevada, New Mexico, Texas, Washington, and Wisconsin. Spouses who acquire property while residing in a community property state are deemed to own the property in equal shares, regardless of who paid for the property or whose names are on the document of title. Spouses who move either in or out of a community property state may need to consider the implications for estate planning, as community property retains it character even when spouses move out of a community property state.

Limited interests in property. For added flexibility in estate planning, ownership of assets may be carved up into limited interests. One example is a life estate, where a life tenant receives use of the property and any income from the property for life, but other individuals, called *remainder persons,* own a future interest in the property.

Prevalence of wills

About 70 percent of Americans die without a will. Those who make a will tend to have certain characteristics in common. According to information from an experimental module of the 1994 Asset and Health Dynamics Among the Oldest Old (AHEAD), higher education and greater wealth increase the probability of having a will. In addition, those who consulted a financial advisor, participated in 100 hours or more of volunteer work in the previous year, or donated more than $500 to religious or charitable organizations in the previous year are more likely to have a will. White households are more likely to have a will than African-American, Hispanic, and other racial groups.

A will is not an estate plan. A will is only one component of a complete estate plan. More sophisticated estate plans usually rely on a combination of estate planning techniques, including a will and trusts, in order to achieve desired objectives. Wills must be carefully coordinated with other estate planning techniques, as there are some things a will cannot do. A will cannot transfer property that is transferred by trusts, title, or contract (will substitutes), so the will must be carefully coordinated with these. A will cannot meet the needs of a person who is incapacitated, but not yet deceased. According to the Mayo Clinic and the Harvard Medical School, a sixty-five-year-old person has at least one chance in four of needing an average of two and one-half years of long-term care. As a result, estate planning often involves the use of *advance directives—* written legal documents that declare an individual's wishes concerning how certain physical and financial matters will be handled, if and when the person loses the capacity to make decisions.

Examples of advance directives are the durable health care power of attorney, the living will, the durable power of attorney (for financial matters), and revocable living trusts. *Durable powers of attorney* are called *durable* because they continue in effect after the onset of incapacity. Confor-

mity to the legal formalities set forth in applicable state law is particularly important relative to advance directives. Finally, a comprehensive estate plan will find a way to communicate important information that doesn't belong in a will and should be shared with appropriate individuals, such as one's personal representative, before death. A letter of last instructions is one way that an individual can communicate his or her feelings about important matters such as funeral instructions and organ donation. The wishes of surviving family members in regard to these matters may be decisive unless the decedent clearly expressed his or her wishes in writing.

Trusts

Trusts are an extremely flexible and useful tool for estate planning. A *trust* is a contract between the donor or grantor and the manager of the trust's assets, called the *trustee.* The trustee holds legal title to the trust property. The trustee has a legal duty to manage the trust property for the benefit of the trust's beneficiaries. The five common elements of all trusts are a grantor, a trustee, a beneficiary, the trust property, and the terms of the trust agreement. Trusts that take effect during the grantor's lifetime are living trusts, while those that take effect upon the grantor's death are testamentary trusts. Testamentary trusts are established by a decedent's will. Trusts may be either revocable or irrevocable. Property transfers to an irrevocable trust are completed gifts; that is, they are no longer owned by the grantor. Property transfers to a revocable trust are not completed gifts, and the grantor retains the power to retrieve the trust property.

There are many different types and uses of trusts. Particular types of trusts are selected based on their usefulness for accomplishing particular estate planning objectives. For example, one use of a *qualified terminable interest property trust* (Q-TIP) is to provide income to a surviving spouse from a second or subsequent marriage, while ensuring that the trust property is ultimately distributed to children from previous marriages. Some objectives can only be accomplished through the use of a particular type of trust. For example, a *qualified domestic trust* must be used to obtain the benefits of the estate tax marital deduction for a nonresident alien spouse of a U.S. citizen. Trusts are particularly useful in dealing with a whole range of situations where the intended beneficiary either is not legally competent to own property, such as a minor, or may become incapable of managing his or her own property.

Federal estate and gift taxes

The federal estate and gift taxes are transfer taxes on the value of property transferred by lifetime gift (gift tax) or from a decedent's estate (estate tax). Every individual has an applicable credit amount against federal estate and gift tax liability. The applicable credit amount is $345,800 in 2002. This is equivalent to a taxable estate of $1,000,000, which is called the applicable exclusion amount. In 2002, the effective marginal estate and gift tax rates range from 37 to 55 percent on taxable estates that exceed the applicable credit amount, which makes minimizing transfer taxes an important objective.

Estate and gift taxes are cumulative. All taxable lifetime gifts made after 1976 are included in the computation of a decedent's federal estate tax liability. Despite this fact, taxable lifetime gifts have one important advantage over testamentary transfers. Taxable lifetime gifts can freeze the value of appreciating properties as of the date of the gift, so that all future appreciation is removed from the donor's estate. Nevertheless, taxpayers generally shouldn't make lifetime taxable gifts that exceed the applicable exclusion amount. One potential disadvantage of lifetime gifts is that the recipient of a gift must take the donor's income tax basis in the gifted property. The effect is to transfer any income tax gain on the property to the recipient. Unlike gifted property, most inherited property receives an income tax basis equal to the fair market value of the property on the date of the decedent's death.

Some gifts are not subject to a gift tax. The most important type is a *present interest gift,* which falls under the annual gift tax exclusion amount of $10,000 per recipient (an amount that is indexed annually for inflation). There is no limit to the number of recipients, so large amounts of money or other valuable property interests can be given to friends or family while using the annual exclusion amount to shield the gifts from being taxed. The gift must convey a present interest in the property; that is, it must be available for the immediate use, possession, or enjoyment of the recipient. The annual exclusion can be used in combination with an irrevocable living trust to permanently remove large amounts of potentially taxable value from an estate. Gifts to

qualified charitable organizations are tax deductible for either gift or estate tax purposes. Lifetime gifts can also reduce income taxes.

The federal *gross estate* includes the fair market value of everything actually owned at the date of death, as well as all property interests deemed to have been owned at the date of death. A life insurance policy given away within three years of death is an example of a property interest that is deemed to have been owned by a decedent on the date of death.

The federal *taxable estate* is computed by first subtracting, from the gross estate, certain allowable deductions such as funeral expenses, administration expenses, debts, taxes, and losses. The value of property left to a surviving spouse or to charity is then deducted, and then the cumulative total of post-1976 lifetime taxable gifts are added. A tentative *federal estate tax* is computed on this amount, which is called the *federal tax base.* Any tentative estate tax payable is further reduced by gift taxes payable on post-1976 lifetime taxable gifts and applicable credits, which include the applicable credit amount explained earlier.

Because federal law allows an unlimited marital deduction for property passing to a surviving spouse who is a U.S. citizen, the estate tax on the estate of the first spouse to die can be eliminated completely by leaving the whole estate to the surviving spouse. This simple approach may not work in the long run, however, because it wastes the first decedent spouse's applicable credit amount. The combined tax bill for both estates may be much larger than it would have been if less of the first spouse's estate had passed to the survivor. Estate plans for married couples with a combined estate valued in excess of one spouse's applicable exclusion amount should use a *bypass trust* or other technique to avoid overqualifying for the marital deduction. A bypass trust, for example, will provide the surviving spouse with the annual income from the trust property and a limited right to invade the corpus, but does not qualify for the marital deduction.

Generation-skipping transfers that do not exceed the generation-skipping transfer tax exemption amount of $1,000,000 per transferor can save money for large taxable estates. These transfers skip over a generation (e.g., from grandparent to grandchild), and thus reduce the incidence of transfer taxation over time. Taxable estates also may benefit from *valuation planning.*

One form of valuation planning involves establishing an entity such as a *family limited partnership* (FLP), spreading the ownership of the FLP among various family members and restricting the transferability of the interests. With proper planning and implementation, the market value of FLP interests will be subject to considerable discounts.

The Economic Growth and Tax Relief Reconciliation Act of 2001 phases in several changes in federal estate and gift taxation from 2002 through 2010. The changes include increases in applicable credit amounts and reductions in tax rates. The act repeals the estate tax in 2010, but not the gift tax. The most important feature of this new law is that it isn't permanent, which means additional changes in federal estate and gift taxation should be expected.

State estate and inheritance taxes

Two kinds of state death taxes may be required: *estate* and *inheritance*. Estate taxes are levied by only a handful of states, with tax rates that vary from 1 percent to 32 percent. The decedent's estate must pay these taxes. About half of the states use a *pickup tax*, which applies only to the estates that pay federal taxes. The tax is designed to obtain, for the state, some of the money that otherwise would go to the federal government. The revenue comes from the federal government's share of the estate taxes, not from the estate of the deceased. In at least sixteen states, heirs must pay state inheritance taxes based on the value of the assets they receive. Inheritance tax rates typically are lowest (and exemptions highest) for the closest kin, and highest (and exemptions lowest) for more distantly related kin and unrelated beneficiaries. Oftentimes, property left to a surviving spouse is completely exempt from tax. Only ten states have a gift tax on lifetime gifts, although state estate and inheritance taxes may apply to gifts made in anticipation of death.

SHARON A. DEVANEY
W. ALAN MILLER

See also ADVANCE DIRECTIVES FOR HEALTH CARE; ASSETS AND WEALTH; BEQUESTS AND INHERITANCES; MEDICAID; TAXATION.

BIBLIOGRAPHY

ADAMS, K., and BROSTERMAN, R. *The Complete Estate Planning Guide.* New York, N.Y.: New American Library, 1998.

ANDERSON, K. E.; POPE, T. R.; and KRAMER, J. L., eds. *Prentice Hall's Federal Taxation 2000, Corporations, Partnerships, Estates, and Trusts.* Upper Saddle River, N.J.: Prentice-Hall, 2000.

BECKER, G. S. "A Theory of Social Interactions." *Journal of Political Economy* 82 (1974): 1063–1094.

BENNETT, J. G. *Maximize Your Inheritance: For Widows, Widowers and Heirs.* Dearborn Financial Publishing, 1999.

BERNHEIM, B. D.; SHLEIFER, A.; and SUMMERS, L. H. "The Strategic Bequest Motive." *Journal of Political Economy* 93 (1991): 899–927.

BOST, J. C. *Estate Planning and Taxation,* 2000 Annual Edition. Dubuque, Iowa: Kendall/Hunt Publishing Company, 2000.

CHANEY, R. L., and FOGARTY, L. S. *Family Limited Partnerships.* St. Louis, Mo.: General American Life Insurance Company/GenMark, 1993.

FONTAINE, C. J., ed. *Fundamentals of Estate Planning,* 5th ed. Bryn Mawr, Pa.: American College, 2001.

FRIEDMAN, M. *A Theory of the Consumption Function.* Princeton, N.J.: Princeton University Press, 1957.

GARMAN, E. T., and FORGUE, R. E. "Estate Planning." In *Personal Finance,* 6th ed. Edited by E. T. Garman. Boston, Mass.: Houghton Mifflin Company, 2000. Pages 554–567.

GOETTING, M. A. *Older Adults, Bequests, and Wills.* Unpublished doctoral dissertation, Iowa State University, Ames, Iowa: 1996.

HARL, N. E. *Farm Estate & Business Planning,* 12th ed., Niles, Ill.: Century Communications, 1994.

HAWLEY, T. H. *The Artful Dodger's Guide to Planning Your Estate,* 2d ed., Carmel-by-the-Sea, Calif.: Linthicum Press, 2000.

HURD, M. D. "Savings of the Elderly and Desired Bequests." *American Economic Review* 77 (1987): 298–312.

LEIMBERG, S. R.; KASNER, J. A.; KANDELL, S. N.; MILLER, R. G.; ROSENBLOOM, M. S.; and LEVY, H. L. "Anatomical Gifts." In *The Tools & Techniques of Estate Planning,* 10th ed., Cincinnati, Ohio: The National Underwriter Company, 1995. Pages 442–443.

LOCHRAY, P. J. *The Financial Planner's Guide to Estate Planning,* 3d ed., Englewood Cliffs, N.J.: Prentice-Hall, 1992.

MASON, J. "Make Sure You Have a Plan for Your Estate." In *Financial Fitness for Life.* Chicago, Ill.: Dearborn, 1999. Pages 279–295.

SCHRADER, S. J. G., ed. *Introduction to Estates and Trusts,* 2d ed. The Philadelphia Institute, St. Paul, Minn.: West Publishing Company, 1992.

SHENKMAN, M. M. *Estate Planning after the 1997 Tax Act.* New York: John Wiley & Sons, 1998.

SHILLING, D. *Financial Planning for the Older Client*, 5th ed. Erlanger, Ky.: National Underwriter, 2001.

ESTROGEN

Menopause, defined as the permanent cessation of menstruation, is the final stage in the process of female reproductive aging. Because of the dramatic increase in life span during the twentieth century, the average woman in this country experiencing menopause has more than one-third of her life ahead of her, and as of the late 1990s, an estimated thirty-five million American women were postmenopausal. In practical terms, menopause can only be diagnosed "after the fact," that is, after a period of twelve months of amenorrhea (absence of menstruation). The average age of menopause is fifty-one, which is preceded by a two- to eight-year period of changing ovarian function, known as perimenopause.

In addition to the variability in the age of menopause and in the length of perimenopause, there is also great variability in the extent of menopausal symptoms. The types of symptoms reported include hot flashes (sensation of warmth, frequently accompanied by skin flushing and perspiration), insomnia, night sweats, depression, headache, backache, painful intercourse, loss of sex drive, vaginal dryness, and problems with short-term memory. Cultural differences may play a role in some of the reporting of symptoms, and it is also possible that different concepts of what is discomfort, or real lifestyle differences, such as exercise and diet, may actually diminish these phenomena in some cultures.

What causes menopause?

The immediate reason that women stop cycling is that their ovaries become depleted of eggs. Humans stop making eggs even before they are born and the seven million eggs contained in the ovaries of a five-month female fetus are all she will ever have. At birth, females have only one to two million eggs, and by puberty, only one-thirtieth of the original seven million remain. During each menstrual cycle, one egg becomes fully developed and will be ovulated. Somewhere between ages thirty-five and forty-five, the constant rate of egg loss suddenly accelerates about two-fold, so that at menopause only

about one thousand eggs are left. It is believed that the alteration in the regularity of cycles compromises the feedback interaction between the ovaries and the neuroendocrine system, ultimately leading to a sharp decrease in the levels of estrogen and progesterone.

The dramatic reduction in the level of estrogen is associated with a wide variety of physiological changes that correlate with menopause. Indeed, as many as four hundred different actions of estrogen have been identified, affecting such diverse systems as circulation, brain activity, sexual behavior, bone biology, sleep patterns, intestinal absorption of food, and immune activity. Although menopause is clearly associated with such negative health effects as osteoporosis and heart disease, not all the alterations of menopause are detrimental. For example, before menopause, the risk of American women developing breast cancer doubles every three years, whereas after menopause it takes thirteen years for the risk to double again.

Effects of menopause

Menopause diminishes the incidence of gynecological cancers because estrogen and progesterone are involved in the development of these cancers in the first place. During the latter part of each menstrual cycle, to prepare the body for possible pregnancy, estrogen and progesterone cause the cells lining the milk ducts in the breast to divide. Every time a cell divides, there is a chance that errors (mutations) can occur in its genetic material, so that the more cycles a woman undergoes that involve cell division of the duct cells, the greater the chance of mutations. Conversely, when these cells become specialized to produce milk during and after pregnancy, they are no longer proliferating and therefore are less likely to undergo mutations. Thus, the rise in breast cancer during the last half of the twentieth century can probably be explained in large part by changes in the length of the total reproductive period, the number of pregnancies and more common delays in having a first child. Ironically, therefore, menopause in its modern context is actually a favorable event for women's health with respect to breast cancer.

In contrast to its beneficial effect on breast cancer incidence, menopause is detrimental to numerous aspects of health. One of the major outcomes of the decline in estrogen is the increased risk of cardiovascular disease and death from heart attacks. In the United States, cardiovascular disease is the number one killer of men starting at age thirty-five, whereas in women, it is not until after the age of sixty that cardiovascular disease becomes the number one cause of death. Indeed, heart and arterial disease kill almost ten times as many postmenopausal women in Western society as do all the gynecological cancers combined.

The second major consequence of the decline in estrogen is osteoporosis, thinning and loss of bone that can ultimately lead to wrist, hip, and vertebral fractures. Both men and women lose bone as they age, but during the first five to ten years after menopause, women experience accelerated bone loss, making them much more likely than men to suffer collapse of vertebrae, wrist fractures, and broken hips. About 20 percent of elderly women with osteoporetic hip fractures die of complications within one year, ranking osteoporosis as the twelfth greatest killer in the United States. Similar to heart disease, osteoporosis is more deadly than all the gynecological cancers combined.

Hormone replacement therapy (HRT)

Most animals in the wild do not live past menopause. By contrast, typical women in industrialized countries can expect to live more than one-third of their lives beyond their reproductive years. If living past menopause is a relatively recent phenomenon, then evolution will not have had time to adjust women's bodies to living with reduced postmenopausal hormone levels. From this perspective, perhaps HRT (used in this entry to designate both estrogen alone or in combination with progesterone) would be advantageous. On the other hand, if menopause arose during evolution as an adaptive mechanism, then women's bodies are likely to be physiologically adjusted to altered hormone levels, and upsetting that delicate balance with HRT might lead to unexpected health-damaging consequences. These two opposing theoretical possibilities are further complicated by an overwhelming amount of often conflicting data on the risks and benefits of HRT, leading to a great deal of confusion and uncertainty, even among experts, as to the optimal strategy for women who reach menopause. In this regard, decisions should also take into account the personal treatment goals, because therapy directed at some symptoms, such as hot flashes, can be

short-term, whereas treatment of a chronic condition, such as osteoporosis, is usually lifelong. It should also be mentioned that the particular doses and routes of HRT can vary according to indication, with different amounts and regimens, including addition of progesterone to prevent endometrial hyperplasia.

The ideal method to scientifically evaluate all of the effects of HRT would be to conduct a randomized trial on a large group of women who are similar in many characteristics, with half the group being given HRT and the other half, a placebo. Indeed, one such study, the so-called Women's Health Initiative, was in progress in 2001, so ultimately, more definitive and comprehensive data on the risks and benefits of HRT will probably become available. At present, however, women reaching menopause are forced to rely predominantly on data from observational, retrospective epidemiological studies. Such studies are subject to a variety of biases, such as educational and socioeconomic backgrounds that might affect the decision of a woman to begin HRT. Nevertheless, it is interesting to note that although the observational studies differ in the details, such as differences in the ages of the subjects and length of estrogen use, virtually all of the analyses demonstrated reduced risk of death among estrogen users. The most comprehensive of these studies, which followed women for more than twenty-five years and had access to all medical records, including precise estrogen doses, showed that the yearly death rate among estrogen users was about half that of nonusers. Nonetheless, because all of these studies were observational, the findings must still be interpreted with caution.

In addition to the overall risk of death, a correlation has been suggested between several specific health parameters and the use of HRT. The most convincing effects are on the process of osteoporosis. Evidence from observational studies indicates that postmenopausal hormone users have fewer fractures than nonusers and show retardation of bone loss. However, the time at which HRT must be initiated in order to protect against fracture is not known. Controversy also exists regarding the maximum age at which HRT can be initiated to be of clinical utility. Although the beneficial effects of estrogen on bone have been demonstrated in women with established osteoporosis, to achieve maximum benefits, HRT should begin at the time of cessation of menses.

The putative beneficial effect of estrogen on cardiovascular status is controversial. Many observational studies on the relation between the use of estrogen and risk events from coronary heart disease suggested lower rates among postmenopausal estrogen users versus nonusers. However, three large prospective studies in the year 2000 concluded that HRT neither prevents cardiovascular problems in healthy women nor protects women with abnormal cardiac function against future cardiovascular episodes. Thus, despite the encouraging suggestions of earlier studies and the biological plausibility of protection against coronary heart disease associated with postmenopausal HRT, the cardioprotective effect of HRT is questionable. Indeed, the American Heart Association has recently issued an advisory statement discouraging the use of HRT in situations where the sole purpose is improvement of cardiovascular health.

Possible beneficial effects of HRT against arthritis, cognitive decline and Alzheimer's disease, periodontal disease, cataract formation, and colon cancer have been proposed based on epidemiological analyses, but further research is required to confirm these results. In any case, it is clear that at the very least, HRT alleviates such non-life-threatening symptoms of menopause as hot flashes, insomnia, and depression.

Precautions regarding HRT

HRT is absolutely contraindicated in women with undiagnosed vaginal bleeding, breast or endometrial cancer, and active deep vein thrombosis. Women with previous clotting disorders, especially in the setting of pregnancy, should be specifically evaluated medically before initiating HRT. Use of HRT after a diagnosis of melanoma remains controversial, and concerns have been raised regarding the use of HRT in women with liver disease or previous gallbladder disease. Other potentially important side effects that have not been adequately analyzed include immunological changes, in light of the presence of receptors for estrogen in various immune cells.

The most controversial aspect of HRT remains the potential increase in breast cancer resulting from long-term estrogen use. There are recognized experts on each side of the debate, but the majority of studies support no significant increase in breast cancer risk in women receiving postmenopausal HRT. Clearly, resolution of this important issue requires a randomized-controlled trial with longitudinal data. In any case, for women who have proven breast cancer or who have a known risk of developing breast cancer, postmenopausal HRT is contraindicated. The safety of HRT after breast cancer remains controversial, with available evidence neither assuring safety nor proving any toxic effects.

Designer estrogens

Estrogen thus appears to be a contradictory molecule, both essential and harmful to women. Because of the dual nature of the effects of estrogen, researchers are actively seeking to identify so-called *designer estrogens,* chemicals that are known technically as selective estrogen receptor modulators (SERM). These substances would behave like estrogen in some tissues but block its actions in others. It is possible that one such compound, raloxifine, now prescribed for maintaining bone density in older women, may be able to protect women from osteoporosis and coronary artery disease as well as endometrial and breast cancer. Long-term studies with this and other SERMs in development may be able to protect women single-handedly from the multiple disorders that increase in prevalence after menopause. For the time being, however, each woman must weigh the known risks and benefits of the available forms of HRT and, together with information and advice from health care providers that takes into account her own health history, make her personal decision regarding whether or not to initiate HRT at the time of menopause.

RITA B. EFFROS

See also CANCER, BIOLOGY OF; ENDOCRINE SYSTEM; HEART DISEASE; LONGEVITY; MENOPAUSE; OSTEOPOROSIS.

BIBLIOGRAPHY

AUSTAD, S. A. *Why We Age.* New York: John Wiley & Sons, 1997.

BELLANTONI, M. F., and BLACKMAN, M. R. "Menopause and Consequences." In *Handbook of the Biology of Aging.* Edited by E. Schneider and J. Rowe. San Diego: Academic Press, Inc., 1996. Pages 415–430.

GREENDALE, G. A.; LEE, N. P.; and ARRIOLA, E. A. "The Menopause." *Lancet* 353 (1999): 571–580.

GRODSTEIN, F.; STAMPFER, M. J.; COLDITZ, G. A.; WILLETT, W. C.; MANSON, J. E.; JOFFE, M.;

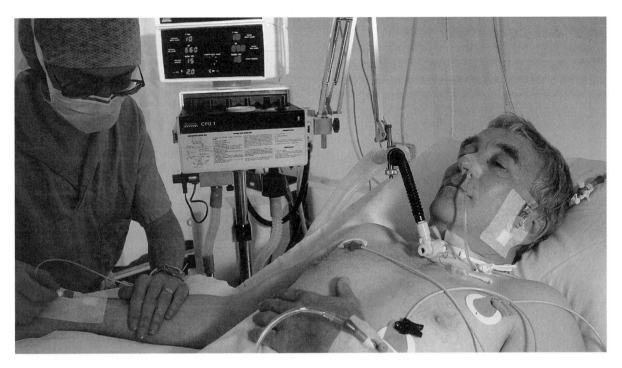

A patient on a life-support system in the intensive care unit of a hospital. Many people feel that disconnecting such life-support machines after a person has stopped breathing on his or her own represents a form of euthanasia that should be allowed, while many others feel such an action is both unethical and immoral. (Photo Researchers, Inc.)

ROSNER, B.; FUCHS, C.; HANKINSON, S. E.; HUNTER, D. J.; HENNEKENS, C. H.; and SPEIZER, F. E. "Postmenopausal Hormone Therapy and Mortality." *New England Journal of Medicine* 336 (1997): 1769–1775.

JORDAN, V. C. "Designer Estrogens." *Scientific American,* October 1998, pp. 60–67.

MOSCA, L. M.; COLLINS, P.; HERRINGTON, D. M.; MENDELSOHN, M. E.; PASTERNAK, R. C.; ROBERTSON, R. M.; SCHENCK-GUSTAFSSON, K.; SMITH, S. C.; TAUBERT, K. A.; and WENGER, N. K. "Hormone Replacement Therapy and Cardiovascular Disease: A Statement for Healthcare Professionals from the American Heart Association." *Circulation* 104 (2001): 499–503.

WISE, P. M.; KRAJNAK, K. M.; and KASHON, M. L. "Menopause: The Aging of Multiple Pacemakers." *Science* 273 (1996): 67–70.

EUTHANASIA AND SENICIDE

"Euthanasia" is a word coined from the Greek language (*eu,* good or noble; *thanatos,* death) in the seventeenth century by Francis Bacon to refer to an easy, painless, happy death. It has now come to mean the active causation of a patient's death through the injection of a lethal dose of medication. Euthanasia differs from assisted suicide, in which the patient self-administers a lethal dose of a compound, usually prescribed by a physician who knows the patient intends to use it to end his or her life.

Assisted suicide and euthanasia differ from a patient's right to refuse or withdraw from unwanted treatment even if that refusal or withdrawal may cause death. The right to refuse or withdraw from unwanted treatment is based on the principle of informed consent that underlies the practice of medicine. That is it is the right of every patient, whether terminally ill or not, and has nothing per se to do with hastening death.

The difference between the two was affirmed by the U.S. Supreme Court in a case in which proponents of assisted suicide challenged a New York law prohibiting it (*Vacco* v. *Quill*). They invoked the equal protection clause of the Fourteenth Amendment to the Constitution to argue that patients denied euthanasia were not being given the same right to hasten death as patients who could do so by choosing to withdraw from life support. The Supreme Court rejected their contention that the right to refuse life-sustaining medical treatment "is nothing more or less than assisted suicide."

The Court based its analysis on intent and causation, two legal principles used to distinguish acts that may have the same result. Under a causation analysis, the Court reasoned that a patient who refuses life-sustaining medical treatment dies from an underlying disease; a patient who self-administers lethal medication prescribed by a physician is killed by the medication. The physician's intent is different in the two situations; a doctor withdrawing or not administering treatment is complying with a patient's wishes, whereas a doctor assisting in a patient's suicide intends that the patient die.

Moreover, a patient who commits suicide with the help of a doctor has the specific intention of ending his or her life; a patient refusing or discontinuing treatment may not. Refusal of life-sustaining treatment is not identical with assisted suicide and *everyone*, regardless of physical condition, is entitled, if competent, to refuse life-sustaining medical treatment, whereas *no one* is allowed to assist a suicide. Thus the law applies evenhandedly to all, and protects all equally.

Historical background

Although throughout history individual philosophers from Plato and Seneca to Montaigne and Hume justified self-induced death for those who were severely sick and suffering, social policies aimed at discouraging suicide have reflected the religious view of life as a divine gift. The waning influence of religion contributed to the questioning of such policies. Physicians, however, were not significantly involved in this questioning until the discovery in the eighteenth century of analgesics and anesthetics that could relieve suffering in dying patients, as well as easily and painlessly end life.

Greater interest in medical euthanasia coincided with the birth in the early twentieth century of the modern hospital as an institution that could provide curative medical and surgical treatment. As medicine learned to control acute infectious disease, life expectancy gradually increased from a norm of forty in 1850 to almost double that figure in 2000. Degenerative and late-onset diseases made the discussion of end-of-life care more urgent, and the role of the physician more important.

Interest in euthanasia at the turn of the twentieth century coincided with the development of the eugenics movement in the United States and Europe. Stimulated by advances in genetics and a misguided attempt to hasten the process of natural selection that had recently been described by Charles Darwin, eugenics envisioned a perfection of the human race, initially through sterilization of the unfit or degenerate, variously defined as criminals, prostitutes, alcoholics, epileptics, and the mentally ill. Thirty states passed sterilization laws; eventually sixty thousand Americans were sterilized; and the movement was embraced by figures ranging from Theodore Roosevelt and Woodrow Wilson to Oliver Wendell Holmes.

Although Germany was not the first country to embrace eugenics, it took hold there more deeply than elsewhere, led by Ernest Haeckel, a famed and respected biologist and social scientist. Haeckel advocated euthanasia for the "hundreds of thousands of incurables—lunatics, lepers, people with cancer etc.. . .artificially kept alive," whom he saw as a drain on the economy and a threat to the health of the Aryan race (Gallagher). Alfred Hoche and Karl Binding, a psychiatrist and an attorney, respectively, built on Haeckel's work to write *The Permission to Destroy Life Unworthy of Life* (1920), an influential book much admired by Adolf Hitler. Hoche and Binding proposed that those who were retarded, deformed, or terminally ill, and those damaged by accident or disease, should be put to death to further racial hygiene and/or because they were a burden to society.

When the Nazis came to power, they legalized voluntary euthanasia, but soon adopted the Haeckel/Hoche/Binding proposals on a scale that even those three men could hardly have imagined. Under the T-4 program (Tiergartenstrasse 4 was the Berlin address from which the program was administered) German doctors ended the lives of several hundred thousand mentally ill children and adults with conditions considered incurable, ranging from schizophrenia to senility.

The postwar revulsion to the holocaust, and to the role of physicians in implementing it, discredited the euthanasia movement. A significant minority of advocates, however, while not stressing the eugenic aspects of euthanasia, continue to see it as a necessary social remedy for the increasing number of old people, the inadequacy of nursing homes, and the economic cost to families and society of caring for the elderly. In the words of Eliot Slater, an English psychiatrist and advocate of euthanasia, "When a chronically sick man dies, he ceases to be a burden on himself, on his family, on the health services and on the community."

In the past some nomadic tribes of Native Americans and Eskimos, such as the Shoshone (Steward) and the Ahtna (De Laguna and McClellan), motivated by the need to move in pursuit of food and other necessities, felt the need to abandon the elderly—a practice known as senicide. Derek Humphry, founder of the Hemlock Society, believes that social and economic necessity will force modern societies in the same direction. He writes, "One must look at the realities of the increasing cost of health care in an aging society, because in the final analysis, economics, not the quest for broadened individual liberties or increased autonomy, will drive assisted suicide to the plateau of acceptable practice." Pietr Admiraal, one of foremost Dutch practitioners of euthanasia, believes that by 2020 Europe may resort to euthanasia to deal with a large population of elderly people. Admiraal says he is glad he will not be alive to see it, but he remains a strong advocate of euthanasia (Hendin).

The revival of interest in euthanasia in the 1970s and 1980s, however, was primarily centered on compassion for suffering patients, most of whom were elderly. It was considered in part to have been a reaction to modern medical technology that permits maintenance of a pointless semblance of life and creates fear of painful and undignified death.

The modern argument

Compassion. Contemporary advocacy for euthanasia centers on compassion for patients whose suffering is considered to be incapable of relief in any other way or who wish to be protected from what they fear will be an undignified death. In the Netherlands, the only country where assisted suicide and euthanasia have long been legally sanctioned, guidelines require that the patient must be experiencing unbearable and unrelievable suffering before the physician can assist in a suicide.

Opponents of legalization point out that the overwhelming majority of patients requesting euthanasia change their mind when their suffering is addressed by a knowledgeable and caring physician. In the exceptional case, sedation may

be necessary to relieve suffering. They see death as becoming undignified when patients are not valued or treated with respect.

Proponents counter that even if it is theoretically possible to provide a painless or dignified death to most or all suffering patients, the trained personnel or the social and medical systems that would permit it are not in place. In the meantime, they claim physician-assisted suicide is needed to end patient suffering.

Compassion can be misdirected, however, and is no guarantee against doing harm. Lewis Thomas, one of the deans of American medicine, wrote insightfully about the sense of failure and helplessness that physicians may experience in the face of death; such feelings may explain why they have such difficulty discussing terminal illness with patients. These feelings may also explain both doctors' tendency to use excessive measures to maintain life and their need to make death a medical decision. By deciding when patients die, and by making death a medical decision, the physician preserves the illusion of mastery over the disease and the accompanying feelings of helplessness. Compassion for the patient can become a rationalization for the physician's own emotional discomfort.

In overburdened families, compassion that requires the death of the patient can also be self-serving. An overburdened spouse justifies ending the life of an infirm husband or wife on the grounds of compassion. A Swedish study (Wasserman) examined the response of relatives to the suicide attempts of elderly patients with somatic illnesses. Family members, overwhelmed by what they felt were the relentless needs of the patient, were likely to delay calling the doctor, to urge nonresuscitation of the patient, and to have expressed wishes that the patient would die. Once help from social and welfare agencies was arranged, families were able to be genuinely compassionate and the patients wanted to live.

Justifying euthanasia by compassion also opens the door to ending the lives of people who appear to be suffering but are not able to make their wishes known, and of those who are capable of consent but do not wish to do so or are simply not consulted. Abuses in all of these categories in the Netherlands have been a cause of concern (Hendin et al., 1997) but are rarely punished. Since there is no objective way of determining what is unbearable pain and suffering, when pain and suffering become all-important as criteria, the decision depends on the doctor's subjective assessment.

Choice. Partly for these reasons, advocates of legalization are increasingly not basing their argument on compassion for those who are suffering, but on the patient's right to choose. Oregon, the only state to legalize assisted suicide, while copying Dutch guidelines in many respects, did not make suffering a criterion for assisted suicide. Simply having a terminal illness, a prognosis of less than six months to live, and a wish to die are enough. How helpful are these criteria and what choice do Oregon patients really have?

When choice is the major determinant, physicians are not encouraged to inquire into the source of the desperation that usually underlies most requests for assisted suicide and euthanasia, an inquiry that leads patients and physicians to have the kind of discussion that often brings relief for patients and makes assisted suicide seem unnecessary. Nor are physicians asked or required by the Oregon law to make such an inquiry (Hendin et al. 1998).

When their suffering is addressed by a knowledgeable and caring physician, the overwhelming number of patients requesting euthanasia change their mind. For the exceptional case sedation may be necessary to provide relief. If confronted with a physician who does not know how to relieve their distress, and the choice is between continuing to suffer and an expedited death, the patient really has little choice. The debate over euthanasia is in part a debate over whether the need to reduce suffering in those who are terminally ill requires the legalization of euthanasia.

The ethical rationale of Peter Singer

The philosopher Peter Singer has attempted to give an ethical justification for euthanasia on the utilitarian principle that approves of actions that enhance the happiness of the individual—in this case the relief from suffering and the exercise of autonomy—as well as the happiness of others who are aware they have that option. Singer assumes that when guidelines are in place, as in the Netherlands, abuses such as nonvoluntary euthanasia are rare; in fact the Dutch government's own sanctioned studies show they are common (Van der Maas et al., 1992, 1996). Moreover, there is substantial evidence that pal-

liative care in the Netherlands has suffered and hospice care has lagged behind other countries because of the easier option of euthanasia. Thus, on purely utilitarian grounds there may be reason to reject euthanasia.

Singer is guided by another principle that influences his thinking on euthanasia. He believes that society has an obligation to protect only sentient persons (i.e., persons capable of reasoning, remembering, and recognizing others). Infanticide of a child with hemophilia is justified when it increases the happiness of the parents. Nonvoluntary euthanasia for the elderly could on the same principle be justified not only on grounds of compassion but also, Keough Singer does not explicitly say so, because it increases the happiness or lessens the burden on children. Philosophers have rejected Singer's position as dealing with the consequences of actions while ignoring the tradition in Western philosophy that judges the morality of actions not just by their consequences but also by the intentions that motivate them.

Conclusion

All relationships in a society are affected when society abandons infirm elderly persons and treats them as expendable. The Eskimo tribes that practiced senicide also were often obliged by the need for good hunters to practice female infanticide; more fortunately situated inland Eskimos, such as the Ihalmiut, who practiced neither, had a sense of their own antiquity, were more socially cohesive, and appear to have led happier lives (Mowat).

Americans are not, nor even with an increase in the elderly population are they likely to be, in the desperate situation of the Shoshone or the Ahnta. Providing the care needed by elderly persons who are seriously or terminally ill will, however, require improving the education of physicians in palliative care, removing regulations that restrict the ways in which physicians can treat pain, widening the availability of hospice care, fostering proper reimbursement for end-of-life care, and passing better-crafted surrogacy laws that, while protecting incompetent patients, also permit proxies to see to it that inappropriate treatments may be withdrawn from them. If all this is done, assisted suicide and euthanasia will not seem a necessary option to elderly patients and the issue of legalization of assisted suicide and euthanasia will become less relevant.

HERBERT HENDIN

See also AUTONOMY; COMPETENCY; PAIN MANAGEMENT; PALLIATIVE CARE; REFUSING AND WITHDRAWING MEDICAL TREATMENT.

BIBLIOGRAPHY

BERKOWITZ, P. "The Utilitarian Horrors of Peter Singer: Other People's Mothers." *The New Republic,* January 10, 2000, pp. 27–36.

DE LAGUNA, F., and MCCLELLAN, C. "Ahtna." In *Handbook of North American Indians,* Vol. 6, *Subarctic.* Edited by June Helm. Washington, D.C.: Smithsonian Institution, 1983. Pages 641–663.

GALLAGHER, H. G. *By Trust Betrayed.* Arlington, Va.: Vandamere Press, 1995.

HENDIN H. *Seduced by Death: Doctors, Patients, and Assisted Suicide.* New York: W. W. Norton, 1998.

HENDIN, H.; FOLEY, K.; and WHITE, M. "Physician-Assisted Suicide: Reflections on Oregon's First Case." *Issues in Law and Medicine* 14 (1998): 243–270.

HENDIN, H.; RUTENFRANS, C.; and ZYLICZ, Z. "Physician-Assisted Suicide and Euthanasia in the Netherlands: Lessons from the Dutch." *Journal of the American Medical Association* 277 (1997): 1720–1722.

HUMPHRY, D., and CLEMENT, M. *Freedom to Die: People, Politics, and the Right-to-Die Movement.* New York: St. Martin's Press, 1998.

MOWAT, F. *The Desperate People.* Boston: Little Brown, 1959.

SINGER, P. *Practical Ethics.* Cambridge: Cambridge University Press, 1993.

SLATER, E. "Choosing the Time to Die." In *Suicide: The Philosophical Issues.* Edited by Margaret P. Battin and David May. New York: St. Martin's Press, 1980. Pages 199–204.

STEWARD, J. H. "Changes in Shoshonean Indian Culture." *Scientific Monthly* 49 (1939): 524–537.

THOMAS, L. "Dying as Failure?" *American Political Science Review* 444 (1984): 1–4.

Vacco v. *Quill.* 521 U.S. 793 (1997).

VAN DER MAAS, P. J.; VAN DELDEN, J. J. M.; and PIJNENBORG, L. *Euthanasia and Other Medical Decisions Concerning the End of Life.* New York: Elsevier Science, 1992.

VAN DER MAAS, P. J.; VAN DER WAL, G.; and HAVERKATE I. et al. "Euthanasia, Physician-Assisted Suicide, and Other Medical Practices Involving the End of Life in the Netherlands. 1990–1995." *New England Journal of Medicine* 335 (1996): 1699–1705.

WASSERMAN, D. "Passive Euthanasia in Response to Attempted Suicide: One Form of Aggression by Relatives." *Acta Psychiatrica Scandinavica* 79 (1989): 460–467.

EVIDENCE-BASED MEDICINE

Evidence-based medicine refers to an approach to the teaching and practice of medicine that developed in the late 1980s and early 1990s. The approach emphasizes that medicine should be practiced according to evidence that can be assayed on the basis of its quality. The idea is that from among competing claims that physicians might face concerning various courses of action they might take, they can choose a course from evidence that has been assessed rigorously and presented systematically.

An influential aspect of the evidence-based medicine approach has been the Cochrane corroboration which is a collaboration of physicians and scientists who undertake detailed, systematic reviews of the evidence surrounding given courses of action. They attempt to gather all relevant information, including research that was conducted to a high standard but its results were not published. (Failure to publish the results of clinical trials appears to be common in the pharmaceutical industry, where there is no incentive and perhaps even a disincentive, to publishing "negative" results, i.e., trials that did not show a given drug to be beneficial.) By assaying all of the information, and prioritizing it by the rigor with which the data were collected, the hope is that a clear picture on which treatment is best will emerge.

For example, consider a patient who is diagnosed with pneumonia, but in whom its cause is not clear (e.g., is it caused by a bacterium? which one?). While almost all physicians will have been taught how to treat pneumonia, in an ideal situation they could rapidly consult an electronic database in which all rigorous studies of treating pneumonia have been reviewed. At present, the highest scientific standard is generally the randomized, blind, controlled trial. In such a trial, patients are assigned to drug A or to drug B, where drug B is either the usual standard (as would be the case in a pneumonia trial) or a placebo (as would be the case in a condition for which no drug has a proven benefit compared with a placebo). Since the patient is randomly assigned to either the new interaction (drug A) or a control group (B), the trial is randomized and controlled. It is also important that the trial be blind, usually double-blind (i.e., neither the patient nor the treating physician is aware of which patient is in which group), so that wishful thinking cannot easily play a part in the decision whether the new drug works better than the existing standard).

For many of the early decades of scientific medicine, the existing standard appeared to be the best available, but as the number of well conducted trials increased, there was a need to aggregate them and summarize the general experience. In consequence. the review article, written by an expert who might have a particular point of view and who might selectively choose evidence, gave way to systematic review in which the evidence is collected in a standard fashion (usually beginning with an electronic literature search) and summarized in a standard way (with procedures known as meta-analyses).

Though no one would argue that doctors should pursue treatments that do not work, there is controversy over how to understand information produced from evidence-based systematic reviews. The controversy is sometimes technical in origin; for example, there are disputes over which is the best way to carry out particular studies or whether it is more important to understand the quality of a given clinical trial than its result, or whether, when the trial experience is aggregated, all trials should count equally. There is also some skepticism that, even using multiple observers, results are still subject to the bias of the reviewers, and thus systematic reviews by different groups can give rise to substantially different conclusions and guidelines.

While these arguments are substantial, there are other areas of controversy that relate to how a given body of information about the average experience of many patients can be translated into a course of action for a given patient. Should the evidence completely determine the course of action, to the extent that another course might be disallowed, or not paid for, or subject to review by a third party? Or should the evidence about what generally works be factored in as one among other important considerations about what to do for a given patient? At this stage, the answer is not clear, and there are thoughtful proponents of each course of action. Nevertheless, the evidence-based medicine movement in seeking to improve scientific standards of clinical inquiry, and in seeking to reduce the arbitrariness of how data are presented, has done much to improve the quality of evidence available to clinicians.

Nawab Qzilibash
Kenneth Rockwood
Meera Thedari

See also Drug Regulation; Geriatric Medicine.

BIBLIOGRAPHY

Ezzo, J.; Bausell, M.; Moerman, D. E.; Berman, B.; and Hadhazy, V. "Reviewing the Reviews. How Strong Is the Evidence? How Clear Are the Conclusions?" *International Journal of Technological Assessment for Health Care* 17, no. 4 (2001): 457–466.

Hart, J. T. "What Evidence Do We Need for Evidence-Based Medicine?" *Journal of Epidemiology of Community Health* 51 (1997): 623–629.

Maasland Ziekenhuis, S. "The Netherlands. Using Health Outcomes Data to Inform Decision-Making: Formulary Committee Perspective." *Pharmacoeconomics* 19, supp. 2 (2001): 49–52.

Maynard, A. "Evidence-Based Medicine: An Incomplete Method for Informing Treatment Choices." *Lancet* 349 (1997): 126–128.

Miettinen, O. S. "The Modern Scientific Physician: 8. Educational Preparation." *CMAJ* 165 (27 November 2001): 1501–1503.

Peveler, R., and Kendrick, T. "Treatment Delivery and Guidelines in Primary Care." *British Medical Bulletin* 57 (2001): 193–206.

Rosser, W. W.; Davis, D.; and Gilbart, D. "Guideline Advisory Committee. Assessing Guidelines for Use in Family Practice." *Journal of Family Practice* 50 (2001): 969–973.

EVOLUTION OF AGING

There are remarkable differences in observed aging rates and longevity records across different biological species (compare, for example, mice and humans). These differences are a result of what is known as the evolution of aging, a result of the processes of *mutation* and *selection*. The attempt to understand the biological evolution of aging and life span was sparked, in part, by the puzzling life cycles of some biological species. For example, a bamboo plant reproduces vegetatively (asexually) for about one hundred years, forming a dense stands of plants. Then, in one season, all the plants flower simultaneously, reproduce sexually and then die. About one hundred years later the process is repeated. This and the observation of other "suicidal" life cycles of various species, such as salmon, promoted the idea that sexual reproduction may come at the cost of species longevity. Thus, in addition to mutation and selection, the reproductive cost, or, more generally, the trade-offs between different traits of organisms, may contribute to the evolution of species aging and longevity. The evolution of aging is also related to the genetics of aging, because it studies the evolution of heritable manifestations of aging in subsequent generations.

For many decades, the evolution of aging was a puzzling phenomenon, especially in light of the Darwinian theory of evolution by natural selection. Darwin's theory is based on the idea of random and heritable variation of biological traits between individuals (caused by mutations), with subsequent natural selection for preferential reproduction of those individuals who are particularly fit to live in a given environment. Therefore, it is expected (and observed) that biological evolution acts to increase the fitness and performance of species evolving in successive generations. From this optimistic perspective, it was difficult to understand why natural selection seemed to result in such bizarrely injurious features as senescence and late-life degenerative diseases, rather than eternal youth and immortality. How does it happen that the developmental program formed by biological evolution—after having accomplished the miraculous success that leads from a single cell at conception, to a subsequent birth, then to sexual maturity and productive adulthood—fails to maintain the accomplishments of its own work? Another theoretical difficulty in understanding the evolution of aging was the timing problem—many manifestations of aging happen after the reproductive period of evolving organisms, at ages that are beyond the reach of natural selection.

The problem of biological evolution of aging has been studied over the years in a purely theoretical and abstract way by August Weismann (1889), Ronald Fisher (1930), Peter Medawar (1952), George Williams (1957), William Hamilton (1966), Brian Charlesworth (1994) and other researchers. The resulting evolutionary theory of aging has been partially tested by direct evolutionary experiments on laboratory fruit flies and on natural populations of guppies. Researchers found that aging and life span do evolve in subse-

quent generations of biological species in the expected direction, depending on particular living conditions. For example, a selection for later reproduction (artificial selection of late-born progeny for further breeding) produced, as expected, longer-lived fruit flies, while placing animals in a more dangerous environment with high extrinsic mortality redirected evolution, as predicted, to a shorter life span in subsequent generations. Therefore, the early criticism of the evolutionary theory of aging as merely a theoretical speculation, with limited and indirect supporting evidence obtained from retrospective and descriptive studies, has been overturned. On the contrary, the evolutionary plasticity of aging and longevity is now an established experimental fact.

The evolutionary theory of aging may be considered as part of a more general *life history theory*, which tries to explain how evolution designs organisms to achieve reproductive success (that is, to avoid extinction). Life history theory is based on mathematical methods of optimization models with specific biological constraints. Among the questions posed and answered by the life history theory are: Why are organisms small or large? Why do they mature early or late? Why do they have few or many offspring? Why do they have a short or a long life? Why must they grow old and die?

The latter two questions represent the entire scientific agenda of the evolutionary theory of aging. Therefore, it could be said that the evolutionary theory of aging is a subset of the life history theory. On the other hand, the evolutionary theory of aging is considered to be the intellectual core of the *biodemography of aging and longevity*. Biodemography is a multidisciplinary approach, integrating methods of biological and social sciences in an attempt to explain demographic data (e.g., life tables) and processes (e.g., mortality trends).

Current evolutionary explanations of aging and limited longevity of biological species are based on two major evolutionary theories: the *mutation accumulation theory* (Medawar) and the *antagonistic pleiotropy theory* (Williams). These two theories are based on the idea that, from the evolutionary perspective, aging is an inevitable result of the declining force of natural selection with age. For example, a mutant gene that kills young children will be strongly selected against (will not be passed to the next generation), while a lethal mutation with effects confined to people over the age of eighty will experience no selection because people with this mutation will have already passed it to their offspring by that age. So, over successive generations, late-acting deleterious mutations will accumulate, leading to an increase in mortality rates late in life (mutation accumulation theory). Moreover, late-acting deleterious genes may even be favored by selection and be actively accumulated in populations if they have any beneficial effects early in life (antagonistic pleiotropy theory).

Note that these two theories of aging are not mutually exclusive—both evolutionary mechanisms may operate at the same time. The main difference between the two theories is that in the mutation accumulation theory, genes with negative effects at old age accumulate passively from one generation to the next, while in the antagonistic pleiotropy theory these genes are actively kept in the gene pool by selection. The actual relative contribution of each evolutionary mechanism in species aging has not yet been determined, and this scientific problem is now the main focus of research of evolutionary biologists.

Interestingly, since the 1950s no fundamentally new evolutionary theories of aging have been proposed. There have been, however, attempts to find a better name for the antagonistic pleiotropy theory, and to specify in more detail how one and the same gene could have both deleterious and beneficial effects. The *disposable soma theory,* which was proposed by Thomas Kirkwood in 1977 and developed further by Kirkwood and Robin Holliday in 1979, considered a special class of gene mutations with the following antagonistic pleiotropic effects: mutations that save energy for reproduction (positive effect) and other accuracy promoting devices in somatic cells (negative effect). The authors of the disposable soma theory argued that "it may be selectively advantageous for higher organisms to adopt an energy-saving strategy of reduced accuracy in somatic cells to accelerate development and reproduction, but the consequence will be eventual deterioration and death." While discussing the disposable soma theory, it is important to keep in mind that it was initially proposed to provide evolutionary justification for another (failed) theory of aging—the *error catastrophe theory,* which considered aging as a result of breakdown in accuracy of macromolecular synthesis within somatic cells. Most researchers agree that the

disposable soma theory is a special, more narrowly defined variant of the antagonistic pleiotropy theory of aging. According to Kirkwood and Holliday, "the disposable soma theory is, in a sense, a special case of Williams's (1957) pleiotropic gene hypothesis [antagonistic pleiotropy theory], the gene in question controlling the switch to reduced accuracy in somatic cells. The good effect of the gene is the reduced investment of resources in the soma, while the bad effect is the ultimate somatic disintegration, or ageing."

In addition to legitimate theoretical and experimental studies of the evolution of aging, there is also a more ambitious pro-evolutionary approach that aims "to overthrow the present intellectual order of gerontology [science of aging], and to replace it with one based on evolutionary and genetic foundations" (Rose).

This ambitious pro-evolutionary approach considers all other theories of biological aging—such as the free-radical theory of aging (Beckman and Ames; Harman), the somatic mutation theory of aging (Morley), the reliability theory of aging (Gavrilov and Gavrilova, 1991; 2001), the mitochondrial theory of aging (Gershon), the waste accumulation theory of aging (Terman), and the error catastrophe theory of aging—as far less important to gerontology: "the evolutionary biology of aging, rather than, for example, cell biology, should be the intellectual core of gerontology" (Rose).

Apparently, this ambitious pro-evolutionary doctrine is based on a literal interpretation of the following statement by Theodosius Dobzhansky (1900–1975) : "Nothing in biology makes sense except in the light of evolution" (Rose).

The claim has been made that a simple evolutionary model can explain even the observed age-trajectory of mortality curves, including the late-life mortality plateaus (the tendency of mortality curves to level off at advanced ages), but other investigators have found these claims to be unsubstantiated. Thus, declarations that the evolutionary theory of aging should have a dominating status among other biological theories of aging remain to be justified.

Evolution of scientific ideas on the evolution of aging

Genetic program for death. August Weismann, the great German theorist of the nineteenth century, was one of the first biologists to use evolutionary arguments to explain aging. His initial idea was that a specific death-mechanism exists, designed by natural selection to eliminate the old, and therefore worn-out, members of a population. The purpose of this programmed death of the old, Weisman thought, was to make space and resources available for younger generations. He probably came to this idea while reading the notes of Alfred Russel Wallace (one of Darwin's contemporaries and a co-discoverer of natural selection), which he later cited in his essay "The Duration of Life" (1889): "Wallace wrote that when one or more individuals have provided a sufficient number of successors, they themselves, as consumers of nourishment in a constantly increasing degree, are an injury to those successors. Natural selection therefore weeds them out, and in many cases favors such races as die almost immediately after they have left successors." Weismann enthusiastically accepted and developed further this idea, which also corresponded well with the hiring practices of German universities of that time, whereby a new candidate had to wait for the death of an old professor to obtain a position.

Suggesting the *theory of programmed death*, Weismann had to think about the exact biological mechanisms executing this death program, and he came to the idea that there is a specific limitation on the number of divisions that somatic cells can undergo. Specifically, he suggested "that life span is connected with the number of somatic cell generations which follow after each other in the course of an individual life, and that this number, like the life span of individual generations of cells, is already determined in the embryonic cell" (Weismann, 1892). Weismann tried to explain "the different life span of animals by making it dependent on the number of cell generations which was the norm for each different species" (1892). Remarkably, his purely theoretical speculation on the existence of a cell division limit was experimentally confirmed many decades later by H. Earle Swim (1959); and this scientific discovery was then successfully developed and publicized by Leonard Hayflick (Gavrilov and Gavrilova, 1991).

Weismann eventually stopped writing about the "injuriousness" of the old and changed his evolutionary views, considering old organisms not to be harmful, but simply neutral for the biological species: "In regulating duration of life, the advantage to the species, and not to the individual, is alone of any importance. This must be obvious to any one who has once thoroughly thought out the process of natural selection. It is of no importance to the species whether the individual lives longer or shorter, but it is of importance that the individual should be enabled to do its work towards the maintenance of the species. . . . The unlimited existence of individuals would be a luxury without any corresponding advantage" (Weismann, 1889).

Subsequent studies confirmed that Weismann's decision to abandon the initial idea of programmed death was a wise one. Many scientific tests of the programmed death hypothesis have been made, and some of them are summarized here.

One way of testing the programmed death hypothesis is based on a comparison of life-span data for individuals of a single species in natural (wild) and protected (laboratory, domestic, civilized) environments. If the hypothesis is correct, there should not be very large differences in the life spans of adult individuals across compared environments. Indeed, for a self-destruction program to arise, take hold, and be maintained in the course of evolution, it must at least have some opportunity, however small, of expression in natural (wild) conditions. Consequently, the age at which such a program is "switched on" cannot be too high, otherwise (because of the high mortality in the wild from predators, hunger, infections, and harsh natural conditions) no one would live to the fateful age, and the self-destruction mechanism would not be able to be expressed. It follows from this that life spans, in even the most favorable conditions, cannot significantly exceed the ages reached by the most robust individuals in the wild—if, of course, the concept is correct.

The analysis of the actual data reveals, however, a picture completely opposite to what would be expected from the programmed death theory: the life spans of organisms in protected environments greatly exceed the life spans observed in natural (wild) conditions. For example, the chaffinch (*Fringilla coelebs*) can live for twenty-nine years in captivity. However, in the wild this is practically impossible, since about a half of all of these birds perish during their first year from hunger, cold, diseases, and attacks by predators, and the mean life span is only about 1.4 to 1.5 years. As a result of this high mortality, only 0.1 percent of the initial number of chaffinches survives to age eleven in the wild. Similar observations were made for field voles (*Microtus arvalis*

Pall). In protected laboratory conditions, the average life span of voles is about seven or eight months, while individual specimens survive to twenty-five months. In the wild, however, the average life span of voles is only 1.2 months, and only 0.1 percent survive to ten months. Observations like these are common for many biological species. Thus, if one attempts to estimate the age of programmed death on the basis of life spans in laboratory conditions, it becomes clear that no death program could arise or be maintained in evolution, if only because it would not be able to come into operation in natural conditions, where practically no individual lives to the required age.

The same conclusion is reached from an analysis of data on the human life span. At present, the mean life expectancy in developed countries is between seventy and eighty years, while the documented record for longevity is 122 years. If we take these figures as an estimate for the age range in which the death program is switched on, we are forced to admit that such a program could not have arisen in human evolution, since, according to paleodemographic data, virtually nobody survived to such an age. For example, only half of those born in the Late Paleolithic era (30,000–10,000 B.C.E.) reached eight or nine years, and only a half of those born in the Neolithic era (6,000–2,000 B.C.E.) reached twenty-six years. Even in the Middle Ages, life expectancy at birth was no greater than twenty-nine years. Investigations of the skeletons of American Indians have shown that just two centuries ago only 4 percent of the population survived to age fifty. Note for comparison, that the probability of surviving to this age in developed countries today is 94 to 96 percent. If these facts are compared, it is difficult to refrain from posing the following question: can the guaranteed destruction of a few old people, who are chance survivors and doomed in the wild, be a sufficient evolutionary basis for the formation and preservation of a special self-destruction program in the human genome? Viewed in this light, the inconsistency of the programmed death hypothesis becomes obvious.

In addition, if the question of whether death is programmed is approached from the evolutionary point of view, it becomes obvious that special mechanisms for the termination of life could hardly help an individual to fight successfully for his survival and the survival of his progeny. On the contrary, those individuals in whom the action of such a program had been impaired by some spontaneous mutation would quickly displace all the remaining individuals, since in their longer life span they would produce more offspring, or at least could increase the survival of their offspring by providing longer parental support.

In 1957, George Williams, the author of another evolutionary theory of aging summarized the critical arguments against the programmed death theory (called *Weismann's theory* for historical reasons). Here is a partial list of his most forceful critical arguments:

1. The extreme rarity, in natural populations, of individuals that would be old enough to die of the postulated death-mechanism
2. The failure of several decades (now over a century) of gerontological research to uncover any death mechanism (the discovery of apoptosis, or programmed cell death, is irrelevant to this discussion, which is focused on the whole organism rather than some of the organisms somatic cells)
3. the difficulties involved in visualizing how such a feature could be produced by natural selection

There is, however, one good reason why this dead theory of programmed death should not be ignored as outdated and should not be forgotten—the ghosts of the theory can still be found in many publications, including the *Encyclopaedia Britannica* which states: "Locked within the code of the genetic material are instructions that specify the age beyond which a species cannot live given even the most favorable conditions," (*Encyclopaedia Britannica*, 15th ed., 1998, p. 424.)

As for August Weismann, he should be credited with at least four significant contributions to aging studies:

1. Suggesting the first evolutionary theory of aging that attracted the attention of other researchers
2. Abandoning his own theory when he understood that it was incorrect—this honest decision allowed new evolutionary theories of aging to develop
3. Correctly predicting the existence of a cell-division limit—without having any data at all
4. Discriminating between germ cells and the somatic cells ("soma"), with a prophetic understanding of "the perishable and vulnera-

ble nature of the soma." (Weismann, 1889); this idea is related to the more recent *disposable soma theory of aging*

Mutation accumulation theory of aging

The mutation accumulation theory of aging, suggested by Peter Medawar in 1952, considers aging as a by-product of natural selection (similar to the evolutionary explanation for the blindness of cave animals). The probability of an individual reproducing depends on his age. It is zero at birth and reaches a peak in young adults, after which it decreases due to the increased probability of death linked to various external (predators, illnesses, accidents) and internal (senescence) causes. In such conditions, deleterious mutations expressed at a young age are severely selected against, due to their high negative impact on fitness (number of offspring produced). On the other hand, deleterious mutations expressed only later in life are rather neutral to selection, because their bearers have already transmitted their genes to the next generation.

Mutations can affect fitness either directly or indirectly. For example, a mutation increasing the risk for leg fracture, due to a low fixation of calcium, may be indirectly as deleterious to fitness as a mutation directly impairing the eggs nesting in the uterus. From an evolutionary perspective, it does not really matter exactly why the organism is at risk not to reproduce—either because many spontaneous abortions occur, or because it becomes an easy prey for a predator (in nature) or for a criminal (in society).

According to this theory, persons loaded with a deleterious mutation have fewer chances to reproduce if the deleterious effect of this mutation is expressed earlier in life. For example, patients with progeria (a genetic disease with symptoms of premature aging) live only for about twelve years, and, therefore, they cannot pass their mutant genes to the next generation. In such conditions, the progeria stems only from new mutations and not from the genes of parents. By contrast, people expressing a mutation at older ages can reproduce before the illness occurs, as it is the case with familial Alzheimer's disease. As an outcome, progeria is less frequent than late diseases, such as Alzheimer's disease, because the mutant genes responsible for the Alzheimer's disease are not removed from the gene pool as readily as progeria genes, and can thus accumulate in successive generations. In other

words, the mutation accumulation theory predicts that the frequency of genetic diseases should increase at older ages.

Mutation accumulation theory allows researchers to make several testable predictions. In particular, this theory predicts that the dependence of progeny life span on parental life span should not be linear, as is observed for almost any other quantitative trait demonstrating familial resemblance (e.g., body height). Instead, this dependence should have an unusual nonlinear shape, with increasing slope for the dependence of progeny life span on parental life span for those with longer-lived parents. This prediction follows directly from the key statement of this theory that the equilibrium gene frequency for deleterious mutations should increase with age at onset of mutation action because of weaker (postponed) selection against later-acting mutations. (The term *equilibrium gene frequency* refers here to the ultimate time-independent gene frequency, which is determined by mutation-selection balance [equilibrium between mutation and selection rates]; see Charlesworth, 1994).

According to the mutation accumulation theory, one would expect the genetic variability for life span (in particular, the additive genetic variance responsible for familial resemblance) to increase with age. (*Additive gene variance* refers to a variance of additive genetic origin; that is, a variation due to additive effects of genes on the studied trait in genetically heterogeneous populations. This variance increases with an increase in mutation frequencies.) The predicted increase in additive genetic variance could be detected by studying the ratio of additive genetic variance to observed phenotypic variance. This ratio (the so-called narrow-sense heritability of life span) can be easily estimated as the doubled slope of the regression line for the dependence of offspring life span on parental life span. Thus, if age at death were indeed determined by accumulated late-acting deleterious mutations, one would expect this slope to become steeper with higher parental ages at death. This prediction was tested through the analysis of genealogical data on familial longevity in European royal and noble families, data well known for their reliability and accuracy. It was found that the regression slope for the dependence of offspring life span on parental life span increases with parental life span, exactly as predicted by the mutation accumulation theory (see Gavrilova et al.). Thus, the current status of the mutation accumulation theory could be characterized as a productive working hypothesis, pending further validation.

Antagonistic pleiotropy theory of aging ("pay later" theory)

The theory of antagonistic pleiotropy is based on two assumptions. First, it is assumed that a particular gene may have an effect not only on one trait, but on several traits of an organism (pleiotropy). The second assumption is that these pleiotropic effects may affect individual fitness in opposite (antagonistic) ways. This theory was first proposed by George Williams in 1957, who noticed that "natural selection may be said to be biased in favor of youth over old age whenever a conflict of interests arises" (Williams, 1957).

According to Williams, this conflict arises from "pleiotropic genes . . . that have opposite effects on fitnesses at different ages. . . . Selection of a gene that confers an advantage at one age and a disadvantage at another will depend not only on the magnitudes of the effects themselves, but also on the times of the effects. An advantage during the period of maximum reproductive probability would increase the total reproductive probability more than a proportionately similar disadvantage later on would decrease it. So natural selection will frequently maximize vigor in youth at the expense of vigor later on and thereby produce a declining vigor (aging) during adult life." (Williams). These verbal arguments were later proved mathematically by Brian Charlesworth (1994).

Williams was suggesting the existence of so-called pleiotropic genes (those demonstrating favorable effects on fitness at a young age and deleterious ones at old age), which could explain the aging process. Such genes are maintained in the population due to their positive effect on reproduction at a young age, despite their negative effects at a post-reproductive age (their negative effects in later life will look exactly like the aging process).

For the purpose of illustration, suppose that there is a gene that increases the fixation of calcium in bones. Such a gene may have positive effects at a young age, because the risk of bone fracture and subsequent death is decreased, but negative effects in later life, because of increased risk of osteoarthritis due to excessive calcification. In the wild, such a gene would have no actual negative effect, because most animals would die long before its negative effects could be observed. There is then a trade-off between an actual positive effect in young individuals and a potential negative one in old individuals: this negative effect may become important only if animals live in protected environments such as zoos or laboratories.

Antagonistic pleiotropy theory explains why reproduction may come with a cost for species longevity, and may even induce death (see the story on bamboo plants and salmon life cycles at the beginning of this article). Indeed, any mutations favoring more intensive reproduction (more offspring produced) will be propagated in future generations even if these mutations have some deleterious effects in later life. For example, mutations causing overproduction of sex hormones may increase the sex drive, libido, reproductive efforts, and reproductive success—and therefore be favored by selection, despite causing prostate cancer (in males) and ovarian cancer (in females) later in the life. Thus, the idea of reproductive cost, or, more generally, of trade-offs between different traits follows directly from antagonistic pleiotropy theory.

The trade-offs between reproduction (reproductive success, fitness, vigor) and longevity were predicted by Williams as "testable deductions from the theory." Specifically, he predicted, "rapid individual development should be correlated with rapid senescence. Reproductive maturation is the most important landmark in the life-cycle for the evolution of senescence. Senescence may theoretically begin right after this stage in development. So the sooner this point is reached, the sooner senescence should begin, and the sooner it should have demonstrable effects." Another prediction of the trade-offs between reproductive capacity (vigor) and longevity was made by Williams in the following way: "successful selection for increased longevity should result in decreased vigor in youth."

These predictions were confirmed later in selection experiments using the fruit fly, *Drosophila melanogaster*. By restricting reproduction to later ages, the intensity of selection on the later portions of the life span was increased. This selection for late reproduction extended the longevity of the selected populations. Furthermore, a reduced fecundity was observed among the long-lived flies, supporting the idea of a trade-off between fertility and survival, as predicted by the antagonistic pleiotropy theory. A similar trade-off between fecundity and longevity was observed when fruit flies were selected directly for longevity. In another selection experiment with different levels of extrinsic mortality, the descendants from populations with low extrinsic mortality demonstrated increased longevity, longer development times, and decreased early fecundity. The general finding from these selection experiments in fruit flies is that increased longevity is associated with depression of fitness (vigor) in early life, just as Williams predicted.

Trade-offs between longevity and reproduction have also been found in experiments with soil-dwelling round worms (the nematode *Caenorhabditis elegans*), where a number of long-lived mutants have been identified. When long-lived mutants were reared together with normal (wild-type) individuals under standard culture conditions, neither of them exhibited a competitive advantage, contrary to theoretical predictions. However, when cultures were exposed to starvation cycles (alternatively fed and starved)—mimicking field conditions in nature—the wild type quickly outcompeted (outnumbered) the long-lived mutant. These findings demonstrate that mutations that increase life span do indeed exhibit some fitness cost, thereby supporting the antagonistic pleiotropy theory of aging.

Studies on humans, however, have been less convincing. One study found that long-lived people (women in particular) did have impaired fertility at a young age—as predicted, in general, by antagonistic pleiotropy theory, and in particular, by disposable soma theory. However, serious methodological flaws were later found in that study, and its findings proved to be inconsistent with findings of many other researchers, including historical demographers analyzing human data (see reviews in Gavrilov and Gavrilova, 1999; Le Bourg, 2001). Therefore, more additional studies on this subject are required.

Implications for aging research

Evolutionary biologists have always been very generous with gerontologists in providing advice and guidance on how to do aging research "in directions that are likely to be fruitful" (Williams). Surprisingly, this generous intellectual assistance proved to be extremely injurious for aging studies in the past. This happened because evolutionary theory was interpreted in such a way that the search for single-gene mutations (or life-extending interventions) with very large pos-

itive effects on life span was considered a completely futile task, destined for failure for fundamental evolutionary reasons. Researchers were convinced by the forceful evolutionary arguments of George Williams that "natural selection will always be in greatest opposition to the decline of the most senescence-prone system" and, therefore, "senescence should always be a generalized deterioration, and never due largely to changes in a single system. . . . This conclusion banishes the fountain of youth to the limbo of scientific impossibilities where other human aspirations, like the perpetual motion machine and Laplace's 'superman' have already been placed by other theoretical considerations. Such conclusions are always disappointing, but they have the desirable consequence of channeling research in directions that are likely to be fruitful."

As a result of this triumphant evolutionary indoctrination, many exciting research opportunities for life span extension were squandered for a half a century, until the astonishing discovery of single-gene mutants with profoundly extended longevity was ultimately made (see Lin et al., 1997; 1998; Migliaccio et al.), despite all discouraging predictions and warnings based on evolutionary arguments.

Recent discoveries of life-span-extending mutations are spectacular. A single-gene mutation (daf-2) more than doubles the life span of nematodes, keeping them active, fully fertile (contrary to predictions of the disposable soma theory), and having normal metabolic rates. Another single-gene mutation, called *methuselah*, extends the average life span of fruit flies by about 35 percent, enhancing also their resistance to various forms of stress, including starvation, high temperature, and toxic chemicals. Finally, a single-gene mutation was found in mice, extending their life span by about 30 percent and also increasing their resistance to toxic chemicals. Researchers involved in these studies came to the following conclusion:

The field of ageing research has been completely transformed in the past decade. . . . When single genes are changed, animals that should be old stay young. In humans, these mutants would be analogous to a ninety year old who looks and feels forty-five. On this basis we begin to think of ageing as a disease that can be cured, or at least postponed. . . . The field of ageing is beginning to explode, because so many are so excited about the prospect of searching for—and finding—the causes of ageing, and maybe even the fountain of youth itself. (Guarente and Kenyon).

Now, when single-gene, life-extending mutations are found, evolutionary biologists are presented with the task of reconciling these new discoveries with the evolutionary theory of aging. They are certain to succeed in this task, however, as evolutionary theories of aging are very flexible and can be adjusted to almost any new finding.

However, gerontologists will also have to learn their lessons from the damage caused by decades of misguided research, when the search for major life-extending mutations and other life-extension interventions was equated by evolutionary biologists with the construction of a perpetual motion machine. Perhaps some leads for getting wisdom from this lesson can be found in the title of a recent scientific review on evolution of aging: "Evolutionary Theories of Aging: Handle With Care" (Le Bourg, 1998).

NATALIA S. GAVRILOVA
LEONID A. GAVRILOV

See also GENETICS; LONGEVITY: REPRODUCTION; LONGEVITY: SELECTION; MUTATION; THEORIES OF BIOLOGICAL AGING.

BIBLIOGRAPHY

BECKMAN, K. B., and AMES, B. N. "The Free Radical Theory of Aging Matures." *Physiological Reviews* 78 (1998): 547–581.

CARNES, B. A., and OLSHANSKY, S. J. "Evolutionary Perspectives on Human Senescence." *Population and Development Review* 19 (1993): 793–806.

CHARLESWORTH, B. *Evolution in Age-Structured Populations.* Cambridge, U.K.: Cambridge University Press, 1994.

CHARLESWORTH, B., and PARTRIDGE, L. "Ageing: Leveling of the Grim Reaper." *Curr Biol* 7 (1997): R440–R442.

FISHER, R. A. *The Genetical Theory of Natural Selection.* Oxford, U.K.: Oxford University Press, 1930.

GAVRILOV, L. A., and GAVRILOVA, N. S. *The Biology of Life Span: A Quantitative Approach.* New York: Harwood, 1991.

GAVRILOV, L. A., and GAVRILOVA, N. S. "Is There a Reproductive Cost for Human Longevity?" *Journal of Anti-Aging Medicine* 2 (1999): 121–123.

GAVRILOV, L. A., and GAVRILOVA, N. S. "The Reliability Theory of Aging and Longevity." *Journal of Theoretical Biology* (2001): 527–545.

GAVRILOVA, N. S., et al. "Evolution, Mutations and Human Longevity: European Royal and Noble Families." *Human Biology* 70 (1998): 799–804.

GERSHON, D. "The Mitochondrial Theory of Aging: Is the Culprit a Faulty Disposal System Rather Than Indigenous Mitochondrial Alterations?" *Experimental Gerontology* 34 (1999): 613–619.

GUARENTE, L., and KENYON, C. "Genetic Pathways That Regulate Ageing in Model Organisms" *Nature* 408 (2000): 255–262.

HAMILTON, W. D. "The Moulding of Senescence By Natural Selection." *Journal of Theoretical Biology* 12 (1966): 12–45.

HARMAN, D. "Free Radical Theory of Aging: Alzheimer's Disease Pathogenesis." *AGE* 18 (1995): 97–119.

HOLLIDAY, R. "The Error Catastrophe Theory of Aging: Point Counterpoint." *Experimental Gerontology* 32 (1997): 337–339.

KIRKWOOD, T. B. L. "Evolution of Aging." *Nature* 270 (1997): 301–304.

KIRKWOOD, T. B. L., and HOLLIDAY, R. "The Evolution of Ageing and Longevity." *Proceedings of the Royal Society London. Series B, Biological Sciences* 205 (1979): 531–546.

LE BOURG, É. "Evolutionary Theories of Aging: Handle With Care." *Gerontology* 44 (1998): 345–348.

LE BOURG, É. "A Mini-Review of the Evolutionary Theories of Aging. Is it the Time to Accept Them?" *Demographic Research* 4, article 1 (2001): 1–28.

LIN, K.; DORMAN, J. B.; RODAN, A.; and KENYON, C. "*daf-16:* An HNF3/Forkhead Family Member That Can Function to Double the Life-Span in *Caenorhabditis elegans*." *Science* 278 (1997): 1319–1322.

LIN, Y.; SEROUDE, L.; and BENZER, S. "Extended Life-Span and Stress Resistance in the *Drosophila* Mutant *methuselah*." *Science* 282 (1998): 943–946.

MEDAWAR, P. B. *An Unsolved Problem of Biology.* London: H. K. Lewis, 1952.

MIGLIACCIO, E.; GIORGIO, M.; MELE, S.; PELICCI, G.; REBOLDI, P.; PANDOLFI, P. P.; LANFRANCONE, L.; and PELICCI, G. "The p66[shc] Adaptor Protein Controls Oxidative Stress Response and Life Span in Mammals." *Nature* 402 (1999): 309–313.

MORLEY, A. A. "The Somatic Mutation Theory of Aging." *Mutation Research* 338 (1995): 19–23.

MUELLER, L. D., and ROSE, M. R. "Evolutionary Theory Predicts Late-Life Mortality Plateaus." *Proceedings of the National Academy of Science U.S.A.* 93 (1996): 15249–15253.

REZNICK, D.; BUCKWALTER, G.; GROFF, J.; and ELDER, D. "The Evolution of Senescence in Natural Populations of Guppies (*Poecilia re-*

ticulata): A Comparative Approach." *Experimental Gerontology* 36 (2001): 791–812.

ROSE, M. R. *Evolutionary Biology of Aging.* New York: Oxford University Press, 1991.

STEARNS, S. C. "Life History Evolution: Successes, Limitations, and Prospects." *Naturwissenschaften* 87 (2000): 476–486.

STEARNS, S. C.; ACKERMANN, M.; DOEBELI, M. and KAISER, M. "Experimental Evolution of Aging, Growth, and Reproduction in Fruitflies." *Proceedings of the National Academy of Science U.S.A.* 97 (2000): 3309–3313.

SWIM, H. E. "Microbiological Aspects of Tissue Culture." *Annual Review of Microbiology* 313 (1959): 141–176.

TERMAN, A. "Garbage Catastrophe Theory of Aging: Imperfect Removal of Oxidative Damage?" *Redox Report* 6 (2001): 15–26.

WACHTER, K. W. "Evolutionary Demographic Models for Mortality Plateaus." *Proceedings of the National Academy of Science U.S.A.* 96 (1999): 10544–10547.

WEISMANN, A. *Essays Upon Heredity and Kindred Biological Problems.* Oxford, U.K.: Clarendon Press, 1889.

WEISMANN, A. *Über die Dauer des Lebens.* Jena: Verlag von Gustav Fisher, 1882.

WEISMANN, A. *Über Leben und Tod.* Jena: Verlag von Gustav Fisher, 1892.

WESTENDORP, R. G. J., and KIRKWOOD, T. B. L. "Human Longevity at the Cost of Reproductive Success." *Nature* 396 (1998): 743–746.

WILLIAMS, G. C. "Pleiotropy, Natural Selection and the Evolution of Senescence." *Evolution* 11 (1957): 398–411.

EXERCISE

There has been a gradually growing awareness among policy makers and health care professionals of the great importance of appropriate exercise habits to major public health outcomes. It has been known for decades that physical activity prevents heart disease, but data now suggest that, on average, physically active people outlive those who are inactive and that regular physical activity helps to maintain the functional independence of older adults and to enhance the quality of life for people of all ages. The basic elements of an exercise prescription for older adults are presented in Table 1.

- Examples of balance enhancing activities include T'ai chi movements, standing yoga or ballet postures, tandem standing and walking, standing on one leg, stepping over ob-

A brochure that urges senior citizens to develop an exercise program to help maintain a healthy lifestyle. (Brochure © Maria Fiatarone Singh. Reproduced with permission.)

jects, climbing up and down steps slowly, turning, and standing on heels and toes.
- Intensity is increased by decreasing the base of support (e.g., progressing from standing on two feet while holding onto the back of a chair to standing on one foot with no hand support); by decreasing other sensory input (e.g., closing eyes or standing on a foam pillow); or by perturbing the center of mass (e.g., holding a heavy object out to one side while maintaining balance, standing on one leg while lifting the other leg out behind the body, or leaning forward as far as possible without falling or moving the feet).

The rationale for the integration of a physical activity prescription into health care for older adults is based on four essential concepts. First, there is a great similarity between the physiologic changes that are attributable to disuse and those

An unidentified 72-year-old woman works out on a treadmill, which is an excellent form of low-impact aerobic exercise. (Corbis photo by Laura Dwight.)

Table 1

General Exercise Recommendations for Older Adults

SOURCE: Author

Modality	Resistance Training	Cardio-vascular Endurance Training	Flexibility Training
Dose			
Frequency	2-3 days/wk	3-7 days/wk	2-7 days/wk
Volume	1-3 sets of 8-12 repetitions, 8-10 major muscle groups	20-60 min	4 repetitions, 30 sec/ stretch, 6-10 major muscle groups
Intensity	15-17 on Borg Scale (80% 1RM), 10 sec/ repetition	11-13 on Borg Scale (45-80% maximal heart rate reserve	Stretch to maximal pain-free distance and hold, relax, and stretch slightly further
Require-ments for safety and maximal efficacy	Slow speed Good form No breath holding Increase weight progressively	Low impact activity Weight-bearing if possible	Non-ballistic movements

which have been typically observed in aging populations, leading to the speculation that the way in which people age may in fact be greatly affected by activity levels. Second, chronic diseases increase with age, and exercise has now been shown to be an independent risk factor and/or potential treatment for most of the major causes of morbidity and mortality in Western societies, a potential that currently is vastly underutilized. Third, traditional medical interventions do not typically address disuse syndromes accompanying chronic disease, which may be responsible for much of their associated disability. Exercise is particularly good at targeting syndromes of disuse. Finally, many pathophysiological aberrations that are central to a disease or its treatment are specifically addressed only by exercise, which therefore deserves a place in the mainstream of medical care, not as an optional adjunct. Therefore, understanding the effects of aging on exercise capacity and how habitual physical activity can modify this relationship in the older adult, including its specific utility in treating medical diseases, is critical for health care practitioners of all disciplines.

Retarding the aging process

In most physiologic systems, there is considerable evidence that the normal aging processes do not result in significant impairment or dysfunction in the absence of pathology, and under resting conditions. However, in response to a stress, the age-related reduction in physiologic reserves causes a loss of regulatory or homeostatic balance. This process has been termed "homeostenosis" (a lessened capacity for fine-tuning of the system). Thus, subtle changes in physical activity patterns over the adult life span cause most people not engaged in athletic pursuits to lose a very large proportion of their physical work capacity before they notice that something is wrong or find that they have crossed a threshold of disability. The second consequence of age-related changes in physiologic capacity is the increased perception of effort associated with submaximal work. Thus a vicious cycle is set up: "usual" aging leading to decreasing exercise capacity, resulting in an elevated perception of effort, subsequently causing avoidance of activity, and finally feeding back to exacerbation of the age-related declines secondary to disuse.

One of the major goals of gerontological research over the past several decades has been to separate the true physiologic changes of aging from changes due to disease or environmental factors, including disuse or underuse of body systems. Numerous studies point out the superior physical condition of those who exercise regularly compared to their more sedentary peers, even in the tenth decade of life. On the other hand, research indicates that years of physiologic aging of diverse organ systems and metabolic functions can be mimicked by short periods of enforced inactivity, such as bed rest, wearing a cast, denervation, or absence of gravitational forces. These two types of studies have led to a theory of disuse and aging which suggests that aging as it is known in modern society is, in many ways, an exercise deficiency syndrome. This implies that people may have far more control over the rate and extent of the aging process than was previously thought.

Minimizing risk factors for chronic disease

Another way to integrate exercise into health care is to view it in light of its potential to reduce risk factors for chronic diseases. As shown in Table 2, the very large potential for exercise to act as a primary prevention tool is obvious from the kinds of risk factors and diseases listed. The major causes of morbidity and mortality (heart disease, stroke, diabetes, cancer, arthritis, functional dependency, hip fracture, and dementia) in the older population, are all more prevalent in individuals who are sedentary as compared to more active peers.

Adjunctive and primary treatment of chronic disease

There are various diseases in which exercise has a potentially valuable role because of its ability to directly treat the pathophysiology of the disease. Examples of this use of exercise are given in table 2. In some cases exercise may provide benefits similar to those of medication or nutritional intervention; in others it may act through an entirely different pathway. The chronic treatment of hypertension and coronary artery disease is clearly a case for management with both standard medical treatments and exercise. Exer-

Table 2
Benefits of Exercise

Physiologic Adaptation	Prevention or Treatment of Disease
Increased bone density	Arthritis
Decreased total body and visceral adipose tissue	Breast cancer
Decreased fibrinogen levels	Chronic insomnia
Decreased sympathetic and hormonal response to exercise	Colon cancer
Decreased LDL, Increased HDL levels	Coronary artery disease
Decreased postural blood pressure response to stressors	Depression
Increased heart rate variability	Hyperlipidemia
Increased neural reaction time	Hypertension
Increased blood volume and hematocrit	Impotence
Increased energy expenditure	Obesity
Increased glycogen storage in skeletal muscle	Osteoporosis
Increased oxidative enzyme capacity in skeletal muscle	Overall and cardio-vascular mortality
Increased glucose disposal rate	Peripheral vascular disease
Increased mitochondrial volume density in skeletal muscle	Prostate cancer
Decreased resting heart rate and blood pressure	Stroke
Increased GLUT-4 receptors in skeletal muscle	Type 2 diabetes mellitus
Decreased arterial stiffness	
Increased maximal aerobic capacity	
Increased stroke volume during exercise*	
Increased capillary density in skeletal muscle	
Increased insulin sensitivity	
Improved glucose tolerance	
Increased cardiac contractility during exercise*	
Decreased heart rate/BP response to submaximal exercise	
Increased oxygen extraction by skeletal muscle	

*Observed only in older endurance-trained men thus far

SOURCE: Author

cise may prevent secondary cardiovascular events as well as minimize the need and risk of multiple drug use or high drug dosages in these conditions.

The benefits of exercise are often most dramatic in individuals in whom medical treatment is already optimized and cannot be pushed further, or when the pathophysiology of the disease itself is not amenable to change. For example, in chronic obstructive pulmonary disease, once bronchospasm has been relieved and oxygen has been supplemented, exercise tolerance may still be very limited due to peripheral skeletal muscle atrophy and inability to effectively extract oxygen and utilize it for aerobic work as a result of years of disuse, poor nutrition, and other factors. However, such peripheral abnormalities can be directly and effectively targeted and treated with progressive endurance training protocols, which have been shown to significantly improve exercise tolerance, functional status, and quality of life in such patients.

The exercise prescription

This section will outline the elements of a prescription designed to stimulate robust adaptation within the major physiologic domains that can be modified by exercise: strength, cardiovascular endurance, flexibility, and balance, as recommended by the American College of Sports Medicine and endorsed by most major medical consensus groups. These elements are discussed separately, because in most cases exercise training is quite specific in its effects, and little crossover will be seen. For example, balance training will not increase one's aerobic capacity or strength. Resistance training is unique in this regard; it has been shown to benefit all of these domains to some extent, with its most powerful effect in the realms of muscle strength and endurance.

Progressive resistance training. Progressive resistance training (PRT) is the process of challenging the skeletal muscle with an unaccustomed stimulus, or load, such that neural and muscle tissue adaptations take place, leading ultimately to increased strength and muscle mass. In this kind of exercise, the muscle is contracted slowly just a few times in each session against a relatively heavy load. Any muscle may be trained in this way, although usually six to twelve major muscle groups with clinical relevance are trained, for a balanced and functional outcome.

The most important element of the PRT prescription is the intensity of the load used. It is evident from many years of research and clinical practice that muscle strength and size are increased significantly only when the muscle is loaded at a moderate or high intensity (60–100 percent of maximum).

The benefits of PRT are both metabolic and functional. It improves sensitivity to insulin and may therefore be important in both the prevention and the treatment of diabetes. It also increases bone formation and density, and has a role in the prevention and treatment of osteoporosis. It significantly improves muscle strength and is associated with muscle hypertrophy, and is therefore useful whenever muscle weakness or atrophy contributes to disease or dysfunction. Such disease or dysfunction includes falls, frailty, chronic heart failure, chronic lung disease, Parkinson's disease, neuromuscular disease, chronic renal failure, arthritis, and other chronic conditions associated with decreased activity levels and impaired mobility. In addition, PRT has marked psychological benefits, having been shown to improve major depression as well as insomnia, self-efficacy, and emotional well-being in older adults.

The potential risks of PRT are primarily musculoskeletal injury and rarely cardiovascular events (ischemia, arhythnias, hypertension). Musculoskeletal injury is almost entirely preventable with attention to the following points:

- Adherence to proper form
- Isolation of the targeted muscle group
- Slow velocity of lifting
- Limitation of range of motion to the pain-free arc of movement
- Avoidance of use of momentum and ballistic movements to complete a lift
- Use of machines or chairs with good back support
- Observation of rest periods between sets and rest days between sessions.

Cardiovascular endurance training. Cardiovascular endurance training refers to exercise in which large muscle groups contract many times (thousands of times at a single session) against little or no resistance other than that imposed by gravity. The purpose of this type of training is to increase the maximal amount of aerobic work that can be carried out, as well as to decrease the physiologic response and

Table 3
Characteristics of Aerobics vs. Resistive Exercise

Feature	Aerobic Exercise	Resistive Exercise
Muscle groups	Most large, appendicular +/- truncal	Any, large or small
Contractions	Many	Few
Mechanical loading of muscle	Low, gravity or or light resistance only	High, Moderate to heavy resistance (60-90% of maximal tolerable load)
Speed of Contractions	Fast	Slow*
Pulse response	Large increase (to 60-85% of maximum)	Small increase, non-sustained between contractions
Blood pressure response	Primarily systolic, diastolic may decrease; dependent on intensity of workload	Systolic, diastolic and mean pressure increase, dependent on intensity of load, mass of muscle involved, duration of contractions; non-sustained between contractions
Primary physiologic responses	Increased maximal aerobic capacity Decreased cardiovascular response, fatigue, and perceived exertion during fixed submaximal workloads	Increased muscle strength, size, and endurance; smaller effect on increased tolerance to aerobic work

*Exception is muscle power training, which requires high force, high velocity contractions

SOURCE: Author

perceived difficulty of submaximal aerobic workloads. Extensive adaptations in the cardiopulmonary system, peripheral skeletal muscle, circulation, and metabolism are responsible for these changes in exercise capacity and tolerance. Many different kinds of exercise fall into this category, including walking and its derivatives (hiking, running, dancing, stair climbing), as well as biking, swimming, ball sports, etc. The key distinguishing features between activities that are primarily aerobic versus resistive in nature are listed in Table 3. Obviously, there may be some overlap if aerobic activities are altered to increase

the loading to muscle, as in resisted stationary cycling or stair-climbing machines. However, such activities are still primarily aerobic in nature, because they do not cause fatigue within a very few contractions, as PRT does, and therefore do not result in the kinds of adaptations in the nervous system and muscle that lead to marked strength gain and hypertrophy.

Overall, walking and its derivations surface as the most widely studied, feasible, safe, accessible, and economical mode of aerobic training for men and women of most ages and states of health. They do not require special equipment or locations, and do not need to be taught or supervised (except in the cognitively impaired, very frail, or medically unstable individual). Walking bears a natural relationship to ordinary activities of daily living, making it easier to integrate into lifestyle and functional tasks than any other mode of exercise. Therefore, it may be more likely to translate into improved functional independence and mobility than other modes of exercise.

The intensity of aerobic exercise refers to the amount of oxygen consumed (VO_2), or energy expended, per minute while performing the activity, which will vary from about 5 kcal/minute for light activities, to 7.5 kcal/minute for moderate activities, to 10–12 kcal/minute for very heavy activities. Energy expenditure increases with increasing body weight for weight-bearing aerobic activities, as well as with inclusion of larger muscle mass, and increased work (force x distance) and power output (work/time) demands of the activity. Therefore, the most intensive activities are those which involve the muscles of the arms, legs, and trunk simultaneously, necessitate moving the full body weight through space, and are done at a rapid pace (e.g.. cross-country skiing). Adding extra loading to the body weight (backpack, weight belt, wrist weights) increases the force needed to move the body part through space, and therefore increases the aerobic intensity of the work performed. The rise in heart rate is directly proportional, in normal individuals, to the increasing oxygen consumption or aerobic workload. Thus, monitoring heart rate has traditionally been a primary means of both prescribing appropriate intensity levels and following training adaptations when direct measurements of oxygen consumption are not available. The relative heart rate reserve (HRR) is the most useful estimate of intensity based on heart rate. Training intensity is normally recommended at approximately 60 to 70 percent of the HRR. It is calculated as is shown below.

HRR = (Maximal heart rate − resting heart rate) + resting heart rate60–70% HRR =.6–.7(Max HR −resting HR) + resting HR

Therefore, a more easily obtainable and reliable estimate of aerobic intensity is to prescribe a level of "somewhat hard," or 12 to 14 on the Borg scale, which runs from 6 to 20. At this level, the exerciser should note increased pulse and respiratory rate, but still be able to talk. All of the major benefits of aerobic exercise (increased cardiovascular fitness, decreased mortality, decreased incidence of chronic diseases, improved insulin sensitivity, blood pressure, and cholesterol, for example) are attainable with this moderately intense level of aerobic training. As is the case with all other forms of exercise, in order to maintain the same relative training intensity over time, the absolute training load must be increased as fitness improves. The workloads should progress on the basis of ratings of effort at each training session. Once the perceived exertion slips below 12, the intensity of the regimen should be increased to maintain the physiologic stimulus for optimal rates of adaptation. As with PRT, the most common error in aerobic training is failure to progress, which results in an early plateau in cardiovascular and metabolic improvement.

Cardiovascular protection and risk factor reduction appear to require twenty to thirty minutes three days per week, as does improvement in aerobic capacity. Epidemiological studies of mortality, cardiovascular disease, diabetes and functional independence suggest that walking about one mile per day (presumably about twenty minutes at average pace) or expending about 2000 kcal/week in physical activities is protective, again pointing to the moderate levels that are needed for major health outcomes. It has been shown that exercise does not need to be carried out in a single session to provide training effects, and may be broken up into periods of ten minutes at a time.

The risks of exercise are summarized in Table 4. The risk of sudden death during physical activity appears to be limited primarily to those who do not exercise on a regular basis (at least one hour per week), which is another reason for advocating regular, moderate periods of exercise rather than periodic high-volume training.

Table 4

The Risks of Exercise in Older Adults

Musculo-skeletal	Cardio-vascular	Metabolic
Falls	Arrhythmia	Dehydration
Foot ulceration or laceration	Cardiac failure	Electrolyte imbalance
Fracture, osteoporotic or traumatic	Hypertension	Energy imbalance
Hemorrhoids*	Hypotension	Heat Stroke
Hernia*	Ischemia	Hyperglycemia
Joint or bursa inflammation, exacerbation of arthritis	Pulmonary embolism	Hypoglycemia
Ligament or tendon strain or rupture	Retinal hemorrhage or detachment, lens detachment	Hypothermia
Muscle soreness or tear	Ruptured cerebral or other aneurysm	Seizures
Stress incontinence	Syncope or postural symptoms	

*Primarily associated with increased intra-abdominal pressure during resistive exercise, but may occur if Valsalva maneuver occurs during aerobic activities

SOURCE: Author

The benefits of aerobic exercise have been extensively studied since the 1960s (the most important of these for older adults are listed in Table 2). They include a broad range of physiological adaptations that are in general opposite to the effects of aging on most body systems, as well as major health-related clinical outcomes. The health conditions that are responsive to aerobic exercise include most of those of concern to older adults: osteoporosis, heart disease, stroke, breast cancer, diabetes, obesity, hypertension, arthritis, chronic lung disease, depression, and insomnia. These physiological and clinical benefits form the basis for the inclusion of aerobic exercise as an essential component of the overall physical activity prescription for healthy aging.

Flexibility training. Flexibility training includes movements or positions designed to increase range of motion across joints. Such range of motion is determined by both soft tissue factors (muscle strength, muscle and ligament length, scarring from surgery or trauma, joint and bursa fluid, synovial tissue thickness and inflammation, ligament laxity, tissue elasticity, degenerative changes of cartilage, temperature of tissues) and bony structure (deformities, arthritic and degenerative changes in bone, surgical devices). Obviously, only some of these abnormalities are amenable to exercise intervention, and these will be discussed below. In general, the effect of stretching the soft tissues around a joint slowly and consistently over time is to increase the pain-free range of motion for that joint.

Flexibility may be enhanced without the use of any specialized equipment. It is often helpful, however, to have a thin mat available for postures that are best done while stretched out on the floor.

The most effective technique for increasing flexibility is to extend a body part as fully as possible without pain, then hold this fully extended position for twenty to thirty seconds. The key requirement is to complete the movement slowly (without any bouncing or ballistic movements). Such bouncing does not increase efficacy and range of motion, but instead may cause muscle contraction that limits the range achievable. A technique known as proprioceptive neural facilitation (PNF) will maximize the stretching effectiveness. The technique is as follows. Once the body part has been stretched as far as possible, the muscle groups around the joint should then be completely relaxed, while maintaining the stretch. Next, an attempt is made to stretch a little further, which is usually possible. This final position is then held for about twenty to thirty seconds before returning to the initial position. PNF serves to counteract the involuntary resistance to overextension of a joint caused by a feedback loop of receptors within the muscle tissue that are activated by mechanical stretch.

Flexibility exercise is part of many other forms of exercise, such as ballet and modern dance, yoga, t'ai chi, and resistance training, because in all of these pursuits the muscle groups are slowly extended to their full range and held before relaxing, just as in PNF. It is not recommended to force a stretch beyond the point of pain, as this may result in injury to soft tissue structures and ultimately worsen function. As with all forms of exercise, as the range of motion increases over time, it is appropriate and necessary to extend the distance the joint is moved so that progress is maintained.

The physiologic benefit of flexibility exercise is increased range of motion across joints. There is some evidence that range of motion is related to functional independence in activities of daily living, posture, balance, and gait characteristics in older adults, as well as to pain and disability and quality of life in arthritis. Flexibility training itself does not result in improved strength or endurance, or marked improvements in balance. Therefore, it is best conceived of as an accessory to other forms of exercise that contributes to overall exercise and functional capacity. To the extent that pain, fear of falling, mobility, and function are improved, quality of life may improve as well. There is a need for much better quantitative research on effective doses and long-term benefits of this mode of exercise in the elderly.

Balance training. Any activity that increases one's ability to maintain balance in the face of stressors may be considered a balance-enhancing activity. Stressors include decreased base of support; perturbation of the ground support; decrease in proprioception, vision, or vestibular system input; increased compliance of the support surface; or movement of the center of mass of the body. Balance-enhancing activities impact on the central nervous system control of balance and coordination of movement, and/or augment the peripheral neuromuscular system response to signals that balance is threatened.

Intensity in balance training refers to the degree of difficulty of the postures, movements, or routines practiced. The appropriate level of difficulty or "intensity" for any balance-enhancing exercise is the highest level that can be tolerated without inducing a fall or near-fall. Progression in intensity is the key to improvement, as in other exercise domains, but mastery of the previous level before progression must be adhered to for safety.

Balance training has been shown to result in improved balance performance, decreased fear of falling, decreased incidence of falls, and increased ability to participate in activities of daily living that may have been limited by gait and balance difficulties. It is expected, although not proven, that such changes ultimately lead to improvements in functional independence, reduced hip fractures and other serious injuries, and improved overall quality of life.

Summary of benefits

Physiologic aging, retirement, societal expectations, accumulated diseases, and medication and nutritional effects conspire to produce deficits in strength, balance, aerobic capacity, and flexibility in older adults. Fortunately, there is increasing evidence for the reversibility of many of these deficits with a targeted exercise prescription. There is still work to be done in refining the prescription, particularly in terms of the amount of flexibility and balance training needed for optimal efficacy. In addition, there is a need for well-controlled, long-term studies on clinically important outcomes, such as treatment of cardiovascular disease and stroke, prevention and treatment of hip fracture, prevention of diabetic complications, reduction in nursing home admission rates, and moderation of disability from arthritis. An "active lifestyle" may be the most desirable public health approach to the maintenance of function and the prevention of disease in healthy persons. However, it is likely that the use of exercise to treat preexisting diseases and geriatric syndromes will always need to incorporate elements of a traditional "exercise prescription," as well as behavioral approaches, to more fully integrate appropriate physical activity into daily life.

MARIA FIATARONE SINGH

See also BALANCE AND MOBILITY; BALANCE, SENSE OF; FRAILTY; HEART DISEASE; LIFE EXPECTANCY; PERIODIC HEALTH EXAMINATION; SARCOPENIA.

BIBLIOGRAPHY

American College of Sports Medicine. "The Recommended Quantity and Quality of Exercise for Developing and Maintaining Cardiopulmonary and Muscular Fitness in Healthy Adults." *Medicine and Science in Sports and Exercise* 22 (1990): 265–274.
American College of Sports Medicine. *Guidelines for Exercise Testing and Prescription.* Philadelphia: Williams & Wilkins, 1995.
BLAIR, S. N.; KOHL, H.; BARLOW, C.; et al. "Changes in Physical Fitness and All-Cause Mortality: A Prospective Study of Healthy and Unhealthy Men." *Journal of the American Medical Association* 273 (1995): 1093–1098.
BORTZ, W. M. "Redefining Human Aging." *Journal of the American Geriatrics Society* 37 (1989): 1092–1096.
DRINKWATER, B.; GRIMSON, S.; CULLEN-RAAB, D.; et al. "ACSM Position Stand on Osteoporosis and Exercise." *Medicine and Science in Sports and Exercise* 27 (1995): i–vii.

FIATARONE SINGH, M. *Exercise, Nutrition and the Older Woman: Wellness for Women over Fifty.* Boca Raton, Fla.: CRC Press, 2000.
HELMRICH, S.; RAGLAND, D.; and PAFFENBARGER, R. "Prevention of Non-Insulin-Dependent Diabetes Mellitus with Physical Activity." *Medicine and Science in Sports and Exercise* 26 (1994): 824–830.
LEE, I.-M.; PAFFENBARGER, R. S.; and HENNEKENS, C. H. "Physical Activity, Physical Fitness and Longevity." *Aging Clinical and Experimental Research* 9 (1997): 2–11.
MAZZEO, R.; CAVANAUGH, P.; EVANS, W.; et al. "Exercise and Physical Activity for Older Adults." *Medicine and Science in Sports and Exercise* 30 (1998): 992–1008.
MILLER, M.; REJESKI, W.; REBOUSSIN, B.; et al. "Physical Activity, Functional Limitations, and Disability in Older Adults." *Journal of the American Geriatrics Society* 48 (2000): 1264–1272.
National Institute of Health, Center for Disease Prevention. "Physical Activity and Cardiovascular Health." *Journal of the American Medical Association* 276 (1996): 241–246.
PATE, R. R.; PRATT, M.; BLAIR, S. N.; et al. "Physical Activity and Public Health: A Recommendation From the Centers for Disease Control and Prevention and the American College of Sports Medicine." *Journal of the American Medical Association* 273 (1995): 402–407.
PROVINCE, M.; HADLEY, E.; HORNBROOK, M.; et al. "The Effects of Exercise on Falls in Elderly Patients." *Journal of the American Medical Association* 273 (1995): 1341–1347.
U.S. Department of Health and Human Services. *Physical Activity and Health: A Report of the Surgeon General.* Atlanta, Ga.: U.S. Dept. of Health and Human Services, Centers for Disease Control and Prevention, National Center for Chronic Disease Prevention and Health Promotion, 1996.

EXPANDED ROLE NURSE

See NURSE PRACTITIONER

EYE, AGING-RELATED DISEASES

The sense of sight, said Aristotle is preferred "to everything else. The reason is that this, most of all the senses makes us know and brings to light many differences between things" (*Metaphysics*, 98A225).

If one looks an eye straight on, several important structures are recognizable, including the pupil, which is the black circle in the center of the eye that dilates and constricts in response to light; the iris, which is the colored muscular structure that allows the pupil to change its size; the transparent cornea, which is really the window of the eye; and the lens. The latter focuses light through the pupil onto the retina at the back of the eye, much as a lens in a camera focuses images onto film. Images are then transformed into electrical signals that are transmitted to the visual cortex at the back of the brain. The space in the eyeball between the lens and the retina is filled with a viscous clear liquid known as vitreous humor (see Figure 1).

With age, many changes (some virtually universal, and others arising from age-related disease) threaten the quality of vision. For instance, tear glands often work less well, leading many older adults to suffer from dry eyes (easily treated with artificial tears). Lax muscles around the eye can result in the lower lid margin rotating away from the eyeball (ectropion) or an inward migration of the eyelashes and eyelid toward the globe (entropion). In the conjunctiva (the skin on the inside of the lid and covering the white part of the eye), tiny blood vessels can rupture, giving rise to localized accumulation of blood akin to a bruise (subconjunctival hemorrhage). Though unsightly, it is not serious and usually does not signify any underlying disorder. It can clear up spontaneously in six to eight days.

Particularly in people who are near-sighted, "floaters" (tiny, condensed debris floating in the vitreous humor) are common and of little consequence. However, any sudden increase in the number of floaters, particularly if accompanied by flashing lights, can herald the onset of serious retinal problems, and requires a thorough eye examination as soon as possible.

Other age-related eye problems can also threaten vision and require evaluation by an ophthalmologist. Corneal ulcers, tumors on or near the eye, inflammation of the structures of the eyeball, occlusion of retinal vessels, and any sudden loss of vision are among them.

Three common sight-threatening disorders are described here in more detail. Each can result in problems sufficient to meet the World Health Organization's definition of visual impairment (i.e., visual acuity less than 20/60 in the better eye). Overall, about 2–4 percent of the population age seventy and over suffers from such impairment.

Glaucoma

Glaucoma is a chronic disorder that when left untreated, will lead to blindness in most cases. The clinical picture usually, but not always, includes elevated intraocular pressure that leads to damage of the optic nerve (optic neuropathy). There are several types of glaucoma: acute and chronic, open- and closed-angle, and secondary. In all cases, treatment is directed toward reducing the intraocular pressure with eye drops, laser, and/or surgery, depending upon the severity of the case and the response to the medical therapy.

Chronic open-angle glaucoma, the most common form, usually comes about insidiously and progresses chronically. Since it is peripheral visual field loss that first occurs, damage can be extensive before the person affected becomes aware of important visual loss.

Theories about the nature and causes of glaucoma are being reevaluated. Early views of open-angle glaucoma as a simple matter of a problem in aqueous outflow have given way to the concept of a more complex neurodegenerative disorder of the optic nerve. New modalities of treatment are being evaluated, including medications that may protect the optic nerve, but the current treatment remains aimed at lowering pressure inside the eyeball. However, it has become clear that a number of other factors play important roles in determining whether a specific level of intraocular pressure will be harmful to a given eye. As these additional factors are identified, new modalities of treatment will arise to address their influence whether these be genetic, vascular, or neuronal.

Age-related macular degeneration

Macular degeneration (the macula is the very central part of the seeing eye) is a common cause of impaired vision in older adults, and often progresses to cause legal blindness. Two types of macular degeneration predominate. The acute "exudative" (wet) form results from proliferation of blood vessels in the macula that subsequently bleed, causing a hemorrhage and scarring in this area. This acute process has devastating effects on vision. In a small percentage of cases (10–15 percent), treatment with either a "hot laser" or, more recently, a combination of a "cold laser" and photodynamic dye, can stabilize the condition and preserve vision.

The more common form of macular degeneration is the slowly progressive atrophic type. While there is no treatment for this form, the clinical development is much slower, and a reasonable degree of vision is often maintained for many years despite the presence of the atrophic lesions in the macula.

Since the macula is necessary for central (in contrast to peripheral) vision, decreased visual acuity and, especially, distortion of the central part of the visual field are important symptoms of this disorder.

Cataracts

A cataract is a clinical condition that describes the opacification (clouding) of the natural lens of the eye. A cataract is not a growth, but a change in the tissue structure of the lens. These changes are very much age-related, and almost physiological, although they occur at much younger ages in some patients than in others, and there are also many ways in which the tissue changes. The most common and physiological change, described as sclerosis of the lens, is similar to a yellowing of plastic after many years of exposure to sunlight. This type of cataract often improves near vision because it helps magnify items, but it reduces distance vision.

Other types of cataracts appear in a spoke-like fashion in the lens or in a membrane type of opacification known as a posterior subcapsular cataract. In all types of cataracts, vision, usually for distance and near, is reduced. Patients often have problems with glare from sunlight, and streetlights and car headlights, and eventually their quality of life deteriorates. As these changes occur, changes in the refractive error, or the power that is needed for eyeglasses, also changes, and in the early stages, a change in lenses can compensate for some of the changes in the eye. Eventually, however, this no longer suffices and more drastic therapy is needed.

Because the lens is an isolated structure with no blood vessels, it has long been known that it could be removed, rather safely, from the eye. Current cataract techniques are called removal by phacoemulsification, and introduction of an intraocular lens. Phacoemulsification is a technique in which a very high-frequency ultrasound probe is introduced into the lens. The lens tissue is then pulverized, as it were, and a second system sucks out the material so that the lens tissue

is removed completely from its very thin membranous sac, known as the capsule. An intraocular lens is then inserted to replace the natural lens. The current standard is to insert a lens that has been folded on itself and will unfold in the eye when it is in place. These techniques allow cataract surgery to be done through a 3 millimeter incision in the clear part of the cornea, and does not require any stitching. Healing is more rapid and safe with this technique. Currently, cataract surgery is an outpatient procedure with only numbing drops put on the eye rather than any other anesthesia or medication being used.

The cataract surgery is one of the great surgical success stories of the late twentieth century. It has permitted millions of people the world over to be rehabilitated to a more functional status and a better quality of life. Nonetheless, cataracts remain the number one cause of blindness in the developing world, and it is simply a matter of resources to get enough cataract surgery done in the developing world to reverse that statistic.

RAYMOND LeBLANC
KENNETH ROCKWOOD

See also ASSISTED LIVING; BRAIN; DRIVING ABILITY; FUNCTIONAL ABILITY; IMAGES OF AGING; NEURODEGENERATIVE DISEASES; REACTION TIME; VISION AND PERCEPTION.

BIBLIOGRAPHY

BUCH, H.; VINDING, T.; and NIELSEN, N. V. "Prevalence and Causes of Visual Impairment According to World Health Organization and United States Criteria in an Aged, Urban Scandinavian Population: The Copenhagen City Eye Study." *Ophthalmology* 108 (December 2001): 2347–2357.

JAENICKE, R., and SLINGSBY, C. "Lens Crystallins and Their Microbial Homologs: Structure, Stability, and Function." *Critical Reviews in Biochemistry and Molecular Biology* 36 (2001): 435–499.

LICHTER, P. R.; MUSCH, D. C.; GILLESPIE, B. W.; GUIRE, K. E.; JANZ, N. K.; WREN, P. A.; MILLS, R. P.; and the CIGTS Study Group. "Interim Clinical Outcomes in the Collaborative Initial Glaucoma Treatment Study Comparing Initial Treatment Randomized to Medications or Surgery." *Ophthalmology* 108 (2001): 1943–1953.

YI, Q.; FLANAGAN, S. J.; and McCARTY, D. J. "Trends in Health Service Delivery for Cataract Surgery at a Large Australian Ophthalmic

Hospital." *Clinical and Experimental Ophthalmology* 29 (October 2001): 291–295.

F

FAINTING

Fainting is a common symptom in the elderly, generally referred to in the medical literature as *syncope*. Fainting is defined as transient loss of consciousness accompanied by loss of postural tone, with spontaneous recovery, not requiring resuscitation. Fainting has multiple underlying causes. This common symptom has potential adverse consequences, such as falls, fractures, brain injury, soft tissue injuries, and anxiety, which particularly in the elderly may lead to loss of independent function. When the reason for fainting is an underlying heart disease, an increased risk of sudden death is suggested; but when fainting is unexplained after thorough initial evaluation and recurrent then there is no such increased risk.

A person who faints may have some convulsions but recovers quickly and is not confused for more than a few minutes, whereas a person with epilepsy will usually have more prolonged convulsions and be confused for a longer time. In coma the heart beats and the person breathes but consciousness is not regained as quickly.

Basic mechanisms and predisposition in elderly people

Fainting results from inadequate energy substrate delivery to the brain. The major energy substrates are oxygen and glucose. Significant lowering of blood sugar tends to result in coma rather than fainting, and a prolonged cessation of oxygen delivery results in death. Thus transient loss of delivery of oxygen to the brain due to decreased blood flow to the brain is the final common pathway in most causes of fainting.

Generalized lowering of oxygen in the blood from heart or lung disease or reduced oxygen-carrying capacity of the blood from anemia are risk factors for fainting, particularly in the elderly, but rarely the sole cause.

Blood pressure lowered enough to decrease blood flow to the brain may cause fainting, and the causes of fainting can be deduced from the blood pressure formula. Blood pressure is the product of cardiac output and total peripheral resistance of the arteries. Cardiac output is the product of stroke volume and heart rate per minute. Stroke volume is the amount of blood that the heart ejects in one beat. Total peripheral resistance is a measure of how constricted the arterial blood vessels are. Thus anything that will reduce the volume of blood that is ejected, impair heart rate, or cause dilatation of the arteries may lead to a fainting spell.

Elderly people are predisposed to fainting by the presence of multiple abnormalities, both age- and disease related. These conditions add up to threaten cerebral blood flow or reduce oxygen content in the blood. A situational stress that further reduces blood pressure, such as standing up from a lying position or straining at stools or voiding, may reduce cerebral oxygen delivery below the critical threshold and result in fainting. Several homeostatic mechanisms that normally preserve blood pressure and cerebral oxygen delivery in the face of stress become impaired with age. These mechanisms include cerebral blood flow autoregulation, blood pressure sensors in the carotid artery (baroreflexes), relaxation of the heart muscle, and sodium conservation by the kidneys.

479

Causes

Multiple studies have shown that 20 to 30 percent of fainting episodes have cardiac causes, 10 to 20 percent have other causes, and 30 to 50 percent remain unexplained in spite of extensive evaluation.

Several cardiac diseases may cause fainting, such as those that cause mechanical obstruction to blood flow such as narrowing of heart valves or abnormal thickening of the heart muscle, called *cardiomyopathy*. Blood clots from veins of the body, most often the legs, may also present with fainting due to obstruction of blood flow through the lungs and heart. Both slow heart rate (less than 40 beats per minute) and rapid heart rate (more than 140 beats per minute) may cause fainting. The rapid heart rate causes fainting by not giving the heart enough time to fill with blood before ejection into the circulation. The causes of these heart rate abnormalities include heart attacks, disease of the conduction system of the heart, and disease—most often seen in the elderly—of the sinus node of the heart, where the origin of the heart beat occurs normally.

Orthostatic hypotension is a term for blood pressure that drops more than 20 mm of mercury on position change, such as standing up from a lying or sitting position. This may cause dizziness when in mild stages but frequently causes elderly people to faint. It is either due to volume depletion or inability to constrict blood vessels under this type of stress. Volume depletion may be caused by fluid loss or blood loss or by too little fluid intake, or by medications such as diuretics, which increase excretion of fluid through the kidneys. Dilatation of the blood vessels may be caused by prolonged inactivity, such as bed rest, or by medications such as blood pressure–lowering medications and the older types of medications prescribed for depression. By only giving the lowest effective dose of medications to the elderly person, these types of adverse effects may be avoided or corrected. Disturbed autonomic function may cause dilatation of the blood vessels and cause fainting. Examples of these are central nervous system diseases—such as Multiple System Atrophy, Parkinson's disease, or Dementia with Lewy Bodies—and peripheral autonomic neuropathies caused by diseases such as diabetes mellitus or amyloidosis. Digestion of food may lead to hypotension and fainting in the elderly person due to inability to compensate for blood pooling in the gut during digestion, so-called postprandial hypotension. Finally, reflexes may cause dilatation of blood vessels, triggered by straining at stools, urination, swallowing, or coughing or by hypersensitivity of the carotid sinus, which is located in the neck.

Evaluation and treatment

The patient's history is the most important part of the evaluation, and the physical examination focuses on blood pressure and heart evaluation to exclude the life-threatening causes of fainting. Therapy should be directed toward minimizing multiple risks of fainting, avoiding toxic interventions, and treating specific symptomatic diseases (for example, with pacemakers for certain conduction diseases in the heart), while basing treatment on the underlying disease, rather than on age per se.

PÁLMI V. JÓNSSON

See also BALANCE AND MOBILITY; DEMENTIA WITH LEWY BODIES; DIZZINESS; EPILEPSY; HEART DISEASE; MULTIPLE SYSTEMS ATROPHY; PARKINSONISM.

BIBLIOGRAPHY

JÓNSSON, P. V., and LIPSITZ, L. A. "Dizziness and Syncope." In *Principles of Geriatric Medicine and Gerontology*, 3d ed. Edited by William R. Hazzard, Edwin L. Bierman, John P. Blass, Walter H. Ettinger, Jr., and Jeffrey B. Halter. McGraw-Hill Inc., 1994. Pages 1165–1181.
LINZER, M.; YANG, E. H.; ESTES, N. A., III; WANG, P.; VORPERIAN, V. R.; and KAPOOR, W. N. "Diagnosing Syncope. Part 2: Unexplained Syncope. Clinical Efficacy Assessment Project of the American College of Physicians." *Annals of Internal Medicine* 127, no. 1 (1997): 76–86.
SHAW, F. E., and KENNY, R. A. "The Overlap between Syncope and Falls in the Elderly." *Postgraduate Medical Journal* 73, no. 864 (1997): 635–639.

FALLS

See BALANCE AND MOBILITY

FAMILY

Although much has been written about the declining importance of the family as a social institution in American society, family relationships continue to be of critical importance in the lives of older people. In fact, research on life course and the family repeatedly finds that people highly value family relationships throughout all of life, and that family ties significantly affect quality of life. Because family roles are such an important aspect of aging, separate entries in this encyclopedia focus on husband-wife, sibling, parent-child, and grandparent-grandchild relationships in later life. Rather than repeating information in these entries, this discussion focuses on how demographic and social changes are affecting family relationships in old age.

Demographic changes affecting family structure

Longevity increased dramatically in the United States over the twentieth century. The average years lived by a person increased from forty-seven in 1900 to seventy-seven in 2000, and the proportion of persons surviving from birth to old age (sixty-five) increased from 39 percent to 86 percent during the twentieth century. This remarkable change in mortality conditions changed the potential for older people to be involved in family relationships, as the following examples illustrate. (1) A growing number of persons have grandparents living when they reach adulthood. The likelihood of a thirty year old having a living grandparent increased from about 20 percent in 1900 to 75 percent in 2000. Thus the potential for being part of a four-generation family has greatly increased over time. (2) More people now have a parent living through their middle years of life. In 1900 only about 8 percent of sixty year olds had a parent still alive, compared to 44 percent of sixty year olds in 2000. This change has greatly increased the probability that parents and children will have a relationship that extends for sixty or more years. It also has increased the likelihood that a woman approaching old age will be called upon to care for a very old parent. (3) The potential for a husband and wife to cosurvive in a first marriage for more than sixty years has increased significantly. However, because of increasing divorce the actual proportion of older people living with their first spouse for this long has not changed much. (4) The odds of older people having a sibling still alive have increased sharply over time. The cosurvival of siblings may be significant because sibling relationships are fre-

quently valued highly by people in their later years of life.

Declining fertility in the United States over the twentieth century also has affected family relationships involving older people. Women who completed their childbearing around 1900 had an average of about five children each, compared to an average of about two for women completing childbearing around 2000. The trend in childbearing was not smooth over the century, however, because of the baby boom from the mid-1940s through the early 1960s. In the mid 1950s women were averaging about 3.5 children each. Because of fluctuating fertility, the proportion of people in later life who have several surviving children varies over time. As baby boomers (who had low fertility and high rates of childlessness) replace the parents of the baby boom as the older population after 2010, the proportion of older people with no or only one child will increase rapidly. This is potentially significant because children have been an important source of social support and caregiving for older people. Declining fertility also means that those who survive to old age now tend to have fewer children and grandchildren than old people in the past. It has been noted that under high mortality conditions grandparents tend to be in short supply, while under low fertility conditions grandchildren are in short supply.

Social changes affecting family relationships

In addition to demographic change, several social changes over the twentieth century have altered family relations involving older people. First, alternative family forms (blended families, single parent families, cohabiting relationships, gay and lesbian unions) have become more common and more accepted. It is not clear how this diversity of "family" forms will affect the lives of older people in the twenty-first century. On the one hand, the plurality of forms may create a broader range of available kinship ties. On the other hand, these alternative kin relationships may not be as strong as the enduring parent-child relationships that have been the primary source of long-term caregiving for disabled older people. The negative effect of divorce on the strength of intergenerational relationships tends to be more significant for males than females.

Second, gender roles have changed as women have surpassed men in educational attainment and have greatly increased their level of participation in the paid labor force. For older people, this means that middle-aged daughters are more likely to be in the labor force and, consequently, less available to provide care for them than in the past (and, as noted above, in the future old people will have fewer adult children). Changing gender roles are also likely to alter marital relationships in later life, as women become less dependent on husbands to manage the family economy and expect more egalitarian and companionate relationships.

Third, the transformation of the American economy has produced a tremendous change in the standard of living over the twentieth century. Increasing affluence has been accompanied by a decline in intergenerational coresidence for older people. In 1900 most older widows resided with an adult child; now most older widows live alone and very few live with a child. The increasing independence in living arrangements does not, however, mean that parent-child relationships have become weak. Almost all older people report having a close relationship with their children, but prefer "intimacy at a distance" to sharing a home. In general, the spread of social security, private pensions, and lifetime savings means that fewer old people are dependent on children for economic support than in the past, so intergenerational relationships are increasingly based on social and emotional bonds.

The future

It is clear that family relationships have been important for older people in the past and continue to be important in the present. As the baby boom ages, the proportion of older people living in marriages will decline and the proportion who are childless will increase. Thus one might anticipate that family relationships would play a smaller role in the lives of older people in the future. Nevertheless, it seems unlikely that the family will lose its place as the most important source of social and emotional support for people as they age through later life.

PETER UHLENBERG

See also GRANDPARENTHOOD; INTERGENERATIONAL EXCHANGES; KIN; MARITAL RELATIONSHIPS; PARENT-CHILD RELATIONSHIP; SIBLING RELATIONSHIPS.

BIBLIOGRAPHY

CHERLIN, A., and FURSTENBERG, F., JR. *The New American Grandparent.* Cambridge, Mass.: Harvard University Press, 1992.

EGGEBEEN, D. P., and HOGAN, D. J. "Giving Between Generations in American Families." *Human Nature* 1 (1991): 211–232.

HAGESTAD, G. "Demographic Change and the Life Course: Some Emerging Trends in the Family Realm." *Family Relations* 37 (1988): 405–410.

PILLEMER, K., and SUITOR, J. J. "Baby Boom Families: Relations with Aging Parents." *Generations* 22 (1998): 65–69.

RILEY, M. W., and RILEY, J. W., JR. "Generational Relations: A Future Perspective." In *Aging and Generational Relations Over the Life Course.* Edited by Tamara K. Hareven. New York: Walter de Gruyter, 1996. Pages 526–533.

ROSSI, A., and ROSSI, P. *Of Human Bonding: Parent-Child Relations Across the Life Course.* New York: Aldine de Gruyter, 1990.

UHLENBERG, P. "Mortality Decline in the Twentieth Century and Supply of Kin Over the Life Course." *The Gerontologist* 36 (1996): 681–685.

FEDERAL AGENCIES ON AGING

A large number of departments and agencies within the federal government administer programs designed to help older Americans. There are multiple reasons why this public responsibility is spread across so many different government bureaucracies (Hudson).

First, older Americans have long had special needs that are absent or less intense among younger people. At advanced ages, people's strength tends to fail, and their health status may decline. Thus, it is often difficult for older people to work and support themselves. If they are ill, they may not be able to pay medical bills or gain access to health care services. It is also true that many older persons, especially very old women, are without family or nearby family members to assist them when they are in need. Thus, there has historically been a need for government to step in and help many people who have problems associated with old age (Binstock).

Second, the needs of older people for governmental assistance were acknowledged in the United States when assistance was not thought to be appropriate for other groups. In other industrial nations, many government programs were begun to assist workers and other working-age people, and were not targeted specifically to the old. The United States, however, proved more reluctant to put in place broad income and health care programs for working-age adults, holding more to a philosophy that such individuals should take care of themselves and their families (Rimlinger).

Third, older people make up a large percentage of the U.S. population today—12.6 percent of Americans are over age sixty-four—and have many of the same needs and demands for government programs that younger people have. Like other Americans, older people want safe streets, good transportation, a clean environment, and healthy food. Because of these interests older people have in common with younger ones, there are many agencies that address the needs of the old and the young on a largely undifferentiated basis.

The government agencies discussed here are confined to ones that devote their attention either exclusively or largely to older Americans. The best example of the first type of agency is the Administration on Aging (AoA) within the Department of Health and Human Services. AoA administers the Older Americans Act, which exclusively addresses the concerns of the 43 million Americans age sixty and above. An example of the second type of agency is the Social Security Administration, which is charged with administering most titles of the Social Security Act. Largely because of its old-age program for retired workers, most Social Security beneficiaries are elderly. However, because survivor, dependent, and disability benefits are also available through Social Security, roughly one-third of Social Security beneficiaries are under age sixty-five. An example of a third type of agency serving elderly and nonelderly is the Federal Transit Administration within the Department of Transportation. Though the elderly are frequent users of mass transit and this agency is very relevant to them, it serves a much broader population than just the old. As such, it is outside the bounds of the agencies discussed here.

Social Security Administration

The Social Security Administration (SSA), an independent agency, administers the largest titles of the Social Security Act, the largest social program in America. The formal name for what is often termed "Social Security" is the Old Age, Survivors, and Disability program (OASDI). Benefits under the OASDI program go to 27 million retired workers, 3 million spouses, 5 million widows and widowers, 2 million children of deceased workers, and 450,000 children of retired workers. OASDI expenditures in 2000 totaled $407 billion. This is the largest single expenditure of the U.S. government. SSA also administers Supplemental Security Income, a smaller program for low-income elderly, blind, and disabled individuals that expended $32 billion in 2000. Unlike OASDI, under which individuals receive benefits related to how much they earned while they were working, SSI beneficiaries receive benefits based on having very low incomes, regardless of their work history. It is because of this difference that OASDI is a "social insurance" program and SSI is a "public assistance" program.

SSA was separated from the Department of Health and Human Services in 1995. Dating to the 1930s, it has a longer and more distinguished history than many government agencies. Over the years its leadership has taken a central role not only in the design of social insurance policy in the United States but also in convincing Americans that Social Security is a needed program and fully in keeping with traditional American values of hard work and self-sufficiency (Derthick).

SSA headquarters are in Baltimore, Maryland, and today it has a staff of over 65,000 employees and 10 regional offices. SSA maintains 1300 field offices, and it is to these offices that individuals go to make inquiries about eligibility and benefits. SSA is one of the few federal agencies that individuals interact with directly; that is, the people serving them are employees of the federal government. (The other major example is the Internal Revenue Service.) The administration of most other government programs involves private nonprofit and proprietary organizations. These organizations contract with the appropriate federal agency, are monitored by that agency, and deliver services for that agency. Among others, this is true of the Medicare program, the Older Americans Act, and the food stamp program.

SSA undertakes a number of activities in support of its principal mission of making payments to beneficiaries under the OASDI and SSI programs. To better inform current workers about how Social Security works, SSA sends individualized statements to them that inform them of the benefits they may receive when they retire. Because a worker's future employment and wages are unknown, these estimates are made on certain assumptions tied to the worker's employment history.

SSA also maintains a research, analysis, and evaluation division. It keeps track of how much money the system is currently expending and currently taking in. In conjunction with the Social Security Advisory Board, created in 1994 as the SSA was becoming an independent agency, SSA staff also undertakes important forecasting activities, advising the president and Congress about the future status of the Social Security trust fund. Because the program is so big and because the American population is aging, these estimates have become very important in discussions about ways in which the Social Security system might be modified or overhauled in the future.

Centers for Medicare and Medicaid Services

The Centers for Medicare and Medicaid Services (CMMS), formerly the Health Care Financing Administration (HCFA), is located in the Department of Health and Human Services and administers Medicare, Medicaid, and the State Children's Health Program. The name was changed in 2001. Medicare and Medicaid were enacted in 1965, and were originally administered by the SSA. HCFA was created as a separate agency within the Department of Health and Human Services in 1977. When Medicare was enacted, it was directed exclusively to people age sixty-five and above; today it serves 33 million older individuals, 4 million disabled individuals, and 162,000 individuals with end-stage renal disease. Medicaid is a federal-state grant program in which the states receive federal reimbursements for expenditures they make on behalf of low-income individuals eligible for Medicaid coverage. Medicaid serves low-income individuals of all ages. However, it is especially important for older people who have long-term chronic illnesses and live in nursing homes or other institutional settings (Coughlin, Ku, and Holahan). Through Medicare and Medicaid, CMMS insures some 75 million Americans.

Medicare beneficiaries may receive their benefits through the traditional fee-for-service system or through a managed care organization,

such as a health maintenance organization. In the former case, CMMS contracts with insurance companies, known as "fiscal intermediaries," that actually process claims from beneficiaries, hospitals, doctors, and other health care providers. Providers receive 80 percent of the fee established by the intermediary, following rules established by CMMS, with the beneficiary responsible for the remaining 20 percent. Prior to 1992, these reimbursements were based on a standard of "reasonable and customary charges;" since that date, reimbursements are based on a fee schedule established by HCFA that reduces reimbursements for surgeries and other selected procedures while increasing them for basic office visits (Moon).

In the case of managed care organizations, CMMS contracts with the managed care organization and provides a fixed amount per beneficiary to that organization, which manages all health care services available to the enrollee. The amounts vary widely around the country, using a complex formula based on 95 percent of the costs per beneficiary under the traditional fee-for-service model (Koff and Park). Other financing and delivery models CMMS is experimenting with include the social health maintenance organization, which includes social as well as health services, and the Program for All-Inclusive Care of the Elderly (PACE), which provides adult day care services for older persons who would otherwise need to be living in nursing homes or other institutional settings.

In purchasing health care services for beneficiaries of these programs, CMMS assures that the programs are being properly run by contractors and states; establishes policies for paying health care providers; conducts research on various aspects of health care management, delivery, treatment, and financing; and assesses and assures the quality of health care being provided through the programs. Of particular concern in recent years have been efforts to rein in fraud and abuse within the Medicare and Medicaid programs, and efforts to assure quality of care.

National Institute on Aging

The National Institute on Aging (NIA) is one of twenty-five separate institutes within the National Institutes of Health (NIH), the principal federal organization sponsoring and conducting scientific research related to health, which in turn is a part of the Department of Health and

Human Services. For many years research on aging was centered within the National Institute of Child Health and Human Development (NICHD). However, those concerned with the particular medical, social, and behavioral problems associated with aging felt that NICHD's principal interests lay elsewhere, as did funding; only about 11 percent of the agency's budget was devoted to research on aging from 1962 to 1974 (Koff and Park). Delegates to the 1961 and 1971 White House conferences on aging pressed for a separate research entity within NIH. Despite the initial opposition of President Richard Nixon to creation of the NIA, he signed legislation authorizing its creation in May 1974.

NIA's missions are (a) to support and conduct high-quality research on aging processes, aging-related diseases, and special problems and needs of the aged; (b) to train and develop highly skilled research scientists; (c) to develop and maintain state-of-the art resources to accelerate research progress; and (d) to disseminate information and communicate with the public and interested groups on ongoing and needed health and research activities (www.nih.gov/nia/about/history).

Because aging-related research is relevant to and conducted by other institutes within NIH, it has been important for NIA to coordinate its activities with them. Put differently, NIA and NICHD are "population focused" (i.e., largely about older people and children, respectively). However, most of the other institutes in NIH are organized around particular diseases (e.g., National Cancer Institute, National Institute on Alcohol Abuse and Alcoholism) or specific organs (National Heart, Lung, and Blood Institute, National Institute of Diabetes, Digestive, and Kidney Diseases). Because all people can contract diseases and all people have bodily organs, there is inevitable overlap between institutes organized around population and around diseases and organs. Thus, NIA has coordinated its activities with other parts of NIH along the following lines, among others: (a) Alzheimer's and related diseases; (b) genetic and environmental bases for differences in the aging process; (c) impact of diet and exercise on health and functioning of older people; (d) means for preventing the need for long-term institutionalization; (e) research to improve the longevity of ethnic and racial minority populations; and (f) cross-cultural comparative studies concerning diverse populations (Koff and Park).

NIA sponsors research on aging through both extramural and intramural programs. The extramural program funds research and training at universities, hospitals, medical centers, and other public and private organizations. The intramural program conducts basic and clinical research in Baltimore and on the NIH campus in Bethesda, Maryland.

Administration on Aging

The Administration on Aging (AoA), within the Department of Health and Human Services, is charged with being an advocate for older people within the federal government and with administering all but one title of the Older Americans Act, which supports a range of socially supportive services for elderly people through a network of state, regional, and provider organizations.

Employment and Training Administration

Two programs administered within the Employment and Training Administration (ETA) of the Department of Labor (DOL) have particular relevance to older people: the Senior Community Service Employment Program (SCSEP) and the Job Partnership Training Act.

SCSEP is Title V of the Older Americans Act (OAA), and it is the only title of the act that is not administered by the Administration on Aging in the Department of Health and Human Services. SCSEP is run by the Employment and Training Administration within DOL. It serves people who are fifty-five or older and have low incomes and poor employment prospects. ETA does not directly oversee the employment of these individuals, but contracts with both national and state organizations to provide employment services. The three principal national contractors are the National Council of Senior Citizens, AARP (formerly the American Association of Retired Persons), and the National Farmers Union (or "Green Thumb," an elder employment program targeting rural America). The state-level contracts are administered through the state units on aging, created through Title III of the OAA.

ETA also administers the Job Partnership Training Act. which is the latest in a series of employment and training programs enacted by the federal government that date back to President John F. Kennedy's administration in the 1960s.

Most of the jobs are intended for younger workers, but provisions in the Title II adult training program require that services be provided to "older individuals on an equitable basis" (Sec. 204).

Employment Standards Administration

A relatively small agency, the Wage and Hour Division within DOL's Employment Standards Administration, is charged with administering and enforcing the Family and Medical Leave Act (FMLA) of 1993. FMLA was the first piece of domestic legislation signed by President Bill Clinton and has been at the heart of heated arguments about what role, if any, the federal government should play in easing the tensions that have emerged between the roles of work and family among today's employees. The growing presence of women in the American labor force has been the impetus behind this legislation. Being at work has made it difficult for many women to meet traditional family obligations; yet allowing these women workers time off for such obligations has put strains on employers (and other employees) in getting jobs completed at the workplace.

FMLA is still in its infancy, but it has the potential in future years of being increasingly relevant to older people. One of the provisions of the law is that a worker can take time off from work to care for "an immediate family member," which includes a parent. As both the overall population and the workforce age, there will be an increasing need for workers to help meet the needs of parents who are frail. If, as has been proposed, FMLA were liberalized to include paid leave, the number of workers helping parents would grow even larger. To this point, implementation of FMLA has been complicated (Scharlach and Grosswald, Hudson and Gonyea) and it will continue to pose challenges for the Wage and Hour Division.

Pension and Welfare Benefits Administration

The Pension and Welfare Benefits Administration in the Department of Labor is charged with enforcing provisions of a very important piece of federal legislation, the Employee Retirement Income Security Act (ERISA), which establishes standards designed to protect private pension funds from collapse or insolvency. In this role it is responsible for protecting $4.3 trillion in pension assets owned by 90 million participants in 700,000 pension plans (www.dol.gov/dol/pwba/public/pubs/factsht1.htm). Prior to ERISA's enactment, several major plans had collapsed, leaving retired participants in those plans unprotected. Changes in the private pension world have made administration of ERISA increasingly complicated, and plans have been presented on ways to simplify its administration (Perun and Steuerle).

ERISA established the Pension Benefit Guaranty Corporation (PBGC), which guarantees certain benefits in the type of pension plan known as a defined benefit plan. PBGC is a federal government corporation established by Title IV of ERISA "to encourage the growth of defined benefit plans, provide timely and uninterrupted payment of benefits, and maintain pension insurance premiums at the lowest level necessary to carry out the Corporation's obligations" (www.pbgc.gov/ABOUT.htm).

Senior Corps

The Corporation for National Service (Senior Corps) was created in 1993 to further the involvement of Americans in strengthening their communities. It merged the activities of two predecessor agencies, ACTION and the Commission on National and Community Service. For two decades ACTION administered VISTA (Volunteers in Service to America) and the three programs that comprise Senior Corps: the Senior Companion Program, the Foster Grandparent Program, and the Retired Senior Volunteer Program (RSVP).

The Senior Companion Program's dual purpose is "to create part-time stipendiary volunteer community service opportunities for low income persons aged sixty and older and to provide supportive person-to person services to assist adults having exceptional needs developmental disabilities, or other special needs for companionship" (Koff and Park, p. 265). Senior Companions can serve twenty hours per week and can receive a stipend based on 1,044 hours of service annually.

Responsibility for the Foster Grandparent Program was transferred from AoA to ACTION in 1971 and to Senior Corps in 1993. Foster grandparents must be fifty-five or older, no longer be in the regular workforce, and have no limitations that would affect their work with children. These older volunteers work with children (up to age twenty-one) in a variety of community and educational settings.

RSVP primarily involves retired professionals, giving them a chance to employ their skills on behalf of local service organizations. They must be available on a regular basis and over age fifty-five; they receive no stipend.

Equal Employment Opportunity Commission

The Equal Employment Opportunity Commission, an independent government agency, is charged with enforcing laws prohibiting job discrimination, including the Age Discrimination in Employment Act (ADEA). There is a long history in the United States of discriminating against older workers (Graebner; Sandell), which ADEA is designed to address. Originally enacted in 1967, ADEA defined the covered ages to be forty to sixty-five; in 1978 coverage was extended to age seventy; and in 1986 the upper age limit was removed entirely. The last action legally eliminated mandatory retirement in the United States (except for select groups of employees). This was considered by advocates for elderly people to be a great civil rights victory equivalent to outlawing discrimination on the basis of race or gender.

Office of Multifamily Housing

The Office of Multifamily Housing (OMH), in the Department of Housing and Urban Development (HUD), administers two major housing programs directed largely to older people: Section 202 of the Housing Act of 1959 and Section 231 of the National Housing Act, originally passed in 1934. Section 202 provides capital advances to nonprofit organizations for financing the construction and rehabilitation of housing that will support very low-income older people, and providing rent subsidies to make the housing affordable. The program grew rapidly in the 1960s, was phased out in the early 1970s, and was reinstated in 1976. Funding support has ranged between $400 million and $700 million in recent years. Through OMH the federal government provides federal loans directly to private nonprofit sponsors (Gelfand). Section 231 insures mortgage loans for construction or rehabilitation of rental housing for elderly persons. Potential sponsors confer with OMH about their project and submit a preliminary application, in-

cluding an application for financing through a HUD-approved lender (www.hud.gov/progdesc/231).

Older people constitute roughly 40 percent of the residents of the 1.3 million units of public housing operated by local governments and funded through HUD. Older people also benefit from smaller grant programs HUD oversees for service coordinators and congregate housing services. Low-income individuals, including elderly people, are eligible for Section 8 rental subsidies—individuals are required to pay no more than 30 percent of their income in rent, with the Section 8 subsidy making up the difference to the landlord.

Food and Nutrition Service

The Food and Nutrition Service of the Department of Agriculture administers the food stamp program, one of the largest federal programs directed toward low-income individuals. Food stamps are a form of voucher which allows individuals to purchase many (but not all) food items from supermarkets and other food stores. Individuals of all ages are eligible for food stamps, and in 1998, 1.5 million elderly households used food stamps, representing 18 percent of all such households.

The Department of Agriculture also makes surplus commodities available to nutrition programs administered under the Older Americans Act by the Administration on Aging.

Department of Veterans Affairs

Nowhere has the aging of America been more notable than in the aging of those who served in the armed forces (Wetle and Rowe). Veterans of World Wars I and II and the Korean War are now all elderly, and many who served in Vietnam are in or are approaching old age. The Department of Veterans Affairs (DVA) is a very large agency which, in most instances, serves veterans directly. Two principal administrative units are especially relevant to older veterans. The Compensation and Pension Benefits Service administers benefits and services for veterans, their dependents, and their survivors, including service-connected compensation; non-service-connected pension, burial, and accrued benefits; and guardianship services. The Veterans Health Administration provides a broad spectrum of medical, surgical, and rehabilitative care to veterans. Pension and health care services are the DVA's services most relevant to older veterans. Non-means-tested pensions are paid to veterans with war-related injuries and disabilities; means-tested pensions are paid to veterans without such injuries and disabilities; and medical services are available on varying bases to all veterans at DVA hospitals throughout the United States.

Conclusion

The federal departments and agencies discussed in this entry are the principal ones serving older people. In dispensing benefits (notably OASDI and Medicare), regulating the private sector (notably ERISA and ADEA), and promoting roles and dignity for older Americans (notably AoA and Senior Corps), these agencies have successfully promoted the interests of older people in American life. Many other "functional" or "generic" agencies also provide benefits for older people in the course of their work involving most or all Americans. The principal administrative challenge to all of these agencies is in coordinating and integrating their activities.

ROBERT B. HUDSON

See also ADMINISTRATION ON AGING; EMPLOYEE RETIREMENT INCOME SECURITY ACT; GOVERNMENT ASSISTED HOUSING; NATIONAL INSTITUTE ON AGING; SOCIAL SECURITY ADMINISTRATION; SOCIAL SERVICES; VETERANS CARE.

BIBLIOGRAPHY

BINSTOCK, R. B. "The Aged as Scapegoat." *Gerontologist* 23 (1983): 136–143.

COUGHLIN, T.; KU, L.; and HOLAHAN, J. *Medicaid Since 1980.* Washington, D.C.: Urban Institute, 1994.

DERTHICK, M. *Policymaking for Social Security.* Washington, D.C.: Brookings Institution, 1979.

GELFAND, D. *The Aging Network: Programs and Services.* New York: Springer, 1999.

GRAEBNER, W. *A History of Retirement.* New Haven, Conn.: Yale University Press, 1980.

HUDSON, R. B., and GONYEA, J. G. "Time Not Yet Money." *Journal of Aging and Social Policy* (2000).

KOFF, T., and PARK, R. *Aging Public Policy.* Amityville, N.Y.: Baywood, 1999.

MOON, M. *Medicare Now and in the Future.* Washington, D.C.: Urban Institute, 1996.

PERUN, P., and STEUERLE, E. *ERISA at 50: A New Model for the Private Pension System.* Washington, D.C.: Urban Institute, 2000.

RIMLINGER, G. *Welfare Policy and Industrialization in Europe, America, and Russia.* New York: John Wiley, 1971.

SANDELL, S. "The Labor Force by the Year 2000 and Employment Policy for Older Workers." In *Retirement Reconsidered.* Edited by R. Morris and S. Bass. New York: Springer, 1988. Pages 107–115.

SCHLARLACH, A., and GROSSWALD, B. "The Family and Medical Leave Act of 1993." *Social Service Review* 71 (1997): 335–359.

WETLE, T., and ROWE, J., eds. *Older Veterans: Linking VA and Community Resources.* Cambridge, Mass.: Harvard University Press, 1984.

INTERNET RESOURCES

National Institute of Health. www.nih.gov/nia/about/history

Pension Benefit Guaranty Corporation. www.pbgc.gov.ABOUT.htm

U.S. Department of Housing and Urban Development. www.hud.gov/progdesc/231

U.S. Department of Labor. www.dol.gov/dol/pwba/public/pubs/factsht1.htm

FEMINIST THEORY

In a 1972 article in the *International Journal of Aging*, Myrna Lewis and Robert Butler asked why feminism ignored older women. A more pertinent question today is: Why are gerontologists ignoring feminism? Aging can be defined as a feminist issue because women make up the majority of older adults, and because older women are disproportionately affected by poverty and chronic illness. In addition, community-based, long-term care of older adults largely depends on the labor of women caregivers who are unpaid (i.e., family, friends), underpaid (i.e., nurses aides, personal aides), and often invisible. The demands of providing such care can have negative consequences for women in old age, particularly low-income women of color. Employment discontinuities created by caregiving across the life span frequently translate into lower retirement and work income in old age. A feminist approach thus seeks to make visible and to validate the importance of women's daily experiences as family caregivers, and to show how this role affects their social, economic, and health status in old age. A feminist analysis of old age cannot be separated from one of older women and, in turn, of caregiving throughout women's lives. Caregiving of older adults is thus one way to illustrate feminist theory related to aging.

Constructs of a feminist theoretical perspective on old age include the following:

- Gender roles are socially constructed, not a biological trait, across the life span
- Women have often been oppressed within the family and undervalued in employment
- The public (employment) and private (family) domains are interconnected
- The personal (private) and political (policy) spheres are interrelated
- Women's experiences differ by race, ethnicity, class, sexual orientation, and age, yet a shared consciousness exists
- Gender justice, implicit within feminism, can benefit both men and women

A more traditional gender-difference approach defines gender as a biological trait of individuals. Accordingly, variations in aging are generally explained as sex differences. For example, researchers typically identify male-female variations in the extent and type of caregiving. Yet sex and age tend to be shaped more by social structure and power relationships than by biology. In a feminist approach, gender exists in socially constructed interactions, not in the individual. It is a property of structures of subordination based on power differentials that shape people's work and family experiences. To illustrate, women frequently provide more care because they generally have a lower income than their male counterparts; because of gaps in long-term care financing; and because of limited choice about whether to, or how to provide care—not because they are naturally more nurturing. Family obligations that may keep women out of the paid labor force, and the resulting restricted opportunities and incomes, can also create negative economic repercussions in old age. Since gender is socially constructed, systemic changes in the structure of work and family across the life span are necessary to ensure gender equity among older adults.

Because of such gender-based structures, family care tends to systematically disadvantage women as a group across the life span. These inequities are often intensified in old age. For example, work discontinuities can mean that women are less likely to have full Social Security

and private pension benefits or private insurance to supplement Medicare. Accordingly, since more older women than older men are poor, they are more likely to depend on Medicaid and Supplemental Security Income, which can translate into a lower quality of care. A feminist perspective thus articulates the interdependence among women who both receive and give care across generations.

The place of women in the social structure fundamentally differs from that of men because most women have experienced oppression and been devalued in both the home and labor market. By articulating women's oppression, feminism differs from other progressive social welfare approaches that advocate structural change, such as the political economy perspective. Under capitalism, the sole operating principle of the marketplace (or public sphere) has historically been profit, not family or community responsibility. Work has typically been defined as measurable output and wages, rather than nurturing and maintenance. By removing production from the home and isolating women within domestic situations, a gender-based division of labor has emerged. Men's work in the labor market has typically been viewed as productive, while women's life work—the nonmonetized and nontechnological work of caregiving—is often regarded as nonwork. Instead, it is seen as a private activity within, and an antidote to, the public marketplace, rather than a central force in shaping it. This can create oppressive conditions and deny women societal power.

When women gain access to the public sphere of employment, their opportunities, income, and access to benefits are often restricted to undervalued, temporary, or contingent service and support occupations. As of 2001, women still had fewer benefits and earned 30 percent less, on average, than men. Low-income women of color, in particular, often provide free labor in the home and inexpensive labor in public settings. Accordingly, society is unaware of the true costs of care by nurses, home health aides, and relatives. The unpaid or underpaid work of women underpins the economy, yet is considered peripheral by traditional economic criteria. As a result, the family obligations that keep women out of the paid labor force for periods of time, and the restricted options and incomes for many of those employed, translate into gender-based economic inequities across the life span, particularly in old age.

Caregiving work thus cuts across the personal and political boundaries of family, employment, and policy. Accordingly, traditional family values affirm a woman's place in the domestic sphere as natural and ideal, and family care as superior to publicly funded care. Public policy has tended to implicitly expect that the family will provide long-term care to older relatives. This occurs because many policymakers define family life as a private matter and care of relatives as an individual responsibility. Feminism thus articulates the interconnections among the values of individualism, independence, and private responsibility that underlie this prevailing policy model where the family is the preferred locus of care. When gender-based elder care is presumed to be nonwork, caregivers are economically penalized and the need for comprehensive long-term care policies is minimized.

While caregiving involves an intensely personal relationship, it cannot be examined apart from the public policies surrounding it. The phrase *personal as political* means that there are no private solutions to women's public problems (Bricker-Jenkins and Hooyman, 1991). Women's experiences in old age—and as caregivers across the life span—are shaped by their interactions with public social service, health, mental health, and long-term care systems and policies. Family, institutional, political, and societal norms, as codified in current long-term care policies, tend to maintain and reinforce gender inequities. This points to the necessity of fundamental structural changes in social institutions and values to accord greater societal recognition to women's work and to ensure flexibility and choice for both those who require and provide care. Under a feminist approach, the aim of such change is to reduce inequities based not only on gender, but also those deriving from class, race, and sexual orientation. This approach recognizes the multiple realities of the aging experience shaped by the social constructs of race, ethnicity, social class, sexual orientation, and age cohort experiences.

A more traditional women's issues approach defines caregiving and its resultant inequities as individual, not societal, responsibilities. For example, caregiving research has typically identified the primary problem to be the subjective stress and burden of caregivers. Individual interventions, such as education, counseling, social support, and incremental changes in services, are viewed as solutions. Yet these interventions may inadvertently blame women for their physi-

cal, emotional, or financial burdens. In contrast, feminism views these problems as being caused by gender-biased policies, structural conditions of economic inequity and occupational segregation, and socially constructed expectations of women. Feminism seeks to alter such expectations and values and to foster policies and practices that promote gender justice. This translates into ensuring a choice of caregiving and employment roles for both men and women across the life span. Feminism targets the whole system, not from the margins, but from the center, with the participation of all men and women. From a feminist perspective, policies need to move away from outdated notions of family toward defining care for older relatives as a collective societal responsibility. This could result in caregiving that is more equitable and humane, and in it being valued by those who give and receive care.

The following principles underlie a possible feminist agenda for both those who receive and give care:

- Caregiving is defined as legitimate work for women and men, a normal part of the family life cycle, and a societal responsibility
- The importance of family care and family relationships are publicly valued, rather than devalued as private responsibilities
- Public policy recognizes both the benefits and costs of family care of relatives across the life span
- The goal is gender justice for women and men that balances the needs of those who receive and those who give care
- Changes must be structural and systemic, not made at the individual level
- Intergenerational alliances across the life span transcend traditional boundaries based on age and type of disability/chronic illness

Components of a feminist approach to care include:

- *Economic supports*, which would attach market value to the socially necessary work of caregiving (e.g., comparable worth for women's work in the marketplace, and adequate compensation for caregiving, both in and outside the home); family-responsive workplace policies would broadly define *family* and *dependent* to recognize the wide variety of contemporary family structures
- *A comprehensive long-term care policy*, which would coordinate integrated community

support services to ensure adequate information, choice, and quality of care for adults across the life span

- Broad-based *cross-generational coalition building*, which would help empower those who receive and give care

Although a feminist approach is not yet feasible, the act of questioning basic assumptions about caregiving and aging can begin to alter societal values, attitudes, and policies.

NANCY HOOYMAN

See also CRITICAL GERONTOLOGY; GENDER; THEORIES, SOCIAL.

BIBLIOGRAPHY

BRICKER-JENKINS, M., and HOOYMAN, N., eds. *Not for Women Only: Social Work Practice for a Feminist Future*, 2d ed. Washington, D.C.: NASW Press, 1990.

BRICKER-JENKINS, M.; HOOYMAN, N.; and GOTTLIEB, N. *Feminist Social Work Practice in Clinical Settings*. Thousand Oaks, Calif.: Sage, 1991.

BROWNE, C. "A Feminist Lifespan Perspective on Aging." In *Feminist Practice in the 21st Century*. Edited by N. Van Den Berg. Washington, D.C.: NASW Press, 1995. Pages 330–354.

BROWNE, C. "Feminist Theory and Social Work: A Vision for Practice with Older Women." *Journal of Applied Social Sciences* 18 (1994): 5–16.

BROWNE, C. *Women, Feminism, and Aging*. New York, N.Y.: Springer Publishing, 1998.

CALASANTI, T. "Feminism and Gerontology: Not Just for Women." *Hallym International Journal of Aging* 1 (1999): 44–55.

CALASANTI, T., and BAILEY, C. "Gender Inequality and the Division of Household Labor in the United States and Sweden: A Socialist-Feminist Approach." *Social Problems* 38 (1991): 31–53.

CALASANTI, T., and ZAJICEK, A. "A Socialist-Feminist Approach to Aging: Embracing Diversity." *Journal of Aging Studies* 7 (1993): 117–132.

ESTES, C. L.; LINKINS, K. W.; and BINNEY, E. A. "The Political Economy of Aging." In *Handbook of Aging and the Social Sciences*, 4th ed. Edited by R. H. Binstock and L. K. George. San Diego: Academic Press, 1996.

GARNER, J. D. "Feminism and Feminist Gerontology." In *Fundamentals of Feminist Gerontology*. Edited by J. D. Gardner. New York: Haworth Press, 1999. Pages 3–13.

GINN, J., and ARBER, S. "Only Connect: Gender Relations and Aging." In *Connecting Gender and Aging: A Sociological Approach*. Edited by S. Arber, and J. Ginn. Philadelphia: Open University Press, 1995.

HOOYMAN, N. "Is Aging More Problematic for Women Than Men?" In *Controversial Issues in Aging*. Edited by L. Kaye and A. Scharlach. Needham Heights: Allyn & Bacon, 1995.

HOOYMAN, N., and GONYEA, J. *Feminist Perspective on Family Care: Toward Gender Justice*. Thousand Oaks, Calif.: Sage, 1995.

HOOYMAN, N., and GONYEA, J. "A Feminist Model of Family Care: Practice and Policy Directions." In *Fundamentals of Feminist Gerontology*. Edited by D. Garner. New York: Haworth Press. Pages 149–170.

LEWIS, M., and BUTLER, R. "Why is Women's Lib Ignoring Old Women." *International Journal of Aging: Human Development* 3 (1972): 223–231.

OVERBO, B., and MINKLER, M. "The Lives of Older Women: Perspectives from Political Economy and the Humanities." In *Voices and Visions of Aging: Toward a Critical Gerontology*. Edited by T. R. Cole, W. A. Achenbaum, P. L. Jakobi, and R. Kastenbaum. New York: Springer, 1993.

RAY, R. E. "A Postmodern Perspective on Feminist Gerontology." *The Gerontologist* 36 (1996): 674–680.

RICHARDSON, V. "Women and Retirement." In *Fundamentals of Feminist Gerontology*. Edited by J. D. Garner. New York: Haworth Press, 1999. Pages 49–66.

FILIAL OBLIGATIONS

The phrase "filial obligations" is generally understood to refer to special duties—specific kinds of actions, services, and attitudes—that children must provide to their parents simply because they are those parents' offspring. Influential in many human cultures throughout history—"Honor thy father and thy mother" is a widely known example from Judaeo-Christian culture—the idea that children have duties to their parents remains familiar today. But filial obligation is also a complicated and controversial notion, involving questions concerning who counts as "parents" and as "children," whether parents can lose their claims to filial obligations by negligence or abuse, just what children are actually obliged to do for their parents, and, most fundamentally, why such obligations should be recognized at all. The questions raised by filial obligations are important not simply because family members can be confused or troubled about what they should do for each other, but also because social policies targeting older people sometimes presuppose that their children, rather than the state, ought to provide certain kinds of support. Without clarity about the nature and limits of filial obligations, both families and societies may expect the other to take the lead in supporting older persons, with the consequence that important needs go unmet.

The focus in this entry will be on duties of adult children to parents. Younger children are also generally thought to have filial obligations—primarily to respect and obey their parents—and such duties are at least somewhat controversial, as the "children's rights" movement attests (Purdy). However, duties assigned to dependent children raise fewer practical or theoretical problems than does the claim that independent adults have obligations to provide not solely respect, but also goods and services, to the people who bore, begot, or raised them.

Threats to filial obligations

The continued recognition of filial obligation is threatened in two general ways, one practical, the other theoretical. While surely many adult children continue to care deeply for their parents, and express their care in how they live their lives, there are signs that children may be finding the needs of parents beyond what they can—or should be expected to—support. In practical terms, adult children and their parents now face a world in which there are, relatively speaking, fewer children to respond to growing and persistent needs of aging parents. Social and technological changes have allowed people greater control over family size, social insurance schemes have made "provision for one's old age" a less compelling reason to have many children, and medical advances have helped more people to live longer, and consequently to face the possibility of prolonged periods of ill health or reduced abilities. Spiraling health care costs in general, and inadequate social support for long-term care for the elderly in particular, indicate that there may be increasing pressure on adult children to take on extensive responsibilities of caring for their parents at a point in history when the burden of care may be heavier and more prolonged, when there are fewer children to do so, and less in the way of cultural supports for undertaking care. A striking illustration of the possible conse-

quence of these trends is provided by The American College of Emergency Physicians, which has reported that as many as 100,000 to 200,000 elderly people are abandoned in emergency rooms in hospitals throughout the United States annually (Pinkney).

Changes in cultural support for filial obligations introduces the more theoretical threat to filial obligations. There is, to start with, concern over how caring responsibilities are handed out within families. "Hands on" care of aging parents has been a task assigned more to daughters and even daughters-in-law, than to sons (Brody); in a culture awakening to the unfairness of disproportionately burdening women, this sexist distribution of labor has made some people suspicious of the very idea of filial obligation. But even more fundamentally, the predominant theoretical understanding of obligation in contemporary Western societies—perhaps particularly in the United States—rests on the ideas of contract and consent, and today's most influential ideas about morality prominently feature the ideal of impartiality. If we owe obligations only when we have agreed to make contracts or promises, it is hard to see why we have any obligations, much less possibly burdensome ones, to our parents. If we should regard all persons with equal moral respect, as the ideal of impartiality seems to require, it is difficult to understand why we have particular responsibilities to help those who just happen to be our parents, when others may have greater needs.

There are other cultural shifts that have made filial obligations more difficult to take with the same seriousness they have enjoyed in the past. Apart from basic questions of fairness in the distribution of the tasks of care across the genders, the latter part of the twentieth century has seen an expansion of possible social roles for at least middle-class women in Western societies; in the United States, for example, more women have full-time, demanding jobs and careers outside the home than has previously been the case. At the same time, young children are dependent on their parents for longer periods of education than had been the case in previous centuries. These developments have strained the caring capacity of adult children. Perhaps, too, the greater prevalence of divorce, resulting in many children not residing with both parents throughout their developmental years, may make it harder for some children to feel a sense of obligation to a parent who has been a missing or distant figure during their youth (although it should be borne in mind that families have always been somewhat unstable—if less threatened by divorce, than more threatened by premature death).

If people are to continue to recognize a special set of obligations to their parents, some kinds of social support may be necessary—for example, more flexibility in the scheduling of work done out of the home, and greater recognition of the significance of the work of children in responding dutifully to the needs of their aging parents. It may also need to be better acknowledged that many older parents continue to make significant contribution to the lives of their grown children, and to those children's families. It would be a mistake to think that older parents are always or even typically on the receiving end of the flow of care.

Moral justifications for filial obligations

However, if society is to provide greater support for the ideal of filial obligation—as opposed, say, to dealing with the needs of vulnerable elderly citizens in more institutional, less family-focused ways—there needs to be some convincing reasons why filial obligations should be recognized, despite the apparent contrary tendency of some contemporary ethical thinking.

It is convenient to divide the kinds of moral justifications for filial obligations into two categories. The first sees filial obligations as based on the marketplace idea of quid pro quo: children are *indebted* to their parents for the many services and goods provided to them in their youth, and perhaps most fundamentally for their parents' having brought them into life in the first place. The ancient philosopher Aristotle argued that "nothing a son may have done [to repay his father] is a worthy return for everything the father has provided for him, and therefore he will always be in his debt" (*Nichomachean Ethics*, section 1163b). The influential medieval theologian and philosopher Thomas Aquinas claimed that since after God our parents are "the principles of our being and government," we owe them respect, reverence and service (*Summa theologica*, Part II-II question 101, article 1.) Some contemporary writers, blending the notion of contract with this sort of "natural indebtedness" have argued that, in our culture, the care that parents provide the young is understood to involve an implicit promise on the part of children that they will provide parents with care in their own turn (see, for instance, Sommers).

But the quid pro quo view—even in its modern formulation—tends not to seem very persuasive today. People are perhaps more inclined to say that it is parents who owe children weighty duties of care since in at least many cases, they have chosen to be parents, while children, famously, "didn't ask to be born." Further, it is parents who have, in effect, brought it about that children are vulnerable to many kinds of possible harm; someone has to step in if that harm is not to occur, and who more appropriate than the adults who have put the children "in harm's way" in the first place? These thoughts tend to support the view that filial obligations arise, not from a quid pro quo relationship ("I cared for you when you were dependent; now it's your turn") but rather out of *affections and attitudes* that children typically have for their parents. The contemporary social philosopher Joel Feinberg has written in support of this view. He believes that filial obligations are based on the gratitude that children should feel to their parents, claiming that gratitude "feels nothing at all like indebtedness." He continues to argue that "my benefactor once freely offered me his services when I needed them. There was, on that occasion, nothing for me to do but express my deepest gratitude to him. . . . But now circumstances have arisen in which he needs help, and I am in a position to help him. Surely, I *owe* him my services now, and he would be entitled to resent my failure to come through" (Feinberg).

However, the connection between gratitude and robust duties of care for parents still strikes some observers as shaky. If parents are merely doing what they are obliged to do in caring for their children, how does gratitude for performance of duties to their children create an obligation for children to provide care to parents that may be equally burdensome in return? The philosopher Jeffrey Blustein claims that when we are grateful, we are not concerned with whether our benefactor owed us the good, but rather what the benefactor's motive was for helping us. This move is interesting because it focuses squarely on the fact that parental duties proceed out of love; ultimately, for Blustein, filial duties are a response to the fact that parents have loved their children. Extending the spirit behind this idea, philosophers Hilde Lindemann Nelson and James Lindemann Nelson have argued that parents are obliged not merely to provide their children with requisite goods and services, but to love and "share themselves" with their children.

In other words, parents are obliged to establish not simply a relationship that reliably provides goods and services to their children, but something more—a relationship of intimacy (Nelson and Nelson). In so loving their children, parents make themselves extremely vulnerable; if their children do not respond by maintaining an intimate relationship with them, parents are likely to suffer significantly. Young, well-nurtured children love their parents "naturally," so to speak. However, when those children mature, and are able to express their own characters through their decisions, the choices they make about their parents represent an opportunity to endorse the loving, noninstrumental character of their earlier relationship. Adult children's choices can also, in effect, declare that, so far as they are concerned, their parent-child relationship was only of value for what they got out of it. If their parents indeed shared themselves with their children, the adult children's ability to repudiate that intimacy by rejecting the relationship will be harmful to the parents, and children's action can be morally assessed as defective if they repudiate the relationship for insufficient reason.

Among the attractive features of accounts of filial obligation based on affection or intimacy is that they provide some basis for understanding what limits there may be to such obligation. Gratitude can be expressed, not in a quid pro quo fashion, but in the maintenance of a relationship that affirms the special significance of those to whom a person is grateful. Adult children can affirm their understanding and acceptance of the intimate character of their relationship with their parents by conveying to their parents a kind of love and concern that reflects their shared history. As an illustration, consider an elderly parent with a terminal illness receiving home-based hospice care. Such a person may have many physical needs: problems with pain control or hygiene, perhaps. But she may also have a need to take stock of her life, to try to come to grips with her own mortality, to celebrate and reconcile with those who have been most important to her. A parent's specifically physical needs might well be seen to by her children, and perhaps would thereby gain a special value. But they are the latter needs—needs that concern the person in her intimate particularity—for which children may be especially required, and for the performance of which they may have a special duty. Generalizing from this example, it might be argued that, while children have filial obligations to attend to

their parents' needs, nothing about those obligations makes it inappropriate for citizens to decide, as a social matter, to make other provisions for them. What filial obligations particularly concern are those parental needs that may not be satisfiable in any way apart from the maintenance of a relation of intimacy with their children.

JAMES LINDEMANN NELSON

See also CAREGIVING, INFORMAL; INTERGENERATIONAL EXCHANGES; INTERGENERATIONAL JUSTICE; KIN; PARENT-CHILD RELATIONSHIPS; PARENTAL OBLIGATIONS.

BIBLIOGRAPHY

AQUINAS, T. *Summa theologica.* Allen, Texas: Thomas More, 1948. The Blackfriars edition. Translated by the Fathers of the English Dominican Province.
ARISTOTLE. *Nichomachean Ethics.* Edited and translated by Martin Ostwald. New York: Macmillan, 1962.
BLUSTEIN, J. *Parents and Children: The Ethics of the Family.* New York: Oxford University Press, 1982.
BRODY, E. M. *Women in the Middle: Their Parent-Care Years.* New York: Springer, 1990.
ENGLISH, J. "What Do Grown Children Owe Their Parents?" In *Having Children: Philosophical and Legal Reflections on Parenthood.* Edited by W. Ruddick and O. O'Neil. New York: Oxford University Press, 1979. Pages 351–356.
FEINBERG, J. "Duties, Rights and Claims." *American Philosophical Quarterly* 3 (1966): 137–139.
NELSON, H. L., and NELSON, J. L. "Frail Parents, Robust Obligations." *Utah Law Review* 1992 (1992): 734–63.
PINKNEY, D. S. "Elderly Straining Emergency Departments." *American Medical News* 12 (October 1990): 3.
PURDY, L.. *In Their Best Interests? The Case against Equal Rights for Children.* Ithaca, N.Y.: Cornell University Press, 1992.
SOMMERS, C. H. "Filial Morality." *Journal of Philosophy* 83 (1986): 446–447.

FINANCIAL PLANNING FOR LONG-TERM CARE

Financial planning for retirement or "old age" is typically based on factors that are fairly well known and more or less under personal control. That is, most people choose when to retire,

Table 1

Aging Changes in ADL rates (per 1000 persons age 65+)

Numbers who need help with:

Bathing	65-74	56	
	75-84	113	
	85+	306	171%*
Dressing	65-74	38	
	75-84	70	
	85+	161	130%*
Toiletting	65-74	20	
	75-84	57	
	85+	142	149%*

*Increase from 75-84 to 85+

SOURCE: U.S. Bureau of the Census. *65+ in the United States.* Current Population Reports, Special Studies, P23–190, 1996. Pages 3–21.

Table 2

Health, Wealth, and Vital Aging

	40-54	55-64	65-69
% worried that I will outlive my pension and savings	51%	45%	32%
% worried that I will spend all my retirement money on long-term care	57%	58%	46%
% yes, there will be medical treatments to get to age 75 and beyond	86%	82%	79%
% worried that I won't be able to afford those medical treatments	57%	59%	47%

SOURCE: National Council on the Aging "American Perceptions of Aging in the 21st Century," national survey (January–February 2000)

know the profile and amounts of their retirement income resources, and more or less know (or can control) many, if not most, expenses. In contrast, planning for *long-term care* is planning for the unknown.

The United Seniors Health Council, a nonprofit organization that advises consumers on long-term care issues, reports that at any one time only 6 percent of people over age sixty-five live in a nursing home, and that only half of people age eighty-five and older need help with everyday *activities of daily living* (ADLs). Very few people, however, can look ahead twenty or thirty years and truly know if they will be one of the fortunate 94 percent or healthier 50 percent who will not need some form of long-term care in old age. Thus, financial planning for long-term care is based on (at least) four interconnected unknowns: (1) How long will I live? (2) Will I be healthy or not? (3) How much will health care and long-term care cost? (4) How will I be able to afford those costs?

In this context it is not surprising that over 80 percent of the American public, middle-agers (ages forty-five to sixty-four) even more than older people, are worried that the unknown costs of long-term care will erode their retirement income and assets. Consequently, this overview of financial planning for long-term care considers the following four topics: (1) Who should plan for long-term care? (2) What are the financial characteristics of long-term care? (3) What are the financial choices and options in paying for

long-term care? (4) What professionals, organizations, and information sources are available to inform this planning process?

Who should financially plan for long-term care?

The old and the old and frail. Over the course of human history most of the improvement in life expectancy has taken place in the past several hundred years, much of it in the past few decades. Improvements in life expectancy at birth (forty-seven years in 1900 vs. seventy-six years in 2000) have been substantial, but the more directly relevant trends are improvements in life expectancy at the older end of the life cycle. For long-term care financial planning a key question is, for example: How likely is it that a sixty-five-year-old will live to age ninety? As reported in a special U.S. Census Bureau analysis of trends in aging, in 1940 the probability that a sixty-five-year-old would survive to age ninety was 7 percent. By 2000 this figure had more than tripled: there was a 26 percent chance that a person celebrating his or her sixty-fifth birthday in 2000 would live to age ninety—and the percentage was estimated to increase to 42 percent by 2050.

As is well documented, however, adding years to life does not always mean adding robust, healthy years. Research using standardized measures of ADLs demonstrates that significant decreases in personal capacity and increased need for regular (e.g., daily) assistance take place as people age from their mid-seventies to mid-eighties and older. Table 1 documents this substantial increase in the need for daily assistance. While the actual percentage of older people requiring such daily assistance is comparatively small—306 per 1,000 (or 30.6 percent) at age seventy-five to eighty-four need daily help in taking a bath—the acceleration of the rate from that age range to age 85+ is substantial: bathing assistance, 171 percent; dressing, 130 percent; and toileting assistance, 149 percent. From the perspective of planning for long-term care, few people know if they will be part of the lucky 69 percent or the unlucky 31 percent who need assistance.

Middle-agers. Although long-term care services are used primarily by people in their eighties and older, financial planning for long-term care is, or should be, largely a task of middle age for two reasons. First, as financial gerontologist Davis Gregg argues, middle age is the stage in the human wealth span when retirement planning should take place. The earlier financial planning takes place, the better, but certainly by age fifty planning should be under way. The relative balance between accumulated income and anticipated expenses should be estimated and examined. The potential costs of long-term care, even if not precisely knowable in numerical terms, should be included in the estimates.

A second middle-age dimension of long-term care financial planning focuses on the middle-agers as the children of elderly parents. One of the less publicized consequences of longer life expectancy is that nowadays many more middle-agers will have surviving parents than was the case in the recent past. As reported by historical demographer Peter Uhlenberg, as recently as 1940 the probability that a fifty-year-old would have both parents alive was only 8 percent, compared with 27 percent in 2000. And the probability that a sixty-year-old child will have at least one parent still alive had increased to 44 percent in 2000 from only 13 percent in 1940.

The public image of middle-agers as a generation "sandwiched" between dual responsibilities to children and to aging parents is much less accurate than it was in 1985 or 1990. Figure 1 shows the ratio of the number of teenage children per middle-ager compared to that of elderly parents per middle-ager. This "support ratio" for teenagers has been declining, while starting

in 2000 the elderly-parent support ratio has increased substantially. As American families move into the twenty-first century, middle-agers appear to have more parents than they have teenage children. Financial planning for long-term care includes planning for parents as well as for oneself.

Financial characteristics of different kinds of long-term care

First and foremost, long-term care is not simply synonymous with nursing homes. Consequently, financial planning for long-term care is not concerned only with nursing homes. As it has developed since 1980, long-term care includes a range of options, and the financial planning process should systematically evaluate the nature of and the trade-offs among the financial and nonfinancial characteristics of these different kinds of long-term care.

"Long-term care" typically refers to chronic, long-lasting care rather than to care that is more or less completed in a few weeks or months following an illness or hospitalization. This time dimension is important to recognize because some of the care services and facilities (e.g., a nursing home) can offer both short-term rehabilitative care after surgery and long-term residential care in the same building. Knowing that "nursing home care" is not identical to "long-term care" and understanding this difference is financially important.

In particular, most health insurance will pay for care in a nursing home that is short-term, posthospital recuperative care but will not pay for chronic long-term care that may be provided in the same facility. The national Medicare program, for example, embraces such a distinction: it pays for short-term care after surgery that can take place in a nursing home but does not pay for chronic care. Because of confusion surrounding this distinction, national studies of financial literacy concerning health, finance, and long-term care have found that many people incorrectly believe that Medicare will pay for chronic long-term care—a mistake which can have severe financial consequences for those who hold this view.

The term "long-term care" most often (but not exclusively) concerns older people whose increasing physical or mental frailty leaves them unable to fully take care of themselves. At its most

Figure 1
Middle-Agers' Support for Their Children vs. Their Parents

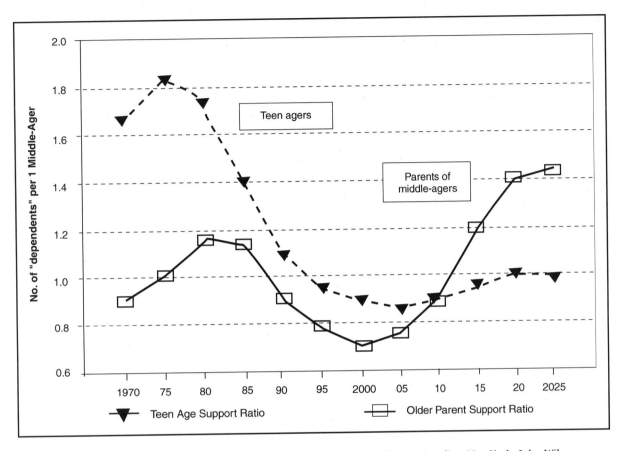

SOURCE: Based on: Cutler, N. E. *Advising Mature Clients: The New Science of Wealth Span Spending.* New York: John Wiley and Sons, 2002.

general level, long-term care refers to a broad range of supportive services that includes personal, social, and residential as well as medical services. Variations on long-term care include the number and intensity of these kinds of services as well as the residential context in which they are delivered. For some older people long-term care may begin and end with assistance with shopping or cooking, and transportation to the doctor as they continue to live in their own home or apartment. For others, long-term care is full-time, medically driven nursing care in a government-licensed residential institution. Different points on this continuum of course imply different levels of cost and financial planning. The following discussion is only an introduction to home care, assisted living, and nursing homes, and is not intended as a complete consumer's guide to the many and increasingly available variations within each general type.

Home care. Most older persons prefer to stay in their own home rather than move to an "institution." The accomplishment of this goal is a function of the older person's needs plus the capacity of the family, community, and financial resources to bring the required personal and medical services into the home setting. While the psychosocial desire to stay at home is often paramount, some people may view home care as a financial question, asking if (or assuming that) home care is substantially less expensive than institutional care.

The most accurate answer to this financial question is "maybe." If family and friends will provide most of the personal, medical, social, home chore, and transportation services, then costs will certainly be lower. If, however, even some of the care is provided by paid caregivers or through a commercial home care service, then the following questions become relevant: Who will identify, screen, and choose the caregivers? Who will monitor caregiver performance and pay the bills? Who will be responsible for tax, insurance, and other legal and procedural details? In sum, home care is not always preferable to institutional care, at least from a financial and administrative perspective. The *Encyclopedia of Home Care for the Elderly* (Romaine-Davis et al.) and *Hiring Home Caregivers: The Family Guide to In-Home Eldercare* (Susik) illustrate the breadth and complexity of the home care approach.

Assisted living.   Between traditional nursing homes and home care is assisted living. In years past such labels as "board and care homes" and "congregate housing" were used to identify residences where older people receive meals, housekeeping services, and some protective oversight, but relatively few health or therapeutic services. In some cases the "facility" was nothing more than the unused bedrooms of an elegant old home, now rented to reasonably healthy and ambulatory older people, with hotel-like rather than hospital-like accommodations.

The growth of assisted living as a separate kind of long-term care is a reflection of the growth and financial resources of the older population, the increasing capacity to remain healthy and reasonably independent at advanced age, and the continuing negative images of nursing homes as "old people's homes" and "institutions." Thus, as the architect and gerontology professor Victor Regnier notes, "assisted living is a long-term care alternative which involves the delivery of professionally managed personal and health care services in a group setting that is residential in character and appearance in ways that optimize the physical and the psychological independence of residents."

The key elements of the definition are "independence" and "residential in character." As the commercial assisted living industry has grown, many facilities provide greater support for higher levels of frailty and dependence; many (depending on state laws and regulations) have professional nurses on site and medical staff on call, and provide regular health monitoring, pharmaceutical management, and physical therapy. While there are many factors that contribute to the various amounts charged by different assisted living facilities (such as location, size of staff, elegance of housing, choices and specialties of meals, availability of health-related services),

two generic financial alternatives should be evaluated.

The hotel model vs. the condo model.   Most assisted living residences operate financially on a residential hotel model, meaning that the resident pays a monthly rental; there may or may not be a binding annual contract. For the monthly fee the resident receives a private (or semiprivate) room including a bathroom with shower or tub; housekeeping and linen service; and two or three meals per day served in a congregate dining room. The cost of the basic monthly room, board, and service may vary within the same facility depending on the size of the room and its location within the building. Some facilities offer rooms to be shared by two roommates or a married couple.

The condo model includes the same range of housing and services, the main difference being that the older person purchases the residence. This model of assisted living is often known as the continuing care retirement community (CCRC). Because the down payment can be quite expensive—from $50,000 to $200,000—these facilities and their services and meals are designed for the more affluent. Within the facility the residential space can vary from a small efficiency apartment to a two- or three-room apartment or town house designed for a married couple.

The "continuing care" feature of CCRC facilities implies that in addition to residential and assisted care services, the resident is purchasing more extended, future-oriented, contractually defined long-term care services. (In earlier years CCRCs were known as life-care communities.) CCRCs typically have hospital or nursing home "wings" as part of the main building (or campus), or have access to such facilities and services nearby.

One unique financial planning issue concerns the facility's rules about the refund of the substantial down payment if the resident dies or moves elsewhere. Some facilities define the buy-in money not as an actual purchase but as advance payment, a kind of mandatory endowment to support the enterprise. They typically offer return-of-payment schedules linked to length of residence. For example, the down payment may be returned minus 2 percent per month; if the resident moves out after twelve months, then 24 percent of the down payment is retained by the CCRC and the remainder is refunded. Given the substantial amounts that are involved, these financial considerations become as important as the personal, location, service, ambience, meal, and other elements of the decision process.

Costs and levels of service. Assisted living facilities charge for personal and health services using either of two basic approaches. In some facilities there is no separate charge for the assistive services; all residents pay the same amount, incorporated into their monthly fee. In this approach healthier, less dependent residents are subsidizing the greater service utilization of the more frail residents. The implied financial and social ethic is that eventually most residents will use additional services, without an increase in their fees, and so the cost-benefit ratio balances out.

Many assisted living facilities use the level of service required as a basis for differential costs per resident. Upon entry to the facility the new resident receives a physical, cognitive, and health assessment, and may enter as a "basic independent services" resident or be assigned to one of three or four higher service levels. The cost of the required level is added to the basic room and board costs.

A hybrid of these two financial approaches is one in which there is a single flat fee for all residents but (like a hotel) with additional charges for services as needed (e.g., requesting room service for meals, asking for additional transportation services, using optional health-related services, etc.).

Some facilities take the view that charging for specific services could inhibit an older person from requesting needed services. Professional assisted living should encourage people to take their meals, to be involved in social activities inside and outside the facility, and to remain as vital and independent as possible. To charge older persons, many of whom are children of the Depression, may encourage them to skip a meal or decline an invitation, in order to save money. Considering the contrasts between these fee for service vs. pooling of risk approaches, careful long-term care planning requires consumers to understand and evaluate the financial consequences as well the psychosocial implications.

Nursing homes. Although long-term care is not synonymous with nursing homes, nursing homes are the most identifiable kind—and symbol—of long-term care, and remain the most prevalent kind of long-term care. According to data reported by the U.S. Health Care Financing Agency (HCFA), in 1997 there were seventeen thousand Medicare/Medicaid certified nursing homes in the United States, representing some 1.8 million beds. A full explanation of the variation in nursing home care is beyond the scope of this entry. Dozens of books are available on how to choose a nursing home, what to look for in a visit to potential residence, and the current rules concerning public payments for nursing home care (through the Medicaid program). Good places to start are the articles on nursing homes in this volume and in the *Encyclopedia of Financial Gerontology*. Both general information and consumer choice guides are presented on the Medicare Web site and on the Web sites (included in the bibliography) of the American Association of Homes and Services for the Aging and the American Health Care Association, whose members include nonprofit and for-profit nursing homes, respectively.

The important financial issue to note at this point is the substantial cost of long-term care in nursing homes. In addition to the residential and personal care provided, as in assisted living facilities, by their very nature nursing homes provide much more intense, higher-level health and medical services to their residents. Nursing homes are licensed by state government agencies, and certified by the Centers for Medicare and Medicaid Services (CMS) to receive Medicare and Medicaid payments. These licenses and certifications determine the medical services that must be present in the nursing home, as well as the staff and licensing requirements for various levels of professional nurses, medical doctors in residence or on call, other health practitioners, and a variety of other health, hospital-like, and protective services.

All of these services are costly, so the monthly cost for nursing home care is substantially greater than for home care or assisted living. Federally collected data show that in 1995 the cost of care in the average nursing home was $127 per day, or over $46,000 per year. It is also important to note that nursing home costs vary substantially from state to state and from city to rural areas within states, including costs of $200 per day in some parts of the country. Clearly, in evaluating the financial dimensions of long-term care planning, average numbers are only vague guides, and consumers should identify the most recent nursing home costs for the specific geographical area that is likely to be chosen.

Financial planning to pay for long-term care expenses

Although the numbers are different, the process of financial planning for long-term care is essentially the same as other financial planning for retirement and older age. At base, financial planning is an exercise (or series of exercises) that compares known and estimated information about various expenses with estimates of the financial resources that are available or expected to be available to cover those expenses. The previous paragraphs focused on the costs-expenditures side of the equation, identifying some of the choices and variables involved in estimating the future costs of home care, assisted living, and nursing homes. It cannot be overemphasized, however, that the costs of all long-term care services and facilities vary and change from year to year, from place to place, and in response to the level of an older person's physical and mental health status. Consequently, all financial planning for long-term care must be continuously re-examined in light of these changing (i.e., increasing) financial costs.

In one sense financial planning for long-term care is relatively easy for people who are already engaged in retirement financial planning. Information for the input side of the equation is already at hand: income from Social Security, employee pensions, continued full-time or part-time employment, other forms of savings and investments, home equity, and possible inheritances are already identified and estimated.

The expenditures or output side of the equation has also been somewhat identified as part of the larger financial planning process, including such items as children's or grandchildren's college education or other kinds of family support, future household expenses, taxes, debt reduction, payment for health insurance above and beyond Medicare, travel and recreation, and bequests.

In other words, the only task at issue is to add in the estimated costs of long-term care. In this context the previous discussion of home care, assisted living, and nursing homes should be of value. Each type of long-term care has its own set of choices, characteristics, and costs. Since the process of financial planning includes the development of alternative scenarios, with alternative estimates of both income and expenditures, long-term care financial planning should consider the desirability, likelihood, and costs of alternative kinds of long-term care.

Personal choices and values. All of the financial options that are examined as part of the alternative long-term care planning scenarios also should be evaluated in terms of nonfinancial personal values. This is especially critical when a middle-age child is involved in long-term care planning with, or for, an elderly parent. The following are just some of the values questions that should be part of the overall long-term care financial planning process. It should be emphasized that since the answers to some of these questions will likely change as the elder (parent or self) becomes less healthy, updated answers should be included as part of the continuing financial planning process.

- Where does the older person want to live? In the same neighborhood as now? Where he or she lived as a young person or was born? Near a child or sibling? Near a current doctor? In the same neighborhood as church or synagogue? In a warmer climate?
- How realistic is it that family and friends can provide some or most of the personal and residential care likely to be needed?
- How devastating would it be if the older person had to leave the house or apartment that is now home? Is the older person willing to sell the house? If able to stay in the house, is he or she willing to apply for a "reverse mortgage," converting home equity to cash in order to pay for home care services, even though this means "going back into debt" as well as spending the equity that might have been bequeathed to children?
- More generally, how important is it to not spend money so as to leave a bequest to family and friends, or to a charity or religious congregation?
- To what extent is the older person willing to rely on public programs usually reserved for people with low income to subsidize his or her long-term care costs?

Overall, because long-term care is a component (albeit a potentially costly future component) of later life expenditures, it should be included in a family's general financial retirement plan. Even though some elements of the planning process, such as future costs and future probability of needing long-term care, are not easily calculated—or perhaps because they are not easily calculated—alternative scenarios that include a comprehensive range of long-term care decisions alongside financial and nonfinancial choices should be part of the overall financial planning process.

At the same time, *financial literacy* in the realm of aging, health, and long-term care is an important element of long-term care planning. It is especially important to understand that "usual" sources of health care finance are not available to pay for long-term care. For example, Medicare does not pay for chronic care in nursing homes. But because Medicare does pay for short-term, posthospitalization rehabilitative care (which can, and often does, take place in a nursing home), the American public continues to believe, incorrectly, that Medicare pays for long-term nursing home care. Similarly, family health insurance, Medigap insurance policies, and HMO health coverage typically do not pay for long-term chronic care. Physician services and medical procedures can continue to be received by older people who live in long-term care facilities and pay for them by Medicare, Medigap, and health insurance; such health insurance does not, however, pay for the residential and personal care that are the hallmark of long-term care. This is clearly a case of "what you don't know can hurt you."

Additional information. The bibliography at the end of this entry provides a fairly broad range of focused long-term care resources, including both general long-term care financial educational and background information, as well as checklists and interactive financial calculators for "testing" alternative financial planning scenarios. In addition, several aspects of long-term care financial planning are discussed elsewhere this volume.

Medicaid is a federal program administered under state auspices and regulations that provides health insurance for people who are low income or *medically indigent.* These health services include long-term care for those who are eligible for Medicaid coverage. Medicaid has become the single largest payer of nursing home bills in the country.

All families are familiar with life insurance, home (fire) insurance, and automobile insurance. In recent years, insurance policies have also become available to pay for some or all the costs of future long-term care. Many people resist long-term care insurance because they question whether they will ever really need it (they might stay healthy forever, or they might die before needing long-term care). Yet fire and auto insurance are purchased with the expectation and hope that they will never have to be called upon. A complete long-term care financial planning process should at least consider the characteristics and costs of such insurance.

Finally, there are several more general considerations that are connected to the financial planning for long-term care, including compiling up-to-date files of all financial and health records; and having a current will or other estate planning processes and documents; and having a health care power of attorney and living will to express preferences for end-of-life treatment.

NEAL E. CUTLER

See also ASSISTED LIVING; CONTINUING CARE RETIREMENT COMMUNITIES; HOME CARE AND HOME SERVICES; LONG-TERM CARE INSURANCE; MEDICAID; MEDICARE; NURSING HOMES; RETIREMENT PLANNING.

BIBLIOGRAPHY

CUTLER, N. E. *Advising Mature Clients: The New Science of Wealth Span Planning.* New York: John Wiley and Sons, 2002.

CUTLER, N. E. "Divine Benefit vs. Divine Contribution Pensions: Approaches to Monitoring Improvements in American Retirement Income Security over the Next Decade." *Journal of Applied Gerontology* 20 (December 2001): 480–557.

CUTLER, N. E. "The False Alarms and Blaring Sirens of Financial Literacy: Middle-Agers' Knowledge of Retirement Income, Health Finance, and Long-Term Care." *Generations* 21 (Summer 1997): 34–40.

CUTLER, N. E. "Geriatric Assisted Living: When Mom and Dad Can't Live Alone Anymore." *Journal of the American Society of CLU & ChFC* 50 (March 1996): 29–33.

CUTLER, N. E. "Money, Health, and Aging Consumers: Ongoing Challenges and New Opportunities for Financial Planning." *Journal of Financial Services Professionals* 55 (March 2001): 52–59.

CUTLER, N. E. "Retirement Planning and the Cost of Long-Term Care: Battling the Fear of the Unknown." *Journal of the American Society of CLU & ChFC* 50 (November 1996): 42–48.

GREGG, D. W. "Human Wealth Span: The Financial Dimensions of Successful Aging." In *Aging, Money, and Life Satisfaction: Aspects of Financial Gerontology.* Edited by Neal E. Cutler, Davis W. Gregg, and Powell M. Lawton. New York: Springer, 1992. Pages 169–182.

Higgins, D. P. "Continuing Care Retirement Communities." In *Encyclopedia of Financial Gerontology*. Lois A. Vitt and Jurg K. Siegenthaler. Westport, Conn.: Greenwood Press, 1995. Pages 90–94.

National Council on the Aging. *American Perceptions of Aging in the 21st Century*. Washington, D.C.: National Council on the Aging, 2002.

Phillips, C. D., and Hawes, C. "Nursing Homes." In *Encyclopedia of Financial Gerontology*. Edited by Lois A. Vitt and Jurg K. Siegenthaler. Westport, Conn.: Greenwood Press, 1995. Pages 385–390.

Regnier, V. A. *Assisted Living Housing for the Elderly: Design Innovations from the United States and Europe*. New York: Van Nostrand Reinhold, 1994.

Regnier, V. A. *Design for Assisted Living: Guidelines for Housing the Physically and Mentally Frail*. New York: John Wiley and Sons, 2002.

Romaine-Davis, A.; Boondas, J.; and Lenihan, A. *Encyclopedia of Home Care for the Elderly*. Westport, Conn.: Greenwood Press, 1995.

Susik, H. *Hiring Home Caregivers: The Family Guide to In-Home Eldercare*. San Luis Obispo, Calif.: Impact Publishers, 1995.

Uhlenberg, P. I. "Mortality Decline over the Twentieth Century and Supply of Kin over the Life Course." *The Gerontologist* 36 (1996): 681–85.

United Seniors Health Council. *Private Long-Term Care Insurance: To Buy or Not to Buy?* Washington, D.C.: USHC, 2001.

U.S. Bureau of the Census. *65+ in the United States*. Current Population Reports, Special Studies, P-23-190. Washington, D.C.: U.S. Government Printing Office, 1996. Figure 3-2.

INTERNET RESOURCES—GENERAL

www.aoa.gov U.S. Administration on Aging, links to all federal programs involving long-term care, and to virtually every national organization involving aging and older Americans.

www.medicare.gov The U.S. Centers for Medicare and Medicaid Services (CMS) Official Medicare Website includes "Nursing Home Compare" online.

www.nlm.nih.gov/medlineplus Free public access to NIH Medline health databases.

www.ElderWeb.com Links to thousands of aging sites, with good organization subsets, including a Living Arrangements section (assisted living, nursing homes) and Financial Planning and Legal Affairs sections.

INTERNET RESOURCES—LONG-TERM CARE PROVIDERS, ANALYSIS, AND INFORMATION

www.UnitedSeniorsHealth.org United Seniors Health Council, excellent nonprofit long-term care educational and counseling organization.

www.nahc.org National Association for Home Care.

www.vnaa.org Visiting Nurses Associations of America.

www.ALFA.org Assisted Living Federation of America.

www.ccal.org Consumer Consortium on Assisted Living.

www.ahca.org American Health Care Association (for-profit nursing homes).

www.aahsa.org American Association of Homes and Services for the Aging (nonprofit nursing home organization).

INTERNET RESOURCES—FINANCIAL AND LEGAL INFORMATION

www.naela.org National Academy of Elderlaw Attorneys.

www.aicpa.org/assurance American Institute of CPAs' new elder assurance specialists.

www.reverse.org National Center for Home Equity Conversion, nonprofit organization for reverse mortgage analysis and education.

www.fpanet.org Financial Planning Association (certified financial planners).

www.usatoday.com/money and www.quicken.com/retirement/planning These two sites include a number of interactive calculators to examine retirement savings, investments, insurance, college tuition planning, and related topics, along with comprehensive discussions of inflation, wills and trusts, taking care of parents, and related topics on financial planning for retirement and later life

FLUID BALANCE

A large part of an individual's body weight is made up of water and chemicals (e.g., sodium, potassium, and chloride), which are called electrolytes. Although the proportions of these electrolytes are tightly regulated throughout life, as people age the relative amount of body weight made up by water changes. In the normal young adult, the capacity of the kidney to regulate fluid and electrolyte balance far exceeds the ordinary demands for conservation and excretion. Even when this capacity is substantially reduced in old age, renal function allows adequate regulation of the volume and composition of the body's fluids under most normal conditions. Inability to maintain normal fluid volumes and electrolyte concentrations is generally due to causes (defects) outside the kidney necessary for their regulation (homeostasis) rather than to insufficient kidney function.

Dehydration, by definition, means a decrease in total body water. Sodium is the primary electrolyte outside the cell (extracellular). This electrolyte has a positive charge (cation) that must be matched to a negatively charged electrolyte (anion), for example, chloride or bicarbonate, and is responsible for maintaining the state of hydration outside the cell. Dehydration may develop from a primary loss of water (insufficient intake of water, excessive sweating, vomiting or diarrhea, or an inability to concentrate the urine), in which case the concentration of sodium in the blood (serum) increases (hypernatremia). Dehydration also may occur when one loses salt (sodium chloride) with its obligated water. This can occur with excessive intestinal and urinary losses containing salt, certain hormone (adrenal) insufficiencies, and with excessive use of diuretic medications. Individuals with this condition become volume depleted, but maintain normal serum sodium concentrations (136–144 mEq/L) until blood volume becomes sufficiently depleted that antidiuretic hormone (ADH) release from the pituitary gland is stimulated. ADH is the hormone primarily responsible for reducing urine volume to conserve water, and for turning a dilute urine into a concentrated urine. If fluid is then replaced, water is retained and the concentration of sodium in the blood falls (hyponatremia).

Older persons are more prone to the development of dehydration. This dehydration is due to a combination of three factors. First, there is an inability of the kidney to conserve sodium when challenged by inadequate intake or excessive losses elsewhere. Second, there is an inability to concentrate the urine as well when similarly challenged by fluid loss. Finally and most importantly, the older person loses normal thirst. Whereas a young person becomes acutely thirsty when dehydrated and drinks to correct for the water loss, an older person often is not similarly motivated. If this becomes severe enough, especially in those with cerebrovascular disease, ingestion of a prescribed amount of water (generally 1–2 quarts) each day may become necessary to prevent recurrent dehydration. Dehydration is most likely to occur after hospital admission for acute illness, for example, infection or emergency surgery, when fluid replacement is often insufficient. Overhydration occurs when an individual retains too much salt and water. This results in edema that can be identified by applying pressure over the shin and creating an indentation that does not quickly return to normal. Usually salt and water are retained in proportionate amounts so serum sodium concentration remains normal. Olderpersons lose the ability to excrete in the urine large amounts of salt.

Older persons also are more prone to the development of low levels of sodium. This can be seen with a decreased (contracted) volume outside the cells (extracellular fluid volume) due to salt depletion followed by stimulation of ADH release to retain water and dilute the blood as described above. Sometimes it is due to dilution, when extracellular fluid volume becomes increased due to an inability to excrete water normally. This is seen with congestive heart failure, and end-stage kidney or liver failure, and is characterized by swelling of the legs (edema) and abdomen (ascites). Most commonly, it is seen when ADH continues to be secreted when the normal stimuli are no longer present. This causes retention of water that, in turn, causes dilution of sodium in the blood. The normal stimuli to secretion of ADH are either a decrease in blood (extracellular fluid) volume, or an increase in the concentration of sodium or solute (osmolality) in the blood. When high levels of ADH persist in the presence of both an increased volume and low concentrations of sodium or solute (both of which should shut off ADH), this is referred to as the syndrome of inappropriate antidiuretic hormone (SIADH). This is often due to pain, but can be due to a tumor (most commonly lung) that independently makes the hormone or something that acts like the hormone; failure of the receptors in the left side of the heart to get the message that blood volume is sufficient, for example, poor blood flow through the lungs due to tuberculosis or pneumonia; or pathology in the brain that abnormally stimulates the release of the hormone. In some cases, generally very old and frail elders, the cause remains unknown (idiopathic). Older persons secrete more ADH in response to any given increase in serum osmolality than younger persons, perhaps helping to explain the greater propensity of older persons to develop hyponatremia. Symptoms consisting of confusion and lethargy progressing to coma and seizures are caused by brain swelling. One can treat this condition with water restriction, or with drugs that interfere with the ability to concentrate the urine (furosemide, lithium, declomycin).

Potassium is the primary cation inside the cell with only 2 percent of total body potassium found outside the cell. Because there is a steep concentration gradient for potassium between inside and outside the cell, the serum concentration (normally between 3.5 and 5.0 mEq/L) is not always an accurate measure of potassium in the body. However, the serum potassium concentration usually determines whether or not there are going to be problems with a deficit or excess of this electrolyte in the body. Low serum potassium concentrations (hypokalemia) can be due to inadequate intake, losses from the intestine (vomiting, diarrhea), or losses from the kidney (renal and adrenal causes). The most common cause is diuretic therapy, but also common in the elderly is excessive use of enemas and purgatives, often overlooked unless the individual is specifically questioned about this. Muscular weakness and pain (cramps) can be early symptoms. Potassium replacement is available in a variety of powder, liquid, and pill forms, but requires a physician's prescription to avoid potentially lethal complications from overdosage.

A high serum potassium concentration (hyperkalemia) can be caused by excessive intake, release of potassium from cells due to tissue breakdown (catabolism), inability of the kidney to excrete potassium, or often a combination of factors. Older persons are much more likely to develop hyperkalemia than younger persons for several reasons. First, they are more likely to have impaired kidney function limiting their ability to excrete potassium in the urine. Second, they secrete less of the adrenal hormone aldosterone into the circulation. This is the hormone that aids secretion of potassium into the urine. A number of medications commonly used by elders (potassium-sparing diuretics; beta-adrenergic blocking agents; nonsteroidal anti-inflammatory agents, or NSAIDs; and angiotensin converting enzyme (ACE) inhibitors) also impair the ability of the kidney to excrete potassium. The symptoms of hyperkalemia are very subtle (anxiety, restlessness, apprehension, weakness), and may precede potentially lethal cardiac arrythymias only briefly, making it important to check serum potassium concentrations periodically if risk is present, for example, during potassium replacement therapy.

Other important electrolytes in the blood and body include calcium and magnesium, both of which can cause symptoms when present in deficient or excessive amounts.

ROBERT D. LINDEMAN

See also DISEASE PRESENTATION; KIDNEY, AGING.

BIBLIOGRAPHY

LINDEMAN, R. D. "Renal and Electrolyte Disorders." In *Practice of Geriatrics*, 3d ed. Edited by E. H. Duthie, Jr. and P. R. Katz. Philadelphia: W. B. Saunders Co., 1998. Pages 546–561.

ZAWADA, E. T., JR. "Disorders of Water and Electrolyte Balance." In *The Merck Manual of Geriatrics*, 3d ed. Edited by M. H. Beersand and R. Berkow. Whitehouse Station, N.J.: Merck Research Laboratories, 2000. Pages 561–571.

FOOT

Attention to foot education and care is especially important as people age. The National Institute on Aging reports high prevalence of lower extremity joint pain among older women. For those relating "severe" pain 17 percent was foot related.

The foot is a complex area consisting of twenty-six bones, thirty-three joints, and several ligaments, muscles, veins, arteries, and nerves. As a primary weight-bearing structure the foot is subject to more deforming forces than any other part of the body. It is estimated that the average person takes eight thousand to ten thousand steps a day and covers about 115,000 miles in an average lifetime. The aging process affects all areas of the foot. With the added insult of normal and abnormal stresses (i.e., shoes, weight bearing, walking, etc.) several foot problems commonly present or are worse in the older population. An outline of common foot deformities found in the aging foot follows.

Nail conditions

Nail ailments are common in the geriatric population. Systemic diseases (i.e., psoriasis, poor circulation, diabetes mellitus, syphilis, reiters syndrome, gout, rheumatoid arthritis, lupus), poor nutrition, and poor circulation can cause changes in nail texture color and presentation. Treatment of underlying disease can help resolution of nail conditions.

Any nail deformity, tight shoes, or improper cutting can lead to painful ingrown nails. In time skin penetration can lead to bacterial infections and chronic inflammation causing a condition referred to as a paronychia. Treatment may consist of nail removal and antibiotics. All nails should be cut straight across to avoid curved edges. If pain is present in nail edges professional help should be sought.

Fungal nail infections, or onychomycosis, are prevalent in older adults. Fungus tends to grow under the nail and cause a discoloration, thickening, and deformed appearance causing pain and nail loss. This condition usually presents at the tip or sides of the nail and progresses to the base. Treatment for onychomycosis can be difficult. In the past topical preparations and removal of the nail produced limited or no results. More recently, oral medications have shown a higher cure rate. Topical preparations have a low risk of side effects but a longer treatment time (about one year). Oral medications have a shorter treatment period (about three months) but present more side effects due to the nature of the treatment. In severe cases, where medications are not appropriate, permanent removal of the nail may be warranted.

Evaluations of nail conditions should include screening for systemic diseases, such as psoriasis, diabetes, gout, and poor circulation, as well as attention to diet and nail cultures to rule out fungus. Although malignancies are rare in the foot, a biopsy of nail or skin changes should be considered.

Skin conditions

Older adults show a high prevalence of dry skin or xerosis due to normal metabolic and nutritional skin changes that causes dehydration and decreased elasticity in skin layers. Severe dry skin can lead to fissures or cuts and predispose the patient to serious bacterial and fungal infections.

To avoid misdiagnosis all initial skin presentations should be evaluated professionally with microbiological tests if necessary. Xerosis and fungal infections can be treated with topical preparations. For severe xerosis, creams used under occlusion (i.e., plastic wrap) have proved helpful. The use of pumice stones are helpful in safely removing skin cells but rarely relieve the condition alone.

Corns and calluses are common in elderly persons. Caused by constant pressure, friction,

or trauma to one area, this skin thickness or hyperkeratosis can be very painful.

Ulcerations or abscesses can occur under these lesions, requiring immediate medical treatment. Footwear should be evaluated for proper fit as tight shoes can contribute to and exacerbate this condition. Periodic scalpel debridement by a podiatrist has been shown to cause immediate relief. Over the counter "corn removers" should be used with caution. They often contain acid and can be dangerous in patients with diabetes or poor circulation.

Joint and bone conditions

In older adults, joint pain, weakness, stiffness, and swelling is often attributed to arthritis. A multitude of factors can contribute to this condition. Cellular metabolism and repair decrease with age contributing to unrepaired lower extremity microtrauma in everyday activities. Progressive weakness and instability and longstanding medical conditions can contribute to further joint destruction. Longstanding arthritis can lead to a breakdown in joint surfaces or cartilage causing painful ambulation. Bone deformity becomes rigid with age, affecting mobility as well as increased areas of skin pressure and contributing to painful hyperkeratotic lesions. In diabetics or individuals with circulatory and neurological problems, skin breakdown or ulcerations can occur.

Treatment for arthritis is dependent on the primary cause. Pain and swelling is often managed with prescription medications. In older persons the dose and amount of medication must be adjusted to accommodate normal decrease in drug metabolism and interactions with current medications. Use of steroid injections can help to alleviate acute pain and swelling but should be limited to avoid destruction of surrounding areas. Elderly persons are often good candidates for more conservative treatment consisting of special molded shoes to decrease skin pressure areas or special padding and/or inserts for existing shoes. Early physical therapy intervention can be helpful in increasing mobility, decreasing long-term rigidity, and helping with stability in the older person.

In addition to arthritis, older persons have a high rate of foot abnormalities such as bunions and hammer toes. A bunion is a deformity or misalignment of the first toe joint or first metatarsal phalangeal joint. This condition causes the toe to deviate toward the second toe and the head of the first bone or metatarsal can be seen as a "bump". With time the joint can become misaligned and stiff. Hammer toes, mallet toes, and claw toes are caused by contractions at joints in the lesser four toes. Pain is often due to the decreased motion in the joint, arthritic changes, and pressure in footwear. Special shoe inserts such as orthotics or shoe modifications may be helpful. If the condition is still painful and debilitating surgical management may be recommended. This could include removing or repositioning bone to decrease the length of the toe and reduce the deformity.

Circulatory conditions

The circulatory system of the lower extremity can be described in two parts, venous (brings deoxygenated blood from the extremity to the heart) and arterial (brings oxygenated blood from the heart to the extremity). Aging affects both components.

Circulatory complications and treatments are system related. In the case of arterial circulation, healing rate, gangrene, ulcerations, and limb loss can occur. The level and degree of arterial insufficiency is important. With venous insufficiency severe swelling and skin ulceration can occur. Long-standing ulceration is an area for potential infection.

The foot is supplied by two major arteries, the dorsal pedius located on the top of the foot and the posterior tibials located on the inner ankle. These arteries should be palpitated at each general medical exam. When these arteries are difficult to feel, special devices know as dopplers can be used to determine the strength rhythm and pressure of these vessels. In the case of arterisclosrosis, special diagnostic exams can visualize and evaluate the interior of the artery for possible occlusions.

Arterial problems are usually caused by an occlusion or blockage of an artery. Atherosclerosis obliterans is the name given to an age-related condition that causes plaque to form inside the vessel walls of arteries. Although any artery can be affected, it is more common in the lower extremities. Common symptoms in arterial disease are ambulatory muscle cramps or pain relieved by rest, coldness, numbness, pain felt while at rest, and skin color changes. Muscle cramps induced by activity and relieved by rest are referred to as intermittent claudication. Common in the calf muscle, this is believed to be caused by decreased oxygen to the muscle.

Rest pain alone is a most likely arterial in nature. When the foot is deprived of blood and oxygen for too long a period, cells start to die. Some elderly persons also suffer from nerve damage or neuropathy and cannot feel the initial symptom of pain. In these individuals, gangrene may be the first sign of trouble. All symptoms should be evaluated for diagnosis and cause.

Veins contain valves to assist in the movement of blood against gravity. Venous problems are often due the incompetence of these valves, a natural process of aging. This incompetence can cause mild to severe swelling in the legs and feet due to the pooling of blood, making ambulation and the wearing of shoes difficult. Long-standing and severe swelling can lead to skin discolorations and ulcerations. Elevating legs, such as in bed, helps in eliminating the fluid and can decrease the swelling.

Special compression stockings can be helpful in "squeezing" the fluid out of the leg and acting as a pump to compensate for the loss of valve function. Older persons sometimes find this stocking difficult to use due to the tightness of the device, arthritis in the fingers, and difficulty in bending. Most companies make compression stockings in a variety of styles and designs and the individual should be fitted and evaluated for the most appropriate one.

Standing, sitting, and walking can increase the amount of swelling. Swelling can occur gradually over the course of a day. Tight shoes, stockings, socks, or garters can cause a painful band and strangulation of the tissue or limb. All socks, shoes, stockings, and garters should be checked periodically for appropriate fit. Elastic bands should be avoided in these individuals.

Individuals with diabetes are more prone to circulatory and neurological problems than the general population. Increased disease duration and severity will affect the presentation of the foot complications. Neurological sensation is a common loss in the diabetic. A simple test determining the ability of one to feel certain pressure thresholds can crudely determine the extent or presence of a neuropathy. Depending on the results of this test, circulatory status, previous foot conditions, and deformities, appropriate follow-up visits can be scheduled. Diabetic people should have their feet thoroughly examined every one to twelve months, depending on their risk categories.

Proper shoe gear and selection

Shoes can both protect and deform. When selecting shoe gear it is important for the shoe to be comfortable at the time of purchase. Certain shoe materials will stretch with time but deformity forces placed on your foot can cause serious conditions. Shoes should be inspected for any areas of rubbing or tightness. It is best to use shoe size as a guide, shop in the middle of the day to account for possible swelling, and bring socks that are normally worn with the shoe. If a special insert or orthotic is worn it should be brought.

People with diabetes need to pay particular attention to the shoes they purchase. Due to their predisposition for neuropathy all shoes should be inspected for foreign objects or areas of irritation before wearing. Going barefoot should be avoided. In some cases special molded shoes are the best option for the diabetic foot. In the case of a short leg, special shoes with lifts may be required.

Feet play an important part in daily activities. As the older population ages, proper foot health will help to maintain quality of life. Keeping active is important and paying attention to and addressing foot ailments is a part of this. With a little prevention and modification and consistent attention, the elderly population should be able to maintain good foot health.

DONNA M. ALFIERI

See also ARTHRITIS; DIABETES MELLITUS.

BIBLIOGRAPHY

ABRAMS, W. B., and BERKOW, R. *The Merck Manual of Geriatrics.* Rahway, N.J.: Merck and Co., Inc., 1990.

Administration on Aging. (1999). "Profile of Older Americans." Available on the Internet at www.aoa.dhhs.gov/

American Podiatric Medical Association. "Foot Facts." Available on the Internet at www.apma.org.faq

GILCHRIST, K. G. "Common Foot Problems on the Elderly." *Geriatrics* 34, no. 11 (1979): 67–70.

HABERSHAW, G. M., and LYONS, T. E. "Foot Health for the Elderly Patient." In *Care of the Elderly Clinical Aspects of Aging*, 4th ed. Edited by W. Reichel. Baltimore, Md.: Williams and Wilkins, 1995. Pages 356–364.

HELFAND, A. E. *Clinics in Podiatric Medicine and Surgery.* 10, no. 1 (January 1993). New York.

LEVIN, M. E.; O'NEAL, L.; and BOWKER, J. H. *The Diabetic Foot,* 5th ed. St. Louis, Mo.: Mobsy Year Book, 1993.

MENZ, H. B., and LORD, S. R. "Foot Problems, Functional Impairment, and Falls in Older People." *Journal of the American Podiatric Medical Association* 89, no. 9 (1999): 458–467.

MUNRO, B. J., and STEELE, J. R. "Foot-Care Awareness: A Survey of Persons Aged 65 Years and Older." *Journal of the American Podiatric Medical Association* 88, no. 5 (1998): 242–248.

National Institute for Health. "Older, Disabled Women Have Trouble Managing Pain." News Release, 15 June 1999. Available on the Internet at http://nih.gov/nia/news/

National Institute for Health. "New Census Report Shows Exponential Growth in Number of Centenarians." Available on the Internet at http://nih.gov/nia/news/

REDMOND, A.; ALLEN, N.; and VERNON, WESLEY. "Effect of Scalpel Debridement on the Pain Associated with Plantar Hyperkeratosis." *Journal of the American Podiatric Medical Association* 89, no. 10 (1999): 515–519.

SPENCE, A. P. *Biology of Human Aging,* 2d ed. Englewood Cliffs, N.J.: Prentice Hall, 1995.

WARD, K., and KOSINSKI, M. "Podiatry." In *Brocklehurst's Textbook of Geriatric Medicine and Gerontology,* 5th ed. Edited by Raymond Tallis, Howard Fillit, and J. C. Brocklehurst. New York: Churchill Livingstone, 1998. Pages 1235–1240.

FRAILTY

Frailty refers to a condition in which older people have multiple, usually interacting, medical and social problems. Such states, with multiplicity and interaction of problems, are complex. Complexity has many consequences, each of which can make the care of a frail older person more challenging. These consequences include complexity of care, making it impossible to do just one thing at once. Every intervention has effects that go beyond the one intended.

Perhaps the most challenging consequence of this complexity is that when frail elderly people become acutely ill, they do not develop the symptoms usually associated with their illness.

Emmer Freeman, 84, prepares to board the van that will take her home after a day at the Alexandrian Brothers Health System facility in St. Louis. The van is part of the All-Inclusive Care for the Elderly (PACE) program, which is designed to keep frail senior citizens in their own homes for as long as possible. (AP photo by James A. Finley.)

Instead, they develop more nonspecific symptoms, such as delirium or falling. This can challenge health care professionals who are typically trained to recognize illness by the characteristic way in which patients describe their complaints. Eliciting these complaints is known as taking a history, and history-taking skills are taught to be as precise as possible, so that many health care professionals come to expect their patients to describe symptoms that specifically fit particular diagnoses. For example, a fit elderly person who develops pneumonia is likely to complain of a fever, cough, shaking chills, and shortness of breath. By contrast, a frail older person who develops pneumonia is more likely to become confused suddenly, or to fall, or simply to take to bed. Symptoms such as these are less specific, and to a health care professional without special training in how illnesses present in older people who are frail, the apparent vagueness of their complaints can be frustrating. The exact mechanism by which so many diseases of older people can present in a nonspecific way is not clear, but it likely reflects the high level of integration of organ systems required to perform such apparently simple, but actually complex, functions such as staying upright, walking about, or being mentally focused.

When an elderly person is frail, their individual organ systems usually are compromised to such an extent that new, additional impairment in one organ system—such as pneumonia, representing an infectious/immunologic impairment that compromises the respiratory system—has effects on other organ systems (such as regulation of blood pressure, or maintenance of alertness and attention). Those caring for frail elderly people must therefore be aware that attention should be paid to problems in several organ systems at once. In consequence, a systematic approach is essential. In addition, the phenomenon of compromise of many organ systems, even if they are not actually failing, increases the likelihood of poor health outcomes when people with such problems become acutely ill. The phenomenon of difficulty in regulating and integrating organ systems to maintain their balance (known as *homeostasis*) has been referred to as *homeostenosis*. The phenomenon of multiple system impairment is also referred to as *allostatic loading*.

Another consequence of frailty is that it alters both how drugs are handled by the body, and how even stable drug levels affect the body. In both cases the result usually is to increase the effect of the drug, so that, frequently, lower than the usual adult doses of most drugs are required. Special vigilance must be taken when prescribing a new medication to an older person who is frail.

A related consequence of multiple medical problems is that frail older people tend to see several different physicians, each specializing in one of the particular problems affecting the older person who is frail. Under these circumstances, the provision of medical care can be fragmented. There often is a need for physicians who can coordinate the overall plan of care.

Another consequence of multiple medical problems is that frail elderly people tend to be on many medications. Sometimes these drugs can interact to produce side effects that themselves require treatment. This problem, known as polypharmacy, is particularly important because the more drugs that a person takes, the higher the chance that they will have an adverse drug reaction.

When older people are frail, they are likely to need assistance to perform daily activities required to remain in the community, such as cooking, shopping, or using the telephone. Special care must be taken to maximize function in these areas, or to provide support should help be needed. Maximizing the function of a frail older person is often the special responsibility of physical and occupational therapists.

People who are frail may also require help with more personal aspects of daily care, such as grooming, toileting, dressing, or even eating. When such dependence occurs, an older person cannot live in the community without a caregiver. This caregiver becomes an essential part of the health picture for those providing health services. How the caregiver feels about their caring role, and how their own health is being affected by having to provide care, become important concerns for both the patient and the health care team. Within a health care team, this aspect is often addressed by a social worker.

The care of older people who are frail requires the specialized skills of many health care professionals. While they each apply their own skills, they face the challenge of doing so in a way that complements the others, and which conforms to the needs and wishes of the patients.

KENNETH ROCKWOOD

See also ASSESSMENT; BALANCE AND MOBILITY; DECONDITIONING; DISEASE PRESENTATION; EXERCISE; GERIATRIC MEDICINE; HOME VISITS; SARCOPENIA.

BIBLIOGRAPHY

PHILIP, J., ed. *Assessing the Elderly.* London: Farrand, 1997.
ROCKWOOD, K.; HOGAN, D. B.; and MACKNIGHT, C. "Conceptualism and Measurement of Frailty In Elderly People." *Drugs and Aging* (2000): 295–302.
ROCKWOOD, K.; SILVIUS, J.; and FOX, R. A. *Comprehensive Geriatric Assessment.* 1998.

FRIENDSHIP

Theorists generally conceptualize "friendship" as a voluntary relationship between equals. This definition of friendship is an abstract conceptualization rather than a description of reality. As Graham Allan observed, in Western society there are no formal rules about who should be friends, but people generally establish relationships with others who are similar to them in terms of race, gender, class, religion, education, and so forth. Although friendships are generally more voluntary than relationships with family and neighbors, this tendency for people to be similar to their friends suggests that there are constraints on friendship choice that are not obvious to the participants. If no hidden rules about what types of friendships are appropriate or desirable existed, friendship patterns would exhibit more variation. Similarly, the statement that friendships are egalitarian is a theoretical rather than an empirical observation.

Older adults define friendship differently than theorists do. Adams, Blieszner, and De Vries found that older adults tend to define friendships in terms of the concrete behaviors involved such as self-disclosure, sociability, day-to-day assistance, and shared activities. Many of them also define friendship cognitively in terms of loyalty, trustworthiness, and shared interests. Not all older adults conceptualize friendship in the same way, however. For example, Paul Wright described women's friendships as face-to-face and men's as side-by-side and concluded that older women emphasize the emotional qualities of friendship. In contrast, older men mention indirect indicators of shared friendship activities such as frequency of contact or length of acquaintance. Lawrence Weiss and Marjorie Lowenthal reported on another source of variation, stage of life course; older adults perceive more complexity than younger people.

Research on the dimensions of older adult friendship

Most of the research on adult friendship has been conducted since the early 1970s. Early studies focused on the number of friends people had and how much time they spent with them. More recently researchers have shifted their focus to the study of other aspects of *friendship structure* such as what proportion of people's friends know each other, whether the friends treat each other as equals, and whether they are demographically similar to each other, to dimensions of *friendship process* such as feelings, thoughts and behaviors involved in a relationship, and finally to the variation in both friendship structure and process across *contexts*. As Adams and Allan discussed elsewhere, these changes in foci reflect the realization that friendships are complex and that they vary tremendously depending on the network, community, and society in which they are formed and maintained.

Gerontologists have examined friendship processes more closely than they have examined friendship structure. In addition to the studies of what people think about their friends, such as those on how older adults define friendship mentioned above, gerontologists have researched how older adults feel about their friends and what they do with and for them. For example, some researchers have reported that older adults feel more satisfied with their friendships when the favors they do for their friends are reciprocated, but Karen Roberto and Jean Scott found that reciprocity was less important among close friends than among casual ones. This finding has implications for the durability of friendships as people age and can no longer help others as much as they could when they were younger.

Most of the research on older friendship, however, has focused on what friends do together, such as sharing companionship, communicating with each other, and especially helping each other. Eugene Litwak noted that in contrast to family members who help older adults with tasks that require long-term commitment, friends are more likely to help older adults with shorter-term tasks or events that they share in common. For example, the friends of older adults might

help them adjust to widowhood, make a decision about when to retire, and decide whether to relocate, whereas family members might nurse older adults with chronic physical problems or manage their finances. The difference in the ways which friends and family members may help older adults may have implications for the welfare of older adults without families.

The research findings on the structural features of older adult friendships are much less conclusive than those about its processes. More research has been conducted on the size of older adult friendship networks and how similar friends are to each other than how likely the friends of an older adult are to know each other. Power and status differentials between older adults and their friends have not been studied at all.

Each study of friendship reports a slightly different average number of friends for older adults. Some of the variation in findings can be attributed to differences in the contexts in which older adults live. For example, researchers commonly report that institutionalized older adults report fewer friends than those who live independently. Differences in the demographic composition of the populations studied also contribute to varied results. For example, like many other researchers, Claude Fisher and Stacey Oliker reported that older men have fewer friends than older women. This suggests that researchers who study samples of older adults in which women are overrepresented will report more friends on the average. The age composition of the sample also affects the average number of friends reported. Many early studies reported that the older adults were, the fewer friends they had. Given these findings, one would expect researchers who study populations in which the average age is high to report a smaller number of friends than those who study younger populations. It would be a mistake, however, to assume that a loss of friends with age is inevitable, universal, and linear, because other researchers such as Colleen Johnson and Lillian Troll and more recently Dorothy Jerrome and Clare Wenger, have demonstrated that some people continue to add new friends to their networks as they age.

The findings regarding the similarity of older adults and their friends and the proportion of the friends of older adults who knew each other also vary by study. It is clear, however, for older adults as well as for people of other ages, that the characteristics of a contest affect the characteristics of the networks embedded within it. For example, Pearl Dykstra and others have reported that during old age the proportion of women's friends who are women is higher than the proportion of men's friends who are men. Although this gender difference exists in all age groups, it is larger in old age, probably because women live longer and thus more of them are available to be friends. The tendency to form relationships with people who are similar to them and the relatively low proportion of men who reach old age suggests that men may be at a disadvantage in establishing new friendships and women may have difficulty developing a diverse network. As Litwak observed, a diverse friendship network is desirable because different types of friends have access to different resources and can help older adults in varied ways.

Studies of the proportion of an older adult's friends who know each other also illustrate the importance of contextual effects. Comparing results in studies of different contexts reveals that the friends of older adults in nursing homes are more likely to know one another than the friends of older adults in age-segregated housing, and that friends of older adults in age-segregated housing are more likely to know one another then the friends living in age-integrated community settings (Blieszner and Adams). The proportion of people's friends who know each other has implications for the types of help they can seek from them. Consider a situation in which an older woman expects to be bedridden for a substantial period of time. If a high proportion of her friends know one another, only one phone call may be necessary to activate a helping network. If, however, her friends do not know each other, then a whole series of phone calls may be necessary. In contrast, imagine an older man with a secret to share. If his friends all know each other, he may worry gossip will spread. If his friends do not know each other, he can be confident that his story will not be retold to anyone who matters to him.

How friends influence the lives of older adults

Studies have suggested that friendships contribute to physical health and longevity, possibly because friendship and happiness are associated with each other. Since the 1960s when Majorie

Lowenthal and Clayton Haven demonstrated that having a confidante was important to older adult mental health, or certainly since the 1970s when Reed Larson summarized the clear connection between friendship activity and psychological well-being, gerontologists have assumed that friendship has positive consequences for older adults. The connection between friendship activity and psychological well-being is one of the most frequently reported findings in the social gerontology literature.

Nonetheless, it is not clear whether friendship leads to happiness or happiness leads to friendship, because researchers have not studied multiple groups born at different times repeatedly as they age. It is only recently that researchers have begun to compare the friendship patterns among older adults of various ages and to examine friendship patterns over time (see Field, for a discussion of some of these studies). It is also not clear how consistently friendship activity and happiness are related to each other in different cultures, because cross-cultural research on older adult friendship has been and is still rare. Until longitudinal studies of multiple cohorts in different contexts have been conducted, the consequences of friendship will be implicit rather than explicit.

REBECCA G. ADAMS

See also KIN; SIBLING RELATIONSHIPS; SOCIAL SUPPORT.

BIBLIOGRAPHY

ADAMS, R. G., and ALLAN, G., eds. *Placing Friendship In Context*. Cambridge, U.K.: Cambridge University Press, 1998.

ADAMS, R. G., BLIESZNER, R.; and DE VRIES, B. "Definitions of Friendship in the Third Age: Age, Gender, and Study Location Effects." *Journal of Aging Studies* 14, no. 1 (2000): 117–133.

ALLAN, G. "Friendship, Sociology and Social Structure." *Journal of Personal Relationships* 15, no. 5 (1998): 685–702.

BLIESZNER, R., and ADAMS, R. G. *Adult Friendship*. Newbury Park, Calif.: Sage, 1992.

DYKSTRA, P. A. *Next of (Non)kin*. Amsterdam: Swets and Zeitlinger, 1990.

FIELD, D. "A Cross Cultural Perspective on Continuity and Change in Social Relations in Old Age: An Introduction to a Special Issue." *The International Journal of Aging and Human Development* 48, no. 4 (1999): 257–351.

FISCHER, C. S., and OLIKER, S. J. "A Research Note on Friendship, Gender, and the Life Cycle." *Social Forces* 62 (1983): 124–133.

JERROME, D., and WENGER, G. C. "Stability and Change in Late Life Friendships." *Aging and Society* 19, no. 6 (1999): 661–676.

JOHNSON, C. L., and TROLL, L. E. "Constraints and Facilitators to Friendships in Late Life." *The Gerontologists* 34 (1994): 79–87.

LARSON, R. "Thirty Years of Research in the Subjective Well-Being of Older Americans." *Journal of Gerontology* 33 (1978): 109–125.

LITWAK, E. *Helping the Elderly*. New York: Guilford, 1985.

LOWENTHAL, M., and HAVEN, C. "Interaction and Adaptation: Intimacy as a Critical Variable." *American Sociological Review* 33 (1968): 20–30.

ROBERTO, K., and SCOTT, J. P. "Friendships of Older Men and Women: Exchange Patterns and Satisfaction." *Psychology and Aging* 1 (1986): 103–109

WEISS, L., and LOWENTHAL, M. F. "Life-Course Perspectives on Friendship." In *Four Stages of Life*. Edited by M. E. Lowenthal, M. Thurner, D. Chiriboga, and others. San Francisco: Jossey-Bass, 1975. Pages 48–61.

WRIGHT, P. "Men's Friendships, Women' Friendships, and the Alleged Inferiority of the Latter." *Sex Roles* 8 (1978): 1–20.

FRONTOTEMPORAL DEMENTIA

Frontotemporal dementia (FTD) is a recently used terminology for clinical Pick's disease (PiD). Arnold Pick (1892) described aphasia and personality changes with progressive frontal and temporal degeneration, but later it became a pathological entity defined histologically by the presence of argyrophilic globular inclusions (Pick bodies) and swollen achromatic neurons (Pick cells). It also became apparent that cases of clinical PiD with frontal and temporal lobe atrophy may not show the typical Pick bodies on autopsy. Constantinidis and colleagues classified PiD as: (1) with Pick bodies; (2) only with swollen neurons; and (3) only scarring, and neuronal loss. They felt "in spite of the dissimilarities between these forms, considering the absence of sufficient knowledge about pathogenesis, it seems prudent at present to maintain the uniqueness of Pick's entity."

With the development of neuroimaging, frontal and temporal atrophy was demonstrated with increasing frequency in vivo. However, instead of shifting the diagnosis of PiD back to the clinic, more recent studies applied new labels such as dementia of the frontal lobe type, or frontal lobe dementia (FLD) (Brun) as new entities, while reserving the diagnosis of PiD for the pathologist. The groups who described dementia of the frontal lobe type further changed the terminology to frontotemporal degeneration (FTD) (The Lund and Manchester Groups), and frontotemporal lobar degeneration (Snowden et al.). Nevertheless, they acknowledged the clinical syndrome was the same whether or not the histology showed Pick bodies. They estimated the incidence at 20 percent of degenerative dementias.

The clinical syndrome of FTD (FLD)

The predominantly behavioral changes of the frontal lobe syndrome often begin under sixty-five years of age with apathy and disinterest, which may be mistaken for depression. On the other hand, the symptoms of disinhibition may suggest a manic psychosis. They may occur paradoxically at the same time. The behavioral manifestations, therefore, are more likely to be presented to a psychiatrist than to a neurologist. Some of the more florid manifestations of disinhibition such as hyperorality (in which patients overeat, or put objects in their mouths) and hypersexuality are interpreted as being due to involvement of both temporal lobes, a phenomenon known as Kluver-Bucy syndrome. Progressive decrease of language output frequently appears later but can be seen at the same time as the behavioral problems. Neuroimaging studies such as CT, MRI, and SPECT scans are important for diagnostic confirmation. Behavioral quantitation may be more useful than cognitive testing. Kertesz and others (1997) constructed a twenty-four-item Frontal Behavioral Inventory (FBI), to ask the caregiver about the most specific behaviors. The FBI is used at the initial interview or for retrospective diagnosis.

At times FTD is associated with motor neuron diseases (MND) such as amyotrophic lateral sclerosis. Recently it was shown that some cases of FTD with or without MND have specific ubiquitin positive, tau negative cytoplasmic inclusions similar to that found in MND.

Primary Progressive Aphasia

Mesulam described a series of cases of slowly progressive language problems (aphasia) and subsequently named the syndrome *primary progressive aphasia*. The clinical and pathological overlap of PPA and FTD is considerable and we suggested the term *Pick complex* (Kertesz et al., 1994) to emphasize the relationship.

The initial presentation of PPA is often word-finding difficulty, or anomia. In this respect, PPA patients are not much different from Alzheimer's patients, except they have relatively preserved memory and nonverbal cognition. Mesulam suggested a two-year period of relatively pure aphasia as the operational definition of PPA, although this may be too restrictive and in many publications it is not adhered to. The more typical clinical picture progresses from anomia to a non-fluent type of aphasia, in which there is increasing word-finding difficulty.

Some patients present with stuttering, slow speech, and articulatory difficulty and errors in speech. These patients are less likely to be mistaken for AD, but unfortunately an unexplained isolated articulatory disturbance in a younger person is often considered to be hysterical. Loss of speech (mutism) used to be considered characteristic of PiD as well, and it tends to be the end-stage of all forms of frontotemporal dementia, even those that start with behavioral abnormalities rather than language disturbance. End-stage mutism also occurs in AD, but usually in a patient who already has a global dementia with loss of comprehension and basic functions of daily living.

Another form of PPA that is different from the more common nonfluent variety was described as *semantic dementia* by Snowden and others (1989). These patients progressively lost the meaning of words, but retained fluency and were able to carry out a conversation.

Corticobasal degeneration

There have been many case descriptions of PiD where the patients had prominent signs of Parkinson's such as slow movements and rigid muscles, known as extrapyramidal features. When Rebeiz and colleagues described selected degeneration of the brain structures they recognized the similarity of the pathology to PiD. This was subsequently confirmed by several investigators who contributed further clinical details and relabelled it corticobasal degeneration (CBD) or corticobasal ganglionic degeneration (CBGD). The asymmetrical extrapyramidal syndrome combined with an inability to perform complete movements (apraxia) and "alien hand," unresponsive to levodopa (the usual treatment for Parkinson's disease), was subsequently described mainly in movement disorder clinics. The interest focused on the extrapyramidal syndrome may have led to the belief that behavioral changes are rare and dementia occurs only in a minority of CBD cases. However, when well-documented case descriptions are specifically reviewed, behavioral, cognitive, and language disturbances suggestive of frontal and temporal lobe involvement seem to be frequent features during the course of the disease.

Pick complex

Pick complex (Kertesz et al., 1994; Kertesz and Munoz) is a unifying concept of the overlapping clinical syndromes of FLD, PPA, CBD, FTD, and associated MND and the underlying neuropathological findings, emphasizing commonalities rather than differences between them. It designates both the pathological and the clinical overlap, avoids the restriction of pathology and clinical symptomatology to the frontotemporal cortex and acknowledges the relationship to PiD. The term *frontotemporal degeneration* or *frontotemporal dementia* does not include the frequent subcortical involvement, parietal pathology, and extrapyramidal symptomatology, and is mostly used for the behavioral syndrome.

Neurogenetics

The discovery of genetic linkage to chromosome 17 q21-22 of several large families with significant resemblance to Pick complex, supports the concept of syndrome (Wilhelmsen). The chromosome region common to all these families, called FTDP-17, contains the gene for the microtubule associated protein tau. At this point, several mutations in the tau gene have been identified in FTDP-17 families (Hutton et al.). Not all families with FTD have tau mutations, but some have ubiquitin-positive, tau-negative inclusions (Kertesz et al., 2000). Genetic biochemical and histochemical distinctions provide further understanding of the syndrome but we must be careful not to lose sight of the clinical, pathological, and genetic cohesiveness, and exercise caution in interpreting the differences.

Treatment

Treatment of FTD is aimed at controlling symptoms pharmacologically. Most of the drugs used were already approved medications, usually used for Parkinson's disease, AD, or depression. Attempts to use levodopa, selegiline, fluoxetine, or similar drugs have not altered the course significantly but may help restless, compulsive, or apathetic behavior. Until proper randomized clinical trials are carried out, these drugs can not be considered efficacious, especially considering the variability and the relatively long clinical course of FTD.

ANDREW KERTESZ

See also ALZHEIMER'S DISEASE; DEMENTIA; DEMENTIA WITH LEWY BODIES; VASCULAR DEMENTIA.

BIBLIOGRAPHY

BRUN, A. "Frontal Lobe Degeneration of Non-Alzheimer Type. I. Neuropathology." *Archives of Gerontology and Geriatrics* 6 (1987): 193–208.

CONSTANTINIDIS, J.; RICHARD, J.; and TISSOT, R. "Pick's Disease—Histological and Clinical Correlations." *European Neurology* 11 (1974): 208–217.

HUTTON, M.; LENDON, C. L.; RIZZU, P.; et al. "Association of Missense and 5'-plice-site Mutations in Tau with the Inherited Dementia FTDP-17." *Nature* 393 (1998): 702–705.

KERTESZ, A.; DAVIDSON, W.; and FOX, H. "Frontal Behavioral Inventory: Diagnostic Criteria for Frontal Lobe Dementia." *Canadian Journal of Neurological Sciences* 24 (1997): 29–36.

KERTESZ, A.; HUDSON, L.; MACKENZIE, I. R. A.; et al. "The Pathology and Nosology of Primary Progressive Aphasia." *Neurology* 44 (1994): 2065–2072.

KERTESZ, A.; KAWARAI, T.; ROGAEVA, E.; et al. "Familial Frontotemporal Dementia with Ubiquitin-Positive, Tau-Negative Inclusions." *Neurology* 54 (2000): 818–827.

KERTESZ, A., and MUNOZ, D. G. *Pick's Disease and Pick Complex.* New York: Wiley-Liss, Inc., 1998.

The Lund and Manchester Groups. "Clinical and Neuropathological Criteria for Frontotemporal Dementia." *Journal of Neurology, Neurosurgery and Psychiatry* 57 (1994): 416–418.

MESULAM, M. M. "Slowly Progressive Aphasia without Generalized Dementia." *Annals of Neurology* 11 (1982): 592–598.

PICK, A. "Über die Beziehungen der senilen Hirnatrophie zur Aphasie." *Prager Medizinische Wochenschrift* 17 (1892): 165–167.

REBEIZ, J. J.; KOLODNY, E. H.; and RICHARDSON, E. P., JR. "Corticodentatonigral Degeneration with Neuronal Achromasia." *Archives of Neurology* 18 (1968): 20–33.

SNOWDEN, J. S.; GOULDING, P. J.; and NEARY, D. "Semantic Dementia: A Form of Circumscribed Cerebral Atrophy." *Behavioral Neurology* 2 (1989): 167–182.

SNOWDEN, J. S.; NEARY, D.; and MANN, D. M. A. *Frontotemporal Lobar Degeneration: Frontotemporal Dementia, Progressive Aphasia, Semantic Dementia.* London: Churchill Livingstone, 1996.

WILHELMSEN, K. "Frontotemporal Dementia is on the MAPt." *Annals of Neurology* 41 (1997): 139–140.

FRUIT FLIES, *DROSOPHILA*

The fruit fly, *Drosophila melanogaster*, has been a leading model for aging research since early in the twentieth century. The benefits of using *D. melanogaster* for research include its short life span (1 to 2 months), ease of culture, and the availability of powerful genetic and molecular biological tools. The latter includes the *Drosophila* "P element," which is a transposable element. Transposable elements are pieces of DNA that can insert into the DNA of a chromosome, and can move from one place in the DNA to another under appropriate conditions. The P element has been engineered so that scientists can control its movement in *D. melanogaster*. For example, it can be used to carry modified or foreign genes into the *D. melanogaster* genome, where they will then be inherited by succeeding generations. Such introduced genes are called *transgenes*, and the resultant strain is said to be *transgenic*. One disadvantage of *D. melanogaster* for aging research is that its small size precludes detailed study of pathology and cause of death. For this reason, life span is still the most reliable measure of the *D. melanogaster* aging rate.

The use of *D. melanogaster* as a model is supported by the numerous similarities between aging in fruit flies and mammals, including a decline in performance of functions such as reproduction, learning, behavior, and locomotion. At the ultrastructural level, similarities include deterioration of muscle and nervous tissue, as well as accumulation of intracellular inclusions such as pigments (lipofuscin), abnormal mitochondria,

A close-up view of the Mediterranean fruit fly. (Corbis Corporation)

and virus-like particles. At the molecular level, similarities include the accumulation of damaged DNA, proteins, and mitochondria. Finally, both fruit flies and mammals exhibit a tight link between stress responses and aging.

An important difference between *D. melanogaster* and mammals is the fact that fruit flies are cold-blooded. Raising the environmental temperature increases the rate of *D. melanogaster* metabolism and aging, and decreases its life span. The ability to manipulate life span in this way has proven to be useful in many studies, and has provided some the first evidence of a link between metabolic activity and life span.

Selection experiments and quantitative trait loci

Current theory suggests that aging exists due to the decreasing force of natural selection as a function of age, and that it has an underlying genetic basis. Much of the experimental support for this theory has come from study of *D. melanogaster*. When an appropriate population of *D. melanogaster* is cultured in the laboratory using only the oldest individuals to reproduce the next generation, the force of selection now acts on the older individuals. Over many generations, this

selection results in populations with significantly increased fertility at older ages and with significantly increased life span relative to control populations. In other words, by experimentally altering "natural" selection in the laboratory, *D. melanogaster* is forced to evolve into a long-lived strain. Such long-lived strains also exhibit increased stress resistance and an increased expression of stress response genes, suggesting that life span and stress resistance are related.

Life span varies quantitatively—either shorter or longer—and for this reason is called a *quantitative trait*. The chromosomal loci, or genes, that affect life span are called quantitative trait loci, or QTLs. QTLs affecting life span have been identified and genetically mapped using appropriate crosses between strains having different life spans.

Changes in gene expression during aging

Aging in *D. melanogaster* is associated with characteristic changes in gene expression. During aging, the expression of certain stress response genes is increased in age-specific and tissue-specific patterns. At least part of this increase appears to be a response to oxidative stress. In contrast, as flies age there is a decreased ability to further increase the expression of these genes and survive acute stresses such as heat shock. Recent data suggests that a similar pattern of stress-response gene expression occurs in aging mammals. In addition, a number of other *D. melanogaster* genes exhibit characteristic dynamic expression patterns during aging. These include several genes with important developmental functions, though the significance of their altered expression during aging is currently unknown.

Transgenics

One way to identify genes that directly regulate aging is to experimentally increase or decrease their expression, and then assay for effects on life span. Decreased life span is problematic, as it is likely to result from novel pathologies that do not normally limit life span. In contrast, increased life span can only result from alterations in limiting processes, and is more likely to identify genes directly related to aging. A strength of the *D. melanogaster* model system is that there are a variety of transgenic methods for increasing or decreasing the expression of specific genes under well-controlled conditions.

Extensive correlative evidence suggests that, for most organisms, oxidative damage may be a primary cause of aging and functional decline. Reactive oxygen species (ROS) are toxic forms of oxygen that are generated as a byproduct of normal metabolism. One of the most common is superoxide, produced as a byproduct of the mitochondria. ROS can damage cellular components, and such oxidatively damaged molecules and organelles have been found to accumulate in all aging organisms, at least those that have been examined, including *D. melanogaster*. Not surprisingly, the genes tested for effects on life span in *D. melanogaster* have been ones involved in preventing or repairing oxidative damage. The gene *hsp70* was originally identified as a gene induced in response to heat and oxidative stress. Hsp70-family proteins can help prevent or repair protein damage caused by heat or ROS by preventing protein aggregation, facilitating protein refolding, and facilitating breakdown of damaged proteins. The enzymes superoxide dismutase (SOD) and catalase work together to detoxify ROS in cells. SOD exists in two forms: cytoplasmic (Cu/ZnSOD) and mitochondrial (Mn-SOD). SOD converts superoxide to hydrogen peroxide, and catalase converts hydrogen peroxide to water and oxygen. Another important defense against ROS involves the enzyme glutathione reductase. This enzyme generates reduced glutathione, which is an abundant small molecule that detoxifies ROS.

If increased expression of a gene increases life span, that gene is, by definition, a positive regulator of life span. Transgenic *D. melanogaster* containing an extra copy of the catalase, CuZnSOD, MnSOD, hsp70, or glutathione reductase genes generally exhibit increased gene expression, but have not been found to exhibit any consistent increase in life span under normal culture conditions. However, extra copies of hsp70 have produced small increases in life span after mild heat stress, and extra glutathione reductase has increased survival in an atmosphere of increased oxygen concentration—a condition known to increase oxidative stress.

Relatively large increases in life span have recently been achieved using more complex methods to control the expression of transgenes. The *GAL4/UAS* system was used to express human Cu/ZnSOD in a tissue-specific pattern during *D. melanogaster* development and aging, with expression in the adult occurring primarily in motorneurons. In other studies a system called *FLP-out* was used to express Cu/ZnSOD specifically in the adult fly. These experiments yielded increases in average life span of up to 48 percent.

At least two negative regulators of *D. melanogaster* life span have also been identified. In these cases, life span is increased when the gene is disrupted or its expression is decreased. A mutation in the *methuselah* gene increases life span by up to 35 percent, and also increases body size and stress resistance. Mutation of the *Indy* gene also increases life span.

The success in identifying genes regulating aging in *D. melanogaster,* each of which is related to genes in humans, suggests that the fruit fly will continue to be a leading model for aging research.

DEEPAK BHOLE
JOHN TOWER

See also ACCELERATED AGING: ANIMAL MODELS; GENETICS; GENETICS: GENE EXPRESSION; LIFE-SPAN EXTENSION.

BIBLIOGRAPHY

ARKING, R.; BURDE, V.; GRAVES, K.; HARI, R.; FELDMAN, E.; ZEEVI, A.; SOLIMON, S.; SARAIYA,

A.; BUCK, S.; VETTRAINO, J.; SATHRASALA, K.; WEHR, N.; and LEVINE, R. L. "Forward and Reverse Selection for Longevity in *Drosophila* is Characterized by Alteration of Antioxidant Gene Expression and Oxidative Damage Patterns." *Expermental Gerontology* 35 (2000): 167–185.

BAKER, G. T.; JACOBSEN, M.; and MOKRYNSKI, G. "Aging in *Drosophila*." In *Cell Biology Handbook in Aging*. Edited by V. Crisotfalo. Boca Raton, Fla.: CRC Press, 1989. Pages 511–578.

KING, V., and TOWER, J. "Aging-Specific Expression of *Drosophila hsp22*." *Developmental Biology* 207 (1994): 107–118.

KIRKWOOD, T. B. L., and AUSTAD, S. N. "Why Do We Age?" *Nature* 409 (2000): 233–238.

KURAPATI, R.; PASSANANTI, H. B.; ROSE, M. R.; and TOWER, J. "Increased hsp22 RNA Levels in *Drosophila* Lines Genetically Selected for Increased Longevity." *Journal of Gerontology: Biological. Sciences* 55A (2000): B1–B8.

LIN, Y.-J.; SEROUDE, L.; and BENZER, S. "Extended Life-Span and Stress Resistance in the *Drosophila* Mutant *methuselah*." *Science* 282 (1998): 943–946.

NUZHDIN, S. V.; PASYUKOVA, E. G.; DILDA, C. L.; ZENG, Z.-B.; and MACKAY, T. F. C. "Sex-Specific Quantitative Trait Loci Affecting Longevity in *Drosophila melanogaster*." *Proceedings of the National Academy of Sciences USA* 94 (1997): 9734–9739.

PARKES, T. L.; ELIA, A. J.; DICKSON, D.; HILLIKER, A. J.; PHILLIPS, J. P.; and BOULIANNE, G. L. "Extension of *Drosophila* Lifespan by Overexpression of Human *SOD1* in Motorneurons." *Nature Genetics* 19 (1998): 171–174.

ROGINA, B., and HELFAND, S. L. "Spatial and Temporal Pattern of Expression of the Wingless and Engailed Genes in the Adult Antenna is Regulated by Age-Dependent Mechanisms." *Mechanisms of Development* 63 (1997): 89–97.

ROGINA, B.; REENAN, R. A.; NILSEN, S. P.; and HELFAND, S. "Extended Life-Span Conferred by Cotransporter Gene Mutations in *Drosophila*." *Science* 290 (2000): 2137–2140.

SOHAL, R. S.; MOCKETT, R. J.; and ORR, W. C. "Current Issues Concerning the Role of Oxidative Stress in Aging: A Perspective." In *Results and Problems in Cell Differentiation*, vol. 29. Berlin: Springer-Verlag, 2000.

SPRADLING, A. C.; STERN, D. M.; KISS, I.; ROOTE, J.; LAVERTY, T.; and RUBIN, G. M. "Gene Disruptions Using *P* Transposable Elements: An Integral Component of the *Drosophila* Genome Project." *Procedures of the National Academy of Sciences USA* 92 (1995): 10824–10830.

SUN, J., and TOWER, J. "FLP Recombinase-Mediated Induction of Cu/Zn-Superoxide Dismutase Transgene Expression Can Extend the Life Span of Adult *Drosophila Melanogaster* Flies." *Molecular Cellular Biology* 19 (1999): 216–228.

TATAR, M. "Transgenes in the Analysis of Life Span and Fitness." *The American Naturalist* 154 (1999): S67–S81.

TOWER, J. "Aging Mechanisms in Fruit Flies." *Bioessays* 18 (1996): 799–807.

TOWER, J. "Transgenic Methods for Increasing *Drosophila* Life Span." *Mechanisms of Ageing and Development* 118 (2000): 1–14.

WHEELER, J. C.; BIESCHKE, E. T.; and TOWER, J. "Muscle-Specific Expression of *Drosophila* hsp70 in Response to Aging and Oxidative Stress." *Proceedings of the National Academy of Science USA* 92 (1995): 10408–10412.

WHEELER, J. C.; KING, V.; and TOWER, J. "Sequence Requirements for Upregulated Expression of *Drosophila hsp70* Transgenes during Aging." *Neurobiology of Aging* 20 (1999): 545–553.

FUNCTIONAL ABILITY

In the course of daily life, people get out of bed, take baths or showers, use the toilet, dress, prepare meals, and eat. These types of basic functions allow people to socialize, work, or engage in a myriad of other productive and social activities. In the lexicon of gerontology, these fundamental self-care activities have been labeled *activities of daily living*, or ADLs. Although mundane and ordinary to most of us, the capacity to perform such activities has been confirmed in numerous studies to have broad implications for functioning, reflecting a person's ability to live independently in the community.

Disability or functional impairment refers to a person's inability to perform these and other basic tasks without assistance, whether due to aging, illness, accident, or conditions at birth. Long-term care services are designed to compensate for an individual's disabilities or functional impairments, or, when possible, to restore or improve functional abilities. In an important sense, functional limitations are the *raison d'etre* for long-term care.

Two basic levels of functional ability are recognized. The most basic ADLs in the areas of personal care and mobility (e.g., eating, bathing, dressing, using the toilet, and transferring from bed or chair) are distinguished from more complex role activities, such as taking medication, managing money, and grocery shopping, which have come to be known as *instrumental ADLs* (IADLs). The basic ADLs were first proposed in 1959 as a cluster of basic physical functions that are useful benchmarks for gauging the effects of rehabilitation. IADL measures were developed in the late 1960s. The IADLS are more heterogeneous than ADLs, and include activities necessary to live independently in the community, such as using a telephone, taking medications, managing money, grocery shopping, meal preparation, shopping, light and heavy housework, doing laundry, using local transportation, and remembering appointments.

The consequences of an assessment of functional ability are extremely personal, and yet they also contain broad policy and practice implications. For many older adults who have entered the formal service system for help, the results often require coming to grips with a loss of, or decline in, functioning in one or more areas where previously they had been independent. At the same time, the use of functional impairment as an eligibility criterion for long-term care services is widespread. Impairment eligibility standards vary from state to state, but are usually defined as needing assistance in two or three ADLs. Most states have created their own ADL measures, although these usually rely on other previously established measures.

A number of comprehensive reviews of functional ability have been completed. Among recent reviews, Mary G. Kovar and M. Powell Lawton provide an excellent review of functional disability (in M. Powell Lawton and Jeanne A. Teresi's edited volume *Focus on Assessment Techniques* [1994]), and Laurence G. Branch and Helen Hoenig offer a succinct review of measures of physical functioning in *Generations* (1997). Another review that has stood the test of time is Rosalie and Robert Kane's *Assessing the Elderly: A Practical Guide to Measurement* (1981).

Measuring functional ability poses a variety of challenges. One important issue is that environmental factors strongly influence responses to ADL and IADL measures. For example, someone who uses a wheelchair may be perfectly able to drive or use local transportation, but may be unable to leave the house due to an inability to negotiate stairs. Whether an individual has difficulty getting to and using the toilet may depend on whether there is a toilet easily accessible, and on whether there are physical aids such as grab rails. In some residential settings, a resident may have the capacity to cook, but have no opportunity to do so. A resident may be able to bathe independently, but may live in a facility in which the rules require that all residents receive assistance with bathing. Asking about a respondent's latent ability to perform a task ("Can you. . .?") has the advantage of addressing barriers in the environment or other contextual factors that may inhibit performance, but such an approach sometimes gives a misleading impression of the respondent's actual performance of ADL tasks. People may not do what they are physically capable of doing because of preferences or cultural reasons. Asking what ADL tasks someone actually does ("Do you. . .?") can provide a better picture of what supports are needed to promote functional ability.

One of the most important dimensions of function ability is dependence. Dependence indicates whether an individual needs or uses the assistance of another person or special equipment to accomplish the task. Dependency, by its very nature, implies the use of formal or informal services that are used in response to disability. One of the most common approaches to determine dependency is to assess how much assistance or help a person requires to perform an activity. Each activity can be rated on a three-point scale of independence: (1) no assistance required, (2) partial assistance required, and (3) total assistance required (or does not do the activity). Another approach is used to assess how difficult or "hard" it is to perform a task or activity. For example, in the Longitudinal Study of Aging (LSOA), a large probability study of the noninstitutionalized elderly, respondents were asked the following question for each activity: "Because of a health or physical problem, do you have any difficulty performing [the activity]." Respondents who reported having some difficulty were asked: "By yourself, and without using special equipment, how much difficulty do you have [performing the activity]: some, a lot, or are you unable to do it?" Respondents were considered functionally impaired if they reported some difficulty or assistance needed in performing one or more tasks.

For programs wishing to assess functional ability, it is preferable to use one of the many already established scales that have been proven to be valid and reliable. Beyond that, a number of additional steps can be taken to improve the accuracy of the assessment and the utility of the results. For example, it is helpful to explicitly include the type of wording that could be used to address the client or respondent in order to standardize the way the questions are asked. It is also important to clearly define in nontechnical language key words or phrases such as *activities of daily living, grooming,* and *transferring.* Assessors too often assume that respondents understand these terms and use them during the course of the assessment, when in fact they are technical terms that may not be clearly understood. Program staff may also need more information than the choices provided in standardized measures. If a client has problems in using the toilet, it will be important to know whether the person has bowel or bladder incidents, whether these occur during the day or night, and how often. This issue can be addressed by allowing space next to each item for comments to describe the problem and what type of assistance is needed, or this type of information can be built into the wording of the items. Additionally, programs may need to add items that address particular service issues or concerns. For example, some IADL measures distinguish between answering the telephone and making a telephone call, and between light housework and heavy housework, and others have added items about laundry, using local transportation, and remembering appointments.

Accurately assessing the functional ability of older adults is a major challenge. The wide use of measures of functional ability belies the difficult measurement issues involved. When properly used, these measures can assure that frail older adults receive the assistance they need to live independently, consistent with their values and preferences. However, all persons are at risk from assessments that they think are accurate, but are not. Clients and their families rely on the accuracy of assessment protocols, and there is a natural tendency to trust formally sanctioned assessments. The term *functional assessment* has a ring of scientific legitimacy, and the results are presumed to be accurate, but this is not always so. Programs use measures of functional ability to determine eligibility for services, and sometimes to justify the need for other important tests, treatments, or interventions. How well this assessment is made has profound implications for the person assessed and for public policy.

SCOTT MIYAKE GERON

See also ASSESSMENT; FRAILTY; LONG-TERM CARE.

BIBLIOGRAPHY

BRANCH, L. G., and HOENIG, H. "Measures of Physical Functioning." *Generations* 21, no. 1 (1997): 37–40.
DOTY, P. "Family Care of the Elderly: The Role of Public Policy." *Milbank Quarterly* 64, no. 1 (1986): 34–75.
DUKE UNIVERSITY CENTER FOR THE STUDY OF AGING. *Multidimensional Functional Assessment: The OARS Methodology,* 2d ed. Durham, N.C.: Duke University, 1978.
JETTE, A., and BRANCH, L. "The Framingham Disability Study, II: Physical Disability Among the Aging." *American Journal of Public Health* 71 (1981): 1211–1216.
JUSTICE, D. *Case Management Standards in State Community-Based Long-Term Care Programs for Older Persons with Disabilities.* Washington, D.C.: National Association of State Units on Aging, 1993.
KANE, R. A., and KANE, R. L. *Assessing the Elderly: A Practical Guide to Measurement.* Lexington, Ky.: Lexington Books, 1981.
KANE, R. A.; KANE, R. L.; and LADD, R. C. *The Heart of Long-Term Care.* Oxford, U.K.: Oxford University Press, 1998.
KATZ, S. C.; FORD, A. B.; MOSKOWITZ, R. W.; JACKSON, B. A.; and JAFFEE, M. W. "Studies of Illness in the Aged. The Index of ADL: A Standardized Measure of Biological and Psychosocial Function." *Journal of the American Medical Association* 185 (1963): 914–919.
KOVAR, M. G., and LAWTON, P. M. "Functional Disability: Activities and Instrumental Activities of Daily Living. In *Focus on Assessment Techniques,* vol. 14. Edited by P. M. Lawton and J. A. Teresi. New York: Springer Publishing Company, 1994. Pages 57–75.
LAWTON, M. P., and BRODY, E. M. "Assessment of Older People: Self-Maintaining and Instrumental Activities of Daily Living." *The Gerontologist* 37 (1969): 91–99.
STONE, R. I. *Long-Term Care for the Elderly with Disabilities: Current Policy, Emerging Trends, and Implications for the Twenty-First Century.* New York: Milbank Memorial Fund, 2000.
VERBRUGGE, L. "The Iceberg of Disability." In *The Legacy of Longevity: Health and Health Care in Later Life.* Edited by S. M. Stahl. Newbury Park, Calif.: Sage Publications, 1990.

FUNERAL AND MEMORIAL PRACTICES

In 1900, it was not uncommon for death to strike at any age. Young children and people over age sixty-five each accounted for about a third of annual deaths in the United States. By the beginning of the twenty-first century, in developed countries, death was largely confined to older adulthood. Three-fourths of annual deaths in the United States now occur to persons over the age of sixty-five. This demographic shift in the age at death, along with urbanization, migration, secularization, and consumerism, have contributed to dramatic changes in funeral and memorial practices in the United States over the past century.

J. J. Farrell, in *Inventing the American Way of Death, 1830–1920* (1980), describes common funeral-related practices that prevailed through the mid-to-late 1800s among people of European descent. Most people died at home during this period, and funerals and burials were handled by the immediate family and neighbors. After the death, women in the family would wash, dress, and prepare the body for burial. Men were responsible for making the plain wood coffin or securing it from the local carpenter. Male survivors dug the grave, and in some cases carved the grave stone. The wake was typically held at home, followed by a committal service at graveside.

As industrialization flourished, American cities grew more crowded, and living spaces became smaller. When death occurred, many families did not have the physical space for a wake in the home. D. C. Sloane (1991) cites three other reasons for the expanding roles of undertakers in the late nineteenth century: (1) the rise in popularity of embalming; (2) a longer distance from the home to the cemetery necessitated someone to organize the procession; and (3) families were concerned about ensuring that all the formalities were followed. The National Funeral Directors Association was established in 1882. The group decided to use the term *funeral directors*, rather than *undertakers*, in an effort to portray a more professional image. During the twentieth century, the role of the funeral director continued to expand into areas previously held by the family and the clergy.

The late twentieth century trend of a few international, profit-seeking funeral chains buying up family-owned funeral homes across the country has led to some concern over the homogenization of the American funeral. There is, however, evidence of a growing movement toward more personally meaningful arrangements, where funeral home personnel function as "facilitators" rather than "directors." Whether homogenization or personalization prevail, three central decisions remain for individuals responsible for final arrangements: 1) what to do with the deceased body?; 2) what type of ceremony will take place to acknowledge the death?; and 3) how shall this person be remembered?

What to do with the body?

Throughout human history, societies have prescribed appropriate final disposition of human remains. Factors affecting final disposition practices include religious beliefs, climate, geography, available space, ethnicity, economics, social customs, and environmental concerns.

Religious beliefs concerning final disposition are influenced by conceptions of what follows death, as well as the role of the physical body. Hinduism and Buddhism require cremation, while Lutherans have no formal position for or against it. The Roman Catholic Church opposed cremation until the latter part of the twentieth century, at which time cremation became permitted, but not encouraged. According to the National Conference of Catholic Bishops, "For the final disposition of the body, it is ancient Christian custom to bury or entomb the bodies of the dead; cremation is permitted, unless it is evident that cremation was chosen for anti-Christian motives" (Order of Christian Funerals, 1990, p. 6).

For both religious and cultural reasons, most Jewish people are buried and not cremated. Many Jews believe in the resurrection, "the return of the soul to the resuscitated body" (Kastenbaum & Kastenbaum, 1989, p.257) and cremation has taken on added negative connotations because of the horrors of the Holocaust.

Several First Nation (American Indian) tribes have the tradition of wrapping the corpse in hides or blankets and setting it out in the air for a year or more. Habenstein & Lamers (1960) explain that, in some tribes, the wrapped body was set in a tree or on a man-made platform. Among Dakota Indians, "at the end of this period of air burial, it was given earth burial" (p. 687).

Table 1
Options for final disposition.
SOURCE: Author

Method	Options
Burial (earth or at sea)	Casketed corpse Uncasketed corpse Cremated remains
Entombment (crypt, mausoleum, or niche)	Casketed corpse Uncasketed corpse Cremated remains
Cremation	Followed by: Earth/sea burial Entombment Scattering of remains Ashes kept in the home Remains stored/left at crematory or funeral home
Body donated to science	Followed by (individual, or more commonly, group): Burial Cremation
Body frozen (Cryogenic suspension)	Unclear

NOTE: Cremation can be a means or an ends to final disposition.

Immigrants to the United States have faced barriers to maintaining traditional body disposition preferences. For example, Hmong refugees to the United States have encountered problems while attempting to make final arrangements because their practices differ from the local norm. They do not wish to be embalmed, do wish to hold the funeral ceremony at home, and desire more control over selecting an auspicious location for burial.

Table 1 lists contemporary final disposition options. Although the cremation rate continues to climb (10 percent in 1960, 24 percent in 1998, and projected 40 percent by 2010), earth burial of casketed remains continues to be the most common form of final disposition in the United States, accounting for about 65 percent of all dispositions. National cremation rates mask the wide variation among the states. Hawaii, Nevada, and Washington have cremation rates over 50 percent, while Mississippi, West Virginia, and Alabama have cremation rates of about 5 percent.

The two remaining forms of final disposition are rarely used. Medical and dental schools around the country accept body donations, or *willed bodies*, for use in research and training. After two years of use, the bodies are generally cremated and either returned to the family or buried in a group grave.

By 1993, about fifty people had opted for cryogenic suspension. Interest in cryogenics was piqued in 1964 when R. C. W. Ettinger published his book, *The Prospect of Immortality*. Ettinger defines cryogenic suspension as "specialized cold storage of clinically dead people. . .in hope of eventual rescue, revival, repair, and rejuvenation by future technology" (Kastenbaum, 1994–1995, p. 159). During an interview with the editor of the journal *Omega*, Ettinger reported the cost of a full-body cryogenic suspension at his Cryogenics Institute was $28,000, compared to $51,000–$60,000 for cryogenic suspension of just the head at other institutes.

Ceremony to mark the death

There are two categories of ceremonies that mark the death of a loved one: a funeral service, in which the body of the decedent is present, generally in a casket; and a memorial service, in which the corpse is not present because it is not available (e.g., lost at sea, destroyed in a fire, missing) or because it has been cremated. Many factors can affect the type of ceremony that follows death, including religious beliefs, ethnicity, local customs, attitudes about the cause of death, age of the person who died, economic circumstances, and perceived social expectations on the part of the person who plans the ceremony.

Dawson, Santos and Burdick report that the social functions of a funeral include: (1) public recognition that a death has occurred; (2) a framework to provide support to those most affected by the death; and (3) a socially accepted way of body disposal. Other functions include: allowing survivors to say good-bye; affirming the worth of one's relationship with the person who died; allowing people to search for meaning in life and death; reinforcing the fact of death in all our lives; and establishing an ongoing helping relationship among mourners. Involvement with funeral rituals may also help with adjusting to the loss, and a funeral can help the community of survivors acknowledge their own mortality while providing social meaning to the passing of a life.

Most of the benefits accrue to individuals and societies from a funeral service are expected to exist for memorial services as well, with the exception of the effects of actually viewing the decedent (which can be, but is not always, part of a funeral service). Some people may benefit more from funeral services, others from memorial services. It may be the contents of the service—rather than the presence of the body—that affects attendees. Research is needed in this area.

A new twist on attending a funeral or memorial service has been made possible by the Internet. In a 2000 *Washington Post* article, Dan Eggen described the funeral service of a seventy-seven-year old woman in Scottsdale, Arizona, "attended" by over twenty people who watched it over the Internet from the East Coast, "many of them elderly relatives who could not make the trip" (Eggen, 2000, p. A01).

How will this person be remembered?

For many centuries, grave markers have served as the primary physical reminder of a life lived. Grave markers and cemeteries have undergone dramatic changes since the mid-1800s. Four places of interment existed in the United States before the nineteenth century: isolated pioneer graves; family farms; churchyards; and potter's fields (for the indigent). In his book, *The Last Great Necessity: Cemeteries in American History* (1991), D. C. Sloane traces the history of the American cemetery including the advent of the rural cemetery of the early 1800s, with its winding lanes and ornate headstones in a natural garden setting; the development of the lawn cemetery, which became popular following the Civil War, with its park-like landscaping and prescribed markers; and the establishment of memorial parks in the 1920s and 1930s, which all but removed the impression of death from the premises by requiring semiuniform flat grave markers that do not interfere with the suburban landscape. (The use of flat markers lowers maintenance costs because lawn mowers can do the work that was previously done by hand). Each type of cemetery reflects the prevailing ideas about the appropriate balance between nature and art, ownership, community inclusiveness, and the relationship between the living and the dead.

Grave-marker inscriptions have also followed trends. Up until the eighteenth century, most burials occurred in churchyards in small towns. Churchyard epitaphs functioned as constant reminders of the transitory nature of human life. "The most common epitaph was 'Where you are now, so once was I. Where I am now, so you will be'" (Jackson and Vergara, 1989, p. 10). By the mid–nineteenth century, Victorian epitaphs reflected more emphasis on the self. "Individual responsibility for the salvation of one's soul, which to some degree supplanted the dominance of the mother church, led to highly individual expressions of faith and grief. . .and a new preoccupation with the grieving family left behind" (Brown, 1994, p. 4).

Contemporary choices for epitaphs run the gamut from simply stating name and birth and death dates to explanations of genealogy and reflections of the decedent's past times. Examples of the latter include the following epitaphs found in a Midwestern cemetery, "I'd Rather be Drag Racing" and also "World's Greatest Trucker" (Brown, 1994).

Aside from grave markers and monuments, there are many other ways in which loved ones have been memorialized both in public and in private. Obituaries continue to notify the community of a death and convey the impact of someone's life and death for the family and community. Memorial photographs of the deceased remain important private possessions, although seldom shared outside the immediate family. Mourning jewelry containing pieces of hair from the decedent was popular in the Victorian era. Today, mourners can purchase a locket containing the cremated remains of a loved one.

Information technology has facilitated changes in memorialization. Video memorial tributes, with family photos set to music, are available through funeral homes, and virtual cemeteries are found on the World Wide Web.

P. Roberts (1999) reports that the emerging Web cemetery is akin to a combination epitaph, obituary, and cemetery. "These sites provide a place to leave words and symbols memorializing the dead among tributes to others who have died" (p. 337). Visitors can leave virtual flowers or stones at markers, and they can sign a virtual condolence book as well. One visitor left this comment at a Web cemetery: "A wonderful idea for one to remember their loved ones. In cyberspace they are everywhere and no where and can be remembered by all" (Roberts, p. 356). Another cyber-visitor wrote: "Thank you for providing me a place where I can go for solace and comfort. . . .I never dreamed I would receive such gratification through cyberspace" (p. 346). Greater use of Web-based memorial practices (and other aspects of final arrangements) are sure to follow in the coming decades as the World Wide Web continues to transform life, and death.

The funeral as a purchase

It is customary to think about funeral, burial, and memorial practices as social, religious, and cultural rituals, but they have become characterized as consumer transactions as well. *The American Way of Death* (1963), a best-selling book detailing the anticonsumer practices of some members of the funeral industry, helped to expand the grassroots Funeral and Memorial Society movement, now known as the "Funeral Consumers Alliance." Currently there are about one hundred local societies dedicated to educating consumers on funeral options and costs.

In 1984, the Federal Trade Commission issued the Funeral Rule, requiring every funeral home in the country to provide accurate, itemized, written price information to anyone who asks for it in person. The rule also prohibits funeral homes from engaging in deceptive or unfair practices. The Funeral Rule applies to both *preneed* and *at need* (after the death) funeral home purchases, but does not cover cemetery, crematory, grave marker, or third-party casket sellers. Consumer advocates are calling for an expansion of the Funeral Rule to include all vendors of funeral-related goods and services.

With most deaths postponed until older adulthood, and funeral directors serving as the repository of final arrangement information, many families face making or overseeing final arrangements without much experience. A 1995 study reported that half the people responsible for final arrangements of a deceased loved one had no idea what the final costs would be before they met with the funeral director. Despite this lack of knowledge, a lot of money is at stake. The mean cost of final arrangements, the study found, was $6,500 (a range of less than $200 to over $14,000).

It is ironic that as the number of funeral and memorial options has increased, the average adult's experience with making final arrangements has decreased. There is also a lack of consensus as to who is responsible for making final arrangements, and when they should be made. Especially in the case of older adults, should decedents make and pay for arrangements before death? Or should this responsibility fall to survi-

vors? These decisions are generally dealt with on a family-by-family basis, though more information, discussion, and options regarding funeral and memorial practices can be expected with the aging of the baby boom cohort.

MERCEDES BERN-KLUG

See also DEATH AND DYING.

BIBLIOGRAPHY

BERN-KLUG, M.; EKERDT, D.; and WILKINSON, D. S. "What Families Know about Funeral-Related Costs: Implications for Social Workers." *Health & Social Work*, 24, no. 2 (1999): 128–137.
BOLTON, C., and CAMP, D. J. "Funeral Rituals and the Facilitation of Grief Work." *Omega* 17 (1986–87): 343–352.
BROWN, J. G. *Soul in the Stone: Cemetery Art from America's Heartland*. Lawrence, Kans.: University Press of Kansas, 1994.
CARLSON, L. *Caring for the Dead: Your Final Act of Love*. Hinesburg, Vt.: Upper Access, 1998.
Cremation Association of North America. *1998 Cremation Data and Projections to the Year 2010*. Available on the World Wide Web at www.cremationassociation.org/html
DAWSON, G.; SANTOS, J. F.; and BURDICK, D. C. "Differences in Final Arrangements Between Burial and Cremation as the Method of Body Disposition." *Omega* 21, no. 2 (1990): 129–146.
EGGEN, D. "Death Finds the Web." *Washington Post*, 17 May 2000, p. A01.
FARRELL, J. J. *Inventing the American Way of Death 1830–1920*. Philadelphia: Temple University Press, 1980.
Federal Trade Commission. *Complying with the Funeral Rule*. Washington, D.C.: FTC, 1995.
FULTON, R. "The Contemporary Funeral: Functional or Dysfunctional?" In *Dying: Facing the Facts*. 3d ed. Edited by H. Wass and R. Neimeyer. Washington, D.C.: Taylor and Francis, 1995. Pages 185–209.
Funeral Consumer's Alliance. Information available at www.funerals.org.
HABENSTEIN, R. W., and LAMERS, W. M. *Funeral Customs the World Over*. Milwaukee, Wisc.: Buffin Printers, 1960.
HAYES, C. L., and KALISH, R. A. "Death-Related Experiences and Funerary Practices of the Hmong Refugee in the United States." *Omega* 18, no. 1 (1987): 63–70.
IVERSON, K. V. *Death to Dust*. Tucson, Ariz.: Galen Press, 1994.

JACKSON, K. T., and VERGARA, C. J. *Silent Cities: The Evolution of the American Cemetery.* New York: Princeton Architectural Press, 1989.

KASTENBAUM, R. "Cryogenic Suspension: An Interview with R. C. W. Ettinger." *Omega* 30, no. 3 (1994–1995): 159–171.

KASTENBAUM, R., and KASTENBAUM, B. *Encyclopedia of Death: Myth, History, Philosophy, Science—The Many Aspects of Death and Dying.* Phoenix, Ariz.: Oryx Press, 1989.

MITFORD, J. *The American Way of Death.* Greenwich, Conn.: Fawcett, 1963.

MURPHY, S. L. "Deaths: Final Data for 1998." *National Vital Statistics Report*, vol. 48, no. 11. Hyattsville, Md.: National Center for Health Statistics, 2000.

Order of Christian Funerals: Study Edition. Chicago: Liturgy Training Publications, 1990.

ROBERTS, P. "Tangible Sorrow, Virtual Tributes: Cemeteries in Cyberspace." In *End of Life Issues: Interdisciplinary and Multidisciplinary Perspectives.* Edited by B. DeVries. New York: Springer, 1999. Pages 337–358.

RUBY, J. *Secure the Shadow: Death and Photography in America.* Cambridge, Mass.: MIT Press, 1995.

SIEGEL, M., ed. *The Last Word: The New York Times Book of Obituaries and Farewells.* New York: The New York Times Company, 1997.

SLOANE, D. C. *The Last Great Necessity: Cemeteries in American History.* Baltimore: Johns Hopkins Press, 1995.

WOLFELT, A. D. *Creating Meaningful Funeral Ceremonies: A Guide for Caregivers.* Fort Collins, Colo.: Companion Press, 1994.

G

GAY AND LESBIAN AGING

Gay men and lesbians (females) are both defined as *homosexuals*. *Homosexual* is defined as a preference for emotional and sexual relationships with persons of the same sex. The terminology used, however, indicates a sense of personal and cultural identity. *Homosexuals* are typically hidden and fearful of disclosure, whereas *gays* and *lesbians* are socially open (*out*) in many walks of their lives (e.g., home, work, and school). Homosexuality as a concept was defined around 1869 and became more widely identified as the "disease of effeminacy" as popularized by the trial of Oscar Wilde. As we enter the twenty-first century, American society views homosexuality as an alternative lifestyle. The social history of homosexuality has seen the status of the entity change from a sin to a crime (either against nature or the state), then to a sickness or disease, and finally to an alternative lifestyle on the margins of society. Homosexuality remains a crime or is considered a disease in many parts of the world. In the United States, for example, many states maintain laws that make sodomy a crime, including consensual relations between adults in private.

Most of the research on homosexuality examines gay men with some scant attention paid to lesbians, and even less research is available on older gays and lesbians. In terms of gays and lesbians, *older* generally refers to those over age fifty. Much of the early research about homosexuality focused on determining the causes or finding an explanation for the homosexual phenomenon. The emphasis was on determining a homosexual's level of normalcy or abnormality. By seeking the causes in order to logically progress toward finding a cure, past research demonstrated the lack of acceptance of homosexuality in American society. More recent research has been devoted to understanding homosexuality and exploring gay and lesbian issues, although homosexuality is still considered deviant by the general population.

With the increasing population of older adults in American society, there will be an increase in the number of older adults who are gay or lesbian. It is important to consider the myths and realities about aging in American society, examine differences between older gay men and lesbians, explore the issues relevant to aging gay men and lesbians, and consider differences in the situation for older homosexuals across cultures and time.

Myths and realities

Many myths abound about gay and lesbian elders. Older gay men are stereotyped as isolated and lonely, increasingly effeminate, and prone to pedophilia. Older lesbians are stereotyped as emotionally cold, lonely, frustrated, and overly masculine. Although a small number of older gays and lesbians fit these descriptions, the vast majority do not. Due to more relaxed gender roles of gays and lesbians, older gays and lesbians may be better equipped to deal with gender role changes (men becoming less masculine and women becoming less feminine) that commonly accompany normal aging.

Most older gay men and lesbians appear to be reasonably well adjusted and integrated into social networks composed primarily of age peers. Commitment to one's sexual orientation and in-

Lesbian couple Lois Farnham (left) and Holly Puterbaugh (shown here at the Vermont Supreme Court in November 1998) were one of three gay or lesbian couples that successfully challenged Vermont's marriage law, which made same-sex unions illegal. Their lawsuit led to the passage of legislation that let gays and lesbians apply for civil union status, which was as legally binding as a marriage certificate. (AP photo by Toby Talbot.)

tegration into the gay community are predictors of good psychological adjustment for gay men. Older lesbians generally expect to grow old gracefully, while remaining interested in life and involved in the social world. Positive adjustment to aging among older gays and lesbians can be attributed to a life course of experience in dealing with problems associated with stigma and society's negative attitude toward homosexuality.

In terms of social support, older gays and lesbians draw more support from friends, and older heterosexuals draw more support from family. Homosexuals often use *fictive kin*, substituting friends for traditional family relationships. These confidant relationships can help to resolve fears associated with aging. Homosexuals also have extensive family ties and long term committed relationships among older gays and lesbians appear to be more common than previously assumed.

Gender differences

Lesbians and gay men represent two distinct communities and the issues of each group differ. Older gay men are likely to either be in a long-term relationship or not in one at all, with a small percentage having numerous short-term relationships. Although they tend to maintain positive attitudes regarding their physical age-related changes, older gay men appear to be more concerned with this than their lesbian counterparts. Furthermore, older gay men are likely to be more financially secure than older lesbians, due to gender inequalities across the life course.

As a result of the virtual invisibility of older lesbians, they are more likely to be ignored at the level of policy and practice. Older lesbians are likely to have practiced serial monogamy. They usually report a positive self-image and positive feelings about their identification as a lesbian and generally do not report fear of changes in physical appearance associated with aging. They express greater fluidity in their sexual orientation, are more likely to have been heterosexually married, and are more likely to have children than gay men.

Major issues with aging

Aging gays and lesbians face the same issues as heterosexual people, such as health and financial concerns. Issues unique to older gays and lesbians relate to society's failure to accept or inability to understand their sexual orientation. Same-sex relationships are generally not legally sanctioned or recognized in the same ways as heterosexual relationships. This can lead to difficulties in managing terminal or chronic illness or partners being unable to collect insurance or pension benefits, because these special rights are reserved for relatives. Similarly, if the gay or lesbian partners or persons significant to either of them have not clearly defined the relationship, others may fail to acknowledge the severity and nature of the loss upon the death of a partner. In addition to the lack of recognition of the emotional needs of the grieving partner, financial and property issues may ensue.

Cultural and subcultural variation

An understanding of homosexuality should be viewed within the cultural context of a particular society. Ritualized homosexuality has been widely reported throughout Melanesia and is understood by anthropologists as age-structured homosexuality. In Sambia, for example, the psychosocial and sexual development in males from middle childhood through old age is regulated through the initiation process controlled through the men's secret society. Adult men initiate boys by inseminating them, but as adults they go on to marry and have children.

Issues typically faced by older gays and lesbians will be exacerbated or mitigated by their cultural or ethnic heritage. In general, gays and lesbians within ethnic groups with particularly strong family ties (e.g., African American, Asian, and Latino/a) and those that place a high value on gender roles may face extreme difficulties—perhaps even being forced to choose between their family and their homosexuality. Traditional Native American cultures, on the other hand, do not tend to divide sexuality into a dichotomy of male and female. Instead, they tend to view people as having both male and female spirits and are generally more tolerant than other subcultures and ethnic groups, especially those coming from European and Eastern cultures.

Historical variation

The experiences of today's older gays and lesbians must be understood within the historical context in which they came of age. Today's older gays grew up in a time of severe homophobia and with a lack of positive role models. Being gay or lesbian put individuals at risk of arrest or institutionalization. Therefore, older gay or lesbian individuals and couples often did not develop a conscious personal identity as gay or lesbian and often do not use that terminology to describe themselves.

Riots following police raids at New York City's Stonewall Inn on June 27, 1969, led to the development of the Gay Liberation Front and the gay rights movement that forced the non-gay society to address homosexuality. Today's younger gays and lesbians tend to encourage *coming out* or *coming out of the closet*. There are a number of different levels and ways that a person comes out, but the process follows a continuum from self-acceptance to general disclosure. Older gays and lesbians have generally been reluctant to embrace this process, especially after a lifetime of successfully hiding their homosexuality. Gays and lesbians who have grown older following the gay rights movement have existed in a social cli-

mate that tends to be somewhat more tolerant of homosexuality (other than the period following the emergence of AIDS, when gays were targeted as the cause).

The future

There have been dramatic social and health changes since the 1980s that will likely have an effect on future generations of older gays and lesbians. Gays and lesbians are much more activist-oriented than in previous decades (other than the initial gay rights movement associated with the 1970s). These advocacy efforts are aimed at policy and legal implications associated with the issues addressed above. Overall, there seems to be a greater social tolerance of same-sex orientation as reflected in the emergence of domestic partnership policies, more realistic portrayal of gays and lesbians in the media, and an overall greater awareness of gays and lesbians in American society. As a result, it is likely that some of the issues faced by older gays and lesbians today will be different for older gays and lesbians in the future, especially those who grew up and grew old after the Stonewall Riots of 1969 and who were involved in the ensuing gay rights movement.

Organizations

A few organizations directed toward older gays and lesbians have emerged, primarily focused on providing for social service needs and advocacy. These organizations include Senior Action in a Gay Environment (SAGE), Pride Senior Network, Lesbian and Gay Aging Issues Network (LGAIN), and Gay and Lesbian Association of Retiring Persons (GLARP).

DENA SHENK
JAMES R. PEACOCK

See also GENDER.

BIBLIOGRAPHY

BERGER, R. M. *Gay and Gray: The Older Homosexual Man*, 2d ed. Binghamton, N.Y.: Harrington Park Press, 1996.
CABAJ, R. P., and STEIN, T. S., eds. *Textbook of Homosexuality and Mental Health*. Washington, D.C.: American Psychiatric Press, Inc., 1996.
DORFMAN, R.; WALTERS, K.; BURKE, P.; HARDIN, L.; KARANIK, T.; RAPHAEL, J.; and SILVERSTEIN, E. "Old, Sad and Alone: The Myth of the Aging Homosexual." *Journal of Gerontological Social Work* 24 (1995): 29–44.

FULLMER, E. M.; SHENK, D.; and EASTLAND, L. J. "Negating Identity: A Feminist Analysis of the Social Invisibility of Older Lesbians." *Journal of Women and Aging* 11 (1999): 131–148.

HERDT, G. H., ed. *Ritualized Homosexuality in Melanesia*. University of California Press, 1984.

KIMMEL, D. C. "The Families of Older Gay Men and Lesbians." *Generations* 17 (1992): 37–38.

LEE, J. A., ed. *Gay Midlife and Maturity*. Haworth Press, Inc., 1991.

PEACOCK, J. R. "Gay Male Adult Development: Some Stage Issues of an Older Cohort." *Journal of Homosexuality* 40 (2000): 13–29.

QUAM, J., and WHITFORD, G. S. "Adaptation and Age-Related Expectations of Older Gay and Lesbian Adults." *The Gerontologist* 32 (1992): 367–374.

SHENK, D., and FULLMER, E. M. "Significant Relationships among Older Women: Cultural and Personal Constructions of Lesbianism." *Journal of Women and Aging* 8 (1996): 75–89.

GENDER

When considering issues of aging, gender must be considered as an integral component. The Census Bureau estimates that the number of women age sixty and older in the world will double between the years 2000 and 2025. In 2000, in developed countries, one in ten persons was a woman age sixty or older. This is projected to increase to one in seven by 2025. While developed countries may have higher percentages of older women, developing countries actually have higher numbers of older women, with faster growth rates for older women than more developed countries.

The different life experiences of women and men are reflected in several key demographic measures. Primary among these is the skewed sex ratio at older ages—there are a far greater number of older women than older men. This phenomenon is directly related to higher life expectancy and lower death rates among women. However, older women do experience their own set of health problems, and older women are more economically disadvantaged than older men. They are also more likely to live alone. On the other hand, women have stronger social support systems than men.

Sex ratios

Figure 1 presents sex ratios for three age groups throughout the world. The sex ratio is the number of males per 100 females. At birth, the sex ratio is generally around 105. In other words, there are more male babies born than female babies. This pattern is found in almost all societies. In the middle ages of the life course, there tends to be almost equal numbers of men and women, but by age sixty-five, the sex ratio is skewed heavily in favor of females. Generally, based on the world average, there are one-third more females than males age sixty-five and older. However, there are regional differences. In Asia, Latin America, and Africa there are about one-fifth more older females than older males, while in Europe there are almost two-fifths more older women. There is more detailed information for the United States, in which the sex ratio falls below 50 for ages eighty-five to eighty-nine, indicating that there are more than twice as many females as males in this age range. For those over one hundred years old, the sex ratio is a mere twenty-one—that is, there are twenty-one males per one hundred females. This pattern of highly skewed sex ratios is the result of gender differences in life expectancy, which are discussed in the next section.

Life expectancy and death rates

It is well known that women live longer than men. Exactly how much longer? And does this advantage continue as people age? In 2000, the average life expectancy for women worldwide was sixty-eight years, while for men it was sixty-four years. Nevertheless, the difference between women and men in life expectancy varies throughout the world. In developing countries women live, on average, three years longer than men. The difference is only two years in sub-Saharan Africa. In contrast, women live an average of seven years longer than men in developed countries. The difference in life expectancy tends to decrease at older ages. At age sixty, the difference ranges from one to four years (see Table 1).

In most countries, there are additional differences in life expectancy based on race, class, and other social-status differences. In the United States, for example, overall life expectancy at birth is 79.2 years for females and 73.6 years for males. However, there are important race differences: life expectancy for white women is 79.8 years; for black women, 74.7 years; for white men, 74.3 years; and for black men, 67.3 years. Therefore, it is white women who have the largest advantage in life expectancy, while black men

Figure 1
Sex ratios for regions of the world: 1995

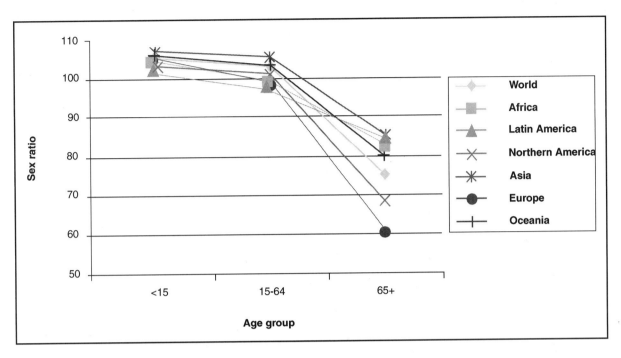

SOURCE: *1997 Demographic Yearbook* (49th issue). New York: United Nations, 1999

lag 12.5 years behind. However, the difference between white women and black men decreases to five years by age sixty-five, when white women are expected to live 19.1 more years and black men 14.2 more years.

Although both black and white women have longer life expectancies than their male counterparts, the differences decrease at later ages, especially among blacks. While black women are expected to live 7.4 years longer than black men at birth, by age sixty-five the advantage in life expectancy is only 3.2 years. Similarly, white women's advantage decreases from 5.5 years at birth to 3.2 years at age sixty-five. It is also interesting to compare the similarities (and differences) between black women and white men. Although life expectancy is similar for these two groups, there are differences in death rates. Black females have higher death rates than white males at ages under five years old, with the difference being especially great under one year old. Black females also suffer higher death rates from thirty-five to sixty-four years old. However, at age sixty-five and older, the death rate for white males surpasses that for black females. Indeed, at age eighty-five and older, black females

have lower death rates than white females and black males have lower death rates than white males.

The importance of the gender difference in life expectancy is obvious: if women live longer than men then there will be more older women than older men. This has several implications for individual women as well as for society. For individual women, it is likely to mean outliving one's spouse, living alone, and poorer economic conditions, as fewer resources are used to cover more years.

These gender differences in life expectancy lead to inquiries about what older men and women are dying from. In the United States, for those forty-five years old and older, the top two causes of death for both women and men are heart disease and cancer, though the death rates from these diseases are higher for men. At the younger ages (forty-five to sixty-four years old), men have higher death rates for nine of the ten leading causes of death, the exception being cerebrovascular diseases (stroke). It is interesting to note that the death rate for causes with large social-behavioral components, such as accidents,

Table 1

Life expectancy at age 60: 1995–2000

	Male	Female
Africa		
Northern Africa	16	18
Sub-Saharan Africa	14	16
Latin America		
Caribbean	19	22
Central America	19	21
South America	17	20
Asia		
Eastern Asia	17	21
Southeastern Asia	16	18
Southern Asia	16	17
Central Asia	16	20
Western Asia	17	20
Oceania	16	19
Europe		
Eastern Europe	16	20
Western Europe	19	23

SOURCE: *The World's Women 2000: Trends and Statistics.* New York: United Nations, 2000.

Table 2

Economic activity rates for men and women 65 years and older: 1997

	Male	Female
Africa		
Northern Africa	31	6
Sub-Saharan Africa	65	35
Latin America		
Caribbean	27	10
Central America	51	13
South America	34	12
Asia		
Eastern Asia	28	12
Southeastern Asia	46	22
Southern Asia	56	20
Central Asia	11	4
Western Asia	30	4
Oceania	55	31
Europe		
Eastern Europe	15	7
Western Europe	9	4

SOURCE: *The World's Women 2000: Trends and Statistics.* New York: United Nations, 2000.

liver disease, HIV infection, and suicide, are two to six times greater for men than women in this age group. For those age sixty-five and older, the leading causes of death are similar for women and men, though men have higher death rates from heart disease, cancer, and pulmonary diseases and women have higher rates from cerebrovascular diseases and Alzheimer's disease.

In addition, although women generally experience lower death rates than men, they suffer from higher rates of several chronic conditions, including arthritis, high blood pressure, cataracts, chronic sinusitis, hay fever, varicose veins, chronic bronchitis, asthma, hemorrhoids, frequent indigestion, and migraines. Men, on the other hand, are more likely to experience hearing impairments, heart conditions, orthopedic impairments, diabetes, visual impairments, tinnitus, and dermatitis.

Why do these differences exist? Surely, part of the reason lies in biology. Males have higher death rates than females at all ages, even before they are born (miscarriages disproportionately occur with male fetuses). These biological differences are likely to be exacerbated by social factors. Men are more likely to engage in risk-taking behaviors, such as driving faster, which lead to higher death rates from accidents. Men are also more likely to smoke and drink alcohol, increas-

ing their risk of lung cancer and liver disease, among other diseases. Finally, men tend to neglect their health more than women, as witnessed by fewer visits to the doctor. The smaller differences that exist in developing countries are likely to be due to harsher living conditions for all.

Economic status and retirement

Men enjoy an economic advantage over women, and older men are no exception. Older men have completed more years of school, are more likely to be in the labor force, and are less likely to be living in poverty than older women. Table 2 shows economic activity rates for older women and men. The economic activity rate is the percentage of people who are engaged in paid activities or are available to work in such activities. In every region, older men are more likely to be economically active than older women. However, in Europe, Canada, the United States, and central Asia, participation rates are low for both men and women. In contrast, sub-Saharan Africa has the highest activity rates for both women and men. Finally, large gender differences in activity among older individuals exist in western Asia, northern Africa, and Central America.

In the United States, labor-force participation rates peak at 93.2 percent for men twenty-five to thirty-four years old while women's participation rates peak at 77.1 percent for thirty-five to forty-four year olds. Between ages fifty-five and sixty-five, men's labor force participation rates drop to 68.1 percent and women's rates fall to 51.2 percent. Finally, those sixty-five years old and older have low rates of participation. Still, men are almost twice as likely to be in the labor force at this age (16.5 percent versus 8.6 percent).

Of those with an income, men have higher incomes than women. When median income peaks (at forty-five to fifty-four years old), women are making 55 percent of what men make. Both men's and women's median income decreases at older ages, though women's decreases faster initially. The big drop in men's median income occurs after age sixty-four. In 1998, men age sixty-five and older earned a median income of $18,166, while the median income for women age sixty-five and older was only $10,504. Related to their lower income, 13 percent of women age sixty-five and older live below the poverty level, compared to 7 percent of their male counterparts.

Among those who are employed, women and men tend to retire at similar ages, with the median age being around sixty-three for both women and men. Often, retirement is hastened by the retirement of one's spouse, though this reason is cited more often by women. An exception is when wives are not employed during the child-rearing years. These wives often retire later than their husbands, perhaps making up for time spent out of the labor force. Husbands also retire faster when they have Social Security income or a pension. On the other hand, wives retire faster when their husbands' income is high. Women's economic well-being does tend to be more influenced by their husbands than vice versa. For example, widowhood is more likely to increase poverty for women than for men. In fact, a man's economic well-being may actually improve when his wife dies.

Marital status, living arrangements, and social support

In every region, at least one-third of older women are widowed (see Table 3). Rates of widowhood are especially high in northern Africa and central Asia, where almost three-fifths of

Table 3

Widowhood rates (percentages) for men and women 60 years and older: 1985/1997

	Male	Female
Africa		
Northern Africa	8	59
Sub-Saharan Africa	7	44
Latin America		
Caribbean	12	34
Central America	12	36
South America	13	37
Asia		
Eastern Asia	14	49
Southeastern Asia	14	49
Southern Asia	11	51
Central Asia	13	58
Western Asia	8	48
Oceania	15	44
Europe		
Eastern Europe	14	48
Western Europe	12	40

SOURCE: *The World's Women 2000: Trends and Statistics*. New York: United Nations, 2000.

older women are widowed. In contrast, widowhood is much less common among men around the world. For example, only 7 percent of men in sub-Saharan Africa outlive their wives. In Africa, older women are over six times more likely to be widowed than older men.

Gender differences in marital status tend to increase with age. In the United States, at ages forty-five to fifty-four years old, the majority of both men and women are married (see Table 4), and only 7 percent of women and 9 percent of men in this age group have never been married. Widowhood is rare for men (1 percent) and very uncommon for women (4 percent). On the contrary, this age range represents the age at which the highest percent of women and men are divorced, with 18 percent of women and 14 percent of men being divorced. The picture changes considerably for those seventy-five years old and over. While the majority of men are still married at this age, only 30 percent of women in this age group are married. Instead, fully 60 percent of women seventy-five and older are widowed. In fact, the percentage of women widowed at ages seventy-five and older is 2.5 times greater than the percentage of men widowed.

Because women tend to be the survivors of marriage, they are also more likely to live alone

Table 4

Marital status of males and females 45 and older: 1998

	Never married	Married	Widowed	Divorced
Male				
45-54	8.9	76.3	0.9	13.9
55-64	5.4	80.2	2.6	11.9
65-74	4.1	79.2	8.8	7.8
75+	3.4	69.2	23.7	3.7
Female				
45-54	7.2	70.8	4.0	18.1
55-64	4.6	67.8	13.2	14.4
65-74	4.3	54.8	31.9	8.9
75+	5.1	29.5	60.4	5.0

SOURCE: *Statistical Abstract of the United States: 1999.* Washington, D.C.: U.S. Census Bureau.

or with someone else. This can be seen by looking at household headship. In every region of the world, women age sixty and older are more likely than older men to be household heads. In fact, almost one-half of older women in Europe are household heads. In the United States, women sixty-five years old and over are as likely to live alone as with a spouse, with 41 percent in each type of living arrangement. In contrast, only 17 percent of men sixty-five and older live alone, while 73 percent live with a spouse. In addition, only 10 percent of these men live with someone other than a spouse, compared to 18 percent of women this age.

Marital status can affect receipt of social support from children. Men who are divorced suffer disruptions in their relationships with their children, especially with their daughters. This may have consequences for caretaking, since disabled parents are more likely to receive care from their daughters. Widowhood may also have negative consequences for men's support networks. Men who are widowed receive less support from their children than those who are still married. In addition, women who are widowed more often develop friendships than men who are widowed, and women are more likely to receive support from friends. Even among older persons who are unmarried and childless, women receive more support than men. Generally, children report better relationships with their mothers than with their fathers. This may be due to the fact that women are more active in maintaining intergenerational relationships. Therefore, although

older women are more likely than older men to find themselves widowed and living alone, they seem better equipped to manage their lives on their own, with some help from family and friends.

Gender roles

Do gender roles relax or persist at older ages? This is an often debated question. It has been argued that men become more feminine and women more masculine as they age, and the idea that men become more sensitive and family-oriented while women become more assertive and confident is a popular one. Many older men tend to look back on their lives and think of such things as time missed with children when they were younger. On the other hand, older women's images of themselves tend to be higher, in terms of self-esteem and confidence, than those of younger women. These women feel that they can be more forceful in doing what they want.

An alternative explanation to reversed roles is the idea that roles may not change that much, but rather that roles may be more easily expressed at older ages. In other words, those who engage in more traditional roles at younger ages will continue to express traditional gender roles, while those who have more egalitarian views at younger ages will find it easier to express these views at older ages. Therefore, older ages provide more flexibility in enacting people's true gender roles. It seems that there is less pressure to behave in ways that conform to gender stereotypes at older ages.

Future gender differences

After decades of widening, the gap between men and women in life expectancy showed some signs of narrowing at the end of the twentieth century. In 2000, the gap in the United States was about two years less than it was in 1970. As a result, a less skewed sex ratio at older ages may emerge, though it will certainly remain weighted toward females for a long time to come.

As for economic roles, it is widely known that women's labor force participation increased dramatically over the last decades of the twentieth century. Female labor force participation rates in the United States increased from 43 percent in 1970 to 60 percent in 1998. The increase was especially dramatic among women forty-five to sixty-four years old, the ages right before retirement. Participation rates for this age group went from around one-half to three-quarters between 1970 and 1998. However, there have also been important changes in men's labor force participation. Over the last few decades of the twentieth century, men's labor force participation rates declined, with larger declines at older ages. Between 1970 and 1998, participation rates for men fifty-five to sixty-four years old decreased from 83 percent to 68 percent, while rates for men sixty-five and older decreased from 27 percent to 17 percent. These changes suggest that more recent and future cohorts of women will be better off economically as they enter old age. Fewer women will be financially dependent on their husbands or other family members. At the same time, more and more men may need, or at least benefit from, their wives working.

Changing family roles may also be important for different cohorts of aging men and women. Although a relatively small number of those sixty-five and older are divorced, the percentage increase between 1980 and 2000 in the United States was fairly large (from 3.4 percent to 7.1 percent for women and from 3.6 percent to 6.1 percent for men). This will likely have important implications—especially for older men, since fathers who are not married to their children's mother tend to receive less support from their children. In addition, it will be interesting to see if changing roles at home among younger couples translate into more egalitarian arrangements among older couples in future cohorts.

GAYLE KAUFMAN

See also FEMINIST THEORY; GENETICS; INEQUALITY; MARITAL RELATIONSHIPS; POPULATION AGING; RETIREMENT.

BIBLIOGRAPHY

AQUILINO, W. S. "Later Life Parental Divorce and Widowhood: Impact on Young Adults' Assessment of Parent-Child Relations." *Journal of Marriage and the Family* 56 (1994): 908–922.
BARER, B. M. "Men and Women Aging Differently." *International Journal of Aging and Human Development* 38 (1994): 29–40.
BELSKY, J. "The Research Findings on Gender Issues in Aging Men and Women." In *Gender Issues Across the Life Cycle*. Edited by B. R. Wainrib. New York: Springer Publishing Company, 1992. Pages 163–171.
BRUBAKER, T. H., and BRUBAKER, E. "Family Care of the Elderly in the United States: An Issue of Gender Differences?" In *Family Care of the Elderly: Social and Cultural Changes*. Edited by J. I. Kosberg. Newbury Park, Calif.: Sage, 1992. Pages 210–231.
BURKHAUSER, R. V.; BUTLER, J. S.; and HOLDEN, K. C. "How the Death of a Spouse Affects Economic Well-Being After Retirement." *Social Science Quarterly* 72 (1991): 504–519.
COONEY, T. M., and UHLENBERG, P. "The Role of Divorce in Men's Relations with Their Adult Children After Mid-Life." *Journal of Marriage and the Family* 52 (1990): 677–688.
DERVARICS, C. "The Coming Age of Older Women." *Population Today* 27 (1999): 1–2.
GENDELL, M., and SIEGEL, J. S. "Trends in Retirement Age by Sex 1950–2005." *Monthly Labor Review* 115 (1992): 22–29.
HARDY, M. A., and HAZELRIGG, L. E. "The Gender of Poverty in an Aging Population." *Research on Aging* 15 (1993): 243–278.
HENRETTA, J. C.; O'RAND, A. M.; and CHAN, C. G. "Gender Differences in Employment After Spouse's Retirement." *Research on Aging* 15 (1993): 148–169.
KOHEN, J. A. "Old but Not Alone: Informal Social Supports Among the Elderly by Marital Status and Sex." *The Gerontologist* 23 (1983): 57–63.
MARKS, N. F. "Midlife Marital Status Differences in Social Support Relationships with Adult Children and Psychological Well-Being." *Journal of Family Issues* 16 (1995): 5–28.

GENERATION

See COHORT CHANGE; AGE-PERIOD-COHORT MODEL

GENERATIONAL EQUITY

Generational equity refers to the concept that different generations should be treated in similar ways and should have similar opportunities. It is often invoked as an issue by those who criticize the share of societal resources that elderly persons consume today and are predicted to consume in the future, when the baby boomers have retired. According to these critics, a trade-off exists between meeting the needs of children and the elderly, and too many resources go to the elderly. This entry presents the history of the debate about generational equity, evaluates the evidence that there is conflict between age groups, and presents an alternative formulation of the notion of generational equity.

History of the debate

Two independent events catapulted the issue of generational equity to visibility in both the policy and the academic communities in 1984. In the policy community, Senator Dave Durenberger (R-Minn.) founded Americans for Generational Equity (AGE). The goal of AGE was to promote the concept of generational equity among America's political, intellectual, and financial leaders. It called into question the prudence, sustainability, and fairness to future generations of federal old age benefit programs. The major vehicles for AGE's message included conferences; books, articles, and op-ed pieces in newspapers; and speeches and comments in the U.S. Congress by a number of prominent AGE leaders who were members of Congress. AGE is now defunct as an organization, but its influence was important in the emergence of the issue of generational equity and in its reshaping of political discourse "so that all future policy choices will have to take generational equity into account" (Quadagno, p. 364). The Concord Coalition, funded by Pete Peterson, an investment banker and former U.S. secretary of commerce, took up where AGE left off. When it was founded, its aim was to bring entitlements (specifically, Social Security and Medicare) "down to a level that's fair to all generations," and its rhetoric was couched in terms of generational equity.

Also in 1984, in the academic community, Professor Samuel H. Preston gave the presidential address to the annual meeting of the Population Association of America, "Children and the Elderly: Divergent Paths for America's Dependents." The address was reprinted in the journal *Demography* and later published in revised form in *Scientific American*. Although Preston never mentioned the term "generational equity" in the address and the subsequent publications, it was clearly his subject. Drawing on large bodies of data on changes in the domains of well-being, the family, and politics, he made the case that conditions have deteriorated for children and improved dramatically for the elderly. Further, he argued that "in the public sphere at least, gains for one group come partly at the expense of another" (Preston, p. 450). According to Preston, U.S. policy makers have made choices that have dramatically altered the age profile of well-being for the young and the old: "Let's be clear that the transfers from the working-age population to the elderly are also transfers away from chil-

dren . . . and let's also recognize that the sums involved are huge" (pp. 451–452).

Since the mid-1980s, references to generational equity have continued. Scholars have held academic conferences; newspapers have carried stories with headlines such as "U.S. Coddles Elderly but Ignores Plight of Children," "America Is at War with Its Children," and "The Tyranny of America's Old" (see Cook et al.); and advocacy groups have debated the issue (see Williamson et al.). The debate that began in the latter half of the 1990s over whether Social Security should be partially privatized offered yet another platform for bringing the issue of generational equity to the foreground (Kingson and Williamson).

Does age conflict exist?

As early as the 1970s, some social scientists warned that one implication of the growing numbers of elders might be a backlash against the old resulting in intergenerational conflict (Neugarten). The emergence of the generational equity debate shows that such concerns were prescient. But is there conflict between age groups either for resources or for support from the public?

Regarding conflict for resources, Preston's argument sparked considerable interest both among scholars and among foundations and agencies to analyze the issue of age group equity in more detail. The National Academy of Sciences, the Alfred P. Sloan Foundation, the Ford Foundation, and the John D. and Catherine T. MacArthur Foundation funded research and a series of conferences and workshops to study the contrasting economic experiences of children and the elderly. Aggregate data from one study compared the experiences of children and the elderly in the United States with those groups in other Western democracies, and replicated one of Preston's major conclusions: the economic experiences of children and elderly persons in the United States diverged widely from the mid-1960s to the mid-1980s. In addition, international comparative data showed that children in the United States have much higher poverty rates than children in most other nations with similar standards of living (Palmer et al.). However, the scholars did not draw the same conclusion as Preston. Instead, they pointed out that it was not at all clear that children's doing worse had enabled the elderly to do better, and showed that U.S. poverty rates for the elderly were on the high side compared with other industrialized nations.

Many professionals dedicated to defending and promoting the interests of America's children see the generational equity debate as a dangerous effort to divide the young and the old and to undercut public support for important government programs such as Social Security. Consequently, they have made a concerted effort to quell the divisive rhetoric of generational equity. Of special importance has been their role in founding Generations United, a group whose goal is to "dispel the myth of competition for scarce resources and reap the benefits of intergenerational collaboration. . .and interdependence" (Generations United, 1990). Further, the organization seeks "to foster intergenerational collaboration on public policy and programs to improve the lives of children, youth, and the elderly" (Generations United, 2001, p. 19). According to David Liederman, former executive director of the Child Welfare League of America, who helped to found Generations United, "What we are trying to say is that the fates of the generations are linked. Obviously, I want better programs for kids. . .but they should not come at the expense of seniors, especially the large number who are poor or near poor" (quoted in Pearlstein).

Is there conflict between age groups in their support for programs for older people? Studies show the answer to this question is no. One of the largest and most visible programs is Social Security. In each congressional election year since 1984, the University of Michigan's National Election Studies (NES) surveys have asked a large, nationally representative sample of Americans whether they would like spending on Social Security increased, decreased, or kept about the same (University of Michigan). In each of the nine election years the question was asked, 90 percent or more of respondents in every age group have said they wanted spending either to be increased or to be kept the same. Less than 7 percent ever said they wanted spending on Social Security decreased. Given the frequent claim that young people do not support Social Security, the most surprising finding is that young people are slightly more likely to support increases in spending than are older persons. For example, in the 2000 NES survey of 1,798 Americans, 62 percent of young adults age eighteen to twenty-nine said they wanted spending for Social Security increased, compared with 60 percent of

respondents age sixty-five to seventy-four and 56 percent of those age seventy-five and over. These findings are similar to earlier research on public support for Medicare and Social Security by Cook and Barrett.

An alternative formulation of generational equity

There is no dispute that America's older citizens receive the lion's share of the income, in cash and in services, that the nation's federal social programs distribute. In 2001, expenditures on the elderly amounted to roughly a third of the entire federal budget (U.S. Office of Management and Budget). But this fact does not imply inequity. That is because the size and distribution of the burdens imposed by children and elderly persons differ. For the most part, parents bear the daily living expenses of children. Their educational costs are borne mostly by state and local governments. The health and income support costs of poor children are shared by the states and the federal government. In contrast, large portions of the income support and health costs of the elderly are borne by the federal government through the Social Security, Medicare, and Supplemental Security Income programs. Thus, as the population ages, the fiscal responsibility of supporting the economically inactive population shifts from families to governments and, within the public sector, from states and localities to the federal government. As Norman Daniels has argued, "Justice between age groups is a problem best solved if we stop thinking of the old and the young as distinct groups. We age. The young become the old. As we age, we pass through institutions that affect our well-being at each stage of life, from infancy to very old age" (p. 18).

From a life course perspective, it follows that an alternative formulation of generational equity is generational interdependence. Kingson et al. discuss the "ties that bind" generations together and stress the high degree of interdependence between individuals and between generations within society. This view emphasizes what different generations have to offer one another as opposed to what one consumes at the expense of the other (Williamson et al.). Such contributions include transfers of income, child care support, personal assistance, formal volunteering, psychological support, and advice.

In line with the notion of generational interdependence, Robert Ball describes Social Security (i.e., Old Age, Survivors, and Disability Insurance) as "America's family protection plan" (p. 11). By this, he means it protects children with the survivors component, working adults under sixty-five with the disability component, and elderly adults with the retirement component. He notes that 98 percent of children under eighteen and mothers and fathers with children under sixteen can count on monthly benefits if a working parent dies; that four out of five people of working age have protection against the loss of income due to sustained disability; and that 95 percent of people sixty-five and older are eligible for Social Security benefits (p. xv).

What of the future? Is generational equity likely to continue as an issue? It is always hard to predict which issues will rise or fall in salience on the agendas of scholars, policy makers, and the media. However, based on the period since the mid-1980s, it would seem that generational equity will continue to be an issue as long as one side or the other in the debate for attention to the reform of social policies and programs thinks its cause is forwarded more by attempts to pit one age group against another than by attempts to find common ground in pursuing the needs of both the elderly and the young.

FAY LOMAX COOK

See also AGE INTEGRATION AND SEGREGATION; INEQUALITY; INTERGENERATIONAL JUSTICE; SOCIAL SECURITY: LONG-TERM FINANCING AND REFORM; WELFARE STATE.

BIBLIOGRAPHY

BALL, R. *Insuring the Essentials.* New York: The Century Foundation, 2000.
COOK, F. L. and BARRETT, E. J. *Support for the American Welfare State: The View of Congress and the Public.* New York: Columbia University Press, 1992.
COOK, F. L.; MARSHAL, V. W.; MARSHALL, J. G.; and KAUFMAN, J. E. "The Salience of Intergenerational Equity in Canada" In *Economic Security and Intergenerational Justice: A Look at North America.* Edited by Theodore R. Marmor, Timothy M. Smeeding, and Vernon L. Green. Washington, D.C.: Urban Institute Press, 1994.
DANIELS, N. *Am I My Parents' Keeper? An Essay on Justice Between the Young and the Old.* New York: Oxford University Press, 1988.
Generations United. *Promoting Cooperation Among Americans of All Ages.* Washington, D.C.: Generations United, 1990.
Generations United. "Generations United Mission." *Together: The Generations United Newsletter* 6, no. 1 (2001): 19.
KINGSON, E. R.; HIRSHORN, B. A.; and CORNMAN, J. M. *Ties That Bind: The Interdependence of Generations.* Washington, D.C.: Seven Locks Press, 1986.
KINGSON, E. R., and WILLIAMSON, J. B. "Why Privatizing Social Security Is a Bad Idea." In *The Generational Equity Debate.* Edited by John B. Williams, Diane M. Watts-Roy, and Eric R. Kingston. New York: Columbia University Press, 1999.
NEUGARTEN, B. L. "Patterns of Aging: Past, Present, and Future." *Social Service Review* 47, no. 4 (1973): 571–580.
PALMER, J.; SMEEDING, T.; and TORREY, B. B., eds. *The Vulnerable.* Washington, D.C.: Urban Institute Press, 1988.
PEARLSTEIN, S. "The Battle over 'Generational Equity': Powerful Spending, Tax Choices Have the Young Calling for the Old to Get Less." *Washington Post* February 17, 1993, p. F1.
PRESTON, S. H. "Children and the Elderly." *U.S. Scientific American* 25, no. 6 (1984): 44–49.
PRESTON, S. H. "Children and the Elderly: Divergent Paths for America's Dependent." *Demography* 21, no. 4 (1984): 435–457.
QUADAGNO, J. "Generational Equity and the Politics of the Welfare State." *Politics and Society* 17, no. 3 (1989): 353–376.
WILLIAMSON, J. B.; WATTS-ROY, D. M.; and KINGSON, E. R., eds. *The Generational Equity Debate.* New York: Columbia University Press, 1999.
U.S. Office of Management and Budget. *Budget of the United States Government, Fiscal Year 2002.* Washington, D.C.: U.S. Government Printing Office, 2001.
University of Michigan. *National Election Studies: Pre-Post-Election Study Dataset.* Ann Arbor, Mich.: University of Michigan, Center for Political Studies, 2001.

GENETICS

Genetics is the branch of biology that deals with heredity—the passing of characteristics (traits) from parents to offspring. The genetics of aging deals with the studies of heredity for traits related to aging, such as life span, age at menopause, age at onset of specific diseases in late life (Alzheimer's disease, prostate cancer, etc.), rate of aging (estimated through tests for biological age), rate-of-change traits, and biomarkers of aging. In practice, most studies are focused on life span, because other reliable markers of aging are lacking or less convenient to use. Therefore, the genetics of aging is closely related to the biology of life span.

Genetics is also the study of the fundamental chemical units of heredity, called *genes*. A gene is a segment of deoxyribonucleic acid (DNA), which carries coded hereditary information. Genes are made up of four types of nitrogenous compounds (called *bases*) known by their first initials: A (adenine), C (cytosine), G (guanine), and T (thymine). The sequence, or code, is the order in which these four bases link up with the sugar deoxyribose and phosphate to form the DNA molecule. To determine the entire sequence of the three billion bases that make up human DNA (the human genome), the U.S. Human Genome Project was initiated in 1990. On 26 June 2000, Celera Genomics announced that it had identified, in general, the sequence of the human genome (with partial use of the Human Genome Project data). The complete sequence is expected to be known by 2003. Many researchers believe that the completion of the Human Genome Project will create a revolution in the identification of the genes involved in the aging process.

The total number of genes in the human genome is still unknown, with estimates around forty-two thousand genes. By comparison, the fruit fly, *Drosophila melanogaster,* has 13,600 genes, while the bacteria *Escherichia coli* has only 4,300 genes. The number of gerontogenes (genes involved in the aging process) remains to be established, but there are no doubts of their existence. For example, in humans, one of the forms of a gene coding for apolipoprotein E (ApoE ε 2) is associated with exceptional longevity and decreased susceptibility to Alzheimer's disease.

Each gene occupies a specific position (locus) on a thread-like structure called a *chromosome*. A chromosome is the linear end-to-end arrangement of genes and other DNA, usually with associated protein and ribonucleic acid (RNA). Chromosomes can be seen in cells with an ordinary microscope. Every human cell (except egg and sperm cells) contains two sets of twenty-three chromosomes—one set from the mother and another set from the father, for a total of forty-six chromosomes. However, the proportion of aberrant cells with "wrong" numbers of chromosomes increases with age, and this may cause cancer and other diseases in later life.

Genetics also involves the study of the mechanism of *gene action*—the way in which genes produce their effect on an organism by influencing biochemical processes during development and aging. The first steps of gene action are well understood in molecular genetics and can be summarized by a simple schema: DNA → RNA → protein. According to this schema, genetic information is first transmitted from DNA to RNA (first arrow corresponding to transcription process), and then from RNA to protein (second arrow corresponding to translation process). In other words, the DNA genetic code ultimately determines the structure (amino acid sequence) of proteins. However, the final steps of gene action in shaping the complex structural, functional, and behavioral traits of an organism, as well as species life span and aging patterns, remain to be understood.

Although genes determine the features an organism may develop, the features that actually develop depend upon the complex interaction between genes and their environment, called *gene-environment interaction*. Gene-environment interactions are important because genes produce their effects in an indirect way (through proteins), and the ultimate outcome of gene action may be different in different circumstances. It is recognized from the effects of diet restriction on mice and other species that gene-environment interactions can greatly modify life span and the rate of aging. Understanding interactions between genes and a restricted diet is important because caloric restriction is known to be the most effective way to extend life span and delay age-related diseases in mammals.

Many of the genes within a given cell are inactive (repressed) much, or even all, of the time. Different genes can be switched on or off depending on cell specialization (differentiation)—a phenomenon called *differential gene expression*. Gene expression may change over time within a given cell during development and aging. Changes in differential gene expression are vitally important for cell differentiation during early child development, but they may persist further in later life and become the driving force of the aging process. Some researchers believe that pharmacological control over differential gene expression in later life may be a feasible approach in the future to slow down the aging process and to increase life span.

Occasionally, changes may occur in a gene or in a chromosome set of a cell, making it different from the original (wild) type. The process that produces such changes is called *mutation*. This term is also used to label the gene or chromosome set that results from mutation process. In many cases, mutations are caused by DNA damage, including oxidative damage or radiation damage (by ultraviolet light, ionizing radiation, or heat). Every time cells divide the risk of mutation increases. This is because mistakes (copy errors) are likely to occur during copying (replication) of a huge DNA molecule in a dividing cell. Accumulation of deleterious mutations with age is one of the possible mechanisms of aging.

Genetics also involves the study of how the aging and life span of progeny depend on parental characteristics, such as parental life span and parental age at conception. Familial resemblance in life span between parents and children is very small when parents live shorter lives (30–70 years) and very strong in the case of longer-lived parents, suggesting an unusual nonlinear pattern of life span inheritance. Also, children conceived by fathers at an older age have more inborn mutations and may be at higher risk of Alzheimer's disease and prostate cancer in later life. Daughters conceived by fathers age forty-five and older live shorter lives, on average, while sons seems to be unaffected in this regard, suggesting the possible role of mutations on the paternal X chromosome (inherited by daughters only) in the aging process.

LEONID A. GAVRILOV
NATALIA S. GAVRILOVA

See also EVOLUTION OF AGING; GENETICS: GENE-ENVIRONMENT INTERACTION; GENETICS: GENE EXPRESSION; GENETICS: LONGEVITY ASSURANCE; GENETICS: PARENTAL INFLUENCE; GENETICS: TUMOR SUPPRESSION; LONGEVITY: SELECTION; MUTATION.

BIBLIOGRAPHY

ARKING, R. *Biology of Aging: Observations and Principles*, 2d ed. Sunderland, Mass.: Sinauer Associates, 1998.
CARNES, B. A.; OLSHANSKY, S. J.; GAVRILOV, L. A.; GAVRILOVA, N. S.; and GRAHN, D. "Human Longevity: Nature vs. Nurture—Fact or Fiction." *Perspectives in Biology and Medicine* 42 (1999): 422–441.
FINCH, C. E., and TANZI, R. E. "Genetics of Aging." *Science* 278 (1997): 407–411.
GAVRILOV, L. A., and GAVRILOVA, N. S. *The Biology of Life Span: A Quantitative Approach.* New York: Harwood Academic Publisher, 1991.
GAVRILOV, L. A., and GAVRILOVA, N. S. "Human Longevity and Parental Age at Conception." In *Sex and Longevity: Sexuality, Gender, Reproduction, Parenthood.* Edited by J.-M. Robine, et al. Berlin: Springer-Verlag, 2000. Pages 7–31.
GAVRILOVA, N. S., et al. "Evolution, Mutations and Human Longevity: European Royal and Noble Families." *Human Biology* 70 (1998): 799–804.
MARTIN, G. M.; AUSTAD, S. N.; and JOHNSON, T. E. "Genetic Analysis of Ageing: Role of Oxidative Damage and Environmental Stresses." *Nature Genetics* 13 (1996): 25–34.
VOGEL, F., and MOTULSKY, A. G. *Human Genetics. Problems and Approaches*, 3d ed. Berlin: Springer-Verlag, 1997.

GENETICS: ETHNICITY

Ethnicity is a term used for categorizing the highly diverse human populations into more homogeneous and distinct *ethnic groups,* based on their common ancestry and cultural characteristics. An ethnic group is defined as a category of people that, in a larger population, is set apart (to some extent) and bound together (through preferential intermarriage) by common ties of race, language, nationality, or culture. Commonly recognized American ethnic groups include American Indians; Latinos; Chinese; African Americans ("blacks"); and Italians, Irish, and other European Americans ("whites"). Ethnic classifications are rather arbitrary—they change over time ("today's ethnicities are yesterday's races"), and they are different in different countries. For example, a person of Pakistani origin is considered *black* or *colored* in the United Kingdom, but would be classified as *white* or *Asian* in the United States. Despite obvious limitations, ethnic classification is useful in aging studies because it allows researchers to explore ethnic differences in aging, longevity, and age-related diseases, as well as the possible role of genetic factors in those differences.

Ethnic groups differ significantly in terms of incidence rates and mortality rates from age-related degenerative diseases, including different types of cancer. For example, black Americans have a three-times higher risk of developing esophageal cancer; twice the risk of developing multiple myeloma, liver, cervical, and stomach cancer; and a 50 percent higher risk for cancers of the oral cavity and pharynx, larynx, lung, prostate, and pancreas. In contrast, white Americans have higher incidence rates for melanoma, leukemia, lymphoma, and cancers of the endometrium, thyroid, bladder (in males), ovary, testes, and brain, as well as postmenopausal breast cancer. These ethnic differences are attributed to interactions between genetic and lifestyle factors, such as genetic susceptibility to carcinogens (different in different ethnic groups) and ethnic variations in exposure to certain pollutants. In the case of Ashkenazi Jews, a specific mutation (185delAG) has been found in this ethnic group that increases twenty-seven-fold the risk of early-onset breast cancer in females (1 percent of this ethnic group carries the mutation).

Significant ethnic differences are found for apolipoprotein-E genetic polymorphisms, which are important determinants of blood-lipid levels, atherosclerosis, and longevity. Specifically, the epsilon 4 allele for this apolipoprotein (ApoE4) is more prevalent in African Americans (21 percent) than in non-Hispanic whites (12 percent) or Hispanics (14 percent). The frequency of this allele is inversely correlated with human longevity, and persons with ApoE4 have a doubled risk of Alzheimer's disease.

Sensational reports have often been published in newspapers and magazines claiming an unusually high percentage of centenarians in some exotic ethnic group, remote geographic area, or isolated religious community. The most famous claims of unusual longevity were made for the Vilcabamba population in Ecuador; for remote Caucasus and Altay populations in the former Soviet Union; and for the Old Order Amish religious communities. Later studies found that these claims were either unsubstantiated or even incorrect because of systematic age exaggeration. Thus, the relationship between ethnicity and exceptional longevity remains to be thoroughly studied. It is interesting to note that the highest scientifically validated longevity world records (122 years and 117 years) belong to women of French ethnicity.

NATALIA S. GAVRILOVA
LEONID A. GAVRILOV

See also ACCELERATED AGING: HUMAN PROGEROID SYNDROMES; EPIDEMIOLOGY; GENETICS.

BIBLIOGRAPHY

CASTRO, E.; OGBURN, C. E.; HUNT, K. E.; TILVIS, R.; LOUHIJA, J.; PENTTINEN, R.; ERKKOLA, R.; PANDURO, A.; RIESTRA, R.; PIUSSAN, C.; DEEB, S. S.; WANG, L.; EDLAND, S. D.; MARTIN, G. M.; and OSHIMA, J. "Polymorphisms at the Werner Locus: I. Newly Identified Polymorphisms, Ethnic Variability of 1367Cy/Arg, and Its Stability in a Population of Finnish Centenarians." *American Journal of Medical Genetics* 82 (1999): 399–403.

GAVRILOV, L. A., and GAVRILOVA, N. S. "Validation of Exceptional Longevity. Book Review." *Population and Development Review* 26 (2000): 40–41.

HAVLIK, R. J.; IZMIRLIAN, G.; PETROVITCH, H.; WEBSTER, R. G.; MASAKI, K.; CURB, J. D.; SAUNDERS, A. M.; FOLEY, D. J.; BROCK, D.; LAUNER, L. J.; and WHITE, L. "APOE-Epsilon4 Predicts Incident AD in Japanese-American Men: The Honolulu-Asia Aging Study." *Neurology* 11 (2000): 1526–1529.

PABLOS-MENDEZ, A.; MAYEUX, R.; NGAI, C.; SHEA, S.; and BERGLUND, L. "Association of Apo E Polymorphism with Plasma Lipid Levels in a Multiethnic Elderly Population." *Arteriosclerosis Thrombosis and Vascular Biology* 17 (1997): 3534–3541.

PERERA, F. P. "Environment and Cancer: Who Are Susceptible?" *Science* 278 (1997): 1068–1073.

GENETICS: GENDER

Most of the differences between human males and females are based on the chromosomal mechanism of sex determination—two X-chromosomes in females and one X chromosome and one Y chromosome in males. There is a gene on the Y chromosome (called Sry) that encodes a protein (called testis differention factor (TDF)) that is required for testicular development. The testes secrete male sex hormones (androgens), which set in motion a cascade that affects both biology and behavior and makes men and women very different creatures.

These differences affect aging, beginning by the fifth decade of life. The death rate, which increases exponentially with age, was 1.7 times higher in males of the fifty-five to fifty-nine age group in 1998 than in females. This difference is largely because of diseases of the circulatory system, in which the male death rate was 2.3 times the female rate in this age group. The estrogenic hormones secreted by the ovaries modulate circulating cholesterol levels, with higher levels of low-density lipoprotein (LDL) cholesterol and lower levels of high-density lipoprotein (HDL) cholesterol in males on the average. The male pattern is associated with greater risk of death from heart disease. At reproductive senescence, with involution of the gonads, the protective effects of estrogens are lost, and eventually the death rate from heart disease in females catches up with that of males. Another consequence of the cessation of estrogen production at reproductive senescence is the gradual demineralization of bone, resulting in osteoporosis, with its attendant fractures. This, plus a likely effect on cholesterol, provide the rationale for taking postmenopausal estrogens.

Another disease contributing in a major way to the higher male death rate is lung cancer, in which the death rate of males in the fifty-five to fifty-nine age group is 1.7 times the female death rate. The difference is related to the greater rate of smoking among males.

A consequence of the differing death rates is a difference in the life expectancies at birth of males and females, with a greater life expectancy seen in females in all developed countries. This gender gap in longevities was 6.7 years in 1998 in the United States (73.5 years vs. 80.2 years). It ranges from 6.5 years to 8.5 years in other developed countries. A social consequence of the gender gap is that the sex ratio, which is 1.05 (males/females) at birth is about 0.33 at age eighty-five. Widows greatly outnumber widowers. In general, men die quickly of catastrophic illnesses while women become older and suffer from more chronic diseases. An important example is Alzheimer's disease. A major part of its greater incidence in women is that they live longer, but there is a greater female prevalence even after adjustment or stratification for age.

Interestingly, those males who survive to an advanced age are, on the average, in better condition than females of the same age.

DAVID W. E. SMITH

BIBLIOGRAPHY

FRATIGLIONI, L.; VIITANIN, M.; VON STRAUSS, E.; TONTODONATI, V.; HERLITZ, A.; and WINBLAD, B. "Very Old Women at Risk of Dementia and Alzheimer's Disease." *Neurology* 48 (1997): 132–138.
KOOPMAN, P. "Sry and Sox 9: Mammalian Testis-determining Genes." *Cellular and Molecular Sciences* 55 (1999): 839–856.
National Center for Health Statistics. "Vital Statistics of the United States: Mortality 1979– 1998." Tables 292a. Available on the Internet at www.cdc/nchs/
SMITH, D. W. E. "Women Live Longer than Men." In *Human Longevity*. Oxford, U.K., and New York: Oxford University Press, 1993. Pages 71–98.
SMITH, D. W. E. "Centenarians: Longevity Outliers." *The Gerontologist* 37 (1997): 200–207.

GENETICS: GENE-ENVIRONMENT INTERACTION

Fundamentally, the science of genetics is concerned with the explanation of differences among organisms. Some theories and methods pertain to the differences among species; others concern the individual differences among members of the same species—the subject matter of this section.

Historically, Mendelian genetics was categorical, dealing with individual differences that could be characterized by assignment of individuals to one or another of two or three categories. Analytic logic compared the observed categorical status of individuals to expectations (hypotheses) derived from Mendel's theory. As long as category assignment was unambiguous, it was a matter of small concern that there might exist individual differences within categories, derived presumably from environmental sources or from genes other than the one under examination. Enormous advances in understanding the basics of inheritance were made from the comfortably simple logical stance of "all and only" causal analysis—all cases of a particular genotype (genetic constitution) were accompanied by the particular phenotype (a measured or observed attribute), and all cases of the phenotype occurred in the presence of that genotype. There were some puzzling exceptions, however. Sometimes, individuals who almost certainly had a particular genotype did not display the associated phenotype. Furthermore, it was observed that the actual manifestation of the phenotype could vary greatly among individuals with the same genotype (with respect to the relevant single locus). Explanations were sought for these cases of reduced penetrance or variable expressivity both in terms of the effects of "modifier" genes or of environmental influence on the phenotype.

The biometrical approach to inheritance concerned phenotypic domains that were not di-

or trichotomous but were instead continuously distributed. Individuality was measured as variance rather than as categorical membership and the logic underlying analysis concerned the degree of phenotypic similarity of individuals of differing degrees of biological relatedness. Initially thought to concern a fundamentally different type of inheritance from the Mendelian, it was shown early in the twentieth century that the basic difference was in the effect size of the relevant genetic factors. Quantitative or continuously distributed phenotypes were theorized to be due to the collective influence of many genes (polygenic inheritance), each of which acted according to Mendelian rules but with individually small effects. The statistical model of quantitative genetics identifies both genetic and environmental sources of individuality, and partitions the variability among individuals into components attributable to these domains. The model also necessarily acknowledges, by means of interaction and covariance terms, the possibilities of interrelationships of factors from these domains.

Thus, with respect both to classical genes of major categorical effect and the polygenes of quantitatively distributed phenotypes, the possibility that the influences of genes are importantly conditioned by environmental context must be considered. This section will provide examples of the interconnectedness of genetic and environmental effects with particular reference to age and aging, including both classical statistical interaction and reciprocal influence between the genetic and environmental domains. It is not intended to be an exhaustive review, but merely to be illustrative of the types of interaction and coaction that can be expected as research on genetic influence on aging processes advances.

Gene-environment interactions

Simply defined, gene-environment interaction refers to situations in which environmental influences have a different effect depending upon genotype, and genetic factors have a differential effect depending upon features of the environment. Such interactions have been found in a wide array of phenotypes in diverse organisms across the phyletic spectrum. Particularly persuasive are data from experimental settings, where different environmental circumstances can be imposed upon groups of differing genotypes. Numerous studies, for example, have shown that different inbred strains of animals re-

spond differently to environmental variables (McClearn et al.). Inbreeding is simply the mating of relatives, which has the effect of reducing genetic heterogeneity in the offspring. Thus, after a number of consecutive generations of inbreeding, the animals within each inbred strain approach the condition of being genetically identical (technically, homozygous in like state at all loci). Because of the stochastic nature of the process through which the homozygosity is achieved, different strains inevitably have different genotypes. Thus, phenotypic differences between strains tested under the same conditions are evidence of genetic influence on the phenotype, even though specific genetic information concerning the number and chromosomal locations of the relevant polygenes is unknown. Similarly, strain differences in the impact of an administered environmental variable reveal a genetic basis for susceptibility to that environmental intervention.

Another genetic procedure available to the animal model researcher is selective breeding. Animals of a genetically heterogeneous population are measured for a particular phenotype; a subset of those with highest values and another subset with lowest values are selected. The "high" animals are mated together, as are the "low" animals. If there is any heritable influence on the phenotype, then offspring from the high-phenotype matings should have higher phenotypic values than that of the entire population from which their parents were selected, and similarly, the offspring from the matings of low-phenotype parents should have lower values. In subsequent generations, with similar continued selection, the increasing phenotypic separation of the high and low lines constitutes clear evidence of the existence of genetic factors affecting the phenotype. By contrast to inbred strains, in which the particular genotypes were simply made homogeneous without regard to any specific phenotype, bidirectionally selected lines represent contrasting groups in which (ideally) all of the genetic factors promoting a high level of phenotypic expression have been concentrated in one group and those promoting a low level in the other group. Such lines are powerful resources for testing hypotheses concerning the physiological mechanisms through which the genes are expressed. Both inbred strains and selected lines offer evidence on gene-environment interaction.

Several investigators have employed selective breeding for early and late onset of reproduction in *Drosophila* in order to generate long-lived and short-lived lines. Luckinbill and colleagues have described a clear example of gene-environment interaction in the course of these selection studies. When selection is attempted from an environment in which larval density is high, the results of selection have been positive; when larval density was thinned, however, no response to selection occurred. The first result gives unequivocal evidence of the existence of genetic variance of the selected trait under the crowded condition, and indicates absence of this genetic variance in the less crowded environment.

Some of the most pertinent mammalian examples concern rodent learning. A classic example is that of Cooper and Zubek, who assessed the influence of different rearing environments on the maze-learning performance of better learners and poorer learners produced by selective breeding. Samples of animals from each line were reared under controlled, environmentally enriched or environmentally impoverished conditions. Overall, the influence of environment was clear, with the number of errors in the test situation declining from the impoverished through the control to the enriched condition. However, the interaction with genotype was notable. The "bright" rats were adversely affected by the impoverished environment, but were not facilitated by the enriched one; the "dull" rats were not affected by impoverishment, but were improved substantially by enrichment. It is clear that the results can be stated equally as (1) the effect of the genotypic differences depending on the environment, or (2) the effect of the environment depending on the genotype.

With animals derived from a similar selective breeding program, McGaugh and Cole added the dimension of age. Samples of the "maze-bright" and "maze-dull" rats were measured at about one month and about five months of age. The environmental feature under examination was the degree of massing of practice during maze learning. When the intertrial interval was only thirty seconds, at the younger age, there were no differences between the lines in performance. When the intertrial interval was thirty minutes, young bright animals performed better than the dull animals. Interaction with sex was also observed: Although all older animals benefitted from distribution of practice, older females

of the two lines did not differ under either degree of massing, but older bright males outperformed older dull males.

Sprott provided similar evidence from a study of passive avoidance learning in inbred mice. At a particular foot shock level, animals of one strain (C57BL/6) were superior to another (DBA/2) at five weeks of age, but were inferior at five months of age. These illustrative results collectively make it clear that the interaction of environments and genes may not be uniform temporally. The existence or nature of the interaction can change across age.

A final example of the use of inbred strains in detecting gene-environment interaction in phenomena of gerontological interest is the study of Fosmire and colleagues. Motivated by the inconsistent evidence that aluminum exposure may be a risk factor for the development of Alzheimer's disease, these investigators examined the effect of an elevated aluminum content in the diet of mice on brain aluminum levels. Five different inbred strains were studied, with a control group and a treatment group within each strain. There were different brain aluminum levels among the control animals who had the regular laboratory diet, showing a heritable basis for differential uptake of the metal under "ordinary" conditions. When exposed to the aluminum enriched diet, the treatment animals of three strains did not differ from the control animals of the same strain. One strain showed a slight effect, and one displayed a large response, with brain aluminum levels over three times that of their controls. These results indicate that there exist genetic factors that influence the physiological processes affecting uptake and distribution of dietary aluminum. Although this study does not address the possible pathophysiological consequences of aluminum, its heuristic value lies in showing a genetic basis of responsivity to environment. By extension, we may presume that the principle applies generally, whether the environmental feature is a putative toxin or a putative therapeutic pharmaceutical.

It will be noted that the above examples have all concerned anonymous complexes of polygenes. The recent advances in characterizing the human genome and those of other model organisms have provided a potent research approach to the individuating of some of the polygenes in such systems, with greatly enhanced insights into the nature of the genetic influence on quantitative traits, and also of the interaction of the genes with environments. The large number of genotype markers now available make it possible to describe the approximate location on the chromosomes of genes of detectable influence on a particular phenotype. These genes, not described in molecular terms, are called quantitative trait loci (QTLs). A remarkable demonstration of the potential of QTL analysis in gerontology has been provided by Vieira and others, who identified QTLs affecting longevity in populations of *Drosophila* maintained under five environmental conditions: three different maintenance temperatures, a single heat shock exposure, or restricted nutrients. The results were a remarkable assortment of interactions. Seventeen QTLs were identified. One has an influence on life span only in the high temperature environment; another only in the starvation environment. Several are specific to one sex only, and in only some environments. One is specific to females and the same allele that has positive influence on life span in the control environment has a negative effect in the high temperature environment. Another has opposite effects in males and females in the heat-shock environment, and one similarly has opposite effects in males and females in the high temperature environment. An overall quantitative genetic analysis revealed that all of the genetic variance was to be found in the interactions of sex X genotype and environment X genotype!

Some loci may have an influence that is substantially additive across the usually encountered environments; others may be so sensitive as to be influencing the phenotype in some environments but not in others, and perhaps in different directions in different environments.

Reciprocal influence of genes and environments

In addition to the types of interaction cited above, there are other ways in which the effects of genes and environments are intertwined: environments can influence gene expression, and genes may affect the array of environments to which an organism is exposed (or exposes itself). These processes can lead to correlation between genotype and environment.

The influence of environment on the expression of genes was classically demonstrated in the operon model of Jacob and Monod, a landmark in the history of molecular genetics. Changes in the nutrient composition of the media of *E. coli* resulted in the "turning on" of the organism's gene that produces the appropriate enzyme for metabolism of lactose. Subsequent research on gene regulation has revealed that the particular genes of an organism that are being expressed may differ from time to time, both developmentally and in response to environmental factors. There has been, for example, a burgeoning of information about the effects of various stressors on gene expression. Described as "heat shock genes" because of the early experimental situations involving brief administration of a high-temperature environment to bacteria and *Drosophila*, this literature now includes examples of various environmental stresses both *in vitro* and *in vivo*, and in several species. As a general summary, these stressors have the effect of inhibiting the typical ongoing protein production of the cells, and promoting the translation of genes that produce a class of proteins that have a protective function in the cells. The rich detail of this research area complements the generalization that has emerged from quantitative genetic analyses in a variety of species, plant as well as animal, that the heritability of quantitatively distributed traits—the portion of the phenotypic variance attributable to genetic differences among the organisms—is often increased under conditions of environmental stress (Hoffman and Parsons).

It has long been appreciated that different loci are expressed in different tissues, and that different loci may be active at different developmental periods. The observations of Rogina and Helfand, who have described a typical life-span pattern of expression of a particular locus in the antennae of *Drosophila*, are particularly pertinent to the conceptualization of genetic and environmental influences on aging. Beginning at low levels, mRNA from this locus rises to a peak at midlife, with a subsequent decline to the initial low levels. In different temperature environments that influence *Drosophila* life span, the rising and falling of the mRNA level is altered, but the form of the function relative to the total life span under the particular environmental circumstances is remarkably preserved. This result can be interpreted as identifying an "intrinsic" pattern of gene expression over the life span, the temporal parameters of which are strongly influenced by environmental temperature. Another age-related illustration of environments affecting gene expression is that of Lee and colleagues, who used a gene array of the gastrocnemius muscle of mice to describe differences in the gene expression profile at five months and thirty months of age. Under conditions of caloric restriction, well established as a life-extending environmental intervention, most of the described gene expression changes were prevented or delayed.

There is also a growing literature concerning the role of genetics in determining the environment to which an organism is exposed. The field of microhabitat selection has provided plentiful illustration of organisms seeking environmental circumstances most suited to some aspect of their gene-influenced physiology. A case in point is that of selection of environments with or without the presence of alcohol by *Drosophila* larvae with different genotypes affecting alcohol dehydrogenase activity (Cavener). The scope for selecting from the array of environmental niches (or making them) is particularly pronounced in human beings (see Bergeman et al.).

Summary

The examples cited here make it clear that conclusions about the effect of a genetic locus must be interpreted cautiously. The detectability, effect size, or even direction of effect may be strongly contingent upon environmental circumstances. It is increasingly clear that the effective genotype—those loci actually being expressed at any given time—may change not only developmentally but also relatively quickly in response to an environmental alteration. It is equally the case that the effect of any environmental influence will depend upon the genotypes of the organisms exposed to that environment. Recognition of the scope for mutuality and reciprocity of genetic and environmental influences is important both for basic understanding of aging processes and for the design and application of interventions intended to extend life span and health span.

GERALD E. MCCLEARN

See also NUTRITION; PATHOLOGY OF AGING, HUMAN FACTORS; STRESS.

BIBLIOGRAPHY

BERGEMAN, C. S.; PLOMIN, R.; PEDERSEN, N. L.; MCCLEARN, G. E.; and NESSELROADE, J. R. "Genetic and Environmental Influences on Social Support: The Swedish Adoption/Twin Study of Aging." *Journal of Gerontology* 45 (1990): 101–106.

CAVENER, D. "Preference for Ethanol in *Drosophila melanogaster* Associated with the Alcohol Dehydrogenase Polymorphism." *Behavior Genetics* 9 (1979): 159–165.

COOPER, R. M., and ZUBEK, J. P. "Effects of Enriched and Restricted Early Environments on the Learning Ability of Bright and Dull Rats." *Canadian Journal of Psychology* 12 (1958): 159–164.

FOSMIRE, G. J.; FOCHT, S. J.; and MCCLEARN, G. E. "Genetic Influences on Tissue Deposition of Aluminum in Mice." *Biological Trace Element Research* 37 (1993): 115–121.

HELFAND, S. L.; BLAKE, K. J.; ROGINA, B.; STRACKS, M. D.; CENTURION, A.; and NAPRTA, B. "Temporal Patterns of Gene Expression in the Antenna of the Adult *Drosophila melanogaster.*" *Genetics* 140 (1995): 549–555.

HOFFMAN, A. A., and PARSONS, P. A. *Evolutionary Genetics and Environmental Stress*. Oxford, U.K.: Oxford University Press, 1991.

JACOB, F., and MONOD, J. "Genetic Regulatory Mechanisms in the Synthesis of Proteins." *Journal of Molecular Biology* 3 (1961): 318–356.

LEE, C.; KLOPP, R. G.; WEINDRUCH, R.; and PROLLA, T. A. "Gene Expression Profile of Aging and Its Retardation by Caloric Restriction." *Science* 285 (1999): 1390–1393.

LUCKINBILL, L. S.; ARKING, R.; CLARE, M. J.; CIROCCO, W. C.; and BUCK, S. A. "Selection for Delayed Senescence in *Drosophila melanogaster.*" *Evolution* 3 (1984): 996–1003.

MCCLEARN, G. E.; VOGLER, G. P.; and HOFER, S. M. "Environment-Gene and Gene-Gene Interactions." In *Handbook of the Biology of Aging*, 5th ed. Edited by E. J. Massoro and S. N. Austad. San Diego, Calif.: Academic Press, 2001. Chap. 16.

MCGAUGH, J. L., and COLE, J. M. "Age and Strain Differences in the Effect of Distribution of Practice on Maze Learning." *Psychonomic Science* 2 (1965): 253–254.

ROGINA, B., and HELFAND, S. L. "Regulation of Gene Expression is Linked to Life Span in Adult *Drosophila.*" *Genetics* 141 (1995): 1043–1048.

SPROTT, R. L. "Passive-avoidance Conditioning in Inbred Mice: Effects of Shock Intensity, Age, and Genotype." *Journal of Comparative Physiology and Psychology* 80 (2000): 327–334.

VIEIRA, C.; PASYUKOVA, E. G.; ZENG, Z.; HACKETT, J. B.; LYMAN, R. F.; and MACKAY, T. F. C. "Genotype-environment Interaction for Quantitative Trait Loci Affecting Life Span in *Drosophila melanogaster.*" *Genetics* 154 (2000): 213–227.

GENETICS: GENE EXPRESSION

Genomes contain all the genetic information needed by an organism, regardless of the circumstance or environment. Generally, however, even single-cell organisms use only a fraction of their genome at any time; that is, cells generally express only a fraction of their genome at any given time. This is especially true among the individual cells that make up multicellular organisms, where cell specialization (differentiation) dictates that only certain genes be expressed in certain cells, and only at particular times during the organism's life span.

Genes and noncoding DNA

In most organisms, genes are composed of discrete segments of DNA. Genes code for all of the proteins and structural RNA molecules used by cells within an organism. The coding segments of genes are often flanked by segments, or elements, that provide regulatory information. Regulatory elements control gene expression—the process that produces a functional protein or RNA molecule from the encoding DNA. Many steps in the control of gene expression are similar between prokaryotes (organisms, such as bacteria, that lack a nucleus) and eukaryotes (organisms that have a nucleus), and between simple and complex eukaryotes, although some features differ among these classes of organisms. Except where noted, the discussion below focuses on complex eukaryotes.

Regulatory DNA. Regulatory DNA includes several types of sequence elements that dictate when and how a gene is expressed. Among the most important of these are the *promoters*—the sequences that direct the start of transcription (the process that transcribes DNA into RNA; discussed below). Regulatory DNA elements also determine under what environmental, developmental, or physiological circumstances a gene is transcribed. Regulatory elements may stimulate or repress transcription by directly binding specific transcriptional activator or repressor proteins. They may also stimulate or repress transcription indirectly by binding proteins that alter the compaction of the DNA, and hence the accessibility of the promoters and other elements to binding proteins. Promoters and some regulatory elements are generally within a few hundred base pairs of the first coding segment of a gene.

Other regulatory elements, particularly those that act indirectly, can be many thousands of base pairs away from genes.

Chromatin. DNA is virtually never naked (devoid of proteins) in cells. Rather, DNA in cells is packaged into *chromatin*—a complex of DNA and protein. Minimally, DNA is bound by *histones,* proteins that form a positively charged core around which 150 to 200 nucleotides of DNA are wrapped. Each core histone-DNA complex defines a *nucleosome.* Nucleosomes are separated by short DNA segments or linkers, which are bound by a noncore histone. Many other proteins bind nucleosomal DNA. Some of these regulate the higher order organization of nucleosomal DNA into secondary coils or folded threads, which in turn are organized into large loops, the bases of which are anchored to the nuclear matrix. Chromatin loops may define domains of *heterochromatin,* which is highly compact and relatively inaccessible to the transcription machinery, or *euchromatin,* which is relatively open and accessible to the transcription machinery.

Noncoding DNA. The coding segments of genes (exons) are often interspersed with relatively large noncoding segments (introns). Introns are initially transcribed into RNA but are subsequently removed by the process of RNA splicing. The functions of introns are not well understood, but at least some introns contain transcriptional control elements. In addition, some introns contain sequences that bind the nuclear matrix, and hence may influence whether genes are in heterochromatic or euchromatic chromatin loops.

Complex eukaryotic genomes contain other large DNA segments that do not encode genes. Some of these are important structural components of chromosomes (e.g., telomeres and centromeres). Others have no obvious structural or regulatory role, though understanding of noncoding DNA sequences is still very incomplete.

Flow of genetic information

Genes are transcribed into RNA by the process of transcription. Some RNA molecules are functional in and of themselves. Examples include the RNA components of certain enzymes (e.g., telomerase); transfer RNA (tRNA), which delivers amino acids to the ribosome for protein synthesis; and ribosomal RNA (rRNA), a structural component of the ribosome. Other RNA

Figure 1

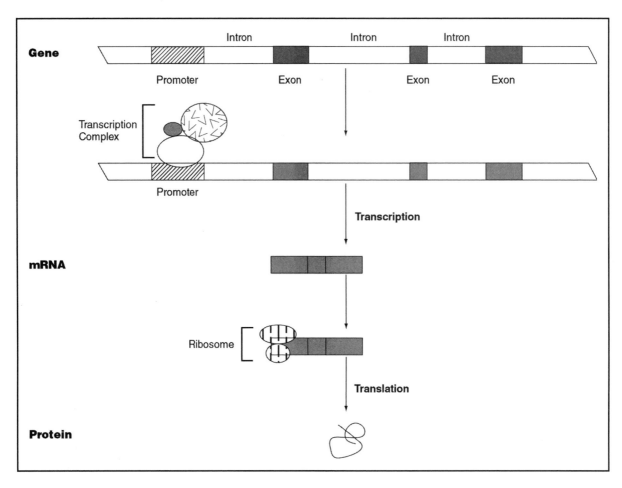

SOURCE: Author

molecules are intermediaries in protein synthesis. Such RNAs are processed in the nucleus into messenger RNA (mRNA) molecules. mRNAs are then exported to the cytoplasm, where they bind ribosomes and direct synthesis of the encoded protein by the process of translation.

Genes are *expressed* when their ultimate products (RNAs or proteins) are produced. Sometimes, genes encoding proteins are considered expressed when they are simply transcribed, but it should be remembered that the proteins, not the transcripts, are the functional products.

Control of gene expression

Gene expression is controlled at multiple levels, including transcription (initiation and elongation), posttranscriptional processing, RNA

stability, RNA export and association with ribosomes, translation (initiation and elongation), and posttranslational processing. Each level tends to be highly regulated and complex. Moreover, each level requires the cooperation of both general and cell-type-specific proteins.

Just as phenotypic differences among species are due to differences in the genes encoded by their genomes, differences among cell types within an organism are largely due to differences with which genes within a genome are transcribed. The genomes of multicellular organisms contain genes that are transcribed in all or most cell types, as well as genes whose transcription is confined to specific cells. From the earliest stages of embryogenesis, transcription is confined to only certain segments of the genome, depending on the cell type and stage of development. Thus, cellular differentiation—the process by which cells acquire and maintain specialized functions—generally entails the differential activation and repression of gene transcription. Differential gene transcription is generally regulated at two broad levels.

Control by transcriptional activators and repressors. All genes are transcribed by the transcription machinery, which consists of a large protein complex. The basal transcription complex contains the core proteins needed to recognize promoter sequences, unwind the DNA duplex, and initiate, elongate, and terminate the primary transcript. This complex also contains proteins that recognize certain types of DNA damage and can recruit proteins to repair the transcribed DNA strand. The basal transcription complex interacts with a large number of specific transcriptional activators and repressors (transcription factors)—regulatory proteins that bind elements outside the immediate promoter region. These regulatory proteins, then, dictate whether or not the basal transcription complex initiates transcription.

Some cells express highly specialized transcription factors that regulate the expression of genes confined to that cell type or its precursors. For example, muscle cells express specific factors that control the transcription of genes encoding muscle-specific proteins. Although these transcription factors can stimulate muscle-specific gene transcription in some nonmuscle cells (e.g., fibroblasts), they cannot activate muscle-specific gene transcription in many other cell types. Moreover, some cell-type-specific genes are controlled by transcription factors that are expressed by many different cell types. Thus, the presence of specific transcriptional activators and repressors alone is generally insufficient for cell-type-specific gene transcription. In addition to the presence of specific transcription factors, the target genes must be in an accessible chromatin state.

Control by chromatin state and epigenetic inheritance. In general, genes located within heterochromatin are inaccessible to the transcriptional machinery, and thus are not expressed, despite the presence of specific transcriptional activators. Such genes are said to be *silenced* in order to distinguish them from unexpressed genes in euchromatin. Unexpressed genes in euchromatin remain accessible to the transcriptional machinery, and thus can readily respond to physiological or environmental signals. Silenced

genes, by contrast, cannot respond to external signals unless the signal includes one to remodel the chromatin (that is, reset the boundaries of heterochromatin and euchromatin). Whether a DNA segment is heterochromatic or euchromatic is generally determined during embryogenesis. The mechanisms that control the state of chromatin are incompletely understood. They include reversible changes to the DNA, such as methylation of cytosine, as well as reversible changes to chromatin proteins, such as acetylation of histones.

The state of chromatin is an important mechanism for initiating and maintaining differential gene expression in multicellular organisms. In adult organisms, the state of the chromatin is generally stably and faithfully maintained, even though chromatin-associated proteins are transiently stripped from the DNA during the processes of replication or repair. Thus, once the pattern of chromatin is established in a differentiated cell, it is stably inherited from one cell generation to the next. This form of inheritance is termed *epigenetic* inheritance, since it does not entail irreversible changes to genomic DNA.

Gene expression and aging

Age-dependent changes in the expression of specific genes have been found in virtually all organisms and tissues that have been tested. These changes have been found to occur at all levels, ranging from the initiation of gene transcription to the posttranslational modification of proteins. In many cases, it has been difficult to decipher which changes in gene expression are responsible for aging phenotypes, as opposed to which changes are responses (whether adaptive or maladaptive) to primary age-related changes in tissues, cells, or molecules.

Despite the many age-related changes in gene expression that have been documented, some general principles and common themes have emerged. First, the expression patterns of many genes do not change with age. This fact has been established by the use of cDNA microarrays, which can assess the levels of mRNA corresponding to hundreds or thousands of genes in a single experiment. The microarray analyses indicate that, at most, only a few percent of the genes expressed by a given tissue or cell type show an age-dependent increase or decrease in mRNA levels.

Second, in many instances, aged cells or tissues appear to be in a chronically stressed state.

The origin of this stress is not clear, but may include exogenous or endogenous oxidative damage or subacute inflammation. Whatever the origin, aged cells and tissues frequently show changes in gene expression that appear to be an adaptive response to stress. In mouse liver, for example, a transcription factor that activates the expression of genes encoding acute-phase proteins increases with age. The acute-phase response is invoked when tissues are inflamed or oxidatively stressed. Similarly, some heat-shock proteins are modestly but constitutively elevated in aged organisms (e.g., *Drosophila*), tissues (e.g., mouse liver), and cells (e.g., senescent human fibroblasts). The heat-shock response is induced by stresses that cause damaged or misfolded proteins to accumulate. The idea that some age-related changes in gene expression are adaptive is supported by microarray analyses of cells and tissues from calorically restricted animals. Caloric restriction extends the life span of many organisms. It also reverses some, but certainly not all, age-related changes in gene expression.

Finally, some aged cells and tissues fail to mount an adequate stress response and therefore are hypersensitive to stress-induced damage or death. Perhaps the best example of this is the heat-shock response. Heat and other stresses induce high levels of heat-shock proteins in young cells and tissues. In aged cells and tissues, by contrast, heat and other stresses fail to induce high levels of heat-shock proteins. The heat-shock response is due to transcriptional activation of the heat-shock genes by a specific transcription factor. Aged tissues and cells apparently contain adequate amounts of the transcription factor. However, for reasons that are not understood, the transcription factor fails to bind the heat-shock gene promoter element in aged cells and tissues.

Gene expression and life span

No single change in gene expression has yet been shown to be responsible for limiting or extending the life span of an organism (or even a tissue, for that matter). However, manipulation of general regulators of gene expression has been shown to alter life span, at least in model organisms. Perhaps the best example of this is the SIR2 protein, which is conserved from yeast to mammals and is responsible for the heterochromatic silencing of genes. In yeast, inactivation of the SIR2 gene results in defective gene silencing,

increased illegitimate recombination at the repetitive loci that encode rRNAs, and a shortening of life span. Conversely, an additional copy of the yeast SIR2 gene, which presumably results in more efficient silencing and suppression of recombination, extends yeast life span. Of greater relevance to complex eukaryotes, an additional copy of the SIR2 gene in the model organism *Caenorhabditis elegans*, a multicellular nematode, also extends life span. SIR2 requires NAD (nicotinamide adenine dinucleotide) as a cofactor. Thus, SIR2 may act to coordinate energy utilization, recombination, and control of gene expression, all of which may strongly influence life span.

JUDITH CAMPISI

See also GENETICS; MOLECULAR THERAPY.

BIBLIOGRAPHY

FINKEL, T., and HOLBROOK, N. J. "Oxidants, Oxidative Stress, and the Biology of Ageing." *Nature* 408 (2000): 239–247.

GUARENTE, L. "Sir2 Links Chromatin Silencing, Metabolism, and Aging." *Genes and Development* 14 (2000): 1021–1026.

HAN, E.; HILSENBECK, S. G.; RICHARDSON, A.; and NELSON, J. F. "cDNA Expression Arrays Reveal Incomplete Reversal of Age-Related Changes in Gene Expression by Calorie Restriction." *Mechanisms of Ageing and Development* 115 (2000): 157–174.

HEDARI, A. R.; YOU, S.; TAKAHASHI, R.; GUTSMANN-CONRAD, A.; SARGE, K. D.; and RICHARDSON, A. "Age-Related Alterations in the Activation of Heat Shock Transcription Factor 1 in Rat Hepatocytes." *Experimental Cell Research* 256 (2000): 83–93.

LEE, C.; KLOPP, R. C.; WEINDRUCH, R.; and PROLLA, T. A. "Gene Expression Profile of Aging and Its Retardation by Caloric Restriction." *Science* 285 (1999): 1390–1393.

PAPACONSTANTINOU, J. "Unifying Model of the Programmed and Stochastic Theories for Aging. The Stress Response Genes, Signal Transduction-Redox Pathways, and Aging." *Annals of the New York Academy of Sciences* 719 (1994): 195–211.

RATTAN, S. I. "Synthesis, Modifications, and Turnover of Proteins During Aging." *Experimental Gerontology* 31 (1996): 33–47.

ROY, A. K. "Transcription Factors and Aging." *Molecular Medicine* 3 (1997): 496–504.

VIJG, J. "Profiling Aging by Gene Arrays." *Mechanisms in Aging and Development* 112 (1999): 1–4.

VILLEPONTEAU, B. "The Heterochromatin Loss Model of Aging." *Experimental Gerontology* 32 (1997): 383–394.

GENETICS: LONGEVITY ASSURANCE

Researchers have identified numerous *longevity genes,* variants of which predispose individuals to a longer life span than the average for a species (see Table 1). These gene variants, or alleles, may occur spontaneously in a fraction of the natural population (e.g., human apoE2) or they be created by researchers in laboratory organisms (e.g., mouse p66shc). A subset of longevity genes extends life span when additional copies are introduced (e.g., worm *sir-2,* yeast *RAS2*). The term *longevity assurance gene,* often used synonymously with *longevity gene,* should not be confused with premature aging (i.e., progeroid) genes, variants of which apparently accelerate aspects of the aging process (e.g., mouse *klotho,* human *WRN*). Longevity genes have been subdivided into two classes. Private longevity genes increase longevity only in certain lineages, populations, or species, whereas public longevity genes are evolutionarily conserved and increase the longevity in a diverse group of species (Martin et al., 1996).

Why do longevity genes exist?

In the 1970s the prevailing view was that aging was the end point of a developmental program that served to remove older individuals from the population. This prompted a search for so-called death genes that dictated the aging process. However, today most scientists believe that there is no selection for aging and that aging is merely a by-product of natural selection. This new paradigm raises a question: If aging provides no selective advantage, how did longevity genes evolve? The answer lies in the distinction between aging and longevity. Although aging is generally believed to be an essentially random process, longevity is evolutionarily adaptive.

This idea was first formulated in the disposable soma theory (Kirkwood and Holliday, 1979), which is based on the premise that all biological activities come at a price. If an organism devotes resources to one activity, those resources are no longer available for other activities. Due to the competing priorities of reproduction, organisms can not afford to allocate the necessary amount of resources to body (i.e., somatic) maintenance to ensure indefinite survival. It follows that a species with a relatively high probability of being killed by extrinsic forces (e.g., starvation, disease, predation, and accidents) will have evolved to invest heavily in reproduction, so that its members develop rapidly and reproduce at a young age (Kirkwood et al., 2000).

Striking the optimum balance between reproduction and survival is as important for species as it is for individuals. During an individual's lifetime the environment is likely to change and, along with it, the optimal balance between reproduction and somatic maintenance. The majority of longevity genes appear to have evolved to boost somatic maintenance during harsh times and to increase growth and reproduction during good times.

An important corollary of the disposable soma theory is that the causes of aging should be primarily species-specific (i.e., private), whereas longevity assurance mechanisms should be evolutionarily conserved (i.e., public). This prediction has been supported by abundant experimental evidence. For example, a major cause of aging in baker's yeast is the accumulation of circular DNA molecules. In contrast, aging in nematode worms is apparently due to the accumulation of cellular damage caused by reactive oxygen species. Despite their having obviously different aging mechanisms, researchers have recently identified at least two public longevity genes that function in both organisms, *SIR2/sir2-1* and *SCH9/akt-1* (Kenyon, 2001). Such findings highlight the potential for experimental organisms to provide clues about human longevity, even if their causes of aging are seemingly unrelated.

Human longevity genes

Although the study of longevity genes in humans is still in its infancy, there is overwhelming evidence that the human life span has a significant heritable component (Caurnil and Kirkwood, 2001). Studies of twins have suggested that genetics accounts for up to 30 percent of the variance in human longevity. An even stronger relationship between genetics and longevity was observed by analyzing the genetics of centenarians and their families. In one study, the siblings of centenarians were three to four times more likely to reach age 100 than were siblings of non-centenarians. Another study showed that the im-

Table 1

Organism	Longevity gene	Relevant function of gene product
Baker's yeast **(S. cerevisiae)**	CDC25	Glucose response signaling pathway
	CYR1	Glucose response signaling pathway
	FOB1	Replication-fork blocking protein, ribosomal DNA instability
	HXK1	Hexose kinase, phosphorylates glucose
	LAG1	Synthesis of ceramides and inositolphosphorylceramide
	LAG2	Transmembrane domain containing protein of unknown function
	NPT1	Nicotinamide adenine dinucleotide (NAD) biosynthesis
	RAS1	Glucose response signaling pathway, deletion extends life span
	RAS2	Glucose response signaling pathway, overexpression extends life span
	SCH9	Protein kinase Akt/protein kinase B (PKB) homolog
	SIR2	Formation of heterochromatin, ribosomal DNA stability
	SIR4	Formation of heterochromatin. Associates with Sir2. Truncated form (Sir4-42p) extends life span
	TPK1	Glucose response pathway
	UTH1	Unknown function, affects gene silencing
	UTH4	Unknown function, affects gene silencing
Nematode worm **(C. elegans)**	age-1	Modulates phosphatidylinostol 3-kinase (PI-3 kinase) in an insulin signaling pathway
	clk-1	Ubiquinone (coenzyme Q) synthesis
	daf-2	Insulin receptor-like protein
	daf-18	phosphatidylinostol 3'-phosphatase, PTEN homolog
	daf-28	Probable DAF-16 phosphatase
	eat-2	Forkhead-like transcription factor
	gro-1	Unknown function
	isp-1	Iron sulfur protein III of mitochondrial electron transport chain
	old-1	Transmembrane tyrosine kinase
	sir-2	Homologue of yeast *SIR2*
Fly **(D. melanogaster)**	chico	Insulin receptor substrate
	indy	Putative membrane transporter protein
	InR	Insulin-like receptor
	methusela	G-protein coupled receptor, modulates stress response
Mouse **(M. musculus)**	p66[shc]	Prevents oxidative-induced cell death (apoptosis)
	GH-R/GHBP	Growth hormone receptor/binding protein
	Pit-1	Pituitary homeodomain transcription factor, mutated in Snell mice
	Prop-1	Pituitary transcription factor, Prophet of Pit-1, mutated in Ames mice
Human **(H. sapiens)**	apoE	apolipoprotein E, removal of cholesterol from blood
	ACE	angiotensin-converting enzyme, regulates blood pressure
	HLA-DR	histocompatability locus antigen
	SOD2	superoxide dismutatse, detoxifies free radicals
	TH	tyrosine hydroxylase, manufacture of hormones and neurtransmitters

SOURCE: Author

mediate ancestors of Jeanne Calment of France (who died at the age of 122, after breaking the record for human life span) were ten times more likely to reach age 80 than was the ancestral cohort (Robine and Allard, 1998).

Examination of the frequency of known gene variants in very old individuals has led to identification of five putative human longevity genes. A major problem in the identification of human longevity genes is that different studies often reach different conclusions. Scientists generally agree that the genes for apolipoprotein E (*apoE*),

angiotensin-converting enzyme (*ACE*), and histocompatibility locus antigen (*HLA-DR*) are genuine longevity genes (see Table 1). Genes for superoxide dismutase 2 (SOD2) and tyrosine hydroxylase (TH) have also been implicated in longevity. Human genes whose association with longevity is debated include those for cytochrome P-450, certain blood coagulation factors, and homocysteine methylation (*MTHFR*). In 2001, Thomas Perls, Luis Kunkel, and colleagues reported the identification in one family of a region on human chromosome IV that predisposes for exceptional longevity (Puca et al., 2001). However, the individual gene or genes responsible have not yet been identified.

There are many genes in humans whose variants reduce life expectancy (e.g., the tumor suppressor gene, *MSH2*). However, these are not true longevity variants because they are known only to reduce the life span, not to extend it. The *apoE* gene, involved in lipoprotein metabolism, has been found to affect longevity most consistently. At least five studies have detected the *apoE*-epsilon2 variant more frequently in centenarians than in the general population. Even so, it has been suggested that the *apoE* is a not a longevity gene, but that the *apoE*-epsilon4 variant causes premature death by promoting atherosclerosis (Gerdes et al., 2000). This matter, which remains to be resolved, illustrates another difficulty in classifying human longevity genes.

Longevity assurance genes in model organisms

Much of what is understood about longevity comes from studies in model organisms such as baker's yeast (*Saccharomyces cerevisiae*), nematode worms (*Caenorhabditis elegans*), and fruit flies (*Drosophila melanogaster*). Genetic screens for long-lived mutants have identified numerous longevity genes, many of which function in a conserved signaling pathway that regulates somatic maintenance and survival in response to environmental stress. In many species, including *C. elegans* and yeast, this regulatory pathway appears to be responsible for the longevity associated with calorie restriction.

Baker's yeast. The aging process and its regulation are better understood for yeast than for any other organism except, perhaps, nematode worms. There are two ways to define longevity in budding yeast. The more common measure is replicative life span, which is the number of offspring, or daughter cells, that a mother cell produces before she dies. Chronological life span is the length of time a population of nondividing yeast cells remains viable when deprived of nutrients. More than twelve yeast longevity genes have been identified. Most of these affect replicative life span, including genes for a sugar-processing enzyme, hexokinase 1 (*HXK1*); cyclic adenosine monophosphate production (*CDC25*); and the silent information regulator 2 (*SIR2*) (Defossez et al., 2001). Variants of these genes extend life span up to twofold by mimicking the effect of low food supply.

Unlike other model organisms, the precise mechanism by which many yeast longevity genes extend life span is known. In 1997, David Sinclair and Leonard Guarente discovered that circular DNA molecules known as ERCs are a primary cause of yeast aging (Sinclair and Guarente, 1997). ERCs are excised from the ribosomal DNA (a highly repetitive region of the yeast genome) by homologous DNA recombination about midway through a yeast cell's life span. ERCs then replicate each cell cycle until they reach toxic quantities (about one thousand per cell). The variants of most longevity genes that extend replicative life span (e.g., *HXK2*, *SIR2*, *CDC25*, *FOB1*, and *NPT1*) do so by stabilizing the ribosomal DNA locus, thus delaying the formation of ERCs.

One of the most interesting yeast longevity genes is *SIR2*. In 1999, Guarente and colleagues discovered that cells with additional copies of *SIR2* enjoy a life span extension of 30 percent (Kaeberlein et al., 1999). *SIR2* binds at various regions of the genome, including the ribosomal DNA, where it suppresses the formation of ERCs. *SIR2* has been shown to encode a type of enzyme known as histone deacetylase (HDAC). HDACs rearrange DNA into a more compact chromatin structure. *SIR2* activity is dependent on the availability of a key metabolite, nicotinamide adenine dinucleotide, which may explain how metabolic activity is coupled to longevity in this organism.

Longevity genes that regulate chronological life span include the gene for adenylate cyclase (*CYR1*) and a protein kinase signaling protein (*SCH9*) (Longo, 1999). Deletion of either of these genes increases resistance to oxidants and extends life span by up to threefold. *SCH9* is considered a public longevity gene because a related worm gene, *akt-1*, also regulates life span and stress resistance in that organism.

Nematode worms. In 1988, Thomas Johnson and colleagues isolated the longevity gene *age-1* from the nematode worm *C. elegans*, the first from any species. Mutations in *age-1* extend life span by about 50 percent. In 1993, Cynthia Kenyon and colleagues showed that worm life span could be doubled by mutating a gene called *daf-2*. More than ten longevity genes have now been identified in *C. elegans* (Braeckman et al., 2001).

The life cycle of *C. elegans* comprises four larval stages prior to the adult stage. In harsh conditions such as starvation or crowding, larvae often enter a developmentally arrested but resistant form called dauer. The majority of longevity genes in *C. elegans* encode components of an insulin-like growth factor (IGF-1) signaling pathway that regulates dauer development (see Table 1). Loss-of-function mutations in dauer formation (*daf*) genes extend the life span by allowing worms to reach maturity and retain some of the traits of dauers, including resistance to heat and oxidative stress.

Not all longevity genes in *C. elegans* are associated with loss-of-function mutations. The *C. elegans sir-2* gene is a relative of the yeast *SIR2* longevity gene. In 2001, Tissenbaum and Guarente reported that additional copies of *sir-2* extended life span in worms by 30 percent. This extension did not occur when the *daf-16* gene was mutated, which suggests that *sir-2* regulates the dauer pathway via *daf-16*. Sir-2 is now considered a significant public longevity gene whose relatives likely regulate longevity in a variety of organisms (Kenyon, 2001).

Certain variants of another *C. elegans* gene, *clk-1*, slow development and extend life span up to 50 percent (Wong et al., 1995). Worms engineered to possess longevity variants of both *clk-1* and *daf-2* live up to five times longer than normal. The *clk-1* gene is implicated in the biosynthesis of coenzyme Q, a component of the mitochondrial electron transport chain. The electron transport chain is a primary source of free radicals that can damage DNA, lipids, and proteins. It was originally thought that *clk-1* increased longevity by reducing free radicals, but recent findings suggest that increased longevity may be attributable to the increased expression of a catalase gene, *ctl-1*, that helps detoxify free radicals (Taub et al., 1999).

Fruit flies. The fruit fly *Drosophila melanogaster* has been used since the 1970s to study the relationship between genetics and longevity, but only recently has there been a concerted effort to identify individual longevity genes in this organism. During winter, *Drosophila* egg development is arrested by downregulating the production of juvenile hormone, which, like worm development, appears to be regulated by an insulin-like growth factor (IGF) signaling pathway (Gems and Partridge, 2001). Mutations in the insulin receptor substrate (IRS) gene, *chico*, and in the insulin/IGF-1 receptor (*InR*) gene allow flies to live up to 80 percent longer than normal by apparently invoking diapausal survival mechanisms.

In *Drosophila*, the insulin/IGF-1 pathway also regulates body size, and many long-lived mutants are small. It is not yet known how the other two *Drosophila* longevity genes, *indy* (I'm not dead yet) and *methusela*, extend life span.

Mice. Although large-scale genetic screens for long-lived mice have not been undertaken because of the cost and labor involved, some longevity mutants have identified in preexisting laboratory stocks of mice, some of which live 60 percent longer than normal mice (Bartke et al., 2001). Snell and Ames dwarf strains of mice are both long-lived and carry spontaneous mutations in the *Pit-1* and *Prop-1* genes, respectively, which are required for the proper development of pituitary cells that produce growth hormone, prolactin, and thyroid hormone, among others. Two other long-lived mouse strains have defects in growth hormone metabolism (i.e., little mice and mice with a targeted disruption of the growth homone receptor gene). All of these mice are small and have very low levels of insulin-like growth factor 1 (IGF-1), which has prompted speculation that an insulin/IGF-1 signaling pathway regulates body size and longevity in mice, as it does in flies.

In 1999, Pier Giuseppe Pelicci and colleagues reported that mice lacking the p66[shc] gene are not small but live one-third longer than normal animals (Migliaccio et al., 1999). p66[shc] encodes a signaling protein that promotes cell death after environmental stress and also seems to promote metabolic activities that generate free radicals.

Implications

The fact that similar pathways regulate longevity in organisms as diverse as flies and mice raises the possibility that humans also possess such a pathway. If they do, there will be an opportunity to develop small compounds that can alter this pathway and possibly delay the onset of age-associated diseases. The greatest obstacle to developing any drug that delays aging is the great length of time it will take to determine its efficacy. At least the discovery that single gene mutations can dramatically increase longevity makes it feasible that one day such drugs will be developed.

DAVID A. SINCLAIR

See also CELLULAR AGING; CENTENARIANS; GENETICS: GENE EXPRESSION; LONGEVITY: SELECTION; MOLECULAR

THERAPY; NUTRITION: CALORIC RESTRICTION; ROUND-WORMS: *CAENORHABDITIS ELEGANS*; THEORIES OF BIOLOGICAL AGING: DISPOSABLE SOMA; YEAST.

BIBLIOGRAPHY

BARTKE, A.; COSCHIGANO, K.; KOPCHICK, J.; CHANDRASHEKAR, V.; MATTISON, J.; KINNEY, B.; and HAUCK, S. "Genes That Prolong Life: Relationships of Growth Hormone and Growth to Aging and Life Span." *Journal of Gerontology Series A: Biological Sciences and Medical Sciences* 56, no. 8 (2001): B340–B349.

BRAECKMAN, B. P.; HOUTHOOFD, K.; and VAN-FLETEREN, J. R. "Insulin-like Signaling, Metabolism, Stress Resistance and Aging in *Caenorhabditis elegans*." *Mechanisms of Ageing and Development* 122, no. 7 (2001): 673–693.

COURNIL, A., and KIRKWOOD, T. B. "If You Would Live Long, Choose Your Parents Well." *Trends in Genetics* 17, no. 5 (2001): 233–235.

DEFOSSEZ, P. A.; LIN, S. J.; and MCNABB, D. S. "Sound Silencing: The Sir2 Protein and Cellular Senescence." *Bioessays* 23, no. 4 (2001): 327–332.

GEMS, D., and PARTRIDGE, L. "Insulin/Igf Signalling and Ageing: Seeing the Bigger Picture." *Current Opinion in Genetics and Development* 11, no. 3 (2001): 287–292.

GERDES, L. U.; JEUNE, B.; RANBERG, K. A.; NYBO, H.; and VAUPEL, J. W. "Estimation of Apolipoprotein E Genotype-Specific Relative Mortality Risks from the Distribution of Genotypes in Centenarians and Middle-Aged Men: Apolipoprotein E Gene Is a 'Frailty Gene,' Not a 'Longevity Gene'." *Genetic Epidemiology* 19, no. 3 (2000): 202–210.

KAEBERLEIN, M.; MCVEY, M.; and GUARENTE, L. "The Sir2/3/4 Complex and Sir2 Alone Promote Longevity in *Saccharomyces cerevisiae* by Two Different Mechanisms." *Genes and Development* 13, no. 19 (1999): 2570–2580.

KENYON, C. "A Conserved Regulatory Mechanism for Aging." *Cell* 105 (2001): 165–168.

KIRKWOOD, T. B., and HOLLIDAY, R. "The Evolution of Ageing and Longevity." *Proceedings of the Royal Society of London Series B: Biological Sciences* 205, no. 1161 (1979): 531–546.

KIRKWOOD, T. B.; KAPAHI, P.; and SHANLEY, D. P. "Evolution, Stress, and Longevity." *Journal of Anatomy* 197, pt. 4 (2000): 587–590.

LONGO, V. D. "Mutations in Signal Transduction Proteins Increase Stress Resistance and Longevity in Yeast, Nematodes, Fruit Flies, and Mammalian Neuronal Cells." *Neurobiology of Aging* 20, no. 5 (1999): 479–486.

MARTIN, G. M.; AUSTAD, S. N.; and JOHNSON, T. E. "Genetic Analysis of Ageing: Role of Oxidative Damage and Environmental Stresses." *Nature Genetics* 13, no. 1 (1996): 25–34.

MIGLIACCIO, E.; GIORGIO, M.; MELE, S.; PELICCI, G.; REBOLDI, P.; PANDOLFI, P. P.; LANFRAN-CONE, L.; and PELICCI, P. G. "The p66^{shc} Adaptor Protein Controls Oxidative Stress Response and Life Span in Mammals." *Nature* 402, no. 6759 (1999): 309–313.

PUCA, A. A.; DALY, M. J.; BREWSTER, S. J.; MATISE, T. C.; BARRETT, J.; SHEA-DRINKWATER, M.; KANG, S.; JOYCE, E.; NICOLI, J.; BENSON, E.; KUNKEL, L. M.; and PERLS, T. "A Genome-Wide Scan for Linkage to Human Exceptional Longevity Identifies a Locus on Chromosome 4." *Proceedings of the National Academy of Sciences* 98, no. 18 (2001): 10505–10508.

ROBINE, J. M., and ALLARD, M. "The Oldest Human." *Science* 279, no. 5358 (1998): 1834–1835.

SINCLAIR, D. A., and GUARENTE, L. "Extrachromosomal Rdna Circles—A Cause of Aging in Yeast." *Cell* 91, no. 7 (1997): 1033–1042.

TAUB, J.; LAU, J. F.; MA, C.; HAHN, J. H.; HOQUE, R.; ROTHBLATT, J.; and CHALFIE, M. "A Cytosolic Catalase Is Needed to Extend Adult Lifespan in *C. elegans daf-C* and *clk-1* Mutants." *Nature* 399, no. 6732 (1999): 162–166.

WONG, A.; BOUTIS, P.; and HEKIMI, S. "Mutations in the *Clk-1* Gene of *Caenorhabditis elegans* Affect Developmental and Behavioral Timing." *Genetics* 139, no. 3 (1995): 1247–1259.

GENETICS: PARENTAL INFLUENCE

Studies examining the factors that affect both longevity and the diseases associated with aging have traditionally focused on the interaction of inheritance (genetics) and lifestyle (environment) on adults. Specific genetic backgrounds have been demonstrated to be risk factors for diseases that occur later in adult life, such as some types of cancers and neurodegenerative diseases. Similarly, certain environmental factors, such as a poor diet, have also been demonstrated to have detrimental physiological effects, leading to an increased incidence of strokes, diabetes, heart disease, or other maladies. Conversely, certain interventions, such as caloric restriction in adult animals, can dramatically extend longevity. However, while the impact of genetics and environment on the occurrence of age-related processes has been extensively studied in adults, the impact of these factors during early developmental events is not so well known. For example, is it possible that parental age at conception can have an influence on the course of aging in the succeeding generation? Can an environmental effect, such as malnutrition, have permanent consequences on offspring if it occurs during or immediately after gestation? What, in fact, are the ramifications of parental age and maternal nutrition on disease and longevity in offspring, and what potential mechanisms underlie these effects?

Parental age

Retrospective studies have reported that older parentage can adversely affect aging in offspring, with some studies reporting stronger contributions from either maternal or paternal sources. For example, in a report by Leonid Gavrilov and colleagues in 1997, analysis of records of European aristocracy revealed that female offspring of older fathers had a significantly reduced life span. Because the effect was related to a paternal source and only influenced female offspring, mutations inherited via the paternal X-chromosome were suspected. As reviewed by Juan Tarin and colleagues in 1998, there are also several diseases associated with older paternal age, including Wilms' tumor, Apert's syndrome, and Marfan's syndrome, among others. Gwen McIntosh, in a 1995 study that controlled for maternal age and known chromosomal abnormalities, found an increased incidence of birth defects as a function of increasing paternal age. Older paternal age has also recently been associated with an increased incidence of prostate cancer and brain cancer. It has been conjectured in the *copy error hypothesis* of L. S. Penrose that spermatozoa are more prone to mutations than oocytes, due to the larger number of divisions they have undergone with age. A review by Crow reports that DNA duplication during gametogenesis is the period when mutations most readily occur.

Aging of female oocyte stocks can also have an effect on the appearance of disease in adult offspring. One of the more familiar circumstances is an aberration in chromosome number, known as *aneuploidy*, which can cause severe developmental problems and compromise life span. Many cases are manifested as trisomy, where three copies of a chromosome (instead of the normal two) occur with increased frequency with advancing maternal age. For example,

Down syndrome (trisomy 21), which results in short stature, mental deficiencies, physiological problems, and a shortened life span, is caused by maternal problems in chromosome separation (nondisjunction), resulting in the appearance of an extra chromosome 21. Trisomy of other chromosomes also occurs in lesser frequencies in newborns, such as chromosome 18 (Edwards' syndrome) and chromosome 13 (Patau's syndrome). In the majority of cases, nondisjunction of maternal origin appears to be responsible for the trisomic condition, although a small percentage of cases involve the paternal source.

Maternal nutrition

The study of long-term effects of maternal nutrition on offspring has a rich and extensive history. The hypothesis, referred to as *fetal origins, fetal programming,* or *metabolic imprinting,* addresses the permanent effect that maternal undernutrition may have on physiological systems in the offspring, reportedly affecting glucose regulation, lipid metabolism, cardiovascular disease, blood pressure, and obesity. Human studies on the *imprinting* effect have been conducted retrospectively, utilizing records to establish vital statistics on newborns. Aspects of health, physiological fitness, and mortality in newborns were followed up many years later, during adulthood. Studies on men born in Herefordshire, England, demonstrated that those with the lowest birth weights were more likely to have higher mortality rates from coronary heart disease. Similarly, low-birth-weight males were more likely to develop noninsulin-dependent diabetes and impaired glucose tolerance, inferring that low-birth-weight babies were deprived nutritionally during development. Data from the Dutch famine of World War II, which resulted in maternal malnutrition, more directly tested gestational malnutrition and demonstrated that glucose tolerance was indeed decreased years later in surviving adults.

Epidemiological studies are limited by their retrospective nature, especially over issues of controls, sampling bias, and concerns over adjustment for confounding factors. In attempts to address some of these concerns, animal studies have been conducted, and in some cases they have supported the fetal origins hypothesis on issues of body composition, cardiovascular disease, and glucose tolerance. However, animal studies must be interpreted with caution, due to questions of species differences in the expression of pathology. Given the large collection of human and animal data on the subject, the fetal origins hypothesis remains topical, though it requires additional research to test its accuracy.

While many of these hypotheses will require elucidation through future study, new technology will greatly assist in the process. Previous studies have also suggested areas of research to help test fetal programming, such as permanent modification of gene expression and alterations in cell number. Epigenetic mechanisms, where heritable changes in gene function occur without changes in DNA sequence, provide another interesting mechanism by which fetal programming can occur. Finally, the techniques of *in vitro* fertilization with gametes from older parents, as well as cloning of differentiated adult cells, may provide new information on the effect of early development on aging in successive generations and help discern the role of genetics and environment on these complex issues.

STEVEN KOHAMA

See also GENETICS; LONGEVITY: REPRODUCTION; MUTATION.

BIBLIOGRAPHY

CROW, J. F. "Spontaneous Mutation in Man." *Mutation Research* 437 (1999): 5–9.
GAVRILOV, L. A.; GAVRILOVA, N. S.; KROUTKO, V. N.; EVDOKUSHKINA, G. A.; SEMYONOVA, V. G.; GAVRILOVA, A. L.; LAPSHIN, E. V.; EVDOKUSHKINA, N. N.; and KUSHNAREVA Y. E. "Mutation Load and Human Longevity." *Mutation Research* 377 (1997): 61–62.
HEMMINKI, K., and KYYRONEN, P. "Parental Age and Risk of Sporadic and Familial Cancer in Offspring: Implications for Germ Cell Mutagenesis." *Epidemiology* 10 (1999): 747–751.
JOSEPH, K. S., and KRAMER, M. S. "Review of the Evidence of Fetal and Early Childhood Antecedents of Adult Chronic Disease." *Epidemiologic Reviews* 18 (1996): 158–174.
MCINTOSH, G. C.; OLSHAN, A. F.; and BAIRD, P. A. "Paternal Age and the Risk of Birth Defects in Offspring." *Epidemiology* 6 (1995): 282–288.
NICOLAIDIS, P., and PETERSEN, M. B. "Origin and Mechanisms of Non-disjunction in Human Autosomal Trisomies." *Human Reproduction* 13 (1998): 313–319.
TARIN, J. J.; BRINES, J.; and CANO, A. "Long-Term Effects of Delayed Parenthood." *Human Reproduction* 13 (1998): 2371–2376.
WATERLAND, R. A., and GARZA, C. "Potential Mechanisms of Metabolic Imprinting That Lead to Chronic Disease." *American Journal of Clinical Nutrition* 69 (1999): 179–197.
ZHANG, Y.; KREGER B. E.; DORGAN, J. F.; CUPPLES, L. A.; MYERS, R. H.; SPLANSKY, G. L.; SCHATZKIN, A.; and ELLISON, R. C. "Parental Age at Child's Birth and Son's Risk for Prostate Cancer: The Framingham Study." *American Journal of Epidemiology* 150 (1999): 1208–1212.

GENETICS: TUMOR SUPPRESSION

Long-lived organisms have had to evolve mechanisms to suppress the development of cancer. These mechanisms are termed *tumor suppression mechanisms,* and the genes that control them are termed *tumor suppressor genes.* Tumor suppressor genes promote the development of cancer when they are lost or inactivated.

Many genes have been shown to function as tumor suppressors. Most participate in normal cellular and developmental processes, where the proteins they encode act to inhibit cell proliferation or promote differentiation or apoptosis. Tumor suppressors also play important regulatory and functional roles in the sensing and repairing of DNA damage, and in the responses to DNA damage; namely, cellular senescence and apoptosis.

Proteins encoded by tumor suppressor genes include growth-inhibitory cytokines and their receptors, such as some members of the TGF-β (transforming growth factor-beta) family and their transmembrane receptors. They also include transmembrane proteins such as E-cadherin, which organizes cells in epithelial tissues and promotes their differentiation. Some nuclear receptors, such as some of those that bind retinoic acid (retinoic acid receptors, or RARs), can also act as tumor suppressors. In addition, proteins that transduce growth-inhibitory signals, such as those that transduce TGF-β and related signals, as well as transcriptional regulators that respond to growth-inhibitory signals, such as the retinoblastoma susceptibility protein (pRB), can be tumor suppressors. Pro-apoptotic proteins comprise another class of tumor suppressors—one example is BAX, which stimulates the opening of the mitochondrial permeability pore, a prelude to apoptosis. Finally, proteins that sense or regulate the repair of DNA damage or that control the cellular response to DNA damage can be tumor suppressors. Examples include ATM (ataxia telangiectasia mutated), a protein kinase that transduces damage signals to p53, and p53 itself, a transcription factor that induces either cellular senescence, apoptosis, or cell-cycle arrest and DNA repair.

Loss or inactivation of tumor suppressor genes can occur by genetic (necessarily hereditary) or epigenetic (not necessarily hereditary) mechanisms. Genetic mechanisms include deleterious mutations or deletion of all or part of the gene. Epigenetic mechanisms include gene silencing, as well as any change in synthesis, degradation, localization, or interaction that prevents the gene product from functioning. Because cancer phenotypes generally result from loss of tumor suppressor gene functions, oncogenic mutations in these genes tend to be recessive, that is, both gene copies must be inactivated before cell behavior is affected.

Because many tumor suppressors function in normal cellular and developmental processes, they tend to be key participants in pathways that control cell growth, death, differentiation, and/or repair.

Two of the most important tumor suppressor pathways are those controlled by the RB and TP53 genes, which encode the pRB and p53 proteins, respectively. Most, if not all, cancers harbor mutations in either the pRB or p53 pathway, or in both.

Both pRB and p53 regulate the transcription of other genes; pRB does so indirectly by binding and regulating transcription factors or transcription modulators. It also inhibits cell-cycle progression, largely by repressing the activity of E2F, a transcription factor that induces the expression of genes needed for DNA replication. By contrast, p53 is a direct transcription factor that induces the expression of cell-cycle inhibitors in response to DNA damage. Consistent with their key roles in tumor suppressor pathways, pRB and p53 are controlled by upstream regulators, and their activities are mediated by downstream effectors. Examples of upstream regulators are p16, which inhibits the cyclin-dependent protein kinase that phosphorylates and inactivates pRB; and ATM, which phosphorylates and activates p53. Examples of downstream mediators are E2F, the transcription factor that is blocked by pRB; and p21, the cyclin-dependent kinase inhibitor whose transcription is induced by p53.

Oncogenic mutations in pRB tend to be deletions, typical for tumor suppressor genes. By contrast, although some p53 mutations are deletions, many cancer cells harbor point mutations in p53. These point mutations alter its functions as a transcription factor, and are dominant.

Tumor suppressor genes are generally identified by their ability to increase the incidence of cancer when one or both copies are defective in the germline, and by their consistent absence in malignant tumors.

Germ-line tumor suppressor gene mutations are rare, and generally heterozygous (only one allele is mutant). This is because, although homozygous mutations favor the growth and/or survival of cancer cells, they are often lethal during embryogenesis. For example, mice lacking both RB genes do not survive to birth, whereas mice carrying one mutant and one wild-type (normal) RB allele develop normally but die of cancer at an early age. The tumors invariably show loss of the wild-type allele, indicating that once development is complete, loss of pRB results in cancer. This is also true in humans—children with one defective and one normal RB allele are normal at birth. However, they have a high incidence of childhood retinoblastoma and other tumors, and the tumors inevitablty have lost the wild-type allele.

Most cancers, of course, develop in organisms with a genetically normal germ line. Nonetheless, tumors generally harbor loss or inactivation of both copies of tumor suppressor genes. One reason that most cancers develop relatively late in life is that it takes time for mutations to develop in both tumor suppressor genes within a single cell.

Not all tumor suppressor genes are critical for normal development. Rather, some tumor suppressors appear to act primarily to suppress the development of cancer during adulthood. For example, genetically engineered mice that completely lack p16 develop normally, but die of cancer during young adulthood. Similarly, mice completely deficient in p53 develop normally, but develop cancer at an early age. When only one p16 or p53 gene is deleted, cancer incidence is lower than in animals that lack both genes, but higher than in wild-type animals. Tumors that develop in these animals invariably lose the remaining gene or, in the case of p53, acquire a dominant mutation in it. Tumor suppressor genes of this type, then, appear to act as longevity assurance genes. That is, they act to prevent the development of cancer during young adulthood or the peak of reproductive fitness. It is not surprising that tumor suppressors of this type also tend to be critical regulators of apoptosis and/or cellular senescence. Cellular senescence and apoptosis are potent tumor suppression mechanisms in mammals that also appear to play important role in the development of aging phenotypes.

JUDITH CAMPISI

See also CANCER, BIOLOGY; CELLULAR AGING: CELL DEATH; CELLULAR AGING: TELOMERES; GENETICS: LONGEVITY ASSURANCE; MOLECULAR THERAPY; MUTATION.

BIBLIOGRAPHY

KAELIN, W. G. "The p53 Family." *Oncogene* 18 (1999): 7701–7705.
MCLEOD, K. "pRb and E2f-1 in Mouse Development and Tumorigenesis." *Current Opinion in Genetics and Development* 9 (1999): 31–39.
OREN, M. "Tumor Suppressors Review Issue." *Experimental Cell Research* 264 (2001): 1–192.

GERIATRIC ASSESSMENT UNIT

When older adults experience changes in their thinking or judgment, their ability to care for their personal or household needs, finances, or physical health, the whole person is negatively changed. Geriatric assessment units (GAUs) can respond with a perspective from the specialty of aging when one or more of these major areas declines. Most GAUs can provide services for older adults in response to at least one of the following three scenarios: (1) when there are multiple medical problems or changes in ability to live independently; (2) because of changes in a variety of age-related areas the older adult would benefit from seeing a variety of specialists who focus on aging; and (3) when an older adult requires a focused evaluation and personal care plan.

GAUs cooperate with the patient's primary care physician to put the GAU's medical care plan into practice. GAUs also make referrals for services and follow-up with the older adult over time.

Generally, a concerned family member makes the GAU appointment. This concerned family member or another individual who knows the older adult well usually attends the appointment. A careful history and description of the present changes help to focus the appointment on the older adult's main problem. Older adults often come to the GAU because family members want to be certain that everything possible is being done to help their older family member live comfortably. The reasons for a GAU appointment may also include questions regarding the older adult's diagnosis, memory loss, depression, and decline in their ability to care for themselves; questions if the older adult needs in-home services or relocation into an assisted living or nursing home setting; confusion regarding multiple medical problems; behavior changes; worries about different effects of taking many medications; and the family's need for education to work with these changes of aging. Increasingly, GAU services are requested to provide an opinion regarding the older adult's judgment and decision-making abilities in legal cases.

The GAU appointment is usually a new experience for older adults and their family members. Most people have experienced short medical evaluations at some point during their lives. In contrast, the GAU often requires several hours or several long appointments to gather the information needed to gain a full picture of the older adult's situation. The GAU generally uses an interdisciplinary team of professionals from different training background. This team usually includes a nurse, social worker, and physician who are specifically trained in working with older adults. The appointment and the interdisciplinary team are costly. These special features of the GAU threaten its very future because policy makers, Medicare, Medicaid, and private insurance companies often fail to recognize the long-term benefit of these services.

The GAU appointment is generally divided into two parts. The medical team meets privately with the family to learn about their concerns, past medical history, and the older adult's ability to care for himself in his present living situation. At the same time, the nurse or social worker meets with the older adult to obtain his or her perception of how the older adult is feeling or getting along at home. In addition, short memory tests and questions regarding mental health issues may be reviewed with the older adult. Next, the interdisciplinary team introduces the physician, who conducts a physical examination. During this time family members receive from the nurse or social worker the testing results that provide appreciated education and explanations for the changes in thinking or behavior by the older adult. Suggestions for providing a safe environment for the older adult are reviewed. These discussions often lead to suggested compromises in both the family's and the older adult's routine. Family members are encouraged to make personal notes of service referral information and a diary of the changes seen in their older family member. The nurse or social worker may also review a family tree to explore additional available sources of personal care and support for the older adult, the health of the patient's family members, or causes of death among family members. GAU appointments generally conclude with a family conference that included the professional team's review of what was learned and recommended for the older adult. Referrals to additional specialists in physical therapy, occupational therapy, nutrition, ministry, pharmacy, as well as community resources are made to meet the different needs of the older adult. Every effort is made to involve the older adult in any suggested plans.

Special geriatric assessment unit locations

Outpatient clinic. Community-based outpatient clinics often provide easy access for older adults. Services such as X-ray and laboratory testing are readily available. It appears that some older adults try harder on memory testing in a clinic-type setting.

Inpatient hospital. Being assessed while hospitalized makes it more difficult for patients to perform at their best since they are already ill. However, all medical services, including laboratory testing and relevant professionals, are available to help make a diagnosis.

Senior housing communities. Providing a GAU within a housing community for older adults provides a comfortable relaxed environment and eliminates transportation problems. The professional team often coordinates easily with home health care services and is aware of the older adult's home environment and thus can better recommend needed in-home care services.

In summary, GAUs review with focused consideration the older adult's entire health and living situation. Mental health professionals are then able to plan a course of action with the older

adult, the family, and primary care doctors, insuring the best possible health, continued independence and, hopefully, avoidance of health crises.

IRENE MOORE

See also ASSESSMENT; MULTIDISCIPLINARY TEAM.

BIBLIOGRAPHY

Agency for Health Care Policy and Research. *Recognition and Initial Assessment of Alzheimer's Disease and Related Dementias: Clinical Practice Guidelines.* Rockville, Md.: U.S. Department of Health and Human Services, November, 1996. AHCPR Publication 97–0702. Page 72.

GALLO, J. J.; FULMER, T. ; PAVEZA, G. J.; et al., eds. *Handbook of Geriatric Assessment*, 3d ed. Gaithersburg, Md.: Aspen, 2000.

GREGANTI, M. A., and HANSON, L. C. "Comprehensive Geriatric Assessment: Where Do We Go From Here?" *Archives of Internal Medicine* 158 (1996): 15–17.

GWYTHER, L. P. "When 'The Family' Is Not One Voice: Conflict In Caregiving Families." *Journal of Case Management* 4 (1995): 150–155.

WEUVE, J. L.; BOULT, C.; MORISHITA, L. "The Effects of Outpatient Geriatric Evaluation and Management on Caregiver Burden." *The Gerontologist* no. 4 (2000): 429–436.

GERIATRIC EVALUATION AND MANAGEMENT

See GERIATRIC ASSESSMENT UNIT; GERIATRIC MEDICINE

GERIATRIC MEDICINE

Geriatric medicine is the study and practice of the medical care of older adults. In the English-speaking world the development of geriatric medicine as a specialty traces its roots to Marjorie Warren in England, in the 1930s. The term "geriatrics" was coined in 1909 by an American, I. L. Nascher, who was struck by parallels with the care of children, pediatrics.

Around the world a number of models of geriatric medicine are practiced, but three predominate. One model, common in the United Kingdom, views geriatric medicine as the comprehensive care of the sick who are over the age of seventy-five years. This care is specialty-based and organized in consultation with family doctors whose practice includes older adults. A second model is similarly directed toward all people over a particular age (some recommend cutoffs at sixty-five, others seventy or seventy-five), but with the roots of the discipline in primary care. A third model does not use an age cutoff, but defines geriatric medicine as the subspecialty care of older adults who are frail. In this context, frailty is generally understood as having multiple, interacting medical and social problems, and geriatric medicine is seen as an alternative to specialties and subspecialties in which care is more focused on the problems of an organ system.

Geriatric medicine is typically contrasted with gerontology, which is the study of phenomena associated with aging. Gerontology is further distinguished by type, such as biological gerontology, social gerontology, and so on. Often the distinction between clinical gerontology and geriatric medicine is more apparent than real, and the two terms are commonly used interchangeably.

The practitioner of geriatric medicine is commonly referred to as a geriatrician, and the formal use of this term is commonly restricted, often by legislation, to people with additional qualifications in geriatric medicine. The work of the geriatrician is carried out in a number of contexts, some of which are increasingly unique to the specialty. The places in which geriatricians work include acute care hospital wards, where a multidisciplinary approach is promoted. Such wards commonly are called geriatric assessment units, or acute care of the elderly units, or geriatric evaluation and management services, to indicate that their focus is more than the medical aspects of care. Such wards emphasize patients' mobility and ability to care for themselves and the social aspects of medical problems. Rehabilitation wards are another common setting for geriatricians, again with an emphasis on integrated, multidisciplinary care. Such focus is also found in geriatric ambulatory care clinics, which serve patients who have acute problems but do not require hospital admission.

The more specialized locales of a geriatrician's practice are geriatric day hospitals and care given in the home. The day hospital has as its focus frail older adults who are able to walk. They commonly attend day hospitals two or three days a week for about six hours a day. Attendance normally is over fairly short and well-defined periods, anywhere from a few weeks to no more than three months. The day hospital particularly targets frail older adults who require investigations that they may not be able to withstand in the compressed time frame of a hospital stay. Typically, those who attend day hospitals have at least two active problems requiring help from any of the disciplines (geriatric medicine, nursing, physiotherapy, occupational therapy, social work, and others) that are represented by the day hospital team.

Geriatricians are among the few specialists who routinely make house calls, and it would not be uncommon for about 10 percent of all geriatric consultations to be carried out in the patient's own home. Indeed, some services seek to see people exclusively in their own homes. House calls require that solutions of patients' problems be tailored to their environments. By contrast, it is possible, when seeing patients in other settings, to propose therapies that are infeasible in the patient's own home. The special skills of the geriatrician include not just competence in the internal medicine of old age, but also the ability to recognize that frail older adults have complex problems. Complex problems are not amenable to single interventions. With complex problems it is not possible to do one thing without taking into account how that might affect other aspects of care. Complexity can range from the need to take into account that treatment for one problem (e.g., a nonsteroidal anti-inflammatory drug for active arthritis) may exacerbate another problem (e.g., congestive heart failure). Equally, some options that are quite feasible for some patients are infeasible for other patients in different social circumstances. The ability to address these problems is formalized in a process known as comprehensive geriatric assessment, and is at the root of what the geriatrician does.

Historically, within medicine, geriatric medicine has not been seen as a glamorous specialty, and recruitment of physicians into the area sometimes can be difficult. Nevertheless, those who practice geriatric medicine typically find that it is an intellectually stimulating and emotionally rewarding specialty well suited to physicians who like to maintain an interest in the whole person.

KENNETH ROCKWOOD

See also ASSESSMENT; DAY HOSPITALS; FRAILTY; GERIATRIC ASSESSMENT UNITS; GERIATRIC PSYCHIATRY; GERON-

TOLOGICAL NURSING; HOME VISITS; MULTIDISCIPLINARY TEAM; PERIODIC HEALTH EXAMINATION; PROFESSIONAL ORGANIZATIONS; REHABILITATION.

BIBLIOGRAPHY

EVANS, J. G. "Marjory Warren Lecture. Service and Research for an Ageing Population." *Age and Ageing* 29, supp. 1 (2000): 5–8.
HOGAN, D. B.; BERGMAN, H.; and MCCRACKEN, P. "The History of Geriatric Medicine in Canada." *Journal of the American Geriatrics Society* 45, no. 9 (1997): 1134–1139.

GERIATRIC PSYCHIATRY

Geriatric psychiatry is the branch of clinical medicine dedicated to the study and the care of mental disorders in older adults. Such disorders include depression, dementia, delirium, other forms of cognitive impairment and behavioral disturbances, psychosis, anxiety, substance abuse, and sleep disorders. Some of these problems may have come on only in the later years; others may have begun in middle age or even have been lifelong. Their causes can range from brain diseases, to diseases or conditions of other parts of the body, to adjustment problems or other emotional/psychological problems. The treatment of these problems begins with the proper diagnosis, and requires not just expertise in geriatric psychiatry but also knowledge of geriatric medicine, neurology, gerontology, abnormal psychology, and psychopharmacology. Often a multidisciplinary approach is needed, involving coordination and teamwork among the primary care physician, psychiatrists, and other specialists.

Research in geriatric psychiatry and related fields focuses on elucidating the epidemiology (how conditions are distributed throughout the population), genetics (inheritance), risk and protective factors, etiology (causal factors), pathophysiology (how the different conditions develop and progress within the body/brain), symptomatology (how different people manifest the conditions), and treatment of mental disorders and psychiatric syndromes that are common in late life. Such research includes identifying genetic risk factors for Alzheimer's disease, and developing new drugs for the safe and effective treatment of depression.

Geriatric psychiatrists are physicians who have completed four years of specialty training in general psychiatry after receiving their M.D. or D.O. degree, followed by at least one additional year of clinical training in geriatric psychiatry. At the completion of their clinical training (typically nine years beyond college), geriatric psychiatrists can become board-certified in psychiatry with added qualifications in geriatric psychiatry. Geriatric psychiatrists diagnose and treat their patients in a variety of practice settings. They see patients admitted to general and psychiatric hospitals on units specializing in the care of older patients suffering from mental disorders. They provide consultation to primary care physicians and medical specialists regarding their older patients who present with psychiatric symptoms. They take care of older outpatients whom they treat with psychotropic medications or psychotherapy in clinics and private offices. They directly manage or provide consultation on residents of nursing homes and other long-term care facilities. Since most older patients with mental disorders also suffer from physical illnesses, geriatric psychiatrists are particularly attuned to the multiple interactions between concurrent mental and physical problems. Some of the life transitions to which older adults must adjust can be stressful and cause coping difficulties, which in turn can lead to more significant problems.

Since the 1950s, through their clinical and research work differentiating "normal aging" from late-life mental disorders, geriatric psychiatrists have contributed to the understanding that the majority of older people are cognitively intact and well adjusted, and they enjoy life. Conversely, "senility" (i.e., dementia), depression, and behavioral disturbances occurring late in life are caused by diseases that can be prevented and treated.

BENOIT H. MULSANT, M.D.

See also ALZHEIMER'S DISEASE; ANXIETY; DELIRIUM; DEMENTIA; DEPRESSION; GERIATRIC MEDICINE; GERONTOLOGY.

BIBLIOGRAPHY

BUSSE, E. W., and BLAZER, D. G., eds. *The American Psychiatric Press Textbook of Geriatric Psychiatry*, 2d ed. Washington, D.C.: American Psychiatric Press, 1997.
SADAVOY, J., ed. *Comprehensive Review of Geriatric Psychiatry II*. Washington, D.C.: American Psychiatric Press, 1996.
SCHNEIDER, L. S., ed. *Developments in Geriatric Psychiatry*. San Francisco: Jossey-Bass, 1997.

SPAR, J. E. *Concise Guide to Geriatric Psychiatry.* 2d ed. Washington, D.C.: American Psychiatric Press, 1997.

GERONTOCRACY

More than any other topic in historical gerontology, gerontocracy forces us to distinguish between valid representations and stereotypic images of age and aging, past and present. Our presumptions about the powers ascribed to long life must be tested in light of what we know today about age-grading in various networks as well as the impact of demographic aging on social norms and societal institutions.

There is abundant evidence to corroborate that gerontocracies—literally, rule by the old ones—existed in ancient times. Compared to today, there were few elders centuries ago. Surviving to one's first birthday was an achievement. One became "middle aged" in the second, not the third, quarter of life. Gray hairs were venerated as icons for attaining advanced ages and for the wisdom that presumably accrued from a rich lifetime of experiences. Knowledge was power. So was the accumulation of wealth (largely through land holdings in agrarian settings, and through commercial wealth in urban areas) that might tantalizingly be dangled before a rising generation who would have to pay obeisance until it, in due course, came of age. Intergenerational tensions are not novel.

So when did old men dominate society? We know that a *gerousia*, a council of elders that included only men over sixty, presided over bellicose Sparta. In the *Laws*, Plato discouraged public service before age fifty. The name of the Roman Senate derives from *senex*, or old. Even if we question the ages at which patriarchs such as Seth, Enoch, and Methusaleh died, Hebrew Scripture in many passages (including the Ten Commandments) attributes long life with virtue. The elders of Israel's twelve tribes were usually described as very old.

Other signs of gerontocracies dot the historical landscape. Sixty was the age in medieval England at which workers became exempt from compulsory labor or military service. Sixty was the average age of the nine men consecrated to be archbishops of Canterbury in the seventeenth century; they died in office at an average age of seventy-three. Ella, Countess of Salisbury, founded a nunnery after she became a widow,

and stepped down as abbess at age sixty-eight. In addition, cross-cultural analyses have brought to light recent examples of gerontocracies. Anthropologists have offered ethnographic studies of tribes in East Africa and villages in southeast Asia in which one's relative standing in a community is primarily reckoned in terms of years, which count for more than even collateral kin ties, number of offspring, or the net value of possessions.

We must be sensitive to the class and gender biases in all these data. Life expectancy at birth was below forty before the twentieth century. It is reasonable to hypothesize that only those who could afford a balanced diet (though not so rich as to cause gout) and avoid back-breaking work (but not so leisurely an existence as to preclude the daily exercise that keeps one limber) could live until their prime. Only those fortunate enough to reach adolescence had any prospects (and then, only with continued good luck) of attaining a "green old age" that made their vital aging integral to the life of the community. Few women past sixty—only exceptionally wealthy widows, daughters of royalty, or indomitable intellects—would have commanded the same degree of power and influence as men of their cohort. Men with endowments ran gerontocracies.

For that reason, we may actually have witnessed more instances of gerontocracy since World War II than before that critical turning point in history. Life expectancies at birth and even at age forty have risen significantly in this century, thus creating a larger pool of older men who potentially can control the political, economic, and social institutions of a given society. Old men ruled the Soviet Union before its demise. These rulers by and large were bureaucrats wily enough to survive purges in their middle age and conservative enough to maintain control over the levers of power as one cohort gave way to the next. (Some claim that the system worked to its own disadvantage: Russia's gerontocracy became sclerotic.) Communist China also entered the modern era under the rule of successive cadres of men and women over sixty.

That youth ruled early America is hardly surprising since the median age in 1790 in the United States was sixteen. Yet the Constitution gave preference to mature leaders: one had to be twenty-five to run for Congress, thirty to become a senator, thirty-five to be elected president. Old men dominated Native American tribal councils. Elders determined who could marry whom and other social activities in slave quarters. Before the twentieth century older American men tended to manage the firms and farms that they had built over the course of their lives. Only infirmity or superannuation forced them to transfer power.

The United States has institutionalized the powers of age in at least two of its three branches of national government. Supreme Court justices have always served for life: few have been tapped for the highest bench before the age of fifty-five. Most then serve for decades. Towards the end of the nineteenth century, moreover, both houses of Congress adopted a "seniority" system which made long service in the House or Senate a prerequisite for committee appointments and chairmanships. People make jokes about nonagenarian Strom Thurmond, but few doubt his power on the Senate floor, which almost matches that of Senator Robert Byrd, a comparative youngster at eighty-one. In the House, Henry Hyde has dominated lawmaking for several decades. Nor has age or increasing concern over debility been impediments to attaining the White House—consider Franklin Delano Roosevelt's victory in 1944, Eisenhower's post-heart-attack landslide in 1956, and public support for Ronald Reagan even after a bout with cancer and the shock of near assassination.

Other current American organizations accord power to their elders. Older men (and occasionally women) who have demonstrated their piety and shrewdness in a succession of administrative offices tend to oversee Protestant, Orthodox, and Roman Catholic churches. Similarly, professional organizations—including gerontological bodies—tend to tap people known for their interpersonal skills and diverse backgrounds for management positions. It takes time to develop a reputation for leadership.

That said, there are no major gerontocracies in post-modern America. Those with the most seniority tend to be older than greenhorns, but rookies can—and do—sometimes rise quickly to the top. Educational attainment matters more than race, gender, geography or (old) age in the acquisition of power.

W. ANDREW ACHENBAUM

BIBLIOGRAPHY

ACHENBAUM, W. A. "Historical Perspectives on Aging." In *Handbook of Aging and the Social Sciences*. 4th ed. Edited by Robert H. Binstock and Linda George. San Diego: Academic Press, 1995. Pages 137–152.
COLE, T. R. *The Journey of Life*. New York: Cambridge University Press, 1992.
EISELE, F. "Gerontocracy." In *The Encyclopedia of Aging*, 2d ed. Edited by George Maddox et al. New York: Springer Publishing, 1995. Page 412.
GUTMANN, D. *Reclaimed Powers*. New York: Basic Book, 1987.
SIMMONS, L. *The Role of the Aged in Primitive Societies*. New Haven: Yale University Press, 1945.

GERONTOLOGICAL NURSING

Gerontological nursing has taken several centuries to become acknowledged as a separate nursing specialty. Its rise should be understood within the context of the emergence and development of the nursing profession generally. Additionally, the growth in the number of older adults, and in the cultural care of elderly persons around the world, must be considered. It is important to note that the preparation of gerontological nurses is dictated somewhat by the cultural strictures and interpretations of a particular society's definition of older persons, which will influence the status of this specialty in different countries.

The beginnings of nursing

The development of nursing has followed the development of mankind. In its most early phases, nurses were almost exclusively female family members. Nursing gained ground toward becoming a profession due to the care provided to the poor, the indigent, the infirm, and the insane; to prisoners and orphans; as well as to women during childbirth and to people during war times. Laywomen who initially tried to fill the demand for more nursing care during the expansion to the New World were ineffective, as they were without role models or training. Religious orders played an important part in the development of nursing care facilities through care provided in their convents, abbeys, and almshouses. In the mid-1850s, the Crimean War provided Florence Nightingale with the necessary outpouring of public support to effect changes in nursing. Nightingale initiated such advances as the establishment of an organized training school and a formalized and standardized organization, thus finally turning nursing into a suitable occupation for women. Nursing was well on its way to being a profession, although it would still take more than one hundred years to become fully acknowledged as a separate health care entity. Nurses now make up the largest international work force in health care.

The impact of world population changes

Reduced infant mortality and death rates, the conquering of major diseases, major medical advances, and better overall health care throughout the world have together resulted in increased life expectancy, and thus more elderly persons, especially those of extreme age (eighty-five years and older). In North America, the immigration boom between 1900 and 1920 also added to the number of older persons at the turn of the century. In modern industrialized societies, old age is identified in terms of chronological age. In other societies, onset of old age is more commonly linked with events such as succession to eldership or becoming a grandparent.

The importance of family life to the well-being of the elderly person can be seen in many cultures. In developing countries, the existence of an extended kin network provides regular and frequent contact as an essential part of the traditional welfare (support) system. In developed countries, even with reduced family size, childless marriages, fewer single adult daughters, and increasing numbers of middle-aged women in the work force (all of which have led to decreasing availability and opportunity for children to care directly for aging parents), the first and major resource for elderly persons is still the family: less than 10 percent of older people are ever institutionalized in these countries.

The field of aging

Gerontology as a field of study was notable in Europe prior to North America because of the earlier maturing of Europe's population while initially North America had a younger population. However, in the early 1930's as North America's war against infectious diseases was won, more focus was placed upon degenerative, chronic diseases—most of which were notable in the growing, older population. Gerontology began as an inquiry into the characteristics of long-lived people. It is defined as the science of

aging, studying the effects of time on human development, specifically aging. Gerontology is the preferred term for the normal aging process including the biologic, psychosocial and spiritual aspects of the older adult. The term *geriatrics* is the area of study related to diseases of the elderly and became popular as geriatric medicine evolved.

The specialty of gerontological nursing

The nursing profession has clearly been affected by the increased aging of the world population, the sheer numbers of elderly people, and the different ways the world's elderly persons are treated. As the population has shifted from *baby boomers* to *senior surge*, the demand for expertise in this escalating population has also intensified. Nurses have long been interested in the care of older persons, and they seemed to have assumed more responsibility than other professions for this segment of the population. With a shift (change of focus from emphasis in children and adolescents towards the elderly) in societal emphasis giving visibility to elderly persons, the nursing community has focused upon this population in terms of increasing their knowledge base and increased education in this neophyte specialty field.

In North America, gerontological nursing began its rise with the acknowledgment of this new nursing specialty by the American Nurses Association in 1962 and the formation of the National Gerontological Nursing Association in 1984. In Canada, the Canadian Nurses Association recognized the Canadian Gerontological Nursing Association as a specialty in 1985. Other nursing specialty organizations developed in Australia and Great Britain. In contrast to the continued use of the term *geriatric*, the term *gerontological nursing* was in use by the early 1980s to reflect the provision of care and the treatment of the whole person, not only care of disease in a medical setting. The assessment of the health needs of older adults, the planning and implementing of health care to meet those needs, and the evaluation of the effectiveness of such care are critical activities in assisting older adults to optimize their functional abilities and thereby maximize independence and promote well-being—a prime directive for gerontological nurses. A more recent term, *gerontic nursing*, refines the sphere of responsibility of gerontological nurses who care for the elderly by encompassing the art and intuition of caring and maintaining the "well elderly" as well as emphasizing illness and scientific principles of care.

During the last half of the twentieth century, there was profound growth in the literature of gerontological nursing. A North American gerontological nursing text was published in 1950, and a monthly journal devoted to gerontological nursing began publication in 1975. The birth of gerontological nursing research to provide a strong, independent knowledge base to link research with the increasing complexity of practice expertise began in the late 1970s.

As the skill and knowledge base of gerontological nurses has continued to accelerate, there has been a corresponding growth in education, with the development of undergraduate baccalaureate, graduate masters, and postgraduate Ph.D. programs in gerontological nursing designed to prepare the necessary clinicians, researchers, educators, and administrators. Specific university-prepared clinical practice streams now include nurse practitioners as clinical nurse specialists and expanded role nurses, among others, providing advanced practice knowledge to older populations. Gerontological nurses must have the knowledge and skill to manage care focused upon normal and abnormal age-related physical changes (e.g., musculoskeletal, sensory, neurological) and age-related psychosocial and spiritual changes (e.g., developmental, intellectual capacity, learning and memory, losses). Gerontological nurses must be educated concerning care strategies about wide-ranging basic and complex physiological and behavioral issues such as pain, pressure ulcers, cognitive impairment, self-esteem disturbance, bereavement, fluid and electrolyte imbalance, and caregiver stress, among other issues. Gerontological nurses must also have expertise in navigating the health care system to act as advocates for their clients.

Standards of nursing practice have been developed in various countries to define the uniqueness and scope of gerontic nursing practice and to provide a foundation for evaluation of nursing practice in all settings where the focus of care is on the older person. Gerontological nurses may also be certified through a written examination available in certain countries, as a recognition of expert professional competency.

The future is secure for gerontological nursing as an acknowledged and well-respected specialty within nursing, as well as a discipline among its interdisciplinary colleagues in efforts to improve care for older persons throughout the world.

DEBORAH A. VANDEWATER

See also GERIATRIC MEDICINE; LONG-TERM CARE; NURSE PRACTITIONER.

BIBLIOGRAPHY

ANDERSEN, H. C. *Geriatric Nursing.* St. Louis: Mosby, 1950.

BARASH, D. P. *Aging: An Exploration.* Seattle: University of Washington Press, 1983.

BURNSIDE, I. M. *Nursing and the Aged: A Self-Care Approach*, 3d ed. New York: McGraw-Hill, 1988.

EBERSOLE, P., and HESS, P. *Toward Healthy Aging: Human Needs and Nursing Response*, 4th ed. St. Louis: C.V. Mosby, 1994.

HOGSTEL, M., ed. *Nursing Care of the Older Adult: In the Hospital, Nursing Home and Community.* New York: John Wiley & Sons, 1981.

Journal of Gerontological Nursing 1, no. 1 (1975): 6.

KANE, R. L.; EVANS, J. G.; and MACFADYEN, D., eds. *Improving the Health Care of Older People: A World View.* Oxford, U.K.: Oxford University Press, 1990.

NOVAK, M. *Aging & Society: A Canadian Perspective*, 3d ed. Toronto: ITP Nelson, 1997.

STEFFL, B. M., ed. *Handbook of Gerontological Nursing.* New York: Van Nostrand Reinhold, 1984.

WOODRUFF, D. S., and BIRREN, J. E., eds. *Aging Scientific Perspectives and Social Issues*, 2d ed. Monterey, Calif.: Brooks/Cole, 1975.

GERONTOLOGY

The quest for explanations for why we age is nearly as old as the written record, going back to long before Ponce de Leon's fabled search for the "fountain of youth" in the early 1500s. It was not until the beginning of the twentieth century, however, that the term *gerontology* emerged. Writing in 1903, the zoologist Élie Metchnikoff noted "it is extremely probable that the scientific study of old age and of death, two branches of science that may be called *gerontology* and *thanatology*, will bring about great modifications in the course of the last period of life" (pp. 297–298). Derived from the Greek words *geront* ("old man") and *logia* ("the study of"), gerontology is defined as the scientific study of aging and of the older population. This dual focus on processes of aging and on the characteristics, conditions, and circumstances of older people is at the heart of the field of contemporary gerontology.

Although the distinction is not always clear in practice, gerontology's concern with the scientific study of aging and old age differs from a related field—geriatrics. *Geriatrics* is the branch of medicine concerned with the treatment and management of diseases and illnesses (e.g., hearing loss, osteoporosis, dementia) that are more prevalent in old age than in the early or middle years. Thus, a geriatrician might be concerned with whether surgical procedures will reverse hearing loss or how an assistive device such as a hearing aid can compensate for declines in a person's ability to hear. A gerontologist might be interested in studying the causes of hearing loss, whether it occurs with greater frequency among older men or older women, and understanding the effects that declining auditory acuity have on an individual's mobility, interaction, and enjoyment of life. Put another way, geriatrics focuses on the clinical diagnosis and treatment of medical conditions that typically occur during the later years, while gerontology involves the scientific understanding of the causes, distribution, and consequences of these conditions.

Gerontological perspectives on aging and old age

Gerontology involves gaining a scientific understanding of processes of aging, processes that take place simultaneously on several levels. Aging occurs at the biological and physiological levels, for example, as the ability of cells to replicate themselves decreases with aging or as respiratory and cardiovascular systems typically become less efficient. Aging is also characterized by a series of interrelated psychological processes that may manifest themselves in changes in the speed with which information is processed or in changes in short-term recall. Aging is also a social process reflecting sequences of roles assumed throughout life and transitions from one role to another (e.g., from employee to retiree, from parent to grandparent, from spouse to widow). When we think of someone as "growing old," we are speaking of the outcomes of these and other processes that take place simultaneously, but at different rates for different people. A thirty-five-year-old grandmother or an eighty-year-old "master" athlete whose cardiovascular system is

functioning at the level of a forty-year-old illustrate how processes of aging may vary from one individual to another.

Although we most often think of aging as an individual phenomenon—as what happens to persons as they grow older—it is also true that both aging processes and what constitutes old age are socially defined or socially "constructed." They are the product of historical, social, political, and economic forces. For administrative purposes, for example, when someone "becomes" old varies widely. One needs to be at least sixty-five years old to be eligible to receive full Social Security benefits (although this changed in 2002, when the eligibility age began to climb gradually to sixty-seven) and sixty to be eligible for programs and services under the Older Americans Act, but only forty to be covered under the provisions of the Age Discrimination in Employment Act. How we conceive of the capabilities of older persons also varies from one time to another. A sixty-five-year-old might be considered too old to work during a recession when unemployment rates are high, but that same person may be a highly desirable employee when the economy is booming, unemployment rates are low, and labor in short supply. As a stage of the life course, old age during America's colonial period was a far different experience from what it is during the first years of the twenty-first century and from what it probably will be when the entire baby boom generation (born between 1946 and 1964) has reached old age in the year 2030. What it is like to be old also varies from one group to another within a society, just as it varies between societies with different cultural traditions. At any particular time, the financial situation of a typical seventy-five-year-old African American woman will differ dramatically from that of a typical seventy-five-year-old white male. And the intergenerational experience of living in a Japanese family, with its tradition of multigenerational living arrangements, will differ from that of the American family where the norm has been "intimacy at a distance."

Because aging is a multilevel passage and because old age is socially constructed, the study of aging and of old age necessarily relies on the contributions of a number of scientific disciplines. For this reason, gerontology is considered a multidisciplinary and interdisciplinary field of inquiry, and professional organizations such as the Gerontological Society of America count among their members researchers and scholars from a wide variety of disciplines.

In the basic sciences, research on the biological aspects of aging is being conducted in such fields as biochemistry, cellular and molecular biology, endocrinology, genetics, immunology, nutrition, pathology, pharmacology, and physiology. Medical and health scientists from specialties such as cardiology, neurology, oncology, and orthopedics are studying the causes, consequences, and treatment of illness and disease; the epidemiology (distribution) of physical well-being; and factors associated with the use of health services by older persons. Social and behavioral research in gerontology similarly includes contributions from scientists with many different disciplinary backgrounds: anthropology, demography, economics, geography, history, political science, psychology, public health, sociology, and statistics. Our understanding of aging and the experience of being an older person is also enhanced by the work of scholars from humanities disciplines such as art, literature, music, philosophy, and religion. Gerontological knowledge has benefited, too, from research conducted by investigators from a variety of professions, such as architecture, nursing, physical therapy, and social work.

Gerontology, then, is a multidisciplinary and interdisciplinary area of scientific inquiry dedicated to increasing our understanding of aging and old age. But just as gerontology comprises a wide array of disciplines permitting research at the intersections of two or more traditional fields, its boundaries are flexible in another important way. We have learned that the nature of old age is often a product of earlier life experiences and that processes of aging begin long before one is old. This recognition has led gerontologists to begin to take a longer view of factors that affect aging and old age and to attempt to locate and identify influences that occur in earlier stages of life. Such an approach is variously known as a life course, life span, or life cycle perspective, and it has drawn our attention to the ways in which late life characteristics may have their origin in events occurring long before old age. Glen Elder, for example, has shown that the current attitudes and values of older persons were shaped by their experience during the Great Depression. And in a fascinating project known as the Nun Study, autobiographies written by nuns when they first entered a convent, at an average age of twenty-three, were examined for their linguistic ability

or idea density. Over sixty years after the autobiographies were written and upon postmortem examination of the brains of deceased nuns, the idea density scores from early life were highly correlated with the presence and severity of Alzheimer's disease in late life (Snowdon, Greiner, and Markesbery). Studies such as these have made gerontologists increasingly aware of the need to examine early antecedents of late-life behaviors, characteristics, and circumstances.

Twentieth-century advances in the gerontological perspective

Foreshadowings of the storyline of twentieth-century gerontology are plentiful. Early Egyptian, Greek, and Roman commentaries on the course of life were known and carefully read by the first of the modern gerontologists. Cicero's *De Senectute* and Soranus of Ephesus's *Gynaecia* and his *Acute Disease* and *Chronic Disease* were frequently echoed. For example, Jean-Martin Charcot's examination of pathological causes of aging captured in his *Diseases of the Elders and Their Chronic Illnesses* (1867) (translated into English in 1881) and the early chapters of G. Stanley Hall's *Senescence* (1922) recounted descriptions from ancient medical tracts.

The decades on either side of the dawn of the twentieth century resounded with innovative efforts to discover first the pattern, then the laws, and finally the causes of aging. Each was seemingly mindful of Adolph Quetelet's 1842 declaration that "Man is born, grows up, and dies, according to certain laws that have never been properly investigated" (quoted in Achenbaum, p. 35). In France, Charcot's search for pathogens associated with aging was particularly influential. In England, Francis Galton sampled nine thousand visitors to the International Health Exposition of the 1880s to identify changes in physical characteristics. In Russia, Botkin surveyed three thousand almshouse residents in an effort to differentiate normal from pathological aging.

In the United States, Charles Minot blended Charcot's focus on cellular changes with those of nineteenth-century cytologist August Weismann and formulated a kind of a proto wear-and-tear theory that saw aging in terms of entropy and fatigue states. The field was given sharper focus with Metchnikoff's 1903 coinage of the word gerontology. Metchnikoff, who was by then director of the Pasteur Institute, focused his own explorations on ways to ward off infectious autotoxicity induced by phagocyte processes (leukocytes that ingest and destroy other cells) carried by intestinal bacteria. He advanced his prescription for hefty helpings of yogurt to quell intestinal disorders thought to engender the debilitations of age in popular and scientific publications and was awarded the Nobel Prize in 1908 for his treatises *The Nature of Man* (1903) and *The Prolongation of Life* (1908).

Thus stimulated, basic biological and physiological research proceeded apace, focusing on such disparate topics as environmental and public health issues, physiological changes, lesions, and cellular-level breakdowns. In 1909, Ignatius Nascher broke ranks and proclaimed that however prevalent pathology might be, old age is not defined by pathological change. Nascher was a true interdisciplinary scientist. Stressing the importance of what might now be called social epidemiology, he dispatched teams of investigators in the New York City area to gather data he then analyzed, using statistical averages to define typical conditions and to contrast one social category with another. With G. Stanley Hall's compendium *Senescence* (1922), the basic parameters of modern gerontology were set as an array of behavior factors and were added to the biological substrate already enunciated. Hall's approach was also significant in that he emphasized positive attributes thought to accompany the aging process (Hendricks and Achenbaum).

Publications: hallmarks and benchmarks

During the early decades of the twentieth century, interest was piqued then quickened again. In 1905, the *Journal of the American Medical Association* printed Stockton's "The Delay of Old Age and the Alleviation of Senility," and the next year Marshall Price's "Ancient and Modern Theory of Old Age" appeared in the *Maryland Medical Journal*. The most influential of these early publications was undoubtedly Nascher's 1909 article in *The New York Medical Record* titled simply "Geriatrics," followed five years later by his volume *Geriatrics: The Diseases of Old Age and Their Treatment, Including Physiological Old Age, Home and Institutional Care, and Medico-Legal Relations* (1914). He coined the term geriatrics to describe a clinical focus and single-handedly launched a new medical specialty. During the same period, Lee Squier's *Old Age Dependency in the United States* (1912) joined Nascher's publications and stands as one of the early efforts in the United States to

survey the conditions of old age. These watershed contributions helped lead to the inauguration of a regular geriatrics section in the *Medical Review of Reviews* in 1917 to promote professionalization of the study of aging. Further impetus came when the *Scientific American* published Genevieve Grandcourt's "Eternal Youth as Scientific Theory" in 1919. Nascher's eye-catching article "Why Old Age Ends in Death" appeared the same year in the *Medical Review of Reviews*.

With G. Stanley Hall's publication of *Senescence*, the behavioral sciences were given clarion voice in the discussion of the causes and implications of aging. Hall was noteworthy because he melded basic research with practical interventions and a critique of societal arrangements. With the publication of Edmund Cowdry's edited handbook, *Problems of Aging* (1939), the broad parameters of gerontological inquiry were pretty well drawn (Hendricks and Achenbaum). Accompanied by financial support by the Josiah Macy Foundation and endorsements from the National Research Council's medical sciences division, Cowdry assembled the best minds of the era to launch a unified fusillade at the problems of aging. Cowdry's encyclopedic reference, which appeared in a second edition in 1942, provided the first widely heard call for a multidisciplinary approach and helped create the collective consciousness of biomedical and behavioral cross-linkages within contemporary gerontology and geriatrics.

Learned societies and other organizational events

A series of organizational events ran parallel to the many scholarly and scientific publications. Together they helped merge gerontology into the scientific mainstream and contributed to the professionalization of the enterprise. No doubt it was fortuitous that Metchnikoff had become affiliated with the Pasteur Institute in Paris in 1888, for his associates there contributed to his thinking just as he contributed to theirs. The seed was fertile and one of his students, V. Korenchevsky, went on to establish the International Club for Research on Ageing in England, succeeded in 1939 by the British Society for Research on Ageing. The club served as a learned society providing scholarly forums to present and exchange ideas. When Korenchevsky came to the United States in 1939 to create a North American branch, his efforts were virtually anticlimactic.

Organizational efforts to promote analysis of aging had appeared on the national agenda as early as 1908 as part of President Theodore Roosevelt's conservation agenda as formulated by the Committee of 100. Members of that group later established the Life Extension Institute in 1914 to promote inquiry into the causes of illness and death. The New York Geriatrics Society was founded in 1915 and other comparable state-based organizations proliferated in short order.

Aging sessions in one guise or another appeared as part of the annual meetings of the American Psychological Association by the turn of the century and other learned societies followed suit. In 1917, the National Conference of Social Work scheduled a plenary session and invited Nascher and a number of speakers to participate in a scholarly exchange on pathological models of aging and to suggest appropriate efforts for social workers.

Attention to the implications of aging grew in the period immediately after World War I. A popular magazine, *Voix du Retraite*, appeared in Paris in 1919 and the Swiss Foundation for the Aging began publishing its *Pro Senectute* in 1923. In 1928, a Japanese organization for the aged, Yokufukai, launched initially in 1925 to help older victims of a major earthquake, began disseminating the *Yokufukai Geriatric Journal*, succeeded in 1930 by *Acta Gerontologica Japonica*. In Eastern Europe, the magazine *Problems of Ageing* (printed in five languages) appeared in 1935 under the auspice of the International Institute for the Study of Old Age and the Romanian government. Meanwhile, in the Soviet Union, I. Fisher and P. Yengalvtchev launched a series of empirical investigations and publications on the role of physical condition, mental status, and environmental factors in promoting longevity. Their efforts led to a major conference in 1938 in Kiev that stands as a milestone for bringing together researchers from Eastern Europe. International interest was accelerating and the number of contributors and publications spread around the globe.

In the same period a number of philanthropic foundations with interests in public welfare and scholarly advancement sponsored various conferences and workshops that led to some of the publications noted above. Among them the W. K. Kellogg Foundation, the Russell Sage Foundation, the Carnegie Corporation, the Josiah Macy Foundation, and the Rockefeller Foundation stand out. None of the efforts were more luminous that the Woods Hole conference that led to Cowdry's *Problems of Aging*. The interdisciplinary message Cowdry and his coauthors promulgated did not gain sweeping acceptance but by 1940, Edward Stieglitz, a newly appointed clinician with the Public Health Service, suggested that the proper study of aging should incorporate no less than geriatrics, the biology of senescence, and sociological perspectives on aging populations. Nathan Shock took over from Stieglitz and continued the same mission for the next thirty years. The same year that Stieglitz began promoting a truly interdisciplinary focus, the National Institutes of Health, founded in 1930, also incorporated a Unit on Gerontology with an edict to enhance knowledge of aging processes.

Although the American Geriatrics Society was founded in midst of World War II (1942), the war years slowed many further developments. However, within a year of war's end, what is now called the Gerontological Society of America was established, with the initial issue of the *Journal of Gerontology* appearing in 1946. Under the auspices of the International Association of Gerontology, which was founded in 1950, international scientific congresses are held to bring together researchers from around the world in an open exchange of ideas.

Despite the publication in 1945 of two important books—Leo Simmons's *The Role of the Aged in Primitive Societies* and Oscar Kaplan's *Mental Disorders in Later Life*—Otto Pollack declared in *Social Adjustment in Old Age* (1948) that insights into aging from the social and behavioral sciences lagged behind those of medicine and biology. Soon a breakthrough contribution began to change that picture. Together with her colleagues from the University of Chicago, Ruth Cavan surveyed three thousand older persons and published the results in *Personal Adjustment in Old Age* (1949). It was only the first of the many contributions made by the Committee of Human Development at the University of Chicago. Perhaps not as well remembered as the famous Kansas City Studies of Adult Aging, or many of the early, seminal contributions of Bernice Neugarten, Ethel Shanas, Robert J. Havighurst, Robert Burgess, Elaine Cumming, William Henry, and others, it nonetheless paved the way for the shape of social gerontology. By the time Elaine Cumming and William Henry published their disengagement interpretation of the results of the Kansas City Studies in their *Growing Old* (1961), gerontology had come of age and advances were occurring along many fronts.

From that point on, the relatively narrow flow of information spread out across the landscape. Programs and certificate training sprang up in California, Michigan, North Carolina and around the country. By the 1960s the Gerontological Society transformed a newsletter into its second journal, *The Gerontologist*, and the first of the White House Conferences on Aging was held. Out of that conference came the establishment of an Office on Aging (under the leadership of Donald P. Kent), later the Administration on Aging, and the momentum that led to both the passage of Medicare and Medicaid (1965) and support via the Older Americans Act for the development of education and training programs in gerontology in the late 1960s and 1970s. The last of the building blocks came in 1975 with the inauguration of the National Institute on Aging to oversee basic research in a wide array of disciplines and to train future researchers. Significant publications continued to emerge, including Clarke Tibbitts's *Handbook of Social Gerontology* (1959), the three-volume *Aging and Society* series under the leadership of Matilda White Riley, and the five editions of the *Handbook of the Biology of Aging*, *Psychology of Aging*, and *Aging and the Social Sciences* under the general editorship of James E. Birren.

Teaching and training

The steadily increasing recognition of the importance of gerontology is reflected in its growing presence in the curricula of institutions of higher education in the United States. In the 1950s, coursework on aging was offered on only a small number of campuses. Data collected in 1957 showed that only fifty-seven colleges and universities offered credit courses in gerontology. The number of campuses with courses on aging increased to 159 in 1967, 607 in 1976, and 1,335 in 1985. By 1992, when the last major survey was conducted, it was estimated that gerontology instruction was offered on 1,639 campuses, or at 55 percent of American institutions of higher education. Of these campuses with credit instruction in 1992, the average number of courses in gerontology was 9.4 and over 40 percent offered a structured program of coursework in gerontology, geriatrics, or aging leading to the awarding of a degree, certificate, special-

ization, concentration, minor, or some other form of credential (Peterson, Wendt, and Douglass.

An important development in graduate education was the establishment of the first Ph.D. programs in gerontology in the late 1980s and early 1990s. A long and continuing debate has centered on the question of whether gerontology is better viewed as a field of specialization or as an emerging academic discipline. Those taking the position that gerontology is a field of specialization contend that doctoral work should take place in one of the more traditional disciplines (e.g., biology, psychology, sociology), but with an emphasis on aging in coursework and research. Those holding the view that gerontology has reached a stage of maturity in its theories, methods, and content argue that doctoral-level work leading to a Ph.D. in gerontology is justified. The merits of each of these positions aside, academic programs leading to a Ph.D. in gerontology existed at a handful of American universities at the outset of the twenty-first century. The debate about whether gerontology is a specialty or a full-fledged academic discipline will doubtless continue, but the emergence of Ph.D. programs attests to the increasing recognition of its importance.

The most comprehensive list of college and university programs in gerontology, geriatrics, and aging has been compiled by the Association for Gerontology in Higher Education (AGHE, now an Educational Unit of the Gerontological Society of America). In its seventh edition, the *Directory of Educational Programs in Gerontology and Geriatrics* (Stepp) provides detailed information on the content, focus, and type and level of credential offered in close to eight hundred programs in the United States, Canada, and other countries.

Applied gerontology

Knowledge accumulated from scientific research on the biological, physiological, psychological, and social processes associated with aging adds to our basic understanding of the human condition. But gerontological research serves another essential purpose. By learning about the nature of aging and old age, we are in a position to use the knowledge to improve the quality of the later-life experience. *Applied gerontology* emphasizes the translation of basic research into the development of services, programs, and interventions for the betterment of the older population. Basic biological research not only illuminates the mechanisms underlying this aspect of the aging process, but also offers clues that have the potential to slow down or reverse deleterious outcomes. Knowing how physiological and sensory processes change with aging provides valuable information that can be used to design environmental modifications to enhance the functional ability of older persons. Gaining a scientifically sound appreciation of the extent and nature of family caregiving can counter the myth of abandonment and allow for the development of an appropriate blend of supportive services to help families cope with the stresses of caring for a frail relative. Studies on the barriers and obstacles people encounter in accessing services and programs enable us to consider ways to restructure their delivery and enable health and human service providers to better meet the needs of target populations.

Gerontology makes a distinction between life expectancy—how many more years one can expect to live at a given age—and "active" life expectancy—or how long one can expect to function well prior to the onset of debilitating conditions. This distinction serves to focus attention on the quality of late life and not simply its quantity. In this sense, the fundamental and complementary objectives of basic and applied gerontology might best be summarized as the pursuit of scientific knowledge to promote and extend the active life expectancy of older persons or, as in the motto of the Gerontological Society of America, "to add life to years, not just years to life."

STEPHEN J. CUTLER
JON HENDRICKS

See also AGING; GERIATRIC MEDICINE; CAREERS IN AGING; NATIONAL INSTITUTE ON AGING; PROLONGEVITY.

BIBLIOGRAPHY

ACHENBAUM, W. A. *Crossing Frontiers: Gerontology Emerges as a Science.* Cambridge, U.K.: Cambridge University Press, 1995.

ELDER, G. H. *Children of the Great Depression*, 25th Anniversary ed. New York: HarperCollins, 1998.

HENDRICKS, J., and ACHENBAUM, W. A. "Historical Development of Theories of Aging." In *Handbook of Theories of Aging.* Edited by Vern L. Bengtson and K. Warner Schaie. New York: Springer Publishing Co., 1999. Pages 21–39.

METCHNIKOFF, É. *The Nature of Man.* New York: Putnam and Sons, 1908. (First published in France, 1903).

PETERSON, D. A.; WENDT, P. F.; and DOUGLASS, E. B. *Development of Gerontology, Geriatrics, and Aging Studies Programs in Institutions of Higher Education.* Washington, D.C.: Association for Gerontology in Higher Education, 1994.

POLLACK, O. *Social Adjustment in Old Age.* New York: Social Science Research Council, 1948.

SNOWDON, D. A.; GREINER, L. H.; and MARKESBERY, W. R. "Linguistic Ability in Early Life and the Neuropathology of Alzheimer's Disease and Cerebrovascular Disease: Findings from the Nun Study." In *Vascular Findings in Alzheimer's Disease.* Edited by Raj N. Kalaria and Paul Ince. New York: New York Academy of Sciences, 2000. Pages 34–38.

STEPP, DEREK D., ed. *Directory of Educational Programs in Gerontology and Geriatrics*, 7th ed. Washington, D.C.: Association for Gerontology in Higher Education, 2000.

GLAUCOMA

See EYE, AGING-RELATED DISEASES

GOVERNMENT ASSISTED HOUSING

Government housing assistance is available to low-income older persons through three major programs: public housing, section 202, and section 8. These programs aim to relieve the housing burden of low-income families, older people, and persons with disabilities (regardless of age). There is no uniform public housing policy solely for older people in the United States. Historically, housing policies and programs were family centered; older people benefited from public subsidies through having low-income or belonging to members of a low-income family. The Housing Act of 1937 resolved to improve the housing standards of those families who could not afford to buy or rent in the private market.

Section 202 and Section 8

The Housing Act of 1937 did not fund housing assistance for older people. The first National

Conference on Aging in 1950 recommended that Congress specifically address housing needs of the elderly, but nine years passed (1959) before enactment of a subsidized housing program known as Section 202.

The Department of Housing and Urban Development (HUD) was created by the Housing and Urban Development Act of 1965 as a cabinet-level agency. Although HUD administers all federal housing programs, the main thrust of its activities traditionally has consisted of urban development. This is reflected in HUD's budget, which in 2000 allocated only 10 percent for housing for the elderly.

The original Section 202 provided loans to nonprofit organizations at a rate of 3 percent to build housing for older low- and moderate-income persons and the disabled. The rate has changed several times due to market conditions. Between 1959 and 1969, approximately forty-five thousand units were constructed. By 1996 there were 7,547 Section 202 facilities housing more than 387,000 persons.

Congress created Section 8 in 1974 to provide subsidized housing assistance to households with incomes too low for them to obtain decent housing in the private market. Under this program, HUD entered into assistance contracts with owners of existing housing and developers of new or rehabilitated housing for a specified number of units to be leased to households meeting federal eligibility standards. Qualified families paid part of the rent and HUD paid the difference directly to owners of the units. In 1999, three million families benefited from Section 8 subsidies; 44 percent of these were older people.

Section 8 includes two forms of subsidy: tenant-based and project-based, each assisting approximately half of the Section 8 units. In the tenant-based programs, vouchers are given to residents, who can choose from the available housing market in the private sector. In the project-based programs, specific properties are subsidized, such as high-rise apartments for older people.

In 1975 HUD entered into twenty-year contracts with the owners of project-based units, resulting in increased owner opt-outs as the contracts expired. With the future of project-based programs threatened, HUD proposed a remedy in 1999, providing vouchers for residents of project-based programs to allow them to remain in the units. This effectively left the decision to accept or reject the vouchers in the hands of the owners, thus putting the future of affordable housing for many older Americans in jeopardy. Since 1996 more than thirty thousand subsidized units have left the Section 8 program. This trend continues; HUD estimates the termination of 900,000 project units by 2004.

Historical phases

Poverty was the main issue in the development of Section 202 and Section 8 programs. During the initial phase (1959–1974) Section 202 housed the moderate-income clientele who did not meet eligibility requirements for public housing. The program was criticized for not being sensitive to the housing needs of the poor, even though it was run by nonprofit organizations. The Housing Act of 1968 allowed the for-profit sector to enter into the building of elderly housing. The Nixon administration terminated funding for Section 202 in 1970, but with enactment of the 1974 Housing Act, funding was reinstated and a new low-income phase began.

"Low income" meant below 80 percent of median income. First-time Section 202 units were also available as Section 8 rentals for eligible low-income persons. For low-income older people, this meant the acceptance of publicly subsidized housing and the realization that they could improve their housing standards by moving to a Section 8 unit. This Section 202 phase also responded to the rural and minority poor and the frail elderly by setting aside up to 25 percent of available funds to improve the conditions of their current housing.

Significant changes occurred between 1984 and 1990. Income eligibility was lowered to 50 percent of the local median income, but the rent contribution for low-income tenants was increased from 25 to 30 percent. Due to significant cuts during the Reagan and Bush administrations, the construction of Section 202 units declined; by 1988 older persons applying for Section 202 housing had to wait eight to eleven years, depending on location. By 1992 there were eight low-income elderly waiting for each vacancy in Section 202 housing. By 1999 over one million families were on the waiting list.

Housing needs in the twenty-first century

HUD used three dimensions (1999) to identify housing conditions of older people: adequacy, affordability, and accessibility. Regarding adequacy, available data suggest that 7 percent of public housing for the elderly and 7 percent of Section 202 housing have moderate deficiencies but better conditions than market-rate rentals. Of the elderly population as a whole, 1.45 million still lack the most basic elements of housing security, such as safety, reliable plumbing, heat sources, or accommodation for those with limitations on activities of daily living (ADL). Nine percent of the units occupied by those with mobility problems are inadequate.

In spite of favorable economic conditions in the 1980s and 1990s, cost continued to be most widespread housing problem for the elderly. Nationally, 7 percent of all older people spent more than 30 percent of income for housing. There are not enough Section 202 and Section 8 funds to provide affordable homes for an eligible 1.5 million elderly.

Accessibility is crucial for older people with functional limitations and disabilities. HUD (1999) reported a need for home modification for 1.1 million older people. Although ADL limitations increase with age, HUD appropriations do not increase proportionately, and sometimes decline. (The $26 billion 2000 HUD budget was called "landmark" by the Clinton administration, when in fact the 1980 HUD budget was $80 billion.)

Perhaps a fourth dimension, appropriateness, is as crucial to recognize as the three just discussed. Lacking the understanding of and sensitivity to the needs of older people and persons with disabilities, both Congress and administrations since the 1950s have ignored needs for services in public housing and subsidized programs by accepting the premise that older persons belong either in a Section 202 or in a Section 8 unit or in a nursing home. Although HUD was mandated to develop services that would help older persons to move on a continuum, the needed services were never developed.

Service needs

As residents in Section 202 units aged, becoming more frail and in greater need of supportive services, few of those services were developed. Although HUD has been required since 1974 to seek assurance that Section 202 projects provide a range of services which, in combination, will prevent premature institutionalization, researchers found that there had been a clear shift away from supportive design features over the history of the 202 program. These features, known as Congregate Housing Service Programs (CHSPs), include the following:

- Provision for nutritional needs by serving two meals a day, seven days a week
- Provision of housekeeping assistance in areas where needed
- Provision of personal assistance to those demonstrating difficulty with ADLs
- Provision of expanded personal counseling services to those experiencing emotional problems due to losses
- Provision for the limited extension of existing transportation services to enable those with physical and mental impairments to meet medical appointments
- Facilitation of optimal utilization of CHSP services through professional case management.

In view of the requirements and the findings, Congress passed the National Affordable Housing Act of 1990 (NAHA), recognizing a need to (1) expand the supply of supportive housing for the elderly and (2) enhance the supportive environment of existing Section 202 projects. One section of the act requires HUD to ensure that projects approved after 30 September 1991 comply with the law. The act also authorizes up to 15 percent of the 202 funds to be spent on supportive services and retrofitting units (e.g., installing ramps or railings) for the frail and disabled. However, these mandates did not carry the needed appropriations. HUD also neglected to comply with the terms of the NAHA. Instead, HUD used random selection to determine in which projects supportive services were placed; selection was not based on need. The decision to initiate and plan supportive services or to convert the Section 202 units to assisted living facilities was left up to the project managers.

Throughout the history of federal housing, project managers were given far greater authority than they were qualified to assume. In the case of service needs for frail older persons, managers lacking necessary training were asked to make needs assessments. Researchers found that the health conditions of the frail elderly were far worse than self-reported to project managers and far worse than residency policy permitted. Fearing nursing home placement, older residents refused to reveal functional problems. Mandated or not, services became very low priority during the Reagan and Bush administrations, when HUD suffered severe budget cuts—from $80 billion in 1980 to $24 billion in 1992. During the same period staff was cut from seventeen thousand to thirteen thousand.

Perhaps the greatest obstacle to linking housing and services lies in the separate jurisdictions of the policy-making arena: building of housing is under the House and Senate Banking Committees, while providing services is under Health and Human Services. The Subcommittee on Housing and Consumer Interests of the House Select Committee on Aging and the House and Senate Appropriations Committees also affect policy decisions. The history of the public housing program showed that the "bricks and mortar" principle prevailed, and high-rise buildings were far more visible to the constituencies of these committee members than the people who resided in them.

Case mix

The service inadequacy is compounded by the case mix of young and old. Traditionally, older and younger persons with physical disabilities lived side by side in the units. Then, due to deinstitutionalization in the 1960s and 1970s, discharged mental patients with no other housing opportunities began to occupy the units. By 1991, 10 percent of the three hundred thousand units housed younger persons with mental disabilities. Interest groups advocating on behalf of younger people with drug and alcohol addiction argued that disproportionate amounts of housing subsidies were spent for the low-income elderly. As the aging network continued to pressure Congress against funding projects with mixed populations, HUD rules and regulations remained ambiguous and the admission of younger and mixed groups continued. Many older residents have reported concerns about physical safety, mental anguish, and loss of quality of life in mixed congregate housing projects.

In spite of the unprecedented economic growth in the 1990s, housing assistance for low-income elderly and persons with disabilities has remained a very low priority. All of the existing programs—public housing, Section 202, Section 8—have been funded at levels far below demonstrated needs.

BÉLA JOHN BOGNÁR

See also HOUSING; HOUSING, ALTERNATIVE OPTIONS; SOCIAL SERVICES.

BIBLIOGRAPHY

American Association of Retired Persons Public Policy Institute. *The Housing Assistance Needs of Older Americans*. Washington, D.C.: AARP, 1995.
U.S. Department of Housing and Urban Development. *Housing Our Elders: A Report Card on the Housing Conditions and Needs of Older Americans*. Washington D.C.: HUD, 1999.
U.S. Department of Housing and Urban Development. *The State of the Cities 2000*. Washington, D.C.: HUD, 2000.

INTERNET RESOURCES

National Resource and Policy Center on Housing and Long Term Care. *Housing Highlights: Government Assisted Highlights*. www.aoa.dhhs.gov/
Picture of Subsidized Households—1998. www.huduser.org.
The State of the Nation's Housing: 2000. www.gsd.harvard.edu.
U.S. Department of Housing and Urban Development. *The FY 2000 Budget of the U.S. Department of Housing and Urban Development*. 1999. www.hud.gov/budget.html.

GRANDPARENTHOOD

Grandparenthood is a significant status in the life of many older adults; more than three-fourths of all people aged sixty-five and older are grandparents. It is a kinship status, and, as such, is dependent on the structure and norms of the kinship system. The contours of the grandparental role have changed dramatically over the last century due to demographic and socio-structural factors, and diversity in grandparent/grandchild (or cross-generational) relationships has become the rule rather than the exception. At the beginning of the twenty-first century, perhaps the most significant single fact gleaned from decades of research about grandparenthood is the heterogeneity of the grandparental experience.

Three generations of an East Indian family in Pomona, California. The grandfather (left) and grandmother (right, in traditional clothing) are pictured with their son and granddaughter. In many non–North American cultures, grandparents play an extrememly important role in the family structure. (Corbis photo by Joseph Sohm.)

The demography of grandparenthood

Demographically, increased longevity, decreased and delayed fertility, and changing patterns of geographic mobility have altered the dimensions of grandparenthood. Longevity is affected by mortality rates, and over the last century, declining death rates have made it more likely that children and young adults will have multiple grandparents in their family networks. Whereas in the nineteenth century few people lived long enough to enjoy the status of grandparenthood for very long, by the end of the twentieth century, grandparental careers spanned several decades. Additionally, changes in mortality have made great-grandparenthood more common; according to Roberto and Skoglund between 40 and 50 percent of all older adults are great-grandparents. Life expectancies that reach into the eighth decade have increased the number of grandparent/grandchild relationships, elongated the grandparental career, and fundamentally altered the interactions between grandparents and grandchildren. Grandchildren increasingly see their grandparents age from young-old to old-old; similarly, grandparents increasingly see

their grandchildren age from childhood to adulthood.

Decreased and delayed fertility during the twentieth century also altered the face of grandparenthood. Twentieth-century fertility, despite significant swings during the Great Depression and post–World War II years, declined from an average of four children per family in 1900 to approximately two children per family in 2000. At the same time, delayed childbearing and increased childlessness have also altered the childbearing experience in ways that have had significant effects on grandparenthood. Although it is still true that the overwhelming majority of older persons are or will become grandparents at some point in their lives, declining fertility means that each grandparent will have fewer grandchildren and that fewer grandparents will attain that status while still raising children of their own. Delayed childbearing has the potential to delay the entrance into grandparenthood, although most who become grandparents do so by age fifty (Uhlenberg and Kilby). Finally, rising levels of childlessness recorded at the end of the twentieth century make it likely that more than a quarter of all older persons will never become grandparents in the twenty-first century.

High rates of geographic mobility, distancing parents from grown children and grandparents from their grandchildren, have also necessitated a change in the way that the cross-generations relate to each other. Over the twentieth century, declining numbers of children lived in extended family households (consisting of a child, a parent, and a grandparent under one roof) and the physical distance between residences increased, with the potential for decreasing interaction opportunities for grandparents and grandchildren. Despite changes in geographic proximity, however, it is also true that even at the end of the twentieth century, more than three-quarters of all older persons who had children lived close to at least one child, which means a greater likelihood of access to grandchildren. Research consistently shows that strong bonds between the generations are maintained despite geographic distance, but the mode of interaction is often something other than face-to-face contact. Technological advances in communication (such as telephones and the Internet) and transportation (rapid rail and air travel) have allowed grandparents and grandchildren to maintain strong relationships despite physical distance.

Socio-structural changes affecting grandparenthood

Major changes in family structure and women's status during the twentieth century also affected the role of the grandparent. Often socio-structural changes had consequences not just for the demographic aspects of grandparenthood but also for the relational aspects as well. Increasing diversity of family structure, manifested in high rates of divorce, single parenthood, and teen parenthood, has created new roles and responsibilities for grandparents. Additionally, as women's status rose throughout the century, grandparents were challenged to adjust from traditional to modern modes of interaction.

In a society where large percentages of children spend at least a portion of their lives in one-parent homes, grandparental roles become more blurred and less well defined. High rates of divorce present grandparents with a variety of possibilities, highly dependent on the attitudes and behaviors of the middle generation. For mater-

nal grandparents, divorce of their adult child often means an added set of instrumental and emotional responsibilities and, therefore, closer ties with grandchildren. This stems, in part, from the common practice of awarding custody to the mother, who then turns to her parents for increased support. For just that reason, the relationships between grandchildren and paternal grandparents tend to suffer after a divorce. Although attention has been focused more on the shrinking ties between the cross-generations after a divorce, remarriage brings with it the possibility of new family roles (such as step-grandparent and step-grandchild) and grandparents often find themselves with additional family roles. The complexities that arise in family constellations as a result of divorce have had another unintended effect on grandparent/grandchild relationships. Divorces among the middle generation have prompted policy action to assure biological grandparents the legal right to maintain ties with their grandchildren.

The steep rise in the divorce rate during the 1970s and 1980s resulted in legislation in all fifty states that allowed grandparents to petition the court for visitation rights with their grandchildren. Although Congress called for a uniform statute as early as 1983, there is, as of 2001, still a wide variety of state policies. At one extreme are several states that allow grandparents to petition for visitation under any circumstances. More frequent are the state policies that specify certain conditions that must be met in order to file, such as the disruption of the child's family through death or divorce, an unfit parent, or a prior custodial role by the grandparent. In virtually all cases, the court must weigh these circumstances against the best interests of the child, and it is such a determination that makes this a complex legal action. At the onset of the twenty-first century, grandparents' rights have become an issue at both the state and federal levels.

One-parent households do not just result from divorce; single, never-married parents and teen parents also contribute to the late-twentieth-century phenomenon of the one-parent household. Traditionally, grandparents have often played the role of family rescuers, and, increasingly, they are being called on to support single and teen mothers during times of family hardship. That support most often takes the form of instrumental aid, such as financial assistance and babysitting, but grandparents are increasingly enlisted as primary caregivers for their grandchildren when crises, such as the illness, death, substance abuse, or incarceration of a parent, occur. The rising number of caregiver grandparents has necessitated a redirection of research and policy efforts to explore and deal with the immediate and long-term consequences for both grandparents and grandchildren.

Over the last century, society moved in the direction of less differentiated gender roles and that trend has significant implications for the role of grandparents. Whereas traditional studies have emphasized the primacy of the grandmother over the grandfather in family relationships and the maternal grandparents over the paternal grandparents, current research challenges or at least refines that conclusion. As the status of women has increased, mothers and grandmothers are more likely to be engaged in jobs and careers than in the past; fathers and grandfathers are more likely to be engaged in family tasks than in the past. A blurring of the division of labor within families may indicate a more balanced perception of grandparental roles in the future.

Grandparent/grandchild relationships

Grandparent/grandchild relationships exist along a number of dimensions: association, affect, role meaning and significance, and exchange. Significantly, the quality of the relationship along these dimensions is often mediated by the middle generation. Just as it is true that a parent only becomes a grandparent because of the actions of his/her child, it is also true that the strength of the cross-generational relationship is dependent on attitudes and behaviors of the middle generation. Adult children who maintain close ties with their own parents provide the norms for strong links between grandchildren and grandparents.

The frequency of contact between grandparents and grandchildren—the associational dimension—depends on a number of factors. Primary among these factors is the geographic proximity of the two generations. Frequency of contact is higher for those who are proximate; interaction is highest for those grandparents and grandchildren who co-reside and lowest for those who are separated by the greatest distance. Although declining proportions of grandparents live in the same household as their grandchildren, the overwhelming majority of older parents live close to at least one of their adult children and opportunities for contact are high.

Studies have shown that interaction between the cross-generations are highest when the grandchildren are young and dependent, presumably because of the intervention of the middle generation. As grandchildren reach their teenage and college years and strive for independence, they are less likely to be in frequent contact with their grandparents, but that pattern is reversed as they reach adulthood and establish their own families. At the end of the twentieth century, patterns of association between grandparents and their grandchildren appeared to be curvilinear.

Despite the physical distance that separates many grandparents from their grandchildren, the affectual or emotional bonds between the generations remain strong. Differentials do exist in the degree of closeness, including whose perspective is recorded, the gender of each generation, and the feelings of the middle generation. For example, grandparents are more likely than grandchildren to report that their relationship is close; studies conclude that the older generation has more at stake in perceiving intimate bonds. But grandchildren of all ages consistently report the warmth of their affection for their grandparents. Gender also appears to be important; grandmothers, and particularly maternal grandmothers, have the closest relationships with their grandchildren. Traditionally, this finding stems from the special kinkeeping role of the woman in the family. This is also connected to the importance that the middle generation plays in establishing and maintaining the closeness of the relationship between grandparents and grandchildren. Because mothers and daughters tend to maintain closer ties as they age than do other family dyads, they foster closer ties with the next generation.

Grandparenthood is a significant and meaningful role for older persons. Research findings consistently show the high levels of satisfaction and pleasure that older persons derive from their grandchildren, and the salience of the relationship is something that is reciprocated. In past centuries, the grandparent was likely to be a figure of authority, based on the economic and social interdependence of family members. But the twentieth century, with its emphasis on independence and autonomy, produced a person more comfortable with a companionate role than an authoritarian one. Nevertheless, grandparents play many different types of roles for their grandchildren, including that of historian, mentor, role model, and surrogate parent. And they carry out these roles by assuming a variety of grandparenting styles, some remote—those who see their grandchildren infrequently and whose interaction is mostly ritualistic; others companionate—those whose focus is on leisure-time activities and friendly interactions, and yet others who are involved—those who take an active role in rearing their grandchildren.

Despite the ideal of independence and autonomy in early twenty-first century families, there is a high degree of obligation and exchange among the generations. Many types of aid flow between the bonds of grandparents and grandchildren. Each generation both gives and receives, depending on life stage, health, and economic circumstances. Significantly, each generation expresses the belief that it has a filial obligation to the other to provide various types of assistance. Instrumental or physical aid includes assistance with chores, financial assistance, and caregiving. Most often, grandparents offer financial help to and babysitting for their grandchildren; in return, grandchildren, when they are old enough, perform chores for their grandparents. Emotional or expressive aid consists of nurturing, social support, and friendship, important commodities that flow both ways throughout the life of the relationship.

At the close of the twentieth century, a new focus on two ranges of exchange emerged. The first was on custodial grandparenting—where grandparents became surrogate parents for young grandchildren because of some catastrophic circumstances surrounding the middle generation, such as death, illness, divorce, drug addiction, or incarceration. On the one hand, studies report that the caregiver grandparent, most often the grandmother, tends to be more stressed, socially isolated, and generally less happy than other, noncustodial, grandparents. But recent research points out some of the more positive effects of the role such as the satisfaction of bettering the life of a grandchild. On the other side of the exchange spectrum is the growing recognition that long life brings the increased likelihood that a grandparent will spend a part of his/her final years in some degree of dependency. Grandchildren are part of the family constellation or the support convoy that may be called upon to offer assistance. Studies show that once they reach young adulthood, grandchildren not only accept their "grand filial" responsibility in theory, but practice it, in fact. Older grandchildren report that they provide both instrumental

and emotional aid to their dependent grandparents.

Diversity in grandparenthood

Given all that has been reported about grandparenthood, the most significant general conclusion is the tremendous heterogeneity of grandparenting experiences. That is due, in large part, to the demographic and sociocultural shifts that have taken place over the last century. Grandparents defy generalizations because they represent such a diverse group. For one, grandparents range in age from persons in their twenties to centenarians; thus they might be men and women who are still in their childbearing years themselves or they might be men and women who have great-great grandchildren. In terms of their life stage, they could be fully employed in the labor force, at the peak of their careers, or retired for decades. Such an enormous age and life-stage range among grandparents is mirrored by a similar age and life-stage range for their grandchildren. Although the predominant image of a grandchild is one of a toddler, the truth is that grandchildren are also young adults in their high school and college years and, increasingly, mature adults forming families of their own.

Diversity also comes in the form of widely different grandparenthood experiences depending on race and ethnicity. Although studies focusing on minority grandparents are limited in number and scope, the conclusions are consistent along several dimensions: specific minority groups are, themselves, very diverse and thus, defy generalization; differentials exist in the grandparenting experience based on whether or not the grandparent was born in the United States; and family structures are affected by the groups' social placement in the larger society and must be analyzed as such.

African-American grandparents are an important resource for their grandchildren, especially given the importance of extended kin networks and intergenerational ties within the social organization of black families. For example, despite increasing heterogeneity in their family structure, African Americans are more likely to live in extended and multigenerational family households than are white Americans, and this experience leads to greater contact with grandchildren. Grandparents are seen as playing a pivotal role in the lives of these children, a role rooted in African-American culture and the socioeconomic realities of their lives.

Hispanics (the term here referring to a number of separate and distinct subgroups including Mexicans, Cubans, Puerto Ricans, and other Latinos coming from Central and South America) differ in their grandparenthood experience from white Americans and African Americans. Acknowledging that there is tremendous diversity within the Hispanic community itself, the limited number of studies that have focused on this population conclude that strong familistic ties translate into frequent contact, high satisfaction, and a high level of social support between the cross-generations.

Asian Americans (the term here referring to subgroups including those from China, Japan, Korea, Vietnam, the Philippines, India, and others coming from Southeast Asia) share an adherence to filial responsibility and gender hierarchy that influences grandparent/grandchild relationships. High rates of coresidence among three generations lead to strong and supportive cross-generational ties, but unlike the case of African Americans, whose extended family structure and households are quite often matrilineal, Asian-American grandparents are more likely to live with their sons than with their daughters. The primacy of age seniority in the traditional cultures represented among Asian Americans makes it likely that grandparent/grandchild interactions are more formal and authoritarian than those of other racial or ethnic groups.

Grandparenthood is a status and an experience that is significant to many older adults. Decades of research have contributed to an understanding of the concept but variations based on age, race, and ethnicity as well as gender, marital, and health statuses make definitions of "grandparenthood" particularly complex. Much in the same way that the U.S. population in the twenty-first century will be defined by tremendous heterogeneity, so, too, will relationships between grandparents and grandchildren.

LYNNE GERSHENSON HODGSON

See also INTERGENERATIONAL EXCHANGES; KIN; PARENT-CHILD RELATIONSHIP.

BIBLIOGRAPHY

ALDOUS, J. "New Views of Grandparents in Intergenerational Context." *Journal of Family Issues* 16 (1995): 104–122.

BENGTSON, V. L., and ROBERTSON, J. F. *Grandparenthood*. Beverly Hills, Calif.: Sage, 1985.
BURTON, L. M., and DILWORTH-ANDERSON, P. "The Intergenerational Roles of Aged Black Americans." *Marriage and Family Review* 16 (1991): 311–350.
CHERLIN, A. J., and FURSTENBERG, F. F. *The New American Grandparent*. New York: Basic Books, 1986.
DRESSEL, P. "Grandparenting at Century's End." *Generations* 20 (1996): 3–78.
FULLER-THOMSON, E.; MINKLER, M.; and DRIVER, D. "A Profile of Grandparents Raising Grandchildren in the United States." *The Gerontologist* 37 (1997): 406–411.
JOHNSON, C. L. *Ex Familia: Grandparents, Parent, and Children Adjust to Divorce*. New Brunswick, N.J.: Rutgers University Press, 1988.
KAHANA, B., and KAHANA, E. "Grandparenthood from the Perspective of the Developing Grandchild." *Developmental Psychology* 3 (1970): 98–105.
KIVETT, V. R. "The Grandparent-Grandchild Connection." *Marriage and Family Review* 16 (1991): 267–290.
ROBERTO, K. L., and STROES, J. "Grandchildren and Grandparents: Roles, Influences, and Relationships." *International Journal of Aging and Human Development* 34 (1992): 227–239.
ROBERTSON, J. F. "Grandparenting in an Era of Rapid Change." In *Handbook on Aging and the Family*. Edited by R. Blieszner and Victoria H. Bedford. Westport, Conn.: Greenwood, 1995. Pages 243–260.
SZINOVACZ, M. E. *Handbook on Grandparenthood*. Westport, Conn.: Greenwood Press, 1998.

GRIEF

See BEREAVEMENT

GROWTH HORMONE

A large body of scientific evidence has accumulated to support the concept that decreases in anabolic hormones that occur with aging contribute to the aging-related decline in tissue function and the aging phenotype. Growth hormone and insulin-like growth factor-1 (IGF-1) are two potent anabolic hormones, and decreases in these hormones have been hypothesized to contribute to the loss of muscle and bone mass, as well as cognitive and immune function, in older adults. In young adults, growth hormone is released in pulsatile bursts from the pituitary gland, with the majority of secretion occurring at night in association with slow-wave sleep. Similar pulses are observed in rodents, except that secretory pulses occur every 3.5 hours in males and hourly in females. The regulation of these pulses involve at least two hormones released by the hypothalamus: first, a growth-hormone-releasing hormone (GHRH), which increases growth-hormone release; and second, somatostatin, which inhibits its release. The dynamic interactions between these hypothalamic hormones regulate high amplitude, pulsatile, growth-hormone secretion. Activation of the hepatic growth-hormone receptor by growth hormone stimulates the synthesis and secretion of IGF-1 into plasma, which, in turn, stimulates DNA, RNA, and protein synthesis and is a potent mitogen for many tissues. Growth hormone and IGF-1 circulating in the blood suppress growth-hormone release from the pituitary in a typical feedback relationship—either directly at the level of the pituitary, or by stimulating somatostatin and/or inhibiting GHRH release from the hypothalamus.

Studies in humans have indicated a substantial decline in the ability of older individuals to secrete growth hormone, and it is now evident that the decline in high-amplitude growth-hormone secretion and plasma IGF-1 concentrations are one of the most robust and well-characterized events that occur with age. Similar to humans, decreases in the amplitude of growth-hormone pulses are observed in rodent models of aging, and these changes, as expected, are closely associated with a decline in plasma IGF-1. Although the specific etiology for the decline in growth-hormone pulse amplitude has not been fully detailed, studies in both humans and animals have documented that, rather than a decline in pituitary response to these hypothalamic peptides, alterations in the secretion of both hypothalamic release and inhibiting hormones appear to be the key factors in the decline in growth-hormone pulse amplitude with age. Since these hypothalamic hormones are controlled by brain neurotransmitters, the concept has evolved that alterations in the regulation of neurotransmitters within the brain are part of the mechanism for the decrease in growth hormone.

Although an attenuation of growth-hormone pulse amplitude is an important contributing factor in the decline in plasma IGF-1, studies have also demonstrated that, in response to growth-hormone administration, the ability to increase

IGF-1 secretion is diminished in elderly individuals. These results indicate that not only a decline in growth-hormone pulse amplitude, but also tissue resistance to growth-hormone action, is responsible for the reduced plasma IGF-1 concentrations. In rodents, a two-fold increase in hepatic growth-hormone receptors has been reported with age, but this increase is unable to compensate for the reduced levels of growth hormone. Thus, there appears to be a failure of circulating growth hormone to activate intracellular signaling pathways that, in addition to the decrease in growth hormone, contribute to a decline in blood levels of IGF-1 in both animals and humans.

Even though a decreased response to growth hormone is an important component of the age-related decline in plasma IGF-1, this deficit can be partially overcome by administration of exogenous growth hormone. Studies in rodents have revealed that the administration of growth hormone increases IGF-1 and restores cellular protein synthesis in the muscle of old animals, indicating that the age-related decline in tissue function results, at least in part, from hormone deficiency. Other reports have been published demonstrating that either growth hormone or IGF-1 could partially reverse the decline in immune function, increase blood vessel elasticity, and increase life span in rodents. These studies were the first indications that the decrease in the concentration of growth hormone has clinical significance and may be responsible for the generalized catabolic state that accompanies normal aging. In the elderly, it has generally been reported that growth-hormone administration increases IGF-1, lean body mass, muscle mass, and skin thickness, and also reduces total body-fat content. In addition, there are reports of elevations in serum osteocalcin (a marker of bone formation) and nitrogen retention, raising the possibility that growth-hormone treatment may delay osteoporosis.

In addition to its role in regulating tissue growth, more recent studies indicate that administration of growth hormone reverses the age-related loss of blood vessels. These and related studies indicating that IGF-1 is produced in microvessels have led to the concept that a reduction in growth hormone and the subsequent decrease in plasma and microvascular-derived IGF-1 lead to a decline in tissue function and/or reduce the capacity of tissues to respond to appropriate stimuli. In fact, raising levels of IGF-1 in old animals has been shown to improve the function of several neurotransmitter systems, glucose utilization and cognition, and also to improve contractility in the heart.

Although there are many potential beneficial effects of growth-hormone therapy in aged animals and humans, the adverse effects of therapy include sodium retention, carpal tunnel syndrome, potential glucose resistance, and hyperinsulinemia. Epidemiological studies also indicate a significant correlation between levels of IGF-1 and prostate, breast, and lung cancer, raising the concern that administration of these mitogenic hormones may initiate and/or accelerate pathological changes in the elderly. These issues have not been directly tested to date, but studies indicate that moderate caloric restriction (60 percent of *ad libitum* food intake), which is capable of decreasing age-related pathology, also lowers plasma IGF-1 levels. Subsequent administration of IGF-1 to these animals removes the protective effects of moderate caloric restriction from specific carcinogens, providing support for the concept that the beneficial effects of moderate caloric restriction are mediated, in part, by decreasing levels of IGF-1. The association between IGF-1 and age-associated pathogenesis remains to be established. Thus, the available evidence suggests that a decline in growth hormone and IGF-1 contribute to the functional decline in tissues with age, but that raising the levels of these hormones may increase the risk of age-related pathology.

WILLIAM E. SONNTAG

See also BIOMARKERS OF AGING; ENDOCRINE SYSTEM; NEUROENDOCRINE SYSTEM; NUTRITION, CALORIC RESTRICTION; THEORIES OF BIOLOGICAL AGING.

BIBLIOGRAPHY

CORPAS, E.; HARMAN, S. M.; and BLACKMAN, M. R. "Human Growth Hormone and Human Aging." *Endocrine Review* 14 (1993): 20–39.
RUDMAN, D.; FELLER, A. G.; NAGRAJ, H. S.; GERGANS, G. A.; LALITHA, P. Y.; GOLDBERG, A. F.; SCHLENKER, R. A.; COHN, L.; RUDMAN, I. W.; and MATTSON, D. E. "Effects of Human Growth Hormone in Men over 60 Years Old." *New England Journal of Medicine* 323 (1990): 1–6.
SONNTAG, W. E.; LYNCH, C. D.; CEFALU, W. T.; INGRAM, R. L.; BENNETT, S. A.; THORNTON, P. L.; and KHAN, A. S. "Pleiotropic Effects of Growth Hormone and Insulin-Like Growth Factor (IGF)-1 on Biological Aging: Inferences from Moderate Caloric-Restricted Animals." *Journal of Gerontology; Biological Sciences* 54A (1999): 521–538.
XU, X., and SONNTAG, W. E. "Growth Hormone and Aging: Regulation, Signal Transduction and Therapeutic Intervention." *Trends in Endocrinology and Metabolism* 7 (1996): 145–150.

GUARDIANSHIP

Ordinarily the person who will be most directly affected by any particular decision about health care, finances, social services, residential issues, or other personal matters is the person who gets to make that decision. There may be times, however, when that individual is not capable of making and expressing difficult personal choices. In those instances, the legal system may need to intervene on behalf of the incapacitated individual. This may be accomplished through a variety of legal devices that vary in terms of their invasiveness into personal autonomy. One of these legal devices is guardianship.

Incapacity to make and express valid decisions is a problem that affects older persons in disproportionate terms. The extent of mental disorders in old age, representing decrements in both intellectual and emotional functioning, is considerable. For some older persons, mental dysfunction may be a carryover from earlier life. For most of the elderly, though, mental health problems develop later in life as a result of organic brain disorders (primary degenerative disorders or multi-infarct dementia), paranoid disorders, drug reactions, excessive use of alcohol, or as the by-product of various physical illnesses. These problems may take the form of cognitive impairment (dementia) in memory, attention, or information processing; emotional lability (psychosis) often manifested as aggression; or pseudodementia (depression). Because of this prevalence of impairment, guardianship is a legal device that disproportionately affects older persons, especially those residing in institutions.

Court-appointed surrogates

Every state has enacted statutes that empower the courts to appoint a surrogate with the authority to make decisions on behalf of a mentally incompetent ward. The terminology for the court-appointed surrogate decision-maker varies among jurisdictions; "guardian" is the most commonly used term, although "conservator" and other terms are employed in some places.

Guardianship statutes are an example of the state's inherent *parens patriae* power to protect those who cannot take care of themselves in a manner that society believes is appropriate. The origins of some form of guardianship based on the state's benevolence toward the dependent stretch back beyond thirteenth-century England.

The terms "capable" or "having capacity" usually are used to describe individuals who, in a health care clinician's professional judgment, have sufficient capacity to make their own choices. The terms "incompetent" or "incompetence" refer to a court's formal ruling on the decision-making status of an individual in the context of an official guardianship proceeding, although some modern guardianship statutes use the term "capable" to refer to a judicial judgment.

Every adult person is presumed to be legally competent to make personal decisions in life. This presumption may be overcome, and a surrogate decision-maker may be appointed, only on a sufficient showing that the individual is mentally unable to participate authentically (i.e., consistent with previously held values) and self-sufficiently in a rational decision-making process.

State guardianship statutes contain a two-step definition of competence. First, the individual must fall within a particular category such as old age, mentally ill, or developmentally disabled. Second, the individual must be found to be impaired functionally—that is, actually unable to care appropriately for person or property—as a result of being within that category. The requirement of functional impairment is emphasized in those states, such as California, whose statutes restrict eligibility for guardianship to those who are "gravely disabled" or the equivalent.

In disputed, adversarial guardianship proceedings, medical and psychological experts usually are called on to testify by each side about the proposed ward's categorical problem and its impact on the proposed ward's functional abilities. In practice, this medical and psychological testimony frequently becomes the primary, if not the sole, basis for adjudicating incompetence.

A court appoints a guardian (referred to in a few jurisdictions as a conservator or committee) as substitute decision-maker for an incompetent person. The incompetent person for whom a guardian is appointed is a "ward," and the relationship created between the guardian/conservator and ward is called "guardianship" or "conservatorship."

Procedural protections

There has been a strong movement since the late 1980s toward greatly strengthening the procedural protections available to prospective wards. In response to widespread public advocacy of greater autonomy and dignity for older persons and sharp criticism of the guardianship system as overly intrusive and paternalistic, most U.S. jurisdictions have adopted extensive revisions to their guardianship statutes. These statutory reforms create or enhance requirements concerning court-appointed legal counsel with adversarial duties, notice to the proposed ward, a hearing, personal attendance of the proposed ward at the hearing, clearly defined standard of proof (varying among states from a preponderance of the evidence test to a higher standard of clear and convincing evidence to the strictest test of beyond a reasonable doubt), explicitly delineated contents of the guardianship petition, and more specificity in the court order finding the ward incompetent and appointing the guardian. In a majority of states, statutes allow for the relaxation of normal procedural requirements to permit the appointment of a temporary or emergency guardian when there is an immediate life-threatening situation or when a permanent guardian can no longer serve.

The guardian who is appointed ordinarily is a private person (relative, friend, or attorney) or institution (bank or trust company); the majority of guardians are relatives of the ward. Many state statutes establish procedures through which competent adults are empowered to nominate in advance the person they wish to serve as guardian for them in the event that guardianship is ordered at some future time, and the courts are required to give strong deference to these preferences.

In a growing number of cases, older individuals are left without any friends or family members who are willing and able to act as a surrogate decision-maker. In response to this significant social phenomenon, some states have devised "public guardianship" systems under which a government agency, acting either directly or through contract with a private not-for-profit or for-profit organization, functions in the guardian role for a ward who has no one else. Elsewhere, some private corporations and organizations offer their services as guardians directly to the courts, either for a fee or on a voluntary, pro bono basis.

Guardian's powers

A court may confer different types of powers on a guardian. Plenary power is complete authority over the ward's person and estate, encompassing virtually every element of the ward's life, including health care and residential choices. Alternatively, guardianship powers may be restricted to control of the ward's estate. In the latter event, the guardian of the estate may make decisions only about the handling of the ward's financial assets—real and personal property—and income. A court may also appoint a *guardian ad litem* who has authority to represent the ward just in a particular legal proceeding, such as a petition for authority to terminate life-sustaining medical intervention.

Courts and legislatures traditionally have treated mental competence as an all-or-nothing concept, even though an older person's functional capacity may wax and wane from time to time and vary widely depending on the kind of choice facing the individual and various environmental factors. In recognition of this reality, all states now allow courts to grant "limited" or "partial" guardianship explicitly delineating the particular, limited types of decisions that the ward is incapable of making and over which the guardian may exercise surrogate authority, with all remaining power residing with the ward. This approach is driven by the constitutional principle that, when the state absolutely must intervene in the life of a person without that person's voluntary permission, the state should engage in the least restrictive or intrusive alternative possible, consistent with accomplishing the state's legitimate goals. Limited or partial guardianship statutes may be permissive, allowing but not requiring courts to carefully tailor the guardian's powers to the ward's needs, or they may mandate that the guardian's powers be drawn as narrowly as possible by the appointing judge.

Any ward, but especially one for whom a plenary guardian has been appointed, inevitably suffers a serious deprivation of decision-making authority. Among numerous kinds of choices taken away, a ward may lose the right to enter into a binding contract, to vote, to hold public office, to marry or divorce, to hold a license (such as a motor vehicle driver's license), to execute a will, to own and sell or give away real and personal property, and to sue and be sued in the courts.

Once a guardianship has been imposed, the appointed guardian is expected to act in a fiduciary, or trust, manner. This responsibility may be fulfilled by performing in a way that is either (1) in accordance with the guardian's judgment of the ward's best interests or (2) consistent with previously expressed or implied values and preferences of the ward. The latter approach is called *substituted judgment*, which is now preferred by most legislatures and courts as most respectful of the ward's own life experiences and deeply held principles. The court retains continuing jurisdiction or power to oversee the guardian's conduct.

Any guardianship may be discontinued when it is no longer needed, and in some states appropriateness must be reviewed at least annually. The successful termination of a guardianship is difficult, because the party arguing for termination bears the burden of proving that competence has been restored.

MARSHALL B. KAPP

See also ADVANCE DIRECTIVES FOR HEALTH CARE; AUTONOMY; COMPETENCY.

BIBLIOGRAPHY

FROLIK, L. A., and KAPLAN, R. L. *Elder Law in a Nutshell*, 2d ed. St. Paul, Minn.: West Group, 1998.

KAPP, M. B. *Geriatrics and the Law: Understanding Patient Rights and Professional Responsibilities*, 3d ed. New York: Springer Pub. Co., 1999.

SCHMIDT, W. C., JR. *Guardianship: The Court of Last Resort for the Elderly and Disabled.* Durham, N.C.: Carolina Academic Press, 1995.

SMYER, M.; SCHAIE, K. W.; and KAPP, M. B., eds. *Older Adults' Decision-Making and the Law.* New York: Springer Pub. Co., 1995.

STRAUSS, P. J., and LEDERMAN, N. M. *The Elder Law Handbook.* New York: Facts on File, Inc., 1996.

ZIMNY, G. H., and GROSSBERG, G. T., eds. *Guardianship of the Elderly: Psychiatric and Judicial Aspects.* New York: Springer Pub. Co., 1998.

H

HAIR

"Hair is the crowning glory"—this old double-play of words emphasizes the significance of hair for men and women. From a physiological point of view, hair provides mechanical protection, insulation, and a wick effect for the dispersal of lubricating sebum and sweat over the adjacent skin. The personalization of hair as a means of defining individual (or group) identity is of equally importance in many societies. It has fundamental social and cultural significance for the individual.

The structure of hair and its growth

The structure of hair is analogous to a plant bulb. The whole unit, with its immediate surrounding, is termed a *follicle* (see Figure 1). The plant bulb is equivalent to the bulbous hair germ, while the sprouting plant is equivalent to the hair. A plant bulb, which is dormant near the soil surface during the winter, begins to sprout in the spring. It moves deeper into the earth and then grows into a full plant, which lasts over the summer. In the fall, the plant shrivels and is detached. The bulb then goes into a resting phase and resprouts the next spring.

The three phases of the hair life-cycle are equivalent (see Figure 1) and are termed *anagen* (growing phase), *catagen* (transitional phase), and *telogen* (resting phase). The lustrous scalps of young adulthood have about 100,000 hairs, blondes having more and redheads less. This number declines in healthy individuals to forty to fifty thousand hairs between the ages of thirty and fifty, at which time the apparent bulk of the hair is 50 percent thinner.

Normally, about 90 percent of hair is in the anagen phase and 10 percent in the telogen phase. Hair is shed daily, with a loss of fifty to one hundred hairs—often found on a brush or pillow as *club* (the small knob on the root end) hairs.

The number of hair follicles is the same in men and women. No new ones develop after fetal life. The juvenile soft hair of childhood becomes the firmer and more lustrous terminal hair of adolescence.

Changes with age

The number of active follicles declines by 30 to 50 percent between the ages of thirty and fifty. This is associated with a decline of male-type hormonal substances. The hair becomes sparser and the sebaceous (grease) gland enlarges. The gland output is reduced by as much as 30 percent in women, but this is more variable and sometimes increased in men.

The graying of hair

Melanin is the brown pigment produced by cells termed *melanocytes*. These cells lie in the bottom layer of the epidermis. The amount of dark pigment that is produced declines with age. At the same time, the central medullary space of the shaft enlarges. Light reflection from the cell surfaces of the cuticle and cortex is also increased. The combination of these changes is generally accepted as the cause of hair graying with age. It is more obvious in dark-haired individuals but appears more complete in lighter haired individuals. The whole process is under genetic control.

There are racial variations. While graying appears as early as twenty years of age in Cauca-

Figure 1
Hair Bulb and Follicle: The Cycle of Hair Growth

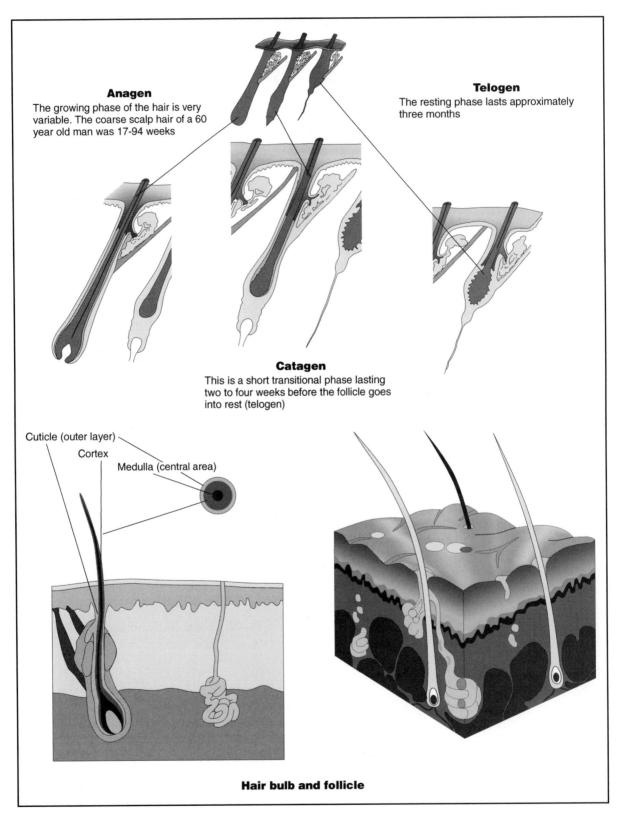

Anagen
The growing phase of the hair is very variable. The coarse scalp hair of a 60 year old man was 17-94 weeks

Telogen
The resting phase lasts approximately three months

Catagen
This is a short transitional phase lasting two to four weeks before the follicle goes into rest (telogen)

Cuticle (outer layer)
Cortex
Medulla (central area)

Hair bulb and follicle

SOURCE: Based on Montagna, W. *The Structure and Function of Skin,* 2nd ed. New York: Academic Press, 1962.

sians and at thirty in Africans, the first appearance of gray hair generally occurs at around thirty-five in Caucasians. By age fifty, 50 percent of the population has some degree of significant graying. The process starts about five years later in Africans, and five years earlier in Japanese. Beard and moustache hair changes before the scalp and body hair. On the scalp, the temple hair grays first, followed by the crown and then back of the scalp. The whole process is a normal physiological change. In any given individual, the age at which graying becomes noticed, and the rate of graying, is not related to the overall rate of biological aging.

Baldness

The most common cause of balding, by far, is physiological. The firm terminal hair of mature adulthood is replaced by soft vellus hair—a relic of the first immature hair of infancy and early childhood. This process is under genetic control, with inherited influence on male-type hormones. The onset can be as young as seventeen in males and in the mid-twenties in females. In general, the areas that are the last to get terminal hair are the first to lose it (see Figure 2). The average of onset in males is in the late twenties and in females in the mid-thirties (see Figure 3).

Reversible hair loss.   Physiological balding is not reversible, but there are other types of balding that are reversible. For example, the hair shaft can break because of fungal infection or from repeated peroxide bleaching.

Hair can fall prematurely from the follicle. This is termed *telogen effluvium*. It can follow an infective illness, or from some other mild toxic process that occurred six to eight weeks beforehand. The hair suddenly falls out in unusual amounts, leaving a thin scalp covering. Previously unnoticed physiological baldness may then be revealed, sometimes causing anxiety. Telogen effluvium is self-limiting, although in some cases the problem continues for a number of years before ceasing spontaneously. Rarer causes relate to hormone irregularity, particularly, thyroid hormones. Dietary factors, such as a general food deficiency, protein deficiency, low blood iron, or, more rarely, low zinc levels, are sometimes responsible. A sudden unexplained onset in older patients always raises concern of an underlying malignancy.

Alopecia areata is a harmless form of patchy baldness that can occur at any time of life. The hair ceases to grow in its mid-anagen cycle and falls out. Usually there are solitary or multiple round patches of baldness, but it can be widespread over the scalp, mimicking other forms of diffuse hair loss. When there is apparent loss of the hair follicle, this condition is termed *scarring alopecia*. Sometimes the follicle opening cannot be seen in normal balding. Burns caused by heat or chemicals can destroy the hair root, as well as some chronic inflammatory conditions. The cause of hair loss can be complex, and assessment by a knowledgeable physician is often required.

Common scalp nuisances of older persons

There are two common irritations of the scalp that may be associated with temporary hair loss: psoriasis and seborrheic dermatitis, which is commonly known as dandruff.

Two percent of the population have psoriasis at any given time. Its cause is not known, although constitutional factors play an important role, as do other trigger factors. Psoriasis can appear at any time in life. It frequently occurs in adults as sharp-edged scaly red patches on the elbows and knees. It can be more extensive over the trunk and limbs, and can also affect the body folds. Discrete patches can occur on the scalp and occasionally involve the whole scalp. Psoriasis can sometimes be itchy. Tar shampoos can give relief if used on a daily basis, and there are other remedies than are available by prescription, though no permanent cure exists.

Seborrheic dermatitis develops after adolescence. With this condition, the scalp is excessively scaly and greasy, and can be intolerably itchy. Those with greasy coarse-pored skin are more prone to seborrheic dermatitis, and older men are affected more than women. Greasy yellowish scales are found in patches, or are diffuse about the scalp. The skin may be red and inflamed. It may also be present on the hairy areas of the face, on the forehead, or down the broad folds at the side of the nose. Its cause is not fully known, but there is a sensitivity in some people to a naturally occurring, common yeast that overgrows in the scalp skin. Tar shampoo used on a regular basis, or a sulphur-releasing shampoo used intermittently, can be helpful.

General care of the older scalp

The scalps of older persons deserve as much attention as those of younger people. Appropri-

Figure 2
Patterns of Male Baldness

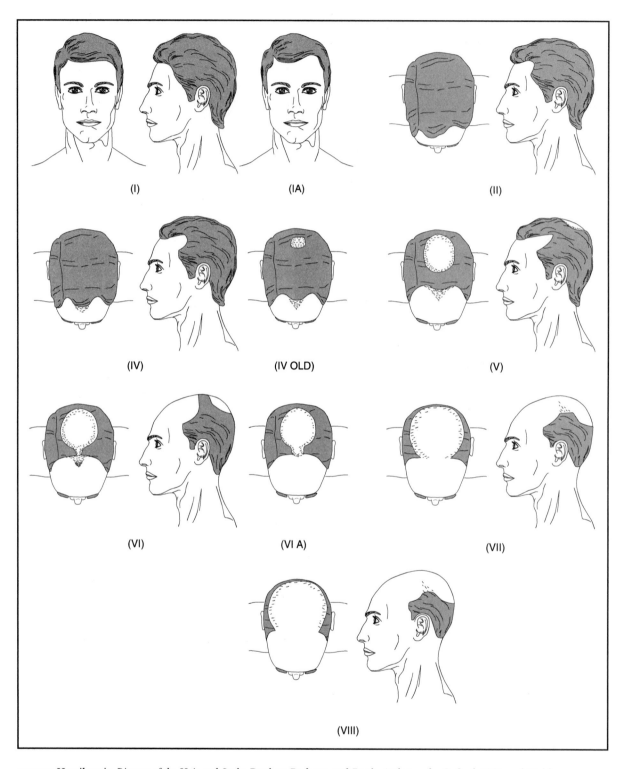

(I)   (IA)   (II)

(IV)   (IV OLD)   (V)

(VI)   (VI A)   (VII)

(VIII)

SOURCE: Hamilton in *Diseases of the Hair and Scalp.* Dawber, Rodney, and Rook, Arthur, eds. Oxford, U.K. and Malden, Mass.: Blackwell Science, 1997.

Figure 3
Balding in Females

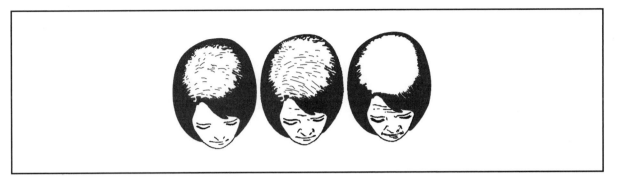

SOURCE: After Ludwig in *Diseases of the Hair and Scalp.* Dawber, Rodney, and Rook, Arthur, eds. Oxford, U.K. and Malden, Mass.: Blackwell Science, 1997.

ate grooming, including washing, combing, and brushing is required for a healthy scalp. Normal cosmetic attention, including waving and setting, should not impair scalp health, so long as there is not undue tension on the hair. Dyeing and other forms of hair coloring can also be used without adverse consequences.

J. BARRIE ROSS

See also ANDROPAUSE; MENOPAUSE; SKIN.

BIBLIOGRAPHY

ARNDT, K. A.; ROBINSON, J. K.; LEBOIT, P. E.; and WINTROUB, B. U. *Cutaneous Medicine and Surgery*, section 8, pages 1245–1294. Philadelphia, Pa.: W. B. Saunders, 1996.

CHAMPION, R. H.; BURTON, J. L.; BURNS, D. A.; and BREATHNACH, S. M. *Textbook of Dermatology*, 6th ed. Edited by Rook/Wilkinson/Ebling. Oxford: Blackwell Science, 1998.

SINCLAIR, R. D.; BANFIELD, C. C.; and DAWBER, R. P. R. *Handbook of Diseases of the Hair and Scalp*. Oxford: Blackwell Science, 1999.

WHITING, D. A. "Chronic Telogen Effluvium: Increased Scalp Hair Shedding in Middle-Aged Women." *Journal of the American Academy of Dermatology* 35 (1996): 899–906.

HEALTH AND LONG-TERM CARE PROGRAM INTEGRATION

The health and long-term care service delivery system is compartmentalized. Physicians, usually the primary care physician, are responsible for outpatient care. Inpatient care is usually under the management of a medical specialist, such as a surgeon, cardiologist, or neurologist. Care after the patient leaves the hospital includes home health care, rehabilitation, and skilled nursing home care. These services, although authorized by a physician, are usually more directly managed by a nurse or therapeutic specialist (e.g., a physical or occupational therapist). Extended care, whether in a nursing home or in the community, is often considered to be long-term care. Long-term care includes "skilled" services provided by a nurse or therapist, as well as the "nonskilled" care provided by a nurse's aide, personal care aide, or housekeeping services. The vast majority of nonskilled long-term care services are provided by family members, but they can also be purchased from private individuals and community agencies. Home or community-based long-term care services, if not directly coordinated by the patient or a family member, are typically planned and monitored by a social services case manager.

The distinctions among these multiple levels of care, and between skilled and unskilled care, are directly connected to the financing and reimbursement processes. The major public insurance program for health care is Medicare. This federally financed program provides coverage for physician, hospital, and skilled home health and skilled nursing home care. Extended or long-term care and unskilled care are usually excluded from Medicare reimbursement. Payment for these services comes either from the patient or the patient's family; or from public programs such as Medicaid or the Veterans Administration (for those who qualify). State governments also use social service programs to finance some unskilled care.

Historically, each level of care and each financing program has operated within its own budget. Under this arrangement, any cost savings from the substitution of lower levels of care for higher ones add costs to the program financing the lower-level services and produce savings for programs financing the higher levels of care. For example, reduced days in a hospital save Medicare costs, and may result in transfers to nursing homes, which have a lower daily cost than hospitals. Nursing home stays of up to one hundred days are likely to be paid by Medicare, but more extended stays usually are paid for privately or through Medicaid. Another example is the decision by a family to keep a member at home rather than place him or her in a nursing home. For those who qualify for Medicaid coverage, the availability of informal family care saves Medicaid costs, and pushes all the cost to the family. For the relatively few persons with private long-term care insurance, this would be a cost savings to insurance as well.

State governments have tried to encourage informal care by permitting persons eligible for Medicaid (who also qualify for nursing home admission) to receive a portion of the funds that would have gone for nursing home care for the purchase of unskilled home care. This is done within the Medicaid program under home and community-based care. This approach begins to solve the problem of limited financing for community-based, long-term care services (for those who have incomes and other assets low enough to qualify for Medicaid), but it does not integrate health care and long-term care.

Several promising approaches to acute and long-term care integration are briefly described here: the Program for All-Inclusive Care for the Elderly (PACE), the social/health maintenance organization demonstration, screening and care coordination in Medicare HMOs, the use of geriatricians and geriatric care teams, and managed care within the Medicaid program.

Program of All-Inclusive Care for the Elderly

The PACE program was initiated in 1986 as a congressionally mandated demonstration. It

has since become a permanent program with authorization for several dozen sites around the United States. PACE offers complete coverage of all Medicare-reimbursed services (including hospital, physician, home health, and skilled nursing homes) and Medicaid-covered services. Medicaid coverage includes the same services reimbursed by Medicare, as well as long-term nursing home care, homemaker services, and adult day health care. The PACE program is targeted exclusively on persons whose needs make them eligible for nursing home placement. These programs are at full financial risk for all Medicare- and Medicaid-covered services used by their members. They receive a fixed monthly payment for each member, regardless of the care received. This is called a capitation payment. Under this reimbursement system the PACE sites can allocate Medicare and Medicaid revenues to whatever services, including non-health care services, deemed most appropriate. Having all services covered under a single budget permits the PACE sites to substitute lower levels for higher levels, when appropriate, and to capture the cost savings. Health and long-term care service integration is further achieved through adult day health care participation of the members, which permits the routine monitoring of functional and health status, medication management, and involvement in physical exercise and other enrichment activities. Care planning is done through multidisciplinary teams who work together rather than through professionals working in isolation.

A difficult challenge for PACE has been maintaining enrollment levels (Irvin, et al.). This is largely the result of program requirements for adult day care participation and the loss of freedom to choose one's physician (participants must use a PACE physician, who is usually a staff doctor). Several sites have been modifying their operations to place less reliance on day care and to give members the option of retaining their own physician.

While this has been a highly popular program with federal and state policy makers, there is still some question about the reimbursement payment levels, and whether the sites are receiving overpayment (Mukamel et al.). This concern arises, in part, because the sites can be selective in the referrals they accept into the program.

Social/health maintenance organization

The first generation of this Medicare demonstration, known as the S/HMO, was implemented in 1985 with the objective of adding a package of chronic care benefits to the acute services and operational structure of the Medicare HMO model. Chronic care benefits included nursing home stays (usually a maximum of thirty days), and personal care, homemaker, and case management services. There was an annual (and in some cases monthly) limit on the amount of services a member could receive. S/HMOs also offered expanded care benefits (such as prescription drugs, eyeglasses, transportation, and preventive dental care) to all members.

The S/HMO demonstration was testing the efficacy of offering and managing access to chronic care benefits (e.g., nonskilled home care), and examining how the expansion of responsibility into community-based care affected the health plan's general approach to its Medicare eligible members. Four sites participated in the initial demonstration. These first generation S/HMOs used a traditional model of outpatient and inpatient physician services and hospital utilization control, with each of these functions operated independently from the functional assessments, and chronic care benefit authorization and case management available to frailty qualified members. Contacts between physicians and case managers were limited—usually to the authorization of Medicare services (Harrington et al.).

In 1995 the Health Care Financing Administration (the agency responsible for the Medicare program) initiated the planning of a second generation model of the S/HMO. The second generation model retains the chronic care benefit package implemented in the first generation plans, and it adds several fundamental refinements intended to better integrate and coordinate primary care and the management of high risk cases. Most important of these was an attempt to develop a strong geriatric service model of care. The "geriatric" approach includes a screening program intended to identify patients at risk for high service costs and disability; timely application of primary care monitoring and treatment to reduce illness and disability; and a geriatric education and consultation program to provide specialty support for complex cases. Care management supports the primary care functions for those requiring home care, those discharged from hospitals or nursing homes, and those who are having difficulty complying with their treatment regimen. Case management efforts are closely integrated with the provision of

primary care, including conferences among the various professionals. The proactive attention to clinical care and preventive services requires the definition of "risk" to include acute and chronic conditions and problems, in addition to the limitations of activities of daily living that have been more typical in the long-term care field (Kane et al.). One second generation plan became operational in 1997.

Screening and service coordination in Medicare HMOs

Surveys of the largest Medicare HMOs show that as early as 1990, plans had begun to establish procedures for identifying high risk patients, assessing and treating multiproblem patients, rehabilitating patients following acute events, reducing medication problems, and expanding benefits to include more home care and case management for nursing home patients (Kramer et al.). These activities incorporate many of the features of the S/HMO model, but without the advantage of a 5 percent higher capitation payment and with no obligation to provide long-term care benefits for those in the community.

Screening and assessment are generally limited to new enrollees or to those who have been hospitalized. High risk cases flagged via this process are referred to primary care (or geriatric assessment) for more in-depth assessments. Screening data are based on self-report questionnaires and telephone interviews. The emphasis in these instruments is given to health conditions and other factors that may be associated with hospitalization, preventable disability, and other avoidable expenditures. The screening of current members has been less formalized. It is generally based on a referral from the primary care physician or triggered by hospitalization (Pacala et al.). Management information systems are becoming more capable of capturing medical records, service encounters, and even prescription refills. Access to these data increases the likelihood of their use to identify and monitor those thought to be at risk for expensive care or avoidable complications, though there are no recent studies documenting the extent or means of implementing such monitoring.

Primary care for post-acute care patients is delivered by a combination of methods (Kramer et al.). For those returning home, most plans rely on the primary care physician. For persons in skilled nursing homes, some plans rely on the primary care physician, others have a medical director who handles all such cases, and still others use a nurse practitioner. Combinations of these approaches may occur, depending on whether the nursing home is a primary referral site for the health plan or a freestanding facility with only a few plan members. The management of other "high risk" but not hospitalized cases largely falls on the primary care physician, although many plans have developed programs targeted to selected diagnoses that include congestive heart failure, diabetes, and chronic obstructive pulmonary disease. Within disease management programs the patient's health care may be managed by a specialist who is supported by a team of professionals responsible for helping the patient monitor symptoms, diet, weight, medication use, and other treatments. The effectiveness of the screening, risk identification, and disease management approaches within health plans has not been formally reported, but experience from clinical trials and other small scale demonstrations leads to expectations of program success (Fama, et al.; Miller and Luft).

Geriatricians and multidisciplinary teams

The extent to which geriatric medicine should, and can, be integrated into the delivery of health care and long-term care is not yet resolved. Historically, some HMOs have used geriatricians as part of their primary care practitioner group but have not allowed these physicians to limit their practice exclusively to geriatric patients. Another model for practice is to have geriatricians (or a geriatric team) provide care and management to the most frail and vulnerable elderly within a system. This is implemented through screening programs, such as those noted earlier, that identify and refer new members who are frail (or current members who have become frail) into this specialty practice for ongoing primary care. Such a model requires a large elderly enrollment to generate a cost-effective practice volume. A variant on this model uses geriatricians as specialist consultants for assessment and advice with ongoing treatment. The patient remains under the care of the regular primary care physician. These two models can be used in combination (Friedman and Kane).

A further variation on the above involves the use of multidisciplinary teams (i.e., nurses, social workers, and/or other health professionals) in conjunction with the primary care physician. This model recognizes that geriatric training is generally more common among nurses and social workers, and it allows for case monitoring to occur through means other than office visits and to encompass care plans that go beyond purely medical treatment. In many cases geriatric nurse practitioners (GNPs) or adult nurse practitioners may assume responsibility for basic primary care, freeing the geriatrician's time for more complex cases. These team models can operate as components in ambulatory care clinics or as adjuncts to the home care program. Such teams are perhaps more common in hospital inpatient and nursing home settings. Under these inpatient circumstances the team likely replaces the patient's primary care physician until the patient returns to the community.

One area where GNPs have been used to good advantage is in providing primary care to nursing home patients. A corporation, EverCare, has developed a cost-effective managed care approach to capitating the acute care of nursing home patients, using GNPs as the major source of primary care. The underlying premise of this approach is that closer attention to the nursing home residents' primary care needs will reduce the use of more expensive hospital care (Kane and Huck). EverCare is being demonstrated at six sites across the country. As it has been implemented, some changes have been necessary. The participating physicians are recruited from those in the community who are already active in nursing home care. Because sufficient numbers of GNPs are not always available, adult nurse practitioners are sometimes used instead.

The relative value of any of these approaches is largely untested, but as a practical matter the choices made by a health plan and medical groups more generally are constrained by the size of their Medicare enrollment and by the limited availability of geriatricians.

Medicaid managed care

Many federal agencies, state governments, providers, and foundations are interested in using managed care for integrating acute care and long-term care. However a number of unresolved practical questions have slowed progress in this area. Two of the most important issues are discussed here. First, combining acute care and long-term care under a single entity raises questions about auspices. Many proponents of long-term care fear that a merged authority will be dominated by a medical mentality and that important social dimensions of long-term care will receive less attention. A second issue has to do with the experience base upon which to establish payment rates for both acute and long-term care services. PACE is the only program that has used a capitation payment blending funds from Medicare and Medicaid. In contrast to this, most state long-term care programs adjust Medicaid payments on the basis of expected Medicare reimbursement. Contractors in these situations are responsible for obtaining the Medicare portion of their payment. On the other hand, if Medicaid is capitated, Medicare usually remains fee-for-service—creating an incentive to shift costs to the fee-for-service payer. If acute care for both Medicaid and Medicare is capitated, then long-term care is usually fee-for-service—creating no incentive for capitated plans to keep members out of the long-term care system because Medicaid will pay for long-term stays. Data systems that can accumulate the full cost (across both Medicare and Medicaid) of the long-term care population or those at risk of entering the long-term care system are only beginning to be implemented.

Recognizing these important knowledge gaps, states have approached acute and long-term care integration in an incremental manner. A handful of states (Arizona, Florida, Minnesota, and Wisconsin) have enrolled elderly persons in Medicaid managed care programs that include varying levels of long-term care coverage (Holahan et al.). Four programs are briefly profiled. An initial common characteristic of these, and the other programs, is that none includes a direct role for the state regarding Medicare reimbursement.

Arizona. Arizona is the only state with a statewide managed care program for persons needing long-term care (Arizona Long Term Care System, ALTCS). The Arizona Health Care Cost Containment System contracts with managed care organizations for the coverage of all Medicaid enrollees. A Medicaid recipient is enrolled in ALTCS only if he or she meets Arizona's long-term care criteria. Through ALTCS the state pays managed care organizations (private companies in the Phoenix and Tucson areas, and county governments in the less populous counties) a capitated rate that covers the full range of community-based long-term care and nursing home care. ALTCS contractors are also responsible for the primary and acute care needs of their members, but this program covers only Medicaid costs; Medicare costs are reimbursed on a fee-for-service basis (McCall and Korb).

Florida. Florida has undertaken demonstration projects in three counties with two managed care organizations to examine the effects of managed Medicaid programs for elderly persons. Only recipients who meet the state's criteria for nursing home care are eligible. During the demonstration only those age sixty-five and older were eligible.

In these projects Medicaid is capitated (similar to the Arizona ALTCS program). State law prohibits the program from enrolling members in a Medicare risk contract. The benefits include in-home care, day care, transport services, supplies, and home adaptations.

Minnesota. Minnesota's Prepaid Medical Assistance Program enrolls elderly persons. It includes some community-based long-term care and up to ninety days of nursing facility care. Any additional long-term care is paid on a fee-for-service basis. Minnesota has initiated a waiver to Medicaid regulations so that it can establish the Senior Health Options Project. This program will integrate a full range of Medicare and Medicaid services for older persons who are dually eligible, regardless of whether they need long-term care. Nursing facility liability under this program will be limited to 180 days, but the rate structure provides incentives to purchase community care.

Wisconsin. The Wisconsin Partnership Program serves persons eligible for nursing facilities. The program currently operates as a Medicaid prepaid health plan (which is partially capitated). Medicare is billed by the providers on a fee-for-service basis. Program planners are seeking federal approval for full capitation of both Medicaid and Medicare services.

ROBERT NEWCOMER

See also CASE MANAGEMENT; DAY HOSPITALS; LONG-TERM CARE; MEDICAID; MEDICARE; MULTIDISCIPLINARY TEAM; VETERANS CARE.

BIBLIOGRAPHY

FAMA, T.; FOX, P.; and WHITE, L. "Do HMOs Care for the Chronically Ill?" *Health Affairs* 14, no. 1 (1995): 234–243.
FRIEDMAN, B., and KANE, R. "HMO Medical Directors' Perceptions of Geriatric Practice in Medicare HMOs." *Journal of the American Geriatric Society* 41, no. 11 (1993): 1144–1149.

HARRINGTON, C.; LYNCH, M.; and NEWCOMER, R. "Medical Services in Social Health Maintenance Organizations." *The Gerontologist* 33, no. 6 (1993): 790–800.

HOLAHAN, J.; ZUCKERMAN, S.; EVANS, A.; and RANGARAJAN, S. "Medicaid Managed Care in 13 States." *Health Affairs* 17, no. 3 (1998): 43–63.

IRVIN, C. V.; MASSEY, S.; and DORSEY, T. "Determinants of Enrollment Among Applicants to PACE." *Health Care Financing Review* 19, no. 2 (1997): 135–153.

KANE, R. L., and HUCK, S. "The Implementation of the EverCare Demonstration Project." *Journal of the American Geriatrics Society* 48, no. 2 (2000): 218–223.

KANE, R. L.; KANE, R. A.; FINCH, M.; HARRINGTON, C.; NEWCOMER, R.; MILLER, N.; and HULBERT, M. "S/HMOs, the Second Generation: Building on the Experience of the First Social Health Maintenance Organization Demonstrations." *Journal of the American Geriatrics Society* 45, no. 1 (1997): 101–107.

KRAMER, A.; FOX, P.; and MORGENSTERN, N. "Geriatric Care Approaches in Health Maintenance Organizations." *Journal of the American Geriatrics Society* 40, no. 10 (1992): 1055–1067.

MCCALL, N., and KORB, J. "Utilization of Services in Arizona's Capitated Medicaid Program for Long Term Care Beneficiaries." *Health Care Financing Review* 19, no. 2 (1997): 119–134.

MILLER, R., and LUFT, H. "Does Managed Care Lead to Better or Worse Quality of Care? A Survey of Recent Studies Shows Mixed Results on Managed Care Plan Performance." *Health Affairs* 16, no. 5 (1997): 7–25.

MUKAMEL, D. B.; TEMKIN-GREENER, H.; and CLARK, M. L. *Health Care Financing Review* 19, no. 3 (1998): 83–100.

PACALA, J.; BOULT, C.; HEPBURN, K.; KANE, R. L.; KANE, R. A.; MALONE, J.; MORISHITA, L.; and REED, R. "Case Management of Older Adults in Health Maintenance Organizations." *Journal of the American Geriatric Society* 43, no. 5 (1995): 538–542.

HEALTH ATTITUDE

Aging naturally entails changes in physical, cognitive, and social capacities. Many of these changes, such as declining strength, difficulty remembering, or bereavement from the death of friends and loved ones, are experienced as a kind of loss. Experiences of loss can affect one's health negatively, but some people maintain a positive *health attitude* despite these unwelcome events, which gives rise to a variety of positive health-related consequences. Like any attitude, which comprises a summary evaluation, favorable or unfavorable, of a concept, object, or situation, one's health attitude is the overall evaluation of one's own health as excellent, good, fair, or poor.

A positive health attitude typically reflects an objective health status that is also positive. Many large-scale surveys of population health, conducted in North America and Europe, have found that respondents' self-evaluations correspond well with more objective measures of their health, such as physician ratings, utilization of health services, diagnosed chronic conditions, or days of reduced activity due to health problems, and poor self-rated health has been shown to predict mortality (Mossey and Shapiro, 1982). A positive health attitude is also likely to be associated with consistent beliefs and behaviors. Someone with a positive health attitude might hold the consistent belief that he or she is not highly susceptible to disease, whereas someone with a negative health attitude might rarely or never engage in health-enhancing behaviors, such as exercise. These relationships are further understood to be bidirectional, that is, engaging in good health practices promotes a positive health attitude and vice versa. Past research has supported theories, such as the health belief model or theory of planned behavior, which describe beliefs as a cause, and behavior as a consequence, of health-related attitudes. Behavior can also be a cause of attitudes, according to research on cognitive dissonance and self-perception theory.

Aspects of an individual's personality, notably his or her optimism and perceived personal control over life events, can contribute to a positive health attitude as well. Highly optimistic people and those with high perceived control consistently view their health more positively, and cope more successfully with health problems, than do highly pessimistic people and those with low perceived control. Finally, the way people explain a health-related event can affect how positively they view their health. When negative events happen (e.g., a heart attack), people who attribute the event to a stable cause (e.g., genetic makeup) will view their health prospects more negatively than do people who attribute the event to an unstable cause (e.g., unhealthy lifestyle). Such characteristic attributions may account for the effects of dispositions such as optimism or perceived control on health attitudes. Moreover, according to research in achievement settings, these attributions may be subject to psychotherapeutic intervention, suggesting one way in which people can adopt a positive health attitude. It remains unclear, however, whether such induced attitudes convey the same protection as those that occur spontaneously.

Positive health attitudes have been associated with mostly desirable health-related consequences, as assessed at a later time. Other circumstances being equal, people who view their health positively live longer, on average, than people who view their health negatively. However, a positive health attitude can also serve a defensive function, leading to undesirable consequences. People may continue a health-damaging behavior, such as smoking, or fail to adopt a health-enhancing one, such as sunscreen use, because their positive health attitude shields them from recognizing the health threat that these choices may pose. Finally, one's health attitude can serve a symbolic function, by reaffirming the increasing value people place on their health as they age.

JUDITH G. CHIPPERFIELD
DANIEL S. BAILIS
RAYMOND P. PERRY

See also CONTROL, PERCEIVED; PERCEIVED HEALTH; PERSONALITY.

BIBLIOGRAPHY

BALTES, P. B., and BALTES, M. M. *Successful Aging: Perspectives from the Behavioral Sciences.* Cambridge, U.K.: Cambridge University Press, 1990.

MOSSEY, J. M., and SHAPIRO, E. "Self-Rated Health: A Predictor of Mortality among the Elderly." *American Journal of Public Health* 72, no. 8 (1982): 800–808.

STROEBE, W., and STROEBE, M. S. *Social Psychology and Health.* Pacific Grove, Calif.: Brooks/Cole Pub. Co., 1995.

TAYLOR, S. E.; KEMENY, M. E.; REED, G. M.; BOWER, J. E.; and GRUENEWALD, T. L. "Psychological Resources, Positive Illusions, and Health." *American Psychologist* 55 (2000): 99–109.

HEALTH INSURANCE

See EMPLOYEE HEALTH INSURANCE

HEALTH INSURANCE, NATIONAL APPROACHES

One key feature of a health system is health insurance. Health insurance allows individuals to share the risk of any large costs due to illness, and provides a structure by which individuals are linked with health care services. Although insured individuals often pay fees to obtain medicine or to see a doctor, health insurance pays for a large portion of medical costs.

Typically, health care insurance systems have a combination of public and private components. However, with the exception of a few countries, such as Germany, the Netherlands, and the United States, most industrialized countries have universal health care for basic health services, funded through the public sector. In a universal system, all citizens or residents, regardless of age, income, or health status, have access to a core set of health care benefits. Australia, Canada, France, Japan, Korea, Sweden, and the United Kingdom all have universal health care systems. Individuals can often supplement the health insurance they receive from the government with private insurance for health services not covered by the public system, or to cover large costs. In France, for example, 84.5 percent of the population purchased supplementary insurance from private sources in 1998. Thus, even in countries with universal health care, it is often the case that not all individuals have the same insurance coverage.

Some countries have mixed systems in which a portion of the population has only public insurance, while others have only private insurance. In Germany and the Netherlands, a majority of the population has public health insurance. Participants in the public insurance program are not allowed to purchase private health insurance that covers the core services already covered under the public system. Thus, among this group, everyone has equal basic health care coverage. Only those who have incomes above a cut-off level have the option to purchase their own private health insurance or go without health insurance.

The health insurance system in the United States is one of the most diverse. About two-thirds of nonelderly individuals in the United States obtain health insurance through an employer. Generally, this insurance is paid for by both the employer and the employee and is heavily subsidized by the income tax system. Some individuals who are working but are not offered employer-subsidized health insurance pay the full cost of their private health insurance. There are also individuals who have public health insurance provided for them by the government. *Medicaid* is a public program that helps some individuals in the United States who have low incomes or who are disabled pay for their health care. *Medicare* is a program that covers health care costs for most of the elderly population. In 2000, 15.8 percent of the nonelderly population in the United States was without health insurance.

In most countries, elderly persons are covered under the same health insurance program or system as other members of the population. One exception is the United States, where the vast majority of older adults are eligible for the public Medicare program. Another important part of a health care system for the elderly is insurance for *long-term care*. Long-term care insurance helps pay for nursing home care if, for example, an individual becomes ill or disabled for an extended period of time. In countries such as Sweden and Denmark, coverage of long-term care is included in the country's general health care system. Germany, on the other hand, has a separate public long-term care insurance program that is mandatory for most of the population. Meanwhile, in the United States, private long-term care insurance is optional and limited. Only the poor are provided with long-term care coverage, via Medicaid. Similarly, France provides free long-term care to the poorest elderly adults, but there is no social long-term insurance under the French system.

Financing

Health care spending varies widely across countries. Table 1 shows health care spending for some industrialized countries. In the United States, almost 13 percent of the *gross domestic product (GDP)* is devoted to health care spending, the highest of any country in the world. At the other end of the spectrum, the Southeast Asian country of Myanmar spends less than 2 percent of its GDP on health care.

High levels of spending do not necessarily guarantee a high-quality health care system. In 2000, the World Health Organization ranked health care systems based on criteria that included measures of overall population health, in-

Table 1
Health Care Expenditures, 1998

	Total expenditure as % of GDP	Per capita public expenditure (U.S. purchasing power parity)
Australia	8.6	2,085
Canada	9.3	2,360
France	9.3	2,043
Germany	10.3	2,361
Japan*	7.5	1,795
Korea	5.1	2,150
Netherlands	8.7	740
Sweden	7.9	1,732
United Kingdom	6.8	1,510
United States	12.9	4,165

SOURCE: OECD Health Data (2001)

equalities within the system, and patient satisfaction. The United States was ranked thirty-seventh out of the 191 countries, despite spending a higher proportion of its GDP on health than any other country. The health status of a population is, of course, determined by many factors outside the health care system itself, such as population wealth and nutrition.

Spending on health care for the elderly makes up a substantial part of health care costs in individual countries (see Table 2). In 1995, the United States spent over $12,000, on average, for health expenditures for each individual age sixty-five and older, as compared to just over $3,000 on average for those younger than sixty-five. Total expenditures on the elderly are particularly high in countries such as Germany, Sweden, and Japan that have a large elderly population. Among the countries shown in table 2, Japan spends the largest proportion of health care expenditures on those sixty-five and older—nearly 50 percent of total expenditures on health in Japan were for older adults in 1997. As the proportion of the elderly population increases in many countries, expenditures on health care for this population may rise even further.

There are numerous regulations that attempt to control the cost of health care. Costs can be controlled by limiting the treatments available to patients, controlling the cost of drugs, or by setting a limit on the amount of money that can be spent on certain health services. In most countries, there are incentives for individuals to purchase, or for doctors to prescribe, cheaper

Table 2
Elderly Expenditures

	Ratio of health spending for persons age 65 and older to persons under age 65	Percent of population 65 and older	Estimated percent of total health spending on the elderly
Australia (1993)	4.09	11.6	35%
Canada (1997)	4.9	12.2	41%
France (1991)	2.96	14.3	33%
Germany (1994)	2.68	15.8	33%
Japan (1997)	4.9	15.7	48%
Korea (1994)	2.38	5.7	13%
Netherlands (1982)	3.59	11.7	32%
Sweden (1993)	2.8	17.6	37%
United Kingdom (1997)	3.35	15.7	38%
United States (1995)	4.6	12.5	40%

SOURCE: OECD Health Data (2001)

generic drugs rather than similar but more expensive medicines. In countries such as Belgium, France, and Italy, fixed budgets are used to limit total expenditures on pharmaceuticals. The prices of drugs are also regulated in some countries, such as Australia.

Countries vary not only in the amount they spend on health care, but also in how they raise funds. Health care can be funded publicly by the government or privately by individuals or firms. Public funding generally comes either from general tax revenues, such as income or sales taxes, or designated tax revenues such as payroll taxes, as in the U.S. Social Security system. Private spending is funded either through voluntary private health insurance or through out-of-pocket expenditures.

Public expenditures. Less than half of United States spending on health comes from public sources (see Table 3). In contrast, Sweden and the United Kingdom each raise funds for over 80 percent of total health care expenditures from public sources. Even within the category of public spending, there is variation in funding sources. Sweden and Australia fund their public spending almost entirely through *general tax revenues,* while France, the Netherlands, and Germany raise funds almost entirely through a *designated tax,* or *social security,* system. In most countries, one scheme dominates.

Under tax-financed health care systems, the government collects general tax revenues (e.g., through sales, income, or property taxes), and decides how much of that revenue to allocate to health care spending and how much to other publicly funded programs, such as education or military spending. In health care systems funded mainly through public insurance, participation in the insurance system is typically mandatory. In general, employers and employees are each required to contribute to a general fund, sometimes known as a *sickness fund,* which is used to pay (in full or in part) for participants' health care services, including doctor visits, pharmaceuticals, and long-term care for the elderly or disabled. In Australia, France, Germany, and the Netherlands, contribution levels are based on income—those with higher salaries are required to contribute at a higher level. Retirees are also frequently required to contribute a percentage of their pension income to social insurance programs. The United States is an important exception—there is no mandatory social insurance contribution imposed on Medicare beneficiaries who are not working.

Private expenditures. Private health care is paid for by individuals, either through private insurance or *as out-of-pocket expenditures* (see Table 4). Even in countries where the entire population is covered by public insurance, some portion of health care costs are funded through out-of-pocket expenditures. These expenditures typically include copayments for pharmaceuticals or physician visits, or spending on treatments not covered by public or private insurance plans, like dental care. High out-of-pocket costs may prevent low-income individuals from obtaining the health care they require. Due to high copayments, out-of-pocket expenditures make

Table 3

Public Health Care Expenditures, 1998

	Public expenditure as % of total expenditure	Social security expenditure as % of public expenditure	Tax funded expenditure as % of public expenditure	Social security expenditure as % of total expenditure	Tax funded expenditure as % of total expenditure
Australia	69.9	0.0	100.0	0.0	69.9
Canada	70.1	1.7	98.3	1.2	68.9
France	76.1	96.8	3.2	73.7	2.4
Germany	75.8	91.6	8.3	69.4	6.3
Japan	78.1	89.2	10.8	69.7	8.4
Korea	46.2	74.5	25.5	34.4	11.8
Netherlands	68.6	94.0	6.0	64.5	4.1
Sweden	83.8	0.0	100.0	0.0	83.8
United Kingdom	83.3	11.8	88.2	9.8	73.5
United States	44.8	33.2	66.8	14.9	29.9

SOURCE: OECD Health Data (2001)

up a particularly high percentage of total health expenditures in Korea. In the United Kingdom, certain groups, such as retirees, are exempt from the copayments required for the rest of the population.

The proportion of private spending on private insurance in the United States is quite high, since most of the population relies solely on private insurance to cover their medical costs. France also has a high proportion of private insurance spending, despite the fact that it relies mainly on public health care spending. This is because individuals covered under the French public system are generally responsible for substantial copayments. Many French people therefore opt to purchase supplementary private insurance policies to reduce out-of-pocket costs.

Medical care resources

The phrase *medical care resources* is used to describe the many parts of the health care system that work together to improve or maintain a person's health. One of the most important resources is the medical workforce. These are the doctors, nurses, pharmacists, paramedics, and other professionals that treat people who seek care. Hospitals and pharmaceuticals are also important medical care resources. Regulatory institutions around the world face a difficult challenge in coordinating the supply of these important resources and allocating them efficiently.

In many countries with universal health care, such as France and the United Kingdom,

the coordination of resources is primarily the responsibility of a central authority or government agency. In other countries, including the United States, many allocation decisions are dictated by economic forces in the marketplace. Nevertheless, even in the United States, many laws are in place to regulate or control medical resources. The characteristics of a health care system and the regulations of the medical workforce, hospitals, and pharmaceuticals impact the medical resources available in a country.

Medical workforce. There are many different types of care in which physicians may specialize. They may also choose whether to live and practice in urban or rural settings, or in hospitals as compared to private clinics. Nurses and other health professionals can typically make similar decisions about their work specialization and location. A health system can provide incentives such as student loans or grants for professionals to enter particular specialties or communities. Alternatively, such choices may be regulated directly by governing institutions.

Rules governing where doctors can practice and which doctors a patient can see vary from country to country. In the United Kingdom and Germany, *general practitioners* are almost always precluded from practicing in hospitals and can only practice in outpatient settings. In these countries, *specialists* provide most of the care in hospitals. In Canada and France, meanwhile, general practitioners can practice in both inpatient and outpatient settings. Such regulations sometimes influence the prevalence of a particu-

Table 4
Private Health Care Expenditures, 1998

	Private expenditure as % of total expenditure	Private insurance as % of private expenditure	Out-of-pocket expenditures as % of private expenditure	Private insurance as % of total expenditure	Out-of-pocket expenditures as % of total expenditure
Australia	30.1	24.8	53.5	7.5	16.1
Canada	29.9	37.5	55.6	11.2	16.6
France	23.9	52.7	43.0	12.6	10.3
Germany	24.2	29.5	52.8	7.1	12.8
Japan	21.9	1.3	77.8	0.3	17.0
Korea	53.8	12.9	77.4	6.9	41.6
Netherlands	31.4	55.7	25.5	17.5	8.0
Sweden	16.2	0.0	100.0	0.0	16.2
United Kingdom	16.7	20.8	66.8	3.5	11.2
United States	55.2	60.7	28.3	33.5	15.6

SOURCE: OECD Health Data (2001)

lar specialty in the medical workforce. In France, for example, the fact that patients can choose either a general practitioner or a specialist as their doctor has created an environment of competition between the two professions. One result is that some doctors that are technically specialists work as general practitioners.

Health care systems also vary in how physicians are paid. Under a *fee-for-service* payment system, physicians are paid for each service they provide. A *capitated* payment system gives physicians a fixed level of payment for each patient that may be treated over a set period of time. Alternatively, physicians can receive a salary. Each of these payment systems is used around the world, often regardless of the universality of their coverage or the level of government involvement. Fee-for-service is the dominant form of physician payment in France, where patients pay up front and are later reimbursed by the public system. In the United Kingdom's National Health Service, physicians are paid on a capitation basis. Meanwhile, physicians in the Swedish health system are paid a salary. Since the United States is dominated by a private system of care, the market has evolved to compensate physicians in each of these three ways depending on their specialty and the environment in which they practice. The different payment schemes may provide different incentives for physicians, thus impacting the availability of certain health care workers in a society.

Hospitals. Hospitals are another medical resource whose regulation varies between health systems. In countries that have public hospitals, such as the United Kingdom, the government can use its central authority to establish hospital capacities and services in a manner that is responsive to the distribution of health needs in the population. In other countries, such as Canada and the United States, hospitals are largely private and guided by the economic forces of the marketplace, though in Canada their budgets are regionally controlled. France, Germany, and Japan, meanwhile, have a more equal share of public and private hospitals.

Pharmaceuticals. The types of drugs that are legal to use in a country are often regulated at the national level. In the United States, the Federal Drug Administration (FDA) determines which drugs are safe and can be made available to patients. It is important to note that insurance providers in the United States and in other countries will often only pay (or help pay) for a portion of legally available drugs. From a patient's point of view, some legal drugs may still be unavailable for use, as the patient may not be able to afford expensive drugs without the help of his or her insurance company. On the other hand, in countries with universal health care, such as Sweden, it is often the case that all legal drugs are made available to all patients.

Health systems also vary in how pharmaceuticals can be obtained. In most countries, physicians prescribe medications but cannot sell them. An interesting exception is Japan, where physicians prescribe and sell drugs to their patients, acting as both physician and pharmacist. By affecting the availability of medical resources, pharmaceutical regulations such as these also affect a patient's use of health care.

The patient's experience

Health care systems exist to serve the patient. Thus, an understanding of the patient's experience is crucial when attempting to compare and evaluate different systems. Rates of health care coverage, degrees of patient choice, amounts of hospital utilization, and types of long-term care vary from country to country, providing patients with vastly different experiences across health care systems.

Coverage. Different types of health care coverage can drastically affect the amount of health care individuals receive. Virtually the entire populations of Australia, Canada, France, Japan, Korea, Sweden, and the United Kingdom have public health care coverage. In contrast, only 45 percent of the population in the United States and 74.5 percent of the population in the Netherlands are covered under public systems. In countries in which large proportions of the population have no coverage, the poor and other at-risk groups may not receive adequate health care. However, it is important to note that even in systems offering universal health coverage, not all patients will necessarily have equal access to care. Patients' experiences may, in fact, vary with factors like income or geographic location. For example, while the Swedish system used to be relatively equitable, rising co-payments have recently increased the gap in services between rich and poor. Because medical resources in France are concentrated in urban areas, residents in rural locations may not have access to the same medical services available in cities.

Health care systems also differ in their coverage of pharmaceutical goods. Elderly individuals are by far the largest consumers of pharmaceuticals, and are thus most affected when drugs are not covered by their health insurance. In Australia, Japan, Korea, Sweden, and the United Kingdom, all people are covered for approved pharmaceuticals. The French public insurance system covers pharmaceuticals at varying rates, with higher rates of reimbursement for drugs considered more essential to patients' health. In Canada, less than half the population receives assistance for pharmaceuticals through the national public system. Most Canadian provinces and territories, however, have developed supple-

mentary programs to help provide pharmaceuticals to the elderly population. In the United States, only 12 percent of the population has public pharmaceutical coverage.

Patient choice. Systems vary in the degree of choice they allow patients. Individuals may have more power to decide how, where, and from whom they receive medical care in some systems than in others. In France, Japan, and Korea, patients are not restricted to any particular set of doctors. Publicly insured individuals in Germany, Sweden, and the Netherlands can choose their doctor from among those affiliated with their sickness fund, or within a specified geographic area. Once patients have chosen a doctor, they can generally change their doctor at will, except in Germany, where they have to complete a three-month period with their current doctor before moving to a new one. In the United States, patients in the managed-care system are typically restricted to a list of medical providers, and some can only change their doctor during specified enrollment periods.

Individuals in the United States managed-care system usually must visit their primary care doctor before seeking care with a specialist. In this way, the primary care doctor serves as a gatekeeper, having complete discretion over patient referrals to specialists. Similarly, in the Netherlands, publicly insured patients can only visit specialists after receiving vouchers from their primary doctor.

In practice, patients' ability to choose a doctor may depend on their level and type of insurance coverage, their income, or the location of their residence. For example, though patients in Canada may typically choose their primary care doctor, the availability of such doctors tends to vary by region. In France, lower-income people are more likely to receive care from general practitioners, while higher-income people tend to receive care from specialists.

Inpatient care. The number and length of hospital stays can also vary greatly between countries. France has the highest hospital admission rate of the countries considered here. Patients in France are frequently checked into the hospital for short stays to undergo procedures that would take place in an outpatient setting in most other systems. Hospital stays are almost completely reimbursed under the French system.

Meanwhile, in Japan and the Netherlands, the average length of stay in hospitals is high—

over thirty days in each country. This is mainly due to the incorporation of long-term care patients in their measure of hospital stays. In comparison, individuals in hospitals in Sweden spend only 6.6 days as inpatients. In Canada, average stays are 8.2 days; while in the United States they are 71 days.

Elderly patients. An elderly patient's experience may differ from that of a younger individual in the same health care system. Even in countries that offer universal coverage, certain groups of patients may receive less care. Elderly persons may be especially affected by this health care rationing. In the United Kingdom, for example, a survey found that the oldest segment of the population rarely received certain health services, including heart transplants, bypass operations, and admission to intensive therapy units.

Another important factor in an elderly patient's experience is long-term care. In the past, older individuals have traditionally received long-term care in hospitals or institutional settings. However, some countries have come to rely increasingly on home care for long-term patients. Table 5 details the share of elderly persons in institutions versus those receiving formal home care. While France, Japan, and the United Kingdom have relatively equal percentages of the elderly population in institutions and receiving formal home care, a greater proportion of the elderly in Australia, Canada, Germany, the Netherlands, Sweden, and the United States receive long-term care in the home. Some countries have passed laws explicitly encouraging this move towards home health care. For example, some localities in Sweden pay family members to provide care in the home. The Netherlands and Germany attempt to provide more flexibility for older adults by offering them an option to receive a lump-sum payment so that they can seek treatment wherever they prefer.

The future of health care

One of the greatest challenges facing health care systems today is the aging of the world population. As noted in the financing section, spending on care for elderly persons already makes up a substantial portion of health care costs. These costs will to continue to rise as the size of the elderly population grows, with people living longer than they ever have before. Most countries are experiencing aging populations, but the most dramatic example of the aging phenomenon is

Table 5
Long-Term Care Usage

	Percent of population age 65 and older in institutions	Percent of population age 65 and older receiving formal home care
Australia (1998)	6.8	11.7
Canada (1993)	6.2	17
France (1997)	6.5	6.1
Germany (1995)	6.8	9.6
Japan (1998)	6	5
Netherlands (1997)	8.8	12
Sweden (1998)	8.7	11.2
United Kingdom (1996)	5.1	5.5
United States (1994)	5.7	16

SOURCE: Jacobzone, S. "Ageing and Care for Frail Elderly Persons: An Overview of International Perspectives." Paris, France: Organisation for Economic Cooperation and Development, 1999.

Japan. Life expectancy at birth in Japan rose from seventy to eighty-four years for women and from sixty-five to seventy-seven years for men between 1960 and 1999. In 1960, 5.7 percent of the Japanese population was age sixty-five and older, while 16.7 percent of the population was age sixty-five and older in 1999. Projections indicate that more than 20 percent of Japan's population will be age sixty-five or older in 2020. Meanwhile, in the United States, the large group of baby boomers will result in a growing proportion of elderly persons beginning in about 2010.

Countries continue to explore new ways of financing and managing their health care systems. In Sweden, for example, efforts have been made to privatize the hospitals. Many of these reforms are aimed at controlling costs, either due to concerns about population aging or because of overall economic and structural shifts in governments. France has instituted a number of reforms intended to reduce soaring health care costs. Most of these have involved increasing patients' contributions for medical services, particularly for pharmaceuticals; however, the wide prevalence of supplementary private insurance schemes to cover these increased payments has limited success of these reforms. In another attempt to control costs, the Netherlands attempted in the early 1990s to implement a system incorporating greater private insurer control. However, since this plan met great opposition from both physicians and the public, these reforms were halted, and the government has instead focused on providing a more efficient public health care system.

Other types of reforms are aimed at improving the quality and availability of health care. In the mid-1990s, the German government passed a law intended to improve equity of care by allowing nearly all insured individuals a choice of sickness funds. Prior to the law's enactment, workers had access to sickness funds of differing quality. In Canada, meanwhile, a recent study showed that a significant number of family physicians are limiting the number of new patients they will accept, signaling an issue in access to care in Canada that will need to be addressed. The one consistent trait across these diverse health systems is that they are all undergoing reform. It remains to be seen how all these changes will effect the provision of health care throughout the world.

ELISE L. GOULD, ET AL.

See also EMPLOYEE RETIREMENT INCOME SECURITY ACT; LONG-TERM CARE FINANCING; MEDICAID; MEDICARE.

BIBLIOGRAPHY

Age Concern England. "New Survey of GPs Confirms Ageism in the NHS." World Wide Web document, 2000. www.ACE.org.uk.

BOCOGNANO, A.; COUFFINHAL, A.; DUMESNIL, S.; and GRIGNON, M. "Which Coverage for Whom? Equity of Access to Health Insurance in France." World Wide Web document, 2000. www.credes.fr/En_ligne/

College of Family Physicians of Canada. "Initial Data Release of the 2001 National Family Physician Workforce Survey." World Wide Web document, 2001. www.cfpc.ca/research/

DIDERICHSEN, F. "Sweden." *Journal of Health Politics, Policy and Law* 25, no. 5 (2000): 931–935.

FRONSTIN, P. "Sources of Health Insurance and Characteristics of the Uninsured: Analysis of the March 2001 Population Survey." EBRI Issue Brief No. 240. Washington, D.C.: Employee Benefit Research Institute.

JACOBZONE, S. "Ageing and Care for Frail Elderly Persons: An Overview of International Perspectives." Paris, France: Organisation for Economic Cooperation and Development, 1999.

JACOBZONE, S. "Pharmaceutical Policies in OECD Countries: Reconciling Social and Industrial Goals," Labour Market and Social Policy Occasional Papers No. 40. Paris, France: Organization for Economic Cooperation and Development, 2000.

Organisation for Economic Cooperation and Development. "OECD Health Data 2001: A Comparative Analysis of 30 Countries." Paris, France: Organisation for Economic Cooperation and Development, 2001.

World Health Organization. "Report on Health, Statistical Annex, Table 10." Geneva: WHO, 2000.

HEALTH, SOCIAL FACTORS

To understand the connection between social factors and health, it is necessary to examine the average level of health of aging people in one social group and then compare this to the average level of health of those in another social group. One's social situation can be examined in several ways including marital status, social class, religiousness, and relationships with others.

If the health of people in one group, such as married individuals, is better on average than the health of those in another, such as widowed persons, one can conclude there is a relationship between that particular marital status and health. Once a relationship is observed, it is important to examine the underlying mechanisms that explain it. First, it is necessary to determine whether health determines one's social position or whether the social position influences health outcomes. If people with certain health problems are not able to attain or remain in a certain social position, researchers say that the underlying mechanism was selection into the social status. In other words, if an existing physical or mental health problem makes it less likely that a person will marry, then that person's health causes his or her marital status. Alternately, if being in a particular social position or group has an effect on one's health, researchers say that something about the social environment associated with that position or group has an effect on health, and they then must investigate further to determine the underlying factors. Information collected at one point in time, however, does not untangle whether one's current social position or one's health status came first. To address this problem, some researchers design studies that follow the same individuals over time, noting the changes in health status and social position over the course of their lives.

Health outcomes are often measured in terms of how a person defines his or her own health, the number of health problems a person has, the amount of disability a person experiences, and the chances a person has of dying—commonly known as *mortality*. Various social factors may have an effect on health and health outcomes.

Social support

Social support includes resources, either practical or emotional, provided by others. A person's social network, which includes the number of relationships and the frequency of contact with others, provides information about how socially integrated an individual is, but does not give information about the quality of the relationships. More in-depth measures of social support include whether the type of support is emotional and provides a feeling of being cared for, or whether it is instrumental and provides practical help with tasks or financial aid. Further, the quality of the interaction indicates whether the social relationship is positive and helpful or negative and conflictual.

Social relationships have a powerful effect on physical and mental health, and on mortality. In one of the earliest studies to note this association, Berkman and Syme (1979) found that even after taking into consideration levels of self-reported health, a social network index comprised of social ties with a spouse, family, and friends; church membership, and other group membership predicted mortality within the next nine years. For people between sixty and sixty-nine years of age, the relative risk of dying over the next nine years for the most isolated men was 1.8 times the risk associated with the most connected men. For women in this age group, those with the least connections had three times the relative risk of those with the most connections. Later studies took into consideration baseline levels of health and found that social integration or isolation added to a prediction of later mortality.

Dean, Kolody, and Wood (1990) found that older individuals who reported higher levels of care and concern from spouses, friends, and children had lower levels of depression than those who experienced little social support. Interestingly, those who reported low levels of expressive support from adult children and spouses had higher levels of depression than those who did not have children or a spouse. This suggests that it is not only the presence of a social tie, but also the quality of the relationship that affects mental health.

Marriage

On average, the health of those who are married is better than the health of individuals who live alone. Further, married individuals live longer than those who are not married. For older adults, the problems associated with being alone are mainly seen in those who are widowed, rather than in those who are divorced or who never married. Goldman, Korenman, and Weinstein (1995) found that for individuals age seventy and older, after taking into consideration self-rated health, functional ability, and medical conditions, widowhood predicts later disability for both men and women, and mortality for men. It is unlikely that the poorer health status of the widowed is due to the crisis of bereavement, because only 7 percent of the widowed in the sample had lost their spouse within two years of the initial interview. Rather, factors associated with being widowed and not remarrying appear to cause poorer health. However, the relationship between widowhood and mortality is only seen for men, and the relationship with disability is much stronger for men than for women. This may be because women are likely to serve as caregivers who monitor their husbands' health behaviors—after their wife's death, men lose an important source of instrumental support.

Marriage does seem to offer a distinct health benefit that the widowed do not enjoy. The protective aspect of marriage could occur because marriage acts as a form of social control that encourages individuals to engage in better health practices and less risky behavior. It could also be due to the social support that a spouse offers. A spouse can serve as a confidant who offers emotional support and practical advice in the face of a problem or stressor. In this way, a spouse serves as a buffer that protects the person from becoming affected by the stress caused by serious life events. Furthermore, support from the spouse can be helpful not only during serious problems, but also during everyday hassles and challenges. Aside from offering emotional and practical support in the face of difficulties, a spouse can serve as someone who offers love, care, and respect, as well as someone who encourages a healthy self-esteem. In addition to these benefits of marriage, it is also possible that the healthiest individuals are better able to remarry after losing a spouse, thereby letting their health status select them into their social position.

Religion

Many studies have found religiosity to have a beneficial influence on the health of older adults. In reviewing the research on the association between religiosity and health, Jeffery Levin (1994) notes that there are several mechanisms through which religion may affect health. First, religious organizations promote behaviors that are congruent with good health outcomes, such as abstaining from smoking; drinking in moderation; and taking care of oneself through exercise and diet. In a study of older adults, Idler and Kasl (1997a) found that those who regularly attended religious services were more likely to engage in physical exercise, to drink only in moderation, and not to have smoked than were those who attended services less frequently or not at all.

Religious involvement may also lead to better health by providing individuals with social support and a feeling of social integration. Compared with individuals who never or rarely attend religious service, those who frequently attend also engage in more leisure activities, have contact with and feel closer to a greater number of friends and kin, and celebrate holidays that involve various social ties.

Social activities and close family relationships do explain some of the relationship between religion and health, but it seems that attendance at religious services also provides something more. Other possible factors linking religion and health involve the psychodynamics of belief systems, religious rites, and faith. Religious rites have a calming effect on members, and religious faith may increase the expectation of positive health outcomes. These factors may serve as a placebo and result in better health outcomes.

Much of the research that finds an association between religion and health cannot determine whether religion causes better health. It is possible that healthy individuals are better able to get to services, while those with worse health and disability are not able to participate. If this is the case, then it is health status that selects individuals into the position of religious participation. Idler and Kasl (1997b) examined data that tracked a group of older adults over twelve years and noted frequency of attendance at religious service and levels of functional ability at different time periods. They found that initial levels of religious participation protected against disability in later years; however, initial levels of disability did not affect attendance three years later. This suggests that religious involvement affects health to a greater extent than health affects religious involvement.

Socioeconomic status

Individuals with lower socioeconomic status (SES)—those who have less education and income—have an earlier onset of illness, more illness overall, and earlier deaths than those with higher SES. Social stratification early in the life course affects the trajectory an individual is likely to follow. Being born with economic advantages is likely to lead to educational success, which is linked to occupational advantage and later financial security. Data from the National Longitudinal Survey of Labor Market Experience: Mature Men, 1966–1990 was used to examine the impact of educational and occupational experiences on premature death. Length of education, type of first job, type of job in middle age, and family wealth in middle age each were found to contribute independently to the risk of a premature death. Data from other countries replicate this importance of social class over the life course for timing of death. When individuals were categorized according to the number of points in their life when they were living with a father who held a manual labor job or they themselves held a manual job, those who never engaged in manual labor had better health than those who did so at all points. While social status in childhood influences later social status through educational advancement, social position at each stage of life has also been found to exert an independent influence on later health.

A large dataset of noninstitutionalized adults in the United States found that in the six years before death, the health status of older respondents varied based on their level of education. In the years before death, those with less education were likely to be more limited in activity, to have multiple chronic health conditions, and to have spent more days in bed and in the hospital. This suggests that those with higher socioeconomic status are likely to live more of their life in good health than those with lower SES.

What is it about lower levels of education and income that leads to declines in health? House, et al. (1994) found that people with lower socioeconomic status are more likely to be exposed to risk factors. Compared with those with more money and education, those with less are at a disadvantage, in terms of drinking, marital status, informal social integration, and chronic financial stress, across all age groups. For other risk factors, including smoking, being overweight, formal social integration, perceived social support, and self-esteem and self-mastery, the disadvantage of those with lower SES increases through middle age and then diminishes later in life. This suggests that early disadvantage based on these risk factors may cause less healthy individuals with lower socioeconomic status to die at earlier ages.

Overall, the health status of older adults is positively related to their social status. Being married, having high levels of social support, attending religious services, and having a high socioeconomic status offers health benefits that the widowed, elderly persons with little social support, those who do not attend religious services, and those of low socioeconomic status do not enjoy. The social position that each older individual occupies, which exerts such strong influence on health, is the result of lifelong processes, and may itself be influenced by earlier health status.

ELLEN L. IDLER
JULIE McLAUGHLIN

See also DIVORCE: TRENDS AND CONSEQUENCES; EDUCATION; INEQUALITY; MARITAL RELATIONSHIPS; MARRIAGE AND REMARRIAGE; RELIGION; SOCIAL SUPPORT.

BIBLIOGRAPHY

BERKMAN, L. F., and SYME, S. L. "Social Networks, Host Resistance, and Mortality: A Nine-Year Follow-up Study of Alameda County Residents." *American Journal of Epidemiology* 109, no. 2 (1979): 186–204.
BLANE, D. "The Life Course, the Social Gradients and Health." In *Social Determinants of Health.* Edited by M. Marmot and R. G. Wilkinson. Oxford, U.K.: Oxford University Press, 1999. Pages 64–80.
DEAN, A.; KOLOGY, B.; and WOOD, P. "Effects of Social Support from Various Sources on Depression in Elderly Persons." *Journal of Health and Social Behavior* 31 (1990): 148–161.
GOLDMAN, N.; KORENMAN, S.; and WEINSTEIN, R. "Marital Status and Health Among the Elderly." *Social Science and Medicine* 40, no. 12 (1995): 1717–1730.
HOUSE, J. S.; LEPKOWSKI, J. M.; KINNEY, A. M.; MERO, R. P.; KESSLER, R. C.; and HERZOG, A. R. "The Social Stratification of Aging and Health." *Journal of Health and Social Behavior* 35 (1994): 213–234.

IDLER, E. L., and KASL, S. V. "Religion Among Disabled and Nondisabled Persons I: Cross-Sectional Patterns in Health Practices, Social Activities, and Well-Being." *Journal of Gerontology: Social Sciences* 52B, no. 6 (1997): S294–S305.
IDLER, E. L., and KASL, S. V. "Religion Among Disabled and Nondisabled Persons II: Attendance at Religious Services as a Predictor of the Course of Disability." *Journal of Gerontology: Social Sciences* 52B, no. 6 (1997): S306–S316.
LEVIN, J. S. "Religion and Health: Is There an Association, Is it Valid, and Is it Causal?" *Social Science and Medicine* 38, no. 11 (1994): 1475–1482.
LIAO, Y.; McGEE D. L.; KAUFMAN J. S.; CAO, G.; and COOPER R. S. "Socioeconomic Status and Morbidity in the Last Years of Life." *American Journal of Public Health* 89, no. 4 (1999): 569–572.
STANSFELD, S. A. "Social Support and Social Cohesion." In *Social Determinants of Health.* Edited by M. Marmot and R. G. Wilkinson. Oxford, U.K.: Oxford University Press, 1999. Pages 155–178.

HEARING

The auditory system changes as a consequence of the aging process, as well as a result of exposure to environmental agents and disease. The cumulative effect of these factors over the life span is a significant hearing loss among a large proportion of adults aged sixty-five years and older. Hearing loss associated exclusively with the aging process is known as *presbycusis.* Deterioration of the auditory system with age leads to changes not only in hearing sensitivity, but also to a decline in processing of speech stimuli, particularly in less-than-ideal listening environments. However, there is large individual variability in the auditory abilities of older people, as well as substantial gender differences in auditory performance. Thus, generalizations about hearing in aging and the impact of decline in the auditory sense must be considered with an understanding of the range of individual differences that may occur.

Prevalence of hearing loss

Hearing loss is the fourth most common chronic health condition reported by individuals who are sixty-five years and over (National Center for Health Statistics). Among males, 33 percent aged sixty-five to seventy-four years, and 43 percent aged seventy-five years and over report a hearing impairment. Comparable figures for females are 16 percent and 31 percent for sixty-five to seventy-four year olds and those seventy-five and older, respectively. A much higher prevalence rate of hearing loss among older people is reported in studies that actually test hearing sensitivity in the population. For example, 83 percent of the 2,351 participants in the Framingham Heart Cohort Study, ages fifty-seven to eighty-nine years, had some degree of hearing loss at one frequency in the speech range (Moscicki, Elkins, Baum, and McNamara). Using a criterion of average hearing sensitivity exceeding 25 decibels Hearing Level (dB HL) as indicating significant hearing loss, the overall prevalence rate in large population-based studies of older adults is about 46 percent.

Source of hearing problems and effects on the auditory system

The principal causes of significant hearing loss among older people are noise exposure, disease, heredity, and senescence. Exposure to industrial noise exceeding 90 dBA for an eight-hour workday over a period of time is known to cause permanent, high-frequency hearing loss. Additionally, a single exposure to very intense sound (exceeding 130 dBA) can also cause a permanent hearing loss that affects either all frequencies or selective, high frequencies. Diseases specific to the ear that affect adults include otosclerosis, Meniere's disease, and labyrinthitis. More than one hundred different abnormal genes causing sensorineural hearing loss have been identified. Although hereditary hearing loss accounts for about 50 percent of congenital childhood deafness, it is also thought to play a role in progressive hearing loss during later adulthood (Fischel-Godshian). At least one report describes a strong family pattern of presbycusis, particularly in women (Gates et al.). Finally, age-related deterioration of structures in the auditory system appears to occur among individuals with no significant history of noise exposure, otologic disease, or familial hearing loss.

The auditory system is housed within the temporal bone of the skull and consists of the outer ear, middle ear, inner ear, nerve of hearing (N. VIII), and central auditory nervous system. Evidence from anatomical studies of temporal bones and physiologic studies of auditory system function in older individuals suggest that age-related changes can occur at each level of the auditory system.

The outer ear consists of the pinna and the ear canal, which collect and amplify acoustic energy as it is transferred toward the tympanic membrane (eardrum). Changes commonly observed in the outer ear of older individuals include an enlargement of the pinnae, an increase in cerumen (earwax) production in the ear canal, and a change in the cartilage support of the ear canals. These factors can affect the sound field-to-eardrum transfer function and thereby alter sound transmission that is received at the tympanic membrane. Excessive cerumen, found in approximately 40 percent of an elderly population, can add a slight-to-mild high frequency conductive overlay to existing hearing thresholds.

The middle ear contains the three tiny bones, or ossicles (malleus, incus, and stapes), that are linked together as the ossicular chain. The principal function of the middle ear is to transmit acoustic energy effectively from the ear canal to the inner ear without an energy loss. The two middle ear muscles, the tensor tympani and stapedius, contract in response to loud sound to protect the inner ear from damage. With aging, the ligaments, muscles, and ossicles comprising the ossicular chain may degenerate, presumably causing a conductive hearing loss. Electrophysiologic measures of middle ear function (tympanometry) further indicate that the middle ear stiffens with age, thereby reducing the transmission of acoustic energy through the middle ear (Wiley et al., 1996).

The inner ear is composed of a fluid-filled bony labyrinth of interconnected structures including the cochlea. The cochlea contains the sensory end organ for hearing (the organ of Corti), which supports the inner and outer hair cells. These microscopic sensory hairs are essential for processing sound. The cochlea analyzes the frequency and intensity of sound, which is transmitted to the nerve of hearing by the inner hair cells. At the same time, the outer hair cells initiate a feedback mechanism resulting in the presence of acoustic energy in the ear canal (otoacoustic emissions). One prominent change in the inner ear with age is a loss of inner and outer hair cells in the basal turn of the cochlea (Schuknecht). Age-related loss of inner hair cells in this region produces a high frequency hearing loss and has been called *sensory presbycusis*. The loss of outer hair cells is expected to alter the feedback mechanism, possibly causing hearing loss and limited capacity to finely tune the frequency of sound. Electrophysiologic measures of outer hair cell function indicate that thresholds of otoacoustic emissions increase linearly with increasing age, although this age effect is confounded by the presence of hearing loss among older subjects (Stover and Norton). Another prominent change in the inner ear with aging is a decrease in the volume of vascular tissue, the stria vascularis, lining the outer cochlear wall. The stria vascularis maintains the chemical balance of the fluid in the cochlea, which in turn nourishes the hair cells. A loss of the vascular tissue produces a permanent hearing loss affecting most frequencies, called *strial presbycusis* (Schuknecht, 1993).

Approximately thirty-five thousand neurons comprise the afferent auditory branch of the eighth cranial nerve (N. VIII) in young, healthy adults. The auditory branch of N. VIII recodes the frequency, intensity, and timing information received from the hair cells and transmits it to the nuclei of the central auditory nervous system. With age, there is a loss of auditory neurons that accumulate over the life span. Considerable evidence demonstrates that the neuronal population comprising the auditory nerve is markedly reduced in aged human subjects compared to younger subjects. The effect on hearing, called *neural presbycusis*, is a mild loss of sensitivity but a considerable deficit in discriminating attributes of sound, including speech.

The nuclei of the central auditory nervous system transmit acoustic signals to higher levels, compare signals arriving at the two ears, recode the frequency of sound, and code other characteristics of the temporal waveform. Final processing of acoustic information is carried out in the primary auditory cortex, located in the superior temporal gyrus. There is a substantial reduction in the number of neurons in each nucleus of the central auditory nervous system with age, with the most prominent decline occurring in the auditory cortex (Willott). These alterations are thought to affect processing of complex acoustic stimuli, including distorted speech signals and sequences of tonal patterns.

Auditory performance

Hearing sensitivity decreases with increasing age among both men and women. A longitudinal study of hearing thresholds among individuals screened for noise exposure, otologic disease, and hereditary hearing loss showed that hearing thresholds decline progressively above age twenty years in men, and above age fifty years in women (Pearson et al.). The decline in hearing thresholds of the men was more than twice as fast as that of the women, at certain ages. Women showed the greatest decline in hearing sensitivity in the low frequencies, whereas men showed the greatest decline in the higher frequencies. For the unscreened population, the average thresholds of older men, sixty-five years of age, show normal hearing sensitivity in the low frequencies, declining to a moderate hearing loss (42 dB HL) at 3000 cycles per second (Hz) and above (Robinson). For women, the average hearing thresholds at age sixty-five years indicate a slight hearing loss (16–25 dB HL) from 500 through 4000 Hz, and a mild hearing loss (30 dB HL) at 6000 Hz. The type of hearing loss typically is sensorineural, indicating that the site of lesion is the sensory mechanism of the inner ear or the nerve of hearing.

Hearing sensitivity in the ultra high audiometric frequencies, above 8000 Hz, shows an age-related decline beginning in middle age that is greater than the decline in the lower audiometric frequencies (250–8000 Hz) (Wiley et al., 1998). These extended high-frequency thresholds are highly correlated with thresholds at 4000 Hz and 8000 Hz, suggesting that early monitoring of extended high-frequency thresholds among young and middle-aged adults may be useful for predicting the onset of presbycusis and for recommending preventive measures.

The ability to detect changes in temporal (timing) characteristics of acoustic stimuli appears to decline with age. Gap detection is the ability to detect a brief silent interval in a continuous tonal stimulus or noise, and reflects the temporal resolving power of the ear. Elderly listeners generally show longer gap detection thresholds than younger listeners (Schneider and Hamstra). Older listeners also require longer increments in tone duration to detect a change in a standard tone duration, compared to younger listeners (Fitzgibbons and Gordon-Salant, 1994). Finally, older listeners' performance for discriminating and identifying tones in a sequence is poorer than that of younger listeners, for tones of equivalent duration (Fitzgibbons and Gordon-Salant, 1998). Taken together, these findings indicate that older listeners have limited capacity to process brief changes in acoustic stimuli. This limitation could affect discrimination of the rapid acoustic elements that comprise speech.

Older people demonstrate difficulty understanding speech. In quiet listening environments, the speech recognition problem is attributed to insufficient audibility of the high-frequency information in speech by older people with age-related, high-frequency hearing loss (Humes). Substantial difficulty recognizing speech in noise also characterizes the performance of older listeners. Some studies have shown that the difficulties in noise are largely associated with the loss of sensitivity (Souza and Turner); other studies suggest that there is an added distortion factor with aging that acts to further diminish performance (Dubno, Dirks, and Morgan). The findings in noise are highly variable across studies and are largely dependent upon the speech presentation level, type of speech material (i.e., nonsense syllables, words, sentences), and availability of contextual cues.

In everyday communication situations, speech can be degraded by reverberant rooms and by people who speak at a rapid rate. Reverberation refers to a prolongation of sound in a room, and causes elements of speech to mask later-occurring speech sounds and silent pauses. With rapid speech, there is a reduction in the duration of pauses between words, vowel duration, and consonant duration. Time compression is an electronic or computer method to simulate rapid speech. Age effects are evident for recognition of both reverberant and time-compressed speech, which are independent and additive to the effects of hearing loss (Gordon-Salant and Fitzgibbons). Moreover, multiple speech distortions of reverberant and time-compressed speech, or either time-compressed or reverberant speech in noise, are excessively difficult for older people. Because both of these types of distortions involve a manipulation of the temporal (time) speech waveform, the recognition problem of older people may reflect a deficit in processing the timing characteristics of sound. An alternative hypothesis is that an age-related cognitive decrement in rapid information processing limits the older person's ability to process speech presented at a fast rate (Wingfield et al.). It should be noted,

however, that older people are able to perform quite well on many speech recognition tasks if given adequate contextual cues (Dubno, Ahlstrom, and Horwitz, 2000).

Impact of age-related hearing loss

Hearing impairment affects the quality of life for older individuals. The principle effects are related to the social and emotional impact of communication difficulties resulting from significant hearing loss (Mulrow et al.). Anecdotal reports of an association between dementia and hearing loss, or between depression and hearing loss, have not been replicated in well-controlled studies with large samples.

Older men and women adjust differently to their hearing loss. Women admit communication problems more often than men and assign greater importance to effective communication than men (Garstecki and Erler). This finding could be associated with differences in marital status between older men and women; older women are more likely to be widowed and thus rely to a greater extent on social interactions outside of the family. Men appear to adjust better to their hearing loss, as reflected by fewer reports of anger and stress associated with their hearing loss compared to reports of women. On the other hand, older men have a higher rate of denial of negative emotional reactions related to their hearing loss than women.

Remediation

Age-related sensorineural hearing loss cannot be ameliorated with medication or surgery. Rather, the principal form of treatment is amplification using a hearing aid. Analog and digital hearing aids are designed to amplify either all or selective frequencies based on an individual's hearing loss, with the goal of bringing all speech sounds into the range of audibility for the hearing-impaired listener. People with sensorineural hearing loss also experience a reduced tolerance for loud sounds. As a result, most hearing aids incorporate amplitude compression circuits to limit the output level of amplified sound without producing distortion. Hearing aids are quite effective for amplifying sound without producing discomfort. Thus, it is not surprising that older hearing-impaired people demonstrate significant benefit from hearing aids for understanding speech in quiet and noisy listening environments and for reducing their perceived hearing handicap (Humes, Halling, and Coughlin). However, there is wide individual variability in the magnitude of hearing aid benefit. The same amplification that hearing aids provide for a target speech signal is applied as well to noise, including the voices of people talking in a background. As a result, older hearing aid users often report less benefit from their hearing aids in noisy environments than in quiet environments. Only about 20 percent of older individuals with hearing loss purchase hearing aids. The prevailing reasons for lack of hearing aid use among older people are stigma, cost, and limited perceived benefit, particularly in noise. Another possible reason for hearing aid rejection by older people is that personal hearing aids do not overcome the older person's difficulties in understanding reverberant speech or rapid speech.

Frequency-modulated (FM) systems are amplification devices that can be beneficial for older listeners when they are located at a distance from a speaker. These can be independent systems or they can be components attached to a hearing aid and used as a selectable circuit. An FM system includes a microphone/transmitter placed near the speaker that broadcasts the sound, via FM transmission, to a receiver/amplifier located on the user. The amplified sound is unaffected by room acoustics, including noise and reverberation. This type of device is particularly helpful for older listeners in theaters, houses of worship, or classrooms, where a long distance between the speaker and the listener can aggravate the detrimental effects of poor room acoustics for older listeners with hearing loss.

Older individuals with bilateral, severe-to-profound hearing loss generally have widespread damage to the cochlea and derive minimal benefit from hearing aids and FM systems for recognizing speech. These individuals are potential candidates for a cochlear implant, a surgically implanted device that delivers speech signals directly to the auditory nerve via an electrode array inserted in the cochlea. Considerable success in receiving and understanding speech, with and without visual cues, has been reported for older cochlear implant recipients (Waltzman, Cohen, and Shapiro).

Regardless of the type of device used by the older hearing-impaired person, a successful remediation program includes auditory training, speechreading (lipreading) training, and counseling. The emphasis in these programs is training the older person to take full advantage of all available contextual cues, based on the consistent finding that older people are able to surmount most communication problems if contextual cues are available. Another principle of these programs is training effective use of nonverbal strategies (e.g., stage managing tactics for optimal viewing and listening) and verbal strategies (e.g., requesting the speaker to talk more slowly).

Prevention

Hearing sensitivity of older individuals in nonindustrialized societies is significantly better than that of older individuals in industrialized societies. This finding strongly suggests that there are preventable risk factors in industrialized societies for apparent age-related hearing loss. Exposure to intense noise and administration of ototoxic drugs are two well-known risk factors for acquired sensorineural hearing loss. The Baltimore Longitudinal Study of Aging has shown that elevated systolic blood pressure is associated with significant risk for hearing loss in men (Brant et al.). In the Beaver Dam epidemiological study, smoking was identified as a significant risk factor for sensorineural hearing loss among the 3,753 participants (Cruikshanks et al., 1998). Nonsmoking participants who lived with a smoker were also more likely to have a hearing loss than those not exposed to smoke in the home. The identification of these modifiable risk factors suggests that an effective program of prevention or delay of adult-onset hearing loss would include use of ear protection in noisy environments, control of hypertension, elimination of cigarette smoking, and monitoring the use of potentially ototoxic medications.

SANDRA GORDON-SALANT

See also BRAIN; HOME ADAPTATION AND EQUIPMENT; VISION AND PERCEPTION.

BIBLIOGRAPHY

BRANT, L. J.; GORDON-SALANT, S.; PEARSON, J. D.; KLEIN, L. L.; MORRELL, C. H.; METTER, E. J.; and FOZARD, J. L. "Risk Factors Related to Age-Associated Hearing Loss in the Speech Frequencies." *Journal of the American Academy of Audiology* 7, no. 3 (1996): 152–160.
CRUICKSHANKS, K. J.; KLEIN, R.; KLEIN, B. E.; WILEY, T. L.; NONDAHL, D. M.; and TWEED, T.

S. "Cigarette Smoking and Hearing Loss: The Epidemiology of Hearing Loss Study." *Journal of the American Medical Association* 279, no. 21 (1998): 1715–1719.

DUBNO, J. R.; AHLSTROM, J. B.; and HORWITZ, A. R. "Use of Context by Young and Aged Adults with Normal Hearing." *Journal of the Acoustical Society of America* 107, no. 1 (2000): 538–546.

DUBNO, J. R.; DIRKS, D.D.; and MORGAN, D. E. "Effects of Age and Mild Hearing Loss on Speech Recognition." *Journal of the Acoustical Society of America* 76, no. 1 (1984): 87–96.

FISCHEL-GODSHIAN, N. "Mitochondrial Deafness Mutations Reviews." *Human Mutation* 13, no. 4 (1999): 261–270.

FITZGIBBONS, P. J., and GORDON-SALANT, S. "Age Effects on Measures of Auditory Duration Discrimination." *Journal of Speech and Hearing Research* 37, no. 3 (1994): 662–670.

FITZGIBBONS, P. J., and GORDON-SALANT, S. "Auditory Temporal Order Perception in Younger and Older Adults." *Journal of Speech, Language, and Hearing Research* 41, no. 5 (1998): 1052–1060.

GARSTECKI, D., and ERLER, S. F. "Older Adult Performance on the Communication Profile for the Hearing Impaired: Gender Difference." *Journal of Speech, Language, and Hearing Research* 42, no. 3 (1999): 735–796.

GATES, G. A.; COUROPMITREE, N. N.; and MYERS, R. H. "Genetic Associations in Age-Related Hearing Thresholds." *Archives of Otolaryngology—Head and Neck Surgery* 125, no. 6 (1999): 654–659.

GORDON-SALANT, S., and FITGIBBONS, P. J. "Temporal Factors and Speech Recognition Performance in Young and Elderly Listeners." *Journal of Speech and Hearing Research* 36, no. 6 (1993): 1276–1285.

HUMES, L. E. "Speech Understanding in the Elderly." *Journal of the American Academy of Audiology* 7, no. 3 (1996): 161–167.

HUMES, L. E.; HALLING, D.; and COUGHLIN, M. "Reliability and Stability of Various Hearing-Aid Outcome Measures in a Group of Elderly Hearing-Aid Wearers." *Journal of Speech, Language, and Hearing Research* 39, no. 5 (1996): 923–935.

MOSCICKI, E. K.; ELKINS, E. F.; BAUM, H. M.; and McNAMARA, P. M. "Hearing Loss in the Elderly: An Epidemiologic Study of the Framingham Heart Study Cohort." *Ear and Hearing* 6, no. 4 (1985): 184–190.

MULROW, C. D.; AGUILAR, C.; ENDICOTT, J. E.; VELEX, R.; TULEY, M. R.; CHARLIP, W. S.; and HILL, J. A. "Association Between Hearing Impairment and the Quality of Life of Elderly Individuals." *Journal of the American Geriatrics Society* 38, no. 1 (1990): 45–50.

National Center for Health Statistics. "Current Estimates from the National Health Interview Survey, 1995." *Vital and Health Statistics* 10 (1998): 79–80.

PEARSON, J. D.; MORRELL, C. H.; GORDON-SALANT, S.; BRANT, L. J.; METTER, E. J.; KLEIN, L. L.; and FOZARD, J. L. "Gender Differences in a Longitudinal Study of Age-Associated Hearing Loss." *Journal of the Acoustical Society of America* 97, no. 2 (1995): 1196–1205.

ROBINSON, D. W. "Threshold of Hearing as a Function of Age and Sex for the Typical Unscreened Population." *British Journal of Audiology* 22, no. 1 (1988): 5–20.

SCHNEIDER, B. A., and HAMSTRA, S. J. "Gap Detection Thresholds as a Function of Tonal Duration for Younger and Older Listeners." *Journal of the Acoustical Society of America* 106, no. 1 (1999): 371–380.

SCHUKNECHT, H. F. *Pathology of the Ear*, 2d ed. Philadelphia: Lea & Febiger, 1993.

SOUZA, P. E., and TURNER, C. W. "Masking of Speech in Young and Elderly Listeners with Hearing Loss." *Journal of Speech and Hearing Research* 37, no. 3 (1994): 665–661.

STOVER, L., and NORTON, S. J. "The Effects of Aging on Otoacoustic Emissions." *Journal of the Acoustical Society of America* 94, no. 5 (1993): 2670–2681.

WALTZMAN, S.; COHEN, N.; and SHAPIRO, B. "The Benefits of Cochlear Implantation in the Geriatric Population." *Otolaryngology—Head and Neck Surgery* 108, no. 4 (1993): 329–333.

WILEY, T. L.; CRUICKSHANKS, K. J.; NONDAHL, D. M.; TWEED, T. S.; KLEIN, R.; and KLEIN, B. E. K. "Tympanometric Measures in Older Adults." *Journal of the American Academy of Audiology* 7, no. 4 (1996): 260–268.

WILEY, T. L.; CRUICKSHANKS, K. J.; NONDAHL, D. M.; TWEED, T. S.; KLEIN, R.; and KLEIN, B. E. K. "Aging and High-Frequency Hearing Sensitivity." *Journal of Speech, Language, and Hearing Research* 41, no. 5 (1998): 1061–1072.

WILLOTT, J. F. *Aging and the Auditory System*. San Diego: Singular Publishing Group, 1991.

WINGFIELD, A.; POON, L. W.; LOMBARDI, L.; and LOWE, D. "Speed of Processing in Normal Aging: Effects of Speech Rate, Linguistic Structure, and Processing Time." *Journal of Gerontology* 40, no. 5 (1985): 579–585.

HEART DISEASE

Cardiovascular disease is the leading cause of mortality worldwide. As cigarette smoking con-

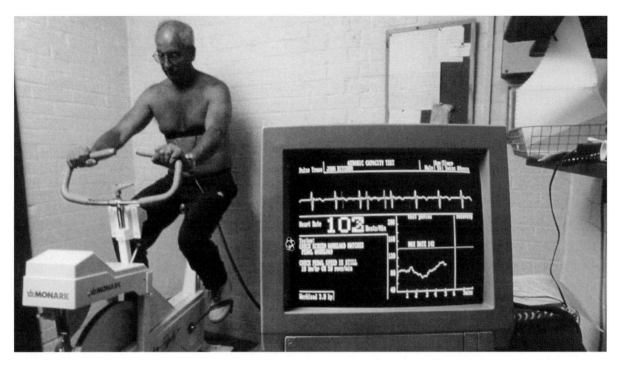

An older man rides an exercise bike while taking an aerobic capacity test, one of a number of cardiac tests that can be used to determine if the warning signs of heart disease are present. (Photo Researchers, Inc.)

tinues to be a status symbol in developing countries, this ranking is expected to continue well into twenty-first century. Heart disease rates increase with age, and older adults have worse outcomes and face special problems, including unusual disease presentation, increasing complications, and particular effects on daily activities and quality of life.

The heart is a muscle in the center of the chest. It is approximately the size of a fist and pumps blood throughout the body, working continuously and requiring a large blood supply. The heart can function through a large range of demands, from sleep to vigorous activity.

Ischemic heart disease

With increasing age, narrowings may develop in the coronary arteries that lead to the heart. This reduced blood supply causes ischemia (insufficient blood supply for the heart's work) and may produce chest pain or angina. Sudden blockages will result in a heart attack, also known as myocardial infarction (MI).

The incidence of heart disease begins to increase in men after the age of forty-five and in women after the age of fifty-five, but the rate for women tends to equal that of men after the age of seventy. It was once believed that hormone replacement therapy would protect women from heart disease, but more recent studies suggest this is not true. The Heart and Estrogen/Progestin Replacement Study (HERS) showed no benefit, as well as an increased risk of blood clots in the leg (deep vein thrombosis) and of gallbladder disease. Along with age, male gender, family history, and ethnicity are nonmodifiable risk factors for heart disease.

The most modifiable risk factor for heart disease is smoking, which leads to increased obstruction of the coronary arteries. Each cigarette also causes spasms in these arteries. Smokers have twice the risk of heart attacks as nonsmokers, and death rates for heavy smokers are two to three times that of nonsmokers. Quitting smoking at any age likely confers benefit. This implies that it reduces disease progression and reduces the risk of MI and stroke; it also leads to a 25 to 50 percent reduction in mortality and recurrent heart attacks (MI).

There are many aids available to help quit smoking. These include nicotine gum (although people with dentures find the gum difficult to use). A nicotine patch is also available. Success rates for quitting using nicotine replacement are 18 to 25 percent, compared to 5 to 10 percent without nicotine replacement. Patients with heart disease may be concerned that nicotine replacement is not safe (potential dangers are dream abnormalities, insomnia, and application site reaction, also known as patch-rash), but if the options are replacement therapy or continued smoking, replacement therapy is probably safer.

Other aids in quitting smoking include medication (e.g., Bupropion, cloridine, mortiptyline) that can help relieve the agitation associated with quitting. Success rates are in the range of 30 percent. Other aids include hypnosis, acupuncture, laser therapy, and relaxation therapy. It is not important which method is chosen; what is important is the need to stop smoking.

The next major modifiable risk factor is diabetes. Diabetes, like heart disease, also increases with age, and prevalence approaches 10 to 20 percent in people over the age of sixty-five. People with diabetes have a two- to four-fold increased risk of coronary artery disease. While good control of diabetes probably reduces risk for heart disease, it seems that control of blood pressure is even more important for diabetics in reducing the risk of developing heart disease.

High blood pressure has also been strongly associated with heart disease, and it also increases with aging. Treating hypertension with low-dose thiazide diuretics and long-acting dihydropyridine calcium channel blockers has been shown to reduce heart attack, stroke, and death for people over the age of sixty.

Cholesterol has also been shown to be a significant risk factor for increasing coronary artery disease (CAD). The HMG-CoA reductase inhibitors (statins) have consistently shown a 20 to 30 percent reduction in heart attacks and death. The cholesterol-lowering trials of statins excluded elderly patients over the age of seventy-five, but the medications are still considered safe. This is because there is wide experience with statins outside the elderly community, randomized trials have proven safe, and side effects have very rarely been reported. In addition, older patients have the greatest risk and suffer the greatest burden from heart attacks and strokes and therefore have the most to gain from the use of these drugs.

Obesity and physical inactivity are also associated with heart disease. Regular physical activity five to seven times per week for twenty to thirty minutes a day can reduce the risk of heart disease by 20 percent. This may pose problems for some older adults, as there is an increase in arthritis in the older population, which can limit their physical ability. The use of a stationary bicycle allows people to sit while exercising and takes the weight off the lower joints, as does swimming and water exercise.

The use of antioxidants such as vitamin E and beta carotene have proven to be of no benefit in reducing heart disease. Fish oil supplements, which contain polyunsaturated fatty acids, have been shown to have a small but significant benefit in those with established heart disease. A Mediterranean-style diet has also been shown to be protective for heart disease. Such a diet includes "more bread, more root vegetables and green vegetables, more fish, less meat (beef, lamb, and pork to be replaced with poultry), no day without fruit, and butter and cream to be replaced with . . . a rapeseed (canola) oil-based margarine" (de Lorgeril, 1994).

Angina is classified into four stages. Functional class I indicates symptoms only with vigorous exertion. Class II indicates symptoms with moderate exertion; such as climbing a flight of stairs, or walking more than two blocks. Functional class III occurs with less activity, and functional class IV occurs at rest or with very low levels of activity such as walking around the room. The classic symptoms of angina are central pressure or chest pain, although the full range of symptoms felt may also include burning; a feeling of heaviness, squeezing, tightness, or fullness; an ache or sharp pain; or even no chest symptoms at all. The chest pain often radiates up into the shoulder and neck and down the arm (the left more so than right). It may also present in the upper abdomen, back, and ears or jaw as well. Other typical features include shortness of breath, a cold sweat (diaphoresis), weakness, nausea and vomiting, or even a loss of consciousness. Typically, these symptoms occur with exertion and are resolved with rest. If there is a change in symptoms with less activity or if they are more severe or prolonged, then the condition is considered *unstable angina*. Worsening of symptoms is related to an increase in the amount of obstruction of the coronary arteries. At the extreme of this spectrum of acute ischemic syndromes or unstable angina is a myocardial infarction, or heart attack. This occurs when the circulation is insufficient to keep the heart muscle alive. Typically, it is associated with a blood clot forming on a partial obstruction in the coronary arteries.

Unfortunately, as people get older they are less likely to present with typical symptoms. They may not have pain or discomfort; problems with nausea, diaphoresis, and weakness may not be attributed to a heart problem; and, frequently, people do not seek attention. Also, diabetics and women are more prone not to have typical symptoms, resulting in misdiagnosis and undertreatment.

More alarmingly, the rates of death from heart attack increase sharply with increasing age. Mortality under the age of sixty-five is probably in the range of 4 percent. Mortality over the age of seventy-five climbs to 20 percent. Complications after an infarct are also increased in the elderly.

When presenting with a heart attack, patients are treated initially with aspirin. Provided there has been no recent surgery or problems with bleeding, they may also be treated with medication to dissolve the clot causing the heart attack. Best results occur if treated within an hour after the onset of symptoms, but benefits are still seen even six to twelve hours after the onset of pain. These thrombolytic medications (e.g., streptokinase, tissue plasminogen activator, reteplase, tenecteplase) have been shown to significantly reduce death, but they are also associated with an increased risk of bleeding. This can be controlled, however, unless there is bleeding in the head, which is almost always fatal. The benefits of the medication outweigh the risks, and, given that older patients have a much greater risk of dying, they also enjoy a much greater absolute benefit from this therapy. For two to three days following an infarct, patients are treated with intravenous medication or an injection of heparin, which keeps the blood thin.

Another possible treatment at the time of a myocardial infarction is angioplasty. Angioplasty has the greatest success for treating MIs, but requires rapid availability and experienced physicians.

Other medications given to patients to reduce mortality after a heart attack are beta blockers and ACE inhibitors. Calcium channel blockers and nitroglycerin under the tongue, in a pill or patch form, or even intravenously, help control pain with acute ischemic syndromes.

With an uncomplicated heart attack, people can expect to be in the hospital five to seven days.

After one to two days of rest, patients start to mobilize. This is done while being monitored. Medications are adjusted as tolerated, and patients generally have an assessment of their heart function by an echocardiogram (ultrasound of the heart) or a wall motion study (a nuclear X-ray). Prior to going home, most patients have an exercise stress test in which they walk on a treadmill while heart rate, blood pressure, and any changes in the electrocardiogram, as well as any recurrence of symptoms, are monitored. If these occur at low levels of activity, there is increased risk and more aggressive investigations or treatment are warranted. If not, the patient is considered low risk and should be safe for discharge.

Following discharge, patients can gradually increase their physical activity, watching for any recurrence of symptoms. Walking for five to ten minutes twice a day, and gradually increasing this up to thirty minutes twice a day, and then to forty to sixty minutes of walking or exercise once a day is recommended.

Congestive heart failure

Congestive heart failure (CHF), or cardiomyopathy, occurs when the pumping action of the heart has been weakened, causing shortness of breath, fatigue, and swelling, particularly in the legs and feet. There is decreased circulation to the major organs, and the kidneys retain more fluid to compensate. There are also neurohormonal factors that tend to stimulate or overdrive the heart. This ultimately can lead to further damage and deterioration of the heart function. Patients with functional class III to IV heart failure, where they are short of breath with low levels of activity or at rest, have a three- to four-year mortality rate of 35 to 45 percent. Mortality may be higher in older patients.

The most common cause of congestive heart failure is ischemic heart disease or prior myocardial infarctions. Older patients with congestive heart failure and coronary artery disease may benefit from revascularization, and they are at higher risk for silent ischemia or missed infarcts. While this accounts for 70 percent of the patients with congestive heart failure, there are numerous other causes, including hypertension, valvular heart disease, viral infection, and arrhythmias. Another age-related problem is chemotherapy (e.g., adriamycin, anthracycline, herceptin, taxanes, and others) for cancer.

With acute congestive heart failure, patients become suddenly short of breath, cannot lie flat, and develop edema. Patients in an emergency room will be treated with oxygen therapy as well as intravenous diuretics and nitroglycerin to help remove the fluid.

CHF can also be more insidious, with a gradual or progressive course of increasing shortness of breath over hours and days. This may be related to a change in fluid or salt intake. CHF patients require polypharmacy (the use of multiple medications, as heart patients often take anywhere from four to twelve drugs a day) to control their symptoms and improve survival. Angiotensin-converting enzyme (ACE) inhibitors have been shown to significantly reduce symptoms, hospitalizations, and mortality. For patients who are intolerant of ACE inhibitors, a reasonable next choice would probably be angiotensin receptor blockers (ARBs).

Beta blockers lower blood pressure, slow the heart rate, and decrease the heart's workload. Previously felt to worsen CHF, studies have shown that beta blockers actually improve survival, reduce symptoms, and improve heart function. Side effects may include fatigue or depression, and it is important that such side effects not be simply blamed on "old age."

Patients with severe heart failure (functional class III to IV) and an ejection fraction less than 30 percent should be treated with spironolactone. This medication is a diuretic with unique neurohormonal-blocking properties that have been shown to significantly reduce mortality. Other diuretics are also useful to help control symptoms of fluid retention.

Digoxin also reduces symptoms and decreases hospitalizations in heart failure. There are other inotropic medications available that make the heart stronger and can temporarily improve symptoms. Unfortunately, these medications decrease survival. Some patients with very severe CHF, however, may feel the benefit of fewer symptoms is worth the risk of not living as long as they would otherwise.

Certain medications are generally contraindicated in heart failure. Most calcium channel blockers worsen heart failure, though amilodipine and felodipine have been shown to be safe. Nonsteroidal anti-inflammatory drugs (NSAIDS) used to treat arthritis may also aggravate heart failure, as can alcohol, which should generally be avoided. Exercise is useful but must be individualized to a patient's physical state. Most lifestyle modifications are probably best coordinated through a heart function clinic run by nurse specialists.

Heart transplantation is an option only if patients have failed all other medical treatments and still have severe heart failure. It is also restricted to patients under sixty-five, as older patients do not do as well with the burden of aggressive immunosuppressive therapy.

Valvular heart disease

The heart consists of four chambers. The two upper chambers, or atria, pump blood into the lower chambers, or ventricles. The right ventricle pumps blood through the lungs, and the blood then returns with oxygen to the left ventricle. The left ventricle pumps blood to the rest of the body and the veins return blood to the right atria. The valves between the atria and ventricle are the tricuspid valve (right) and the mitral valve (left). The valves out of the heart are the pulmonary valve (right) and the aortic valve (left). These prevent blood from going backwards, optimizing pumping efficiency. There are two possible malfunctions with any valve. The valves can become stenotic, or tight, and cause a flow obstruction, or the valves can become loose or floppy and allow backward flow, or insufficiency. Most valve disease in adults involves the mitral valve or the aortic valve. Rheumatic fever is probably the most common cause of valvular heart disease worldwide. Caused by untreated streptococcal infections, rheumatic fever can cause either stenosis or insufficiency. This is much less common where antibiotics are widely available. The aortic and the mitral valve are also prone to calcification, or thickening, and stenosis with aging.

Mild-to-moderate mitral insufficiency does not require any surgical intervention, but if the insufficiency becomes severe, or if there are signs of worsening heart failure, then repair or replacement of the mitral valve may be necessary. If the mitral valve is too tight, it can cause CHF. This is diagnosed by an echocardiogram. Mitral stenosis can be repaired either by surgery or with a balloon (valvuloplasty). The balloon prevents the need for invasive surgery but may result in some mitral insufficiency. If a patient is not a good candidate for open heart surgery, a valvuloplasty is an attractive option.

Artificial valves are either tissue or metal. Tissue valves are frequently used on older patients because they do not require anticoagulation and cause less risk of stroke, but they tend to wear out within ten to fifteen years. Metal or mechanical valves require special blood thinners (e.g., warfarin) to prevent the valve from clotting up and blocking, and to prevent strokes. These blood thinners do increase the risk of bleeding and require regular monitoring.

The aortic valve occasionally shows significant leaking. If this is mild or moderate, it can be treated with medication. Nifedipine has been shown to reduce the progression and the need for surgery. If regurgitation is severe, valve replacement may be necessary. Aortic stenosis causes an increased strain on the pumping action of the heart. This can lead to angina, CHF, or loss of consciousness (syncope). Surgery is the only definitive treatment with severe aortic stenosis.

The risks of valvular surgery is increased in elderly patients, including an increased rate of perioperative mortality, increased postoperative infection, stroke and renal failure, prolonged hospital stay, and postoperative disability. Operative risks also depend on other comorbidities. Surgical consideration must be individualized for each patient and a balanced discussion of all reasonable risks and benefits is necessary for making the right decision.

Patients with valvular heart disease or artificial heart valves are at increased risk for developing endocarditis—an infection on the heart valve. Antibiotics are needed to prevent such infections when undergoing surgery and dental work.

Arrhythmias

The sinus node is the pacemaker of the heart. It sits high in the atria and sends out a regular signal for the heart to beat. This signal is controlled by neurological and hormonal triggers that make the heart speed up and slow down as needed. There is a delay switch between the atria and ventricle that is called the *AV node*. Arrhythmias occur when the heart is either beating too fast (tachycardia) or too slow (bradycardia). The most common arrhythmias consist of isolated and premature atrial contractions (PACs), and extra beats, called *premature ventricular contractions* (PVCs). These are normal. Some people are quite sensitive and can feel the heart skip or flip in their chest, followed by a brief pause before

the heart returns to its normal rhythm. Most people notice this when sitting quietly or lying in bed. Triggers include smoking, alcohol, coffee, tea, chocolate, or other stimulants. These are not life threatening and do not require treatment.

PVCs are also associated with CHF. While frequent PVCs may be a sign of increased risk in patients with ischemic heart disease and congestive heart failure, treating these with antiarrhythmic medication has been proven to increase mortality. Treatment is therefore reserved only for symptomatic and sustained ventricular tachycardia (VT), which causes symptoms of weakness, lightheadedness, or syncope. Sustained VT can cause sudden death and requires defibrillation with electrical paddles. This is commonly depicted in television and movies, with survival rates on television of approximately 75 percent. In reality, survival rates are generally less than 20 percent.

Unfortunately, medications that have been used to treat ventricular tachycardia have had modest success at best. Newer automatic implantable cardiac defibrillators (AICD) are special pacemakers, and they can be programmed to give a shock to restore normal rhythm when VT is detected. These devices are very expensive, but very effective.

Other common arrhythmias in the upper chamber of the heart include supraventricular (SVT) or atrial tachycardias. If prolonged, these can cause palpitations, shortness of breath, fatigue, weak spells, and even syncope.

Atrial fibrillation is an irregular SVT that can occur intermittently or continuously. Increasing age is a major risk factor for atrial fibrillation, which occurs in 5 percent of people over sixty-five and as many as 10 percent of people over the age of eighty. Patients who have infrequent atrial fibrillation lasting only a few minutes may not require any antiarrhythmic medication. If atrial fibrillation causes weakness, shortness of breath, angina, or heart failure, treatment with medication is warranted.

If patients do not convert (from abnormal to normal rhythm) with medication or are unstable, they may require electrical cardioversion, in which patients are sedated ,or asleep, and then shocked with external paddles to restore normal rhythm.

Frequently, patients are not symptomatic with atrial fibrillation, and it may be picked up incidentally. This can happen when a patient undergoes an electrocardiogram (ECG) as part of a routine or presurgical check-up and atrial fibrillation is discovered as a result. In this situation, there is no clear benefit to trying to restore sinus rhythm, as many antiarrhythmic medications carry significant side effects. Beta blockers or calcium channel blockers may be used to control heart rates with atrial fibrillation. The other important risk is stroke. Patients who have atrial fibrillation and no valvular disease, as well as no other risk factors, have a risk of stroke of 1 percent per year. Risk factors include age greater than seventy-five, prior stroke or transient ischemic attack (TIA), diabetes, and hypertension. These risks increase the annual stroke rate to 4 to 5 percent per year. Anticoagulation using warfarin reduces the risk of stroke by 70 to 80 percent. The major risk associated with using this medication is an increased risk of bleeding. If warfarin is deemed unsafe, aspirin reduces the risk by 35 percent.

Bradycardia, or slow heart rate, is caused by sinus node disease, AV node disease, or heart block (which means the electrical impulse fails to reach the ventricle; heart block is caused by AV node disease). It also increases in frequency with increasing age. Symptoms include weakness or lightheadedness, fatigue, shortness of breath, or syncope. Bradyarrhythmias can be diagnosed by an ECG at the time of symptoms. Additionally, a holter monitor (a small device worn for twenty-four to forty-eight hours to record all heart beats) can detect and record arrhythmias.

Several cardiac medications, such as beta blockers, calcium channel blockers, and digoxin, can cause bradyarrhythmias and may need to be stopped. A pacemaker is used to treat bradycardia, and is generally inserted in the operating room or in a cardiac care unit. Pacemakers have a single wire in the ventricle and sometimes a second one in the atria. Modern pacemakers are no longer affected by interference caused by microwaves, metal detectors, or store security systems, though there has been some interactions noted with cellular phones. As the world becomes more electronically busy, the potential for interference with pacemakers changes, and pacemaker manufacturers must continue to strive to keep ahead of new potential hazards.

Driving and heart disease

Regulations regarding driving and heart disease vary in different locations. Patients who are functional class IV should not drive, while those who are functional class III or better may drive, provided their doctor agrees. Following unstable angina or a heart attack, patients should be stabilized one month before driving. Patients should also wait one month after bypass surgery or insertion of a pacemaker before driving. Patients with AICD and documented episodes of VT should probably not drive if spells or shocks are frequent.

Sex and heart disease

Sexual activity is an important part of people's lives, including both older adults and patients with heart disease. Many of the problems that give rise to heart disease, such as diabetes, hypertension, and various medications, can also give rise to sexual dysfunction. More commonly, patients and their partners may be afraid to engage in sexual intercourse for fear it may trigger a heart attack, though the risk of precipitating a heart attack or heart disease during intercourse is quite low.

The first question to be asked is whether the heart can cope with the physical exertion involved. A middle-aged person uses approximately four to five METS (metabolic equivalent units) during intercourse. This is the equivalent of a brisk walk or of climbing two to three flights of stairs. An exercise stress test is measured in METS, and this is an easy way to determine if the work of intercourse will bring on angina. In general, it is safe to resume sexual activity two to three weeks after a heart attack. While elderly patients likely exert less energy than younger individuals during sexual intercourse, if symptoms such as angina or excessive shortness of breath develop, then the activity should be stopped and, if necessary, nitroglycerin may be used to relieve angina.

The question of patients with heart disease using Viagra raises some serious concerns. While Viagra is a highly effective and popular medication to treat erectile dysfunction, it is contraindicated in patients who are using nitroglycerin. This includes patients who are using nitroglycerin pills or patches, or people who need to use nitroglycerin by spray or pills under the tongue to relieve angina. Viagra and nitroglycerin taken together may cause significant and severe drops in blood pressure. This effect may occur up to twenty-four hours after using Viagra, and the potential exists for these effects occurring even later in elderly patients.

Glossary of cardiac medication

Angiotensin-converting enzyme (ACE) inhibitors improve survival with congestive heart failure and ischemic heart disease, reduce complications and incidence of diabetes, and lower blood pressure. They may decrease kidney function, increase potassium levels, and cause a dry cough. Also present the rare risk of angioedema.

Angiotensin receptor blockers are useful to lower blood pressure and for congestive heart failure with no cough. However, they may cause renal failure or elevated potassium levels.

Aspirin is a blood thinner that reduces death from heart attacks and angina and reduces the chance of strokes. It does present a very small increased risk of bleeding and ulcer irritation may occur.

Beta blockers improve survival following heart attacks with congestive heart failure and with hypertension, lower blood pressure, have antiarrhythmic benefits, and also improve heart function. Side effects include possible fatigue, depression, erectile dysfunction, and bradycardia. Beta blockers are contraindicated in asthmatics.

Calcium channel blockers are used to reduce blood pressure and help with angina. May be associated with constipation or reflux. Constipation may be a bigger problem with older patients, especially if immobility is present. Edema is another possible problem associated with these drugs.

Clopedigrol is a blood thinner used to reduce heart attack or stroke and may be used with or instead of aspirin.

Digoxin is used in the treatment of heart failure and reduces symptoms and hospitalizations. Adverse effects include nausea, GI upset, and bradycardia.

Diuretics are useful for lowering blood pressure and treating symptoms of congestive heart failure. May be associated with postural hypotension. Also can cause electrolyte abnormalities, including low potassium. May increase uric acid and precipitate gouty attacks.

Nitroglycerin is used to treat symptoms of angina. It may cause headaches, but tolerance develops.

Spironolactone is used to treat severe congestive heart failure, but may increase potassium and decrease renal function. It also may cause gynecomastia and increased hair growth.

Statins (HMG-CoA reductase inhibitors) are useful in reducing cholesterol and decreasing the risk of heart attacks and strokes. Very rare problems with liver abnormalities or muscle pain sometimes occur.

Warfarin is used to prevent strokes with valvular heart disease and with atrial fibrillation. Negative effects include the increased risk of bleeding.

PAUL MACDONALD

See also AGING; CHOLESTEROL; DEMENTIA; DEMENTIA WITH LEWY BODIES; DIABETES MELLITUS; DISEASE PRESENTATION; EXERCISE; FAINTING; HIGH BLOOD PRESSURE; REVASCULARIZATION: BYPASS SURGERY AND ANGIOPLASTY; STROKE; VASCULAR DEMENTIA; VASCULAR DISEASE; VITAMINS.

BIBLIOGRAPHY

ACE Inhibitor Myocardial Infarction Collaborative Group. "Indications for ACE Inhibitors in the Early Treatment of Acute Myocardial Infarction." *Circulation* 97 (1998): 2202–2212.

ALLHAT Collaborative Research Group. "Major Cardiovascular Events in Hypertensive Patients Randomized to Doxazosin vs. Chlorthalidone." *Journal of the American Medical Association* 283, no. 15 (2000): 1967–1975.

Antiarrhythmics Versus Implantable Defibrillators (AVID) Investigators. "A Comparison of Antiarrhythmic-Drug Therapy With Implantable Defibrillators in Patients Resuscitated From Near-Fatal Ventricular Arrhythmias." *New England Journal of Medicine* 337 (1997): 1576–1583.

ANTMAN, E. M.; COHEN, M.; RADLEY, D.; et al. "Assessment of the Treatment Effect of Enoxaparin for Unstable Angina/Non-Q-Wave Myocardial Infarction." *Circulation* 100 (1999): 1602–1608.

Atrial Fibrillation Investigators. "Risk Factors for Stroke and Efficacy of Antithrombotic Therapy in Atrial Fibrillation." *Archives of Internal Medicine* 154 (1994): 1449–1457.

BONOW, R. O.; CARABELLO, B.; DE LEON, A. C. JR.; et al. "ACC/AHA Guidelines for the Management of Patients With Valvular Heart Disease." *Journal of the American College of Cardiology* 32 (1998): 1486–1588.

CANTO, J. G.; SHLIPAK, M. G.; ROGERS, W. J.; et al. "Prevalence, Clinical Characteristics, and Mortality Among Patients With Myocardial Infarction Presenting Without Chest Pain." *Journal of the American Medical Association* 283 (2000): 3223–3229.

Cardiac Arrhythmia Suppression Trial (CAST) Investigators. "Effect of Encainide and Flecainide on Mortality in a Randomized Trial of Arrhythmia Suppression After Myocardial Infarction." *New England Journal of Medicine* 321 (1989): 406–412.

CIBIS-II Investigators and Committees. "The Cardiac Insufficiency Bisoprolol Study II (CIBIS-II): A Randomised Trial." *Lancet* 353 (1999): 9–13.

COHEN, M.; DEMERS, C.; GURFINKEL, E. P.; et al. "A Comparison of Low-Molecular-Weight Heparin With Unfractionated Heparin For Unstable Coronary Artery Disease." *New England Journal of Medicine* 337 (1997): 447–452.

CURB, J. D.; PRESSEL, S. L.; CUTLER, J. A.; et al. "Effect of Diuretic-Based Antihypertensive Treatment on Cardiovascular Disease Risk in Older Diabetic Patients With Isolated Systolic Hypertension." *Journal of the American Medical Association* 276 (1996): 1886–1892.

DAJANI, A. S.; TAUBERT, K. A.; WILSON, W.; et al. "Prevention of Bacterial Endocarditis." *Circulation* 96 (1997): 358–366.

DE LORGERIL, M., et al. "Mediterranean Alpha-Linolenic Acid-Rich Diet in Secondary Prevention of Coronary Heart Disease." *Lancet* 343 (1994): 1454–1460.

DE LORGERIL, M.; SALEN, P.; MARTIN, J.; et al. "Mediterranean Diet, Traditional Risk Factors, and the Rate of Cardiovascular Complications after Myocardial Infarction." *Circulation* 99 (1999): 779–785.

Digitalis Investigation Group. "The Effect of Digoxin on Mortality and Morbidity in Patients With Heart Failure." *New England Journal of Medicine* 336 (1997): 525–533.

DOWNS, J. R.; CLEARFIELD, M.; WEIS, S.; et al. "Primary Prevention of Acute Coronary Events with Lovastatin in Men and Women with Average Cholesterol Levels." *Journal of the American Medical Association* 279 (1998): 1615–1622.

GIBBONS, R. J.; CHATTERJEE, K.; DALEY, J.; et al. "ACC/AHA/ACP-ASIM Guidelines for the Management of Patients with Chronic Stable Angina: Executive Summary and Recommendations." *Circulation* 99 (1999): 2829–2848.

GILL, T. M.; DIPIETRO, L.; and KRUMHOLZ, H. M. "Role of Exercise Stress Testing and Safety Monitoring for Older Persons Starting an Exercise Program." *Journal of the American Medical Association* 284 (2000): 342–349.

GISSI-Prevenzione Investigators. "Dietary Supplementation with N-3 Polyunsaturated Fatty Acids and Vitamin E after Myocardial Infarction: Results of the GISSI-Prevenzione Trial." *Lancet* 354 (1999): 447–455.

HAKIM, A. A.; CURB, J. D.; PETROVITCH, H.; et al. "Effects of Walking on Coronary Heart Disease in Elderly Men." *Circulation* 100 (1999): 9–13.

HANSSON, L.; LINDHOLM, L. H.; EKBOM, T.; et al. "Randomised Trial of Old and New Antihypertensive Drugs in Elderly Patients: Cardiovascular Mortality and Morbidity the Swedish Trial in Old Patients with Hypertension-2 Study." *Lancet* 354 (1999): 1751–1756.

HAYES, D. L.; WANG, P. J.; REYNOLDS, D. W.; et al. "Interference with Cardiac Pacemakers by Cellular Telephones." *New England Journal of Medicine* 336 (1997): 1473–1479.

Heart Outcomes Prevention Evaluation Study Investigators. "Effects of an Angiotensin-Converting-Enzyme Inhibitor, Ramipril, on Cardiovascular Events in High-Risk Patients." *New England Journal of Medicine* 342 (2000): 145–153.

HJALMARSON, A.; GOLDSTEIN, S.; FAGERBERG, B.; et al. "Effects of Controlled-Release Metoprolol on Total Mortality, Hospitalizations, and Well-Being in Patients with Heart Failure." *Journal of the American Medical Association* 283 (2000): 1295–1302.

HULLEY, S.; GRADY, D.; BUSH, T.; et al. "Randomized Trial of Estrogen Plus Progestin for Secondary Prevention of Coronary Heart Disease in Postmenopausal Women." *Journal of the American Medical Association* 280, no. 7 (1998): 605–613.

ISIS-2 (Second International Study of Infarct Survival) Collaborative Group. "Randomised Trial of Intravenous Streptokinase, Oral Aspirin, Both, or Neither Among 17,187 Cases of Suspected Acute Myocardial Infarction: ISIS-2." *Lancet* (1988): 349–360.

JORENBY, D. E.; LEISCHOW, S. J.; NIDES, M. A.; et al. "A Controlled Trial of Sustained-Release Bupropion, a Nicotine Patch, or Both for Smoking Cessation." *New England Journal of Medicine* 340, no. 9 (1999): 685–691.

KIRKLIN, J. K.; NAFTEL, D. C.; BLACKSTONE, E. H.; et al. "Risk Factors for Mortality After Primary Combined Valvular and Coronary Artery Surgery." *Circulation* 79, suppl. 1 (1989): 185–190.

LOGEAIS, Y.; LANGANAY, T.; ROUSSIN, R.; et al. "Surgery for Aortic Stenosis in Elderly Patients." *Circulation* 90 (1994): 2891–2898.

Long-Term Intervention with Pravastatin in Ischaemic Disease (LIPID) Study Group. "Prevention of Cardiovascular Events and Death with Pravastatin in Patients with Coronary Heart Disease and a Broad Range of Initial Cholesterol Levels." *New England Journal of Medicine* 339 (1998): 1349–1357.

Medical Research Council Working Party. "Medical Research Council Trial of Treatment of Hypertension in Older Adults: Principal Results." *British Medical Journal* 304 (1992): 405–412.

PAUL, S. D.; O'GARA, P. T.; MAHJOUB, Z. A.; et al. "Geriatric Patients with Acute Myocardial Infarction: Cardiac Risk Factor Profiles, Presentation, Thrombolysis, Coronary Interventions, and Prognosis." *American Heart Journal* 131 (1996): 710–715.

PITT, B.; POOLE-WILSON, P. A.; SEGAL, R.; et al. "Effect of Losartan Compared with Captopril on Mortality in Patients with Symptomatic Heart Failure: Randomised Trial—The Losartan Heart Failure Survival Study ELITE II." *Lancet* 355 (2000): 1582–1587.

PITT, B.; ZANNAD, F.; REMME, W. J.; et al. "The Effect of Spironolactone on Morbidity and Mortality in Patients with Severe Heart Failure." *New England Journal of Medicine* 341 (1999): 709–717.

RYAN, T. J.; ANTMAN, E. M.; BROOKS, N. H.; et al. "ACC/AHA Guidelines for the Management of Patients with Acute Myocardial Infarction." *Journal of the American College of Cardiology* 34 (1999): 890–911.

SACKS, F. M.; PFEFFER, M. A.; MOYE, L. A.; et al. "The Effect of Pravastatin on Coronary Events after Myocardial Infarction in Patients with Average Cholesterol Levels." *New England Journal of Medicine* 335 (1996): 1001–1009.

SCHLANT, R. C., and ALEXANDER, R. W. *Hurst's the Heart*, 8th ed. New York: McGraw-Hill, 1994.

SHAPIRA, O. M.; KELLEHER, R. M.; ZELINGHER, J.; et al. "Prognosis and Quality of Life after Valve Surgery in Patients Older than 75 Years." *Chest* 112 (1997): 885–894.

SHEPHERD, J.; COBBE, S. M.; FORD, I.; et al. "Prevention of Coronary Heart Disease with Pravastatin in Men with Hypercholesterolemia." *New England Journal of Medicine* 333 (1995): 1301–1307.

SOLVD Investigators. "Effect of Enalapril on Survival in Patients with Reduced Left Ventricular Ejection Fractions and Congestive Heart Failure." *New England Journal of Medicine* 325 (1991): 293–302.

SPAF III Writing Committee for the Stroke Prevention in Atrial Fibrillation Investigators. "Patients with Nonvalvular Atrial Fibrillation at Low Risk of Stroke During Treatment with Aspirin." *Journal of the American Medical Association* 279 (1998): 1273–1277.

STAESSEN, J. A.; FAGARD, R.; THIJS, L.; et al. "Randomised Double-Blind Comparison of Placebo and Active Treatment for Older Patients with Isolated Systolic Hypertension." *Lancet* 350 (1997): 757–764.

Tobacco Use and Dependence Clinical Practice Guideline Panel, Staff, and Consortium Representatives. "A Clinical Practice Guideline for Treating Tobacco Use and Dependence." *Journal of the American Medical Association* 283 (2000): 3244–3254.

U.K. Prospective Diabetes Study Group. "Tight Blood Pressure Control and Risk of Macrovascular and Microvascular Complications in Type 2 Diabetes: UKPDS 38." *British Medical Journal* 317 (1998): 703–713.

YUSUS, S. *Evidence Based Cardiology*, 1st ed. London: British Medical Journal Publications, 1998.

ZIJLSTRA, F.; HOORNTJE, J. C. A.; DE BOER, M.; et al. "Long-Term Benefit of Primary Angioplasty as Compared with Thrombolytic Therapy for Acute Myocardial Infarction." *New England Journal of Medicine* 341 (1999): 1413–1419.

HERBAL THERAPY

For thousands of years, plants have been a source of medicinal agents. Many of the drugs we use today still come from plants, for example, morphine (opium poppy), digoxin (foxglove), and atropine (datura) to mention a few.

In recent years, there has been much interest on the part of the general public about herbalism, often as part of an alternative/complementary form of health care. A renewed interest in herbal remedies and natural products has placed additional responsibility on consumers and health professionals to know:

• why common medicinal herbs are used;
• the potential for undesirable side effects, interactions, or allergic reactions;
• if the claims being made are correct;
• the quality of available products; and
• if the cost is reasonable.

Foxglove

The attraction of herbal/natural remedies reflects on interest in a "back to nature" philosophy. While attractive, it is important for the public to know that there may be problems associated with the use of some herbs. For example:

- "If it is natural, then it must be safe." Strychnine, a natural product once used in tonics, is a violent poison. Tobacco has been positively linked to lung cancer.
- "Herbs are not drugs." Oregano added to pasta for flavoring is a herb, but the opium poppy, also an herb, contains the very powerful drug morphine.
- "Herbs cannot do any harm, they can only cure." This is clearly incorrect when you consider plants such as poison ivy!
- "If it has been used for centuries it must work." The age of a statement is not proof it is correct. Bloodletting was used for centuries, but that did not make it effective. The effectiveness of medicinal agents, whether herbal/natural or man-made, old or new, must be determined through careful study.

Nevertheless, there is a trend toward the use of herbal products to treat just about any condition. A maze of herbal/natural products ranging from vitamins to cancer treatments promoted by advertising is available to consumers. It becomes important to ask about the content, regulation, efficacy, uses, and safety of these products. What do these herbal products contain? How much? What are they used for? How long should they be taken? Are they safe? Do they really work? Are there active chemical ingredients? What are the dosages and warnings for a given herbal/natural product?

How are herbal/natural products regulated?

The difference between herbal/natural products and approved drugs is their regulatory status. Prescription products (for example, morphine) and nonprescription or over-the-counter (OTC products such as senna tablets) must meet strict requirements. The manufacturer must provide:

- scientific evidence to prove that the product is safe and effective;
- proof that it follows good manufacturing practices (GMP) in a clean (sanitary) facility that meets all the quality control standards set by the Food and Drugs Administration (FDA) in the United States or Health Canada in Canada; and
- full label disclosure to indicate medicinal and nonmedicinal ingredients and directions for safe use that include cautions and contraindications.

Scientific evidence requires that the product undergoes careful scrutiny to see whether it is of benefit in treating or curing a given medical condition. This involves treating people in a carefully designed and controlled study that is monitored by health professions to see whether the product is safe and whether it works (i.e., is effective). These studies are referred to as double-blind placebo-controlled clinical trials. This is how researchers determine the effects, side effects, and adverse reactions of a product. If the product is shown to be of benefit, the information or evidence from the study is forwarded to the FDA for further scrutiny and approval for marketing.

If the product is deemed safe, effective, and compliant, it receives a unique Drug Identification Number (DIN) that is clearly printed on the product label. This allows the public to know that they are consuming a product that has been evaluated as being safe and effective for a given medical condition.

In the United States most herbs are sold as "dietary supplements" under the Dietary Supplement Health and Education Act (DSHEA) of 1994. Under this law they are considered safe, unless proven unsafe by the FDA. In other words, the manufacturer does not have to prove the product is safe. Rather, it is up to the government to prove the product is harmful. This is in contrast to prescription and nonprescription products that must be proven safe and effective by the manufacturer before they are marketed.

The DSHEA prohibits making medical claims on dietary supplement labels, but it allows for publications to be used in connection with their sale. Therefore, products are required to bear the words "This statement has not been evaluated by the Food and Drug Administration. This product is not intended to diagnose, treat, cure or prevent any disease." The FDA does not scrutinize dietary supplements or literature used to promote their sale. This waiver serves to warn the public that the product or literature has not been approved as a regulated drug.

With a similar twist, in Canada most herbs are sold as a "food" without any labeled disclosure, health claim, or quality control. Marketing a product with a health claim places it under the category of "drug." This would require meeting strict requirements under the "drug" part of the Food and Drugs Act of 1953. Selling it as a "food" avoids any testing for safety and efficacy. Unfortunately, this leaves all consumers and health professionals wondering about the quality, safety, and efficacy of the product.

What kinds of products are we concerned about?

Chronic conditions such as Alzheimer's disease, arthritis, high blood pressure, depression and problems with the prostate gland become more common with advancing age. Consequently products such as, ginkgo biloba, glucosamine, garlic, St. John's Wort and saw palmetto, are frequently promoted as treatments for these health problems.

***Ginkgo biloba*, L. (Ginkgoaceae).**   Ginkgo has been prescribed in Europe for illnesses associated with reduced blood flow in the brain in elderly persons. These include depression, short-term memory loss, ringing in the ears (tinnitus), and Raynaud's disease.

Gingko Biloba

Researchers are still studying ginkgo to find out how it works. It may work as an anticoagulant (blood thinner), vasodilator (opens up blood vessels) or as an antioxidant (a chemical that has a protecting effect in the body) (Desmet). The anti-stress and anti-anxiety activity may be due to its effect on an enzyme in the brain (White, Scates, and Cooper; Letzel, Haan, and Feil).

Because of the way ginkgo may work, patients taking aspirin, anticoagulants (blood thinners, for example, Coumadin®), vasodilating agents (drugs that open up blood vessels), anti-inflammatory, or antidepressant drugs should not add ginkgo to their medicines without first consulting with their doctors. Side effects of ginkgo have included stomach upsets, headache, dizziness, and vertigo. Ginkgo seeds and fruit pulp are toxic if eaten (*Pharmacist's Letter*).

Clinical studies in humans for symptoms associated with decreased blood flow to the brain, used dosages of 120 to 160 mg per day of a ginkgo biloba extract, with treatment lasting for at least four to six weeks. Results showed that ginkgo may have some benefit but that this needs to be studied further. Ginkgo does not seem to be of benefit for treating tinnitus (World Health Organization).

Figure 1

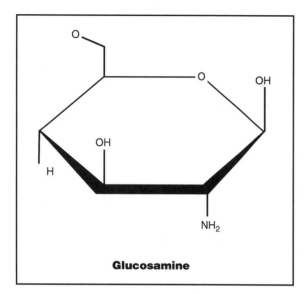

Glucosamine

SOURCE: Author

Glucosamine.   Glucosamine is a sugar derivative that occurs naturally in the body (see Figure 1). It is an essential nutrient used in the formation of specialized sugar polymers called glycosaminoglycans. These polymers are used to form bone, cartilage, heart valves, ligaments, nails, tendons, and synovial fluid (a lubricating fluid found in weight-bearing joints).

As the human body ages, cartilage, which cushions the ends of bones, begins to lose elasticity, shrinks, and cracks. Sometimes pieces of cartilage break off into joint space and irritate the surrounding tissue. This inhibits movement and causes inflammation that results in decreased movement and pain. The muscles that hold the joints together weaken due to their lack of use, and the joint may change its shape and function. After a long period the bones may rub together causing more pain and the formation of spurs. This condition is known as osteoarthritis (OA).

It has therefore been suggested that supplementation with glucosamine may relieve symptoms of OA. The usual oral dosage reported in the scientific literature is 500 mg, three times a day. Glucosamine is a by-product of the shellfish industry and obtained from the exoskeletons of crustaceans (lobsters). Pharmacists and physicians should ask the consumer if they have any allergies to shellfish. Glucosamine is well tolerated and adverse reactions or drug interactions have not been reported.

Large-scale, long-term clinical studies are needed to evaluate the efficacy of glucosamine in the treatment of OA (McAlindon et al.). It is important for the patient to understand the nature of OA, risk factors (heredity, injury to the joint, and excess body weight), and current therapy, which includes diet, exercise, and physiotherapy. Appropriate lifestyle changes may eliminate or limit the need for medications.

***Serenoa repens* (Bart.) or saw palmetto.**   In men the urethra is surrounded near its base by the prostate gland, which secretes part of the semen. When this gland enlarges, as it often does in older men, urination may become difficult. Symptoms of urinary frequency, urgency, and hesitancy are common in urinary tract infections, cancer of the prostate, or prostate enlargement. Therefore, it is very important for patients to see their doctor to find out the nature of the underlying problem.

Saw palmetto extract, has been used to treat symptoms associated with prostate enlargement ("Sabal fructus"). Clinical studies using an oral dose of 160 mg of extract twice daily indicate that it may help the symptoms associated with an enlarged prostate (Brinker). The most common adverse effects are nausea and stomach pain. Headache, increased blood pressure, urinary retention, and back pain have been reported (Nemecz).

Saw palmetto has not been shown to reduce enlargement of the prostate gland, and patients with symptoms should be encouraged to see their physician for routine checkups.

Conclusion

A herbal/natural product can have effects and side effects. It is best for individuals to check with their doctor or pharmacist to see whether it is safe and effective for them. Individuals should use the same caution as they would with any medication, by consulting their pharmacist or doctor.

MEERA B. THADANI

See also ARTHRITIS; DRUGS AND ARTHRITIS; EVIDENCE-BASED MEDICINE; PROSTATE; VITAMINS.

BIBLIOGRAPHY

BRINKER, F. "An Overview of Conventional, Experimental and Botanical Treatments of Nonmalignant Prostate Conditions." *British Journal of Phytoerhapy* 3, no. 4 (1993/1994): 156–176.

DESMET, P. A. G. M. *Adverse Effects of Herbal Drugs*, vol. 3, Berlin: Springer Verlag, 1997.

LETZEL, H.; HAAN J.; and FEIL, W. B. "Nootropics: Efficacy and Tolerability of Products from Three Active Substance Classes." *Journal of Drug Development and Clinical Practice* 8, no. 2 (1996): 77–94.

MCALINDON, T. E.; LAVALLEY, M. P.; GULIN, J. P.; et al. "Glucosamine and Chondroitin for Treatment of Osteoarthritis: A Systematic Quality Assessment and Meta-Analysis." *Journal of the American Medical Association* 283 (2000): 1469–1475.

NEMECZ, G. "Saw Palmetto." *U.S. Pharmacist* (January 1998): 97–102.

Pharmacist's Letter No. 97-005, Vol. 97, no. 4, Therapeutic Research Centre, Stockton, Calif.: 1997.

SCHULZ, V.; HANSEL, R.; and TYLER, V. E. *Rational Phytopathy: A Physicians' Guide to Herbal Medicine*. Berlin: Springer-Verlag, 1998.

WHITE, H. L.; SCATES, P. W.; and COOPER, B. R. "Extracts of Ginkgo Biloba Leaves Inhibit Monoamine Oxidase." *Life Sciences* 58, no. 16 (March 1996): 1315–1321.

World Health Organization. "Ginkgo." *World Health Organization Monographs on Selected Medicinal Plants*, vol. 1. Geneva, Switzerland (1999): 154–167.

HIGH BLOOD PRESSURE

Although diastolic blood pressure is considered an important risk factor for cerebrovascular disease, congestive heart failure, and coronary heart disease, it is now clear that isolated systolic hypertension and elevated pulse pressure also play an important role in the development of these diseases, which are the major causes of cardiovascular morbidity and mortality among subjects over sixty-five years of age. The benefit of antihypertensive therapy in reducing the incidence of cardiovascular and cerebrovascular complications has been shown for systolic and systolo-diastolic hypertension. Essential hypertension (no discoverable organic cause) is the main cause of hypertension in the elderly population. In addition, secondary hypertension—especially that associated with kidney disease—is more common in older than in younger adults.

Definition of hypertension

Blood pressure is defined by two values: systolic (contraction of the heart), the highest value, and diastolic (dilation of the heart), the lower. "The Sixth Report of the Joint National Committee on Prevention, Detection, Evaluation, and Treatment of High Blood Pressure" (JNC-VI) and the World Health Organization/International Society of Hypertension Guidelines subcommittees have agreed that both systolic and diastolic blood pressure should be used to classify hypertension. Systolo-diastolic hypertension is diagnosed when systolic and diastolic blood pressure are over 160 and 90, respectively. Isolated systolic hypertension refers to systolic blood pressure over 160 and diastolic blood pressure under 90.

Misdiagnosis may be more frequent in the elderly due to various factors, including inappropriate length of the cuff due to obesity or very low weight, fluctuations in blood pressure due to postural hypotension, and/or anxiety (white coat effect). The difficulty of measuring blood pressure in elderly persons should encourage the development of ambulatory blood pressure measurement.

Ambulatory blood pressure measurement is most useful for identifying patients with white-coat hypertension, also known as isolated clinic hypertension, which is arbitrarily defined as a clinc blood pressure of more than 140 mmHg systolic or 90 mmHg diastolic in a patient with daytime ambulatory blood pressure below 135 mmHg systolic and 85 mmHg diastolic.

Blood pressure changes and hypertension

Both systolic and diastolic blood pressure increase with age. However, diastolic blood pressure increases with age until the age of fifty or sixty and then tends to remain stable or even decrease slightly, whereas systolic blood pressure rises progressively until the age of seventy or eighty. This combination of changes probably reflects stiffening of the blood vessels and reduced arterial elasticity and leads to a large increase in pulse pressure (the difference between the systolic and diastolic pressures) with aging (Burt et al.). In persons over eighty, a decrease in both diastolic and systolic blood pressure has been found in some studies, and may be due to poor health in this very frail population. The global prevalence of both diastolic and systolic hypertension in people over sixty-five is about 45 percent. Hypertension is more frequent in black than white persons, and in women than men. The prevalence of isolated systolic hypertension is about 7, 11, 18, and 25 percent in people aged sixty to sixty-nine, seventy to seventy-nine, eighty to eighty-nine, and over ninety, respectively. Isolated systolic hypertension is more frequent in women than men.

The mechanisms of hypertension in elderly persons involve an increase in thickness of aortic and large artery walls and a decrease in vessel elasticity, which raises systolic blood pressure. Hypertension also increases peripheral vascular resistance, because of the reduced elasticity of these arteries. In addition, it reduces the sensitivity of nerve endings stimulated by pressure changes, resulting in the impairment of postural reflexes, which makes elderly persons with hypertension prone to hypotension when standing erect. The vasoconstriction due to changes in the balance between beta-adrenergic vasodilatation and alpha-adrenergic vasoconstriction raises peripheral vascular resistance and blood pressure. Increased sodium intake and decreased sodium excretion induce sodium retention. In contrast to hypertension in younger adults, the renin-angiotensin system is not thought to play a major role in hypertension in older adults.

Risk of hypertension

Hypertension stands out as the major risk factor for cardiovascular disease and mortality in elderly persons (Forette et al., 1982). Both systolic and diastolic blood pressure are involved, but with advancing age, systolic blood pressure has been identified as a better predictor of cardiovascular risk than diastolic blood pressure, in both men and women (Kannel and Gordon, 1978). Since at any given level of systolic blood pressure, mortality was found to increase as diastolic pressure decreased, pulse pressure must also be considered a risk factor (Staessen et al., 2000).

Systolic, diastolic, and combined hypertension increase the risk of stroke. Data from the Framingham Study have shown that apart from this risk, elevated systolic blood pressure is a major risk factor for all cardiovascular diseases, including left ventricular hypertrophy, congestive heart failure, ischemic cardiopathy, and peripheral artery diseases. High midlife blood pressure has been shown to be a strong independent predictor of later cognitive impairment.

However, some authors who studied very old patients reported a J curve profile with higher cognitive impairment in subjects with low blood pressure. The decrease in blood pressure may be due to pathological processes that also affect cognitive functioning or, alternatively, it may be a consequence of dementia. In addition, hypertension appears to be the strongest risk factor for vascular dementia and possibly for Alzheimer's disease.

A correlation between mortality and high blood pressure has been widely shown. This excess mortality is mainly correlated with systolic blood pressure (Kannel et al., 1976). However, in people over eighty years old, some authors have reported either no association between blood pressure and mortality or an inverse association, which disappears after adjustment for indicators of poor health.

Benefits of antihypertensive therapy

Several randomized, double-blind, placebo-controlled intervention studies have provided strong evidence in favor of treating hypertension in elderly patients. Reports of first outcome trials published in 1985 and 1991 that focused attention on systolo-diastolic hypertension showed a reduction in cardiovascular and cerebrovascular morbidity and mortality in patients over sixty-five years old (Amery et al.; Dahlöf et al.; Medical Research Council).

More recent trials have specifically addressed the problem of isolated systolic hypertension. A meta-analysis by Staessen et al. (2000) showed that in 15,693 patients with isolated systolic hypertension who were included in eight trials, antihypertensive treatment reduced stroke by 30 percent. Total mortality decreased by 13 percent, cardiovascular mortality by 18 percent, all cardiovascular complications by 26 percent, and coronary events by 23 percent. Treatment prevented strokes more effectively than it prevented coronary events.

An important finding in the investigation of systolic hypertension in Europe (Syst-Eur; Forette et al., 1998) was that in older people with isolated systolic hypertension, antihypertensive treatment that started with the calcium-channel blocker nitrendipine significantly reduced the incidence of dementia, from 7.7 to 3.8 per 1000 person-years. The incidence of Alzheimer's disease dropped even more after such treatment than that of vascular or mixed dementia. By contrast, in the Systolic Hypertension in the Elderly Program (SHEP), active treatment based on diuretics and beta-blockers failed to reduce the incidence of dementia significantly. These negative results argue against conferring protection simply by lowering blood pressure. In the mechanism of dementia prevention, calcium-channel blockers might have a neuroprotective effect. The potential importance of the Syst-Eur results for public health policies warrants confirmation by other trials.

Should very old people be treated?

The value of antihypertensive treatment is well established for patients age sixty years and over. The results are mixed for the oldest age group, eighty years and over. The European Working Party on High Blood Pressure in the Elderly Trial failed to demonstrate that antihypertensive treatment was significantly beneficial above the age of eighty (Amery et al.). In the STOP-Hypertension trial (Dahlöf et al.), this treatment resulted in a smaller reduction in the number of deaths from stroke, myocardial infarction, and other cardiovascular diseases in older than in younger patients. By contrast, in the SHEP trial the positive effect of active treatment, compared with placebo, on the relative risk of stroke increased with age, and reached its maximum in the group of patients age eighty years or older. In the Syst-Eur study, a significant reduction was found in morbidity, but not in mortality, in the oldest patients (Staessen et al., 1997). In a meta-analysis of data from 1,870 participants over age eighty, Gueyffier et al. suggested that treatment reduced the rates of stroke, major cardiovascular events, and heart failure by 30 percent. On the other hand, there was no reduction in mortality due to cardiovascular disease or in total mortality. The results of this meta-analysis, which were favorable for morbidity, argue against the existence of a threshold age beyond which hypertension should not be treated.

What should be the goal blood pressure ?

Although the benefit of treating hypertension in elderly subjects is now well established, controversy still exists regarding the goal blood pressure. Indeed, according to the J curve hypothesis, a major reduction in diastolic blood pressure to less than 65 mmHg might jeopardize

appropriate blood flow in the brain, heart, and kidneys during the diastole, and might be associated with an increase in mortality. However, in the SHEP study low diastolic blood pressure did not increase mortality.

As an intermediate goal, most studies recommended either reducing systolic blood pressure to under 160 mmHg and diastolic pressure to under 90 mmHg, or reducing the initial systolic and diastolic blood pressures by 20 mmHg. The benefit of a larger decrease (≤140 mmHg) remains to be determined by the results of ongoing studies.

Drug therapy

Most trials have been run with diuretics and beta-blockers as first-line drugs. Since the 1980s, the efficacy and safety of these two classes of drugs have been demonstrated in elderly subjects (Amery et al.; SHEP; Dahlöf et al.; MRC). The benefit of calcium-channel blockers (Staessen et al. 1997; Hansson, Lindholm, Ekbom et al.) and angiotensin-converting-enzyme inhibitors (Hansson, Lindholm, Niskanen et al.) has been shown for the prevention of cardiovascular and cerebrovascular complications in older patients.

Because age- and disease-associated factors affect the metabolism and distribution of pharmacologic agents, antihypertensive therapy should be given at low doses, which should be increased gradually. However, despite alterations in metabolism, most elderly patients tolerate medication without a significant increase in adverse events compared to younger patients or control groups. First-line treatment should consist of diuretics or beta-blockers (JNC-VI). In isolated systolic hypertension, diuretics and calcium-channel blockers are recommended (SHEP; Staessen et al., 1997).

Concomitant diseases may influence the choice of therapy. In patients with coronary artery disease, beta-blockers may be useful, but peripheral artery disease, heart failure, or obstructive bronchopathy may limit their use in elderly persons. In older patients with coronary artery disease, use of calcium-channel blockers may be discussed. In cardiac dysfunction and congestive heart failure, prescription of diuretics, angiotensin-converting-enzyme inhibitors, or both is an appropriate initial choice. In older adults, fixed-dose combination therapy has the advantage of increasing compliance, reducing the cost of antihypertensive therapy, and achieving a higher response rate.

Nonpharmacologic interventions

Older hypertensive patients can also benefit from nonpharmacologic interventions designed to lower blood pressure (JNC-VI), including weight control, reduction of excessive alcohol consumption, cessation of smoking, and increased exercise. Any reduction of sodium intake in elderly people should be cautious because it can reduce food intake.

Management of hypertension

Despite the evidence that treatment is beneficial in terms of reducing morbidity and mortality, hypertension is still poorly controlled in elderly persons. Both in the United States and in Europe, less than 30 percent of patients on hypertensive drugs attain the JNC-VI goal blood pressure (<140 and <90 mmHg) (JNC-VI; Burt et al.). Achieving the goal is relatively easy for diastolic blood pressure, but much harder for systolic blood pressure. Moreover, the new indication of pulse pressure as the most powerful risk factor must now lead doctors to consider systolic rather than diastolic blood pressure when determining treatment goals. Consequently, the development of drugs that lower systolic blood pressure more effectively should be promoted (Staessen et al., 2000). Blacher et al. have emphasized the need for randomized trials with antihypertensive drugs that act differently on the pulsatile component of blood pressure. These authors suggested that vasopeptidase inhibitors and nitric oxide donors might increase the distensibility of large arteries and reduce pulse pressure.

ANNE-SOPHIE RIGAUD

See also HEART DISEASE; STROKE; VASCULAR DISEASE.

BIBLIOGRAPHY

AMERY, A.; BIRKENHÄGER, W.; BRIXKO, P.; BULPITT, C.; CLEMENT, D.; DERUYTTERE, M.; DE SHAEPDRYVER, A.; DOLLERY, C.; FAGARD, R.; FORETTE, F.; FORTE, J.; HAMDY, R.; HENRY, J. F.; JOOSSENS, J. V.; LEONETTI, G.; LUND-JOHANSSEN, P.; O'MALLEY, K.; PETRIE, J.; TRASSER, T.; TUOMILEHTO, J.; and WILLIAMS,

B. "Mortality and Morbidity Results from the European Working Party on High Blood Pressure in the Elderly Trial." *Lancet* 1, no. 8442 (1985): 1349–1354.

BLACHER, J.; STAESSEN, J. A.; GIRERD, X.; GAZOWSKY, J.; THIJS, L.; LIU, L.; WANG, J. G.; FAGARD, ROBERT; and SAFAR, MICHEL. "Pulse Pressure Not Mean Pressure Determines Cardiovascular Risk in Older Hypertensive Patients." *Archives of Internal Medicine* 160 (2000): 1085–1089.

BURT, V. L.; WHELTON, P.; ROCCELLA, E. J.; BROWN, C.; CUTLER, J. A.; HIGGINS, M.; HORAN, M. J.; and LABARTHE, D. "Prevalence of Hypertension in the U.S. Adult Population: Results from the Third National Health and Nutrition Examination Survey, 1988–1991." *Hypertension* 25 (1995): 305–313.

DAHLÖF, B.; LINDHOLM, L. H.; HANSSON, L.; SCHERSTÉN, B.; EKBOM, T.; and WESTER, P. O. "Morbidity and Mortality in the Swedish Trial in Old Patients with Hypertension (STOP-Hypertension)." *Lancet* 338 (1991): 1281–1285.

FORETTE, F.; DE LA FUENTE, X.; GOLMARD, J. L.; HENRY, J-F.; and HERVY, M-P. "The Prognostic Significance of Isolated Systolic Hypertension in the Elderly. Results of a Ten-Year Longitudinal Survey." *Clinical Experimental Hypertension* A4 (1992): 1177–1191.

FORETTE, F.; SEUX, M-L.; STAESSEN, J. A.; THIJS, L.; BIRKENHÄGER, W. H.; BARBASKIENE, M-R.; BABEANU, S.; BOSSINI, A.; GOL-EXTREMERA, B.; GIRERD, X.; LAKS, T.; LILOV, E.; MOISSEYEV, V.; TUOMILEHTO, J.; VANHANNEN, H.; WEBSTER, J.; YODFAT, Y.; and FAGARD, R. "On Behalf of the Syst-Eur Investigators. Prevention of Dementia in Randomized Double-Blind Placebo-Controlled Systolic Hypertension in Europe (Syst-Eur) Trial." *Lancet* 352 (1998): 1347–1351.

GUEYFFIER, F.; BULPITT, C.; BOISSEL, JEAN-PIERRE; SCHRON, ELEANOR; EKBOM, TORK; FAGARD, ROBERT; CASIGLIA, EDOARDO; KERLIKOWSKE, K.; and COOPE, J. "Antihypertensive Drugs in Very Old People: A Subgroup Meta-Analysis of Randomised Controlled Trials." *Lancet* 353 (1999): 793–796.

Guidelines Subcommittee, World Health Organization-International Society of Hypertension. "Guidelines for the Management of Hypertension." *Journal of Hypertension* 17 (1999): 151–183.

HANSSON, L.; LINDHOLM, L. H.; NISKANEN, L.; LANKE, J.; HEDNER, T.; NIKLASON, A.; LUOMANMÄKI, K.; DALHÖF, B.; DE FAIRE, U.; MÖRLIN, C.; KARLBERG, B. E.; WESTER, P. O.;

and BJÖRK, J-E. "Effect of Angiotensin-Converting-Enzyme Inhibition Compared with Conventional Therapy on Cardiovascular Morbidity and Mortality in Hypertension: The Captopril Project (CAPPP) Randomised Trial." *Lancet* 353 (1999): 611–616.

HANSSON, L.; LINDHOLM, L. H.; EKBOM, T.; DAHLÖF, B.; LANKE, J.; SCHERSTÉN, B.; WESTER, P. O.; HEDNER, THOMAS; and DE FAIRE, ULF. "Randomised Trial of Old and New Antihypertensive Drugs in Elderly Patients: Cardiovascular Mortality and Morbidity the Swedish Trial in Old Patients with Hypertension-2 Study." *Lancet* 354 (1999): 1751–1756.

KANNEL, W. B., and GORDON, T. "Evaluation of Cardiovascular Risk in the Elderly: The Framingham Study." *Bulletin of the New-York Academy of Medicine* 54 (1978): 573–591.

MRC WORKING PARTY. "Medical Research Council Trial of Treatment of Hypertension in Older Adults: Principal Results." *British Medical Journal* 304 (1992): 405–412.

SHEP COOPERATIVE RESEARCH GROUP. "Prevention of Stroke by Antihypertensive Drug Treatment in Older Persons with Isolated Systolic Hypertension. Final Results of the Systolic Hypertension in the Elderly Program (SHEP)." *Journal of the American Medical Association* 265 (1991): 3255–3264.

"The Sixth Report of the Joint National Committee on Prevention, Detection, Evaluation, and Treatment of High Blood Pressure." (JNC-VI) *Archives of Internal Medicine* 157 (1997): 2413–2446.

STAESSEN, J. A.; FAGARD, R.; THIJS, L.; CELIS, H.; ARABIDZE, G. G.; BIRKENHÄGER, W. H. BULPITT, C.; DE LEEUW, W.; DOLLERY, C. T. FLETCHER, A. E.; FORETTE, F.; LEONETTI, G.; NACHEV, C.; O'BRIEN, E. T.; ROSENFELD, J.; RODICIO, J. L.; TUOMILEHTO, J.; and ZANCHETTI, A. "Randomised Double-Blind Comparison of Placebo and Active Treatment for Older Patients with Isolated Systolic Hypertension." *Lancet* 350 (1997): 757–764.

STAESSEN, J. A.; GAZOWSKI, J.; WANG, J. G.; THIJS, L.; DEN HONDE, E.; BOISSEL, J-P.; COOPE, JOHN; EKBOM, TORK; GUEYFFIER, FRANÇOIS; LIU, L.; KERLIKOWSKE, K.; POCOCK, S.; and FAGARD, R.. "Risks of Untreated and Treated Isolated Systolic Hypertension in the Elderly: Meta-Analysis of Outcome Trials." *Lancet* 355 (2000): 865–872.

HIP FRACTURE

Hip fractures, particularly in frail elderly persons, have a profound effect on morbidity, mortality, and length of hospitalization, and they are a significant risk factor for institutionalization. With the age of the world's population ever increasing, hip fractures will constitute an increasingly large health, social and economic burden. A coordinated multidisciplinary approach, including orthopaedic surgeons, geriatricians, nurses, physiotherapists, occupational therapists, and social workers will be required to provide optimal management of persons who suffer hip fractures.

Etiology

The majority of hip fractures are caused by a simple fall inside the home. Frail, elderly people are particularly susceptible to falls, given their many coexisting medical conditions that influence gait, balance, and coordination. Fracture incidence is directly related to age, doubling with each decade beyond age fifty. Women are much more commonly affected than men, by a ratio of 2.5 or 3 to 1. The white population in the United States is much more commonly affected than the African-American, Hispanic, or Asian populations. Other factors associated with injury include osteoporosis and osteomalacia, a history of smoking, excessive use of alcohol and caffeine, physical inactivity, and previous hip fracture.

Diagnosis

The clinical diagnosis of a displaced hip fracture is often readily apparent due to the so-called down and out posture, with the affected limb being shortened and externally rotated. In nondisplaced fractures there may not be an obvious deformity. The diagnosis in such cases is made based on the history of fall (a single fall) and subsequent inability to bear weight, as well as pain when the hip is moved either actively by the patient or passively by the examining clinician.

Routine radiographs of the hip, usually taken in two views (front and side) are sufficient to confirm the diagnosis. Occasionally a fracture may not be apparent radiographically, so if the clinical suspicion is strong, further investigations should be carried out. Radionuclide imaging with technicum bone scanning is most commonly used, but even with this tool diagnosis can be difficult. Particularly in an elderly person, a fracture may not become apparent on bone scan for two to five days after an injury. More recently, MRI has been shown to be more accurate and, if hospitalization of the patient is required, more cost effective. These techniques would only be used in the exceptional case where the diagnosis is not clear. For example, metastatic cancer frequently affects the proximal femur. Specific attention to bone quality on the radiograph is required to detect an occult lesion indicating a pathologic fracture. (A fracture through abnormal quality bone, generally a metastatic diseased bone. Certain cancers commonly metastasize to the proximal femur, especially lung, breast, prostate, thyroid and renal cancers.) The likely primary cancer sites are breast, lung, prostate, thyroid, and kidney.

Principles of management

The primary goal of management is to return patients to their prefracture ambulatory status and level of function. Initial treatment is directed toward pain control, and small, frequent doses of analgesics can be utilized. In displaced hip fractures, splinting of the limb is helpful. Simple splinting, such as bunny-boot traction with five pounds, or skin traction can be utilized. In the undisplaced fracture traction is unnecessary, but care must be used when moving the patient. Skin breakdown can occur within hours, and it is therefore important that the patient position is changed frequently. Only in rare instances is nonsurgical management appropriate. Nonsurgical management may be considered for the stable impacted hip fracture when the patient has already walked following the fall and has minimal or no pain with passive range of motion of the hip; minimal pain with active range of motion of the hip; or nearly full range of motion. Radiographs should demonstrate a stable fracture pattern. Nonoperative management can also be considered in the severely debilitated, cognitively impaired, and previously nonambulatory patient who does not appear to be having any significant discomfort.

Preparation for surgery

A complete history and physical examination with specific concern for any anaesthetic risk is required prior to surgery. Previous infections about the hip or history of venous thromboembolism (blood clots) should be specifically applicable to hip surgery. A careful review of current medication is also necessary. Specific emphasis on the history of malignancies to help rule out occult pathologic fractures is required. In addition, careful note should be made of the patient's cognitive and functional status prior to surgery. This information is helpful in making prognosis for recovery after surgery and for assessing the need for postoperative rehabilitation. Cross matching of blood is necessary, as transfusion frequently will be required perioperatively.

Unnecessary delay of a patient's operative intervention appears to worsen the outcome. Ideally, elderly patients should undergo surgery within the first forty-eight hours of injury, as delay beyond this appears to decrease their overall recovery. As these patients often have significant medical problems, the focus should be on correcting any reversible medical condition within twenty-four to forty-eight hours. Similarly, because of the periods of fasting (once admitted into hospital, patients are not permitted to eat or drink prior to surgery. If there are delays prior to surgery this might prolong the period of fast or there may be multiple fasts depending on delays), care must be taken to optimize the patient's nutrition and hydration prior to surgery.

Hip fractures are often clinically obvious, but other causes of groin pain and leg deformity need to be considered, including fractures of the pubic rami, lumbar spine disease, trochanteric bursitis, osteoarthritis or inflammatory arthritis of the hip, or, rarely, a septic hip joint.

Classification of fractures

A simple classification of hip fractures can direct surgical management and indicate prognosis. In general, hip fractures can be divided into two types: intracapsular fractures and extracapsular fractures (see Diagram 1). The reason for this dichotomy concerns the blood supply to the femoral head. Blood flow arises chiefly from branches of the medial circumflex femoral artery that runs along the posterior superior aspect of the femoral neck with the capsule (fibrous covering of the joint that maintains the joint's synovial fluid and with the hip joint maintains it's blood supply) to form a ring of blood vessels around the femoral head. Therefore, if the fracture is intracapsular and the femoral head is displaced it can tear or disrupt the blood supply. This gives rise to a condition known as *avascular necrosis*. In addition, a displaced fracture gets bathed in the synovial fluid capsule of the hip joint. This does not lead to an optimal healing environment. The fracture, therefore, is at a greater risk for nonunion.

Diagram 1
Anatomy of the Proximal Femur

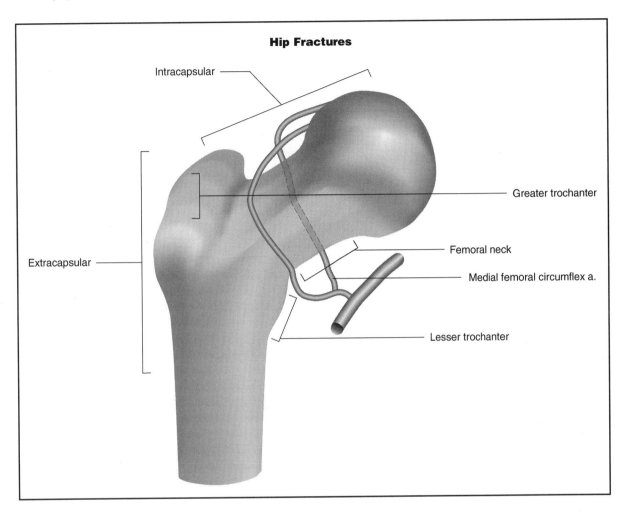

Hip Fractures

Intracapsular

Extracapsular

Greater trochanter

Femoral neck

Medial femoral circumflex a.

Lesser trochanter

SOURCE: Author

Displaced intracapsular fractures have, at least, a one in three risk of avascular necrosis and an additional one in three risk of nonunion. Therefore, in an elderly person, management usually consists of prosthetic replacement of the hip joint. By contrast, undisplaced hip fractures have much lower rates of avascular necrosis and nonunion and are usually treated with multiple screw fixations.

Extracapsular fractures consist of intertrochanteric fractures and subtrochanteric fractures. These can be further classified as stable or unstable. Unstable fractures have loss of bone continuity posteromedially along the proximal femur, which is where most weight bearing occurs. If there is significant disruption of bone

here these fractures are inherently unstable. In general these require anatomic reduction and fixation.

Subtrochanteric fractures comprise approximately 15 percent of hip fractures. In the elderly population there are two groups of patients who sustain this injury. The first includes those whose femurs are quite osteoporotic and break from a minor fall. The second group may have pathologic lesions in the proximal femur, and a fracture may occur to the weakened pathologic bone. Special care needs to be taken in evaluating these patients clinically and radiographically. These fractures, because of the high biomechanical stresses in this region of the femur, tend to be unstable and often require intramedullary fixation.

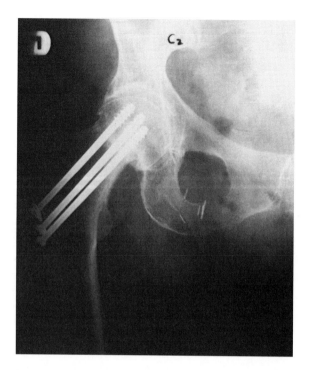

Figure 1. Multiple screw fixation in situ compressing fracture fragments (AO cannulated screws synthesis). (X-ray provided by P. Rockwood.)

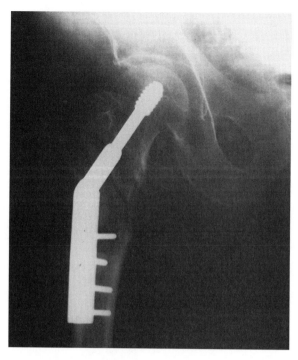

Figure 2. Displaced subcapital hip fracture treated with unipolar prosthesis (Austin Moore: Howmedica). (X-ray provided by P. Rockwood.)

Displaced pathologic fractures may require prosthetic replacement.

Specific surgical management

Patients who sustain an undisplaced subcapital hip fracture (a fracture occurring beneath the femoral head at the head neck junction; it is an intracapsular fracture of the hip) have a lower risk of avascular necrosis and nonunion, and the fracture is therefore best managed by in situ fixation of the fracture. This consists primarily of partially threaded screws that can grip the cancellous bone of the femoral head and are placed in a parallel position along the axis of the femoral neck to allow compression of the fracture site. This compression will enhance stability and progression to union. Three or four pins are generally utilized (see Figure 1).

The displaced subcapital hip fracture continues to be somewhat of an enigma and challenge, and there is no specific ideal treatment program. In general, in elderly people, high rates of avascular necrosis and nonunion mean that no attempt is made to salvage the hip. Agreement exists that a prosthetic replacement will be uti-

lized, but the specific type of prosthesis has been controversial. The traditional method uses an uncemented unipolar prosthesis. This consists of a single-size femoral stem that is placed into the femoral canal with the diameter of the head size of the ball varying according to patient size (see Figure 2). This is a cost-effective, straightforward management of these fractures. However, questions about this device concern its ability to achieve fixation and its potential for long-term acetabular erosion. Both conditions may lead to pain and require revision surgery. More recent evidence suggests that a cemented unipolar replacement maybe superior in outcome to the uncemented type, although acetabular erosion remains a potential problem.

Bipolar hip replacement consists of a femoral stem, similar to that used in total hip replacement, which allows matching of size to the femoral canal (usually with cement techniques) to fix it to the proximal femur. The bipolar component allows a floating acetabulum or second head to fit on top of the standard total hip head, and this allows, in theory, for motion to occur at the smaller head to the larger head (the standard total hip femoral head articulates with the longer acetabular head), as well as the larger head to the acetabulum. One theoretical advantage of the bipolar design has been that it can be converted relatively easily to a total hip replacement—the bipolar larger head can be removed and a cup placed into the acetabulum without replacing the femoral component. The significant disadvantage, compared to unipolar replacement, has been that it is substantially more expensive.

Total hip arthroplasty has also been utilized in the management of displaced subcapital hip fractures. However, long-term outcomes are poor compared to total hip arthroplasty for osteoarthritis of the hip. There are numerous variables for this, including that patients tend to be more frail, the bone stock is less, and patients tend to have a higher dislocation rate. Overall, it has higher morbidity and mortality rates than the same procedure for osteoarthritis.

Extracapsular intertrochanteric fractures

Surgical management of the intertrochanteric fracture requires a sliding hip screw. This consists of a plate and barrel firmly fixed to the proximal femur with a large lag screw that enters into the femoral head and is connected to the plate through the barrel. The fracture site is compressed, as the screw is able to collapse inside the barrel, and compression of osteoporotic bone at the fracture site affords increased stability and enhances bone union. If there is comminution (multiple bone fragments) at the posteromedial aspect of the proximal femur, the fixation can be unstable and may reduce the patient's ability to walk after surgery until bone union occurs (see Figure 3).

Extracapsular subtrochanteric fractures

These fractures are associated with increased blood loss and increased risk of pathologic origin. They are generally treated with intramedullary devices or sliding hip screws with long side plates. Intramedullary devices are rods that insert through the canal of the bone and have interlocking screws that pass through both sides of the bone and the rod to stabilize the fracture. In the case of pathologic fracture, the surgeon may choose to utilize methyl methacrylate (bone cement) and/or prosthetic replacement to enhance stabilization.

As bone becomes more osteoporotic, fracture patterns can become more complex and extra-

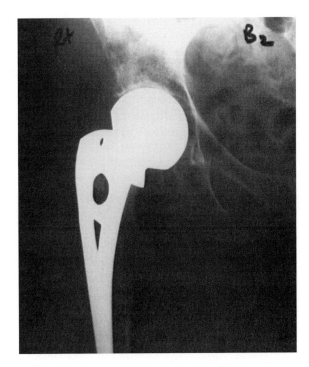

Figure 3. Displaced unstable intertrochanteric fracture fixed with hip compression screw (DHS: Dynamic Hip Screw, synthesis). (X-ray provided by P. Rockwood.)

capsular fractures can consist of intertrochanteric fractures with subtrochanteric extension. These fractures can be very unstable and technically challenging to fix. The specific choice of implant will vary from surgeon to surgeon and center to center. Since their introduction, cephalomedullary interlocking femoral nails have been utilized as an intramedullary nail, with screws that lock into the femoral head through the nail. The hardware is also locked with screws distally in the nail through the bone. These devices have been successful in treating such complex fracture patterns.

Postoperative rehabilitation

Postoperative management (of hip fracture patients) requires multidisciplinary coordination, with the combined goal of returning the patient to prefracture status and back to independent living. A large number of patients lose independence and end up being institutionalized after hip fracture because of general disability and loss of ambulation.

Functional recovery after hip fracture can be variable. Only 40 to 60 percent of patients recover their full prefracture ambulatory function, and only 25 to 35 percent regain their full independence in activities of daily living prior to fracture. Factors contributing to these low rates include older age, cognitive impairment, and few outside social contacts.

Early discussion with patients and their families is needed so that everyone is well versed in the intended rehabilitation goals. This is especially important for patients returning home, as structural adjustments may be needed to the house, such as the installation of handrails and grab rails or moving the patient to a single level accommodation. Other home support systems may also need to be implemented. Occupational therapy services and social services can be very valuable. With respect to physiotherapy, the goal is to mobilize patients quickly, and the surgeon needs to make the decision on their weight-bearing status. Medications to prevent thromboembolic disease (blood clots) are required.

Morbidity and mortality

The one-year mortality after hip fracture ranges from 12 to 36 percent. The highest risk of mortality appears to be in the first four to six months, and there is also significant intrahospital mortality. These rates are significantly higher than age-matched controls. Following one-year postfracture, the mortality rate appears to drop back to age-matched control rates. Factors associated with increased mortality include advanced-stage impaired cognition, institutionalization, cardiovascular disease, and male gender.

Morbidity rates are also quite significant. In the early hospital course, patients are at risk for *fracture disease*. This includes pneumonia, urinary tract infections, decubitus ulcers, and thromboembolic disease. Additionally, cognitive impairment can be exacerbated. This is often multifactorial in nature, with analgesic medication and other polypharmacy effects, complications of the fracture disease, and even the sudden change in environment all implicated.

PETER ROCKWOOD, M.D.

See also ARTHRITIS; BALANCE AND MOBILITY; MULTIDISCIPLINARY TEAM; OSTEOPOROSIS; PRESSURE ULCERS; REHABILITATION; SURGERY IN ELDERLY PEOPLE.

BIBLIOGRAPHY

BEATY, J. H. *Orthopedic Knowledge Update 3-Home Study Syllabus.* American Academy of Orthopaedic Surgeons, 1999.

CRENSHAW, A. H. *Campbell's Operative Orthopedics,* vol. 2, 8th ed. St. Louis, Mo.: Mosby Year Book, 1992.

ROCKWOOD, CHARLES A., and GREEN, DAVID P. *Rockwood and Greene's Fractures in Adults,* 5th ed. Philadelphia: Lippincott-Williams & Wilkins, 2001.

ROCKWOOD, PETER R.; ROCKWOOD, KENNETH J.; and EATON, WILLIAM H. "Elderly Long-Stay Surgical Patients." *Canadian Journal of Surgery* 31, no. 1 (1988): 62–64.

ROCKWOOD, PETER R., and HORNE, J. GEOFFREY. "Hip Fractures: A Future Epidemic?" *Journal of Orthopedic Traumatology* 4 (1990): 388–393.

WIESEL, SAM. W., and DELAHAY, JOHN N. *Essentials of Orthopedic Surgery,* 2d ed. Philadelphia: W.B. Saunders Company, 1997.

HIV/AIDS

See SEXUALITY

HOME ADAPTATION AND EQUIPMENT

As people get older, two major challenges impact on their ability to engage in everyday tasks. The first is a gradual decline in hearing, vision, and mobility (which includes walking, and movement of the arms and body). The second challenge is a high probability, which increases with age, of having one or more chronic diseases, such as arthritis, cataracts, or heart disease. These chronic diseases often lead to additional impairment. In many cases, the impact of impairment on doing everyday tasks (functional performance) can be overcome or reduced through the design of the places where people live, work, study, play, and worship, and through the use of assistive technology devices (also called assistive technology or assistive devices—all three terms are used interchangeably). Assistive technology is a relatively new term but is now widely used. The Technology Related Assistance for Individuals with Disabilities Act of 1988 defined an *assistive technology device* as "any item, piece of equipment, or product system, whether acquired commercially off the shelf, modified or customized, that is used to increase, maintain, or improve functional capabilities of individuals with

Figure 1. A remote control device with large buttons is easier to use for people who have arthritis or other difficulties with their hands.

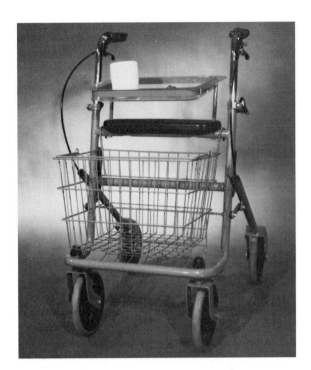

Figure 2. A walker such as this one makes walking easier and safer for millions of elderly persons.

disabilities." This is a broad definition that includes *low-tech devices* (i.e., those traditionally recommended by rehabilitation specialists—occupational therapists and physical therapists—such as buttonhooks and reachers). Assistive technology devices also include *high-tech devices*, which often have microprocessor components, and include computers with voice output, print enlargement systems for persons with low vision, and environmental control units.

Another important concept is *universal design*. The best device is one that is designed for all people, not just for people with disabilities. Universally designed devices, such as phones and computers, are easier to locate, lower in price, and easier to get repaired. Universal design relates to another simple term, *tool*. Humans are "tool users," and with the exception of sea otters, which use rocks to break shells, and chimpanzees, which use sticks to dig up insects, no other species uses objects, or tools, to make doing things easier. Humans' tools range in complexity from shovels to space shuttles and from rulers to supercomputers. If we think of assistive devices as tools, as extensions of persons that enhance performance, we can also view disabilities as a set of challenges to provide the right tools to overcome the impact of the disabling condition.

While we usually think of assistive devices, or tools, as objects that are held or controlled, we also need to consider our "built" environment—buildings, sidewalks, and landscaped areas—and the things placed or included in them—cabinets, doors, and curb cuts. It is possible to design environments to maximize functional performance by building in features that make it possible for people with disabilities to use the environment in the same way as nondisabled people. The concept of universal design can be applied to the environment, as well as to assistive devices, with the goal of reducing the impact of chronic illness and the declines associated with the aging process.

Assistive devices for older adults

Many assistive devices are available for older persons with disabilities. Abledata, a computerized database of over twenty thousand assistive devices, is an excellent resource for searching for information on assistive devices. Searches can be conducted by product type, impairment type, and company. Abledata is available on the World Wide Web at www.abledata.com/.

In discussing assistive devices for older people, this entry covers the following categories of assistive devices: devices for persons with mobility and/or motor impairments (including environmental control devices and seating or walking aids, and wheelchairs) and those with vision, hearing, cognitive, and communication limitations. Older adults often have more than one chronic condition and resultant impairments, and may benefit from devices in several categories. Multiple impairments may also require modification of devices. For many of these devices, an occupational therapist or physical therapist should assist with evaluating the person, determining the needs and the best devices, and training and follow-up on the use of the devices.

Devices for persons with mobility impairments. The first type of these devices to be considered is environmental control devices.

Environmental control devices. Some environmental control devices help people who have difficulty moving about. They are also helpful in certain situations for people with cognitive or visual impairments. An environmental control device can increase a person's ability to operate almost any device that runs on electricity—radios, computers, phones, lights, and security systems—and can be used in a home setting, an assisted living facility, or a nursing home. A handheld remote control for a television is an example of an environmental control device that is widely used. However, the remote controls typically sold with television sets are not designed with the needs of older persons in mind. Though they offer many features, the buttons are typically small and the symbols are difficult for many older adults to read. However, there are several universal remote control devices that offer larger buttons and strong color contrast between the symbols on the buttons and the background—a good example of universal design. Figure 1 provides an example of a universal remote control that has useful features for older people.

A study of older adults living in nursing homes compared two groups, one of which was given handheld environmental control devices connected to their radio and the other was not. Participants in both groups had radios, but the group with the environmental control devices used their radios significantly more than the group who relied on nursing home staff, or themselves, to operate their radios (Mann). This study used the simple X-10 type of handheld en-

vironmental control devices, available for under $35 at most consumer electronics stores. This study illustrates how designing the environment with the right tools results in more independent interaction with the environment.

Other examples of low-cost environmental control devices include (1) a touch-lamp device that allows a person to turn a lamp on or off simply by touching any metal part on the lamp; (2) voice-activated wall switches that simply require the person to say "on" or "off" rather than physically manipulate the switch; (3) movement detection switches that will turn lights on or off by sensing movement (or lack of movement) in the room. For a person who has difficulty getting up to turn lights on or off, these devices can make the task much easier.

In choosing an environmental control device there are many considerations, but simplicity of operation is perhaps the most important. The examples cited above are all relatively easy to install and to use. Reliability and durability are also important considerations. Are the features of the device appropriate for the intended user? Some environmental control devices require training in their use, especially those that are integrated into a computer system. The amount of training required to ensure that the user will operate it successfully is another important consideration.

Mobility devices. About 6 percent of noninstitutionalized people over sixty-five years old have difficulty walking, and almost 8 percent have difficulty "getting outside," according to the National Health Interview Survey (Prohaska, et al.). Canes, crutches, and walkers are examples of mobility devices that are used to assist with walking and getting outside by providing support and balance. Mobility devices are used by more people than any other category of assistive device. The cane is one of the oldest assistive devices and is second only to eyeglasses in popularity and numbers used. People who experience some loss of balance may decide on their own to purchase a cane. For those with more serious mobility impairments, a variety of canes and walkers are available to make walking easier and safer. Some of the newer walker designs come with a built-in seat, which allows the person to sit and rest when tired. Figure 2 illustrates a walker that has both a seat and a basket to carry items. Usually when people go from one place to another, they are carrying something. If they have to use both hands to grasp a walker, a basket or bag or tray is needed to carry items.

Though canes and walkers are widely used, many people have difficulty using them. Almost half of the identified problems relate to difficulty and/or risk with the use of the cane. A primary physician, often through a referral to a physical therapist, can play an important role in identifying problems people are having with walking and using the cane and walker For those who might benefit from a cane or walker, a careful evaluation should be performed, in the setting where the person will most frequently use the device (Mann, et al.).

The wheelchair is another category of assistive devices that can provide independent mobility and make assisted mobility possible. Advances in wheelchair design have led to lighter, more comfortable products. There are many considerations in selecting an appropriate wheelchair, including type of cushions, armrests, wheels, tires, hand rims, and power. It is important to have a trained professional, typically a physical or occupational therapist, involved in evaluating and recommending the most appropriate wheelchair. Therapists also make recommendations for wheelchair accessories, which include devices for transferring into and out of the wheelchair, trays, safety belts, clothing guards, and bags and pockets. Several references provide detailed information on wheelchairs (Mann and Lane; AARP).

Reachers. Reachers are assistive devices that extend a person's reach and enable grasping and movement of objects at a short distance—but a distance longer than would be possible without the device. Reachers are inexpensive and very useful for many older adults with disabilities. They can be helpful for people with lower back problems, arthritis, and heart conditions. People who use wheelchairs find that a reacher can make it possible to pick up things they could not access while in the wheelchair. With a reacher people do not need to bend over or stretch up as much, which can reduce the possibility of causing further physical impairment. Unfortunately, many older people practice the unsafe procedure of standing on a chair or stool to reach into high cabinets or other places; reachers can help eliminate the need to do this, and thus reduce the potential for a fall. In a study of older people with disabilities who were living at home, 20 percent of participants owned and used a reacher, and almost 10 percent considered their reacher their most important assistive device. Another study of reachers determined the tasks for which

older persons used reachers, and tested performance of these tasks using three reachers selected for their potential to meet the needs of older persons with disabilities most satisfactorily. The criteria for evaluating reachers were developed by older persons who used reachers, and included adjustable length, one-hand use, lifetime guarantee, lock system for grip, forearm support, light weight, and lever-action trigger. The Winchester Reacher was rated highest by consumers who tested three reachers that best met the consumer criteria (Chen, et al.).

Reachers can be purchased from durable medical suppliers (listed in the Yellow Pages under "Medical Equipment and Supplies"), catalogs of special products, and, more recently, in some department stores. In hospital or rehabilitation programs, occupational therapists often recommend reachers for elders.

Phones. More and more is being said about universal access to the Internet. It is easy to forget how relatively recently another important communication device became available. Phones are in virtually every home and office in America, but it has been only a century or so that they have been available at all, and now the phone is considered a necessity for work and leisure. For older people with disabilities, phones provide opportunities for talking to other people when it is difficult to get out of the home. More than 30 percent of people over sixty-five years old live alone, and over 50 percent of people over age seventy-five live alone. For elders with disabilities the phone also represents a safety device, a tool for calling for help if they have fallen, if they are ill, or if someone is trying to intrude into their home.

There is a wide range of special features available on phones today that assist elders with sensory, physical, or cognitive impairments. Many people with disabilities are easily able to use phones with such features as large buttons, single-button dialing, and, more recently, voice-activated operation. Phones are a good example of a device available in the larger marketplace that can help people with disabilities (as opposed to many assistive devices that are targeted at a much smaller segment of the population). Having a larger market results in lower prices. Most of the special phone features that can be helpful for a person with a disability can be found on phones sold in electronics and department stores.

Assistive devices for the visually impaired. Vision declines with age, and many elders have significant vision impairment. In fact, one out of five elderly persons has difficulty reading as a result of vision impairment. One out of twenty people over sixty-four years of age cannot see words or letters on a page (U.S. Bureau of the Census). Vision loss can result from a number of conditions, such as diabetic retinopathy, cataracts, and macular degeneration. Vision loss is also related to a decrease in mobility: people with severe vision loss tend to get out of their homes less than those without vision loss (Long).

Many people with vision loss use eyeglasses. In fact, eyeglasses are the most common assistive device, and are typically provided by an optometrist. For people who require other vision devices or devices that provide stronger magnification, occupational therapists often participate in providing assistive devices. In addition to assistive devices, there are some general rules that should be followed when with a visually impaired person:

1. In speaking to a person with a visual impairment, don't talk more loudly than usual unless the person also has a hearing impairment. Be sure to tell the person who you are. Tell the person when you are leaving.
2. Ask the person if assistance is needed; do not wait to be asked.
3. When guiding a person with a severe vision loss, allow the person to hold your arm and follow a few steps behind.
4. When assisting with setting up activities, provide larger images when possible. For example, you can set the enlargement feature on a photocopy machine to increase the size of print or pictures.
5. Position the person close to the objects involved in the task.
6. Increase the amount and/or intensity of light, but at the same time reduce glare.
7. Provide contrasting colors, for example, dark objects on a light surface. This may require placing a cloth on the table for activities.

There are many low-cost, simple assistive devices for people with vision impairments: magnifying glasses, pens that write with a bold line, and writing guides. Bookstores and libraries carry materials in large print. Checks can be printed with large characters, and games are available with enlarged playing boards. As discussed above, stores carry phones with large buttons, large numbers, and backlit displays. Thermometers, clocks, watches, and blood sugar monitors are all available with either large-print or voice output features.

Since the 1980s, computer and video-based technology have made it possible to develop a number of special products to assist people with visual impairments. The features offered by these devices make them very appropriate for older adults. Stand-alone print enlargement systems increase the size of any written material or picture. The systems include a monitor (usually fourteen to nineteen inches) and a viewing table where the book or other material is placed. Some viewing tables are automated and can be controlled with a foot pedal. For older adults with visual impairments, a print enlargement system often makes it possible to read newspapers and books. In fact, a study found that reading was one of the two activities that visually impaired elders most missed doing (Mann, et al.).

Braille provides a way for people who are blind to read print on paper. Software is available that, together with a Braille printer, permits Braille printing of text produced on a computer with a word processor. Refreshable Braille displays are available on a device called the Navigator. Available in twenty- or forty-character-long strings, tiny pins move up and down to produce the Braille characters, representing a portion of the computer screen. While a smaller percentage of visually impaired persons is now learning Braille, a significant portion of older adults who have been blind since their youth are benefiting from these computer-based Braille output devices.

Voice output with a computer allows a person to write into a word processor, spreadsheet, or database file and then check the accuracy and content of the file. Existing files and E-mail messages can be spoken by the computer for the visually impaired person. Together with a scanner, which takes text that is already printed and converts it into a computer file, printed material becomes available to the person with a visual impairment. For elders with severe vision loss, a talking computer may make it possible to continue work, leisure reading, and carrying out household tasks that require writing and reading.

Devices for persons with hearing impairments. Like vision, hearing declines with age. Many older people have difficulty hearing, and background noise becomes more of a problem as people age. About one-third of people age sixty-five or older have some hearing impairment and the figure increases to almost half in persons over age eighty-five (Hotchkiss). While many older adults accept hearing loss as a normal part of aging and do nothing about it, there are assistive devices that can improve hearing for some people.

Tinnitus is a significant hearing problem for over 90 percent of persons over age sixty-four (U.S. Public Health Service). With tinnitus people experience a ringing sound in their ears. There is no cure, but "maskers" are sometimes used to provide a more acceptable sound than that produced by the tinnitus. Hearing aids are used to offset the effect of the hearing loss that often accompanies tinnitus. Surgery is sometimes employed to reduce tinnitus, as are drugs, relaxation techniques, and biofeedback.

Hearing aids. The most common assistive device for hearing loss is the hearing aid, typically prescribed by an audiologist. Many older people have difficulty using hearing aids due to vision impairment and loss of dexterity in the fingers: they have difficulty replacing batteries, positioning the device, or adjusting the controls. Of all assistive devices, hearing aids have the highest rate of dissatisfaction among people who own them. This is due in part to the fact that many people get their hearing aids without an audiological assessment.

Assistive listening devices. When hearing aids do not provide adequate sound amplification, *assistive listening devices* (ALDs) may be used. Some people use both a hearing aid and an ALD, depending on the situation they are in. The components of an ALD include a microphone for the person(s) speaking, an amplifier to capture and "enlarge" the sounds, and, for the person with the hearing loss, a headset. ALD systems are hardwired or use either FM radio waves or infrared signals. Churches and theaters are installing ALD systems, usually FM and infrared systems. The hardwired system is more often used in a home.

Telecommunication devices for the deaf (TDDs). For people who are deaf, TDDs are designed to provide the means to use the telephone. They are actually small microprocessor-based devices that have a screen, keyboard, and modem. With a TDD at both ends of a telephone line, messages can be typed in and read at each end. Relay services are available in every state so that a person with a hearing impairment can type in a message to an operator, who in turn provides the final receiver with the spoken message. TDDs are now available in public places such as airports.

Amplification and other signaling devices. There are a number of assistive devices that provide amplified sound. Electronics and phone stores carry phones that offer amplified sound and devices that can be added to an existing phone in order to provide amplification. Closed-captioned television provides text at the bottom of the screen on television sets equipped with a special decoding device. All new televisions have this feature installed. Other devices include smoke detectors that provide a visual alert, such as a flashing light. A number of these low-cost devices can make it possible for older adults with hearing loss to continue their involvement in important life roles.

Devices for persons with cognitive impairments. Persons with cognitive impairments can benefit from devices that assist with writing and retaining information, and performing simple household chores.

Note writing and electronic notebooks. Memory loss can occur as a result of a number of diseases associated with aging, including Alzheimer's disease. One low-tech solution to memory impairment is to write reminder notes on paper and post them in appropriate places. An alternative, high-tech solution is to use a small electronic notebook. Many digital wristwatches now offer features such as alarms that can be used as reminders for taking medications.

Other devices. Other helpful devices include automatic turn-off switches for stove burners, automatic timers for lights, movement-sensitive light switches that turn lamps on when a person enters a room, and security systems that sound an alarm when someone attempts to open a secured door.

Summary

Assistive devices can help older people remain independent. Many of these devices are simple to use and/or install, and can be purchased at neighborhood stores. Others, such as mobility and hearing aids, require professional assistance in evaluating the need, recommending the most appropriate device, and providing training and follow-up in their use.

WILLIAM C. MANN

See also HEARING; HOUSING; HOUSING AND TECHNOLOGY; HUMAN FACTORS; LONG-TERM CARE; TECHNOLOGY; VISION AND PERCEPTION; WALKING AIDS; WHEELCHAIRS.

BIBLIOGRAPHY

American Association of Retired Persons. *Product Report. Wheelchairs.* Washington, D.C.: AARP, 1990.

CHEN, L.-K. P.; MANN, W. C.; TOMITA, M.; and BURFORD, T.. "An Evaluation of Reachers for Use by Frail Elders." *Assistive Technology* 10, no. 2 (1998): 113–125.

HOTCHKISS, D. *The Hearing Impaired Elderly Population: Estimation, Projection, and Assessment.* Monograph Series A, no. 1. Washington, D.C.: Gallaudet Research Institute, 1989.

LONG, R. G. *Effects of Age and Visual Loss on Independent Outdoor Mobility.* Rehabilitation R & D Progress Report. Baltimore: Department of Veterans Affairs, 1989.

MANN, W.; HURREN, D.; KARUZA, J.; and BENTLEY, D. "Needs of Home-Based Older Visually Impaired Persons for Assistive Devices." *Journal of Visual-Impairment and Blindness* 87, no. 4 (1993): 106–110.

MANN, W. C. "Use of Environmental Control Devices by Elderly Nursing Home Patients." *Assistive Technology* 3, no. 4 (1992).

MANN, W. C.; GRANGER, C.; HURREN, D.; TOMITA, M.; and CHARVAT, B. "An Analysis of Problems with Canes Encountered by Elderly Persons." *Physical & Occupational Therapy in Geriatrics* 13, no. 1/2 (1995): 25–49.

MANN, W. C., and LANE, J. P. *Assistive Technology for Persons with Disabilities: The Role of Occupational Therapy.* Rockville, Md.: American Occupational Therapy Association, 1991.

PROHASKA, T.; MERMELSTEIN, R.; MILLER, B.; and JACK, S. "Functional Status and Living Arrangements." In *Vital and Health Statistics, Health Data on Older Americans.* Hyattsville, Md.: U.S. Department of Health and Human Services, 1992.

U.S. Bureau of the Census. *Disability, Functional Limitation, and Health Insurance Coverage: 1984/85.* Current Population Reports, series p-70, no. 8. Washington, D.C.: U.S. Government Printing Office, 1986.

U.S. Public Health Service. *Prevalence of Selected Chronic Conditions, United States, 1983–1985.* Advance Data from Vital and Health Statistics, no. 155. DHHS publication no. (PHS) 88-1250. Hyattsville, Md.: Public Health Services, 1988.

HOME CARE AND HOME SERVICES

Services delivered in the homes of older adults have become an increasingly popular form of care in recent years. Such services allow older persons to remain in the familiar surroundings of their homes and neighborhoods, thus avoiding the trauma that can be associated with relocation and entry into a nursing home or related facility. In-home services, by definition, are based in the community and represent a desirable alternative in many cases to the health and social services provided to incapacitated older adults in institutional settings such as nursing homes, homes for the aged, and other long-term care facilities. Not only are such services usually preferred by older individuals, they can also be provided, in many cases, more cheaply than would be the case in institutional settings. Home care services can also provide important temporary respite for family members and others providing care to incapacitated older persons.

Home care origins

The first documented home care program, the Boston Dispensary, was created in 1796. Boston University's Home Medical Service, founded in 1885, is considered to have been the first hospital-based home care program. Beginning in the 1920s, interest in home care was sparked by those directing attention to the treatment of the increasing number of chronically ill patients. While it was agreed that such patients were not best served in acute care hospitals, disagreement persisted through the 1930s and 1940s as to whether they were better served in institutional settings or in their homes.

More recently, the financial benefits accruing to home care have been emphasized. In the 1970s and early 1980s, proponents of home care argued that home-delivered services were a legitimate substitute for costly hospitalization and increased public money being spent on nursing home care. At the same time, expanded coverage of home care services was legislated through the Medicare and Medicaid systems, the primary government programs supporting this category of service. These regulatory changes, especially those under the federal Omnibus Budget Reconciliation Act of 1980 (OBRA), fueled the expanded use of home health care services. Hospice care for the terminally ill, also delivered in the home, was included in Medicare for the first time in 1982.

Throughout the 1980s, the number of proprietary or for-profit providers of home care grew at a particularly rapid pace because Medicare amendments under OBRA allowed such providers to be Medicare certified. It should be noted that although home care has grown considerably since 1980, it continues to represent a small proportion of spending for all personal health care costs (less that 10 percent of Medicare and Medicaid benefit expenditures are for home care services). The third most common source of payment for home care services is out-of-pocket payments by consumers themselves (Kaye, 1995, 1992).

The growth of home care

It is estimated that anywhere from 14 to 18 percent, or five to six million older adults living in the community could benefit from home care services. These numbers reflect those persons who are functionally impaired to varying degrees (that is, unable to perform one or more of their major activities of daily living such as cooking, shopping, cleaning, and dressing). Some of these older adults are totally confined to their homes and even their beds. It has been argued that additional numbers of older persons who now reside in nursing homes and similar such facilities could also be better served in their homes were in-home services more widely available.

Reflecting the current popularity of home care, the number of organizations providing in-home services to incapacitated persons has increased significantly in recent years. The home care service industry has grown from only eleven hundred such programs in 1965 to more than twenty thousand currently (National Association for Home Care, "Basic Statistics," March 2000). While a substantial proportion of patients served by home care programs are older adults, women in particular, it is important to remember that home care services are also provided to a wide variety of individuals in need of help, including those with chronic health conditions, terminal and acute illness, and those with permanent disabilities. Home care services are also provided by a broad array of organizations including hospitals, visiting nurse associations, hospices, Area Agencies on Aging, senior citizen centers, and even some nursing homes that have moved toward diversifying the services they offer older adults in the community. The fastest growing segments of home care have been hospital-based programs and those that operate for a profit and are unaffiliated with other agencies or organizations. Freestanding for-profit agencies comprise 41 percent of Medicare-certified home care programs, followed by hospital-based agencies, which represent 30 percent (National Association for Home Care, "Basic Statistics").

It should be noted that since 1997 there has actually been a decline in the number of Medicare-certified home health agencies due, at least in part, to changes in home health reimbursement regulations enacted as part of the Balanced Budget Act of 1997. Approximately 2,500 home care agencies ceased to operate between 1997 and 2000, and Medicare home care expenditures actually declined by 4 percent in 1998, making it the only segment of health care to experience a decline during that period (National Association for Home Care, "Report Confirms Medicare Cuts"). More restrictive Medicare reimbursement requirements continue to challenge the capacity of some programs to operate on sound financial footing. At the same time, home care personnel continue to be in short supply, especially home care aides, who occupy positions of relatively low status within the human services sector, as reflected by their limited career advancement opportunities and low salaries.

Changing face of home care services

A steadily expanding array of services are now available to older individuals that experience a health or long-term disability and wish to be cared for at home. Accompanying our improved ability to miniaturize and make portable a variety of medical and communications technologies has been the continuous expansion in the range of high-tech medical care that can be provided in the home (Kaye and Davitt). Presently available home environmental and medical devices include: personal emergency response and auto-dialing and alarm systems signaling the need for help; in-home computers for self-instruction on taking medications and operating medical equipment; telehealth and telemedicine systems that allow patient health monitoring and assessment from remote locations; intravenous therapy equipment, including artificial nutrition and hydration; mechanical ventilation; and even robots able to assist the patient in performing certain basic activities of daily living.

There are several types of organizations providing home care services to the aged, some of which offer one type of service exclusively while others provide a variety of integrated services. Most home care services are available twenty-four hours a day, seven days a week throughout the year. The designation *home health agency* usually refers to a Medicare-certified service provider that complies with governmental requirements and is highly regulated. Such an organization may focus on the provision of nursing services while others may offer a broader range of care including physical and occupational therapy, social work, housekeeping, and durable medical equipment.

There are numerous home care services that offer exclusively homemakers and home health aides. Although not equipped to provide nursing services, the home health aides offer hands-on care such as patient bathing and dressing in addition to bearing responsibility for household tasks, including meal preparation and light housekeeping. Housekeeper services exclude hands-on care. Both home health aides and housekeepers serve as companions for their patients.

Hospice care, which may be offered as an inpatient service or in the home, is designed to provide integral medical, psychosocial, and spiritual care to the terminally ill as well as offer support to their families. It is typically available to persons with a life expectancy of no more than six months. Providers of hospice care in the home furnish the necessary services, equipment, and medications to allow the patient to die in his or her own home, in the company of loved ones, and without unnecessary pain. Care is palliative, alleviating pain without curing. Hospice services are typically Medicare certified.

In addition to home health care and hospice agencies, registries, specialized employment agencies, and private-duty agencies are sources for hiring home care workers, particularly nurses and aides. Unlike their Medicare-certified counterparts, they are not usually regulated or li-

censed by a government body and they do assess a fee for placement of staff. All types of home care personnel—nurses, aides, therapists, social workers, companions, and others—may be privately employed by individuals without a mediating organization. These home care workers, however, are not regulated by an outside party unless they receive government funding.

As a result of the trend toward providing in-home services to the more infirm, durable medical equipment suppliers, pharmaceutical companies, and infusion therapy companies have become regular features of the home care landscape. Providers of durable medical equipment offer a variety of products, including respirators, wheelchairs, catheters, and walkers, and typically provide delivery and set up. Some pharmaceutical, respiratory therapy, and infusion therapy companies provide nursing staff as well to administer medications and train patients in proper self-management techniques for the medical equipment provided.

Not only are home care services available in a number of forms, they are also provided by an array of professionals and paraprofessionals as described below.

- Companions, as their name would suggest, provide companionship to home care patients who are socially isolated and, in doing so, also increase the patient's safety by visiting on a regular basis.
- Dieticians who are trained in the nutritional needs of patient populations offer dietary assessments and counseling.
- Home health aides assist patients who cannot manage their activities of daily living alone. They may provide help with toileting, dressing, meal preparation, and transferring as well as offer companionship to the isolated.
- Housekeepers or homemakers offer chore services such as light housekeeping, laundering, and shopping. Unlike home health aides, they do not provide hands-on patient care.
- Occupational therapists (OTs) help patients with their daily living activities by providing skills, specialized adaptive equipment, and retraining. They address tasks such as bathing, meal preparation, dressing, and household maintenance.
- Physical therapists (PTs) work with patients to relieve pain or restore mobility through the use of exercise, massage, and specialized equipment.

- Physicians, as independent professionals, may make visits to the home to diagnose and treat patients or they may provide these services as a member of a home care service interdisciplinary team. Physicians may also oversee patients' care plans and prescribe medications.
- Registered nurses (RNs) and licensed practical nurses (LPNs) provide skilled services such as wound care, injections, and intravenous therapy that cannot be provided by paraprofessional and nonprofessional staff.
- Social workers, who often serve as case managers in home care, tend to the emotional and social well-being of patients by providing counseling services and establishing relationships between patients and other types of needed service providers.
- Speech therapists address the needs of patients with communication disorders that hinder their ability to speak. They are also qualified to provide assistance with muscle control in and around the mouth area that may affect breathing and swallowing.
- Volunteers can play a critical role by offering a variety of services including friendly visiting, transportation service, meal delivery, and running errands.

Paying for home care services

Home care services may be paid for out-of-pocket, meaning paid privately by the recipient of service or family members, or by third parties (e.g., insurance companies). In many cases, home care services are covered by both a third party and the patient, with the patient covering the difference between the amount reimbursed and the actual cost of care. According to the Health Care Financing Administration (HCFA), in 1997 out-of-pocket expenditures represented approximately 22 percent of all home care payments. Among third-party payers, Medicare was the primary single source of home care payments, covering about 40 percent, followed by Medicaid at almost 15 percent and private insurance at approximately 11 percent (National Association for Home Care, "Basic Statistics"). HCFA projects that the portion paid by Medicaid will increase and Medicare's share will decrease through the year 2008.

Medicare, a federal program providing benefits to most Americans sixty-five years of age and older, will cover home care services for home-bound persons with medical conditions requiring skilled nursing or therapy services. To qualify for reimbursement, the patient must be under the care of a physician, who authorizes and periodically reviews the patient's plan of care. The patient must receive service from a Medicare-certified home health agency. In addition to skilled nursing care, Medicare may provide coverage for home health aide services, physical therapy, occupational therapy, speech therapy, medical social work, and medical equipment and supplies. Medicare coverage is also available for hospice care for the terminally ill.

Medicaid, a program for low-income individuals, is a joint federal-state medical assistance program. Because it is administered by individual states, there are differences in eligibility requirements and covered services from state to state. All states, however, are mandated by federal Medicaid guidelines to cover part-time nursing, home health aide services, and medical equipment and supplies. States may optionally provide payment for a variety of therapies and medical social work services. The majority of states also provide Medicaid-covered hospice care.

Various types of private insurance policies provide home care benefits, each with its own eligibility requirements and array of covered services. Commercial health insurance companies often provide some coverage for short-term acute care in the home, but availability of reimbursement for long-term home care is less common. Such policies frequently have cost-sharing provisions requiring that the insured pay some part of the cost of home care services.

Long-term care insurance, which has grown in popularity in recent years, varies greatly from company to company. While initially intended to provide benefits for extended nursing home care, such policies now routinely offer benefits for a variety of in-home services.

Medigap insurance, as the name implies, is designed to bridge many of the gaps in Medicare coverage. Medigap policies vary with regard to eligibility and benefits, but do often provide coverage for short-term in-home recovery care. Medigap insurance policies are typically not designed for long-term care.

Veterans in need of in-home care due to a service-related disability or condition are eligible for home health care benefits through the Veterans Administration (VA). These home care services must be provided by one of the VA's own home care programs.

Other smaller sources of home care payments include the Older Americans Act which provides federal funding to state and local programs serving frail and disabled older adults; federal social services block grants to states; managed care organizations; Civilian Health and Medical Program of the Uniformed Services (CHAMPUS); and workers' compensation.

Questions for consumers to ask

Selecting an agency that will provide you with home care services is an important and often difficult decision. Generally speaking, the agency must have the necessary experience in providing the kind of care that is needed and be able to provide it effectively. The agency must be able to demonstrate that it has properly trained and supervised staff to care for the patient. Talking to trusted relatives, friends, and professionals (such as one's doctor) about the agency can help with decision-making. The National Association for Home Care (1996) offers the following checklist of questions to ask when determining which home care provider to use.

- How long has this provider been serving the community?
- Does this provider supply literature explaining its services, eligibility requirements, fees, and funding sources? Many providers furnish patients with a detailed "Patient Bill of Rights" that outlines the rights and responsibilities of the providers, patients, and caregivers alike. An annual report and other educational materials also can furnish helpful information about the provider.
- How does this provider select and train its employees? Does it protect its workers with written personnel policies, benefits packages, and malpractice insurance?
- Are nurses or therapists required to evaluate the patient's home care needs? If so, what does this entail? Do they consult the patient's physicians and family members?
- Does this provider include the patient and his or her family members in developing the plan of care? Are they involved in making care plan changes?
- Is the patient's treatment course documented, detailing the specific tasks to be carried out by each professional caregiver? Does the patient and his or her family receive a copy of this plan, and do the caregivers update it as changes occur? Does this provider take time to educate family members on the care being administered to the patient?
- Does this provider assign supervisors to oversee the quality of care patients are receiving in their homes? If so, how often do these individuals make visits? Who can the patient and his or her family members call with questions or complaints? How does the agency follow up on and resolve problems?
- What are the financial procedures of this provider? Does the provider furnish written statements explaining all of the costs and payment plan options associated with home care?
- What procedures does this provider have in place to handle emergencies? Are its caregivers available twenty-four hours a day, seven days a week?
- How does this provider ensure patient confidentiality?

The following checklist of questions recommended by the National Association for Home Care are to be asked of those individuals and organizations whose names were given as references by the home care provider.

- Do you frequently refer clients to this provider?
- Do you have a contractual relationship with this provider? If so, do you require the provider to meet special standards for quality care?
- What sort of feedback have you gotten from patients receiving care from this provider, either on an informal basis or through a formal satisfaction survey?
- Do you know of any clients this provider has treated whose cases are similar to mine or my loved one's? If so, can you put me in touch with these individuals?

Particularly in the case of high-tech home care that necessitates the importation of various technical devices and services into the home, it may be difficult to determine whether this type of arrangement is appropriate for a particular patient or home setting. The decision will be based on factors including: the adequacy of space, electrical capacity, and power backup for the required medical equipment; the ability of the patient or his or her designee to operate and maintain the devices in the absence of trained personnel; the availability of third-party coverage or adequate private funds to cover associated expenses; and an assessment of all viable alternatives. Individuals respond differently to the prospect of turning a home into a high-tech hospital room, making the choice of doing so largely a personal one (Kaye and Davitt).

Patient rights

Home care patients, like hospital patients, have certain rights and protections that must be documented in a written patient bill of rights and provided by the agency to all recipients of service. The federal government requires that all home care patients be informed of their rights, which are also enforced by the law.

LENARD W. KAYE

See also HOME HEALTH THERAPIES; HOSPICE; LONG-TERM CARE; MEDICAID; MEDICARE; MEDIGAP; PERSONAL CARE.

BIBLIOGRAPHY

KAYE, L. W. *Home Health Care.* Newbury Park, Calif.: Sage Publications, 1992.
KAYE, L. W., ed. *New Developments in Home Care Services for the Elderly: Innovations in Policy, Program, and Practice.* New York: The Haworth Press, Inc., 1995.
KAYE, L. W., and DAVITT, JOAN K. *Current Practices in High-Tech Home Care.* New York: Springer Publishing Company, 1999.
National Association for Home Care. *Basic Statistics About Home Care.* News release. Washington, D.C.: 2000.
National Association for Home Care. *How to Choose a Home Care Provider.* News release. Washington, D.C.: 1996.
National Association for Home Care. *Report Confirms Medicare Cuts Hurting Frailest Home Care Patients.* News release. Washington, D.C.: 2000.

HOME HEALTH THERAPIES

As health care costs continue to increase and the trend toward consumerism in health care accelerates, older adults are seeking more information about the health care options available to them. In many cases they are also thinking about how they will handle their future long-term care needs. Though home health care can address many short-term and long-term health problems, it is often overlooked or not fully understood.

Benefits of home care

Home health care or "home care" offers many advantages to patients, particularly older adults. For the chronically ill and disabled, home care allows the patient to live at home—a home that is usually familiar and comfortable. Studies show that patients recuperating from an acute illness or accident recover faster in a home environment. At home, family and friends can play a vital role in the person's recovery process and mental well-being. What is more, home care gives an older adult a sense of independence by offering an important measure of control over day-to-day events.

Home care improves the quality of care provided and increases patient satisfaction. When it is available, patients often have shorter stays in inpatient settings. Home care ensures a safe discharge to the home while providing continuity of care.

The comparably low cost of home care is another benefit. In 1998, the average Medicare cost for a home visit from a professional nurse was $93, which makes it an economical alternative compared to inpatient hospitalizations and nursing home stays. Combined with good outcomes and high quality, the cost of home care can make it a practical and favored option for many people.

Limits of home care

While twenty-first century technology allows many services to be performed at home that were impossible even a few years ago, there are limits to what home care can do. In some cases a person is simply too ill or has needs that are too complex to be cared for safely in a private home. In other cases a person cannot be cared for at home because the home environment is unsafe (e.g., no one in the home can help care for the patient). The need for informal caregiver support as a supplement to home care is especially important for people with cognitive impairments.

There is also a question of paying for care. Under many insurance plans home care coverage is limited or does not exist. If a person cannot afford to pay for home care, the only option may be to return to a hospital or nursing home where services are covered by insurance. Many areas of the country are also experiencing a shortage of home care providers (especially nurses and home health aides), which can prevent home care from being a feasible alternative.

Home health therapies

Home care includes a wide range of therapies that can be curative, palliative, or restorative. These therapies are delivered in a person's residence, whether it is a private or a group home (e.g., an assisted living facility or other type of senior housing). Home health therapies include medical, nursing, social, and rehabilitative treatments. These therapies are classified as "skilled needs" and must be provided by a health care professional. Registered nurses (RNs) and licensed practitioner nurses (LPNs) provide skilled nursing care and home infusion care. RNs also serve as case managers, perform the home care assessment on the first home visit (or in the hospital or nursing facility before discharge), and create and manage the care plan. Physical therapists, occupational therapists, and speech pathologists all provide rehabilitation therapy. Social workers help patients to deal with social and emotional issues, such as living arrangements, family problems, and financial matters.

In addition to skilled needs some people need help with the essential activities of daily living (ADLs)—bathing, dressing, getting around inside, toileting, transferring (e.g., from bed to chair), and eating. People also have difficulties with activities that are less basic than ADLs. These instrumental activities of daily living (IADLs) include paying the bills, shopping, cleaning, and doing laundry. Both home health aides and personal care attendants provide personal care (assistance with ADLs) and homemaker services (assistance with IADLs). In addition, home health aides are trained paraprofessionals who change dressings, help with medications, and provide other services that support skilled care.

The major services involved in each of the therapies are outlined in Table 1.

Home care patients

Anyone requiring treatment, assessment, or education is a candidate for home care. Home care patients range from premature babies to people over one hundred years old. Most people receiving home care fall into one of the following categories:

- People who are recuperating from an acute illness
- The chronically ill
- The physically/mentally disabled
- People diagnosed with a terminal illness.

Various home care programs are available, depending on a person's needs. Most home care patients are in "post-acute care" programs, in which they receive services for a limited period of time (e.g., after a hospital stay). Some agencies may have special acute care programs for adults, children, or maternal/child health.

There are also long-term care (LTC) programs, many of which are government-sponsored (often through Medicaid), and their availability varies by location. Examples of LTC programs include the Program for All-inclusive Care for the Elderly (PACE) programs, and long-term home health care programs (also known as "nursing homes without walls"), and managed long term care programs.

The last major type of home care program is hospice. Hospice programs provide palliative care and counseling to patients who are terminally ill, as well as counseling and bereavement services to family members. Because of the nature of the program, care is provided for a limited period of time (from a few weeks to one year).

Home care providers

The RNs, LPNs, therapists, social workers, home health aides, and personal care attendants who provide home health services work for a variety of organizations that are authorized to provide home care. The main differences between the types of home care providers are the specific services/programs offered, the types of healthcare workers who provide them, and the types of insurance coverage accepted.

Certified home health agencies (CHHAs) are certified by Medicare to provide nursing and home health aide services, and provide or arrange for other services, such as physical therapy, home infusion, and social work. Services are generally paid for by Medicare or Medicaid, and are provided for a limited period of time. Long-

Table 1

Nursing
- Home care/health status assessments
- Injections
- Wound care
- Instruction about disease treatment/prevention
- Coordination of care through case management services
- Blood tests
- Oxygen administration

Social Work
- Evaluation of social and emotional factors
- Counseling
- Assistance with entitlements

Personal Care
- Assistance with ADLs

Homemaker Services
- Assistance with IADLs

Paraprofessional Services
- Services such as dressing changes and other activities that support skilled needs, under the supervision of an RN or physical therapist

SOURCE: Author

Rehab

Physical (PT)
- Restoration of mobility/strength
- Restoration of injured/atrophied muscles
- Teaching transfer and walking techniques

Occupational (OC)
- Improving/restoring function in ADLs
- Cognitive retraining

Speech Language Pathology
- Developing/restoring speech (as a result of trauma, surgery, or stroke)
- Retraining in breathing, swallowing, muscle control

Home Infusion
- Intravenous drug therapies (e.g., chemotherapy)
- Pain management
- Other drug treatment modalities

term home health care programs are similar to CHHAs, except that they provide long-term care (with no specific limitations on the duration of treatment). Licensed home health agencies (LHHAs) are licensed by the state to provide nursing, home health, and personal attendant services, but are not certified to provide Medicare- or Medicaid-financed home care. LHHA services are available only to patients who pay privately or have private insurance.

Other sources of home care include social welfare agencies, community organizations, and adult day care centers, as well as nurse registries and staffing and private duty agencies.

Paying for care

There are a number of sources for paying for home care, depending on the insurance coverage available, the primary diagnosis, and the type of services needed. In 1997 over $32 billion was spent on home care in the United States. Table 2 shows the breakout by payer.

The types of services that are covered vary by payer, and approval of all services depends on the needs of the patient. Though coverage varies, common payment requirements are that the patient is under a physician's care, and that the services ordered are reasonable and necessary to

treat the patient's condition. In many cases the patient must also be homebound.

Please note that the information in this article is a general guide to what different types of insurance cover, and should be used for reference purposes only. Because of the potential for financial liability, both a physician and the insurance provider should be consulted before a person receives home care.

Medicare is a national health insurance program designed primarily for people age sixty-five and over. Limited home care coverage is available under Medicare Part A. Medicare provides home care only if there is a need for intermittent skilled nursing care or physical, speech, or occupational therapy. In addition a physician must certify that the patient is homebound. (Medicare's definition of "homebound" is that the condition of the patient is such that there is a normal inability to leave home and, consequently, that leaving home would require a considerable and taxing effort.) The patient has to be under the care of the physician who certifies that care in the home is necessary. All home care services must be provided through a CHHA. There is no copayment for home care services under Medicare, though any related durable medical equipment is subject to a 20 percent copayment. No Medicare coverage is available for people who require only personal care.

Table 2

National Home Care Expenditures, 1997

Out-of-pocket	22%
Private health insurance	11%
Other private	12%
Total private	**45%**
Medicare	40%
Medicaid	15%
Other public	<1%
Total public	**55%**

SOURCE: *National Health Expenditures Projections 1998–2008.* Health Care Financing Administration, Office of the Actuary.

Medicaid is a program, jointly funded by the federal and state (and in some cases local) governments, that provides comprehensive medical care coverage for people whose income and assets fall below a specific level. Each state administers its own Medicaid program, so eligibility requirements and the specific benefits vary by state. In some cases, Medicaid may provide a more generous home care benefit than Medicare. Coverage is often available for unskilled needs over longer periods of time.

Private health insurance, usually administered through employers, typically covers only relatively short periods of post-acute home care. Managed care organizations (e.g., HMOs) usually have strict precertification requirements for all nonemergency services, including home care. Many managed care plans require a copayment for each home care visit (e.g., $10 per visit) and limit the number of home care visits allowed in a plan year. Coverage is usually limited to a post-acute benefit focused on skilled nursing or rehabilitation therapies.

Since the 1990s, long-term care (LTC) insurance has become increasingly popular. Many LTC policies provide some compensation for home care within a specified period of time. The actual amount paid for each home care visit, the limit on the number of visits, and what triggers the LTC payments vary widely, depending on the policy. Therefore the LTC policy that is chosen determines the extent of the home care benefit (as well as how using that home care benefit affects the nursing home benefit).

Persons who are not covered by insurance or who need care in addition to what is covered by insurance, can pay for home care themselves. Home care costs vary by location and agency, so it is important to find out the cost of care beforehand. It may be helpful to compare the costs of different agencies and to check with the local department of health or aging to get a better understanding of home care prices.

Important questions

Someone who is a candidate for home care should have the following questions answered—by a doctor, a hospital, a home care agency, or a state or local health agency—before starting care.

1. What kind of agency is providing the care?

- Find out the full name of the agency and what type of agency it is (e.g., a CHHA or hospice).
- Ask if the agency is accredited (e.g., through the Joint Commission on Accreditation of Health Organizations (JCAHO) or Community Health Accreditation Program (CHAP)).
- Call the state licensing agency (usually the state Department of Health) to find out if there are any outstanding complaints against the agency.

2. Who will provide the care?

- Ask for the credentials and experience of the person(s) who will provide the care.
- If the patient has a rare or difficult-to-treat problem, find out if the health care provider has received specialized training.

3. Who is in charge?

- Find out who is responsible for coordinating care and how to contact them.
- Ask who the home health aide reports to.
- Find out what kind of backup system exists if the home care provider does not show up.
- Ask for phone numbers to call to (1) contact the case manager, (2) report a no-show or other urgent problem, (3) report a nonurgent problem, and (4) make a complaint.

4. What services will the patient receive?

- Ask the case manager for the care plan after the first assessment visit is made.

The plan of care should include the condition the patient is being treated for, the expected outcome when service ends, the type of therapies that will be received and from whom, the frequency of visits, and when the home care is expected to end.

- Be sure to ask the case manager or the doctor any questions about the plan of care.
- Ask the case manager to update the patient, the doctor, and the insurance company if the plan of care changes or is expected to change.

5. How much will the patient pay?

- Ask the insurance company if precertification or any other requirements must be met before beginning care.
- Ask the insurance company what the patient will be obligated to pay, based on the plan of care. Call the insurance company directly; benefit booklets, Web sites, and other sources may be out-of-date or may not be specific enough.
- Ask the agency about the option of paying out of pocket for extra care or for care after the insurance coverage runs out.
- Ask the agency if the patient is eligible to receive any charitable care dollars or is eligible for Medicaid or any special government programs or long-term care plans.

6. Is home care the best choice?

- Ask the case manager or doctor what can be done to get the most out of the home care experience.
- Ask the case manager or doctor what the alternatives to home care are.
- Find out what should be done when home care ends.

The future of home care

Home care will continue to be an integral part of the health care system in the future. In fact, its importance is expected to grow as a result of the aging population and the increasing number of frail older adults living at home. In 2000 there were approximately thirty-five million people age sixty-five or older in the United States.

The size of this group is expected to double to seventy million by 2030.

At the same time there is also an increasing number of people with chronic illnesses. In 1995 there were ninety-nine million people of all ages with some type of chronic disease. This number will increase to one hundred and forty-eight million by 2030. Almost one-third of the people in this group have a major limitation as a result of their chronic condition.

Finally, the continued emphasis on providing cost-effective health care options and the growth of consumer choice are working to move home care into a more prominent light.

CAROL RAPHAEL, MPA
JOANN AHRENS, MPA

See also HEALTH AND LONG-TERM CARE PROGRAM INTEGRATION; HOME CARE AND HOME SERVICES; LONG-TERM CARE.

BIBLIOGRAPHY

Health Care Financing Administration, Office of the Actuary. "Home Health Care Expenditures and Average Percent Change, by Source of Funds: Selected Calendar Years 1970–2008." www.hcfa.gov
Health Care Financing Administration, Office of the Actuary. "Home Health Care Expenditures, Percent Distribution and Per Capita Amounts by Source of Funds: Selected Calendar Years 1970–2008." www.hfca.gov
Health Care Financing Administration and the Office of Strategic Planning. *A Profile of Medicare Home Health*, August 1999, 80.
National Association for Home Care. "Basic Statistics About Home Care." www.nahc.org
RWJ Foundation. *Chronic Care in America: A 21st Century Challenge*. August 1996. (1995 data).
U.S. Bureau of the Census. "Projections of the Total Resident Population by 5-Year Age Groups, and Sex with Special Age Categories: Middle Series, 1999 to 2100." www.census.gov
Visiting Nurse Service of New York. *Finding Home Health Care for Seniors in New York*. 2000.

HOMELESSNESS

Prior to the current crisis (which began in 1980 when the number of homeless persons started to increase dramatically), definitions of *homelessness* included persons residing in substandard housing, such as single-room occupancy

A homeless elderly woman is assisted by a Salvation Army volunteer at one of that organization's many food centers throughout the United States. For many senior citizens who have lost their homes, such charity operations are their only means of obtaining food. (Visual Unlimited)

(SRO) hotels, cheap boarding houses, and skid row flophouses. More recently, however, the term has been used solely to describe the plight of persons sleeping in shelters or public spaces; that is, the "visible" or "literal" homeless. Many persons are at-risk for homelessness on account of their being doubled-up with other persons in one apartment, having excessive rent burdens, or having very low incomes—an estimated one in ten New Yorkers fall into these risk categories.

The literature has used ages 40, 45, 50, 55, 60, and 65 as markers of aging among homeless persons. Increasingly, however, there has been a consensus that the definition of *older homeless* should include those age 50 and over, because many homeless persons who are in this age group look and act ten to twenty years older.

Two reviews of surveys of homeless people, and a nationwide survey of soup kitchens and shelters, identified substantial homelessness among the older adults, although they produced a wide range of estimates (between 2.5 percent and 27.2 percent) as the result of heterodox methods and definitions of old age. Between 1980 and 2000 the proportion of older persons among the homeless declined, though their abso-

lute number grew. Moreover, the proportion of older homeless persons is expected to increase dramatically as baby boomers begin to turn fifty. Thus, with an anticipated growth of over 50 percent in the general population of those age fifty to sixty-four between 2000 and 2015, and a near doubling of those age fifty and over by 2030, it is likely that by 2030 the number of older homeless persons in the United States will grow from its 2000 level of between 60,000 and 400,000 to an estimated 120,000 to 800,000. (These large variations in numbers are due to different methods of enumeration.)

Risk factors for homelessness

Carl Cohen has proposed a model of homelessness in which various biographical and individual risk factors accumulate over a lifetime. Except in the case of extremely vulnerable individuals, homelessness is not likely to occur unless several of these factors coexist. In most instances, however, the ultimate determinants are the unavailability of low-cost housing and insufficient income to pay for housing. Finally, the length and patterns of homelessness reflect a person's ability to adapt to the street or shelter, along with individual and system factors that may prolong homelessness. The principal risk factors that have been found to increase vulnerability to homelessness among older individuals are described below.

Race. While the proportionate representation of Caucasians is higher among older than younger homeless persons, African Americans are still over-represented among older homeless persons in the United States.

Age 50–64. Because of the entitlements available to persons at age sixty-five (e.g., Social Security), their proportion among the homeless is roughly one-fourth of their representation in the general population. Conversely, persons between fifty and fifty-nine years old are disproportionately represented among the homeless, compared with their representation in the general population (about one and one-half to two times).

Extremely low income (current and lifetime). Older homeless persons are likely to come from poor or impoverished backgrounds and to spend their lives in a similar economic condition. More than three-fifths work in unskilled or semiskilled occupations, with current income roughly one-half the poverty level.

Disruptive events in youth. Consistent with reports of high prevalence of childhood disruptive events among younger homeless persons, about one-fifth of older homeless persons have had disruptive events such as death of parents or placement in foster care.

Prior imprisonment. Roughly half of older homeless men and one-fourth of older homeless women report prior imprisonment.

Chemical abuse. Although prevalence rates of alcoholism vary, the levels are about three to four times higher among older men than among older women, and levels are higher among homeless men and women than among their age peers. Illicit drug abuse falls off sharply in homeless persons over fifty, but this may increase with the aging of the younger generation of heavy drug users.

Psychiatric disorders. The rates of psychiatric illness among older homeless persons have been biased by the difficulty that such persons encounter in attempts to be rehoused. Levels of mental illness have been found to be consistently higher among women than men, with psychosis

more common among women and depression slightly more prevalent among men. Studies of homeless people in New York City have found that 9 percent of older men and 42 percent of older women displayed psychotic symptoms, whereas 37 percent of older men and 30 percent of older women exhibited clinical depression. Levels of cognitive impairment range from 10 to 25 percent, but severe impairment occurred in only 5 percent of older homeless persons, which is roughly comparable to the general population.

Physical health. Older homeless persons suffer a level of physical symptoms roughly one and one-half to two times the level of their age peers in the general population, although their functional impairment is not worse than their age peers.

Victimization. Both younger and older homeless persons report high rates of victimization. Studies have found that nearly half of older persons had been robbed and one-fourth to one-third had been assaulted in the previous year. More than one-fourth of women reported having been raped during their lifetime.

Social supports. Compared to their age peers, social networks of older homeless persons are smaller (about three-fourths the size), more concentrated on staff members from agencies or institutions, more likely to involve material exchanges (e.g., food, money, or health assistance) and reciprocity. Older homeless persons also have fewer intimate ties than their age peers. Although not utterly isolated, older homeless persons lack the diverse family ties that characterize older adults in the general population. Only 1 to 7 percent are currently married, versus 54 percent in the general population. Nevertheless, various studies have found that about one-third to three-fifths of older homeless persons believed that they could count on family members for support.

Prior history of homelessness. One of the key predictors of prolonged and subsequent homeless episodes is a prior history of homelessness. Lengths of homelessness are higher among older men than older women.

Once a person is homeless, evolution into long-term homelessness involves a process in which the individual learns to adapt and survive in the world of shelters or streets. Furthermore, certain persons (e.g., men, the mentally ill, those with prior homeless episodes) are more apt to remain homeless for extended periods, most likely reflecting impediments at the personal and systems levels.

The two principal systemic factors that create homelessness are lack of income and lack of affordable housing. In cities where there may be adequate housing supplies, high levels of poor-quality jobs, unemployment, and low incomes make most housing unavailable to the poor. Conversely, in cities where incomes may be higher and jobs are more plentiful, tight rental markets stemming from middle-class pressure and escalating living costs also makes housing less available to lower-income persons. Both these conditions can push some people over the edge into homelessness.

Although it is now recognized that a majority of homeless persons do not suffer from severe mental illness, the closing of mental hospitals (*deinstitutionalization*) has been often cited as playing a critical role in causing homelessness. There is strong evidence that deinstitutionalization does not exert a direct effect on homelessness, as there is usually a time lag between a person's discharge from a psychiatric hospital and subsequent homelessness, and many homeless people with mental illness have never been hospitalized for psychiatric illness. Thus, whereas mental illness may at times lead to homelessness, it is also apparent that the disproportionately large numbers of homeless mentally ill persons also reflect systemic factors such as the unavailability of appropriate housing and inadequate entitlements for this population.

At the service level, there has been a paucity of programs for homeless and marginally housed older persons. Age-segregated drop-in/social centers, coupled with outreach programs, have been shown to be useful with this population. Unfortunately, while many agencies proclaim an official goal of rehabilitating the homeless person and reintegrating them into conventional society, the bulk of their energies go into providing accommodative services that help the person survive from day to day.

Another potentially useful modality is a mobile unit, of the type developed by Project Help in New York City, to involuntarily hospitalize persons. Used judiciously, and being mindful of civil rights, such units can assist those elderly homeless who are suffering from moderate or severe organic mental disorders or from mental illness that is endangering their lives. Advocacy is

also important. For example, in Boston, the Committee to End Elder Homelessness consists of a coalition of public and private agencies working to eliminate elder homelessness and to provide options for this population.

Based on the model of aging and homelessness described above, it is likely that the imminent burgeoning of the aging population will result in a substantial rise in at-risk persons. Prevention of homelessness among older persons will depend primarily on altering systemic and programmatic factors. In some geographic areas, where income supports and employment opportunities are greater, it will mean ensuring that there is adequate low-income housing stock. Conversely, in areas where cheaper housing may be available, it will be necessary to boost entitlements to levels sufficient to make existing housing affordable. Finally, for people who become homeless, there must be an expansion of programs targeted to the needs of older persons that work seriously towards reintegrating these persons into the community.

CARL COHEN

See also BABY BOOMERS; HOUSING; LIVING ARRANGEMENTS; MENTAL HEALTH SERVICES.

BIBLIOGRAPHY

COHEN C. I. "Aging and Homelessness." *The Gerontologist* 39 (1999): 5–14.
COHEN, C. I., and SOKOLOVSKY, J. *Old Men of the Bowery. Strategies for Survival Among the Homeless.* New York: Guilford Press, 1989.
CRANE, M. *Understanding Older Homeless People.* Buckingham, U.K.: Open University Press, 1999.
KEIGHER, S. M., ed. *Housing Risks and Homelessness Among the Urban Elderly.* New York: Haworth Press, 1991.
WARNES, A., and CRANE, M. *Meeting Homeless People's Needs. Service Development and Practice for the Older Excluded.* London: King's Fund, 2000.

HOMEOSTASIS

See FRAILTY; STRESS

HOME VISITS

For most of history medical care has been provided in the home, in most cases by family

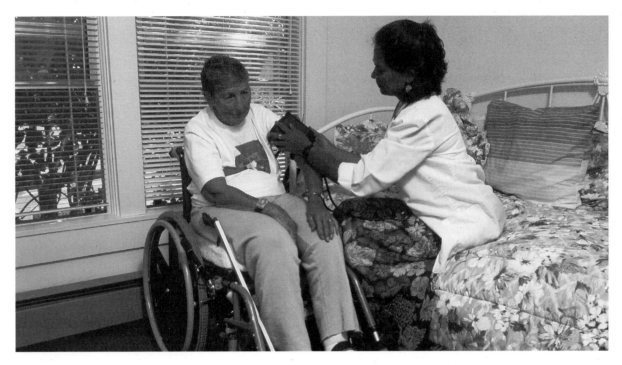

A home health care worker leans forward to take the blood pressure of an elderly woman in a wheelchair. Home visits make it much easier for many older people to receive medical care. (Corbis Corporation)

members or neighbors and in more dire situations by physicians. With the rise of the modern hospital in the early part of the twentieth century, together with the increasing mobility offered by the automobile, patients began to come to physicians rather than the other way round. In the United States, for example, a precipitous drop in the number of home visits after World War II occurred, from 40 percent of all patients encounters in 1930 to no more than 10 percent by 1950. By 1980 house calls made up only 0.6 percent of such contacts. In Canada and the United Kingdom, especially in large cities, the practice of home visiting has also declined.

However, for a significant minority of older persons, care today should still be provided in the patient's home. One may divide up the kinds of care broadly between acute and ongoing (long-term) services.

Home-based services ("hospitals without walls" as the most extreme example) have evolved since the early 1980s in response to two pressures: the first financial, the second relating to quality of care and patient choice. In some cases (for example the provision of intravenous antibiotics for the treatment of pneumonia), at least in the United States, it is often although not always cheaper to look after such patients in their own homes. In addition, the acute hospital can be a dangerous place for patients, especially the frail elderly. Thus there is the approach by many jurisdictions toward the transferring of hospital care back to the community as well as the frequently heard complaint that elders are being discharged home "quicker and sicker."

That being said, this kind of hospital-at-home acute care system requires careful and frequent monitoring of the patient, and at least daily visits by a physician and usually more than once daily visits from nurses. In the case of home rehabilitation (for example, stroke or fracture of the hip) physiotherapists and occupational therapists may also be involved in home visiting.

Midway between this acute kind of home care and long-term home care for the chronically ill sits the traditional medical home visit usually supplied by a physician, although sometimes a nurse may be involved. Here the main purpose of the visit is assessment, either of an acute illness or for examination of patient function within the home as part of the process of comprehensive geriatric assessment. Many experts in geriatric medicine believe there is no better place than the senior's home to examine the four principal domains of geriatric assessment: functional ability, physical health, psychological health, and socio-environmental factors.

The very act of entering the older person's domain instantly provides the visitor with a wealth of data. The physician (or other assessor) can quickly take in the family constellation and other support systems, as well as the safety of the physical environment. The physician can examine the medications that the patient says that she is taking and might even find others that have not been reported. Can the patient get in and out of her home or does her arthritis preclude the use of stairs and render her a shut-in? The patient's nutritional status can sometimes be determined by merely opening the refrigerator door.

The third model of visiting involves the care of the chronically ill for ongoing care in their own homes. Most older people, in the face of chronic, severe, and even terminal illness prefer to be looked after and to stay in their own homes as long as possible. Family members usually concur and many are willing to take on the load ("informal care"). However, such caregivers require the support of a formal network in order to avoid the inevitable burnout that can accompany such a "thirty-six hour day" (as has been so well described in caring for the Alzheimer's patient).

A well-organized and publicly funded system is best for the provision of such ongoing care. Various models exist and organization, use of personnel, and funding mechanisms will differ from country to country and may even differ within countries. For example, while Canada's health care system is supervised and regulated by the federal government, each province maintains responsibility for the day-to-day functioning of its health care system. Thus home care plans differ from province to province. An interesting experimental model in the province of Quebec involves an attempt to integrate home, hospital, and long-term services.

In the United Kingdom there is a split between the nationally run National Health Service and the "district" that is responsible for social services. Thus once can find various models of home care throughout the United Kingdom.

In Israel, the National Insurance Institute (Social Security) provides homemaker services to more than 90,000 of Israel's 600,000 seniors for a maximum of sixteen hours weekly in a nationally run program. The four sick funds (similar in function to nonprofit health maintenance organizations) provide medical and nursing care, but not always in coordination with the homemaker program.

Other countries provide different models of service. An excellent review of the literature can be found in an annotated bibliography from the World Health Organization.

Hospice care is an excellent example of the use of medical and nursing home visits. The patient qualifying for such care will have a terminal disease and usually less than three to six months to live (although it is notoriously difficult to make such accurate predictions). Such home care utilizes a multidisciplinary care team made up of a physician, nurse, and social worker. Other professions are called in as required.

The "elderly" are a very heterogeneous group including both vigorous and frail people found at any age from 65 to 120. The "young-old" (65–84) and even the vigorous "old-old" (85+) senior may well utilize health services in the usual way and not require home visits.

However, for the frail, the chronically ill, the housebound, and especially the terminally ill older person, care should be provided at home whenever possible. A well-organized health and social service system can help provide such care, keep health care costs within reasonable limits, and, above all, contribute to a higher quality of life and satisfaction for such people.

A. MARK CLARFIELD
SUSAN GOLD
HOWARD BERGMAN

See also ASSESSMENT; FRAILTY; GERIATRIC MEDICINE; PERIODIC HEALTH EXAMINATION.

BIBLIOGRAPHY

BERGMAN, H.; BELAND, F.; LEBEL, P.; CONTANDRIOPOULOS, A. P.; TOUSIGNANT, P.; BRUNELLE, Y.; KAUFMAN, T.; LEIBOVICH, E.; RODRIGUEZ, R.; and CLARFIELD, A. M. "Care of the Frail Elderly in Canada: Fragmentation or Integration?" *Canadian Medical Association Journal* 157 (1997): 1272–1273.
KOREN M. J. "Home Health Care." In *The Merck Manual of Geriatrics*, 2d ed. Edited by W. B. Abrams, M. H. Beers, R. Berkow, and A. J. Fletcher. Whitehouse Station, N.J.: Merck Research Laboratories, 1995. Pages 303–313.
MEYER, G. S., and GIBBON, R. V. "House Calls to the Elderly—A Vanishing Practice Among

Physicians." *New England Journal of Medicine* 337 (1997): 1815–1820.

MORGANSTIN, B.; GERA, R.; and SCHMELZER, M. *Long-Term Care Insurance in Israel, 1999.* Jerusalem: National Insurance Institute, 1999.

PUSHPANGODAN, M., and BURNS, E. "Caring for Older People." *British Medical Journal* 313 (1996): 805–808.

SOROCHAN, M. "Home Care in Canada." *Caring* 14 (January 1995): 12–19.

TENNSTEDT, S. L.; CRAWFORD, S. L.; and McKINLAY, J. B. "Is Family Care on the Decline? A Longitudinal Investigation of Formal Long-Term Services for Informal Care." *Milbank Quarterly* 71, no. 4 (1993): 601–624.

World Health Organization. *Home-Based and Long-Term Care: Annotated Bibliography.* Geneva: World Health Organization, 1999.

HOMOSEXUALITY

See GAY AND LESBIAN AGING

HORMONE REPLACEMENT THERAPY

See ESTROGEN; MENOPAUSE

HOSPICE

Hospice care was introduced in the United States in 1974 in response to the growing concern about the medicalization of dying. The first hospice in the United States was the Connecticut Hospice in New Haven. At that time, within health care, the emphasis was on curing illnesses and prolonging life, often at tremendous cost and with limited input from the seriously ill person. Patients typically viewed physicians as "experts" and deferred to their judgment.

The lay community, and some health care professionals, were growing increasingly concerned about their family members, friends, and neighbors dying in hospitals across the United States. There was general consensus that there had to be a better way to assure that persons at the end of life did not die alone and in pain.

Hospice emerged as an alternative to traditional health care, with the majority of care being provided by volunteers. The services provided by hospice programs were typically free, since health care insurers did not recognize hospice as part of the larger health care system. In order to be eligible for hospice, a patient's physician had to specify that the person was expected to live a year or less and that the focus of care would shift away from cure to palliation of symptoms. During the early years of the movement, it was emphasized that hospice was a concept, not a place.

Initially, the expectation was that, in order to receive hospice care, a terminally ill person would have at least one family member or friend who was willing to assume responsibility for his or her personal care. This criterion has evolved over time to provide greater flexibility for persons who are single, providing an option for such individuals to hire a caregiver or to move into a more structured environment when personal-care needs warrant additional assistance.

The Medicare benefit and other insurers

In 1984, hospice care was formally recognized as a benefit under the Medicare program. This was an important turning point for the hospice movement in the United States, demonstrating that hospice care had evolved from being largely a volunteer model to a recognized component of the health care delivery system, and therefore reimbursable. "In 1997, Medicare spent approximately $2 billion of its roughly $200 billion budget on hospice services provided to 382,989 patients who received over 19 million days of hospice care" (NHPCO, p. 1).

With the hospice Medicare benefit came increased regulation and additional restrictions on who was eligible for this benefit. For example, physicians had to give a seriously ill person a prognosis of six months or less to live for that person to be eligible. This admission criterion continues to be problematic, since determining a person's prognosis is not an exact science. In addition, patients (and their families) have to acknowledge that they are likely to die within the next six months. Consequently, patients are often referred to hospice very late in their illness trajectory and, therefore, do not receive the full benefit that the interdisciplinary hospice team is able to offer. In 1999, the average number of days that persons received hospice care prior to their death was forty-eight days; the median length of stay was twenty-nine days. Depending on the health care market, the length of stay in hospice can vary considerably. For example, in 1999 in Oregon the average length of stay was forty-two days and the median was sixteen days.

Figure 1

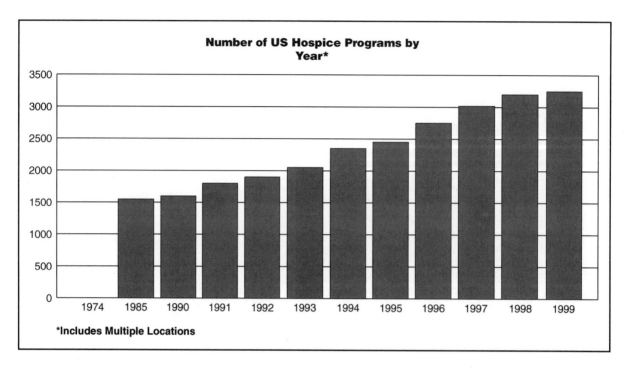

SOURCE: National Hospice and Palliative Care Organization website (www.nhpco.org)

According to the National Hospice and Palliative Care Organization (NHPCO), Medicaid also covers the cost of hospice care in forty-three states and in the District of Columbia. Health care insurance plans cover "80 percent of employees in medium and large businesses. Eighty-two percent of managed care plans offer hospice benefits, along with most private insurance plans and the federal Civilian Health and Medical Program of the Uniformed Services program" (NHPCO, p. 1).

Hospice services

In 2001, NHPCO estimated that there were "3,139 operational or planned hospice programs in the U.S. . . . .including the District of Columbia, Puerto Rico, and Guam" (NHPCO, p. 1). Just under half of the operational programs in 1999 were independent freestanding agencies (44 percent), followed by hospital-based (33 percent), and home health agency-based (17 percent). Figure 1 summarizes the growth in hospice programs since 1974.

In 1999, an estimated 700,000 patients were admitted to hospice and 600,000 died while receiving hospice care. Hospices provided care to 29 percent of Americans who died in 1999. "For those who were served by hospice care, 78 percent were able to die at home or under hospice care in a nursing home" (NHPCO, p. 1). Figure 2 summarizes the growth in hospice admissions from 1985 to 1999.

During the early years of the hospice movement, there were only a handful of inpatient hospice units in the United States. This was in contrast to the model of hospice inpatient care that emerged in England under the leadership of Dame Cicely Saunders, who opened Saint Christopher's Hospice in 1967. Individuals who are cared for in hospice inpatient units may be there because their family caregivers are not able to provide the needed care at home, or because they are experiencing uncontrolled symptoms and need a higher level of skilled care than can be provided in the home.

Trained volunteers, clergy, and health care providers from a variety of disciplines (e.g., medicine; nursing; occupational, physical, and speech therapy; social work) make up the hospice interdisciplinary team. This team develops, and continually updates, the care plan in collaboration with the patient's primary physician. Care

Figure 2
More Patients and Families Choose Hospice Care Each Year

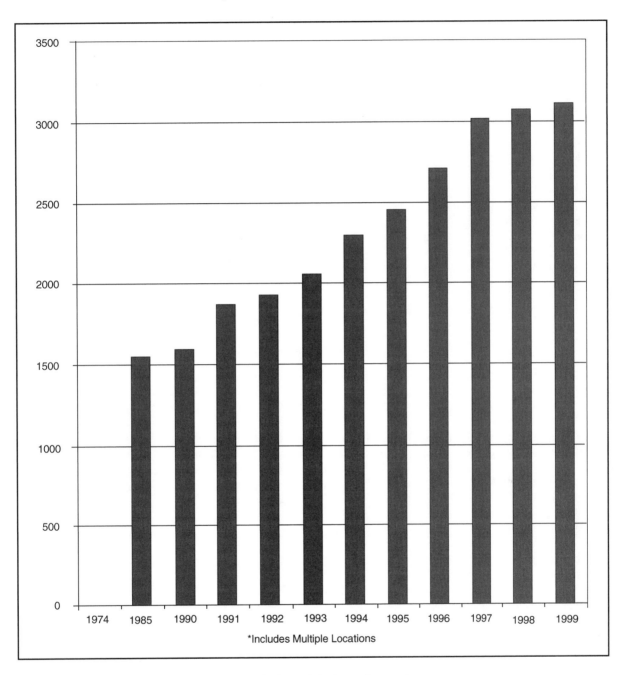

*Includes Multiple Locations

SOURCE: National Hospice and Palliative Care Organization website (www.nhpco.org)

plans include both terminally ill persons and their families. The majority of hospice care is provided in nonhospital settings by registered nurses and home health aides.

When a terminally ill person is being cared for in a home environment, hospice nurses make routine home visits to evaluate the effectiveness of the care plan, to recommend to the primary physician what medication changes are needed in order to better control symptoms, and to support the family caregiver. Home health aides provide personal care when the person's condition warrants it, or when the family caregiver is unable to assume this responsibility seven days a week. Other members of the interdisciplinary team, such as social workers, make home visits as appropriate.

"Considered to be the model of quality, compassionate care at the end of life, hospice care involves a team-oriented approach to expert medical care, pain management, and emotional and spiritual support expressly tailored to the patient's needs and wishes" (NHF, p. 1). The team pays particular attention to symptom management, including working aggressively to lessen pain at the end of life. Although the management of pain remains a challenge, in the early years of the hospice movement team members experienced considerable resistance because of fears of addiction and hastening death, as well as the general lack of knowledge about pharmacological and nonpharmacological interventions for pain.

Under the Medicare benefit, hospices have to include a volunteer component within their service package (e.g., persons to run errands, pick up medications, sit with the patient), which recognizes the important role that volunteers can play in supporting dying persons and their family caregivers. Medicare-certified hospices also provide bereavement support following a death, although the benefit does not include financial reimbursement for bereavement services.

The family as the unit of care is also an important component of hospice care. The interdisciplinary team works closely with family caregivers to assure that they have the knowledge and skills to care for their dying family members, and that they have access to the team's expertise twenty-four hours a day, seven days a week. As the dying person's disease progresses and care needs increase, the burden of care can, at times, be overwhelming to family caregivers. In some situations, it does become necessary to admit the dying person to an inpatient facility in order to better manage problematic symptoms and/or provide the family caregiver with relief from caregiving responsibilities.

The majority of hospice patients are elderly persons who have been diagnosed with cancer. NHPCO estimates that "hospices now care for over half of all Americans who die from cancer, and a growing number of patients with other chronic, life-threatening illness, such as end-stage heart and lung disease" (2001, p. 1). It is important to note that hospices provide care across the age continuum and that specialized hospice programs for children have been developing in more urban areas of the United States.

Future perspectives

Hospice care in the United States has experienced tremendous growth since 1974, and it served as the forerunner to the health care community's current focus on palliative care. Although there isn't a universally accepted definition of palliative care, it is often described as "a way to meet the physical, mental, and spiritual needs of chronically ill and dying patients. . . (with) attention to relieving symptoms and meeting patient goals" (Lynn, Schuster, and Kabcenell, p. 134). In contrast to hospice care, where the patient must have a limited prognosis and a terminal illness, patients receiving palliative care must have a disease that is life limiting. This criterion broadens the number of patients who can benefit from palliative care. At the foundation of both hospice and palliative care is the effort to improve an ill person's quality of life through expert symptom management.

The challenges that hospices face are not unique to this area of health care. Americans' growing concern with the cost of health care means that hospice programs need to continually provide the highest quality end-of-life care at the lowest cost, whether the care is provided in the home, in another community-based setting, or within a hospice inpatient unit. In the future hospices will also be confronted with shortages of registered nurses as nurses and other health care providers from the baby-boom generation retire.

Finally, hospices must also continue to aggressively educate the public about the services that they provide. In 1999, the National Hospice Foundation conducted a public opinion survey of people age forty-five or older and found that:

- Only 24 percent of Americans put into writing how they want to be cared for at the end of life. A substantial proportion (19 percent) have not thought about end-of-life care at all, while 1 percent have thought about it, but not told anyone their wishes.
- Of those people who experienced the terminal illness of a loved one in the past year, only 22 percent used hospice services.
- Eighty percent of the respondents said that they did not know the meaning of the term *hospice*.

- People do know what they want from end-of-life care: 83 percent believe that making sure a patient's wishes are enforced is extremely important. Being able to choose among the types of available services was also extremely important, according to 82 percent of the respondents.
- People are willing to have an outside organization come into their homes and assist with care for a family member in the last stage of life. Fully 66 percent would welcome help from an outside organization, while 24 percent would prefer to take care of the family member themselves, with the help of family and friends. (NHPCO, p. 2).

Hospice care makes a difference in the lives of persons who are experiencing the end of their lives. With the graying of America, it is expected that the demand for hospice care will continue to increase. Hospice professionals and volunteers support persons with terminal illnesses (and their families) to optimize quality of life during this difficult transition. It is essential that referrals for hospice care are made in a timely manner in order to maximize the benefits of hospice care both prior to, and after, the death of a family member.

JANE MARIE KIRSCHLING

See also CAREGIVING, INFORMAL; HOME CARE AND HOME SERVICES; MEDICALIZATION OF AGING; PAIN MANAGEMENT; PALLIATIVE CARE.

BIBLIOGRAPHY

CONNOR, S. R. *Hospice: Practice, Pitfalls & Promise.* Philadelphia, Pa.: Taylor & Francis, 1997.

JAFFE, C., and EHRLICH, C. H. *All Kinds of Love: Experiencing Hospice.* Amityville, N.Y.: Baywood, 1997.

LATTANZI-LICHT, M.; MILER, G. W.; and MALONEY, J. J. *The Hospice Choice: In Pursuit of a Peaceful Death.* New York: Simon and Schuster, 1998.

LYNN, J.; SCHUSTER, J. L.; and KABCENELL, A. *Improving Care for the End of Life: A Sourcebook for Health Care Managers and Clinicians.* New York: Oxford University Press, 2000.

National Hospice and Palliative Care Organization. *Facts and Figures on Hospice Care in America..* Alexandria, Va.: NHPCO, 2001. Available at www.nhpco.org

National Hospice Foundation. *How to Select a Hospice Program.* Alexandria, Va.: NHF, 2001.

Available at www.nhpco.org, click on How to Select a Hospice Program.

Oregon Hospice Association. *Summary Report: Program Data 1998.* Portland, Ore.: OHA, 1999.

Oregon Hospice Association. *Summary Report: Program Data 1999.* Portland, Ore.: OHA, 2000.

SANKAR, A. *Dying at Home: A Family Guide for Caregiving.* Baltimore, Md.: John Hopkins University Press, 2000.

SMITH, S. A. *Hospice Concepts: A Guide to Palliative Care in Terminal Illness.* Champaign, Ill.: Research Press, 2000.

HOUSING

Housing plays a vital role in the lives of older adults due to the amount of time they spend at home and their desire to age in place. The features of housing are strong determinants of safety and ability to get out into the community. In addition, the cost of housing is a major expenditure for most older adults. The aging of the population necessitates a broad array of housing alternatives that provide different levels of on-site services, supervision, sociability, privacy, and amenities. These housing options range from single-family homes and apartments to nursing homes. The following sections describe the wide array of housing options available.

Independent housing

Private sector housing. Most independent older persons reside in private sector homes or apartments. Over three-quarters (77 percent) of older adults own their own home. While rates of home ownership decrease with advancing age, 67 percent of adults over age eighty-five still own their own homes. Certain groups, however, have lower rates of home ownership (HUD). For example, home ownership rates are highest for whites and lowest for black (64 percent) and Hispanic households (57 percent) (Naifeh). Older renters differ from homeowners in that they have somewhat lower incomes, have lived in their units for relatively shorter periods of time, and occupy housing in somewhat worse condition.

Accessory units. Accessory units and elder cottage housing opportunity (ECHO) housing (i.e., granny flats), are private housing arrangements in or adjacent to existing single-family homes. These units are complete, self-contained units, usually with a separate entrance. Older adults who are frail and need to be close to their children or other family members can benefit from this option. Another possibility is that older homeowners can rent these units to younger persons at below market rent in return for certain services, such as shopping and meal preparation. Homeowners may also benefit from this situation because it provides an extra source of income to help with living expenses. Zoning in communities designed for single-family housing generally prohibits accessory apartments or ECHO housing, so a special use permit may be needed. Such impediments have restricted the growth of this option.

Shared housing. Shared housing is an arrangement in which two or more unrelated people share a house or apartment. Each person usually has his or her own sleeping quarters, and the rest of the house is shared. Surveys suggest that 2.5 percent of older adult households have at least one nonrelative living in their home, and almost 20 percent of older adults would consider living with someone who was not a family member or a friend. This living situation may occur naturally when individuals decide to form a household, through matches facilitated by an agency, and in small group homes operated by nonprofit or private organizations. In certain cases, agency-sponsored shared housing in small group homes may include services such as meal preparation, housekeeping, and shopping.

However, there are problems and considerations that arise in shared housing, especially in small group homes. Planning and zoning commissions may categorize shared housing with residential care homes, nursing homes, and other types of homes for older adults, all of which are excluded from residential areas zoned for single-family housing. A second problem is that elderly living in shared housing situations who receive food stamp benefits or Supplemental Security Income (SSI) may lose a portion of their benefits or be declared ineligible altogether. Nevertheless, shared housing can provide a source of additional income, reduce housing costs, and provide social, emotional, and physical support.

Government-assisted housing. Since 1959 the federal government has played a major role in increasing the housing supply for low-income older persons through financing housing for the elderly and reducing rents through tenant subsidy programs. Approximately 1.7 million older persons live in federally subsidized housing nationwide. The largest program serving low-income older persons is public housing, in which approximately half a million elderly reside, primarily in special housing for the elderly. Section 202 housing, initially authorized under the 1959 Housing Act to serve moderate-income older persons, has provided the funds for nonprofit sponsors to develop about 325,000 units in which about 387,000 tenants live. Sections 515 and 516 of the Housing Act of 1949 provide housing assistance to rural residents and farm laborers through tenant subsidies.

In addition, older persons live in a variety of housing developed through other federal programs (e.g., Section 236 of National Housing Act of 1968, Section 8 new construction), that have reduced the interest rate on loans for developers. Such programs have generally produced shallower subsidies than public housing. In order to make these programs affordable by low-income persons, many residents receive Section 8 rental certificates or vouchers, which reduce housing expenses to 30 percent of income and can be used to rent units in the private sector.

Supportive housing options

Because frail older persons are likely to need a more physically supportive dwelling unit, greater supervision (e.g., with medications) or services, or more companionship than can be efficiently provided in conventional homes or apartments, a number of supportive housing options have developed since the 1980s. Estimates of the absolute and relative sizes of the populations that live in supportive housing vary considerably because of inconsistent definitions of supportive housing, the difficulty in identifying unregulated facilities, and problems that older persons have accurately answering survey questions about the type of housing they occupy.

Estimates of the number of older persons living in supportive housing settings range from one million to two million. By all accounts, however, the stock of supportive housing is still insufficient to meet the needs of a growing population of frail older persons; much of it remains unaffordable to those with low and moderate incomes, and its quality remains difficult to judge.

Continuing care retirement communities. Also called life care communities, continuing care retirement communities (CCRCs) are unique in that they offer various levels of care within one community to accommodate residents who have changing needs. Most CCRCs offer independent living areas, assisted living, and skilled nursing care. Services that are offered include transportation, meals, housekeeping, and physician services. Some communities provide most of their own services, whereas others obtain many of them through contracts with outside organizations.

Each community houses between four hundred and six hundred older persons, often in a campus-type setting. CCRCs generally require, as a condition for entry, that new residents be in reasonably good health. Once a person is admitted, however, CCRCs are the most accommodating of all settings because residents can remain and obtain services in the community even if they experience physical or mental limitations.

The typical age of entrants is seventy-nine and the majority are women (75 percent). The primary reason that older persons select CCRCs is security, represented most clearly by the assurance of high quality nursing care and personal care services.

By 1992 there were approximately a thousand CCRCs, housing approximately 350,000 to 450,000 older persons. It is predicted that the number of facilities could double by 2010, though growth may be tempered by an increase in other options, such as home care and assisted living.

Most CCRCs require residents to pay an entrance fee and monthly fee, for which the community guarantees a dwelling unit, services, meals, and nursing care. Entrance fees typically range from $20,000 to $400,000 with an average of $40,000; monthly fees range from $200 to $25,000. Generally, CCRCs are an option affordable only by middle- and upper-income older persons, for most residents must pay out of pocket. Residents generally are required to have Medicare parts A and B. In order to reduce their potential liability for long-term care, some CCRCs offer or require long-term care insurance.

As of 2000, thirty-five states have regulations in place for CCRCs; though they vary greatly in stringency. Government involvement usually takes the form of measures to improve the ability of residents to make informed decisions and to guard against the bankruptcy of these facilities. CCRCs, fearing overinvolvement by the government, have formed their own regulating agency, the Continuing Care Accreditation Commission, which adopts basic standards that focus on finance, residential life, and health care.

Board and care homes. Board and care homes are residential facilities that generally offer on-site management, supervision, a physically accessible environment, meals, and a range of services for physically or mentally vulnerable older people and younger disabled people who cannot live independently. In facilities serving primarily seniors, the average age is approximately eighty-three, about eight years older than residents of government-assisted housing.

Data from a 1991 survey suggest that over thirty thousand board and care homes exist in the United States, more than double the number of nursing homes (Sirrocco). However, owing to their smaller size (usually between five and twenty dwelling units), board and care facilities house only about one-fourth as many residents (about four hundred thousand persons) as nursing homes, and include about two hundred thousand persons under age sixty-two.

The cost of living in this type of facility varies with location and the services provided, but in general the average monthly fee ranges from $450 to $2,000. Many of the older residents in board and care homes are subsidized by state governments, which add an amount to the Supplemental Security Income (SSI) that many residents use to pay for their accommodations and care. Most board and care homes are very modest in nature and require that residents share rooms. Though theoretically licensed and regulated by state governments, many of the smaller board and care homes remain unlicensed and enforcement is lax.

Congregate housing. Congregate housing refers to a wide range of multiunit living arrangements for older persons in both the private and the public sector. Older persons who live in this type of housing generally have their own apartments that include kitchens or kitchenettes and private bathrooms. Most of this housing has dining facilities and provides residents with at least one meal a day (frequently included in the rent). There are common spaces for social and educational activities, and in some cases transportation is provided. Congregate housing generally does not offer personal care services or health services. It is therefore not licensed under regulations that apply to residential care facilities or assisted living.

In line with the physical characteristics of the buildings and the limited provision of services, congregate housing attracts older persons who can live independently. It especially appeals to older persons who no longer want the responsibility of home maintenance or meal preparation, and positively anticipate making new friends and engaging in activities. Problems may arise later, however, as residents age in place and need more assistance than the facility provides.

Residents, who are usually sixty-five to eighty-five years old and widowed, typically live in a one- or two-bedroom unit in a facility with fifty to four hundred units. Units are rented monthly, for from $700 to $2500 a month, and paid for out of pocket. Nonprofit facilities are usually subsidized by government agencies or religious organizations, and therefore are less costly than for-profit facilities. Most Section 202 housing falls in the congregate housing category.

Assisted living. During the 1990s assisted living (AL) was the fastest growing segment of the senior housing market. Assisted living is a housing option that involves the delivery of professionally managed supportive services and, depending on state regulations, nursing services, in a group setting that is residential in character and appearance. It has the capacity to meet scheduled and unscheduled needs for assistance and is managed in ways that aim to maximize the physical and psychological independence of residents (see Table 1). AL is intended to accommodate physically and mentally frail elderly people without imposing a heavily regulated, institutional environment on them (Kane and Wilson).

The typical AL resident is female, age eighty-three or over, and widowed. In 1999 there were approximately thirty thousand to forty thousand facilities in the United States housing approximately one million individuals (ALFA). Costs vary from $383 per month to $6,150, with an average of $2,206 in 1998 (ALFA). Most residents must pay out of pocket for their care (see Figure 1). An individual's health insurance program or long-term care insurance policy is another possible source of funding. As of 2000, there are few governmental funding sources for ALs. Some states and local governments use Supplemental Security Income along with Medicaid to pay for low-income residents, or the Medicaid waiver

Table 1
Services Generally Provided by Assisted Living Facilities

Services:
Meals
Housekeeping
Transportation
Assistance for persons with functional disabilities
24-hour security
Emergency call systems in living unit
Health maintenance, wellness, exercise programs
Medication management
Personal laundry services
Social and recreational activities
Short-term respite care
Therapy and pharmacy services
Special programs for persons with Alzheimer's disease or other forms of dementia

SOURCE: Author

program to reimburse for services. In addition, the Department of Veterans Affairs and the Department of Housing and Urban Development, and the Independent Agencies Appropriations Act of 2000 allow HUD vouchers to be used in certain AL complexes and provide grants to convert some Section 202 buildings into AL facilities.

Varying definitions of ALs around the nation have produced difficulties with regulation and accreditation. With little leadership from the federal government, states have established regulations on their own. By the beginning of 1999, 25 states had regulations in place, with three more states pending (ALFA, 1999). In 2000, both the Rehabilitation Accreditation Commission (CARF) and the Joint Commission on the Accreditation of Healthcare Organizations (JCAHO) developed an accreditation process to promote quality care and outcomes for AL residents.

Aging in place

Although the continuum of housing identifies a range of housing types, there is increasing recognition that frail older persons do not necessarily have to move from one setting to another if they need assistance. Semidependent or dependent older persons can live in their own homes and apartments if the physical setting is more supportive and affordable services are ac-

Figure 1
Average Monthly Rent and Fees in Assisted Living Facilities

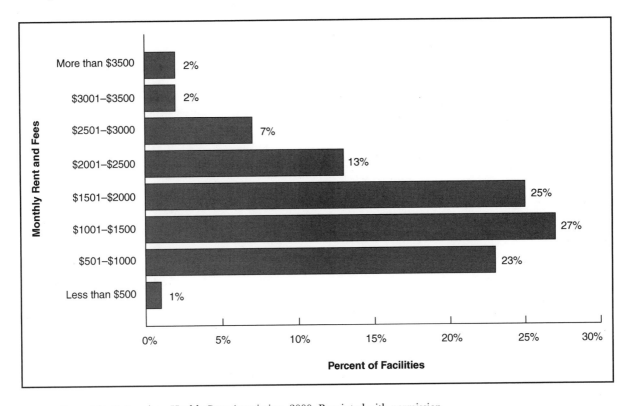

cessible. Indeed, most older adults express a strong desire to age-in-place in their own homes and communities. Yet often, these older adults live in physically unsupportive environments, disconnected from services. Instead of facilitating older persons' ability to grow old safely, independently, and with dignity, many settings have instead become a source of the problem itself. The following section examines various methods and programs that enable older adults to age-in-place.

Home modifications. Home modifications are adaptations to home environments that can make it easier and safer to carry out activities such as bathing, cooking, and climbing stairs. Increasing evidence suggests that home modifications can have an important impact on the ability of chronically ill or disabled persons to live independently (Mann, 1999). In addition, environmental factors such as lack of privacy or insufficient space may impede family and formal caregiving (Newman, 1985; Newman et al., 1990).

Estimates by the National Center for Health Statistics indicate that 7.1 million persons live in homes that have special features for those with impairments (La Plante et al., 1992; see Table 2). In conventional homes and apartments of persons 70 and older, grab bars and shower seats are the most common home modifications at 23 percent, followed by wheelchair access inside the home such as wide hallways (9 percent), special railings (8 percent), and ramps at street level (5 percent) (Tabbarah et al., 2000). However, a large number of older persons who report health problems, mobility limitations, and dependency in ADLs and IADLs (instrumental activities of daily living), live in housing without adaptive features. It is estimated that at least 1.14 million households occupied by older persons need additional supportive features (HUD, 1999).

The overall low incidence of supportive features in the home is due to three major barriers. First, there is a lack of professional and consumer awareness concerning problems in the home environment. For example, several studies have

Table 2

Frequent Home Adaptations by Numbers of Households

Adaptation	Total Number of Elderly Households
Handrails	3 million
Ramps	2.1 million
Extra-wide doors	1.7 million
Raised Toilets	1.3 million

SOURCE: La Plante, M. P.; Hendershot, G.;E.; and Moss, A. J. "Assistive Technology Devices and Home Accessibility Features: Prevalence, Payment, Need and Trends." *National Center for Health Statistics. Advance Data* 217 (1992): 1–12

found that many disabled persons, especially among the elderly, have a low level of awareness of the risks that the environment presents or a lack of knowledge of how home adaptations might make living safer and easier. In fact, older persons are often reported as having adapted their behavior to the environment (e.g., stopped taking baths or showers because of the danger of falling) rather than having adapted their environment to their changed capabilities (e.g., installing a handheld shower, adding a grab bar). Among professionals such as doctors, knowledge about home adaptation also is low. Concern has been expressed that even case managers, the gatekeepers for many long-term care services, may overlook home modifications.

Second, some home modifications may be unaffordable. The cost of home adaptations ranges from less than $100 for the purchase and installation of a simple handrail or grab bar to more than $1000 for a roll-in shower or several thousand dollars for a stair lift.

A third barrier reported by individuals and social service agencies in obtaining home modifications has been the delivery system (Pynoos). Simple home adaptations are often made by persons with disabilities and their family members. However, many persons lack the ability to identify environmental problems and make adaptations. Even installing an uncomplicated grab bar on a wall requires the ability to attach it to a stud and locate it at the correct angle and height in relation to the person using it. It is often necessary to employ a provider to assess problems and make changes, especially those that are complex, such as a roll-in shower. Overall, the modest nature of many jobs, the need for specialized skills, the low income of many persons who need adap-

tations, concerns about the reliability of private providers, and the difficulty of accessing specialists, such as occupational therapists, contribute to service delivery problems in home modifications.

Clustering services. Clustering services involves consolidating fragmented services for multiple clients. This strategy can reduce travel time and costs, enable more efficient worker assignment, and lead to service of more consumers. Since the 1990s, there has been a growing realization that economies of scale, as well as opportunities for peer support, exist in providing services to large numbers of frail elders living in one place. In addition to assisted living, several demonstrations and programs have been carried out in more conventional housing settings to test models of planning, organizing, and providing services.

One of the earliest of these demonstrations, the Congregate Housing Services Program (CHSP), authorized under Title IV of the Housing and Community Development Act of 1978, provides a service-enriched setting for frail older persons. Advocates for the CHSP promoted it on the basis that it would prevent "premature" institutionalization of elderly and handicapped residents of federally subsidized housing. The CHSP was carried out initially in sixty-three public housing and Section 202 sites, using HUD funds to pay for services such as meals, homemaking, and transportation to select groups of tenants with three ADL and/or IADL needs. A service coordinator and professional assessment team oversaw eligibility for and organization of the services. Between 1979 and 1985, approximately $28 million was spent on services to 3,500 residents of sixty-three public housing and Section 202 projects.

Because of controversy about whether the CHSP actually prevented institutionalization and HUD's continued reluctance to pay for services, the program did not expand until the early 1990s (Redfoot and Sloan) with the passage of the National Affordable Housing Act of 1990. By this time the CHSP, initially funded solely by HUD, required a significant state and local match that discouraged many sites from applying. Nevertheless, by 1994 the program had grown to more than one hundred sites.

The concept of clustering services has been the basis of several other innovative delivery systems. For example, the New York City Visiting Nurses Association (VNA) has used Medicaid waivers to provide services to groups of residents living in government-assisted housing. Personnel and health care staff are assigned to clusters of frail residents in senior housing. Staff can therefore move from one resident to another, performing various tasks, rather than spending long blocks of time with individual residents. An evaluation of the VNA project found that it saved money, although residents were somewhat less satisfied because individually they received less service (Feldman et al.).

Service coordination. The concept of service coordination is an outgrowth of the CHSP and the Robert Wood Johnson Foundation's Supportive Services Program in Senior Housing demonstration. Through the Housing and Community Development Act of 1992, Congress authorized expenditures for a service coordinator program. Service coordination is often described as the glue that holds a program together or the linking mechanism between residents of housing complexes and services. It is a less intensive model than the CHSP and relies more on linking residents up with services rather than providing them directly.

Services coordinated for residents include meals-on-wheels, in-home supportive services, hospice care, home health care for those who eligible for Medicare or Medicaid, transportation services, on-site adult education in areas of interest, and monthly blood pressure checks. There is also assistance with locating other living arrangements, such as an assisted living facility or a nursing home, when it becomes necessary, but the primary focus is on assisting residents to continue living in their current apartments.

Though the coordinators in this program do not have budgetary authority for services, they can serve a broad group of frail older residents. By 1999 there were approximately a thousand service coordinators connected with public and Section 202 housing complexes across the country. An evaluation of the program revealed that service coordinators successfully marshal a number of new services for residents, who report high levels of satisfaction with the program.

In 1999 HUD acknowledged responsibility for adapting its stock of housing for the elderly into more supportive settings linked with services. HUD's Housing Security Plan for Older Americans, approved by Congress as a part of its 2000 budget, includes $50 million to expand the service coordinator program and $50 million to convert some existing Section 202 housing for the elderly into assisted living.

A comprehensive system of community-based care. The Program of All-inclusive Care for the Elderly (PACE) is a major health care–based demonstration project that provides a range of services to older adults in the home. PACE, which is expected to include approximately fifty sites and ten thousand participants by 2005, attempts to replicate the On Lok Senior Health Services Program in San Francisco, which integrates Medicare and Medicaid financing and provides medical and long-term care services to frail persons who are eligible for a nursing home in a daycare setting. Participants in the program are assigned to an interdisciplinary team for regular needs assessment and care management. PACE's purpose is to address the needs of long-term care clients, providers, and payers. The comprehensive service package allows clients to continue living at home while receiving services, rather than in institutional settings. Nevertheless, many PACE sites have added housing, having found that a number of participants live in deficient settings or need more supervision and help with unscheduled needs than can be provided in individual home settings.

The challenges to incorporating housing into an integrated continuum of care are evident. Much must be done to develop housing as an environment that supports health, particularly as people age and/or become disabled. Conversely, health care providers and payers must recognize the impact that housing situations can have on health. Then, efforts can be made to integrate housing and health services. Housing settings can begin to develop informal affiliations and strategies that enable services to be coordinated on a client-specific as well as a buildingwide basis, taking advantage of the economies of scale inherent in delivering or "clustering" services for groups of older people living together. The organizations that have integrated housing with health care should be examined as models of how such integration works and what the potential would be to increase the integration in the future.

Conclusion

It is increasingly becoming recognized that housing plays an important role in the lives of the elderly. While new strategies and approaches have been developed to increase housing options, a range of affordable supportive housing choices for older persons remains an elusive goal. Progress in this area necessitates the recognition that housing should be an integral part of long-term care policy, and that more can be done to encourage aging in place.

JON PYNOOS
CHRISTY MATSUOKA

See also AGING IN PLACE; ASSISTED LIVING; BOARD AND CARE HOMES; CONGREGATE HOUSING; CONTINUING CARE RETIREMENT COMMUNITIES; GOVERNMENT-ASSISTED HOUSING.

BIBLIOGRAPHY

American Association of Retired Persons (AARP). *Understanding Senior Housing into the Next Century: Survey of Consumer Preferences, Concerns, and Needs.* Washington, D.C.: AARP, 1996.

Assisted Living Federation of America (ALFA). *The Assisted Living Industry 1999: An Overview.* Fairfax, Va.: ALFA, 1999.

FELDMAN, P. H.; LATIMER, E.; and DAVIDSON, H. "Medicaid-Funded Home Care for the Frail Elderly and Disabled: Evaluation of the Cost Savings and Outcomes of a Service Delivery Reform." *Health Services Research* 31, no. 4 (1996): 489–508.

KANE, R. A., and WILSON, K. B. *Assisted Living in the United States: A New Paradigm for Residential Care for Frail Older Persons?* Washington, D.C.: American Association of Retired Persons, 1993.

LA PLANTE, M. P.; HENDERSHOT, G. E.; and MOSS, A. J. *Assistive Technology Devices and Home Accessibility Features: Prevalence, Payment, Need and Trends.* Advance Data no. 217. National Center for Health Statistics, 1992. Pages 1–12.

MANN, W.; OTTENBACHER, K.; FRAAS, L.; TOMITA, M.; and GRANGER, C. "Effectiveness of Assistive Technology and Environmental Interventions in Maintaining Independence and Reducing Home Care Costs for the Frail Elderly." *Archives of Family Medicine* 8: (1999): 210–217.

NAIFEH, MARY L. *Housing of the Elderly: 1991.* Current Housing Reports, Series H123/93-1. Washington, D.C.: U.S. Government Printing Office, 1993.

NEWMAN, S. J. "Housing and Long-Term Care: The Suitability of the Elderly's Housing to the Provision of In-Home Services." *The Gerontologist* 21, no. 1 (1985): 35–40.

NEWMAN, S. J. et. al. "Overwhelming Odds: Caregiving and the Risk of Institutionalization."

Journal of Gerontology: Social Sciences 45, no. 5 (1990): S173–S183.

PYNOOS, J. "Towards a National Policy on Home Modification." *Technology and Disability* 2, no. 4 (1993): 1–8.

REDFOOT, D. L., and SLOAN, K. S. "Realities of Political Decision-Making on Congregate Housing." In *Congregate Housing for the Elderly: Theoretical, Policy, and Programmatic Perspectives.* Edited by L. W. Kaye and A. Monk. Binghamton, N.Y.: Haworth Press, 1991. Pages 99–110.

SIRROCCO, A. *Nursing Homes and Board and Care Homes.* Advance Data No. 244. Hyattsville, Md: National Center for Health Statistics, 1994.

TABBARAH, M.; SILVERSTEIN, M.; and SEEMAN, T. "A Health and Demographic Profile of Noninstitutionalized Older Americans Residing in Environments with Home Modifications." *Journal of Aging and Health* 12, no. 2 (2000): 204–228.

U.S. Department of Housing and Urban Development (HUD) Office of Policy Development and Research. *The Challenge of Housing Security: Report to Congress on the Housing Conditions and Needs of Older Americans.* Washington, D.C.: HUD, 1999.

HOUSING, AGE-SEGREGATED

Any discussion of the advantages and disadvantages of age-segregated housing must be placed within the context of several important facts. Ninety percent of older adults live independently in age-integrated communities. Age-segregated housing options are marked by great diversity, ranging from inner-city housing projects to trailer parks to upscale continuing care retirement communities. Elders who moved to age-segregated settings generally express satisfaction with their housing situation, but so do older adults living in age-integrated settings. The vast majority of community-dwelling older adults would prefer to remain in their current home and never move (American Association of Retired Persons, 1992).

The debate

Given the great heterogeneity of age-segregated housing types, an abstract and global discussion of the pros and cons of such settings is of limited value because the debatable issues vary greatly from setting to setting. (For a detailed description of the advantages and disadvantages associated with each type of living arrangement for older adults, see Folts and Yeatts; Golant, 1992; and Tilson). One of the overarching themes in the debate has centered around older persons' ability to face their own aging.

Golant (1985) identified three types of elders whose attitude toward their own aging does or does not make them good candidates for age-segregated living. Those who strongly identify with age peers and who cannot relate to a youth culture would feel comfortable in an age-segregated setting. Elders of the second type, too, would prefer an age-segregated setting, but for very different reasons: Comparing themselves to younger persons and trying to measure up to their standards, these elders escape such unfavorable comparison by preferring to live among age peers. Elders of Golant's third type flat-out deny their oldness and can continue to do so by avoiding association with age mates and by seeking out age-integrated settings. Foster and Anderson present a similar argument in which they contrast the "escape-the-system" model of adaptation with the "confront-the-system" model of adaptation. They argue that elders who seek age-segregated settings try to ignore or deny old age by living in places that foster "pseudoactivity" although the authors concede that such settings may enhance the self-image of elders. While both of these models stress individual characteristics and make sense intuitively, they beg the question of why elders might have these feelings.

Jaber Gubrium's socio-environmental model stresses the fit between the level of functioning (activity resources) of a person and the environmental demands (activity norms) of a setting and provides some clues as to why elders might seek out or avoid settings with a given age composition. Age-integrated settings have high activity norms, that is, expectations for a wide variety of activities, while age-segregated settings have low activity norms. Older adults with high activity resources (health, money, social relations, social support, physical mobility) would feel comfortable in a setting with high activity norms but bored in one with low activity norms. Similarly, older adults with low activity resources would feel overwhelmed in a setting with high activity norms but comfortable in one with low activity norms. This model assumes that old persons living in either setting restrict their activities to that setting, which is clearly not the case. Elders living

in age-integrated settings often form age-based subgroups, and many elders living in retirement communities have far-reaching ties beyond their housing environment.

Critics of age-segregated settings for older adults argue that such arrangements reflect the profound agism of our society, which pushes elders out of the mainstream of society and causes them to retreat into safe havens, thus isolating them from the rest of society, depriving them of community, preventing them from sharing their skills and wisdom, causing them to lead sad and lonely lives with low morale and no purpose, discouraging them from interacting with young people, and accelerating their mental and physical decline.

Such assertions reflect uninformed prejudice and ignorance of the empirical evidence. Most older persons living in age-segregated settings experience none of these problems. In some sense, many experience the best of two worlds: continued contact with the "outside world" and the benefits of living in a community of persons who have many other things than age in common. Age-segregated housing environments are most successful when their residents come from similar backgrounds and have had similar life experiences. For example, Arlie Hochschild's ethnography of Merrill Court, a congregate housing complex for working class widows, is one of many accounts we have of such settings. Hochschild's study revealed Merrill Court as offering its residents many opportunities for community creation: a rich life of social relations, subgroup formation, continued adherence to the work ethic, shared reminiscence, the freedom of joking about their own aging and impending death as well as continued contact with family and friends outside of Merrill Court.

All age-segregated settings provide opportunities for activities, and many are increasingly incorporating the concept of wellness, which encompasses physical functioning, and psychological, emotional, and spiritual well-being. The presence of age-mates mitigates the suffering caused by some of the losses associated with aging. Elders within age-segregated communities of all types develop networks of informal support. Continuing care retirement communities attract active and well elders who do not end their vital engagement in the community at large. Many find meaning in volunteering, travel, and continued involvement in political activities and civic matters. Early literature on the subject suggested that one of the attractions of retirement communities was that they allowed elders to escape from the world of the work ethic and to pursue leisure activities without being criticized. Subsequent research has shown that there are many other motivating factors for such a move, the most important one being the assurance of long-term care down the road.

Of course, service-rich age-segregated settings will have a considerable number of elders in ill or declining health. It would be absurd to suggest, as some early critics have done (Mumford), that age segregation accelerated such decline. Anticipation of and preparation for the need for care is one major reason older persons move to age-segregated settings. Similarly, studies comparing residents in age-segregated and age-integrated settings on such variables as social cognition (Cohen, Bearison, and Muller) or emotional closeness (Adams) hardly warrant the conclusion that any observed differences are the result of the setting rather than of a variety of individual attributes.

Age-segregated settings bestow on residents a sense of security and a lessened fear of crime, although age segregation by itself is no guarantee for safety. A very visible concentration of elders may actually invite attacks on persons considered easy victims if the housing is located in an unsafe neighborhood. Another benefit of age-segregated living is elders' ability to talk about and even prepare for death in the company of age-mates. On the physical-practical side, such settings offer an array of services and amenities all in one place—transportation, social activities, physical exercise, religious services, chore services, health care—that would be difficult and costly to obtain by frail elders in the community. Residents in such settings also look out for each other, and many derive a sense of well-being by helping frailer residents.

Types of age-segregated housing

One way of exploring the advantages and disadvantages of age-segregated housing is to ask who moves to such settings and why. A brief overview of the array of housing options for older adults will make it clear that the age structure of a setting is probably not the only consideration elders take into account when they choose among the many options available on the housing market. Resources and preferences

(health, functional abilities, economic resources, informal support, embeddedness in community) and housing characteristics (availability, location, cost, amenities) are as important as age. One could even argue that for some older adults' age segregation is the accidental result of having opted for a number of amenities—most often the assurance of nursing care in the future—that happen to attract other older adults.

The continuum of housing options for older adults is most often described in terms of levels of independence, ranging from independent households at one end to nursing homes at the other end of the continuum, with each offering different levels of supportive services (Atchley, 1999). This difference in supportive services is reflected in the definition of three categories of retirement housing: age-segregated communities for active retirees with minimal or no services; congregate housing with a service package that most typically includes meals and socialization; and life care communities offering extensive long-term care (Stockman and Fletcher). Settings vary also in their willingness to accommodate residents' increasing frailty and thus allow them to age in place (Tilson).

Another important distinction is that between publicly and privately sponsored settings. Recent developments in the market for senior housing have largely been limited to the private sector while already inadequate public housing programs have experienced even greater losses, much to the detriment of poor elders who have few real choices amid the proliferating array of new options in senior housing (Golant, 1992). Among the five major types of affordable housing identified by Golant, low-rent apartment projects, either with or without some congregate services, are low-income elders' only age-segregated housing option. The demand for such housing vastly exceeds the supply and has resulted in long waiting lists of eligible elders who have few other options. Finally, there is the distinction between planned and naturally occurring (Hunt and Ross) or *de facto* age-segregated settings (Golant). While the former are quite visible and receive most of the publicity, the latter are evolving slowly and often imperceptibly in many places throughout the United States, shaped by demographic forces such as out-migration of the young, elders choosing to age in place or moving into apartment complexes where many older adults already reside (Sykes), and by other push and pull factors such as proximity to friends, physical features of the building, and increasing dissatisfaction with previous housing (Hunt and Ross).

Settings designed for active and independent retirees include continuing care retirement communities (CCRCs), retirement villages, and retirement towns of varying sizes, with a selection of housing type and cost. Settings designed for frail elders include a number of types of congregate housing variously described as board and care homes, group homes, personal care homes, or adult care facilities, many of which provide adult care services in a home-like setting at relatively low cost. The recently developed concept of assisted living facilities is rapidly gaining in popularity. Designed for elders of varying levels of frailty, such facilities provide the level of care that meets individual needs short of continuous nursing care.

Future trends in senior housing

It is uncertain how the aging baby boomers will affect the housing market, given analysts' conflicting views of boomers' levels of savings and debts (Benjamin and Anikeeff). Demand for specific types of senior housing will vary by age, as it does now, with young, well, active, and mostly married elders opting for retirement communities and frail elders seeking more service-rich environments. During the first two decades of the twenty-first century, assisted living facilities will experience the largest growth in demand (Edelstein and Lacayo). Need or desire for care is the first and major housing decision elders have to make before they select a specific type of housing. This second decision will depend on a number of economic, demographic, sociological, and health factors. Edelstein and Lacayo predict that while up until 2020, the senior housing demand will grow considerably, there will be a shift from "intensive personal service [to] less personal-intensive congregate care and assisted living housing types" (p. 215). Growing attention to design issues exemplified by the concept of universal design and home modification, combined with a proliferation of in-home services, may widen elders' housing choices (Lanspery and Hyde). As in the past, preference for age-segregated or age-integrated settings will be one of many considerations entering into older adults' housing decisions.

LISA GROGER

See also AGE INTEGRATION AND AGE SEGREGATION; CONTINUING CARE RETIREMENT COMMUNITIES; LONG-TERM CARE; RETIREMENT COMMUNITIES.

BIBLIOGRAPHY

ADAMS, R. G. "Emotional Closeness and Physical Distance Between Friends: Implications for Elderly Women Living in Age-Segregated and Age-Integrated Settings." *International Journal of Aging and Human Development* 22 (1985–1986): 55–76.

American Association of Retired Persons (AARP). *Understanding Senior Housing for the 1990s.* Washington, D.C.: AARP, 1992.

ATCHLEY, R. C. *Social Forces and Aging—An Introduction to Social Gerontology,* 9th ed. Belmont, Calif.: Wadsworth Pub. Co., 1999.

BENJAMIN, J. D., and ANIKEEFF, M. A. "Primer on Key Issues in Seniors Housing." In *Senior Housing.* Edited by M. A. Anikeeff and G. R. Muller. Norwell, Mass.: Kluwer Academic Publishers, 1998. Pages 5–19.

COHEN, F.; BEARISON, D. J.; and MULLER, C. "Interpersonal Understanding in the Elderly: The Influence of Age-Integrated and Age-Segregated Housing." *Research on Aging* 9 (1987): 79–100.

EDELSTEIN, R. H., and LACAYO, A. J. "Forecasting Seniors Housing Demand." In *Senior Housing.* Edited by M. A. Anikeeff and G. R. Mueller. Norwell, Mass.: Kluwer Academic Publishers, 1998. Pages 205–235.

FOLTS, W. E., and YEATTS, D. E. *Housing and the Aging Population—Options for the New Century.* New York: Garland Publishing, Inc., 1994.

FOSTER, G. M., and BARBARA, G. A. *Medical Anthropology.* New York: Wiley, 1978.

GOLANT, S. M. *Housing America's Elderly—Many Possibilities/Few Choices.* Newbury Park, Calif.: Sage Publications, 1992.

GOLANT, S. M. "In Defense of Age-Segregated Housing." *Aging* 348 (1985): 22–26.

GOLANT, S. M. "Locational-Environmental Perspectives on Old-Age Segregated Residential Areas in the United States." In *Geography and the Urban Environment.* Edited by D. T. Herbert and R. J. Johnston. New York: Wiley, 1980. Pages 257–294.

GUBRIUM, J. F. "Toward a Socio-Environmental Theory of Aging." *The Gerontologist* 12 (1972): 281–284.

HOCHSCHILD, A. R. *The Unexpected Community—Portrait of an Old Age Subculture.* Berkeley: University of California Press, 1973.

HUNT, M. E., and ROSS, L. E. "Naturally Occurring Retirement Communities: A Multiattribute Examination of Desirability Factors." *The Gerontologist* 30 (1990): 667–674.

LANSPERY, S., and HYDE, J., eds. *Staying Put—Adapting the Places Instead of the People.* Amityville, N.Y.: Baywood Publishing Company, 1997.

MUMFORD, L. "For Older People: Not Segregation But Integration." In *Housing the Elderly.* Edited by J. A. Hancock. New Brunswick, N.J.: Center for Urban Policy Research, 1987. Pages 39–47.

STOCKMAN, L. E., and FLETCHER, J. "Retirement Housing: A Maturing Market." *Builder* 8 (1985): 70–91.

SYKES, J. T. "Living Independently with Neighbors Who Care: Strategies to Facilitate Aging in Place." In *Aging in Place: Supporting the Frail Elderly in Residential Environments.* Edited by D. Tilson. Glenville, Ill.: Scott, Foresman and Company, 1990. Pages 53–74.

TILSON, D., ed. *Aging in Place: Supporting the Frail Elderly in Residential Environments.* Glenview, Ill.: Scott, Foresman and Company, 1990.

HOUSING: ALTERNATIVE OPTIONS

A long time ago a wise woman said, "Everybody needs a place to stay." That includes the elderly members of society. Housing for older people is often ill defined and poorly understood; most people think of high-rise buildings or subsidized projects that older people move into when their neighborhoods are lost to urban development. In reality, there exists great diversity among senior housing arrangements, extending from privately owned dwellings and age-segregated housing to mobile home parks, retirement villages, congregate housing retirement hotels, granny flats, single room occupancies (SROs) and homelessness by choice or necessity. These alternatives are grouped into three main categories: (1) nonplanned or ordinary housing owned or rented by older people, accommodating 90 percent of the elder population; (2) specialized housing, accommodating 4 percent; and (3) nursing homes, accommodating 5 percent of the frail elderly.

Aging in one's own home

In 1994 there were 20.8 million U.S. households headed by older persons; 78 percent were homeowners and 22 percent were renters. Older males and married couples were more likely to be owners (86 percent) than were older females (67 percent). Home owners without mortgage payments spent 16 percent of their monthly incomes on housing in 1993, compared with 29 percent for those with mortgage payments. Owning a home provides by far the least expensive housing for most elderly, particularly for those whose homes are mortgage-free or close to being paid for. Staying in one's own home is the preferred alternative for the majority of older adults, provided that the neighborhood remains free of social and environmental deterioration.

Most of the recent literature referring to older community residents *aging in place* concentrates on the poor elderly who are low-income home owners, or renters, or who live in publicly subsidized housing. The greater number of older people who are aging in place do not fall into these categories, but live in diverse types of structures in varied physical settings. An emerging social policy aimed at helping older persons remain in their current housing as long as possible is a further component of the choice to age in place.

In order to meet the ever increasing needs of older persons who are aging in place, an array of community services developed during the 1980s and 1990s. The public sector invested huge amounts of funds to deliver health and social services to eligible community residents, and private, fee-for-service enterprises cater to those who can afford to pay.

Renting

In 1995 the Public Policy Institute reported that only 1.9 million vacant rental units had rent low enough to be affordable for the 5.1 million poor renters. The federal government defines expenditures for housing that exceed 30 percent of income as excessive; 71 percent of poor households experience excessive housing cost burdens. (Poor households includes owners and renters.) About 40 percent of the older poor households spend half or more of their income on housing. The incidence of excessive housing cost is particularly high among those age seventy-five and above and among older women living alone. Renters are particularly affected by excessive housing costs: 77 percent of older renters spend more than 30 percent of their income on housing.

Because older renters have few opportunities to raise their incomes through employment and because poverty in old age is more likely to be permanent, it appears that there will be a continued need for housing assistance. In 1999 almost one million older renters with worst-case needs did not receive any housing assistance. Worst-case households are those whose incomes are below 50 percent of the area median and who pay more than 50 percent of their income for rent, or who occupy substandard housing, or are displaced involuntarily. The incidence of worst case housing is highest among the oldest and youngest renter households, and they must wait for several years for housing assistance.

Shared housing

Shared housing can be best defined as facilities accommodating at least two unrelated individuals, at least one of whom is over sixty years of age, and in which common living spaces are shared. It is a program that targets single- and multifamily homes and adapts them for elderly residents. The typical number of elderly is three or four. The most easily recognized benefit of shared housing is that of companionship. It is also a means of keeping the elderly in their own homes while helping to provide them with the economic means to maintain there.

Shared housing may be forbidden by zoning laws in some suburban communities, especially wealthy ones. Often, however, local housing authorities promote shared housing by matching applicants.

Benefits include decreasing loneliness, maintaining the helping role, saving money through shared costs, having a greater sense of security, avoiding institutionalization, providing an alternative to living with children, and maintaining normal neighborhood living and freedom of activities.

Mobile homes

According to the U.S. Census, over two million persons age sixty-five and older lived in manufactured housing. This housing alternative is an important source of affordable housing for older Americans. On the average, mobile homes cost less than $35,000; more than half of them are bought by middle-aged and younger persons who grow older in these homes.

According to the 1999 AARP survey of mobile homes, there are critical deficiencies in the construction of manufactured housing. Strict housing and safety standards have existed since 1974 but have not been enforced by HUD. The AARP survey found that 77 percent of homeowners reported problems with the construction or installation of their homes, and 57 percent reported more than one problem. Even though 95 percent of the homes were covered under warranty, only 35 percent of the deficiencies were repaired.

In spite of the ongoing problems mobile home owners encounter with maintaining their homes, 80 percent expressed high levels of satisfaction with their living arrangements, and they planned to age in place.

Elder cottage housing opportunities

Elder cottage housing opportunities, or ECHO (also called granny flats and modular housing) are movable trailer houses that can be attached to existing homes and removed when no longer needed. The Administration on Aging renamed these accessory units in 1998. The concept originated in the state of Victoria, Australia, in 1972, traveled to the Scandinavian countries, and then to Canada (in the 1980s) and the United States (by the 1990s).

These units are designed to meet the physical needs of the elderly and provide the opportunity for them to live independently or semi-independently, but still be near family or friends. Although usually installed on the property of adult children, ECHO units can also be used to form housing clusters for the elderly on small tracts of land that are leased by nonprofit corporations or local housing authorities.

The major barriers to the development of this form of housing are rigid zoning laws, lack of public information, and concern about decreases in neighborhood property values.

Despite attention from the media and from housing professionals, granny flats have been successful only in part. Use and acceptance have been greater in other countries than in the United States. It is possible that the concept will become more agreeable to Americans as the proportion of elderly persons increases to an expected 20 percent of the population by 2030.

Single-room occupancies

A type of housing that has long been an important source of affordable housing is the single-room occupancy (SRO). The term single room occupancy describes not only the structure but also the common lifestyle characteristics of the residents. SRO units differ depending on the structures where the rooms are located: they may be rented in a rooming house or an old hotel, with or without shared kitchen and bath facilities, or they may be rented in a single-family structure.

By a 1987 estimate, four hundred thousand elderly individuals lived in SROs nationwide. Single elderly often face housing problems more difficult than those faced by the elderly in families; they are likely to live in rental housing, and a disproportionate number are poor. They face a risk of social isolation after the roles and responsibilities of the workplace are no longer part of their lives. Their lower incomes are more often compounded by lack of an assets cushion in the form of home equity, and they have no spouse helper available if they become impaired.

The SRO is an acceptable part of the housing stock. Generally inexpensive, it is one option for the community's very poor, unattached citizens, who include a disproportionate number of the elderly. SRO does not constitute planned housing for the elderly in the same sense that continuing care retirement centers serving the more affluent do.

A related option for those with more income is the retirement hotel, which can be inexpensive, expensive, or in between. Some older hotels in central cities specialize as senior citizens' hotels in order to maintain reasonable occupancy. In some cases, meals and a few organized activities (e.g., bingo and cards) are provided. The hotels are particularly appropriate for self-reliant elderly who wish to continue an independent lifestyle with the amenities of a city—including public transportation—but without the responsibilities of housekeeping.

Continuing care retirement communities

Continuing care retirement communities (CCRC), also referred to as life-care communities, are planned communities that combine housing and a range of services (including independent living, assisted living, and nursing home care), and serve primarily the middle- and upper-middle-class elderly. There were close to 2,000 CCRCs, housing some four hundred thousand to five hundred thousand residents, operating in the United States at the end of the 1990s.

Nearly all CCRCs charge an entry fee plus a monthly fee, a structure which appeals to facility operators because it links revenue to the resident's longevity as well as to the rate of inflation. There are two basic types of contracts. An all-inclusive plan provides an independent living unit, residential services, amenities, health-related services, and long-term nursing care in return for a specific price (paid as entry fee plus monthly payments). A fee-for-service plan provides an independent living unit, residential services, and amenities. It guarantees access to nursing care—for which residents pay a per diem rate, except for minimal services such as twenty-four-hour emergency care. Between these two plans are various other arrangements known as modified plans.

Besides possessing educational and economic advantages, CCRC residents represent a relatively healthy segment of the older age group. This is not surprising, because CCRCs have health status entrance requirements for persons applying for independent living units.

Homelessness

The homeless are defined as persons lacking a permanent residence. Their accommodations at night may be a public or private shelter or a place not intended to be a shelter, such as a train station. Nationwide, 6 percent of homeless people are between fifty-five and sixty-four years of age, and 2 percent are sixty-five or older.

Most homeless elderly have an unstable residential history over a period of years. The majority of homeless elderly are males who have experienced lifetime alcohol abuse, lived alone, had cognitive problems, moved from shelter to shelter, and refused to seek institutionalization. Even if placement in a nursing home would improve their lives, they are unwilling to seek help from traditional health and social service agencies. Homeless older people are likely to remain on the streets and continue their lifestyle. Whether by choice or by necessity, homelessness for these elderly persons is a fact of life, and so far society has not found another housing alternative for them.

Although the housing alternatives described above are available to older people and persons with disabilities, the choice of any one of them depends largely on affordability, willingness to relocate, physical and mental functioning, socioeconomic status, race, and gender. If the present trend continues, even more diverse alternatives will have to be developed to accommodate individual income levels and lifestyle choices of the future aging population. The new demographics will likely force the public and private sectors to cooperate and develop housing alternatives until the ultimate goal of community living is achieved and institutions become the last alternative living arrangement for older Americans.

BÉLA JOHN BOGNÁR

See also CONTINUING CARE RETIREMENT COMMUNITIES; HOMELESSNESS; HOUSING; LONG-TERM CARE.

BIBLIOGRAPHY

American Association of Retired Persons (AARP). *National Survey of Mobile Home Owners—Executive Summary*. Washington, D.C.: AARP, 1999.

GOLANT, S. *Housing America's Elderly*. Newbury Park, Calif.: Sage, 1992.

HARE, P. "The Echo Housing/Granny Flat Experience in the U.S." In. *Granny Flats as Housing for the Elderly: International Perspectives*. Edited by N. Lazarowich. New York: Haworth Press, 1991. Pages 57–70.

PYNOOS, J., and REDFOOT, D. "Housing Frail Elders in the United States." In *Housing Frail Elders: International Policies, Perspectives, and Prospects*. Edited by J. Pynoos and P. Liebig. Baltimore: Johns Hopkins University Press, 1995. Pages 187–210.

SHERWOOD, S.; RUCHLIN, H.; and SHERWOOD, C. "CCRCs: An Option for Aging in Place." In *Aging in Place: Supporting the Frail Elderly in Residential Environments*. Edited by D. Tilson. Glenview, Ill.: Scott, Foresman and Company, 1990. Pages 125–164.

HOUSING AND TECHNOLOGY

Anticipating the future needs of older adults

Predicting the future of technology is very similar to predicting the weather. The further forward in time one speculates about technological developments, the less reliable those predictions will be. There are lessons to be learned in this regard from those who looked forward from the nineteenth century into the twentieth. Railroads, mass public transportation within cities, and huge steamships were all technological marvels that were the basis for predictions about the future of technology into the twentieth century and beyond. However, under pressure from the emerging automobile companies, urban public transportation was largely relegated to bus transit in most cities. Automobiles supplanted railroads and the urban public transit systems of America by the 1930s, owing to preferences for personal transportation. America's railroad system is a very efficient method for hauling freight, but it carries very few passengers today. After numerous catastrophes at sea and the advent of air travel, steamships disappeared as a major intercontinental conveyance, and the largest moving objects ever built by man became recreational cruise ships by the 1970s.

On the other hand, the computer, a device that was a laboratory oddity built by the U.S. armed services in the 1940s, was transformed into one of the most significant consumer and business products ever devised, and no one predicted the emergence of the Internet from another defense department technology, a form of communications called *Arpanet*. Initially, Arpanet electronic communications was devised to provide a means of emergency connectivity between defense department installations if other forms of communication were cut or out of service in time of war. The use of Arpanet for personal communications, and its extension to university campuses, led to today's Internet. The Internet was never, in fact, invented, it evolved. Looking backward into the past, the reliability of technology prediction has been uneven—akin to driving an automobile into the future by looking only into the rearview mirror.

The level of reliability for predicting what might be available to serve the needs of older adults has been very high, however, at least for predictions of up to ten years away. It is difficult, however, to accurately envision the technologies the world will have at its disposal when the population of older adults peaks at midcentury. One very interesting aspect of all the technology that is either under development or can be envisioned is that it will depend upon energy to run. Ever-increasing applications of technology in the home will use increasing amounts of electrical and other forms of energy. This has important consequences for older adults who purchased their homes while working and are now balancing energy costs against health care requirements. Fortunately, most predictions foresee a world requiring products with lower power utilization requirements and homes that should be able to shift between energy from a grid and some level of naturally generated power, such as solar or wind.

The automobile can be seen as an extension of the home, and it is a very important part of the lives of older adults. It is unlikely that the automobile will disappear as a major form of conveyance, as the horse did in the early twentieth century. It is more likely that the use of motor vehicles as personal transportation will continue at least through 2050. It is also likely that the automobile will become more efficient through the use of alternative fuels, otherwise they will become useless as oil supplies become unavailable. Hybrid engines, combining gasoline and electric energy, are already in production, and it is likely that their adoption will be rapid within the first decade of the twenty-first century.

There is a connection that must be made between population trends and the evolution of technology that should, and must, meet human needs. There is virtual certainty about the inexorable growth of the population of older adults well into midcentury. According to census data, the inexorable growth of the total population of the United States will result in an unprecedented 50 percent increase in population between 2000 and 2055. Significantly, this population will be living largely near urban centers which will affect the type, density, and life-long requirements for housing. The fastest growing segment of this population is, and will continue to be, people over the age of sixty-five, with an increase of over 26 million people in this age group between 2000 and 2030. The profile of this population is also increasing in its diversity, becoming more multiracial, multi-ethnic, and multilingual.

Each generation or cohort of aging individuals reaching older adulthood will also bring their experience, education, lifestyle, human associations and connections, and their needs and desires with them as they age. Computerphobia, and technophobia in general, will eventually evaporate, even if it remains in the post–World War II generation. Indeed, discretionary income among older adults is generally high, and housing purchases of single-family dwellings at the upper end of the price spectrum is, and will remain, a purchase made mainly by older adults.

With those housing purchases come all of the opportunities for technology; both that which is part of the original purchase and that acquired after purchase. Technology and affluence go hand-in-hand. The acquisition of goods and services, however, is made by older adults only if they meet certain lifestyle requirements.

Have the product development professions, technology innovators, and the homebuilders begun to anticipate new markets for houses, consumer products, and technologies? Those who generate technology have begun, albeit late in the game, to see the demographic changes that are coming, and they have established a variety of approaches to make their product development efforts inclusive. *Universal design* is an approach that recognizes the diversity of the world population. This philosophy of designing encompasses the diversity brought about by recognizing aging, the expansion of the racial and ethnic base, and the increasing prevalence of individuals with both moderate and severe disabilities, in the population (Covington and Hannah). Another philosophy of design is referred to as *transgenerational design* (Pirkl). Transgenerational design extends the human factors associated with product development to include characteristics of normal age related change. Theoretically, inclusiveness of this kind offsets disability. In both philosophic approaches, disability can be measured as the difference between a person's ability to cope with his or her environment with and without the support of technology. For many older adults, technology can be the difference between continuous participation in all forms of activity or exclusion from the spectrum of activities that give meaning and enhance and invigorate all people throughout life.

The federal government has recognized universal design as a theme for additions to civil rights legislation and is creating law parallel to the response from the technology producers and the design and engineering communities. The Rehabilitation Act of 1990, Section 508, and the new Information Technology Act of 2001 (in effect in June of 2001) Section 255, both mandate the development of universal products for all communications technology—including hardware and software products, Internet web sites, media productions, etc. Inclusiveness has become a watchword of a movement to extend accessibility to all (Hypponen). The focus on needs of the technology user is called *human centered design* within the manufacturing industry. Used as a general reference in the development of technology, human centering is another way to state that all technology and its manifestation in products can only be effective in the future if they respond to a broadening base of human capabilities and characteristics. Recognizing this diversity means attempting to understand differing needs and differing human capabilities and characteristics.

Technology trends

Matching technology trends to the wide range of human capabilities and characteristics may be an easier prospect than one would initially think. An important trend is the movement in industrial production from mass production to mass customization. By the 1960s, American industry was responding to a theoretically homogeneous population with massive quantities of individual product technologies. A mass-production line has little variability, however, and efforts to market such technologies requires a focused approach defining the American population in terms of limited stereotypes. Running parallel to the increasing diversity of the population, automated, robotic, and computer-controlled machining and manufacturing permit single production lines to produce as many as three hundred different products. In this way, smaller quantities of goods can be produced profitably, permitting the manufacturer to address diverse consumer needs. Additionally, manufacturing has moved from stockpiling goods in an inventory that must be sold over time to a form of production called *just-in-time production*, in which goods are produced only as they are required. Older Americans are more divergent in their characteristics than are younger adults. If housing, building products, appliances, and consumer products are going to be successful, they must address varying individual requirements—and do so quickly. Emerging production technologies and methods for product distribution are at hand that will address the new trend toward mass customization.

One of the most significant technologies related to this form of production may soon be seen in the apparel industry. As of 2001, several manufacturers of full-body scanning devices were planning to launch their technologies. This technology will make it possible to manufacture clothing within days of a person being measured by a computer-controlled imaging system. Various forms of full-body scanning technology presently exist, including laser-light, photo-optical, and holographic scanning. Since the technology is just emerging, advances are rapid and prices are dropping. So-called scanning salons have appeared in California and are in use by the catalogue distribution company Lands End. The scanning process takes seconds, and automatic computer-driven software determines the measurements required for a specific garment. The data are transferred to computer-controlled pattern and fabric cutters, and custom-fitted clothing is returned to the consumer in a matter of days. It is possible to speculate that such technology could eventually drop in price and increase in resolution, speed, and capacity to the point where it will become a built-in part of a dressing room in the home. Scanning will permit all clothing to be accurately tailored to fit any individual, and scanning on a continuous basis will permit accurate sizing as people change through time.

This technology has applications well beyond the provision of clothing. It can also be used to monitor overall healthfulness and the effectiveness of a person's diet. Body conformation and composition, differences in body shape over time, even determining measurements of static positioning and reach could be important aspects of determining early onset of osteoarthritis and osteoporosis. Indeed, full-body scanning could revolutionize the design and development of furniture, automobile interiors, and other products where fit is critical for support, healthfulness, and comfort.

With regard to overall trends in technology development, it is important to understand that technology development at the beginning of the twenty-first century shows no sign of reaching a plateau. There are more individuals and organizations than ever before generating technology and instantaneously sharing information about what they create. The combination of expanded technology generation and worldwide electronic communication has accelerated the rate at which technology can advance. Innovation and information can be dispersed on a global scale.

One source on innovation and technology trends is the Battelle Memorial Institute, an independent laboratory for technology development in numerous areas of activity, including energy supply, transportation, housing, and consumer product development. Battelle has issued forecasts of technology development, many of which will directly impact the home environment and the lives of older adults. They include wearable, voice-actuated microcomputers and the integration of sensor systems in the home and in appliances permitting communication between people and technology, and between products. Battelle also predicts important advances in energy and alternative fuels, such as fuel-cell development and alternative power sources for home environmental heating, ventilation, and air conditioning, as well as many more manifestations of current technologies—and new ones just ahead.

On the immediate horizon are many forms of wireless, miniaturized, interactive computer technologies that will be worn by a person rather than sit on a desktop. Computer sensors combined with a fitted garment called the *Smartshirt* is a next step in continuous monitoring of vital health signs in and away from the home. Smart clothing is being developed for the armed services to monitor the condition of armed-services personnel operating in battlefield conditions. An array of computer-controlled sensors imbedded in a T-shirt will provide continuous information on vital signs. If wounded, the smart clothing will provide data on the wound to a base station so that medical personnel will be adequately prepared to deal with the trauma once in the field.

Applications of this technology for civilian use and health care are already underway at the Georgia Institute of Technology. Older Americans, especially those enduring the long-term effects of heart disease and other cardiovascular problems will be among the first to benefit from this technology. Wireless communications will permit continuous monitoring of an individual's condition, including location, by a home computer. The base station in the home will automatically signal either the individual or a health care professional if any change, especially an injurious or life threatening change, takes place. Since voice input of data and synthetic voice output from computers is already at hand, the technology will be interactive in the most user-friendly way possible. Other means of communicating a condition will be possible for the deaf and hearing impaired.

Advanced residential technology—the house that learns

The instantaneous communication of information immediately begs questions of security and privacy. These issues are genuine and pro-

found. Setting privacy issues aside, the benefits of nonintrusive continuous monitoring technologies are clear. Wearable, wireless, miniaturized computer technologies actuated by voice that permit sensor-detected organic changes or self-initiated body and vital-function scans allow the creation of a dramatic change in the dynamic of health care and extended independence. Clothing that is fit-mapped to the individual, containing an array of sensors that are tracked from home computing systems, will alter the long-term prognosis for extended independence among older adults.

Technology for monitoring the individual is already moving forward. Another step in the process is the elimination of hard-wired home electronics and the development of invisible technologies that not only monitor the individual but also control and regulate the home environment in response to individual needs. Heating, ventilation, and air conditioning systems will become both *smart* and *aware*, sensing individual changes and conditioning air through antibacterial filters. Antibacterial impregnations of carpeting have been available for over thirty years. The next step will be wall, floor, and ceiling surface treatments that are antiallergenic and antibacterial.

Gardening is an important activity among older adults, but asthma and other allergic reactions to both lawn and garden flora, and also to chemical treatments of lawns and gardens, can inhibit continuous gardening as susceptibility to allergic conditions increases. There is the possibility of the development of genetically engineered lawn and garden products that eliminate both the sources of allergy and the need for chemical treatments.

The major change on the horizon for the home environment is the development of invisible products and technologies. The development of communications between the home and the homeowner, and also between product technologies, with no interface except *awareness*, gives rise to a fundamental change in the way everyone interacts with their built environment. An *aware house* has been built at the Georgia Institute of Technology. It is fitted with nonobtrusive electronic monitoring devices that allows the home, through its computer technology, to sense the behaviors and patterns of the daily lives of individual adults. There are imaging devices implanted in the walls and ceiling, as well as worn on a person's body, that can observe daily routines, and the performance of tasks, and even learn to read gestures. One important area of the research is an attempt to understand changes in memory through observation of individual task performance. Specific experimentation is underway that will have older adults performing household tasks such as food preparation while there are intrusions of other adults during the process. By interfering with the performance of tasks, the focus required through short-term memory can be monitored. This awareness may render clues about the early onset of short-term memory loss and early onset of dementia. Knowing the patterns of an individual and monitoring the changes that occur over time may give rise to the interventions necessary to offset confusion and withdrawal. The goal becomes provision of subtle and progressive supports, technological as well as through the intervention of others, that will sustain an individual's ability to remain in his or her own home for as long as possible.

Transfer of this level of technology to applications in the realm of housing production is likely several years, if not decades, off. This research, using nonobtrusive computer-controlled monitoring, has just begun. However, the implications for future home development are clear. The technology is currently available, and will improve over time, that will not only permit monitoring of the physiological status of an individual, but will also permit observation and knowledge of the psychological, cognitive, and behavioral health of an individual. These developments are specifically directed at understanding older adults and providing support to aging in place.

Retirement, work, education, and leisure

Working at home is now a reality for a substantial number of Americans. The home office, with its computer, facsimile machine, and telephone, is now a definitive part of the household environment. The relationship between work and retirement is variable and flexible. Retirement for many may occur more than once or twice, and many that have left careers are at least partially employed. Clearly, new generations of older Americans can anticipate longer careers, several forms of employment, more changes of career, and intermittent work roles mixed with periods of retirement. This is a very different picture from the image of a person working for one company for three decades, being given a gold watch, and picking up a fishing pole with no thought of continuing in any form of active employment. Older adults in the twenty-first century may experience a much later onset of formal retirement and never be fully removed from the workforce until health changes alter their ability to continue working. The home office will grow in importance as this societal change inexorably moves forward. Many professional women will experience the ebb and flow of work, family, and retirement—all related to the options afforded through the home office.

The home is also becoming a primary location for education. America is at the beginning of a new age of life-long learning. The University of Phoenix has been among the leading institutions offering distance education and degree programs to a global student body. Before the end of the first decade of the twenty-first century, many institutions of higher education will be offering courses to more students off-campus than are residents in dormitories on campus. The home is also a learning center for a growing number of older Americans. They may become involved in educational programs for intellectual stimulation, but many will be involved in degree programs through distance education.

Asynchronous education is the term applied to self-learning at one's own pace. Once again, computing permits an extension of many forms of learning without the presence of teachers. The classroom of the future may well be a large flat screen connected to a robust home-computing system that connects students all over the world. Windowing onscreen will allow real-time discussion. Instantaneous translations will permit a history teacher in India to offer a history course to a class of young and old students on campuses, at other locations, and in their own homes. Broadband technology will provide the teacher (and the student) the ability to call up still photographic visual materials and streaming video in electronic form. After the lecture, course notes, the lecture itself, and support materials will be available on an on-call basis. Indeed, the class itself will likely be prerecorded for logging on at any time, with prescribed times for exchanges with the teacher. It may not be possible to tell the difference between much of what will become available in the form of educational materials, actual courses, and entertainment. There are a variety of terms now applied to these mixed forms of presentation, including *infotainment* and *edutainment*. The presence of computer technology has already changed the classroom and the approach to teaching almost every subject.

For older adults, the implications of these changes in education, work, and entertainment may blur the distinction between activities. It will also be a means for continuous involvement and intellectual stimulation that could have a beneficial effect upon well-being and health and wellness. Computing could be used to support memory as well as continuing education. Repetition requires patience on the part of a teacher, but a computer doesn't care and can be called upon to repeat information continuously.

Home technologies and daily life

Imaginative films have depicted many forms of robotic assistance, most of them anthropomorphic in character, conducting household chores. This represents the visible technology that is less likely in the future, unless preferences among American consumers call for a walking, talking robot with a name. The 1999 film, *Bicentennial Man*, featuring the noted actor and comedian Robin Williams, explores a well-worn (some might argue threadbare) theme in movie making about such anthropomorphic robots. In actuality, robotic assistance in the performance of tasks is more likely to be dispersed among product technologies and appliances in areas such as lawn care, household surface cleaning, cooking, and home maintenance. The house will be aware, and the products within the house will be smart and able to communicate. Computer technologies imbedded within food-storage containment areas and refrigeration units will be able to read bar-coded supplies, determine dates of expiration, alert the homeowner about potential spoilage, and even communicate alternative menus to electronic display units or voice output devices. Smart appliances will augment the preparation of food by sensing the degree of cooking completion. Recycling in the kitchen will be accomplished with the assistance of trash sorting and compacting units. Water quality will be continuously monitored, as will all of the systems of the home, through on-call maintenance and service programs that will enhance the overall healthfulness of the home environment. Virtually all of this technology is at hand, and applications will soon emerge in the marketplace.

For older adults, the acquisition, monitoring, and use of medications is of great importance. Medication containment units will be available that will not only keep track of quantities, but will also read bar-coded information provided with the medication and provide appropriate reminders to the resident about medication intervals and dosage. Detoxification from drug interactions is a widespread problem among older adults. Technology applied to the appropriate control and dispensing of medications will be of great importance. Over time, these products can become part of a system of health care that is supported by technology and a new form of health care system that sustains individual independence, helps control the costs of health care through emphasis on awareness and preventative measures, and provides the appropriate interventions only when necessary.

Conclusions

Of the many assumptions made in predicting the future, one that is implied almost every time the future of technology is discussed is that technology is beneficial. Technology is benign, and the intention is to create benefit through the use of technology. But, is more of it better than less? In the end, older adults will choose what they want and inform the world about technology's viability and benefit. The unobtrusive characteristic of the technology to come is most appealing. However, its application and the interface with people are clearly significant. A house that is constantly attempting to communicate with its resident regardless of that individual's receptivity or desire to interact seems to be a future for domestic living that few would care to contemplate. A house that is a machine is also less than desirable. Thoughtful integration of smart and aware technologies that also manifest sensitivity about the user is the sort of quality that must be imparted to a living space. Currently, computers display none of this quality. Today, users are confronted with computer crashes that signal *fatal errors* and other admonitions as if the failings imbedded in the complexity of the machine are somehow the fault of the owner/operator. A house that is continually experiencing electronic crashes that have the user both mystified and worried will be unacceptable.

This phenomenon in computing systems is addressed in the book *The Humane Interface* (2000) by Jef Raskin. Raskin states that the future relationship of advanced computing to the novice user must be one of a much more friendly interface; one that does not present complexity in order to do the simplest operation. While the technology is at hand, or nearly within our grasp, to provide extended independence to older adults, the difficulty in creating this sophisticated home of the future does not lie in developing capacity, it is in making that capacity easily usable, with seamless transitions of interface from person to machine, machine to machine, and home to homeowner. Quality of life has always been the ultimate issue of aging. Americans will be spending more time in their lives as older adults than they will in any other time of life. The potential in the technological future of the home holds great promise for sustaining quality as well as maintaining independence.

JOSEPH A. KONCELIK

See also AGING IN PLACE; HOME ADAPTATION AND EQUIPMENT; HUMAN FACTORS; TECHNOLOGY.

BIBLIOGRAPHY

Battelle Memorial Institute. *The Business of Innovation: Technology Forecasts*. BMI, 1995. Available at www.battelle.org/forecasts/technology.stm.

CAMPBELL, P. "Population Projections: States, 1995–2025." In *Current Population Reports: Population Projections*. Washington, D.C.: U.S. Bureau of the Census, 1997.

COVINGTON, G. A., and BRUCE, H. *Access by Design*. New York: Van Nostrand Reinhold, 1997.

DYCHTWALD, K., and FLOWER, J. *Age Wave*. New York: Bantam Doubleday Dell, 1990.

HYPPONEN, H., ed. *Handbook on Inclusive Design of Telematics Applications*. Helsinki, Finland: Stakes, 1999. Available at www.stakes.fi

PIRKL, J. J. *Transgenerational Design: Products for an Aging Population*. New York: Van Nostrand Reinhold, 1994.

RASKIN, J. *The Humane Interface*. Reading, Mass.: Addison-Wesley, 2000.

HUMAN FACTORS

Although most older people live active and relatively healthy lives, increased age is associated with changes in certain abilities, such as vision, hearing, and memory, that make it difficult for some older people to perform tasks such as driving, using equipment such as computers, or remembering to take medications. Furthermore, older people are more likely to suffer from some type of chronic disease such as arthritis, high blood pressure, or dementia. People with these conditions often require assistance with basic activities such as preparing meals, bathing, or finding their way. Aging is also associated with positive changes, such as increased wisdom, knowledge, and experience, and thus older people represent an extremely valuable resource to the community, the workplace, and the family. There are numerous examples, such as senior mentoring, of how older adults continue to make productive contributions to society.

The challenge confronting researchers, designers, and policy makers is to develop strategies to maximize the ability of older people to reach their potential and remain healthy and productive. In addition, strategies are needed to help older people who are frail or disabled receive needed care and support. *Human factors engineering*, the multidisciplinary science that focuses on user-centered design, can make valuable contributions toward accommodating an aging population and enhancing the lives of older adults. Relevant applications of human factors include: housing design, transportation, equipment and product design, and work

Human factors engineering

Human factors engineering is the study of human beings and their interactions with products, environments, and equipment in the performance of tasks and activities. The field of human factors is interdisciplinary, encompassing the disciplines of engineering, psychology, computer science, physiology, and biomechanics. The focus of human factors research is the study of human capabilities, limitations, and characteristics in relation to real world activities and systems. Relevant research projects might include understanding the implications of age-related changes in vision for the design of visual displays or how age-related changes in memory impact the ability of seniors to learn to use new technologies.

The objectives of humans factors are to improve the fit between people and the designed environment so that performance, safety, comfort, and user satisfaction are maximized. To achieve these goals, human factors engineering uses a systems approach to design, where the capabilities and limitations of the user are evaluated relative to the demands generated by products and tasks. An example of this approach would be evaluating the force requirements necessary to operate a hand control, such as door knob, relative to the grasping and strength capabilities of the intended user population.

The focus on user-centered design makes human factors engineering a natural discipline to address the problems of older adults and help them retain and enjoy independence in their later years. Using the techniques and methods of human factors it is possible to understand the impact of age-related changes in abilities on the performance of everyday tasks and activities, identify areas where problems and difficulties arise, and discover solutions to address them. These solutions might include redesign of equipment or environments, interface design solutions, training solutions, or suggestions for the development of new products or technologies.

Areas in which human factors engineering can be used to improve the lives of older people include: mobility/transportation, living environments, and information technology (for a discussion of health care applications see Czaja, 2000).

Mobility and transportation

It is fairly well known that many older people, because of difficulty walking, using stairs, driving, or using public transportation, have difficulty getting from place to place. Problems with mobility often make it difficult for older people to get to stores, banks, and physicians' offices; to participate in community activities; or to maintain contact with family and friends. These problems are exacerbated for older adults who live in suburban or rural communities where public transportation is often minimal or nonexistent and driving is the only option. Driving is problematic for many older adults, making this a topic of great interest to policy makers, researchers, and the elderly themselves.

In this regard, issues related to the safety and mobility of older drivers has received considerable attention within the human factors community. This research has been directed toward understanding the difficulties experienced by older drivers and the reasons for these difficulties, as well as identifying potential design solutions. Several researchers have found that problems with driving are related to deficits in vision and aspects of cognition (see Ball and Owsley, 1991). It is also known that certain tasks,

such as left-hand turns, or certain environments, such as driving in construction zones, are difficult for older people. Many older people also report difficulty adjusting to changes in automobile design.

Proven areas of effective intervention include redesign of roadway signs and warnings, modifications in the design of the automobile, and training. It has been shown, for example, that providing older people with training on abilities important to driving, such as visual attention, offers the potential of improving driving performance. Strategies such as increasing the contrast of roadway signs so that they are easier to read or providing drivers with additional signs about upcoming traffic or roadway demands can also help enhance the safety of older drivers.

Other important areas of human factors intervention include identifying alternative solutions, such as modifications in public transportation systems to make them more easily available, so that the need for driving is reduced. Older people commonly report problems using buses or subways due to inefficient design. Common problems include difficulty getting on and off, crowding, lack of security, and lack of availability of transportation systems. Other problems relate to understanding schedules and maps. Many of these problems are amenable to human factors solutions.

Living environments

Another area where human factors engineers can make important contributions is the design of living environments. Contrary to popular belief, most older people live in the community, either alone or with a relative. Many older people also spend a great deal of time at home. However, living at home is often challenging for older adults, as they find it difficult to perform tasks such as bathing, cooking, and cleaning. The rate of home accidents is high among older people. Problems with home activities and home safety are often linked to inappropriate housing design.

Falls among elderly people are common, and in fact represent a frequent cause of accidental injury and death. Furthermore, many older people restrict their activities because of fear of falling. Reasons for falls among the elderly include losses in vision, balance, and reaction time, and changes in gait. Common locations or sources of falls include stairs and steps; bathtubs and showers; ladders and stools; and tripping or slipping on throw rugs, runners, or carpets. Understanding the reasons for these falls will help uncover design solutions. Many falls on stairways occur because older people, due to declines in vision, fail to perceive the first or last step. This problem might be addressed by installation of more lighting in stairways and highlighting, through the use of color, the beginning and ending of steps. Handrails can also help remedy the problem. A more radical solution is to design housing without stairs, or to design in a way that minimizes the need for people to go up and down stairs. Strength and balance training has also been shown to reduce the risk of falls among the elderly and to reduce the consequences if a fall should occur. In all of these examples, the goal is to help insure a match between the capabilities of the older person and the demands of the task and the environment.

Computer technology and information systems

Computer and information technologies offer the potential of enhancing the independence and improving the quality of life of older people. These technologies make it possible to bank and shop at home, maintain contact with family and friends, access physicians and health care providers, access information about community resources, and participate in educational programs. Despite popular stereotypes, older people are interested and willing to use new technologies. However, because of lack of familiarity with technology, lack of training, and difficult-to-use systems, technology is often a source of frustration for many older adults and the potential benefits of technology for this population are not realized. This is another area where human factors engineers can, and do, make significant contributions.

An excellent example relates to automatic teller machines (ATMs). A recent survey showed that older people use ATMs far less frequently than younger people because they don't feel safe using them, don't feel they need them, or do not know how to use them. They also indicated that they would be more likely to use ATMs if someone showed them how to use them. Researchers at Georgia Institute of Technology have discovered effective ways of teaching older people to use ATMs. Specifically they found providing

older adults with an on-line tutorial that provided hands-on interactive experience with an ATM system and practice on actual ATM tasks improved their ability to perform ATM transactions. They also discovered that simple changes in system design, such as improving the visual display and the content of on-screen messages, greatly enhance the ability of older people to successfully use ATMs. It is also important to understand that these types of design changes are usually effective for people of all ages.

Several researchers (e.g., Charness, 2000; Walker, Philbin, and Fisk, 1997; Smith, Sharit, and Czaja, 1999) have shown that current input devices, such as the computer mouse, also make it difficult for older adults to use technology. These problems are related to age changes in movement control. Tasks such as double-clicking or cursor positioning are particularly difficult for older people. Some of these difficulties can be eliminated by making the interface easier by changing the gain and acceleration of the mouse, or by switching to alternative input devices such as a light pen. Current findings also suggest that voice control may be beneficial for older people, as it minimizes the need for use of the hands and fingers.

Software that is complex also causes problems for older people. For example, many older people are interested in learning to use the World Wide Web (WWW), but find it difficult because of poor interface design. Strategies such as changing the structure of the network and menu characteristics so it is easier for people to find information have been found to be effective for both younger and older people. Other techniques, such as providing on-screen information regarding search history ("where one is and where one has been") also aid performance, as the demands on memory are reduced.

The topic of aging and information technology is becoming increasingly important, as the use of technology is permeating most aspects of society. The challenge for human factors engineers is to help insure that technology is useful to, and useable by, older adults. Much needs to be done in the area of training and interface design in order to meet this challenge.

Conclusion

Human factors engineering can be used to help design tasks, products, equipment, and environments to help accommodate an aging population. Research in this area has demonstrated the importance of attending to the needs of older people in system design, and also that training and design solutions can be beneficial for older people. The basic premise of human factors is that successful performance results from user-centered design and a fundamental understanding of user capabilities, needs, and preferences. Improving the health and quality of life of older people requires that knowledge of aging be applied to the design of products and environments.

SARA CZAJA
CHIN CHIN LEE

See also BALANCE AND MOBILITY; DRIVING ABILITY; FUNCTIONAL ABILITY; HEARING; HOME ADAPTATION AND EQUIPMENT; HOUSING AND TECHNOLOGY; INTELLEGINCE; MEMORY; TECHNOLOGY; VISION AND PERCEPTION.

BIBLIOGRAPHY

BALL, K., and OWSLEY, C. "Identifying Correlates of Accident Involvement for the Older Driver." *Human Factors* 33 (1991): 583–595.

CHARNESS, N. "Aging and Communication: Human Factors Issues." In *Aging and Communication: Opportunities and Challenges of Technology.* Edited by N. Charness, D. C. Park, and B. A. Sabel. New York: Springer, 2000.

CZAJA, S. J. *Human Factors Research for an Aging Population.* Washington, D.C.: National Academy of Science Press, 1990.

CZAJA. S. J. "Ergonomics and Older Health Care for Older Adults." In *The Encyclopedia of Care of Elderly.* Edited by M. D. Mezey. New York: Springer, 2000.

CZAJA, S. J., and SHARIT, J. "Age Differences in Attitudes Towards Computers: The Influence of Task Characteristics." *The Journals of Gerontology: Psychological Sciences and Social Sciences* 53B (1998): 329–340.

FISK, A. D. "Human Factors and the Older Adult." *The Magazine of Human Factors Applications* 7, no. 1 (1999): 8–13.

KALASKY, M. A.; CZAJA, S. J.; SHARIT, J.; and NAIR, S. N. "Is Speech Technology Robust for Older Populations?" *Proceedings of the 43rd Annual Meeting of the Human Factors and Ergonomics Society.* (1999).

LAMBERT, L. D., and FLEURY, M. "Age, Cognitive Style, and Traffic Signs." *Perceptual and Motor Skills* 78 (1994): 611–624.

LAWTON, P. "Aging and the Performance of Home Tasks." *Human Factors* 32 (1990): 527–536.

ROGERS, W. A.; FISK, A. D.; MEAD, S.; WALKER, N.; and CABRERA, E. F. "Training Older Adults to Use Automatic Teller Machines." *Human Factors* 38 (1996): 425–433.

ROGERS, W. A.; MEYER, B.; WALKER, N.; and FISK, A. D. "Functional Limitations to Daily Living Tasks in the Aged: A Focus Group Analysis." *Human Factors* 40 (1998): 111–125.

SMITH, M. W.; CZAJA, S. J.; and SHARIT, J. "Aging, Motor Control, and the Performance of Computer Mouse Task." *Human Factors* 41 (1999): 389–397.

STAPLIN, L., and FISK, A. D. "A Cognitive Engineering Approach to Improve Signalized Left-Turn Intersections." *Human Factors* 33 (1991): 559–571.

U.S. Department of Transportation. *Traffic Safety Facts.* Washington, D.C.: National Center for Statistics and Analysis, 1994.

WALKER, N.; PHILBIN, D. A.; and FISK, A. D. "Age-Related Differences in Movement Control: Adjusting Submovement Structure to Optimize Performance." *Journal of Gerontology: Psychological Sciences* 52B (1997): P40–P52.

HYPERTENSION

See HIGH BLOOD PRESSURE

I

IMAGES OF AGING

The mass media's neglect of older people—and the often distorted presentation of elders as uniformly robust "golden years" retirees on the golf course—is generally regarded as regrettable, but financially understandable. Economic interests in news, entertainment, and advertising are used to rationalize the marketplace bias against anything more than an incidental inclusion of older age groups. This bottom-line approach is driven by the quest for dollars that slip through youthful fingers. Young families are considered to be more easily swayed by brand appeals than affluent but tight-fisted seniors, who are supposedly set in their consumerist ways. Yet, those who have taken a harder look have seen the ageism pervading the media as a tangled skein of stereotypes dyed by unfounded assumptions that are threaded with financial and political conflicts of interest. The devaluing of older people in the media is reinforced by the acrid image of *geezers*, a disparaging term that has become commonplace in major-media descriptions of elders.

Geezer bashing

The provocative phrase, *greedy geezers*, was embossed on generational politics by a dramatically illustrated cover of the *New Republic* (see Figure 1). It showed a fearsome old man leading a charge of elders evidently bent, as the accompanying article would claim, on draining the nation's economy through massive entitlement spending for their own comfort. Since then, the term *geezer* has been increasingly applied to older adults, despite the word's obvious use by proponents of one side of a political controversy who

want to diminish sympathy for the beneficiaries of public policies they would like to reverse. Principal examples in the year 2000 included crass references to "geezers" and the "old farts in Washington" by conservative syndicated newspaper columnist Michelle Malkin and an acerbic description of "increasingly fat, rested and healthy. . .geezers" by *The New Republic*'s "TRB" columnist Andrew Sullivan. These negative political associations are reinforced by the frequently invoked image of elders as an unstoppable force—*San Francisco Chronicle* Washington correspondent Carolyn Lockhead described them as "probably the most powerful voting bloc in America."

There is no mistaking that the stream of images depicting generational greed, profligate political potency, and economic impotency among older adults have political consequences. For example, public-policy analysts Merril Silverstein, Fay Lomax Cook, and colleagues compared public opinion data from 1990 to 1997, "a period characterized by the intensification of generational politics." Their study found much good news for advocates of existing social policies, such as that 74 percent of all Americans still supported Social Security and Medicare "as an earned right." However, the researchers also discerned that "the public has grown more apprehensive about the value of government programs serving the elderly." The report showed, in part, that "perceptions of the elderly as well-off increased over the period. Where 33 percent of the public agreed in 1990 that people over sixty were well-off, this increased to 39 percent in 1997. Interestingly, about the same proportion of the population saw children as well-off in 1990, but by 1997

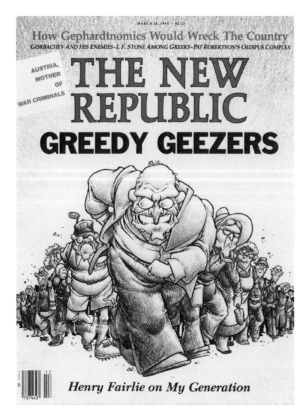

Figure 1. Cover of New Republic *magazine from March 28, 1988 picturing the onslaught of the "Greedy Geezers."* (Reprinted with permission.)

only 19 percent saw children as well-off. . .This dramatic twenty-point shift suggests that a considerable number of people have come to view the elderly as having a material advantage over children in society." Silverstein and his colleagues noted that most of the increase in this viewpoint came from elders themselves, 53 percent of whom believed that those sixty or older were well-off in 1997.

The image of idle, affluent elders has been reinforced by the limited presentations of older people in advertising. Marc Freedman, in his book, *Prime Time*, describes "a classic illustration" of idealized retirement that appeared "ironically, in the middle of Peter G. Peterson's May 1996 *Atlantic Monthly* cover story, 'Will America Grow Up Before it Grows Old?'" According to Freedman, the article lambasts the older population as a bunch of shiftless freeloaders. Among its pages was a glossy full-page ad for the insurance company ITT/Hartford depicting a smartly dressed, youthful-looking older couple dancing on the deck of a boat, kicking up their heels, and laugh-

ing like joyous teenagers. Accompanying the idyllic scene was the message: "One day you'll get to act like a kid again, but for now, let's discuss your allowance." Freedman did note a hopeful trend in financial industry advertising toward depictions of social engagement by older people. For example, he cites a 1999 American Express ad showing a trio of elders helping to build a house for Habitats for Humanity. Yet in the year 2000 the relatively few images of elders in advertising continued to show people who are well-heeled and self-absorbed.

Invisible elders

Media images of older people today alternate sharply between the figure of the geezer, who is to be feared and satirized, and of the sweet and vulnerable, if ineffectual, senior citizen. Older women, in particular, are cast in diminished roles or dismissed entirely, not only in the United States but worldwide. The attitude that elders constitute a group not needing to be seen or heard was addressed at the United Nations in New York City during a conference held on 13–15 October 1999, titled "The Impact of Globalization on the Images of Older Women." In one presentation, veteran BBC news anchor Nigel Kay reported that his network's recently completed second annual survey of older people in its news and entertainment programming found that even though 20 percent of the British population are sixty or older, only 7 percent of the BBC onscreen population were of that age. "Even more distressing," Kay emphasized, "on television older men significantly outnumber older women by about 70 percent to 30 percent," in spite of the women's holding a 57 percent majority among the country's older citizens.

Kay explained that the network began conducting the yearly television census in cooperation with Age Concern, England's principal nongovernmental organization (NGO) involved with issues in aging, as part of the broadcaster's process of developing policies concerning its treatment of elders.

At one session of the U.N. conference, O. Burtch Drake, president and CEO of the American Association of Advertising Agencies, spoke of women's media image with sharp irony. "Older women are not being portrayed at all; there is no imagery to worry about." Political scientist Hamideh Sedghhi commented that "images of older women differ globally. Perceptions of the aged range from positive traits such as sweet, pleasant, giving, and caring, to negative characteristics like slow, feeble, cranky, and repetitive." She went on to surmise, "Antiaging pursuits and gender stereotyping are economically profitable," especially in the marketing of cosmetics and plastic surgery. Sedgahhi added that often "businesses replace older employees with younger ones in an effort to give the failing organization a more youthful image."

The general absence of older women in the media was underscored at the conference by results of a survey of public broadcasters in six northern European countries (the Netherlands, Norway, Sweden, Finland, Denmark, and Germany). Bernadette van Dijck, who heads the Gender Portrayal Department of the Netherlands Broadcasting Organization in Utrecht, said the 1997–1998 study revealed that both women and men aged sixty-five or older represented merely 2 percent of the television populations in those nations, and older women "were mainly invisible."

Furthermore, a 1999 British study titled *Older Generations in Print* surveyed 3,686 articles appearing in 1,096 local, regional, and national news outlets. Its authors state that "older people these days often lead full and active lives, but this rarely is acknowledged in the media." The investigators claim that despite their documenting good coverage of the primary social and political issues regarding Britain's aging demographics, "when it comes to the actual portrayal of older people there is a problem with the identification of old age with vulnerability, epitomized in the predominance of the frail-victim story." The authors continue: "We are not bidding for what is often called a 'positive image' of ageing [sic], since this would suggest something like PR for older people, and that would be just another kind of distortion. We are suggesting that news values need to be more imaginative and diverse."

"Old warhorses" in U.S. newsrooms

In the United States, the attitude of the news media's most highly placed executives toward older audiences was documented by Nancy Hicks Maynard. Maynard came to disturbing conclusions after conducting interviews during more than two years with two hundred of the most influential executives in the media, under a grant from the Freedom Forum, which is sponsored by the Gannett Foundation. Her study was summarized in a series of columns in the *Columbia Journalism Review.*

Maynard bemoans the dwindling audiences for news and lays the blame squarely on a "generation gap" in newsrooms. She writes that in the last two decades of the twentieth century both the audience and newsroom staffs aged beyond the point where they respect the more lucrative and modern interests in the news industry. "The gray-haired set has captured the news business," she writes. "This generational domination is far more complete than gender or even racial gaps, and it may be a factor in young adults' news consumption patterns and the shrinking audience for traditional news." The negative impression of older audiences, as viewed by Maynard's informants, is reflected in one solution for increasing younger audiences. According to Maynard, many journalists "preparing the news shy away from today's tools and rules" of high-tech interactivity. She writes that "Journalists with these sensibilities don't connect with the young, and neither does their coverage. Some news executives are beginning to understand this. As they do, in the finite world of print, they unceremoniously ax the old warhorses to make way for something new. In 1999, the *New York Times* fired from its op-ed page both humorist Russell Baker and former executive editor Abe Rosenthal. They were replaced by clever baby boomers. . . ."

Old warhorses, dead wood, and related images suggesting that older people place a drag on productivity and momentum toward future growth are routinely expressed in policies of the entertainment and advertising industries—often in ways that directly affect how, or whether, more mature themes or images are represented on movie or television screens. For example, in October 2000, a group of twenty-eight highly successful Hollywood screenwriters (who were later joined by many other screenwriters) filed a federal class-action suit against the major networks, studios, and talent agencies claiming they participated in a "systematic" pattern of age discrimination. The *Los Angeles Times* reported (24 October 2000) that the lawsuit, which was later dismissed by the court, cited a 1998 study commissioned by the Writers Guild of America "showing the decreased rate of writers forty and older on broadcast-network sitcoms and dramas. According to the report, for instance, nearly 75 percent of writers within the guild age thirty or younger were employed in 1997, versus 46 percent of those in their 40s and 32 percent of those in their 50s."

The ageism affecting older screenwriters and actors runs so deep in the media's impressions about its economic interests that a television network's bottom line is most heavily damaged if it is identified as attracting an "old audience," a phrase used by the *New York Times* in referring to CBS. In his "Television" column, *Times* writer Bill Carter reminded readers that CBS was "once the butt of jokes by all its rivals for having a core audience of viewers who signed on to see Jack Benny and haven't quit yet." Later that month, the *Wall Street Journal* (24 October) reported in a front-page story that NBC had lost ground in competition for "the coveted 18 to 49 age group." The article stressed, "In the past three years, the median age of NBC's audience has risen to forty-five from forty-one, a bad omen for advertising revenues."

Advertising rates trump ratings

What neither the *New York Times* nor the *Wall Street Journal* article explained is that attracting older viewers loses money—even if the older audience for a show is significantly larger than that of a competing show drawing younger viewers. For example, Lawrence K. Grossman, former president of both NBC News and PBS, wrote "Newscasts tend to attract older audiences, a serious deficiency in an industry dedicated to the single-minded pursuit of the young adults advertisers prize most. TV time buyers pay $23.54 per thousand viewers to reach 18 to 35 year olds and only $9.57 per thousand for those over the age of 35, according to industry sources." (Grossman).

Grossman's article also contradicts Maynard's assertion that the interests of older new consumers are already fulfilled in current programming. According to Grossman, "to lower their audience's age level and raise profitability, TV news producers, national and local alike, keep lightening the content of their newscasts, filling them with titillating tabloid items about crime, celebrities, and gossip, while playing down serious reporting about government, international affairs, and major public issues, whose appeal is thought to be confined mainly to older viewers." Grossman goes on to admit, "When I ran NBC News. . .I was as guilty of the age myopia as anyone."

The connection between advertising and what audiences see of older people, if they see

them at all, was examined by Anna Nolan Rahman and Elyse Salend when they conducted media research during the early and mid-1990s. In an article for the American Society on Aging newspaper, *Aging Today* (January-February 1995, page 11), they explained that highly successful programs featuring older actors, such as CBS's "Murder She Wrote" with Angela Lansbury, earned lower advertising revenue per minute than its more youth-attracting rival, "Lois and Clark," even though "Murder She Wrote" was rated number sixteen among all television shows in the May 1995 "sweeps" (twice-yearly periods when ratings are used to adjust ad rates), and "Lois and Clark," a romantic Superman adventure series, landed in the ninety-eighth spot. The same demographic bias, according to Rahman and Salend, causes "most of the major-market stations in the syndication arena" to turn down opportunities to replay even highly successful programs appealing to mature viewers.

Rahman and Salend traced "a key reason" for the television industry's dogged pursuit of younger audiences to a development in the early 1950s. They explained that "when ABC was launched, the fledgling network, concentrated mostly in urban areas, had difficulty attracting older viewers, who were tuned to CBS and NBC. ABC was popular, however, among 18-to-34 year olds. Desperate for a sales hook, ABC decided to turn what was then considered a negative into a positive. Rahman and Salend quote Arnold Becker, who worked at ABC in its early years and was later vice president of Entertainment Research at CBS, as saying that ABC linked the young-adult market with adults 35 to 49 and "started singing the praises of the 18-to-49-year-old group." Becker told them that the ABC pitch used such phrases as, "Get them to buy when they're young, you'll get them for life." Or, "The young will try new things," and the refrain, "The old are set in their ways." Becker added that these age-based statements are "baloney . . . they're not true."

Advertisers' misconceptions

Maynard echoes another common misconceptions about older consumers: "While older people have the most money and spend a lot of it, mass media advertising influences them the least." This assertion is coming under increasing fire from others in advertising and marketing. Maynard goes on, "A number of high-end or specialty magazines cater to their tastes. The young women who control the family purse are the biggest target for the mass media, so advertisers pay a premium to get their attention." This convention of the advertising industry was criticized by Richard A. Lee. According to his 1995 study, "Advertising industry denial of changes in family structure that make per capita spending more important than household spending is a major contributor to ageism in advertising."

Lee describes the advertising industry's adherence to household spending "as a fixation on life as it was with the Cleavers," where mom buys all of the food and kids' clothes and dad buys the family car. He suggests that they would be better served by focusing on per capita spending, which the field's own data shows is more lucrative. He dismisses the "Leave it to Beaver" model of marketing to households as the primary consumer unit, calling this approach "a useful myth." He explains, "If the industry starts shifting toward per capita spending as the measure of consumer potential, [it] will be obligated to shift away from media advertising where economies of scale are based on the presence of household buying units."

Lee's research, conducted in cooperation with the Association of Advertising Agencies International, included 206 employees at thirty-eight advertising agencies in distinct markets across the United States. The study found that those surveyed generally ignore older audiences, even though one of their most commonly available sources of economic and demographic data, the *Official Guide to Household Spending* shows that "per capita consumer spending peaks in the 55 to 64 age range, and 65 to 74 year olds outspend 35 to 44 year olds." Lee found, however, that 80 percent of ad agency staff who completed the survey overestimated the number of consumers over age fifty; "75 percent underestimated the discretionary spending power" of older consumers, and 85 percent fell short in guessing the personal net worth of aging Americans.

According to Lee, advertising-agency professionals erroneously visualize mature audiences as "A lot of poor people with little consumer potential." Moreover, 54 percent of respondents agreed with false statements that "seniors buy price" or are mainly cost conscious, and "seniors don't switch brands."

Careful not to point blame at young ad executives, Lee criticizes industry leaders for unfounded notions revealed in statements such as: "We need to hire some young punks with attitude," and "the only thing that sells in America are youth, sex, and protection against aging."

Increasingly, the view that older consumers are under-appreciated is gaining support in the advertising and marketing industries. An article by the American Advertising Federation titled "Senior Spending" notes that, "while Generation Y is appealing to marketers, focusing on the senior population, an oft-forgotten group, also can be highly profitable." This article cites findings of a 1999 survey of six hundred people aged five and older conducted by Research 100 of Princeton, N.J. This proprietary study found that seniors are "neither frugal nor set in their ways" and spend "more time considering new brands and products than other age groups." Further, according to the article, Zona Research, Inc. "reports that seniors fifty-five and older spent three times as much on Internet purchases during the 1998 holiday season than the average holiday shopper." The article concludes that "To capitalize on this senior market, advertisers need to shed their misconceptions and age biases. . . . This exploding market can be of great benefit to advertisers, if only they take the initiative and target them." Brad Edmondson, former editor of American Demographics, emphasizes that ". . .The boomers are not the only market in America.. . .In particular, our data also show that generations older than the baby boom are gaining consumer power, so that robust spending on some products may be emerging among householders in their 70s and 80s."

Hopeful signs

There are, however, hopeful signs for a more representative presentation of older people in the U.S. media. For example, Lawrence K. Grossman describes the emergence of the *age beat* in journalism in many parts of the United States. Unlike other single-focus assignments in newsrooms, he writes, the agebeat is "not a special interest beat, or what in current media jargon is called a 'niche' beat, but one of the most important general interest beats of the coming century."

The age beat began to emerge in earnest in the United States in the early 1990s. In 1993, a half-dozen reporters among those covering the American Society on Aging (ASA) Annual Meeting in Chicago met to form the Journalists Exchange on Aging (JEoA), a group that has since then produced the *Age Beat* newsletter and has developed and cosponsored educational programs for journalists with a range of organizations, including the University of Minnesota School of Journalism and Communication, the Freedom Forum, the AARP Andrus Foundation, and the International Longevity Center. Based at ASA in San Francisco, it has provided networking opportunities for journalists and an informal information exchange for background and sources on the complexities of covering issues in aging. By summer 2001, the group listed almost seven hundred media journalists who follow the concerns of the aging population enough to want to receive the group's information.

Results from the Third National Survey of Journalists on Aging, cited in *Aging Today* (March-April 2001), showed that the 149 respondents are "seasoned and sensitized" to issues of growing older. The typical reporter covering aging is a woman (61 percent of respondents) who has been a professional journalist for 22.4 years and has produced stories on aging during the past 8.5 years for at least part of her editorial work. The study, conducted by JEoA, found that 95.5 percent of participants had "experienced aspects of issues in aging" themselves or through their families. More strikingly, 98.4 percent of those who have been touched personally by facets of aging agreed that their experience had affected their "journalistic perspective." This affirmed that their personal experience informed their perspective, rather than compromised their objectivity. Of 115 respondents to the question, "Do you feel most other reporting you see/hear on issues (such as Social Security and Medicaid) is accurate and balanced," 40 percent said no.

These respondents represented a growing corps of veterans of the age beat that has developed at such news organizations as *Minneapolis Star-Tribune, Orange County Register, The Oregonian, Richmond Times-Dispatch, Arizona Republic, Consumer Reports, Consumer Digest, Pittsburgh Post Gazette, Washington Post, Los Angeles Times, The Oklahoman*, and numerous dailies in Florida.

In *Life in an Older American* Grossman observed, "It can only be hoped that with more journalism training, education and experience, coverage of generational issues will become more practiced and therefore more intelligent and sophisticated. As older people lead younger life-

styles, society will have little choice but to adopt patterns of relationships that reflect not generational battles but integrated living among generations. Generational separation and segregation should give way to community models in which vigorous older people serve as valuable resources for the young. . ."

PAUL KLEYMAN

BIBLIOGRAPHY

CUMBERBATCH, G.; GAUNTLETT, S.; LITTLEJOHNS, V.; WOODS, S.; and STEPHENSON, C. *Too Old for TV? A Portrayal of Older People on Television: A Report for Age Concern England*. Birmingham, England: The Communications Research Group, 1999.

EDMONDSON, B. "Do the Math." *American Demographics*. October, 1999.

FREEDMAN, M. *Prime Time: How Baby Boomers Will Revolutionize Retirement and Transform America*. New York: Perseus Books/Public Affairs, 1999.

"Going for Youth, CBS Attracts Attention." *New York Times*. October 1, 2000.

GOOMBRIDGE, B.; SEYMOUR, E.; and CASS, B. *Older Generations in Print: A Report from Media Age Network*. London, U.K.: Secretariate for the International Year of Older Persons, 2000.

GROSSMAN, L. K. "Aging Viewers: The Best Is Yet to Come." *Columbia Journalism Review*. 36 no. 5 (January/February, 1998): 68.

GROSSMAN, L. K., and BUTLER, R. N "The Media's Role." In *Life in Older America*. New York: The Century Foundation Press, 1999. Pages 231–238.

KLEYMAN, P. "The Media's Role: Beyond the Medical Model of Reporting on Aging." In *Health Aging: Challenges and Solutions*. Edited by K. Dychtwald. Gaithersburg, Md.: Aspen Publishers, 1999. Pages 303–314.

LEE, R. A. *Ageism in Advertising: A Study of Advertising Agency Attitudes Toward Maturing and Mature Consumers*. High Yield Marketing: 1995.

LOCKHEAD, C. *San Francisco Chronicle*, Washington Bureau, September 10, 2000.

MAYNARD, N. H. *Megamedia: How Market Forces Are Transforming the News*. New York: Maynard Partners, 2000.

Prime Time: How Baby Boomers Will Revolutionize Retirement and Transform America. New York: Perseus Books/Public Affairs, 1999.

RAHMAN, A. N., and SALEND, E. *Aging Today*. January/February, 1995.

"Senior Spending." *American Advertising*. New York: American Advertising Federation (Winter 1999–2000).

SILVERSTEIN, M., and COOK, F. L. "Solidarity and Tension Between Age-Groups in the United States." *International Journal of Social Welfare* 9 no. 4 (2000): 270–284.

SMITH, J. *The Impact of Globalization on the Images of Older Women: Report of International Symposium.* October 13–15, 1999. Edited by Jeanne Smith. New York: AARP International Activities Office, 2000.

SULLIVAN, A. "TRB from Washington: Old Guard." *The New Republic* (October 9, 2000): 6.

IMMIGRANTS

Immigration had an important influence on the American population during the last third of the twentieth century comparable to peaks in the earliest decades of the century. In 1997, for example, nearly 800,000 persons immigrated legally to the United States. In that year, the mean age of native-born American adults eighteen and over was virtually identical to that of long-term immigrants (45.1 and 45.0 years, respectively), while recent immigrants averaged 33.5 years of age. Since people usually immigrate when they are young, immigration offsets the effects of population aging, but only in the short run. Because immigrants also grow older, 10.8 million new immigrants would be required annually to maintain year-2000 support ratios (the ratio of persons age fifteen to sixty-four to those sixty-five and older) until 2050. Since recent immigrants are largely from Asia and the Western hemisphere, the older population will grow more diverse in its ethnic and racial composition as young immigrants age.

Types of older immigrants

Persons age sixty-five and older made up only 3 percent of immigrants who entered the United States between 1990 and 2000, as compared to 14 percent of immigrants who arrived before this period and 12 percent of the native-born population. Older people are less likely to move, if only because they have stronger ties to their place of residence. Despite this propensity to *age in place*, 41,780 immigrants age sixty-five and older were admitted to the United States as permanent residents in 1996. The majority of older immigrants in 1996 (57 percent) were women. While most of the older men were married (84 percent), the women were more evenly divided between the married (45 percent) and the widowed (40 percent).

The percentage of immigrants age sixty-five and older has climbed steadily—from 2 percent in the early 1960s to 4 to 5 percent in the late 1990s. Because overall immigration increased markedly, this period also saw an eight-fold increase in the number of elderly immigrants. Most older immigrants settled in states that already had large immigrant populations (e.g., California, New York, Texas, Florida, Hawaii).

In addition to immigrants admitted as permanent residents, many older people who entered the country earlier adjust their visas to permanent resident status. In 1996, adjustments included 6,230 refugees and asylees, age sixty-five and older who had sought protection from persecution in their countries of nationality. Furthermore, many older adults are among the tourists and visitors admitted to the United States on a temporary visa each year. Of the 1.4 million elderly nonimmigrant visitors in 1996, nearly half came from the United Kingdom, Japan, Germany, or Mexico.

Older people who immigrate permanently do so largely for family reasons, particularly to be close to children living in the United States. There are no numerical limits placed on immigrants who are immediate relatives of U.S. citizens, provided they are twenty-one years of age or older. In 1996, 87 percent of newly admitted immigrants, age sixty-five and older entered the country as parents of U.S. citizens. Another 11 percent of older immigrants entered under some other family reunification provision of U.S. immigration law (e.g., as spouses of U.S. citizens or permanent residents). Apparently, illegal immigration is unusual for those admitted as parents. Fewer than 2 percent of parents who immigrated to the United States in 1996 had been illegal immigrants at some point, as indicated by self-reports or visa documents, but almost 20 percent of all permanent immigrants had such irregularities.

Origins of older immigrants

The major countries that are departure points for older immigrants include China, Russia, Cuba, the Philippines, Mexico, India, Vietnam, and Iran. When the Immigration and Nationality Act Amendments of 1965 ended the system of national origin quotas, which favored European immigrants, there was a marked increase in Asian immigration. According to Immigration and Naturalization Service data, in 1991

Rose Lagunoff, 102, holds an American flag moments after being sworn in as a United States citizen on August 6, 1997 in Silver Spring, Maryland. Lagunoff came to the United States from Russia when she was fifteen years old. (AP photo by Gail Burton.)

over half of the permanent legal immigrants age sixty-five and older entered the United States from Asia. China and the Philippines each contributed over 10 percent of the older immigrants in 1991. Asia was the birthplace of nearly two-thirds of older people immigrating as parents of U.S. citizens. To become eligible to sponsor a parent's immigration, immigrant children must become naturalized citizens. Asians have high naturalization rates. In contrast, Mexican immigrants have relatively low naturalization rates, so the large Mexican immigrant population has proportionately fewer elderly immigrants than it might otherwise have.

Few Europeans, except for those from formerly socialist countries such as Russia, immigrate to the United States today. In contrast, Europeans dominated immigration in the first two-thirds of the twentieth century. These immigrants became naturalized citizens, raised their families in the United States, and assimilated economically. Today, in advanced old age, their social and economic circumstances look very much like that of their native-born American counterparts, particularly in terms of their receipt of Social Security and Supplemental Security Income (SSI).

Economic circumstances

Although they are generally younger than seniors from the earlier European immigration waves, recent older immigrants are not as well-off economically. In the sixty-five-and-older population, in 1990, those who immigrated during the 1980s were twice as likely to live in poverty as were all older Americans. By and large, recent elderly immigrants lack the human capital—education, English fluency, U.S.-based work experience, and good health—that would make them employable in the skills-based U.S. economy. In 1991, immigrating parents of U.S. citizens had completed only 7.4 years of schooling, on average, versus 12.7 years for all immigrants age 25 and older. Not surprisingly, less than 1 percent of permanent immigrants age fifty-five and older was admitted on an employment preference visa in 1996. Of those age sixty-five and older, almost nine out of ten immigrants are not in the labor force, a figure comparable to that for native-born seniors.

Lacking U.S. employment experience, older immigrants are not likely to qualify for Social Security, except perhaps as dependents of U.S. workers. According to the 1998 and 1999 Current Population Surveys, only 31 percent of persons age sixty-five and older who immigrated after 1990 received Social Security, compared to 78 percent of older long-term immigrants and 91 percent of native-born seniors. Since Social Security is a mainstay of retirement income, it is not surprising that older immigrants rely more heavily on public assistance—the surveys found that among recent immigrants, 24 percent received means-tested Supplemental Security Income (SSI), compared to 13 percent of their long-term counterparts and only 3 percent of native-born seniors.

In response to the growing numbers of aliens collecting SSI, Congress tightened eligibility requirements with the 1996 welfare reform legislation. Assuming they meet strict income and asset limits, legal aliens who are blind, disabled, or sixty-five years of age and older are eligible for SSI only if they are recent refugees or have worked forty quarters under Social Security-covered employment. SSI rules create an incentive for legal aliens to become citizens, but the requirements, particularly the knowledge of English, discourage older immigrants from naturalizing. In 1990, 41 percent of older people who had immigrated during the 1980s spoke no English. Whether the new SSI provisions will actually discourage elderly immigration remains to be seen.

Family ties

Because of their limited economic resources, people who immigrate in old age usually depend on their children for support. Beginning in December 1997, new immigration rules reinforced family support obligations. Not only must the household income of those sponsoring a family member's immigration be at least 125 percent of the poverty line, but also the required *affidavit of support* is now a legally enforceable contract. Shared housing is one way for kin to support elderly immigrants. In contrast to the *intimacy at a distance* that characterizes native-born seniors, elderly immigrants are apt to live with offspring rather than independently. Coresidence may benefit the younger generation as much as, or more than, the older generation, because the older immigrant often assumes responsibility for childcare and housekeeping in a child's home.

Some parents are, in fact, invited to immigrate by their grown children so that they can help out around the house. Cultural expectations for family togetherness and kin eldercare may also dictate that aging parents and grown children live in close proximity. Immigrant families are more likely than native-born Americans to rely on family care of the dependent aged, as opposed to formal means of support. Hispanic and Asian immigrants age sixty and older are even more likely than older, non-Hispanic white immigrants to reside with other family members. This relation is independent of economic resources, English-language fluency, and disability.

Although older immigrants maintain close family ties, their adjustment to life in the United States can be slow, and is sometimes painful. Older people who are recent immigrants are at particular risk of depression. Age-related cognitive and physical limitations (e.g., mobility restrictions) can impede assimilation and acculturation. Structural aspects of the life course also contribute to elderly isolation. Unlike younger people, older immigrants are not exposed to the

English language or to American customs in the school and workplace. Ethnic communities, where older immigrants can interact with other elderly people from their native land, can offer a comfortable accommodation for those who immigrate late in life. A growing number of older immigrants require specialized social service programs to address their particular needs in a culturally appropriate manner.

JUDITH TREAS
MICHAEL TYLER

See also AGING IN PLACE; INTERGENERATIONAL EXCHANGES.

BIBLIOGRAPHY

BLACK, S. A.; MARKIDES, K. S.; and MILLER, T. Q. "Correlates of Depressive Symptomatology among Older Community-Dwelling Mexican-Americans: The Hispanic EPESE." *Journals of Gerontology* 53 (1998): S198.

GOLD, S. J. *Refugee Communities: A Comparative Field Study.* Newbury Park, Calif.: Sage, 1992.

JASSO, G.; MASSEY, D. S.; ROSENBERG, M. R.; and SMITH, J. P. "The New Immigrant Pilot (NIS-P): Overview and New Findings about U.S. Legal Immigrants at Admission." *Demography* 37 (2000): 127–138.

KRITZ, M. M.; GURAK, D. T.; and CHEN, L. W. "Elderly Immigrants: Their Composition and Living Arrangements." *Sociology and Social Welfare* 27 (2000): 85–114.

MIN, P. G. *Changes and Conflicts: Korean Families in New York.* Boston, Mass.: Allyn Bacon, 1998.

MOON, A.; LUBBEN, J. E.; and VILLA, V. "Awareness and Utilization of Community Long-Term Care Services by Elderly Korean and Non-Hispanic White Americans." *The Gerontologist* 38 (1998): 309–316.

TREAS, J. "Older Americans in the 1990s and Beyond." *Population Bulletin* 50 (1995): 1–45.

TREAS, J. "Older Immigrants and U.S. Welfare Reform." *International Journal of Sociology and Social Policy* 17 (1997): 8–33.

TREAS, J., and TORRECILHA, R. "The Older Population." In *State of the Union: America in the 1980s,* Vol. 1. Edited by Reynolds Farley. New York: Russell Sage Foundation, 1995. Pages 47–91.

U.N. Department of Economic and Social Affairs, Population Division. *Replacement Migration: Is It a Solution to Declining and Ageing Populations?* New York: United Nations, 2000.

U.S. Immigration and Naturalization Service. *Statistical Yearbook of the Immigration and Natu-*

ralization Service, 1996. Washington, D.C.: U.S. Government Printing Office, 1997.

VAN HOOK, J. "SSI Eligibility and Participation among Elderly Naturalized Citizens and Noncitizens." *Social Science Research* 29 (2000): 51–67.

WILMOTH, J. "Living Arrangements Among Older Immigrants in the United States." *The Gerontologist* 41 (2000): 228–238.

IMMUNE SYSTEM

The immune system provides the body with resistance to disease. *Innate immunity* is furnished by relatively nonspecific mechanisms, such as the rapid inflammation experienced shortly after injury or infection. In contrast to innate mechanisms that hinder the entrance and initial spread of disease, *adaptive immunity* is more selective in its activity, and upon repeated exposures to pathogens can often prevent disease. There are two kinds of adaptive immune responses. *Humoral* immune responses are effective against agents that act outside of cells, such as bacteria and toxins. During humoral immune responses, proteins called *antibodies,* which can bind to and destroy pathogens, are secreted into the blood and other body fluids. In contrast, *cell-mediated* immune responses are important in resisting diseases caused by pathogens that live within cells, such as viruses. During cell-mediated responses, immune cells that can destroy infected host cells become active. Furthermore, cell-mediated immunity may also destroy cells making aberrant forms or amounts of normal molecules, as in some cancers.

Numerous aspects of adaptive immunity differ substantially in aged individuals from what is seen in young adults. For example, aged individuals often have attenuated or otherwise impaired immune responses to various bacterial and viral pathogens. Indeed, this general trend forms the basis for recommended immunizations against infectious agents that younger individuals resist easily. Aged individuals often respond differently to vaccination, however, sometimes resulting in a lack of protective immunity. In addition, untoward immune phenomena, such as certain forms of autoimmunity, as well as cancers involving cells of the immune system, show increased incidence in aged individuals. A complete understanding of these age-associated changes in immune status and function remains elusive, requiring knowledge of the mechanisms underlying maintenance, activation, and control of the immune system.

Lymphocytes, clonal selection, and antigen recognition

Lymphocytes are central to all adaptive immune responses. They originate from stem cells in the bone marrow. Cells destined to become lymphocytes either mature in the bone marrow or exit the marrow and mature in the thymus (because they are sites of lymphocyte production, the bone marrow and thymus are termed the *primary lymphoid organs*). Lymphocytes that mature in the bone marrow make antibodies and are called *B lymphocytes* (B cells); whereas lymphocytes that mature in the thymus are called *T lymphocytes* (T cells). The T lymphocytes are further subdivided into functional subsets: *cytotoxic T lymphocytes* (Tc cells) generate cell-mediated immune responses and can destroy other cells that have pieces of antigen on their surface; *helper T lymphocytes* (Th cells) regulate the immune system, governing the quality and strength of all immune responses. Tc and Th cells are often termed CD8+ and CD4+ T cells, based on so-called "cluster designation" (CD) molecules found on their surface.

The notion that specificity in adaptive immune responses derives from a clonal distribution of antigen receptors, coupled with requisite receptor ligation for activation, is the central argument of the generally accepted *clonal selection hypothesis.* Simply put, while billions of different antigen receptors can be made (in terms of antigen-binding specificity), each lymphocyte makes only one kind. Engagement of this receptor is requisite for lymphocyte activation, so a given antigen activates only those lymphocytes whose receptors bind well, yielding appropriate specificity in the overall response.

Antigen recognition by lymphocytes. The B lymphocyte's antigen receptor is a membrane-bound version of the antibody it will secrete if activated. When activated, a B lymphocyte's secreted antibodies enter the blood and other body fluids, where the bind the antigen and help destroy it. In contrast, a T lymphocyte's antigen receptor (TcR) is not secreted, but instead binds antigen displayed on the surface of other cells. Further, while B lymphocytes can bind native antigens directly, T lymphocytes can only bind an antigen when it is degraded and *presented.* Antigen presentation occurs when degradation products of protein antigens become attached to molecules encoded by a group of genes called the Major Histocompatibility Complex (MHC) and displayed on cell surfaces. All vertebrates have a homologue of this gene complex; for example, the human MHC is named HLA. When proteins either are made within a cell or are ingested by phagocytosis, they may be degraded by a variety of systems. The resulting small peptides become associated with binding clefts in MHC molecules. This peptide-MHC molecule combination is then displayed on the cell's surface for recognition by T lymphocytes. Different categories of MHC molecules exist, encoded by different genes within the MHC. Class I MHC molecules tend to become associated with the degradation products of proteins that were synthesized inside the cell. Further, class I molecules generally present antigen to cytotoxic T cells, so if a cell makes class I MHC molecules, it can present antigen to cytotoxic T cells. Most kinds of cells in the body express MHC class I molecules, so nearly any cell that is synthesizing nonself proteins (such as those from a viral infection) can be destroyed by cytotoxic T cells. In contrast, class II MHC molecules present antigen to helper T cells, so a cell that makes class II MHC molecules can present antigen to helper T cells. Only a few kinds of cells, including dendritic cells, macrophages, and B lymphocytes, normally express class II MHC molecules and present antigen to Th cells.

Lymphocyte development, production, and receptor diversity. Since antigen receptor specificities are clonally distributed, the selectivity of immune responses relies on the constant availability of a large and diverse pre-immune lymphocyte pool. Towards this end, millions of lymphocytes are produced daily in the marrow and thymus. As lymphocytes develop and mature, they begin to express their surface-bound antigen receptor. The receptor's expression and specificity are established through a series of DNA rearrangement and splicing events that yield functional antigen receptor genes. Because the portion of the receptor molecule that will interact with antigen derives from such pseudorandom gene-splicing mechanisms, the number of permutations available to afford diversity among clonally distributed antigen-combining sites is enormous—in the range of 10^{12}.

Age-associated changes in lymphocyte development and selection. Lymphocyte production and selection changes with age. For example, the rate at which lymphocytes are generated in the thymus and bone marrow, which will dictate the turnover of mature lymphocytes in the periphery, has been shown to decrease with age. These shifts appear to reflect a combination of factors, which may include a lower frequency of successful antigen-receptor-gene expression, reflecting intrinsic changes in B cell progenitors. Further, failure or diminution of stromal trophic elements necessary for the survival of developing lymphocytes may occur with increasing age. Finally, shifts in the representation of various differentiation subsets, likely reflecting changes in the homeostatic processes that govern steady state numbers, shift with age. The mechanistic bases for these changes remain unclear, and are the subject of intense investigation.

In addition to changes in lymphocyte production, the degree of receptor diversity within both mature and developing lymphoid compartments may become truncated with age. This may alter the frequency or breadth of available primary clones that can engage in immune responses, affecting the outcome of immunization or vaccination. Similar to the factors contributing to reduced production rates, the basis for truncated antigen receptor diversity appears manifold. For example, it likely involves downstream effects precipitated by altered lymphocyte production and selection; but probably also originates from the life-long accumulation of expanded *memory* clones, which are the result of antigen-driven expansion, and perforce less diverse.

Secondary lymphoid organs and immune responses

Lymphoid organs, vessels, and recirculation. Mature lymphocytes constantly travel through the blood to the lymphoid organs and then back to the blood. This constant recirculation insures that the body is continuously monitored for invading substances. The major areas of antigen contact and lymphocyte activation are the secondary lymphoid organs. These include the lymph nodes, spleen, and tonsils, as well as specialized areas of the intestine and lungs. Appropriate recirculation and compartmentalization is essential to vigorous immune function, since this provides appropriate surveillance of the host for antigens, as well as the appropriate juxtaposition of all cellular elements to insure fruitful interaction.

Cell interactions in immune responses. Although antigen binding is necessary to activate a B or T cell, that alone is insufficient to induce an immune response. Instead, both humoral and cell-mediated responses require interactions between three cell types: antigen-presenting cells (APCs), Th cells, and either a B cell or Tc cell. Generally, the interaction between the APC and Th cells involves not only the binding of the TcR by the antigenic peptides in association with the MHC, but a series of *second signals*. These requisite second signals are afforded by the interactions of both membrane-bound ligand receptor pairs, known collectively as *costimulators,* as well as a variety of soluble growth and differentiation factors secreted by the antigen-presenting cells.

Humoral immune responses involve several events following the entry of antigen. First, antigen-presenting cells take up some of the antigen, attach pieces of it to Class II MHC molecules, and present it to T-helper cells. Binding the presented antigen activates T-helper cells, which then divide and secrete stimulatory molecules called *interleukins*. These stimulatory molecules in turn activate any B lymphocytes that have bound the antigen, and these activated B cells then divide, differentiate, and secrete antibody. Finally, the secreted antibodies bind the antigen and help destroy it through a variety of so-called effector mechanisms, including neutralization, complement fixation, and opsonization.

Cell-mediated immune responses involve several events following the entry of antigen. Helper T cells are required, so some of the antigen must be taken up by APCs and presented to T-helper cells. Binding the presented antigen activates the T-helper cells to divide and secrete interleukins. These in turn activate any cytotoxic T cells that have bound pieces of the antigen presented by class I MHC molecules on infected cells. The activated cytotoxic cells can then serially kill cells displaying antigen presented by class I MHC molecules, effectively eliminating any cells infected with the antigen.

Age-associated changes in recirculation, interaction, and immune responses. The patterns of compartmentalization and recirculation may vary with age, and again likely reflect a combination of factors. These probably include relative increases in memory-cell populations, whose recirculation and compartmentalization properties differ from primary lymphocytes, as well as alterations in the efficacy and structure of the lymphatics caused by either intrinsic or extrinsic factors. Of course, these shifts may alter the han-

dling and recognition of antigens by APCs and lymphocytes, consequently impacting heavily on all negative and positive selective processes. It is also clear that the strength and duration of immune responses can change with age. Most reports of such changes are largely descriptive and subject to great variability.

Immune tolerance and autoimmunity

The immune system generates significant numbers of lymphocytes whose antigen receptors bind "self" molecules strongly enough to engender immune activity against self components. Indeed, the random processes responsible for antigen receptor diversity, coupled with genetic polymorphism in most structural genes, makes generation of such "autoreactive" receptors unavoidable. The random processes responsible for antigen-receptor diversity, coupled with genetic polymorphism in most structural genes, makes generation of such autoreactive receptors unavoidable. The avoidance of pathogenic autoreactivity, despite this likelihood of developing receptors capable of binding to self molecules, is collectively termed *immunologic tolerance.*

How cells bearing potentially autoreactive receptors are controlled remains an area of intense investigation, but several mechanisms clearly play important roles. Many autoreactive clones are eliminated before they mature in the marrow and thymus, because when immature B or T cells have their antigen receptor occupied they undergo *deletion* via apoptotic cell death. In contrast, mature lymphocytes resist death induced via receptor ligation. Regardless of the exact mechanisms involved, these so-called *central deletion* mechanism provide a means to screen and eliminate incipient autoreactive cells before they completely mature. However, these central tolerance mechanisms, while clearly an important element of immunologic tolerance, are insufficient to fully explain the lack of autoreactivity. For example, some self molecules are expressed only in tissues found outside of the thymus or bone marrow, precluding exposure of developing lymphocytes. Thus, a variety of *peripheral tolerance* mechanisms are believed to be important in successful avoidance of self reactivity. These include the functional inactivation of lymphocytes through *anergy,* the blockage or prevention of appropriate second signals, discussed above, and the sequestration of certain self components in areas where lymphocytes do not recirculate, such as the chamber of the eye.

If the immune system fails to appropriately eliminate or control self-reactive cells, they may cause life-threatening autoimmune disease. These diseases may involve cell-mediated responses, humoral responses, or both. Examples of autoimmunity include: type I diabetes, where individuals make an immune response against their insulin-producing cells, destroying them and resulting in abnormal sugar metabolism; myasthenia gravis, where one makes antibodies against normal molecules that control neuromuscular activity, resulting in weakness and paralysis; and systemic lupus erythematosus, where antibodies to many normal body constituents are made, resulting in widespread symptoms. Some autoimmune diseases lead to the deposition of antibody-antigen aggregates called *immune complexes* in the kidney, lungs, or joints. Because these complexes will trigger complement and other inflammatory processes, they can result in severe damage to the affected areas.

Age-associated changes involving immune tolerance. Age-associated changes in the susceptibility to autoimmune phenomena are well-established. Indeed, epidemiological evidence shows that the incidence of various autoimmune diseases peaks at certain ages. Thus, while many other risk factors are also involved, elucidating the links between various autoimmune syndromes and age forms an important immunologic problem. Because the mechanisms that mediate immune tolerance *per se* are poorly understood, it is even more difficult to establish how age-associated factors can influence susceptibility. Clearly, shifts in the production, selection, and homeostatic processes that govern lymphocyte activity may play a role, but causal relationships await further research.

MICHAEL P. CANCRO

See also IMMUNOLOGY, HUMAN; IMMUNOLOGY: ANIMAL MODELS.

BIBLIOGRAPHY

HODES, R. J. "Aging and the Immune System." *Immunology Review* 160 (1997): 5–8.
JANEWAY, C. A., JR.; TRAVERS, P.; WALPORT, M.; and SHLOMCHIK. *Immunobiology*, 5th ed. New York: Garland Publishing, 2001.
KLINE, G. H.; HAYDEN, T. A.; and KLINMAN, N. R. "B Cell Maintenance in Aged Mice Reflects Both Increased B Cell Longevity and Decreased B Cell Generation." *Journal of Immunology* 162, no. 6 (1999): 3342–3349.
KLINMAN, N. R. and KLINE, G. H. "The B-Cell Biology of Aging." *Immunology Review* 160 (1997): 103–114.
LERNER, A.; YAMADA, T.; and MILLER, R. A. "Pgp-1hi T Lymphocytes Accumulate with Age in Mice and Respond Poorly to Concanavalin A." *European Journal of Immunology* 19, no. 6 (1989): 977–982.
LINTON, P., and THOMAN, M. L. "T Cell Senescence." *Front Biosci.* 6 (2001): D248–D261.
MILLER, R. A. "Effect of Aging on T Lymphocyte Activation." *Vaccine* 18, no. 16 (2000): 1654–1660.
MOUNTZ, J. D.; VAN ZANT, G. E.; ZHANG, H. G.; GRIZZLE, W. E.; AHMED, R.; WILLIAMS, R. W.; and HSU H. C. "Genetic Dissection of Age-Related Changes of Immune Function in Mice." *Scand J Immunol.* 54, no. 1–2 (2001): 10–20.
PAUL, W. *Fundamentals of Immunology*, 4th ed. New York: Lippincott-Raven, 1999.
STEPHAN, R. P.; SANDERS, V. M.; and WITTE, P. L. "Stage-Specific Alterations in Murine B Lymphopoiesis with Age." *Int Immunol.* 4 (1996): 509–518.

IMMUNOLOGY: ANIMAL MODELS

Observations in animal models have substantially advanced our knowledge of immune system adaptation, changes during the aging process, and age-associated degenerative diseases with autoimmune characteristics.

Animal models of immune adaptation

Animal models provided early proof that discrimination of *self* (that which the immune system identifies as belonging to the body) and *nonself* (that which the immune system identifies as foreign to the body) is determined not entirely at conception, but, to a large extent, during early fetal development by a process called *immune adaptation*. In 1945, Ray D. Owen reported that nonidentical cattle-twin embryos frequently share a common placenta, resulting in the exchange of blood between the fetuses. Owen discovered that this chimerism led to immune tolerance of skin grafts between the adult cattle. Their immune systems did not recognize allogeneic cells shared during the period of immune adaptation, when the immune system identifies cellular and molecular components of the body and memorizes them as self. Later, Milan Hasek connected the circulatory systems of chicken embryos and demonstrated tolerance of the adult birds to each other's tissues. In 1953, Peter B. Medawar and his colleagues demonstrated that the injection of foreign spleen cells into newborn mice resulted in adult tolerance of skin grafts from these foreign donors. These animal experiments confirmed the premise that immune adaptation is determined by the fetal or neonatal environment, rather than inherited.

Immunologic aspects of aging

Most immunologic activities decline with age, but some show an increase, and a few show no significant change. In principle, two types of cellular changes could alter immune functions: changes in the number of immune cells (quantitative change), and changes in the functional efficiency of immune cells (qualitative change).

Quantitative change. A modest loss of circulating lymphocytes (15 percent) has been observed in aging humans, but in mice the total number of immune cells does not change appreciably with age. Thus, cell loss does not appear to contribute significantly to changes in immune function with age.

Qualitative change. Metabolic, morphologic, and genetic studies present impressive evidence for age-related qualitative changes in immune cells. An important role in the regulation of immune reaction belongs to monocyte-derived cells (MDCs). These cells originate from monocytes, which leave the blood and differentiate into various types of tissue macrophages. Lymphocytes are the mediators of immunity, but their function is under the control of MDCs. The MDC system not only activates lymphocytes, it also makes lymphocytes tolerant or unreactive to self antigens, lymphocytes to self-antigens, thereby minimizing autoimmune reactions.

Studies in mice have shown that, with age, MDCs have a reduced capacity to stimulate proliferation and differentiation of lymphocytes. These results suggest an age-related shift in the regulatory activities of MDCs in the absence of a change in their numbers.

Age-associated diseases

Normal aging is inevitably associated with an overall decline of functional performance of all tissues (systemic change). However, some individuals develop degenerative diseases with autoimmune characteristics, resulting in the aging of tissue-specific cells (organ-specific change).

Systemic change. Although the complex mechanisms of the primary processes of aging are unknown, many theories have been proposed. The most popular concern pertubations of biologic systems, such as neuroendocrine or immune systems, or of the genetic program, as well as phenomena such as somatic-cell mutation, error accumulation and repair, entropy, and cell loss. The maximum life span of mammals (the life span of the longest-lived survivors) shows marked variations among species. Figure 1 shows that the extent of skin aging, as determined by the pentosidine level in skin collagen, substantially increases with the maximum life span for each species. Yet, the progressive increase begins with the onset of immune senescence, i.e., dimunution of T lymphocyte function accompanying age-associated involution of thymus and coinciding with the decline of immune-system function. These observations indicate that the onset of both immune senescence and skin aging are not dependent on time, but are genetically programmed for each species.

Studies of animal models have also shown that epigenetic factors, i.e., exogenous (environmental) substances and influences, which may silence or enhance the activity of genes, can influence longevity of individuals and prevent systemic changes. Early caloric restriction significantly extends the life span, retards the aging rate, and delays immunologic, biologic, and pathologic changes. The immune system of long-lived mice matured more slowly and declined later in life when subjected to a life-extending, calorically restricted (but nutritionally adequate) diet.

Organ-specific change. Along with gradual systemic aging, some individuals exhibit an accelerated organ-specific aging known as *degenerative diseases with autoimmune characteristics*. These diseases may affect virtually any tissue, but most frequently affected are neural tissues (multiple sclerosis and presenile dementia), the cardiovascular system (atherosclerosis), synovial tissue (rheumatoid arthritis), and the pancreas (diabetes mellitus). Degenerative diseases may have different etiologies, but they have in common an accelerated aging of tissue-specific cells caused by an inappropriate relationship of the immune system toward self.

Figure 1

Maximum Lifespan, Immune Function, and Skin Aging Schematic. The correlation among maximum lifespan (solid line), immune system performance (blocks), and skin aging (dashed line) in various species. Immune system performance increases during childhood (ch), full immune competence (IC) is attained at the beginning of reproductive period (rp; 12 to 14 years of age in humans), and declines in aging individuals (ag) from the onset of the immune senescence (IS; 42 to 46 years of age in humans). Note that skin aging is not time-dependent, but accelerates with the onset of the immune senescence in a species-specific manner.

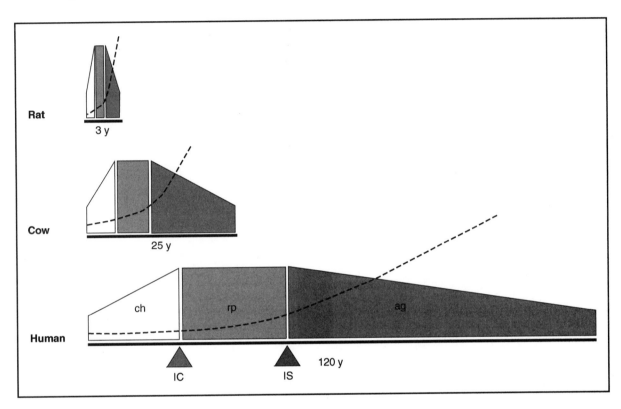

SOURCE: Data obtained from the following sources: 1) Geokas M. C.; Lakatta E. G.; Makinodan T.; Timiras P. S. "The Aging Process." *Annals of Internal Medicine* 113 (1990): 455–466. 2) Klein J. *Immunology: The Science of Self-Nonself Discrimination.* New York: John Wiley & Sons, Inc., 1982. 3) Sell D. R.; Lane M. A.; Johnson W. A.; Masoro E. J.; Mock O. B.; Reiser K. M.; Fogarty J. F.; Cutler R. G.; Ingram D. K., et al. "Longevity and the Genetic Determination of Collagen Glycoxidation Kinetics in Mammalian Senescence." *Proceedings of the National Academy of Science.* 93 (1996): 485–490.

In normal individuals, the first organ affected by aging is the ovary. Ovarian aging is not only of major importance in its own right, but is also of interest for its relationship to the general biology of senescence. There is a striking correlation between the period at which an organ is present during early ontogeny and that organ's functional longevity (see Figure 2). For instance, the liver, which differentiates very early, can (in human beings) function for over one hundred years. However the ovary, which differentiates much later, does not function for more than a half of that period.

Animal models have shown that additional restriction of ovarian development in early on-togeny, for instance by injection of androgens during immune adaptation, results in the premature aging of the ovary. Hence, epigenetic (or, in certain individuals, inherited) restriction of organ development prior to the end of immune adaptation can result in the reduction of tissue's functional longevity.

Conclusion

Animal models have substantially enhanced our understanding of the role of the immune system in tissue physiology and pathology. The dominant role belongs to MDCs, which influence the function of lymphocytes. The relationship

Figure 2

Tissue Development and Longevity—the relationship between the period of tissue differentiation during immune adaptation (ia) and determination of adult tissue longevity. The liver differentiates from early stages of ontogeny, and functions throughout the life. The ovary differentiates later, and its normal function is limited (until the end of the reproductive period). If differentiation of the ovary is delayed toward the end of the immune adaptation (EIA, which is the end of the second trimester of intrauterine life in humans and the beginning of the second postnatal week in rats and mice), premature aging of the ovary (PAO) follows.

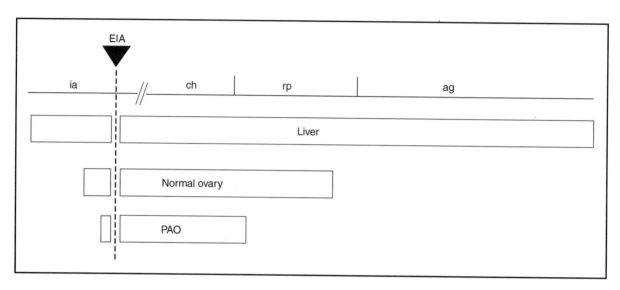

Legend: ch = childhood; rp = reproductive period; ag = aging
SOURCE: Based on: Bukovsky A.; Ayala M. E.; Dominguez R.; Keenan J. A.; Wimalasena J.; McKenzie P. P.; Caudle M. R. "Postnatal Androgenization Induces Premature Aging of Rat Ovaries." *Steroids* (2000) 65:190-205.

between immune system and self is determined during immune adaptation, when the immune system may be programmed to ensure preservation of normal mature cells in self tissues. Epigenetic (environmental), or inherited alteration to early tissue development may contribute to the manifestation of organ-specific degenerative disease later in life. The knowledge gained from animal models offers hope for future modification of the human immune system to combat a number of disease processes.

ANTONIN BUKOVSKY
MICHAEL R. CAUDLE

See also IMMUNE SYSTEM; NUTRITION, CALORIC RESTRICTION; THEORIES OF BIOLOGICAL AGING.

BIBLIOGRAPHY

BANCHEREAU, J., and STEINMAN, R. M. "Dendritic Cells and the Control of Immunity." *Nature* 392 (1998): 245–252.
BUKOVSKY, A.; AYALA, M. E.; DOMINGUEZ, R.; KEENAN, J. A.; WIMALASENA, J.; ELDER, R. F.; and CAUDLE, M. R. "Changes of Ovarian Interstitial Cell Hormone Receptors and Behavior of Resident Mesenchymal Cells in Developing and Adult Rats with Steroid-Induced Sterility." *Steroids* (2001a): (in press).
BUKOVSKY, A.; CAUDLE, M. R.; KEENAN, J. A.; UPADHYAYA, N. B.; VAN METER, S.; WIMALASENA, J.; and ELDER, R. F. "Association of Mesenchymal Cells and Immunoglobulins with Differentiating Epithelial Cells." *BMC Developmental Biology* 1 (2001b): 11.
BUKOVSKY, A.; AYALA, M. E.; DOMINGUEZ, R.; KEENAN, J. A.; WIMALASENA, J.; ELDER, R. F.; MCKENZIE, P. P.; and CAUDLE, M. R. "Postnatal Androgenization Induces Premature Aging of Rat Ovaries." *Steroids* 65 (2000a): 190–205.
BUKOVSKY, A.; CAUDLE, M. R.; and KEENAN, J. A. "Dominant Role of Monocytes in Control of Tissue Function and Aging." *Medical Hypotheses* 55 (2000b): 337–347.
GEOKAS, M. C.; LAKATTA, E. G.; MAKINODAN, T.; and TIMIRAS, P. S. "The Aging Process." *Annual of Internal Medicine.* 113 (1990): 455–466.

KIRKWOOD, T. B. "Ovarian Ageing and the General Biology of Senescence." *Maturitas* 30 (1998): 105–111.

KLEIN, J. *Immunology: The Science of Self-Nonself Discrimination.* New York: John Wiley and Sons, 1982.

RANDOLPH, G. J.; BEAULIEU, S.; LEBECQUE, S.; STEINMAN, R. M.; and MULLER, W. A. "Differentiation of Monocytes into Dendritic Cells in a Model of Transendothelial Trafficking." *Science* 282 (1998): 480–483.

SELL, D.R.; LANE, M. A.; JOHNSON, W. A.; MASORO, E. J.; MOCK, O. B.; REISER, K. M.; FOGARTY, J. F.; CUTLER, R. G.; INGRAM, D. K.; et al. "Longevity and the Genetic Determination of Collagen Glycoxidation Kinetics in Mammalian Senescence." *Proceedings of the National Academy of Sciences U.S.A.* 93 (1996): 485–490.

IMMUNOLOGY, HUMAN

The immune system is an intricate network of cells and tissues that resists invasion from infectious agents (pathogens) and combats environmental stresses that induce allergic reactions, viral infections, infectious diseases, autoimmune syndromes, and cancer. The body eradicates foreign substances using innate (natural or nonspecific) and adaptive (acquired or specific) immune responses. Innate immunity refers to the body's initial nonspecific response to the invading substance using natural defensive barriers (skin, mucous membranes, temperature, and chemical mediators) and cells (macrophages, neutrophils, and natural killer [NK] cells) to limit or clear the foreign substance.

During an adaptive immune response, the body engages immune cells (T and B lymphocytes) that specifically recognize and selectively eliminate foreign substances. Adaptive immunity has four major characteristics: 1) antigen specificity, 2) diversity, 3) immunologic memory, and 4) ability to differentiate self from nonself. Antigen specificity is mediated by receptors on immune cells that recognize defined peptides called *antigens*. Receptor development is a spontaneous and random process that begins during fetal development so that the repertoire of receptors is present on lymphocyte membranes at birth. This large array of receptors, each having its own specificity for a particular antigen, is the basis for the diversity of the adaptive immune response. When a lymphocyte binds a peptide specific for its receptor, it becomes activated. Activation is multifaceted and induces proliferation and subsequent expansion of cells with that particular receptor. This clonal expansion of antigen-specific lymphocytes is the basis for immunologic memory. Immunologic memory enables immune cells to "remember" a previous encounter with a pathogen so that a more rapid response of higher magnitude can be produced after re-exposure to that same peptide. An absolutely critical feature of adaptive immunity is that immune cells must distinguish self from nonself. This recognition phase not only ensures that a specific immune response against only the invading pathogen is produced, but also prevents nonspecific responses against cells of the body that would result in autoimmunity.

Adaptive immunity consists of humoral and cell-mediated immune responses. The primary cells in adaptive immunity are B and T lymphocytes. B lymphocytes, which are principal mediators of humoral responses, originate in bone marrow and mature in the liver during fetal development, and subsequently in gut-associated mucosal lymphoid tissue. The antigen receptor on the B cell membrane is the immunoglobulin (Ig) molecule, which confers both specificity and diversity to humoral responses. During a humoral immune response, B cells differentiate into plasma cells, which secrete antibodies specific for the invading pathogen. T lymphocytes are responsible for the cell-mediated response. T cells originate in bone marrow and mature in the thymus. Upon exiting from the thymus, T cells will have differentiated into two subpopulations: helper (CD4+) T cells and cytotoxic (CD8+) T cells. These two populations facilitate cell-mediated immunity in two ways: CD4+ T cells produce cytokines (they are soluble factors that are released from cells after contact with specific antigens), enhance innate immunity, and induce antibody responses, while CD8+ T cells directly kill tumors or virus-infected cells.

Despite the presence of B and T cells at birth, neonates cannot produce a maximal adaptive immune response because their immune system has not yet fully matured. Maturational changes in the immune system continue after birth and are fairly complete by two years of age. However, subtle changes do occur until about puberty, at which point the immune response is fully developed.

Age-related changes in immunity

The incidence of infectious diseases, autoimmune syndromes, and cancers is increased in older adults and may be related to environmental and genetic factors. However, strong evidence also indicates that an overall dysregulation of the immune system may at least partially account for the increased incidence of these disorders in older adults.

Innate immunity. Changes in the innate immune response of older adults have received relatively little attention, and data thus far are inconclusive. Currently, the consensus is that NK activity does not dramatically change in older adults. However, lymphokine-activated killer-cell activity is decreased, at least to a limited extent, in older adults. Assessment of phagocytosis (process by which foreign substances (e.g., cells, bacteria, cell debris) are engulfed and destroyed) and cytokine production by cells of the innate response system has yielded inconsistent results, making it difficult to assess their role in the age-related decline in immune function. Clearly, additional controlled studies are necessary to define changes in innate immunity of older humans.

Adaptive immunity. Age-related changes in adaptive immunity have been studied extensively. Decreased antibody production after immunization or infection, reduced affinity of antibodies, and increased production of autoantibodies have been reported. However, these changes in B cell function cannot be explained by alterations in B cell numbers. The mechanism of age-related changes in B cell function has not yet been elucidated. Most evidence suggests that decreased B cell function probably reflects a decrease in help (i.e. cytokine production) from helper T cells, although some intrinsic changes in B cells have been identified.

There is a plethora of information regarding age-related changes in human T cell function. One of the earliest changes occurs in the thymus, the site of T cell maturation, which begins to involute at puberty. Involute refers to the atrophy of the thymus, resulting in a loss of collularity and a decrease in thymic function. However, the contribution of this change to decreased immune function of older adults is debatable, as involution occurs decades before decreased T cell responses are apparent. One of the most consistent findings is that proliferative responses of T cells to both nonspecific (mitogenic) and antigenic

stimuli are decreased in elderly adults. A similar decrease is observed in both delayed-type hypersensitivity reactions and cytotoxic T cell activity.

To elucidate possible mechanisms for these age-related changes in T cell function, total cell number, distribution among various subsets, and cytokine production have been evaluated. Most, but not all, reports concur that the circulating number or percentage of T cells is not dramatically affected by age. However, investigators generally agree that a shift from a naïve to a memory phenotype is seen with advancing age in both CD4+ and CD8+ T subpopulations. This shift in phenotype could explain the reduced ability of older adults to produce immune responses to antigens that they have not encountered previously. The effects of age on T cell cytokine production have been variable and dependent on the cytokine measured and the stimulus (i.e., mitogen (substance that induces proliferation (cell division) of T and B cells, regardless of antigen specificity) or antigen) used for induction. The most consistent observation among human studies is that mitogen-induced interleukin (IL-2) production is decreased in elderly individuals. In contrast, IL-4, IL-6, IL-10 and interferon-γ levels after stimulation with either mitogen or antigen have been observed to increase, decrease, or not change with age. Collectively, however, current data clearly indicate that aging preferentially and consistently affects T cell function. This suggests that maintenance and/or restoration of T cell function are critical for sustaining immune function in older adults.

Theories of aging

General theories of aging have been postulated to explain the decline in immune function of older adults. Among these many theories, the *free radical* (a free radical is an atom, molecule, or compound with one or more unpaired electrons in its outer orbit. When oxygen is utilized during oxidative metabolism, oxygen intermediates, such as superoxides, hydrogen peroxide, and hydroxyP radicals, are formed due to the partial reduction of oxygen. Although most of these oxygen intermediates will react with hydrogen to form water, some will remain as free radicals. These free radicals can cause damage to cell membranes by reacting with nearby molecules in the cell.) theory of aging is one of the most popular and well documented. This theory states that the production of free radicals increases with age, and that these molecules permanently modify the structure of lipids, proteins, DNA, and cells; and thus impairs their function. Although this theory seems plausible, there is little direct evidence that the accumulation of free radicals is causally related to decreased immune responsiveness in humans. Reduction of free radical levels has improved some, but not all, indices of immune function, and the effects seemed to be indirect.

A second general theory of aging is that age-related changes in physiologic and biologic processes are due to changes in the composition of cell membranes, rendering them dysfunctional. Proponents of the free radical theory of aging believe that these alterations in membrane composition result from increased free radicals, which attack membrane phospholipids, increase the cholesterol to phospholipid ratio, and increase cell membrane rigidity. Although limited in scope, studies have shown that lymphocyte membranes of aged donors are more rigid and less fluid. Reports have also shown that a more rigid membrane impairs receptor movement within the cell membrane, and therefore inhibits activation and proliferation of lymphocytes and other immune cells. In addition, these changes in the cell membrane could affect cognate interactions between immune cells, or between immune cells with target cells. It is likely that a combination of several interrelated but independent theories of aging will ultimately explain the age-related decline in the immune response of elderly humans.

Dietary supplementation

Dietary supplementation with antioxidant micronutrients—such as beta-carotene, vitamin E, zinc, and vitamin A—to offset the age-associated decline in immune function of older adults has received much attention in the media. The premise of these studies is that supplementation with antioxidants reduces the deleterious effects of increased free radical production and, thereby, minimizes the age-related decline in the immune response and decreases the incidence of infections and cancer. Several studies have supported this view by showing positive effects of micronutrient supplementation on cell-mediated and humoral immunity and a decrease in the duration of infection. However, equally well-controlled studies have indicated that micronutrient supplementation in older adults produced only transient positive effects, adverse effects, or

no effect on indices of immune function and protection from infectious disease. Differences in study design (i.e., the micronutrient tested, the dose given, and the duration of supplementation) probably account for these discrepant results. Although most evidence suggests that supplementation with moderate doses of micronutrients is not harmful, studies must be conducted to determine whether long-term supplementation produces any deleterious effects on the immune response of older adults. Likewise, future studies must investigate whether or not positive effects of these micronutrients are mediated by their antioxidant properties or by acting to maintain or enhance immune function in older adults by other mechanisms. Such studies are necessary so that the lay public, particularly older adults, understands the implications, and possible consequences, of using micronutrient supplementation as a method to offset the age-related decline in immune function.

In summary, an age-related decrease in immune function is well established in humans and several other mammalian species. This decrease has been consistently observed in T cell proliferation and is associated with a shift to a memory T-cell phenotype. Alterations in cytokine production, antibody responses, and innate immunity have also been observed in some cases. However, the dependence of these changes on T cell alterations must be established to clearly elucidate possible mechanisms of age-related changes in the immune response of elderly humans.

DONNA M. MURASKO
ELIZABETH M. GARDNER

See also IMMUNE SYSTEM; IMMUNOLOGY, ANIMAL MODELS; NUTRITION; THEORIES OF BIOLOGICAL AGING.

BIBLIOGRAPHY

BERNSTEIN, E. D., and MURASKO, D. M. "Effect of Age on Cytokine Production in Humans." *Age* 21 (1998): 137–151.
HIGH, K. P. "Micronutrient Supplementation and Immune Function in the Elderly." *Clinical Infectious Disease* 28 (1999): 717–722.
KUTZA, J.; KAYE, D.; and MURASKO, D. M. "Basal Natural Killer Activity of Young Versus Elderly Humans." *Journal of Gerontology: Biological Sciences* 50A (1995): B110–116.
MEYDANI, S. "Vitamin/Mineral Supplementation, the Aging Immune Response, and Risk of Infection." *Nutrition Review* 51 (1993): 106–109.

MILLER, R. A. "The Aging Immune System: Primer and Prospectus." *Science* 273 (1996): 70–74.

MILLER, R. A. "Biology of Aging and Longevity." In *Principles of Geriatric Medicine and Gerontology,* 4th ed. Edited by W. R. Hazzard, J. P. Blass, W. H. Ettinger, Jr., and J. G. Ouslander. New York: McGraw-Hill, 1999. Pages 3–20.

MURASKO, D. M., and BERNSTEIN, E. D. "Immunology of Aging." In *Principles of Geriatric Medicine and Gerontology,* 4th ed. Edited by W. R. Hazzard, J. P. Blass, W. H. Ettinger, Jr., and J. G. Ouslander. New York: McGraw-Hill, 1999. Pages 97–116.

MURASKO, D. M., and GOONEWARDENE, I. M. "T Cell Function in Aging: Mechanisms of Decline." *Annual Review of Gerontological Geriatrics* 10 (1990): 71–96.

SOHAL, R. S., and WEINDRUCH, R. "Oxidative Stress, Caloric Restriction, and Aging." *Science* 272 (1996): 59–63.

INCOME SUPPORT FOR NONWORKERS, NATIONAL APPROACHES

Means-tested and social insurance programs have evolved to provide income support to people who cannot, or are not expected to, support themselves. Thanks to old-age income protection schemes, typically referred to as social security, growing numbers of men and women around the world face an economically secure old age free of work. Between 1940 and 1999, the number of countries with programs that provide cash benefits to older persons, the disabled, and survivors rose from 33 to 167 (U.S. Social Security Administration, 1999).

Social security programs take a variety of forms. They may be non-contributory and paid for out of general revenues, or they may require contributions from workers and employers. They may be defined benefit plans that use a formula to calculate benefits based on some combination of earnings and years of employment or defined contribution plans whose benefits depend on plan contributions. Some provide a flat-rate benefit to all residents of a country, subject to certain conditions; others are based on work histories and years of earnings. Programs may be targeted to individuals or families with income and/or assets below a certain level; others pay benefits to anyone who has met the contribution

requirements. Mandatory savings programs, such as provident funds, are found in a number of countries; and in a few countries, mandatory private pensions add another layer of income protection in old age.

In the more developed countries of the world, social security coverage is nearly universal. Coverage in the less developed countries is generally far more limited, often restricted to public sector employees or workers in urban areas. Though still young, these countries are aging rapidly, causing governments to examine how best to extend old-age protection to vast numbers of people who lack access to a public old-age support system.

Canadian and American models

The continued aging of the more developed countries is prompting many of them to reassess their social security systems in light of rising old-age dependency ratios and concern that the public sector might not be able to maintain current levels of support without substantially higher taxes. In many countries, efforts to reduce the rate of growth of social security expenditures have resulted or are likely to result in the reform of old-age social protection schemes. This has been the case in Canada and the United States, countries whose approaches to old-age support share a number of important features and differ in fundamental ways.

Both Canada and the United States have public, mandatory, contributory, earnings-related pension programs covering almost all workers that provide a portion of the income workers will need in retirement. Disability benefits are available in both countries. Both countries also offer tax incentives to encourage employers to provide private pensions and residents to save for their own retirement. Canada, however, provides a universal benefit, known as a demogrant, that can be supplemented by payments to persons with inadequate income. The United States lacks this universal benefit, but it, too, offers extra protection to very low-income elderly through a separate, means-tested program of income support.

Income support for older nonworkers in Canada

Two national programs help protect older Canadians from destitution in old age: (1) the

Old Age Security program, which includes the Old Age Security pension (OAS), the Guaranteed Income Supplement (GIS), and the Allowance and Allowance for the Survivor and (2) the Canada Pension Plan (CPP). Canadian law allows the provinces to opt out of the CPP if they offer a similar pension plan. The province of Quebec has chosen this route and established the Quebec Pension Plan (QPP), which is comparable, but not identical, to the CPP.

The Old Age Security pension is a universal monthly benefit available to persons aged sixty-five or older, regardless of employment history, who are either Canadian citizens or legal residents who have resided in Canada for at least ten years since turning age eighteen. The full Old Age Security pension is paid to persons who have lived in Canada for at least forty years since turning eighteen; partial benefits are paid for shorter residency. Benefits, which are financed from general revenues, are paid monthly and adjusted quarterly based on increases in the Consumer Price Index. Pensioners with individual net income above a certain level must repay all or part of the OAS.

The Guaranteed Income Supplement (GIS) is an income-tested monthly benefit paid to recipients of an Old Age Security pension who have little other income. The amount of the GIS depends on marital status as well as income; any money other than the Old Age Security pension is defined as income for the purpose of determining the GIS amount. The GIS is indexed quarterly to reflect increases in the Consumer Price Index. The government bears the whole cost of these benefits, which may be supplemented by income-tested benefits in the provinces.

The Allowance and Allowance for the Survivor may be paid to spouses, partners, including common-law and same sex partners, and survivors. These benefits are based on need and limited to persons between the ages of sixty and sixty-four who have lived in Canada for at least ten years since turning eighteen. These benefits are converted to an Old Age Security pension when a recipient turns sixty-five.

The Canada Pension Plan is an earnings-related pension program that pays full retirement benefits at the age of sixty-five. Early reduced benefits may be paid starting at age sixty; late increased benefits are available up to age seventy. Beneficiaries must have made at least one year of contributions to qualify for this pension.

All workers, including the self-employed, between the ages of eighteen and seventy must contribute to the Canada Pension Plan or the Quebec Pension Plan. Benefits between the CPP and QPP are portable.

In 2001, Canadian workers and their employers in both the CPP and QPP each paid 4.3 percent of the worker's earnings up to a maximum, C$38,300, that is indexed to average wage growth. The first C$3,500 of earnings is exempt from taxation; this amount is not indexed. Self-employed workers contribute the employer's and the employee's share. The employer-employee contribution rate is rising to 4.95 percent of wages by 2003, where it is scheduled to remain.

Legislation enacted in 1998 introduced changes that move the Canada Pension Plan from pay-as-you-go financing, where contributions in any one year are largely paid out in benefits that year, to a system with greater funding. Designed to help pay future pension benefits in an aging Canada, the reserves are to be invested in a diversified portfolio of securities, rather than solely in provincial bonds, which was the practice until recently.

The formula used to calculate benefits at the time of retirement in Canada adjusts previous earnings to make them comparable to earnings at the time of retirement. The adjustment is based on the maximum pensionable earnings for the past five years. Up to 15 percent of low-income years may be deducted from the pension calculation, as may be years when someone was caring for a child under the age of seven. The resultant pensions, which amount to about 25 percent of a worker's average monthly earnings over his or her working life, are fully indexed annually.

Spousal benefits are not paid under the Canada Pension Plan. However, survivors' benefits are payable to legally married and common-law survivors. These benefits amount to 60 percent of the spouse's retirement pension, up to a maximum and are reduced for retirement below the age of sixty-five.

The Canada Pension Plan provides credit splitting upon divorce or separation. Based on the premise that marriage or a common-law relationship is an economic partnership, credit splitting acknowledges that both partners are entitled to share the pension credits earned by either partner during their marriage or cohabitation. Upon divorce or separation, pension credits earned during the relationship are combined and divided equally between the partners. Such splitting generally works to the advantage of the lower earner in a partnership, typically the wife, and produces a higher retirement benefit than she would otherwise have received.

Canadian workers may be eligible for disability benefits if they have worked and contributed to the Canada Pension Plan or Quebec Pension Plan for a specified period. To qualify for disability benefits, a worker must have "severe and prolonged incapacity for any gainful activity" (U.S. Social Security Administration, 1999). At age sixty-five, disability benefits are converted to a retirement pension. Access to health insurance is an important component of financial well-being in old age, and virtually all Canadians are eligible for publicly funded health care in Canada.

Income support for older nonworkers in the United States

The primary public retirement program in the United States is the Old-Age, Survivors, and Disability Insurance (OASDI) program. OASDI, referred to by almost everyone simply as Social Security, now covers almost all U.S. workers, regardless of age. The primary exceptions include workers enrolled in some state and local pension plans and federal government employees hired before 1984.

The U.S. Social Security system is a mandatory contributory program under which workers and their employers each pay 6.2 percent of a worker's earnings up to a maximum, which in 2001 was US$80,400. This "taxable maximum" is adjusted annually based on increases in average wages. Self-employed workers pay the combined employer-employee amount. U.S. workers and their employers each contribute an additional 1.45 percent on all earnings to the Medicare program, the federal health insurance program for persons aged sixty-five and older.

For the first six decades of the OASDI program, full retirement benefits were payable at age sixty-five. Early actuarially reduced benefits have been available at age sixty-two since 1956 for women and 1961 for men. For workers turning age sixty-two in 2000, the age of eligibility for full benefits began to increase gradually; it will reach sixty-seven in 2027. Benefits will still be available at age sixty-two when the higher full benefit age is fully in effect; however, workers will experience a greater reduction in benefits. Workers who postpone collecting retired worker benefits between full retirement age and age sixty-nine receive a delayed retirement credit. This credit has not represented a full actuarial increase in benefits and has not been instrumental in prolonging the worklife. However, the credit is increasing and will reach the full actuarial increase of 8 percent per year for workers delaying retirement after 2008.

Social Security benefits are indexed according to changes in the Consumer Price Index for Urban Wage Earners and Clerical Workers and adjusted once a year. To be eligible for benefits, workers must have at least forty quarters of credits, or ten years of earnings. Benefits are based on thirty-five years of highest indexed covered earnings out of a total of forty. The five years of lowest earnings are deducted before the benefit is calculated. There are no child-care credits or exclusions. Years of zero earnings, up to a maximum of five, serve as de facto child care credits for many workers who leave the labor force to care for children. Long-term low-income workers may be eligible for a minimum benefit.

Upon reaching retirement age, workers may be eligible for Social Security benefits based on their own earnings as workers, on the earnings of a spouse, or on a combination of the two. Most men and a growing number of women collect retired worker benefits based on their own work histories and earnings. Many spouses—predominantly women—still lack the requisite forty credits of coverage and are entitled to a spousal benefit that amounts to 50 percent of their husband's retired worker benefit. Workers whose retired worker benefit amounts to less than 50 percent of their spousal benefit are dually entitled, that is, they are entitled to benefits as retired workers and as spouses. However, they can only receive one benefit. Technically, they receive their own retired worker benefit that is "topped up" to the spousal benefit to which they are entitled. In effect, they receive the same benefit they would have received had they never contributed to Social Security. Though Social Security is gender neutral, most recipients of spousal benefits and dually entitled beneficiaries are women.

A divorced spouse who has been married for at least 10 years is also eligible for spousal benefit of 50 percent of the other spouse's retired worker benefit. A surviving spouse—whether a widow or divorce who had been married 10 or more years—will collect 100 percent of the former spouse's benefit if that is higher than her own benefit. Common law partners may also be eligible for spousal and survivor benefits in states that recognize those marriages. Earnings sharing, as it is called in the United States, has been proposed for Social Security. Although extensively studied in the 1980s (U.S. House of Representatives; Congress of the United States; Fierst and Campbell), it has not advanced legislatively.

The weighted benefit formula used to calculate Social Security benefits redistributes income from higher earners to lower earners by replacing a greater percentage of the pre-retirement earnings of a low earner than a high earners Social Security replaces about 40 percent of the pre-retirement earnings of a life-time average earner.

Social Security disability benefits may be paid to workers with sufficient quarters of coverage who are unable to engage in "substantial gainful activity due to impairment expected to last at least one year or result in death." At age sixty-five, disability benefits convert to retired worker benefits. Medicare is the national health insurance program for persons sixty-five and older who are eligible for Social Security. Part A, which is non-contributory, covers hospital expenses. Part B, which requires a premium contribution from beneficiaries, primarily covers physician expenses.

Supplemental Security Income (SSI) is a means-tested program administered by the Social Security Administration that provides income support to needy persons aged sixty-five or older and blind or disabled adults and children. The level of benefits, however, keeps many of these recipients below the poverty level. Twenty percent of the recipients, or about 1.3 million persons, are receiving benefits based solely on age; another 11 percent are blind or disabled and sixty-five or older. The majority also receive Social Security (U.S. Social Security Administration, 2000a). Federal SSI payments, which are paid from general revenues, may be supplemented by payments from the States.

In recent years, the Social Security Trust Funds have been building up sizable reserves, which under current law are invested in special U.S. Treasury bonds guaranteed by the government. The growing demands that baby boomers will place on the U.S. Social Security system as they retire have led to numerous proposals for reform, including calls to invest a portion of the reserves in equities, as has occurred in Canada.

Summary

Canada refers to the three floors of its retirement income system. The first floor is the Old Age Security program, the second the Canada Pension Plan, and the third is private savings, which includes individual savings and employer-sponsored pension plan (Human Resources Development Canada, 2000a). In the U.S. retirement income system, reference is made to the three legs of the retirement income stool—Social Security, employer-provided pensions, and individual savings. The most significant difference between these two systems is that Canada offers a universal pension, and the United States does not. The key similarity between the two systems is the mandatory, earnings-related component that covers workers in the two countries and that requires contributions from both workers and their employees. Both systems provide relatively modest replacement rates that are adjusted to keep pace with inflation. There is a greater use of general revenues to support older persons in Canada than in the United States. Benefits are also available at a younger age in Canada and after shorter tenure.

Neither the Canadian publicly financed retirement income system nor the one in the United States provides all of the income middle-income retirees are likely to need in old age. Both countries attempt to have these benefits supplemented by employer-provided pensions and individuals savings. Both countries provide benefits to the needy elderly, although the programs that do this are very different from one another.

Despite differences in the public retirement income systems of Canada and the United States, both contribute roughly the same amount to total retirement income, though less of the total comes from the earnings related pension in Canada than in the United States (Gunderson, Hyatt, and Pesando). About 40 percent of the aggregate income of persons sixty-five and older in Canada in 1997 came from the OAS (29 percent) or the CPP/QPP (21 percent), while about 46 percent of the aggregate income of the sixty-five-plus population in the United States in 1998 came from publicly funded pensions, mainly Social Security (Human Resources Development Canada, 2000b; U.S. Social Security Administration, 2000b). Canada's Guaranteed Income Supplement goes to a much higher proportion of older persons than does the American SSI, although GIS is not, according to Turner, a poverty program like the U.S.'s Supplemental Security Income program.

Another significant difference between the Canada Pension Plan and the U.S. Social Security Program is the diversified investment of reserves currently permitted in the CPP but not in the U.S. Social Security program. Credit splitting and payment of certain benefits to same-sex common law partners also distinguish the publicly financed income retirement system in Canada from that in the United States.

Improvements in both systems over the years have resulted in sharp declines in the proportion of poor or low-income elderly. Though economic security continues to elude many retirees, the availability of indexed benefits guaranteed for life have gone a long way toward enhancing the economic security of older nonworkers in the United States and Canada. As a result, retirement in comfort and dignity is a reality for growing numbers of retirees in both countries.

Detailed information on income support for older nonworkers in Canada can be found at the web site of Human Resources Development Canada: www.hrdc-drhc.gc.ca. Comparable information for older nonworkers in the United States can be found at the web site of the Social Security Administration: www.ssa.gov.

SARA E. RIX

See also CANADA; CANADA, RETIREMENT INCOME; PENSIONS, PLAN TYPES AND POLICY APPROACHES; PENSIONS, PUBLIC PENSIONS; SOCIAL SECURITY ADMINISTRATION; SOCIAL SECURITY, AND THE U.S. FEDERAL BUDGET; SOCIAL SECURITY, LONG-TERM FINANCING AND REFORM; SUPPLEMENTAL SECURITY INCOME.

BIBLIOGRAPHY

Congress of the United States, Congressional Budget Office. *Earnings Sharing Options for the Social Security System.* Washington, D.C.: Congressional Budget Office, 1986.
FIERST, E. U. and CAMPBELL, N. D., eds. *Earnings Sharing in Social Security: A Model for Reform.* Washington, D.C.: Center for Women Policy Studies, 1988.
GUNDERSON, M.; HYATT, D.; and PESANDO, J. E. "Public Pension Plans in the United States and Canada." Iin W. T. Alpert and S. A. Woodbury, eds., *Employee Benefits and Labor Markets in Canada and the United States.* Kalamazoo, Mich.: W. E. Upjohn Institute for Employment Research, 2000. Pages 381–411.
Human Resources Development Canada. "Did You Know? The Three Floors of the Retirement Income System." News Room: Old Age Security and Canada Pension Plan, 2000a. www.hrdc-drhc.gc.ca
Human Resources Development Canada. "Facts, Impact, and Context—Canada's Public Pensions." News Room: Old Age Security and Canada Pension Plan, 2000b. www.hrdc-drhc.gc.ca
TURNER, J.. "Risk Sharing Through Social Security Retirement Income Systems." In J. Turner, ed., *Pay at Risk: Risk Bearing by U.S. and Canadian Workers.* Kalamazoo, Mich.: Upjohn Institute for Employment Policy, 2001.
U.S. House of Representatives, Committee on Ways and Means, Subcommittee on Social Security. *Report on Earnings Sharing Implementation Study.* Washington, D.C.: U.S. Government Printing Office, 1985.
U.S. Social Security Administration. *Highlights of Supplemental Security Income Data, September 2000.* Washington, D.C.: Office of Policy, Social Security, 2000a. www.ssa.gov/
U.S. Social Security Administration. *Income of the Population 55 or Older.* Washington, D.C.: U.S. Government Printing Office, 2000b.
U.S. Social Security Administration. *Social Security Programs Throughout the World—1999.* Washington, D.C.: U.S. Government Printing Office, 1999.

INDIVIDUAL RETIREMENT ACCOUNTS

An Individual Retirement Account (IRA) provides some form of tax advantage to assets held by an individual until retirement, with certain exceptions. Despite the recent trend toward the use of the 401(k) and similar plans, the IRA is still a valuable tool for retirement planning and other goals. The types of IRAs are traditional, Roth, education, SEP, and SIMPLE; all of them use one of two forms of preferential tax treatments affecting contributions and gains. Individuals, small businesses, and the self-employed can all potentially use IRAs. The Internal Revenue

Service (IRS) does not dictate the type of investment held in an IRA; investors can use stocks, bonds, mutual funds, and others (Preston). The investment choice should be determined by investment horizon, risk tolerance, and possibly investment savvy (Hanna and Chen).

The traditional IRA has been available for some time. The Roth IRA was born out of the 1997 Taxpayer Relief Act and provides a different tax advantage than other types of retirement savings vehicles, which will be discussed later. The 2001 Taxpayer Relief Act (2001 TRA) brought changes to contribution limits and will be in effect beginning in 2002. These changes will be highlighted where applicable.

Traditional IRA

The traditional IRA allows an individual to place up to $2,000 per year in an account on a tax-deferred basis. This means that the contribution is not counted as taxable income the year it is contributed and will not be taxed until it is withdrawn. This also applies to any earnings on the contributions. Each member of a married couple may have his or her own IRA and may contribute as much as $2,000 per person. The 2001 TRA has provided for increases in this amount. The contribution allowed per person increases to $3,000 between 2002 and 2004, increases again to $4,000 from 2005 to 2007, and finally reaches $5,000 for 2008 and beyond. The contribution amount will be indexed for inflation after 2008 and will increase in increments of $500. A special catch-up provision is instituted for taxpayers age fifty and over. Taxpayers who are fifty or over during 2002 may make an additional $500 contribution between 2002 and 2005 and an additional $1,000 beginning in 2006.

A qualified contribution reduces the amount of income that will be used in computing the total income tax owed because the contribution is not taxable income. The investment gains and the principal will be taxed as the distributions are taken. The actual reduction in tax liability is equal to the amount of the contribution multiplied by the marginal tax rate, the tax rate on the last dollar earned. For example, if Matt can contribute $2,000 to an IRA and he is in the 28 percent marginal tax bracket, he would save about $560 (2000 × 0.28) on his tax bill by contributing to a traditional IRA.

Households can contribute some amount to a traditional IRA as long as the taxpayer will not be seventy and one-half by the end of the year and has earned income for the year. The exception to the earned income rule is a nonworking spouse, who may contribute to an IRA provided that the couple's combined income less IRA contributions is greater than $2,000. This spousal IRA allows for a contribution to be made by one spouse on behalf of the other, who has little or no monetary compensation. The amount of the allowable contribution can be reduced or phased out as the household's modified adjusted gross income (MAGI) increases. The MAGI is the adjusted gross income plus exempt qualified interest, such as interest from a municipal bond. The rules for the phaseout are determined by whether or not the individual is participating in an employer-provided retirement plan. In the case of a married couple where one spouse is covered by such a plan and the other is not, the allowable contribution is based on each spouse's own situation. Employer-provided retirement plans include 401(k), SEP, SIMPLE, tax-sheltered annuities, and defined benefit plans.

In addition to annual contributions, three types of transfers can fund traditional IRAs. The first is a transfer from one IRA provider to another. This does not involve any direct payment or distribution to the investor, and hence there are no tax implications. A transfer from a traditional IRA or defined contribution plan to another IRA, also known as a rollover, must be declared, but if it is contributed within sixty days of the distribution, the rollover is tax-free; otherwise there will be a penalty on any distribution that was not frozen during that time. Frozen assets are those that cannot be withdrawn from the financial institution because the institution is insolvent or the state where the institution is located restricts withdrawals because of insolvency. Further, if the distribution is not a direct rollover, or is paid to the owner, 20 percent must be withheld and is taxable. Only the amount in the account that could be taxed can be rolled over. Last, the amount of an IRA transferred into another IRA because of a divorce settlement is tax-free.

Distributions from the traditional IRA can begin without penalty after the account holder reaches age fifty-nine and one-half. Withdrawals prior to that age incur a 10 percent federal tax penalty unless they meet one of the criteria determined by the IRS. One is payment of medical costs. These medical expenses must not be reimbursed and must exceed 7.5 percent of adjusted gross income (AGI). Second, withdrawals are allowed before fifty-nine and one-half when funds are needed because of recent disability. A third situation that avoids the 10 percent penalty is if a person is the beneficiary of an inherited IRA. Fourth, withdrawal of a sum not in excess of qualified higher education expenses, such as tuition and books, is permitted. An additional provision allows up to $10,000 to be withdrawn and applied toward purchasing or building a first home. Distributions from an IRA must begin by April 1 in the year after the account holder reaches seventy and one-half. If the entire amount is not withdrawn, then a schedule based on the owner's life expectancy must be followed for the distributions. Under this provision, annuity payments taken prior to fifty-nine and one-half are not penalized.

IRAs can be passed to heirs (more than one) and are included in the estate of the deceased. However, only the spouse of the decedent can take over the IRA; others cannot contribute to, roll over, or roll over assets into the IRA. Inherited IRAs must be withdrawn entirely within the first five years after the owner's death or over the life expectancy of the beneficiary. If this person is not the spouse, the serial withdrawals begin after the first year following the death of the IRA owner; a spouse can wait until the time at which the deceased would have been seventy and one-half.

Roth IRA

As part of the 1997 Taxpayer Relief Act, the Roth IRA was introduced to provide taxpayers with a unique means of saving for retirement and other goals. The principal difference between the Roth and the traditional IRAs is related to the taxation of contributions and distributions. While a deduction can be taken for contributions to a traditional IRA, there is no deduction for contributions to a Roth IRA. Instead, the earnings grow tax-exempt. This means that when money is withdrawn, there will be no taxes to pay. Therefore the key difference between Roth and traditional IRAs is that with the Roth, taxes are paid on contributions but not in retirement, and the opposite is true for the traditional IRA.

The Roth IRA may be preferable to a traditional IRA. The question one must answer to determine which one is best is at what rate the individual would like to pay taxes. While this may require making some assumptions about one's income sources in retirement, and assuming that tax laws will not change, it is still a reasonable approach to deciding which choice is best. If one expects his or her tax rate to increase in retirement, then a Roth IRA is preferable. This might be the situation for many young individuals, especially those just finishing college. If one expects it to decrease in retirement, then a traditional IRA is preferable. This may be the case for one who is making this choice later in life and is more established in his or her career.

As with a traditional IRA, individuals can place $2,000 into a Roth IRA each year ($4,000 for married couples). The increases provided by the 2001 TRA discussed for the contributions to a traditional IRA are also applicable to the Roth IRA. The rules regarding spousal Roth IRAs are the same as those for the traditional spousal IRA. The phaseout for allowable contributions for a Roth IRA is the same as that for those not participating in employer-sponsored retirement plans for the traditional IRA. Contributions to a Roth IRA can be made at any age, even beyond seventy and one-half.

Generally the rollover provisions of a Roth IRA are similar to those of a traditional IRA. In order to be eligible for a traditional-to-Roth rollover, certain conditions must be met. Failure to meet these guidelines subjects the rollover to a 6 percent federal tax for excess contributions as well as the 10 percent federal tax penalty; it also is included in ordinary income, and thus is subject to income taxes. Prior to 1999 the traditional-to-Roth rollover distribution could be taken over a four-year period, but this is not the case for new or current rollovers.

Distributions from a Roth IRA will be tax-free as long as they have been held in the IRA for five years or more and are withdrawn for appropriate reasons (the same as those for a traditional IRA). Otherwise, the early withdrawal penalty applies to the total amount withdrawn in that year. Unlike the traditional IRA, the rule requiring distributions to begin by age seventy and one-half does not apply to the Roth IRA. However, the rules regarding distributions after the owner's death are the same as those for the traditional IRA.

Education IRA

The education IRA, although similar to a Roth, has several important differences. Like the Roth, the education IRA does not provide a current tax deduction but does allow for tax-free growth of the investment principal, and has the same phaseout rules for allowable contributions. The purpose of the education IRA is to save for qualified higher education expenses for the named beneficiary. These expenses include tuition, fees, books, and room and board for students enrolled at least half-time, and as of 2002 will also include expenses for elementary and secondary schools. The contributions to this IRA must be made before the beneficiary reaches eighteen years of age and must be made in cash. The cash stipulation differs from other IRAs, for which the contributions can also be in the form of securities. Another important difference is that the contribution for an education IRA cannot exceed $500 per year per child. However, this limit increases to $2,000 after 2001. Excess contributions face the same rules as the Roth IRA, but if there are contributions made on the child's behalf to a qualified state tuition program, such as a Section 529 plan or prepaid tuition plan, then any amount contributed to the education IRA is considered excess. Excess contributions must be withdrawn by year-end or face a 10 percent penalty.

The distributions from an education IRA in any year cannot exceed the amount of qualified higher education expenses. Otherwise, the same rules apply for withdrawal and bequests that exist for traditional and Roth IRAs. The only exception is that the funds must be distributed by the time the beneficiary is thirty years old or, if the beneficiary dies, the assets must be distributed to that person's beneficiaries within thirty days from the time of death. If the person is a minor or does not have a will then state laws of intestacy will dictate the beneficiary.

SEP-IRA

The fourth type of IRA is a Simplified Employee Pension (SEP-IRA), which allows employers to make contributions on behalf of qualified employees. To qualify, an employee must be at least twenty-one years old, have worked three out of the five previous years for the employer, and earned at least $400 of compensation in the year contributions are made.

The contribution by the employer on behalf of an employee for the SEP-IRA is limited to the lesser of $30,000 or 15 percent of the employee's compensation, excluding the employer contribution to a tax-deferred account; a SEP-IRA cannot be a Roth IRA. Although employees can also contribute to this account, the same rules for contributions apply as in a traditional IRA. Further, the SEP-IRA is considered an employer-sponsored plan, and thus any contributions by the employee are subject to the same phaseout rules that govern the traditional IRA. Rules regarding distributions are the same as those for a traditional IRA.

SIMPLE IRA

The fifth type of IRA is the Savings Incentive Match Plan for Employees (SIMPLE). A SIMPLE plan allows an employee to allocate a portion of his or her income to an IRA as long as the employee received at least $5,000 in compensation in one of the previous two years and will receive at least $5,000 during the current year. Further, employees whose benefits are covered by a union, who are nonresident aliens, or who would not have been eligible if not for an acquisition, disposition, or similar activity do not need to be included in the SIMPLE plan.

The contribution is limited to $6,000 per year. As part of the 2001 TRA, the annual contribution increases to $7,000 in 2002, and will increase in $1,000 increments per year, up to $10,000 in 2005. After 2005, the contribution will be indexed to inflation and increase in $500 increments. Employers are required to contribute between 1 and 3 percent of the individual's compensation, but the amount can be only 1 percent for two of the five years following the election period. Rules regarding distributions are the same as those for a traditional IRA. A SIMPLE IRA cannot be a Roth IRA.

Who is using IRAs?

Results from the 1998 Survey of Consumer Finances (SCF) show that almost 49 percent of U.S. households have some type of retirement account, an increase of more than three percentage points over 1995 (Kennickell et al.). The SCF provides more specific data regarding ownership of IRAs (Kennickell). Additional statistics were computed using data from the 1998 SCF to determine the percentage of individuals between nineteen and ninety-five years of age using IRAs during 1997. Over 28 percent owned an IRA in 1997, and the average balance was $20,209. The proportion of those owning IRAs increases with age, then decreases for those approaching retirement. The amount invested also increases with age, then begins to decrease, which is consistent with the fact that when a person retires, he or she is receiving distributions.

The overall strategy when deciding on an IRA is determining the best time to pay taxes, which is when the marginal tax rate is lowest. Further information can be obtained from Publication 590 of the U.S. Department of the Treasury.

MICHAEL STEVEN GUTTER

See also RETIREMENT PLANNING.

BIBLIOGRAPHY

HANNA, S., and CHEN, P. "Subjective and Objective Risk Tolerance: Implications for Optimal Portfolios." *Financial Counseling and Planning* 8, no. 2 (1997): 17–26.
HOFFMAN, W. H.; SMITH, J. E.; and WILLIS, E., eds. *Individual Income Taxes: 2001 Edition.* Cincinnati: South-Western College Publishing, 2001.
KENNICKELL, A. B. *Codebook for 1998 Survey of Consumer Finances.* Washington, D.C.: Federal Reserve System, 1997.
KENNICKELL, A. B.; STARR-MCCLUER, M.; and SURETTE, B. "Recent Changes in U.S. Family Finances: Results from the 1998 Survey of Consumer Finances." *Federal Reserve Bulletin* 86, no. 1 (2000): 1–29.
PRESTON, R. "The Dos and Don'ts of IRA Investing." *Journal of Accountancy* 189, no. 4 (April 2000): 45–53.
U.S. Department of the Treasury. "Individual Retirement Arrangements." Publication 590, 1999. http://www.irs.ustreas.gov/

INEQUALITY

Social inequality encompasses relatively long-lasting differences between groups of people and has considerable implications for individuals, especially "for the rights or opportunities they exercise and the rewards or privileges they enjoy" (Grabb, 1997, pp. 1–2). Most studies of social inequality consider gaps in income and assets between advantaged and disadvantaged groups of people. However, important considerations in the study of social inequality also include issues of status, power, housing, and health, as well as the relationship between these factors and economic well-being.

Economic well-being, status, power, housing, and health are influenced by many factors, including age. In most research on inequality in later life researchers organize age-based systems of inequality on the basis of whether one is old, middle aged, or young. Comparisons are made between these age groups, or *strata,* to determine whether one group is disadvantaged relative to another.

Other factors that influence social inequality include gender, class, ethnicity, and race. Increasingly, researchers are recognizing that to fully explore the complexities of inequality, all of these factors must be considered. Yet, there remains disagreement among scholars about how class, age, gender, ethnicity, and race influence one another, and about which among these is most important to inequality. In the literature on aging, researchers have approached this issue in various ways. Central to these approaches are debates between multiple-jeopardy and leveling hypotheses, studies of heterogeneity and cumulative advantage/disadvantage, and discussions of diversity.

Multiple bases of inequality: conceptual issues

Research on the relationship between inequality and class, gender, age, ethnicity, and race has often addressed the question of whether the disadvantages associated with class, gender, ethnicity, and race increase in older age (multiple-jeopardy hypotheses), stay the same, or whether the gap between these groups diminishes in later life (leveling hypotheses). Multiple-jeopardy hypotheses argue that class, racial, ethnic, and gender inequalities carry on in later life and that groups who are disadvantaged by these dimensions of inequality in midlife (e.g., women or people of color) face increasing disadvantage in older age. Alternatively, the leveling hypothesis suggests that people who are privileged in early life have more to lose in later life, and that a leveling out of resources takes place. Furthermore, social security policies serve to enhance the resources of those who are disadvantaged earlier in life, which further reduces the gap between the haves and the have-nots among older people. There has been mixed support for both types of hypotheses, depending on what dimensions of inequality are considered and the particular inequality outcome that is of concern. However, after reviewing many diverse studies that consider either the combination of class and age, gender and age, or race and ethnicity and age, Fred Pampel (1998) concluded that there is more support for the multiple-jeopardy hypothesis than for the leveling approach.

Related to multiple-jeopardy arguments are life-course discussions of heterogeneity and cumulative advantage/disadvantage. The key distinction between these two perspectives is the latter's emphasis on time. According to the cumulative advantage/disadvantage hypothesis, the heterogeneity between groups of people increases over time. This hypothesis suggests that individuals have specific class, gender, and racial/ethnic characteristics that provide them with a certain amount of advantage or disadvantage. Initially, there is little separation between the haves and the have-nots on the basis of these distinctions. However, as time passes, the separation between the advantaged and disadvantaged grows and age cohorts become increasingly heterogeneous. The reason that this occurs is because the economic and social value that is attached to productive work in most Western societies differs depending on one's gender, race/ethnicity, class, and age. For the most part, research on cumulative advantage/disadvantage has found support for the hypothesis, but most of the research has focused on income inequality rather than on status, power, housing, or health.

Recent theoretical work on aging and inequality has also considered the issue of diversity. Although the terms *heterogeneity* and *diversity* have been used interchangeably, the distinction between them is an important one. Both of these concepts are about difference, but the theoretical emphasis on power relations varies between the two. While *heterogeneity* can refer to any meaningful group or individual difference, *diversity* is about "examining groups in relation to interlocking structural positions within a society" (Calasanti, 1996, p. 148). This requires that class, age, gender, and ethnicity/race be conceptualized as "sets of social relations, characterized by power, that are fundamental structures or organizing features of social life" (McMullin, 2000, p. 525), and not as individual attributes. Furthermore, social class, age, gender, and ethnicity/race must be viewed as interlocking sets of power relations. This emphasis on power relations in diversity research prompts a consideration of what is meant by *power,* and by the related concept *status.*

Status and power

Put simply, status refers to one's position in society. Sociologists often make a distinction between *ascribed status* and *achieved status.* Ascribed status refers to characteristics of individuals over which they have little control, such as their sex, age, race, or ethnicity. Achieved status, on the other hand, refers to positions in society that an individual may achieve, such as level of education or occupational status. Although ascribed and achieved status have received considerable research attention, the *status group* concept is more relevant to the discussion presented here, because it is directly tied to issues of power. A status group refers to a set of people who "have a subjective sense of common membership and a group awareness that is relatively well defined" (Grabb, 1997, p. 50). Status groups are clearly demarcated in society on the basis of their prestige, honor, and the resulting power that they have.

What then, is meant by *power?* There are many sociological definitions of power but perhaps the most widely cited view reflects the ability of individuals or groups in social relationships to impose their will on others regardless of resistance (Weber, 1922). Economic resources are often thought to be associated with power. However, as the preceding discussion of status groups suggests, power may also be derived from prestige and honor.

Because status moves away from the idea that power is largely based in economic relationships, it is tempting to consider issues of aging and inequality in this light. This is because most older people do not have direct associations with the economy (i.e. they do not work for pay), and therefore must derive their status and power, if they have any, from other means. Hence, one question that arises is whether age groups might well be evaluated with regard to their status, and, in turn, whether honor, prestige, and power vary across age groups.

The extent to which age is associated with power and status varies depending on the specifics of the culture or society in question. In some societies, high levels of status and power are found in older age groups relative to younger groups, but in other societies older adults are afforded very little status or power.

In early twenty-first-century Canada and the United States, the relationship between age, status, and power is complex. In these societies, very rarely are young children or teenagers afforded higher levels of status and power than are adults. Regardless of levels of maturity, dexterity, or intellectual ability, teenagers who live in North America must turn a certain chronological age before they are legally able to drive a car, vote, or consume alcohol. Wage scales are established for teenagers, not on the basis of what they do, but on their chronological age. Hence, a twenty year old and a seventeen year old could be working at the same job and the seventeen year old could legally be paid less for doing the same work. All of this suggests that the status and power of younger people in North America lags far behind that of middle-aged or older persons. This assessment is too simplistic, however. A counter pressure to these facts exists which has been referred to as the "cult of youth." This refers to the ideology in North American culture that favors young over old and suggests that to be young is to be vibrant, beautiful, and happy, whereas to be old is to be tired, unattractive, and grim. These cultural views do little to take away from the status and power that middle-aged adults have. However, for older adults these views are especially detrimental because, combined with the loss of their youthful appeal, they have also lost the power and status associated with middle-aged activities such as working for pay and raising families.

The status and power associated with age is influenced by other dimensions of inequality, including class, gender, and ethnicity/race. Yet researchers have not tended to consider these intersections in their discussions of status and power. Anecdotally, however, we can imagine that an older, retired, white man who had a successful career as the president of a large multinational company will likely maintain some status and power despite his age. One way in which men in these circumstances do this is by retaining their memberships on the executive boards of companies or public organizations (e.g., universities). Alternatively, there would be very little status and power associated with being an aging, Hispanic housewife.

As this discussion on status and power illustrates, research on aging tends to insufficiently deal with the intersections between class, age, gender, and ethnicity/race. Where possible, the ensuing discussions will present information on class, age, gender, and ethnicity/race, while maintaining a focus on aging and later life. Nota-

bly, very little research has simultaneously and systematically considered all of these dimensions of inequality, thus limiting the extent to which the intersection of these factors can be discussed. Further, most of the available information on health and housing assesses income differences rather than social-class differences and focuses on black/white racial comparisons to the neglect of other racial and ethnic groups. In the following discussion, therefore, income will be used as a proxy for social class and racial comparisons will be limited to discussions of older black and white Americans.

Housing

Contrary to popular opinion, the majority (95 percent in the United States) of older people (age 65 and over) live within the community and not in institutional settings such as nursing homes. Among those older people who live in communities, most live in homes that they own (77 percent in the United States).

The structural factors that the U.S. government uses to evaluate housing problems include whether a household has adequate heating and cooling systems, plumbing, and kitchen facilities; whether it has structural defects; and whether there is equipment in need of repair. These structural issues are a significant concern for older people living within a community, because almost 8 percent of them live in dwellings that have moderate to severe structural problems. The U.S. government also assesses housing on the basis of whether it is overcrowded, and on whether there are excessive shelter costs. Very few older adults live in overcrowded households, but one-quarter of older homeowners and one-third of older renters are considered to spend too much of their income on housing. In other words, between one-quarter and one-third of older people spend over 30 percent of their income on housing, and people in this situation are not thought to have enough money available to spend on food, medical expenses, transportation, and clothing.

Low-income households are at higher risk of housing problems than are high-income households, regardless of age. This fact has led some commentators to conclude that housing policies that target older adults should be abandoned for housing policies that focus more specifically on income. Others argue that older adults are in unique situations that require specific housing-policy initiatives. For instance, to the extent that older adults are more frail than younger adults, their housing deficiencies may not be well captured by typical measures of housing problems. As an example, a significant housing problem for an older adult may be the need for assistive devices installed in the bathroom. If an older adult cannot afford such devices, then they are at risk of injury and their home does not meet their basic safety needs. This is an issue that most younger adults do not face. Furthermore, older adults may suffer the negative consequences of living in substandard housing more so than younger adults do. The fact that every year there are North American news reports of older people dying from the summer heat or the winter cold is a point that attests to this claim.

There are also subgroups of older people, the very old (eighty-five+) and black older adults in particular, that are at heightened risk of occupying poor housing (Golant & LaGreca, 1995).This suggests that researchers must carefully consider how age and race intersect in assessments of housing deficiencies and that diversity among those aged sixty-five and older is an important issue in this regard. Assessments of gender differences are rare in the literature on housing deficiencies in later life. This seems a bit odd in light of the fact that higher proportions of older women than older men live alone and that living alone likely increases one's risk of suffering negative consequences of poor housing because there may be no one available to help in times of crisis. Furthermore, because there are well established relationships between poverty and gender and between poverty and poor housing, neglecting potential gender differences in housing seems particularly odd. However, studies on housing often use the household as the unit of analysis and rely on census information that defines household heads on the basis of the name that appears on the lease or land title. Hence, problems with data may make it difficult to fully capture gender inequality in housing.

Health

According to the World Health Organization, health is broadly defined as "a state of complete physical, mental, and social well-being and not merely the absence of disease or infirmity" (World Health Organization, 2000). This definition suggests that many measures of health must be explored to fully understand health and in-

equality. Older persons are more likely than younger persons to experience chronic health problems, functional impairments, and death. This being said, it is inaccurate to assume that all, or even most, older people are sick to the point that they have trouble functioning. Although the majority (85 percent) of adults age sixty-five or older have one or more chronic illness, only about 20 percent of older adults have trouble providing their own personal care or living independently as a result of functional impairment. Nonetheless, among the older population, health does vary on the basis of age, with those over the age of eighty-five having significantly poorer health than those between the ages of sixty-five and eighty-five.

In general, research suggests that rates of clinical mental disorder are higher among younger than among older adults (Krause, 1999). On the other hand, rates of cognitive impairment and suicide are higher among older than among younger adults (Krause, 1999). Unlike these findings from the psychiatric perspective, sociological research on mental health tends to focus on depressive symptomatology rather than clinical assessments of mental disorder. This research, although still inconclusive, suggests that the relationship between age and depressive symptomatology is nonlinear, decreasing from young to middle adulthood and then increasing at age 60 and thereafter (Krause, 1999).

Gender significantly influences health in later life. On average, women live seven to eight years longer than men. However, older women experience more chronic illnesses and functional impairments, report more depressive symptoms, experience higher levels of psychological distress, and have higher rates of prescription drug use than do older men. Notably, while there is a higher prevalence of depressive disorders among women at all ages when compared to men, this gap decreases with increasing age.

Beyond these age and gender differences, there is further diversity in physical health among older adults on the basis of class and race. One well-known and consistent finding is the relationship between socioeconomic status (SES) and health. Research on physical health generally shows that individuals from lower socioeconomic strata have worse health than do those from higher socioeconomic strata. In general, however, class differences in health are smaller in older age than they are in younger age. Indeed, when education and income are used as measures of SES, the inverse relationship between SES and health is not always supported among samples of older adults. Yet, if occupation is the SES measure used, class differences in health in later life are usually found. For instance, older persons who were previously employed in skilled, white-collar work have fewer health problems and lower rates of mortality than those who were employed in unskilled, blue-collar work (Pampel, 1998).

Regarding mental health, older persons with lower levels of education and income tend to report more depressive symptoms than do those with higher levels of education and income. In contrast, relationships between either education or income and depressive disorder in later life appear to be weak.

Such a strong and consistent relationship between SES and health exists because people with lower levels of income, lower levels of education, and bad jobs are more likely to experience malnutrition, to disproportionately lack knowledge of health care practices, and because they are more often exposed to dangerous working and living environments. All of these things negatively affect health status. Furthermore, research has shown that SES is associated with access to health care services. In particular, older people with higher incomes and who have private health insurance go to the doctor more often and spend more nights in the hospital than do older people who have lower incomes or who do not have private health insurance, regardless of their overall health (Mutchler & Burr, 1991).

The relationship between race and health in later life is complex. For the most part, research suggests that, compared to older white Americans, older black Americans report more chronic health problems, have higher levels of functional decline, and have higher rates of mortality. Yet, even though physical and mental health are often correlated, older black Americans and older white Americans tend to have similar levels of mental health.

The physical health gap between white Americans and black Americans does not increase in later life, but instead remains consistent or declines. In fact, there appears to be a crossover in health after the age of eighty-five, whereby older black persons gain a slight health advantage.

The most reliable data for this crossover effect come from mortality statistics. The ratio of black men and women to white men and women who die in each ten-year age group declines steadily from age twenty-five onward. American data from 1992 show that the black to white mortality ratio for twenty-five-year-old to thirty-five-year-old males is 2.39, and for females it is 2.72. These ratios decline for each successive age group until a crossover occurs in the eighty-five and older age group. In this age group the ratio is .99 for women and .95 for men, suggesting that among the oldest old, black men and women have a slight advantage over white men and women regarding mortality.

Selectivity in survival is the most common explanation given for the age-based decline in the racial health gap and the crossover effect in mortality ratios. This selectivity explanation suggests that the reason the gap in health status between older white and black adults remains the same or declines in later life has to do with the fact that black Americans are at greater risk of dying than are white Americans at each life-course stage. Hence, only the healthiest black persons live into old age, thereby reducing the health distinction between white and black Americans in later life.

Conclusion

To the extent that status, power, housing conditions, and health reflect overall well-being, the information presented above suggests that, all things considered, older adults tend to have lower levels of well-being than younger adults. However, the relationship between age and well-being is very complex. Indeed, there is notable diversity among older adults, with class, age, gender, and ethnicity/race intersecting to structure inequality in later life. The first letter of each of these bases of diversity forms the word CAGE. A lot of imagery comes to mind when one thinks of the word *cage,* and for certain groups of people this imagery is quite accurate. However, one must also recognize that there also is a great deal of variation in inequality. Not all working class, racial, or ethnic minority women suffer from low levels of well-being, even though they are at heightened risk. Hence, a task of future gerontological work on inequality is to assess what contributes to such variation and how individuals make choices that either amplify or diminish the effect of structural circumstances on inequality.

JULIE ANN MCMULLIN

See also Economic Well-Being; Generational Equity; Health, Social Factors; Housing.

BIBLIOGRAPHY

Belgrave, L. L.; Wykle, M. L.; and Choi, J. M. "Health, Double Jeopardy, and Culture: The Use of Institutionalization by African-Americans." *The Gerontologist* 33 (1993): 379–385.

Calasanti, T. "Incorporating Diversity: Meaning, Levels of Research, and Implications for Theory." *The Gerontologist* 36 (1996): 147–164.

Dannefer, D., and Sell, R. R. "Age Structure, the Life Course and 'Aged Heterogeneity': Prospects for Research and Theory." *Comprehensive Gerontology B* 2 (1988): 1–10.

Fry, C. L. "Age, Aging, and Culture." In *Handbook of Aging and the Social Sciences*, 4th ed. Edited by R. H. Binstock and L. K. George. New York: Academic Press, 1996. Pages 117–136.

George, L. K. "Social Factors and Illness." In *Handbook of Aging and the Social Sciences*, 4th ed. Edited by R. H. Binstock and L. K. George. New York: Academic Press, 1996. Pages 229–252.

Golant, S. M., and La Greca, A. J. "The Relative Deprivation of the U.S. Elderly Households as Judged by Their Housing Problems." *Journals of Gerontology*, Series B, 50B, (1995): S13–S23.

Grabb, E. G. *Theories of Social Inequality: Classical and Contemporary Perspectives*, 3d ed. Toronto, Canada: Harcourt Brace & Company, 1997.

Krause, N. "Mental Disorder in Late Life: Exploring the Influence of Stress and Socioeconomic Status." In *Handbook of the Sociology of Mental Health*. Edited by C. S. Aneshensel and J. C. Phelan. New York: Kluwer Academic/Plenum Publishers, 1999. Pages 183–208.

Markides, K. S., and Black, S. A. "Race, Ethnicity, and Aging: The Impact of Inequality." In *Handbook of Aging and the Social Sciences*, 4th ed. Edited by R. H. Binstock and L. K. George. New York: Academic Press, 1996. Pages 153–170.

McMullin, J. A. "Diversity and the State of Sociological Aging Theory." *The Gerontologist* 40 (2000): 517–530.

McMullin, J. A. "Theorizing Age and Gender Relations." In *Connecting Gender and Ageing: A Sociological Approach*. Edited by S. Arber and J. Ginn. Buckingham, England: Open University Press, 1995. Pages 30–41.

McMullin, J. A., and Marshall, V. W. "Ageism, Age Relations, and Garment Industry Work in Montreal." *The Gerontologist* 41 (2001): 111–122.

McMullin, J. A., and Marshall, V. W. "Structure and Agency in the Retirement Process: A Case Study of Montreal Garment Workers." In *The Self and Society in Aging Processes*. Edited by C. Ryff and V. W. Marshall. New York: Springer, 1999. Pages 305–338.

Moen, P. "Gender, Age, and the Life Course." In *Handbook of Aging and the Social Sciences*, 4th ed. Edited by R. H. Binstock and L. K. George. New York: Academic Press, 1996. Pages 171–187.

Mutcher, J. E., and Burr, J. A. "Racial Differences in Health and Health Care Service Utilization in Later Life: The Effect of Socioeconomic Status." *Journal of Health and Social Behavior* 32 (1991): 342–356.

O'Rand, A. "The Cumulative Stratification of the Life Course." In *Handbook of Aging and the Social Sciences*, 4th ed. Edited by R. H. Binstock and L. K. George. New York: Academic Press, 1996. Pages 188–207.

O'Rand, A. "The Precious and the Precocious: Understanding Cumulative Disadvantage and Cumulative Advantage Over the Life Course." *The Gerontologist* 36 (1996): 230–238.

Pampel, F. C. *Aging, Social Inequality, and Public Policy*. Thousand Oaks, Calif.: Pine Forge Press, 1998.

Pynoos, J., and Golant, S. "Housing and Living Arrangements for the Elderly." In *Handbook of Aging and the Social Sciences*, 4th ed. Edited by R. H. Binstock and L. K. George. New York: Academic Press, 1996. Pages 302–324.

Turner, B. S. *Status*. Minneapolis: University of Minnesota Press, 1988.

Weber, M. *Economy and Society*. New York: Bedminster Press. 1922; reprinted in 1968.

World Health Organization. "Definition of Health." World Wide Web document. www.who.int/

INFLATION

See Consumer price index and COLAs

INFLUENZA

Influenza is an acute respiratory illness caused by infection with influenza type A or B virus. It typically occurs in outbreaks over a five- to six-week period each winter. Each year, hundreds of thousands of excess hospitalizations, tens of thousands of excess deaths, and billions of dollars in health care costs can be attributed to influenza and its complications. Attack rates can

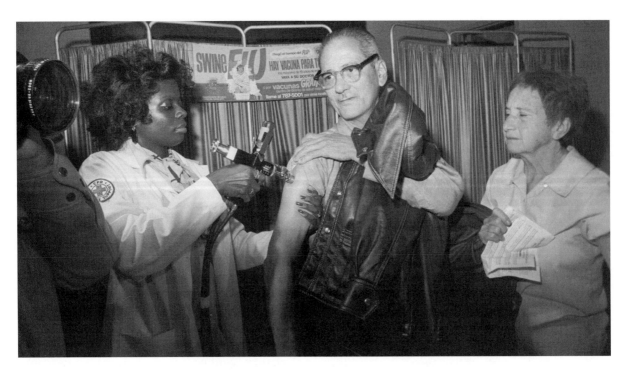

Nurse Jacqueline Spaky delivers an swine flu injection to an elderly patient in New York City in 1976. The city set up 45 sites at which to give the shots free of charge in an attempt to limit the spread of the deadly disease. Older adults are more susceptible to catching the flu, and its affects can often be much more harsh than in younger patients. (Corbis/BETTMAN photo.)

be as high as 10 to 40 percent in the community, and examination of influenza epidemic curves typically reveals a bimodal pattern, with attack rates highest in the young and morbidity and mortality highest in the elderly population. In most studies, elderly persons with chronic respiratory conditions account for up to 80 percent of patients with such serious complications as hospitalization and death.

Influenza can be a particularly difficult problem for people who live in long-term care facilities (LTCFs), where case fatality rates during outbreaks often exceed 5 percent. Up to 22 percent of residents that acquire influenza will develop complications of infection severe enough to result in hospitalization. Once influenza is introduced into a LTCF by staff and visitors, these relatively closed communities are an ideal setting for the rapid spread of influenza by droplet transmission. Attack rates among residents can exceed 40 percent.

Clinical findings

Influenza is typically characterized by the abrupt onset of fever, chills, headaches, severe myalgias (muscle pains), malaise, and loss of appetite. These are evident after an incubation period of one to two days. In the first three days of illness, headache and muscle pain are usually the most bothersome symptoms, with the severity of these complaints reflecting the magnitude of the fever. Dry cough, severe sore throat, and nasal obstruction and discharge are usually also present, although they may be overshadowed by the systemic complaints. The fever typically resolves after approximately three days, but the cough, sore throat, and hoarseness may persist for three to four days after the fever resolves. It is important to remember that in frail older adults disease presentation can be atypical. For example, some individuals might present only with fever, lack of energy, or confusion, and without any evidence of respiratory illness. Influenza should be considered in any illness characterized by fever in an elderly person during influenza season.

Without complications, influenza is a self-limited illness lasting five to eight days. Elderly patients and patients with high-risk medical conditions, including chronic lung or heart disease, kidney disease, problems with the immune system, cancer, or other chronic medical problems are at risk for developing complications from influenza. Pneumonia caused by the influenza virus itself and secondary bacterial pneumonia are the most common and serious complications of influenza. Patients with influenza pneumonia, a complication which is fortunately quite rare, will present with typical signs and symptoms of influenza but go on to develop severe cough, shortness of breath, and cyanosis. Chest X-rays will usually show bilateral findings most consistent with adult respiratory distress syndrome, and gram stains of sputum will not identify a bacterial pathogen. Death, due to diffuse hemorrhagic pneumonia, is high even with prompt antiviral therapy.

Secondary bacterial pneumonia is indistinguishable from community-acquired pneumonia in the absence of influenza, except that it typically occurs in elderly patients or patients with chronic heart or lung problems after recovery from a classic influenza illness. Patients will usually describe a recurrence of fever, cough, and sputum production four to fourteen days after their initial recovery from influenza. Physical examination and chest X-ray usually reveal a focal area of lung infection. Microbiological examination of the sputum often shows bacteria such as *Streptococcus pneumoniae* or *Haemophilus influenzae*. Treatment of community-acquired pneumonia as a secondary complication of influenza infection is not different than in any other setting, and requires antibiotic drugs.

Diagnosis

Influenza virus can be readily isolated from nasal swabs, throat swabs, nasal washes, and sometimes sputum. A throat swab alone is less sensitive than nasal or throat washes, and thus washes are preferred. Specimens should be placed into containers of viral transport medium and transported to the laboratory for viral culture. Two-thirds of positive cultures will be detected within seventy-two hours, with the remainder within five to seven days. However, particularly for influenza detection in long-term care facilities, faster methods of detection are needed. A variety of rapid detection methods for influenza virus exist that detect viral antigens by immunofluorescence or ELISA in as little as one hour, with reasonable sensitivity and specificity under optimal conditions. At present though, viral culture remains the gold standard for diagnosis of influenza infection.

Treatment

In otherwise healthy children and adults with uncomplicated influenza infection, antiviral therapy is not generally warranted. Bed rest, adequate fluid intake, and treatment with analgesics, cough suppressants, and decongestants may improve symptoms. In patients at significant risk for the development of complications of influenza, or in those with influenza pneumonia, the use of antiviral medications may decrease morbidity and mortality. Until recently, therapy for influenza typically involved the use of amantadine or rimantadine, antiviral drugs active against influenza A. Most studies examining the efficacy of these drugs have shown a reduction in clinical symptom scores, a faster resolution of fever, and a decrease in the level and duration of infectivity. Most authorities support the use of amantadine in the treatment of complicated influenza A virus infection, even late in the course of illness. Treatment with antiviral medications is also generally recommended for outbreaks of influenza A virus infection in LTCFs, although whether these drugs prevent illness, relieve symptoms, or reduce the duration of illness or complications in this setting is not clear.

These drugs can lead to complications. Confusion, delerium, seizures, falls, insomnia, or fractures occur in 22 to 47 percent of residents of LTCFs treated with amantidine, and drug resistance develops readily. Side effects can be reduced in the elderly by reducing the dose of amantadine to 100 mg or less daily in the presence of renal insufficiency. Central nervous system side effects are less problematic with rimantadine than with amantadine.

The neuraminidase inhibitors are a new class of antiviral medications with activity against both influenza A and B virus. These agents, although expensive, offer a much better side-effect profile and are better tolerated in the elderly than amantadine. Although resistance to these agents has been reported, it is not yet a significant problem. The role of these agents in the prevention and treatment of influenza infections in the elderly has not yet been established, but there is mounting evidence to suggest that they may play a key role in the management of influenza in LTCFs in the near future.

Prevention

Influenza vaccination represents the safest, most cost-effective means of prevention of morbidity and mortality from influenza virus. Current guidelines recommend influenza vaccine yearly in all individuals over age sixty-five, all residents of LTCFs, children or adults with chronic pulmonary or cardiovascular illness, children requiring chronic aspirin therapy, and women in the second or third trimester of pregnancy during influenza season. Yearly influenza vaccine is also recommended in health care workers, employees of LTCFs who come in contact with patients, and home care providers or others who have household contact with high-risk individuals.

At present, an inactivated vaccine directed at three viruses (influenza A H1N1, H3N2, and influenza B) is currently used. This vaccine can reduce the incidence of confirmed influenza, influenza-like illness, all respiratory infections, exacerbations of cardiopulmonary disease, hospitalization, and death in both community-dwelling elderly persons and in residents of LTCFs. Although the vaccine has only 30 to 40 percent efficacy in preventing influenza in residents of LTCFs, severe illness, hospitalization, and death are significantly reduced. High vaccination rates among residents of a LTCF significantly reduce the chances of an outbreak occurring in that facility, and should an outbreak occur, vaccination will decrease hospitalizations by 50 to 60 percent and mortality by as much as 80 percent. In order to maximize the effectiveness of the vaccine in the prevention of influenza-associated morbidity and mortality in residents of LTCFs, it is critical that high staff vaccine rates be maintained in hopes of reducing and delaying introduction of influenza into these facilities. A newly developed but not yet licensed cold-adapted, live, attenuated, trivalent, intranasal influenza vaccine has been shown to increase serum, mucosal, and cell-mediated immunity when given in combination with the currently available intramuscular vaccine.

SHELLY MCNEIL

See also LUNG, AGING; PNEUMONIA.

BIBLIOGRAPHY

BRADLEY, S. F., et al. "Prevention of Influenza in Long-Term Care Facilities." *Infection Control Hospital Epidemiology* 20 (1999): 629–637.
LIBOW, L. S.; NEUFELD, R. R.; OLSON, E.; BREUER, B.; and STARER, P. "Sequential Outbreak of Influenza A and B in a Nursing Home: Efficacy of Vaccine and Amantidine." *Journal of the American Geriatric Society* 44 (1996): 1153–1157.
"Prevention and Control of Influenza: Recommendations of the Advisory Committee on Immunization Practices." *Morbidity and Mortality Weekly Report* 47 (1998): 1–16.
TREANOR, J. J. "Influenza Virus." In *Principles and Practices of Infectious Diseases*, 5th ed. Edited by G. L. Mandell, J. E. Bennett, and R. Dolin. New York: Churchill Livingstone, 2000. Pages 1823–1849.

INSULIN

See DIABETES MELLITUS

INTELLIGENCE

Empirical work in geropsychology began in the early part of the twentieth century with the observation that there were apparent declines in intellectual performance when groups of young and old persons were compared on the same tasks. This early work was done primarily with measures designed for assessing children or young adults. The intellectual processes used in the development of cognitive structures and functions in childhood, however, are not always the most relevant processes for the maintenance of intelligence into old age, and a reorganization of cognitive structures (for example, mental abilities) may indeed be needed to meet the demands of later life. Nevertheless, certain basic concepts relevant to an understanding of intelligence in childhood remain relevant at adult levels. Changes in basic abilities and measures of intelligence must therefore be studied over much of the life course, even though the manner in which intellectual competence is organized and measured may change with advancing age.

This section will first review the historical background for the study of adult intelligence. Alternative formulations of the conceptual nature of intelligence will then be described. Next, changes in intellectual competence that represent actual decrement that individuals experience will be differentiated from the apparently lower performance of older persons that is not due to intellectual decline, but instead reflects a maintained, but obsolescent, functioning of older cohorts when compared to younger peers. This is the distinction between data on age differences gained from cross-sectional comparison of groups differing in age and data acquired by means of longitudinal studies of the same individuals over time. This discussion will also include information on the ages at which highest levels of intellectual competence are reached, magnitudes of within-generation age changes, and an assessment of generational differences. Some attention will be given to the distinction between academic and practical intelligence. Finally, the influences of health, lifestyles, and education will be considered. This will provide an understanding of why some individuals show intellectual decrement in early adulthood while others maintain or increase their level of functioning well into old age.

Intellectual development from young adulthood through old age has become an important topic because of the increase in average life span and the ever-larger number of persons who reach advanced ages. Assessment of intellectual competence in old age is often needed to provide information relevant to questions of retirement for cause (in the absence of mandatory retirement for reasons of age), or to determine whether sufficient competence remains for independent living, for medical decision making, as well as for the control and disposition of property. Level of intellectual competence may also need to be assessed in preparation for entering retraining activities required for late-life career changes.

Historical background

Four influential theoretical positions have had a major impact on empirical research on intelligence and age. The earliest conceptualization came from Sir Charles Spearman's work in 1904. Spearman suggested that a general dimension of intelligence (g) underlied all purposeful intellectual pursuits. All other components of such pursuits were viewed as task or item specific (s). This view underlies the family of assessment devices that were developed at the beginning of the twentieth century; particularly the work of Alfred Binet and Henri Simon in France. Thinking of a single, general form of intelligence may be appropriate for childhood, when measurement of intellectual competence is used primarily to predict scholastic performance. However, a singular concept is not useful beyond adolescence, because there is no single criterion outcome to be predicted in adults. Also, there is

convincing empirical evidence to support the existence of multiple dimensions of intelligence that display a different life-course pattern.

The notion of a single dimension of intelligence became popular during World War I, when Robert Yerkes constructed the Army Alpha intelligence test for purposes of classifying the large number of inductees according to their ability level. Because of the predominantly verbal aspects of this test, it was soon supplemented by performance measures suitable for illiterate or low-literate inductees. Assessing a single dimension of intelligence also widely influenced educational testing. It was around this time that Lewis Terman, a psychologist working at Stanford University, adapted the work of Binet and Simon for use in American schools and introduced the Stanford-Binet test, which dominated educational testing for many decades. Terman was also responsible for the introduction of the IQ concept. He argued that one could compute an index (the *intelligence quotient*, or IQ) that represents the ratio of a person's mental age (as measured by the Stanford-Binet test) divided by the person's chronological age. An IQ value of 100 was assigned to be equivalent to the average performance of a person at a given age. The IQ range from 90 to 110 represented the middle 50 percent of the normal population. Because there is no linear relation between mental and chronological age past adolescence, however, the Stanford-Binet approach did not work well with adults (see below).

An early influential multidimensional theory of intelligence was Edward. L. Thorndike's view that different dimensions of intelligence would display similar levels of performance within individuals. Thorndike also suggested that all categories of intelligence possessed three attributes: power, speed, and magnitude (see Thorndike & Woodworth, 1901). This approach is exemplified by the work of David Wechsler. The Wechsler Adult Intelligence Scale (WAIS) consists of eleven distinct subscales of intelligence, derived from clinical observation and earlier mental tests, combined into two broad dimensions: verbal intelligence and performance (nonverbal-manipulative) intelligence. These dimensions can then be combined to form a total global IQ. The global IQ (comparable to the Stanford-Binet IQ) is statistically adjusted to have a mean of 100 for any normative age group. The range of the middle 50 percent of the population is also set to range from 90 to 110. The Wechsler scales were used in the clinical assessment of adults with psychopathologies, and some of the subtests are still used by neuropsychologists to help diagnose the presence of a dementia.

The Wechsler verbal and performance scales are highly reliable in older persons, but measurable differences between the two are often used as a rough estimate of age decline, a use that has not proven to be very reliable. A more significant limitation of the test for research on intellectual aging, however, has been the fact that the factor structure of the scales does not remain invariant across age. As a consequence, most recent studies of intellectual aging in community-dwelling populations have utilized some combination of the primary mental abilities.

Factorially simpler multiple dimensions of intelligence were identified in the work of Louis Leon Thurstone during the 1930s, which was expanded upon by J. P. Guilford in 1967. (The primary mental abilities described by Thurstone and Guilford have also formed the basis for this author's own work; see Schaie, 1996b.) Major intellectual abilities that account for much of the observed individual differences in intelligence include verbal meaning (recognition vocabulary), inductive reasoning (the ability to identify rules and principles), spatial orientation (rotation of objects in two- or three-dimensional space), number skills (facility with arithmetic skills), word fluency (recall vocabulary), and perceptual speed. Further analyses of the primary intellectual abilities have identified several higher-order dimensions, including those of fluid intelligence (applied to novel tasks) and crystallized intelligence (applied to acculturated information).

The introduction of Piagetian thought into American psychology led some investigators to consider the application of Piagetian methods to adult development. However, Jean Piaget's (1896–1980) original work assumed that intellectual development was complete once the stage of formal operations had been reached during young adulthood. Hence, this approach has contributed only sparsely to empirical work on adult intelligence.

There are also discernable secular trends that cut across theoretical positions on different aspects of adult intelligence. Diana Woodruff-Pak has identified four stages: (1) until the mid-1950s, concerns were predominantly with identifying steep and apparently inevitable age-related decline; (2) the late 1950s through the mid-1960s saw the discovery that there was stability as well as decline; (3) beginning with the mid-1970s, external social and experiential effects that influenced cohort differences in ability levels were identified; and (4) in the 1980s and 1990s the field has been dominated by attempts to alter experience and manipulate age differences. Successful demonstrations of the modifiability of intellectual performance has led researchers to expand definitions of intelligence and to explore new methods of measurement.

Conceptualizations of intelligence

Past approaches to the study of intelligence (from its origin in work with children) were primarily concerned with academic or intellectual performance outcomes. Current conceptualizations of intelligence, by contrast, often distinguish between academic, practical, and social intelligence. All of these, however, are basically manifestations of intellectual competence. The contemporary study of intellectual competence has been largely driven by three perspectives: The first sees competence as a set of latent variables (latent variables are not directly observable but are inferred by statistical means, e.g., factor analysis, from sets of observed variables that are related to the "latent variables") that represent permutations of variables identified by studies of basic cognition. This perspective has been characterized as a *componential* or *hierarchical* approach. The second perspective views competence as involving specific knowledge bases. The third focuses on the "fit" or congruence between an individual's intellectual competence and the environmental demands faced by the individual.

Componential/hierarchical approaches to intelligence.   The three major examples of such approaches are: Robert Sternberg's triarchic theory of intelligence; Paul Baltes' two-dimensional model; and the hierarchical model linking intellectual competence with basic cognition proposed by Sherry Willis and K. Warner Schaie.

Sternberg proposed a triarchic theory of adult intellectual development that involves metacomponents, and experiential and contextual aspects (a metacomponent is a necessary component required for the others). The metacomponential part of the theory involves an information-processing approach to basic cognition, including processes such as encoding, allocation of mental resources, and monitoring of thought processes. The second component of the theory posits that these processes operate at different levels of experience, depending upon the task—the basic components can operate in a relatively novel fashion or, with experience, they may become automatized. For example, identifying a driver's response pattern under a specific traffic condition; this response then becomes automatic whenever a similar condition is encountered. According to Sternberg, the most intelligent person is the one who can adjust to a change in a problem situation and who can eventually automate the component processes of task solution. The third aspect of the theory is concerned with how the individual applies the meta-components in adjusting to a change in the environment.

Baltes proposed a two-dimensional componential model of cognition. The first component is identified as the *mechanics of intelligence,* which represent the basic cognitive processes that serve as underpinnings for all intelligent behavior. The second component of the theory is labeled the *pragmatics of intelligence.* This is the component that is influenced by experience. Baltes argues that the environmental context is critical to the particular form or manifestation in which pragmatic intelligence is shown. The concept of wisdom has been linked with, and studied within, the pragmatics of intelligence.

Willis and Schaie conceptualized a hierarchical relationship between basic cognition and intellectual competence. Basic cognition is thought to be represented by domains of psychometric intelligence, such as the second-order constructs of fluid and crystallized intelligence and the primary mental abilities associated with each higher-order construct. The cognitive abilities represented in traditional approaches to intelligence are proposed to be universal across the life span and across cultures. When nurtured and directed by a favorable environment at a particular life stage, these processes and abilities develop into cognitive competencies that are manifested in daily life as cognitive performance.

Intellectual competence, as represented in activities of daily living, is seen in the phenotypic expressions of intelligence that are context- or age-specific. The particular activities and behaviors that serve as phenotypic expressions of intelligence vary with the age of the individual, with a person's social roles, and with the environmen-

tal context. Problem solving in everyday activities is complex and involves multiple basic cognitive abilities. Everyday competence also involves substantive knowledge, as well as the individual's attitudes and values associated with a particular problem domain.

Age changes in intelligence

A number of longitudinal studies have been conducted in the United States and in Europe covering substantial age ranges. An important new addition is the initiation of longitudinal studies in the very old, providing hope for better information on age changes in the nineties and beyond.

Longitudinal studies of intelligence usually show a peak of intellectual performance in young adulthood or early middle age, with a virtual plateau until early old age and accelerating average decline thereafter. However, it should be noted that different intellectual skills reach peak performance at different ages and decline at different rates. Figure 1 provides an example from the Seattle Longitudinal Study, a large scale study of community-dwelling adults. This figure shows age changes from twenty-five to eighty-eight years of age for six primary mental abilities. Note that only perceptual speed follows a linear pattern of decline from young adulthood to old age, and that verbal ability does not reach a peak until midlife and still remains above early adult performance in advanced old age. Similar patterns have been obtained in meta-analyses of the WAIS (cf. McArdle, 1994).

It should also be noted that there are wide individual differences in change in intellectual competence over time. For example, when change in large groups of individuals was monitored over a seven-year interval, it was found that the ages 60 to 67 and 67 to 74 were marked by stability of performance, while even from ages 74 to 84 as many as 40 percent of study participants remained stable. However, it was also found that by their mid-sixties almost all persons had significantly declined on at least one ability, while remaining stable on others.

Age differences in intelligence

Findings from age-comparative (cross-sectional) studies of intellectual performance are used to compare adults of different ages at a single point in time. Because of substantial genera-

Figure 1
Longitudinal age changes on six latent intellectual ability dimensions.

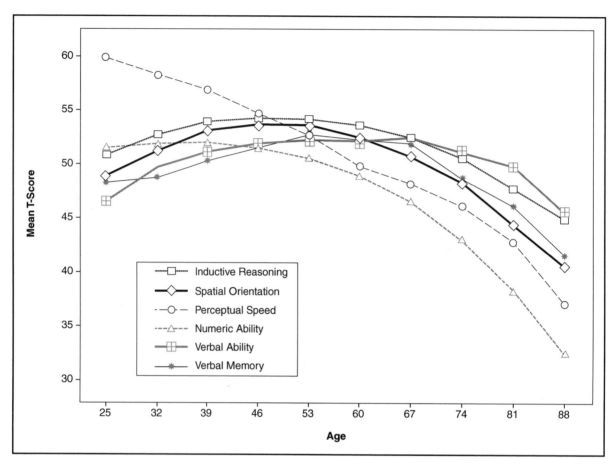

SOURCE: Schaie, K. W.."The Course of Adult Intellectual Development." *American Psychologist* 49 (1994): 304–313.
Reprinted with permission of the American Psychological Association.

tional differences, these studies show far greater age differences than the within-individual changes observed in longitudinal data. Ages of peak performance are found to be earlier (for later-born cohorts) in cross-sectional studies. Modest age differences are found by the early fifties for some, and by the sixties for most, dimensions of intelligence. On the WAIS, age differences are moderate for the verbal part of the test, but substantial for the performance scales. Because of the slowing in the rate of positive cohort differences (a later-born cohort performs at a higher level than an earlier-born cohort at the same ages), age difference profiles have begun to converge somewhat more with the age-change data from longitudinal studies. Both peak performance and onset of decline seem to be shifting to later ages for most variables.

Figure 2 presents age differences over the age range from twenty-five to eighty-one for samples tested in 1991, found in the Seattle Longitudinal Study, which can be directly compared to the longitudinal data presented in Figure 1. Particularly noteworthy is the fact that cross-sectional age differences are greater than those observed in longitudinal studies—except for numerical skills, which show greater decline when measured longitudinally.

More recent studies of the WAIS with normal individuals (the WAIS has been widely applied to samples with neuropathology or mental illness, so it is important to state that the work referred to is on normal individuals) use approaches that involve latent variable models (see McArdle & Prescott, 1992; Rott, 1993), while other analyses have been conducted at the item

Figure 2
Cross-sectional age differences on six latent intellectual ability dimensions.

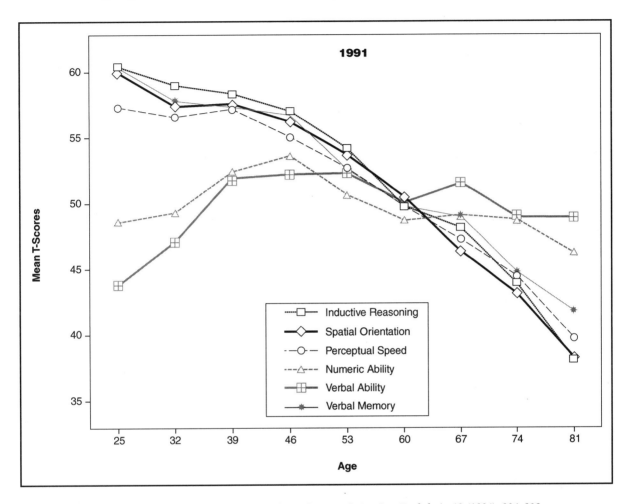

SOURCE: Schaie, K. W.."The Course of Adult Intellectual Development." *American Psychologist* 49 (1994): 304–313.
Reprinted with permission of the American Psychological Association.

level. A study by Sands, Terry, and Meredith (1989) investigated two cohorts spanning the age range from 18 to 61. Improvement in performance was found between the ages of 18 and 40 and between 18 and 54. Between ages 40 and 61, improvement was found for the information, comprehension and vocabulary subtests, while there was a mixed change (gain on the easy items and decline on the difficult items) on picture completion and a decline on digit symbol and block design (with decline only for the most difficult items of the latter test). The discrepancies between the longitudinal and cross-sectional findings on the WAIS, as well as on the primary mental abilities, can be attributed largely to cohort differences in attained peak level and rate

of change arising as a consequence of the different life experiences of successive generations.

Since women, on average, live longer than men, one might ask whether there are differential patterns by sex. Most studies find that there are average-level differences between men and women at all ages, with women doing better on verbal skills and memory, while men excel on numerical and spatial skills. The devel-opmental course of intellectual abilities, however, tends to have parallel slopes for men and women.

Cohort differences in intellectual abilities

Cohort differences in psychometric abilities have been most intensively examined in the Seattle Longitudinal Study. Cumulative cohort dif-

Figure 3
Cumulative cohort differences on six latent intellectual ability dimensions for cohorts born from 1897 to 1966.

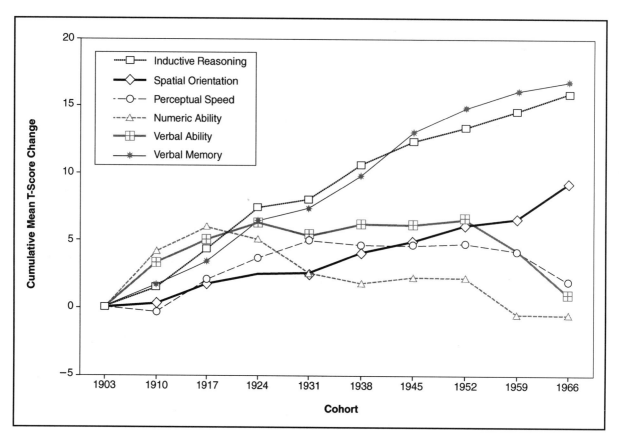

SOURCE: Schaie, K. W.."The Course of Adult Intellectual Development." *American Psychologist* 49 (1994): 304–313. Reprinted with permission of the American Psychological Association.

ferences for cohorts born from 1897 to 1966 are shown in Figure 3 for the abilities discussed above. There is a linear positive pattern for inductive reasoning and verbal memory, a positive pattern for spatial orientation, but curvilinear or negative patterns for numeric ability and perceptual speed. Factors thought to influence these cohort differences include changes in average educational exposure and changes in educational practices, as well as the control of early childhood infectious diseases and the adoption of healthier lifestyles by more recent cohorts. Similar differences have also been found using biologically related parent-offspring dyads compared at approximately similar ages.

The effect of these cohort differences is to increase age differences in intelligence between young and old for those skills where there have been substantial gains across successive generations (e.g., inductive reasoning), but to decrease age differences in instances were younger generations perform more poorly (e.g., number skills). Hence, it should be kept in mind that some older persons seem to perform poorly when compared with their younger peers not because they have suffered mental decline, but because they are experiencing the consequences of obsolescence.

Practical intelligence

Much of the work done by psychologists on intelligence has concerned those aspects that are sometimes called *academic intelligence*. However, an equally important aspect of intelligence is concerned with the question of how individuals can function effectively on tasks and in situations encountered on a daily basis. It has been shown that individual differences in performance on everyday tasks can be accounted for by a combination of performance levels on several basic abilities.

Competence in various everyday activities (e.g., managing finances, shopping, using medications, using the telephone) involve several cognitive abilities or processes that cut across or apply to various substantive domains. But the particular combination or constellation of basic abilities varies, of course, across different tasks of daily living. It is important to note that the basic abilities are seen as necessary (but not sufficient) antecedents for everyday competence.

Other variables, such as motivation and meaning, and in particular the role of the environment or context, determine the particular types of applied activities and problems in which practical intelligence is manifested. Everyday competence also involves substantive knowledge associated with the particular everyday-problem domain, as well as attitudes and values with regard to the problem domain. Both the sociocultural context and the microenvironment determine the expression of practical intelligence for a given individual. For example, while the ability to travel beyond one's dwelling has been of concern through the ages, comprehending airline schedules and operating computer-driven vehicles are only recent expressions of practical intelligence. The environment also plays an important role in the maintenance and facilitation of everyday competence as people age. Environmental stimulation and challenges, whether they occur naturally or through planned interventions, have been shown to be associated with the maintenance and enhancement of everyday competence in the elderly. Practical intelligence appears to peak in midlife and then decline, following closely the changes observed in the underlying cognitive abilities associated with specific everyday problems.

Influences upon intellectual development

Intellectual competence does not operate within a vacuum. It is affected both by an individual's physiological state (i.e., the individual's state of health and, in old age particularly, the presence or absence of chronic disease), as well as the presence or absence of a favorable environmental context and adequate support systems. Figure 4 provides a conceptual schema of the influences that impact the adult development of cognitive/intellectual competence.

Adult cognitive functioning must, of course, be initially based upon both heritable (genetic) influences and the early environmental influences typically experienced within the home of the biological parents. It has been suggested by some behavior geneticists that much of the early environmental influences are nonshared (i.e., not shared by all members of a family). However, there is retrospective evidence that some early shared environmental influences may affect adult intellectual performance (see Schaie & Zuo, 2000). Both genetic and early environmental factors are thought to influence midlife cognitive functioning. Early environmental influences will, of course, also exert influences on midlife social status. Genetic factors are also likely to be implicated in the rate of cognitive decline in adulthood. Thus far, the best-studied gene in this context is the apolipoprotein E (ApoE) gene, one of whose alleles is thought to be a risk factor for Alzheimer's disease. ApoE status is therefore also considered a factor in cognitive development (the expression of this gene is probably not important prior to midlife).

Influence of health. Considerable information is available on the reciprocal effects of chronic disease and intellectual abilities. It has been observed that decline in intellectual performance in old age is substantially accelerated by the presence of chronic diseases. Conditions such as cardiovascular disease, renal disease, osteoarthritis, and diabetes tend to interfere with lifestyles that are conducive to the maintenance of intellectual abilities, while they also have direct effects on brain functioning. One study found that individuals free of chronic disease perform intellectually at levels that are characteristic of those seven years younger who are suffering from such diseases. However, it has also been shown that the age of onset of chronic disease is later, and the disease severity is less, when it occurs in individuals functioning at high intellectual levels.

Influence of lifestyles. Many studies have related individual differences in socioeconomic circumstances (and resultant lifestyles) to the maintenance of high levels of intellectual functioning into old age. In particular, it has been shown that individuals who actively pursue intellectually stimulating activities seem to decline at lower rates than those who do not. Such pursuits may include travel, intensive reading programs, participation in clubs and organizations, and cultural and continuing-education activities. Conversely, those individuals whose opportunities for stimulating activities have been reduced due to the loss of a spouse or other factors restricting

Figure 4

Conceptual model of health and environmental factors influencing the adult development of intellectual/cognitive competence.

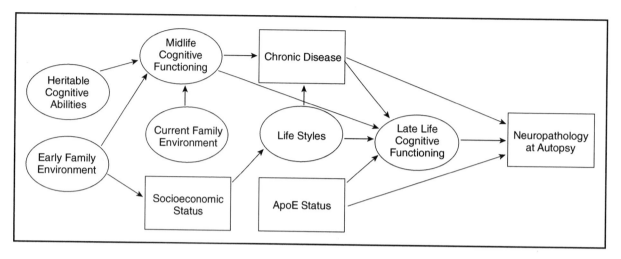

SOURCE: Schaie, K. W. (2000). "The Impact of Longitudinal Studies on Understanding Development from Young Adulthood to Old Age." *International Journal of Behavioral Development* (2000). Reprinted with permission.

their social networks may be at greatest risk for decline.

Influence of education. Both the maintenance of intellectually stimulating activities and the pursuit of healthful lifestyles appear to be dependent to a considerable extent on an individual's level of attained education. Over the course of the twentieth century, in the United States, there was an average increase in educational exposure amounting to approximately six years for men and five years for women. This societal shift may be largely responsible for many of the favorable cohort differences in intellectual abilities described in this article. Those advantaged educationally are also more likely to be engaged in intellectually stimulating work experiences. These, in turn, have been shown to have favorable effects on the maintenance of intellectual functions into old age. Finally, it should be noted that while there is eventual age-related decline in intelligence for both the educationally advantaged and disadvantaged, those who start at a high level are likely to retain sufficient intellectual competence to last throughout life.

K. WARNER SCHAIE

See also AGE-PERIOD-COHORT MODEL; CREATIVITY; FUNCTIONAL ABILITY; LEARNING; PROBLEM SOLVING, EVERYDAY; WISDOM.

BIBLIOGRAPHY

ARBUCKLE, T. Y.; MAAG, U.; PUSHKAR, D.; and CHAIKELSON, J. S. "Individual Differences in Trajectory of Intellectual Development over 45 Years of Adulthood." *Psychology and Aging* 13 (1998): 663–675.

BALTES, P. B. "The Aging Mind: Potentials and Limits." *Gerontologist* 33 (1993): 580–594.

BALTES, P. B.; MAYER, K. U.; HELMCHEN, H.; and STEINHAGEN-THIESSEN, E. "The Berlin Aging Study (BASE): Overview and Design." *Ageing and Society* 13 (1993): 483–533.

BINET, A., and SIMON, T. "Methodes Nouvelles pour le Diagnostic du Niveau Intellectuel des Anormaux." *L'Annee Psychologique* 11 (1905): 102–191.

BOSWORTH, H. B., and SCHAIE, K. W. "Survival Effects in Cognitive Function, Cognitive Style, and Sociodemographic Variables in the Seattle Longitudinal Study." *Experimental Aging Research* 25 (1999): 121–139.

BUSSE, E. W. "Duke Longitudinal Studies of Aging." *Zeitschrift für Gerontologie* 26 (1993): 123–128.

CARROLL, J. B. *Human Cognitive Abilities: A Survey of Factor-Analytic Studies.* New York: Cambridge University Press, 1993.

CUNNINGHAM, W. R., and OWENS, W. A., JR. "The Iowa State Study of the Adult Development of Intellectual Abilities." In *Longitudinal Studies of Adult Psychological Development.* Edited by K.

W. Schaie. New York: Guilford, 1983. Pages 20–39.

EICHORN, D. H.; CLAUSEN, J. A.; HAAN, N.; HONZIK, M. P.; and MUSSEN, P. H. *Present and Past in Middle Life.* New York: Academic Press, 1981.

GRIBBIN, K.; SCHAIE, K. W.; and PARHAM, I. A. "Complexity of Life Style and Maintenance of Intellectual Abilities." *Journal of Social Issues* 36 (1980): 47–61.

GUILFORD, J. P. *The Nature of Human Intelligence.* New York: McGraw-Hill, 1967.

HORN, J. L., and HOFER, S. M. "Major Abilities and Development in the Adult Period." In *Intellectual Development.* Edited by R. J. Sternberg and C. A. Berg. Cambridge, U.K.: Cambridge University Press, 1992.

HULTSCH, D. F.; HERTZOG, C.; SMALL, B. J.; MCDONALD-MISZLAK, L.; and DIXON, R. A. "Short-Term Longitudinal Change in Cognitive Performance in Later Life." *Psychology and Aging* 7 (1992): 571–584.

MATARAZZO, J. D. *Wechsler's Measurement and Appraisal of Adult Intelligence,* 5th ed. Baltimore: Williams & Wilkins, 1972.

MCARDLE, J. J. "Structural Factor Analysis Experiments with Incomplete Data." *Mutivariate Experimental Research* 29 (1994): 404–454.

MCARDLE, J. J., and PRESCOTT, C. A. "Age-Based Construct Validation Using Structural Equation Modeling." *Experimental Aging Research* 18 (1992): 87–115.

PLOMIN, R., and DANIELS, D. "Why Are Two Children in the Same Family So Different from Each Other?" *The Behavioral and Brain Sciences* 10 (1987): 1–16.

POON, L. W.; SWEANEY, A. L.; CLAYTON, G. M.; and MERRIAM, S. B. "The Georgia Centenarian Study." *International Journal of Aging and Human Development* 34 (1992): 1–17.

ROTT, C. "Intelligenzentwicklung im Alter [Development of Intelligence in Old Age]." *Zeitschrift für Gerontologie* 23 (1990): 252–261.

SANDS, L. P.; TERRY, H.; and MEREDITH, W. "Change and Stability in Adult Intellectual Functioning Assessed by Wechsler Item Responses." *Psychology and Aging* 4 (1989): 79–87.

SCHAIE, K. W. "Midlife Influences upon Intellectual Functioning in Old Age." *International Journal of Behavioral Development* 7 (1984): 463–478.

SCHAIE, K. W. "The Hazards of Cognitive Aging." *Gerontologist* 29 (1989): 484–493.

SCHAIE, K. W. "The Course of Adult Intellectual Development." *American Psychologist* 49 (1994): 304–313.

SCHAIE, K. W. "Generational Differences." In *Encyclopedia of Gerontology.* Edited by J. E. Birren. San Diego, Calif.: Academic Press, 1996a. Pages 567–576.

SCHAIE, K. W. *Intellectual Development in Adulthood: The Seattle Longitudinal Study.* Cambridge, U.K.: Cambridge University Press, 1996b.

SCHAIE, K. W. "The Impact of Longitudinal Studies on Understanding Development from Young Adulthood to Old Age." *International Journal of Behavioral Development* (2000).

SCHAIE, K. W.; PLOMIN, R.; WILLIS, S. L.; GRUBER-BALDINI, A.; and DUTTA, R. "Natural Cohorts: Family Similarity in Adult Cognition." In *Psychology and Aging: Nebraska Symposium on Motivation, 1991.* Edited by T. Sonderegger. Lincoln: University of Nebraska Press, 1992.

SCHAIE, K. W., and WILLIS, S. L. "Theories of Everyday Competence." In *Handbook of Theories of Aging.* Edited by V. L. Bengtson and K. W. Schaie. New York: Springer, 1999. Pages 174–195.

SCHAIE, K. W., and WILLIS, S. L. "A Stage Theory Model of Adult Cognitive Development Revisited." In *The Many Dimensions of Aging: Essays in Honor of M. Powell Lawton.* Edited by B. Rubinstein, M. Moss, & M. Kleban. New York: Springer, 2000. Pages 175–193.

SCHAIE, K. W., and ZUO, Y. L. "Family Environments and Adult Cognitive Functioning." In *Context of Intellectual Development.* Edited by R. L. Sternberg and E. Grigorenko. Hillsdale, N.J.: Erlbaum, 2001.

SCHOOLER, C.; MULATU, M. S.; and OATES, G. "The Continuing Effects of Substantively Complex Work on the Intellectual Functioning of Older Workers." *Psychology and Aging* 14 (1999): 483–506.

SPEARMAN, C. "General Intelligence: Objectively Determined and Measured." *American Journal of Psychology* 15 (1904): 201–292.

STEEN, B., and DJURFELDT, H. "The Gerontological and Geriatric Population Studies in Gothenburg, Sweden." *Zeitschrift für Gerontologie* 26 (1993):163–169.

STERNBERG, R. J. *Beyond IQ: A Triarchic Theory of Human Intelligence.* Cambridge, U.K.: Cambridge University Press, 1985.

TERMAN, L. M. *The Measurement of Intelligence.* Boston: Houghton, 1916.

THORNDIKE, E. L., and WOODWORTH, R. S. "Influence of Improvement in One Mental Function upon the Efficiency of Other Mental Functions." *Psychological Review* 8 (1901): 247–261, 384–395, 553–564.

THURSTONE, L. L. *Primary Mental Abilities.* Chicago: University of Chicago Press, 1938.

WILLIS, S. L., and SCHAIE, K. W. "Everyday Cognition: Taxonomic and Methodological Considerations." In *Mechanisms of Everyday Cognition.* Edited by J. M. Puckett and H. W. Reese. Hillsdale, N.J.: Erlbaum, 1993.

WOODRUFF-PAK, D. S. "Aging and Intelligence: Changing Perspectives in the Twentieth Century." *Journal of Aging Studies* 3 (1989): 91–118.

YERKES, R. M. "Psychological Examining in the United States Army." *Memoirs of the National Academy of Sciences* 15 (1921): 1–890.

INTERGENERATIONAL EXCHANGES

One of the most salient aspects of the relationship between aging parents and their adult children is the nature and extent of exchanges of goods, services, and support. No matter what their age, parents and children occasionally need help; most of time, family members are asked first. Exchanges between parents and children are embedded in family and kinship relationships. The focus here will be on routine or normative kinds of exchanges between American parents and children, rather than on caregiving, which involves more systematic, extraordinary, and extensive help.

Consequences of social and demographic changes for exchanges between generations

Scholars have become particularly fascinated with exchanges between parents and children, in part because there have been a series of social changes that have altered the context of relations between parents and children and probably heightened the salience of intergenerational exchanges. First, the fact that individuals are living longer has led to several important changes to later-life family relationships. Not surprisingly, the potential for long-lasting family relationships has greatly increased. Certainly the prospects for long-lasting marriages is greater. However, these marriages have not become as commonplace as one would suppose, due to the sharp rise in divorce in the post–World War II era. The other family relationship that has been profoundly affected by declines in mortality has been parent-child relationships. It is not unusual for parents

and children today to accrue fifty years or more of interwoven biographies. The majority of individuals today will spend most of their lives in a relationship with parents where they are not minors. Indeed, in an aging society like the United States, parents and children will share key adulthood transitions such as work, parenthood, retirement, and, for some, grandparenthood. These extended years of shared lives form a very different context for exchanges of support than was the case for the first half of the twentieth century. Finally, increases in longevity have changed the experience of grandparenthood—for both generations. Grandparents are much more likely to be alive and in good health for a significant part of their grandchildren's lives. Grandparenthood is also much more likely to a part of the life course of aging adults.

Second, declines in family sizes have altered the generational structure of families. The pool of potential family members "down" the generational ladder has become smaller, while the declines in mortality have worked to maintain the number of family members "up" the generational ladder. It is increasingly common today for middle-aged adults to have more living parents than children. The true force of this social change will not be felt, however, until the baby-boom generation (those born in the decade after World War II) has entered old age. The question is, will there be "enough" children available to care for this generation

Finally, the large increase in divorce has posed challenges for intergenerational exchanges. Divorced adult children often have many needs, and they often turn to their parents for help. As divorce became commonplace among young adults, intergenerational support, in the form of parent's helping children with financial assistance, housing, childcare, and emotional support became crucial. However, the proportion of aging parents who are divorced is also growing, and these parents often do not have the resources to provide needed assistance to their adult children.

Why do individuals give?

There are two theoretical explanations for why individuals give. Some scholars argue that intergenerational support can best be understood by using social exchange theory (Homans, 1958; Thibaut & Kelly, 1959), while others point to altruism as the key theoretical construct

(Deutsch, 1975). A basic premise of social exchange theory is that social exchanges and interactions will continue as long as they are seen as beneficial. Intergenerational exchanges of support happen where perceived rewards are seen to offset the costs to an individual. In other words, parents give help to children with the understanding that they will get something back that is "worth" the costs of what they give. Several studies have found patterns in data on routine assistance that are consistent with this theory. For example, Glenna Spitze and John Logan (1989) found that women's investment in caregiving (direct and intensive care to a family member in need) and kin keeping activities (a range of activities from keeping in touch, relating news, or visiting, to activities that encompass exchanges of help like babysitting, loaning money, or providing emotional support) in their early and middle life course creates obligations in men and children that lead to assistance in later life. However, conclusive tests of hypotheses drawn from this theory have not yet happened, in part due to the great demands on data a careful test would require.

A second explanation of patterns of intergenerational support suggests they are largely explained by altruism. The idea is that parents and children care about each other, or at least feel some sense of responsibility toward each other, and this concern motivates parents to monitor the well-being of their children (and children to monitor the well-being of their parents) and offer assistance when they perceive that there is a need. This theoretical approach has been behind a good deal of the quantitative models of assistance rendered across generations; that is, the modeling intergenerational resource flows is largely built around variables measuring the resources and needs of each generation. However, despite the intuitive appeal of this theory, the empirical support is mixed. Research to date indicates that needs are certainly an important part of the explanation of exchanges, but providing support, and the motives behind these acts, appear to be more complex than this theory would suggest. In short, no unified theoretical explanation for intergenerational exchanges has emerged.

Factors that affect exchanges

The availability during the 1990s of large, nationally representative surveys with good questions on exchanges of support between generations has led to considerable advances in our understanding of the overall patterns of support, as well as the characteristics of families, parents, and children that effect the giving and receiving of assistance. From the perspective of the adult child, routine exchanges with parents are not all that common. The 1987–1988 National Survey of Families and Households (NSFH) found that only 17 percent of adult children received money (at least $200 given or loaned in the past five years) from their parents, and only 4 percent gave money to their parents. In the month before the interview, only 13 percent of adult children received childcare, 17 percent received household assistance, and 32 percent gave household assistance. Advice and emotional support are the most common forms of exchange, with 27 percent of respondents receiving such support, and 25 percent giving such support to their parents.

This picture looks somewhat better when we take the perspective of aging parents. Parents age fifty-five and older with at least one adult child living independently report higher levels of giving and receiving assistance than their adult children report. This is to be expected, of course, given that children typically have only one set of parents with whom to engage in exchanges, while most parents can potentially draw support from several children. Giving advice and emotional support is most frequently exchanged (42 percent), followed by giving money to children (33 percent) and receiving advice and giving childcare (both 29 percent). Only one in five aging parents received assistance with household chores, transportation, or household repairs from any of their adult children during the previous month. Receiving monetary assistance is virtually unheard of (3 percent). At any given point in time, more than one-third of older adults are not involved in giving, and over 60 percent have not received anything from any of their adult children.

These relatively modest levels of routine exchanges are not due to children being unavailable—a strong majority of parents (72 percent) have at least one adult child living within twenty-five miles. Neither is it because parents and children are not in regular contact or maintain good relations—studies have shown repeatedly that parents and children maintain a high level of contact via visits, phone calls, and letter writing, and that both parents and children generally rate their relationship as positive. Rather, these levels of help appear low because routine assistance, at least in American families, tends to be episodic rather than continuous, contingent more on a particular need that suddenly arose.

These general trends obscure significant variations. Researchers have given considerable attention to race and ethnic variations in exchanges. Ethnographic studies and specialized surveys document extensive social support networks among African-American families. These findings have led some researchers to conclude that African Americans have stronger family networks than Americans of European descent. However, recent work based on nationally representative data that systematically compare kin assistance of African Americans and European Americans have generally not found superior support networks among minority families, even when socioeconomic differences are taken into account. Other scholars, noting the strong familism of Mexican Americans, have concluded from specialized surveys documenting involvement in mutual support activities that Mexican Americans have stronger kin networks than whites. However, studies that have systematically compared kin assistance among representative samples of Hispanic groups and whites have not found significant differences.

Intergenerational exchanges are affected by the gender of the participants. A large number of studies show that women are more involved than men in kin-keeping activities that structure family events and maintain contact among family members. Across generations, there is evidence that the mother-daughter tie is stronger than other parent-child relationships. However, it is not the case that men are uninvolved in exchanges. Rather, their giving tends to mirror traditional gender-role expectations—men are found to be more likely to give financial help and less likely to be providing childcare or emotional support.

Assistance that involves face-to-face interactions, such as childcare or the performance of household tasks, diminishes with physical distance. It would seem plausible that certain forms of intergenerational help, such as financial assistance or advice and emotional support, would not be affected by distance; however, research has found that distance remains a significant barrier to the exchange of aid given to children by parents, but less so for children giving aid to

their parents. Perhaps children are more adept at using modern means of transportation and communication than their parents to reduce geographic barriers to rendering assistance.

Finally, one of the strongest predictors of exchanges is parental resources. Parents with the most resources (e.g., married, highly educated, high income or wealth) are significantly more likely to render help to their children.

Changes over the life course

Exchanges of assistance vary in patterned ways over the life course of both parents and children. One of the surest ways to receive parental support is to have a child. Giving to children is also affected by changes in the lives of parents. Most significantly, as parents age, they tend to give less to their children. Much of this decline in giving can be explained by factors associated with aging (e.g., declines in health, death of spouse, changing needs of children). Yet, there is evidence that this gradual decline in the likelihood of giving help to children persists even when these other factors are taken into account.

Finally, and inevitably, the death of the parent leads to an inheritance of the parent's estate. This "final" intergenerational transfer has received significantly less attention from researchers. Available evidence indicates that parents typically treat their children equally in bequests. However, at least one study shows that those who did not give equally did not systematically give more to children with lower earnings.

DAVID EGGEBEEN

See also BEQUESTS AND INHERITANCES; FILIAL OBLIGATIONS; PARENTAL OBLIGATIONS; PARENT-CHILD RELATIONSHIP.

BIBLIOGRAPHY

COONEY, T. M., and UHLENBERG, P. R. "Support from Parents over the Life Course." *Social Forces* 71 (1992): 62–84.

COX, D., and RANK, M. R. "Inter-Vivos Transfers and Intergenerational Exchange." *Journal of Political Economy* 82 (1992): 305–314.

DAVEY, A., and EGGEBEEN, D. J. "Patterns of Intergenerational Exchange and Mental Health." *Journals of Gerontology: Psychological Sciences* 53 (1998): P86–P95.

DEUTSCH, M. "Equity, Equality, and Need: What Determines Which Value Will Be Used as the

Basis of Distributive Justice?" *Journal of Social Issues* 31 (1975): 137–149.

DILWORTH-ANDERSON, P. "Extended Kin Networks in Black Families." *Generations* 14 (1992): 29–32.

EGGEBEEN, D. J. "Family Structure and Intergenerational Exchanges." *Research on Aging* 14 (1992): 427–447.

EGGEBEEN, D. J., and HOGAN, D. P. "Giving Between Generations in American Families." *Human Nature* 1 (1990): 211–232.

EGGEBEEN, D. J., and WILHELM, M. O. "Patterns of Support Given by Older Americans to Their Children." In *Aging and Active: Dimensions of Productive Engagement Among Older Americans.* Edited by S. A. Bass. New Haven, Conn.: Yale University Press. Pages 122–168.

HOGAN, D. P.; EGGEBEEN, D. J.; and CLOGG, C. C. "The Structure of Intergenerational Exchanges in American Families." *American Journal of Sociology* 98 (1993): 1428–1458.

JAYAKODY, R. "Race Differences in Intergenerational Financial Assistance." *Journal of Family Issues* 19 (1998): 508–533.

LOGAN, J., and SPITZE, G. *Family Ties: Enduring Relations Between Parents and Their Grown Children.* Philadelphia, Pa.: Temple University Press, 1996.

MARKIDES, K. S.; BOLDT, J. S.; and RAY, L. A. "Sources of Helping and Intergenerational Solidarity: A Three-Generational Study of Mexican Americans." *Journal of Gerontology* 41 (1986): 506–511.

McGARRY, K., and SCHOENI, R. F. "Transfer Behavior Within the Family: Results from the Asset and Health Dynamics Study." *The Journals of Gerontology Series B* 52B (Special Issue), (1997): 83–92.

MENCHIK, P. L. "Primogeniture, Equal Sharing, and the U.S. Distribution of Wealth." *Quarterly Journal of Economics* 94 (1980): 299–316.

ROSSI, A. S., and ROSSI, P. H. *Of Human Bonding: Parent-Child Relations Across the Life Course.* New York: Aldine de Gruyter, 1990.

SPITZE, G., and LOGAN, J. "Helping as a Component of Parent-Adult Child Relations." *Research on Aging* 14 (1992): 291–312.

STACK, C. *All Our Kin: Strategies for Survival in the Black Community.* New York: Harper & Row, 1974.

WILHELM, M. O. "Bequest Behavior and the Effect of Heirs' Earnings: Testing the Altruistic Model of Bequests." *American Economic Review* 86 (1996): 874–892.

WILSON, M. "The Black Extended Family: An Analytical Consideration." *Developmental Psychology* 22 (1986): 246–258.

INTERGENERATIONAL JUSTICE

The term *intergenerational justice* refers to the ethical problem of distributing scarce resources between different age groups in a society. For example, intergenerational justice is at stake when societies debate how much of their scarce resources should be devoted to areas such as education that primarily benefit the young, versus programs such as social security or Medicare that benefit older members of the population. Similarly, the problem of justice between generations arises when societies consider limiting health care resources to the elderly in order to increase health care resources available to the young.

Historical background

While the problem of allocating scarce societal resources among age groups has always existed, during the past two centuries this problem has gained prominence in many developed nations. Greater attention to intergenerational justice is in part due to the fact that the societies of many developed nations are aging. Unlike the aging of individuals, which occurs in a progressive, chronological fashion, societies are said to age whenever their number of older members increases relative to their number of younger members. Most industrial nations, including the United States, have been aging since at least 1800. In 1800, the demographic makeup of developing countries resembled that of today's Third World countries: roughly half the population was under the age of sixteen, with few people living beyond the age of sixty. Since that time, these countries have become developed nations, and have witnessed increases in life expectancy and decreases in fertility rates. Thus, since 1950, the ranks of Americans age sixty-five and older has more than doubled, while the number of persons over the age of eighty-five has more than quadrupled. These trends are forecast to continue until around the middle of the twenty-first century. At the other end of the age span, developed countries have seen a decline in the proportion of young people. After 1964 the total fertility rate began to plummet, reaching a low of 1.7 in 1976, a figure below the replacement rate of the population. These twin phenomena have dramatically increased the proportion of older persons in developed nations. At the same time, the age profile of many Third World countries remains heavily weighted toward younger age groups.

A relatively larger number of older citizens increases the demand for a variety of services used primarily, or disproportionately, by older individuals. For example, consumption of health care services rises sharply with age. In the United States, persons sixty-five and over represent 12 percent of the population, yet they account for 33 percent of the country's total personal health care expenditures, exclusive of resource costs. Between 1980 and 2040, the demand for health care among the oldest Americans (those seventy-five and over) is forecast to increase at a dramatic rate. There will be a 265 percent increase in physician visits, a 291 percent increase in days of hospital care, and a 318 percent increase in nursing-home residents among this age group.

Contemporary debates over intergenerational justice frequently focus on the problem of whether society should limit the share of scarce resources it devotes to the elderly. For example, in the United States, where the old increasingly outnumber the young, debates about limiting health care expenditures for older individuals have emerged in political and philosophical discussions during the latter part of the twentieth century.

Philosophical and ethical background

It is revealing to consider what form discussions about intergenerational justice might take if the young outnumbered the old. Would such concerns be expressed in terms of setting limits to publicly financed health care for the young? If not, perhaps there is more at stake here than the proportion of old persons compared to young persons within society. If a society would be relatively less willing to curtail resources to younger people, this might suggest that its sense of justice somehow includes the idea that the young are inherently more morally deserving of scarce resources than older persons are. It is unclear that any ethical basis can be found to support such a position.

The philosopher Daniel Callahan argues that it is not unjust to deny persons access to publicly financed life-extending medical care once they reach a natural life span. Callahan's reasoning is that once individuals reach old age, death may be an occasion for sadness, but should also be thought of as a relatively acceptable event. To clarify this idea, Callahan asks people to imagine the death of both an older person and a younger person they know, and to consider how they will feel about their deaths twenty or thirty years after the fact. According to Callahan, while the death of any individual is a loss, we perceive the deaths of young and old persons differently. When viewed in distant retrospect, people continue to feel despair and moral outrage about the death of young persons because such persons were deprived a full and meaningful life. By contrast, over time the deaths of old persons are regarded as philosophically and ethically tolerable because death in old age does not rob persons of living their full or "natural" lifespan.

If these judgments are correct, perhaps society's obligation to prevent the death of younger persons is not the same as the obligation to prevent the death of older persons; perhaps more of its scarce resources should be devoted to preventing premature deaths, and comparatively less devoted to preventing death in old age. Callahan proposes that society can ethically ration publicly financed life-extending health care to people who have reached a "natural lifespan." Most people will reach a natural span of life by age sixty-five, or certainly by their late seventies or early eighties. After this age, individuals remain free to use personal resources to pay for life-extending care in old age, yet society is not obligated, according to Callahan, to devote scarce resources to this end.

Contractarian approaches to intergenerational justice

Social-contract theories of justice offer us a quite different way of looking at intergenerational justice. According to this school of thought people incur morally binding obligations of justice only by virtue of their consent or agreement. Whereas for Callahan the concept of a natural lifespan defines what expectations for health care are reasonable at different stages of life, for the contractarian normative judgments are solely a matter of rational choice by unfettered individuals. Rather than viewing ethical obligations as unalterable dictates imposed by God, nature, or by one's station in life, the contractarian regards the source of ethical obligation to be free and rational agents. The social contract view is sometimes put forward as a comprehensive ethical theory, and sometimes presented as an account of justice and social obligation.

Working in this tradition, philosopher Norman Daniels frames the problem of intergenerational justice as a problem of choosing what resources we should devote to old age. Yet rather than calling for a consensus among members of the society, as social contract views typically do, Daniels casts intergenerational justice as a first-person problem of prudential choice. Intergenerational justice is thus viewed as a problem of distributing scarce resources between the older and younger stages of each person's own life. In other words, we should stop thinking about intergenerational justice as arising between distinct groups of people. The young and old are one and the same—in the sense that each person passes through youth, adulthood, and old age.

Before choosing how to allocate resources across our life span, Daniels introduces a procedural constraint aimed at ensuring fair and impartial conditions for choosing. To prevent people from biasing the distribution of resources to the stage of life they currently occupy, they must be blind to their own actual age, and then imagine that they will live out their whole lives with the result of their choice. In other words, people should expect to experience firsthand the advantages and disadvantages of their distributive choices for youth, adulthood, and old age.

With this background, Daniels goes on to argue that people would opt for a scheme that improved their chances of reaching a normal life expectancy, rather than one that gave them a greater chance of living beyond a normal life expectancy. In the area of health care, for example, it is just for a society to impose age-based restrictions on health care in order to free up resources devoted to improving people's chances of reaching normal life expectancy. Daniels emphasizes that rationing medical care by age is consistent with treating persons equally. This is because, unlike sexism or racism, differential treatment by age equalizes over time. If we treat the old one way and the young another, over time each person is treated both ways.

Utilitarian approaches

Whereas contractarian approaches take as their starting point the idea of rational choice by individuals, utilitarian theories begin with the premise that all human conduct should promote, to the greatest extent possible, the welfare of all. Whereas Daniels places emphasis on the long-term prudential interest of the individual, utilitarianism is concerned impartially with the interests of all. Thus, utilitarianism sometimes requires substantial sacrifice on the part of individuals as a means to producing the greatest good for everyone. Rather than inviting people to calculate their own prudential interests, utilitarians instruct people to consider the interests of all conscious beings who may be affected by what they do.

How are problems of intergenerational justice settled within a utilitarian framework? Often this approach requires age-based rationing of scarce resources in order to maximize the achievement of some important goal. For instance, it might be argued that to maximize public welfare, scarce health care resources should be aimed at prolonging the life of young persons who are relatively more productive and efficient in their contributions to society. Older individuals contribute to society in fewer areas and function less efficiently where they do. They cease professional work and take leave of active participation in other social roles, such as parenting. Alternatively, working within the utilitarian tradition, it might be argued that older persons should be excluded from scarce medical resources in order to maximize cost savings. As noted already, elderly individuals, on average, consume a disproportionate share of health care. Finally, utilitarian thinking might support age-based rationing in order to yield the greatest possible return on society's health care dollars. The young have, on average, many more years ahead to live than older people do. Therefore, life-extending health care distributed to younger people will tend to yield a greater return on investment in terms of life-years saved.

Libertarian approaches

Whereas utilitarian approaches tend to grant societies authority to require substantial sacrifices from individuals to promote the public welfare, libertarians reject state authority altogether, or at least want to see it substantially reduced. Libertarians underscore individual liberty and individual rights to private property. While bearing affinities to social-contract theories, which also place emphasis on free choice by rational individuals, libertarians tend to emphasize the free market approach to distributing scarce resources. According to one prominent libertarian view, what makes a distribution of scarce resources just or unjust is not its outcome, but how it was arrived at. So long as individuals are free to acquire and exchange goods on a free market, whatever distribution of goods results is just.

What are the implications of libertarian thinking for intergenerational justice debates? First, one cannot say in advance how much of society's scarce health care resources the old and the young deserve. Rather than viewing health care as a right, the libertarian views private property as a right. Thus, people are free to exchange private property for health care, or for other goods, in a free market. According to this conception, inequalities in health care are fair if they were historically acquired through fair acquisitions and exchanges, rather than through blatantly unfair means such as stealing, enslaving, defrauding, or otherwise coercing people. Society is not justified in establishing health care policies that require, through taxing or other means, individuals to sacrifice justly acquired goods. When elderly or other groups in a society lack access to basic health care, the libertarian calls upon a principle of charity, rather than social justice, to improve their plight.

Summary

The distribution of scarce resources between the young and the old will continue to attract widespread attention in scholarly and public-policy discussions. Different philosophical approaches to justice yield very different answers to the question of how these concerns should be settled. The philosophical assumptions inherent in proposals for rationing based on age, for example, derive little support from libertarian schools of thought, yet fit well within the framework of utilitarian and contractarian viewpoints. Gaining clarity about the problem of intergenerational justice in health care and other areas will require paying closer attention to the philosophical and ethical assumptions that underlie different policy proposals.

NANCY JECKER

See also GENERATIONAL EQUITY; POPULATION AGING.

BIBLIOGRAPHY

CALLAHAN, D. *Setting Limits: Medical Goals in an Aging Society.* New York: Simon and Schuster, 1987.

DANIELS, N. *Am I My Parents' Keeper?: An Essay on Justice Between the Young and the Old.* New York: Oxford University Press, 1988.

GAUTHIER, D. *Morals by Agreement.* New York: Oxford University Press, 1986.

JECKER, N. S. "Aging and the Aged: Societal Aging." In *Encyclopedia of Bioethics,* vol. 1. Edited by W. T. Reich. New York: MacMillan Publishing Company, 1995. Pages 91–94.

RAWLS, J. *A Theory of Justice.* Cambridge, Mass.: Harvard University Press, 1971.

INTERGENERATIONAL RELATIONS

See PARENT-CHILD RELATIONSHIP

INTERNET RESOURCES

The large number of Internet sites related to aging has both simplified and complicated electronic information retrieval. Many government, professional, trade, and consumer organizations maintain informational pages on aging on the World Wide Web. In addition, nearly every institution of higher learning has its own site—with links to countless others. Commercial websites are available, ranging from those promoting specific services, products, and materials to those offering a virtual shopping mall of items.

Medical and pharmaceutical sites vary in quality, with some offering sound scientific advice and others promoting questionable "cures" and nostrums that raise concerns about Internet quackery. Caution is needed when researching information from unknown commercial sites.

Rather than inundate the reader with am extensive index of sites, the following selections offer a basic list of reliable sources of information from well-established agencies and organizations in aging. Each of these sites have links to many other locations. In addition, many of the entries in this encyclopedia refer the reader to Internet sites that are specific to that topic.

AARP (formerly the American Association of Retired Persons; http://www.aarp.org/). This thirty million member organization has tremendous influence on aging policy and legislation in the United States and around the world. The AARP promotes the interests of people age fifty and older, particularly on issues of health and economic well-being. The "Research and Reference" section in the topic guide index on AARP's home page opens into a wealth of articles, data, and information on aging.

Administration on Aging (AoA; U.S. Department of Health and Human Services;

More and more elderly people are learning to use computers and the Internet, which has a wealth of information of interest to older people. Clare Meadows (right) receives assistance from thirteen-year-old Dominic Penn during Meadows's senior computing class at the Chestnut Ridge Middle School in Washington Township, New Jersey. (AP photo by Allen Oliver.)

www.aoa.dhhs.gov). The AoA was established as the agency with primary responsibility for programs initiated under the Older Americans Act (1965). The AoA's website offers information to various audiences, including older people, caregivers, practitioners, and researchers. The home page "Quick Index" provides direct access to various programs that provide caregiver assistance, including the "Eldercare Locator," a directory service that assists people in finding local support resources for older persons. The site also provides information about the characteristics and needs of older Americans and about government programs that provide their welfare.

Alzheimer's Association (www.alz.org). The Alzheimer's Association is a voluntary organization that funds research on causes and treatments of Alzheimer's disease. Through a national network of local chapters, the organization serves as an educational and support resource for persons with Alzheimer's, and for those who care for them. The site has information tailored to persons with Alzheimer's, their families, health care workers, and the media.

American Geriatrics Society (AGS; www.americangeriatrics.org). The AGS is a professional society for physicians and other health providers. The AGS website describes the organization, its publications, and its activities, but also includes consumer education and health information, as well as numerous links to other professional and trade organizations and consumer aging and health.

American Society on Aging (ASA; www.asaging.org/). A source of information and training for persons working in the field of aging, the San Francisco–based national organization brings together professionals engaged in services, research, education, and policy. The site links to numerous constituent groups, such as the Business Forum on Aging; Forum on Religion, Spirituality and Aging; Healthcare and Aging Network; Lesbian and Gay Aging Issues Network; Lifetime Education and Renewal Network; Multicultural Aging Network; Mental Health and Aging Network; and the Network on Environments, Services and Technologies.

Canadian Association on Gerontology (CAG; www.cagacg.ca/). This national multidisciplinary organization promotes research, education, and policy on issues of aging. The site offers information concerning CAG conferences and publications, as well as links to Canadian educational programs in gerontology and geriatrics.

Elderhostel (www.elderhostel.org). A nonprofit organization founded in 1975, Elderhostel offers short-term educational travel experiences for persons age fifty-five and older. The website explains participation and registration, and also lists catalogs of learning and service programs conducted in most U.S. states and Canadian provinces and in many countries around the world.

Gerontological Society of America (GSA; www.geron.org). The GSA is the foremost U.S.-based organization promoting research and scholarship in aging. Members come from the biological sciences, clinical medicine, behavioral and social sciences, policy and practice fields, and arts and humanities. The GSA publishes prestigious scholarly journals, and its website features links to recent research findings and to many other organizations in aging, including sources for research funding. Allied units of the GSA include a policy institute, the National Academy on an Aging Society, and the Association for Gerontology in Higher Education.

GeroWeb (geroserver.iog.wayne.edu/Gero-Webd/GeroWeb.html). This "virtual library," sponsored by the Institute of Gerontology at Wayne State University, will provide the user with a list of Internet sites in response to search terms, or in relation to predefined categories such as biology/genetics, local resources, mental health, employment, grants/funding, sociology, and retirement. All the sites included in the virtual library are oriented towards those "interested in gerontology, geriatrics, the process of aging, services for the elderly, or the concerns of senior citizens in general."

Healthfinder   (www.healthfinder.gov/). Sponsored by the U.S. Department of Health and Human Services, this site leads users to sound health information, including "selected online publications, clearinghouses, databases, web sites, and support and self-help groups, as well as government agencies and not-for-profit organizations that produce reliable information for the public." The homepage is organized with links in categories such as "Hot topics," "Health news" and "Just for you," under which there is a special category for seniors.

InfoAging (www.infoaging.org/). Site is sponsored by the American Federation for Aging

Research (AFAR), an organization that promotes biomedical research, this educational site is organized like an E-zine, featuring interesting, up-to-date articles on biology, advances in medicine, and health concerns of older persons.

International Longevity Center—USA (IL-CUSA; www.ilcusa.org). This multinational, nonprofit institute is dedicated to research, education, and policy about longevity and population aging. ILCUSA emphasizes positive ways that greater life expectancy can impact nations around the world. The site lists the educational symposiums and workshops sponsored by ILCUSA, and also posts reports, working papers, and other articles.

Medicare (www.medicare.gov). This official site offers both basic and detailed information on the Medicare health insurance program. The site describes health-plan choices, the location of facilities, and participating physicians. There is information about Medigap policies and prescription drug assistance programs. The site has Medicare-related news and updates, as well as links to various types of health care resources.

National Archive of Computerized Data on Aging (NACDA; www.icpsr.umich.edu/NACDA). This research-oriented site is located in the Inter-University Consortium for Political and Social Research (ICPSR) at the Institute for Social Research at the University of Michigan. NACDA acquires, preserves, and distributes scientific data sets relevant to studies in aging. NACDA provides free access to over one hundred such data sets, as well as providing links to other ICPSR data sets. NACDA provides user and technical support and also conducts educational programs to promote secondary data analysis in research on aging.

National Center for Health Statistics: Aging Activities (www.cdc.gov/nchs/agingact.htm). This site provides access to "Trends in Health and Aging," an electronic data warehouse that describes the health status, behaviors, utilization, and cost of health care for older Americans; to "Longitudinal Studies of Aging," a set of surveys of health status and behaviors across two cohorts of older persons; and to the Federal Interagency Forum on Aging Related Statistics; as well as to such forum products as *Older Americans 2000: Key Indicators of Well Being, Wallchart on Aging, 65+ in the United States,* and *Trends in the Health of Older Americans.*

The National Council on the Aging (NCOA; www.ncoa.org/). The NCOA is an association of organizations and professionals engaged in advocacy and service provision for older people. Its primary activities include assisting community organizations; program development and implementation; and promoting aging-friendly public policies, legislation, and practices. The NCOA website describes research and demonstration projects, policy initiatives, and activities of the ten constituent units of the organization. The site also provides resources specifically oriented toward the aging worker.

National Institute on Aging (NIA; www.nia.nih.gov/). The NIA conducts and supports biomedical and behavioral research on aging processes. An agency within the National Institutes of Health, it was founded in 1974 to conduct research within its own laboratories and clinics, as well as fund research on aging at universities, medical centers, and scientific institutes. The site provides access to information regarding research funding and training opportunities, intramural and extramural research programs, research conferences, workshops, and meetings. The site also contains an authoritative section on "health information," which provides links to the NIA's Alzheimer's Disease Education and Referral Program. Copies of public service ads are also included, as well as access to a large number of NIA fact sheets on medical and lifestyle topics.

Social Security Administration (www.ssa.gov). This is the agency that administers the Social Security program of retirement, survivors, and disability benefits. The website has information about taxes, eligibility and benefits, and instructions about how to apply for benefits. There is also a section with information for employers. The site describes the operations and history of the program, its financing, and the future of Social Security. Links to Medicare are included.

SeniorNet (www.seniornet.org/php/). A nonprofit organization that provides access to, and education about, computers and the Internet to persons age fifty and older. SeniorNet offers computer classes and workshops at hundreds of local "Learning Centers," which are reviewed on their site. The site also sponsors "Roundtables," senior discussion groups on a variety of topics, and "Enrichment Centers," with content in areas of special interest.

Seniors Canada On-line (www.seniors.gc.ca/). A Canadian government site that provides easy on-line access to a wide range of information and to the services offered by multiple governmental offices. The site includes articles related to health, family, housing, and legal issues. In the category of "Employment," one can find information regarding various federal assistance programs, resources, and regulations for employers, as well as employment services. The site also contains key information about old age security and the Canada Pension Plan.

United Nations Programme on Ageing (www.un.org/esa/socdev/ageing/index.html). The UN Programme on Ageing, which focuses on the aging of the world population, gathers information on national, international, and nongovernmental programs and policies. The site includes articles about the aging of the world population, describes the World Assembly on Ageing, and lists other international activities. There is a global database of policies and programs that can be searched by year, country, issue, or certain population characteristics.

The U.S. Census Bureau (www.census.gov and www.census.gov/population/www/socdemo/age.html). This site provides an abundant amount of data on any number of population topics. By selecting "Age Data" or "Elderly/Older Population Data" at the "Subjects A to Z" index, users can view data tables and other governmental publications regarding older populations. The links are not only organized by geographic level of data (county, state, national, international), but also by specific older populations, such as baby boomers, persons 55+, and persons 65+.

CHARLES HUYETT

INTERPERSONAL PSYCHOTHERAPY

Interpersonal psychotherapy (IPT) is a time-limited psychotherapy originally developed for the treatment of major depressive disorder (MDD). Since its development, it has also been used as a treatment for other psychiatric disorders. IPT focuses on interpersonal relationships because clinical observations and research have documented that depression can be triggered by problems in human relationships. Once people become depressed they may then also have additional problems in close relationships—most often with spouses—because of the symptoms of MDD. Problems in close relationships, however, can make it much harder to recover from depression.

734 INTERPERSONAL PSYCHOTHERAPY

IPT was first developed as part of a large study of the effectiveness of psychotherapy and antidepressant medication for depression in adults. Because IPT was first used in a research study, it was important that research therapists conducted IPT in the same way. IPT was therefore *manualized*—that is, the rationale, goals, and structure of the sessions were all outlined (Klerman, Weissman, Rounsaville, and Chevron, 1984; Weissman, Markowitz, and Klerman, 2000). The original manual still forms the foundation for conducting IPT with depressed people.

IPT is usually conducted over sixteen sessions, and there are three phases of treatment. In phase one (sessions one through three) the patient's symptoms are reviewed, a psychiatric diagnosis is given, and MDD is characterized as an illness. Patients are educated about depression and its treatment, and a determination is made as to whether the patient should be referred for antidepressant medication. Since seriously depressed people often blame themselves for their inability to complete daily responsibilities, they are counseled that this is common in MDD and that a temporary reduction in responsibilities may be best. Next the therapist reviews the patient's most important personal relationships to get a sense of the positive and negative aspects of them and what the patient might want to change in these relationships. The therapist then determines what the likely focus of the psychotherapy will be. IPT usually focuses on one or two of four interpersonal problem areas: role transition (a major life change), grief (problems in coming to terms with the death of a significant other), interpersonal dispute (conflict with a significant other), and social skills deficits (individuals who lack social skills to develop and maintain ongoing relationships with other people). At the end of phase one, the therapist summarizes the patient's concerns and outlines a treatment plan and goals for treatment. The patient is also reminded that IPT primarily focuses on current problems and concerns, in contrast to some psychotherapies in which early family issues are frequently discussed.

In phase two of IPT (sessions four through thirteen) the focus is on achieving the goals that were established in the problem area(s) selected for treatment. Overall goals and specific strategies to achieve those goals have been outlined in IPT for each of the four interpersonal problem areas. The patient continues to be educated about MDD, encouraged to think about and try out different options to achieve therapeutic goals, and, when needed, provided with support, guidance, and encouragement. Overall, the role of the therapist is as an active collaborator and facilitator.

In phase three of IPT (sessions fourteen through sixteen) there is an explicit discussion of the coming end of treatment, clarification of how the patient feels about this, and education that ending therapy can be difficult for some. There is also a review of the patient's progress, including any reduction in depressive symptoms and to what degree treatment goals have been met.

In younger adults, IPT has been found to be effective in the treatment of an episode of MDD, alone or in combination with antidepressant medication. It has also been found to be effective in longer-term studies of the usefulness of IPT and antidepressant medication to keep previously depressed people from having another episode of depression (see Frank and Spanier 1995).

Most people experience significant life changes at some point during old age. Health problems, the deaths of a spouse, siblings, or friends; retirement; adjustment to new social circumstances; and reduction of finances are some of the stressful circumstances older people confront. Most older adults successfully contend with these stresses and do not become depressed. A minority of older people do experience MDD and can benefit by psychotherapy and/or antidepressant medication. Given the interpersonally relevant changes of late life, IPT appears especially well-suited for depressed older adults.

A growing body of research indicates that IPT is useful in the treatment of depressive symptoms as well as MDD in older people. One study found IPT as useful as antidepressant medication in treating an episode of MDD (Schneider, Sloane, Staples, and Bender 1986). In another study, Charles Reynolds and his colleagues used IPT, antidepressant medication, and combinations of these treatments with older adults experiencing MDD who also had prior episodes of MDD. After successful initial treatment with IPT and antidepressant medication, older adults received one of several treatments or combinations of treatments and were followed for up to three years to determine which treatment(s) reduced the likelihood of a recurrence of MDD. Overall, it appeared that the combination of monthly IPT and antidepressant medication best reduced the likelihood of a recurrence of depression (see Reynolds, et al. 1999). In other research, a brief form of IPT reduced symptoms of depression in older people with medical problems (Mossey, Nott, Higgins, and Talerico, 1996).

Research studies and clinical reports indicate that IPT requires relatively little adaptation for older adults. The brief, problem-focused, collaborative nature of IPT is appealing to many elderly people. Role transition and interpersonal dispute are the most common interpersonal problems areas in IPT with older adults. Consistent with research studies, clinical reports indicate that 75 percent of older people with depression-related diagnoses treated with IPT alone or in combination with antidepressant medication evidence a significant reduction in depressive symptoms (see Hinrichsen 2000).

Further research is needed to examine the success of IPT in the treatment of late life depression. However, it appears that IPT is a promising psychotherapy, particularly for depressed older adults who are experiencing interpersonal problems.

GREGORY A. HINRICHSEN

See also DEPRESSION; PROBLEM SOLVING THERAPY; STRESS AND COPING.

BIBLIOGRAPHY

FRANK, E., and SPANIER, C. "Interpersonal Psychotherapy for Depression: Overview, Clinical Efficacy, and Future Directions." *Clinical Psychology: Science and Practice* 2 (1995): 349–369.

HINRICHSEN, G. A. "Interpersonal Psychotherapy for Treating Late Life Depression." In *Innovations in Clinical Practice: A Sourcebook*, vol. 18. Edited by L. Vandecreek and T. L. Jackson. Sarasota, Fla.: Professional Resource Press, 2000. Pages 21–31.

KLERMAN, G. L.; WEISSMAN, M. M.; ROUNSAVILLE, B. J.; and CHEVRON, E. S. *Interpersonal Psychotherapy of Depression*. New York: Basic Books, 1984.

MOSSEY, J. M.; KNOTT, K. A.; HIGGEN, M.; and TALERICO, K. "Effectiveness of a Psychosocial Intervention, Interpersonal Counseling, for Subdysthymic Depression in Medically Ill Elderly." *Journal of Gerontology: Medical Sciences* 51A (1996): M172–M178.

REYNOLD, C. F.; FRANK, E.; PEREL, J. M.; IMBER, S. D.; CORNES, C.; MILLER, M. D.; MAZUMDAR, S.; HOUCK, P. R.; DEW, M. A.; STACK, J. A.; POLLOCK, B. G.; and KUPER, D. J. "Nortriptyline and Interpersonal Psychotherapy as Maintenance Therapies for Recurrent Depression: A Randomized Controlled Trial in Patients Older than 59 Years." *Journal of the American Medical Association* 281 (1999): 39–45.

SCHNEIDER, L. S.; SLOANE, R. B.; STAPLES, F. R.; and BENDER, M. "Pretreatment Orthostatic Hypotension as a Predictor of Response to Nortriptyline in Geriatric Depression." *Journal of Clinical Psychopharmacology* 6 (1986): 172–176.

WEISSMAN, M. M.; MARKOWITZ, J. C.; and KLERMAN, G. L. *Comprehensive Guide to Interpersonal Psychotherapy*. New York: Basic Books, 2000.

INTERVENTIONS, PSYCHO-SOCIAL-BEHAVIORAL

An intervention involves actions that alter, or are intended to alter, relationships between observable phenomena. Prototypical characteristics of intervention studies include a clearly defined starting and ending point, a detailed manual describing the intervention protocol, one or more postintervention outcome measures, and a baseline measure or comparison group against which individuals exposed to the intervention can be compared. Intervention studies typically occur in real world settings, as opposed to the laboratory, and if well designed, yield strong causal conclusions about the relationships between the intervention and the observed outcomes.

Intervention studies with older adults have been commonplace for at least three decades, but there has been an explosion of intervention research since the early 1990s and the pace of research continues to accelerate. This growth was in part stimulated by the vast quantities of descriptive and observational data collected in prior decades and the desire to effectively address the needs of older adults in American society. The majority of psychosocial and behavioral interventions targeted at older adults aim to maintain or enhance physical health, mental health, or cognitive functioning. Such interventions are commonly an outgrowth of research which has identified factors that have a significant impact on older adults and that seem to be amenable to change. Psychosocial and behavioral interventions are increasingly used as an alternative or supplement to surgical or pharmacological approaches due to their general efficacy and relative cost effectiveness (Schulz, Lawton, and Maddox).

Physical health and functioning is the most common target goal of interventions for older adults, as illustrated by interventions to reduce falls, increase muscle strength necessary for independent functioning, enhance urinary continence, lower blood pressure, detect prostrate cancer, lower cholesterol levels, increase bone mineral density, enhance self-care behaviors (e.g., medication compliance, exercise) and decrease the frequency of unhealthy behaviors (e.g., smoking, alcohol use). Mental health interventions for older adults are often aimed at reducing anxiety and depressive symptomatology, enhancing sleep quality, and increasing feelings of global or domain-specific satisfaction and perceived control. Some psychosocial interventions are directed at improving quality of life in individuals suffering from psychiatric illness whereas other interventions are directed at individuals who are at risk for psychiatric illness due to common late-life stressors such as chronic illness, spousal caregiving, and bereavement. Other common goals of psychosocial interventions are enhanced relationship quality, increased recreational or leisure activity, and improved cognitive functioning. Although most intervention studies are primarily focused on physical health, mental health, or cognitive functioning, improvements obtained in any one of these domains are likely to carry over to the other domains.

Common intervention approaches include cognitive or behavioral training; physical activity training; peer support for dealing with specific stressors; education; and counseling or psychotherapy that is provided in an individual or group setting. Educational interventions are perhaps the most general approach, in that individuals can be educated in regard to a multitude of issues, such as how to manage medications, how to cope with grief, and how to modify their home to make it more accessible. Other approaches include preventive health screening, special packaging of medications, pet therapy, music therapy, light therapy, intergenerational programs, adult day care, and cognitive training. It is becoming more common to target older adults both directly and indirectly through changes in their environment or to target multiple entities within a single intervention (e.g., the older adult, informal or formal caregivers, and the physician) (Council on Scientific Affairs, American Medical

Association). Important synergies are likely to be achieved by such simultaneous targeting of multiple individuals with intervention strategies that focus both on the pragmatic and psychological aspects of a given health-related problem.

A critical aspect of psychosocial interventions is the evaluation of these approaches for their ability to effect change in targeted outcomes. Interventions that have demonstrated efficacy include educational interventions for the management of chronic illness, behavioral interventions for incontinence, relaxation training for insomnia, and physical activity interventions for reduction of falls and bone fractures.

LYNN M. MARTIRE
RICHARD SCHULZ

See also SOCIAL SERVICES.

BIBLIOGRAPHY

Council on Scientific Affairs, American Medical Association. "Physicians and Family Caregivers: A Model for Partnership." *Journal of the American Medical Association* 269 (1993): 1282–1284.

SCHULZ, R.; LAWTON, M. P.; and MADDOX, G., eds. *Annual Review of Gerontology and Geriatrics.* Vol. 18, *Interventions Research with Older Adults.* New York: Springer Publishing Company, 1999.

IRA

See INDIVIDUAL RETIREMENT ACCOUNT

ISRAEL

The State of Israel was established after the Holocaust, in 1948, as a Jewish and democratic state. One of its declared goals was to become the renewed homeland, open to Jews from all over the world. Since then, Israel has absorbed immigrants from about one hundred countries. Most of them came in large waves during short periods of time as other countries opened their gates for emigration. The demographic composition of these immigrant waves has thus been a significant factor in shaping Israel's demography.

Aging population

When Israel was established, it was a young society with just 4 percent of its population age sixty-five and over. The first large immigration wave was composed mainly of European Jews, most of whom were young people who had survived World War II. The most recent wave of immigrants began in 1989 from the former Soviet Union. Since then, approximately 730,000 people have arrived in Israel, increasing its population by about 20 percent. The relatively high percentage of elderly people among them (16 percent) significantly increased the absolute number of elderly people in Israel, as well as their proportion in the general population.

In addition to the effect of immigration on Israel's demography, its population has grown older over the years due to a constant decrease in the fertility rate and increase in life expectancy. The aging of the population has been quite rapid. The percentage of elderly people age sixty-five and over grew from 4 percent in 1948 to 9.85 percent in 1998. The population of people age seventy-five and over (the old-old) grew even more rapidly. Thus, not only has the general population been aging, but also the old population itself has been growing older. By the end of 1998, the group of the old-old comprised 42.5 percent of people age sixty-five and over.

These trends are expected to continue. At the end of 1999 the Israeli population numbered 6,041,400 persons, with about 600,000 (almost 10 percent) elderly. In 2020 elderly people will make up close to 12 percent of the general population, and the old-old will constitute about one-half of the total elderly population.

Heterogeneity is a dominant characteristic of Israel's population. About 80 percent of Israelis are Jews, the remaining 20 percent are mostly Moslem Arabs. Elderly Jews comprise 11.5 percent of the Jewish population, while Arab elderly comprise only about 3 percent of the Israeli Arab population. Elderly Arabs are younger than elderly Jews, have less education, and lower income.

Significant diversity also exists among elderly Jews. In 1998, almost two-thirds of them were born in European or American countries, about 26 percent were born in Asian or African countries, and only 8 percent were born in Israel. In general, Israeli-born elderly persons and elderly of western origin have more education and higher levels of income than people of Asian or African origin. However, elderly immigrants who arrived to Israel in the 1990s from the former Soviet Union, although younger and more educated than the Israeli veteran elderly, are physically and economically weaker (Carmel and Lazar).

Gender differences are found in all the cultural groups of elderly Israelis. Similar to other industrialized societies, Israeli women live longer than men. In 1999, their life expectancy at birth was 79.9 years, while that of men was 76.2 years. Despite living longer, women's general well-being is worse than that of men in terms of health and socioeconomic status. More women than men also live alone and a significantly lower percentage of them is married (40.3 percent versus 78.7 percent in 1999).

Social services

Awareness of needs of the large and rapidly growing group of elderly population intensified in the 1980s. Israel responded to these needs by passing new welfare laws and developing new services. Israel ensures by law a minimal level of income to its older population. In addition to a pension received from the workplace, Israeli citizens above the official retirement age (women at the age of 60 and men at the age of 65) are eligible to receive an old-age pension from the National Insurance Institute (NII). In 1998, about one-third of the elderly population received a supplementary income because this was their only income, or because their overall income was lower than the poverty line. In general, elderly Israelis have lower socioeconomic status than younger age groups. This situation is expected to change in the twenty-first century as younger and better-educated cohorts reach old age.

Since the establishment of Israel, health care services have been available to the vast majority of the population. In 1995, Israel passed the National Health Care Law, under which all Israeli citizens have health care coverage, regardless of income. This insurance covers ambulatory and hospitalization services, including medications which are provided by four sick funds. Elderly Israelis consume more than 30 percent of the national expenditure on health services.

The dominant orientation that has guided Israel's health and welfare policies in meeting the needs of frail and disabled persons is to enable them to continue living in their own homes and communities as long as possible. Accordingly, a wide network of welfare and long-term health services has been established throughout the country by public and private agencies.

For independent elderly persons, many municipalities have opened social clubs. Public and private sheltered housing units have been built in many settlements for persons who want to live independently and for those who need limited services.

The needs of disabled elderly persons have been addressed in part by the Nursing Law, which was passed in 1988. Under this law, people who live in the community and who have difficulties in performing activities of daily living (ADL) are eligible to receive up to sixteen hours per week of help at home, providing for personal needs as well as cooking, house cleaning, and shopping. These trained care providers are paid directly by the state through private manpower agencies.

Community services for the disabled elderly are also provided in numerous public day-care centers. These centers provide a variety of services to people who need assistance in ADL. Services include transportation, meals, nursing surveillance, dentistry and physiotherapy, workshops, social activities, and help in bathing, foot care, and hair styling.

Large municipalities provide subsidized hot, nutritionally balanced meals to the home through the Meals on Wheels service. In addition to regular welfare services, many localities have also developed a wide range of voluntary community services including home visits to ill or lonely persons, information and counseling services, loan of medical equipment and devices for disabled persons, supportive neighborhood programs, and home repair projects. Due to this network of community services, only 22.4 percent of the elderly people who were defined as disabled lived in institutions in 1999.

Long-term institutional care is provided by a variety of public and private organizations such as nursing homes for independent, frail, and nursing-care elderly. These services are financed partly by the government and partly by the patient and the patient's children, depending on their income. Long-term, institutional complex nursing care is financed by the sick funds. The total number of beds for elderly persons in long-term care institutions in 1998 was 43 per 1,000 elderly persons. Only about 5 percent of the elderly population lived in institutions in that year.

Challenges

Despite this rich network of services, at the beginning of the twenty-first century Israel has to find responses to a number of emerging issues. Because of the growing number of elderly persons who are healthy and independent, programs must be developed to increase their involvement in the workplace, community, and family life in order to improve their health and quality of life and to reduce their needs for social and health services. Israel must also address the challenge of providing appropriate services for a large number of elderly people with diverse cultural backgrounds and languages who live in the same communities. Developing and expanding training programs for formal care providers in order to ensure the quality of services is another important social challenge.

The multiple various services which differ in ownership, responsibility, and financing result in duplications, inefficiency in the provision of services, and fragmentation in the continuity of care. This situation is confusing to the disabled persons, their families, and to formal caregivers. Changes in financing arrangements and the establishment of coordinating mechanisms, which will ensure access to comprehensive, continuous, and efficient care to all are critical (Clarfield et al., 2000).

Families have a dominant role in caring for elderly people in Israel. Most of the main caregivers are women, either spouses or daughters. With the decrease in the number of children per family, and increases in longevity, the number of dependent parents will significantly increase. This load will become heavier with the years, when the middle aged and young-old women, many of whom will be frail themselves and still working outside home, will have to care for a number of older relatives, as well as for their husbands, children, and grandchildren. In 1999 about 10 percent of the Israeli population over age sixty-five had older parents, and 42 percent of them took care of their parents on a daily basis. The parent support ratio (persons eighty and over divided by population age fifty to sixty-four) increased from 57 per thousand in 1961 to 192 in 1997. The development of supportive services for family and other informal caregivers will become one of the goals of the future. The increasing ratios of dependency on the national level will also have economic implications for the whole society, which will require such changes as raising the age of retirement and revisions in the pension system.

SARA CARMEL

See also MIDDLE EASTERN COUNTRIES; POPULATION AGING.

BIBLIOGRAPHY

CARMEL, S., and LAZAR, A.. "Health and Well-Being Among Elderly Persons: The Role of Social Class and Immigration Status." *Ethnicity & Health* 3 (1998): 31–43.

CLARFIELD, M. A. M.; PALTIEL, A.; GINDIN, Y.; MORGINSTIN, B.; and DWOLATZKY, T. "Country Profile: Israel." *Journal of the American Geriatrics Society (JAGS)* 48 (2000): 980–984.

Statistical Abstracts of Israel 1999. Jerusalem: Central Bureau of Statistics, no. 50, 1999.

World Health Organization. *The World Health Report 2000—Health Systems: Improving Performance.* Geneva: WHO, 2000.

J

JAPAN

At the start of the twenty-first century, 17 percent of the Japanese population was age sixty-five or older—a proportion matched only by Belgium, Greece, Italy, and Sweden, and surpassed by Monaco with 22 percent. What sets Japan even further apart from the rest of the world is the speed with which this aging has occurred. For example, it took Sweden eighty-five years to increase from 7 percent to 14 percent sixty-five and older, whereas in Japan it took only twenty-six years. The reason for the extraordinary pace of aging in Japan is the much shorter period during which Japanese women shifted from having five or more children to fewer than two and the dramatic improvements in survival, especially after World War II. In response to the rapid pace of aging in Japan, public and political attention there has become more focused on the issue of aging perhaps than in other developed countries. This entry will review the demographic factors influencing past and future aging in Japan, the circumstances of today's elderly population, and the challenges of developing policies to accommodate the rapid change in age structure.

Demographic determinants of aging

In its earliest stages, population aging is most influenced by fertility decline rather than by mortality decline, which tends to be concentrated at the youngest ages as the importance of infectious, parasitic diseases declines and that of chronic, degenerative diseases increases. In 1925, Japanese women gave birth to an average of 5.1 children each, but by 1950 fertility had fallen to 3.7 children and by 1960 to below the re-

placement level of 2.1 children per woman (the number of children needed to just replace a couple in the population). Japan did not experience the long postwar baby boom that the United States did.

In 2000, Japanese women were having on average fewer than 1.4 children each. Although fertility within marriage and ideal family size declined very little in the last two decades of the twentieth century, increases in educational and work opportunities for women in that period were associated with later ages of marriage, and thus with reduced overall fertility. Such low fertility, even combined with lower mortality, means that the absolute size of the Japanese population will likely begin to decline between 2005 and 2010; the size of the cohort of twenty to twenty-four year olds who might be expected to enter the labor force has already begun to decline.

Now that Japan has progressed so far in its demographic transition, mortality decline is the primary force behind aging. Life expectancy at birth increased from about forty-five years in 1925 to sixty years in 1950 and to eighty-one years in 2000, the highest on earth. As in all richer countries, women outlive men; their life expectancies are eighty-four and seventy-seven years, respectively. A major contributor to increased survival in Japan has been the significant decline since 1970 in the death rate from cerebrovascular disease, which until 1980 was the leading cause of death. In the late 1990s, Japan was atypical of richer countries in that cancer was the number one cause of death instead of heart disease.

This rapid increase of survival means that the coming decades will see even greater aging

An elderly Japanese postman wears the kimono and straw hat that was still a traditional part of the mailman's uniform in 2000. (Corbis photo by Peter Wilson.)

in Japan. In its 1998 update, the United Nations projected that in 2050 the proportion of individuals age sixty-five and over would be 36 percent, assuming that life expectancy increased to eighty-four years and fertility remained at 1.4 children per woman. A fertility rebound to 1.8 children would result in only 32 percent sixty-five and over; an even greater increase to replacement-level fertility would result in 29 percent of the population age sixty-five and over. The proportion of people age eighty and over would increase from less than 4 percent in 2000 to 10, 12, or 13 percent in 2050, depending on the fertility scenario. Thus, the stage is set for continued dramatic aging of the Japanese population. Other countries in Asia, especially those in East and Southeast Asia, will also experience significant aging in the first half of the twenty-first century, but Japan has a substantial head start due to its earlier fertility decline and its remarkable success in reducing mortality.

Characteristics of the older population

The older Japanese population is similar to other older populations around the world in that it is predominantly female, and older men are more likely to be married than older women—both patterns that are influenced by the sex differences in life expectancy. But Japan differs in two important respects—in patterns of labor force participation and of living arrangements.

In their late fifties and their sixties, Japanese men are much more likely to be working than their counterparts in other rich countries. In 1998, 85 percent of men ages fifty-five to sixty-four and 36 percent of men age sixty-five and over were in the labor force. The percentages for women were 50 and 15, respectively. In the United States, similar proportions of older women work, but older men are less likely to be in the labor force. In 1998, participation rates were only 68 percent for those ages fifty-five to sixty-four and 17 percent for those sixty-five and over. Labor force participation at older ages in most European countries is even lower. There are several possible reasons for the higher rates in Japan. Some have pointed to Japan's strong work ethic and work-group orientation. Others have emphasized the relative immaturity of the Japanese pension system until the last part of the twentieth century. Gruber and Wise have highlighted the relatively low penalty in terms of reduced pension benefits associated with continued work in Japan.

Labor force participation of the sixty-five and over population declined in Japan from 1980 to 1998, as it did in other richer countries, but the trend for the fifty-five to sixty-four population has been flat for Japanese males and upward for females. These time trends around the prime retirement ages likely reflect increases in the age of eligibility for public pensions and the efforts by the Japanese government to encourage firms to retain older workers or hire them anew.

The second significant characteristic of older Japanese is that they are much more likely to be living with their adult children than are their peers in other more developed countries. In 1990, 59 percent of the sixty-five and older population coresided with children, while 25 percent lived with spouses only, 4 percent with others, and 11 percent alone. Although the percentage coresiding is high by Western standards, it is low for Asia, where in recent decades roughly 75 percent coresidence has been the pattern. In fact, the figure for Japan in 1990 represents an 18 percentage point drop from 1970, when Japan was more typical of Asian societies. This decline in Japan likely reflects the increased survival of spouses, a change in preferences among family members for coresidence, and perhaps increased resources that allow the actualization of a preference for living apart from children. Not surprisingly, cross-sectional analysis based on Japanese data from 1988 indicate that older people with more education and a surviving spouse are less likely to live with their children than are people with less education and those who are widowed.

Hirosima's projections of living arrangements based on past trends in population, marital status, and propensity to coreside indicate that living with children will likely continue to decline to about 40 percent in 2010 with 36 percent of males coresiding and 43 percent of females doing so. The proportion living alone is expected to increase from 5 to 8 percent among males over the same period and from 15 to 16 percent among females. The biggest changes will likely be in the category of living with spouse only: from 36 to 50 percent for males and from 17 to 32 percent for females. Although coresidence is not necessary or sufficient for intergenerational support, these projections are consistent with the decline in the proportion of women of reproductive ages who expect to depend on their children once they reach old age, from 65 percent in 1950 to 18 percent in 1990.

Moreover, it would appear that on average older Japanese in the early 1990s were relatively well-off financially in comparison to younger Japanese and similar in circumstance to older people in other developed countries. As a result of a greater number of years of working and saving, it is not surprising that the net worth of older Japanese is larger than that of younger Japanese. Home ownership is an important component of wealth among older Japanese. Data from the Organization of Economic Cooperation and Development indicate that rates of home ownership among Japan's older population are over 75 percent, which is comparable to or even higher than some European countries. Of course, there is some decline in income with retirement. Even so, the ratio of income at age sixty-seven to income at age fifty-five in Japan is similar to the ratios in many European countries, about 75 to 80 percent. Public pension benefits are an important component of income for older Japanese. It remains to be seen how the bursting of the so-called bubble economy and the subsequent economic slowdown in the 1990s will ultimately affect the overall economic well-being of older Japanese,

especially those at the low ends of the income and wealth distributions. Furthermore, serious questions about the future of the public pension system are a source of concern.

Policy challenges

Like other more developed countries, Japan is facing the prospect of increasing costs of its public pension and health systems, and it is considering what response, if any, is appropriate to the coming declines in population and work force.

There has been particular concern that the increased ratio of retirees to workers would require unbearably high contribution rates to maintain the fiscal viability of the public pension systems. At the same time, the government has recognized the importance of pensions to older people. The options for pension reform are basically to increase contributions, decrease benefits, or increase the age of eligibility for benefits, and the Japanese government used all three mechanisms in a series of reforms in the 1980s and 1990s.

In March 2000, the Japanese parliament passed legislation that is forecasted to limit the increase in premiums from 17.4 percent of monthly pay (shared equally by employee and employer) in 2000 to 25.2 percent in 2025, as opposed to 34.5 percent if the law had not been changed. To accomplish this goal, benefits for new retirees are being cut by 5 percent, and it is estimated that lifetime retirement benefits will be cut by about 20 percent for a typical worker who is forty years old in 2000. The age of eligibility is being gradually increased from sixty to sixty-five, semiannual bonuses received by workers will for the first time be included in the pay used to calculate their contributions, and the adjustment of benefits for inflation will be based on consumer prices instead of wages. Some critics have argued that even these significant changes are not enough and that the government forecasts of the viability of the system are based on fertility assumptions that are too high.

In 2000, the Japanese government also implemented a new long-term care insurance system that requires monthly contributions of roughly $20 to $30 from persons age forty and over. Those who are already retired pay at the upper end of that range. Also a copayment of 10 percent is paid by all but the lowest-income beneficiaries of services. In 2000, the government was also considering adjusting its broader medical insurance system and requiring older people to pay a percentage of their costs of care (up to a limit), as opposed to the current system of nominal fees.

Increasing the size of the working-age population relative to the retired population would help improve the fiscal health of the pension and medical insurance systems. Possible mechanisms include allowing more immigration, increasing the labor force participation of older people and women, and—over the long run—increasing fertility. Japanese society has not been nearly so open to newcomers as the United States, so unless there is major social change, immigration is unlikely to make much difference. Although Japan's older population is already relatively active in the labor force, improvements in health combined with financial need and job opportunities might well lead to even greater participation. Women are truly in the middle, since they are typically the caretakers of those in the older and younger generations who may need assistance, and many young women are choosing to opt out of this role or at least delay it. Making work more compatible with family responsibilities for both men and women will be a key element of accommodating the dramatic changes in age structure that are to come in Japan.

LINDA G. MARTIN

See also CHINA; SOUTH ASIA.

BIBLIOGRAPHY

GENDELL, M. "Trends in Retirement Age in Four Countries, 1965–1995." *Monthly Labor Review* 121 (August 1998): 20–30.
GRUBER, J., and WISE, D., eds. *International Comparison of Social Security Systems.* Chicago: University of Chicago Press, 1999.
HIROSIMA, K. "Projection of Living Arrangements of the Elderly in Japan: 1990–2010." *Genus* 53, no. 1–2 (1997): 79–111.
MARTIN, L. G. "The Graying of Japan." *Population Bulletin* 44 (July 1989): 1–41.
RETHERFORD, R. D.; OGAWA, N.; and SAKAMOTO, S. "Values and Fertility Change in Japan," In *Dynamics of Values in Fertility Change.* Edited by R. Letee. Oxford, U.K.: Oxford University Press, 1999. Pages 121–147.
TSUYA, N. O., and MARTIN, L. G. "Living Arrangements of Elderly Japanese and Attitudes Toward Inheritance." *Journal of Gerontology: Social Sciences* 47 (March 1992): S45–S54.

JOB PERFORMANCE

What is the relationship between age and job performance? The average age of people in the workforce is getting higher, with increasing numbers of middle-aged and older workers employed in many different jobs (Fullerton; Johnston and Packer). Thus, it is important to know whether job performance is higher or lower for older workers in comparison with younger workers. Most reviews of empirical research on this issue have concluded that although individual studies differ, averaging across available studies reveals virtually no relationship between age and job performance (McEvoy and Cascio; Rhodes; Salthouse and Maurer; Warr). The fact that there is no observable relationship is interesting to many people because it is known that age-related declines can occur in important mental and physical abilities (as documented elsewhere in this encyclopedia). If abilities that are important for performing work do decline with age, but job performance is not lower for older workers, this seems paradoxical.

When considering this issue, it is important to realize that two different but related questions can be asked about the job performance–age relationship. First, one could ask whether, at the same point in time, younger workers in a given job perform differently than older workers in the same job. This type of question is answered through cross-sectional research in which people of different ages are compared against each other (for example, people age twenty-five versus people age sixty). However, a second question that can be asked is whether workers who are twenty-five years old today will perform better or worse after thirty-five years in a particular job. That is, would performance in that job increase or decrease over time for the same people? This type of question is answered through longitudinal research, in which the same people are tracked across time to observe age-related changes in behavior. Perhaps for obvious reasons, research conducted on the age–job performance relation has thus far been largely cross-sectional (Warr). It is difficult and expensive to conduct research on the same people across many years, and of course people change occupations, switch companies, and take other actions that make this impractical. Therefore, there is not a great deal of data on whether job performance changes with age. There is mostly research to show whether there are differences across age groups in the performance of various jobs. And cumulative research shows that there are essentially no differences in observed performance as a function of worker age.

In reaching this conclusion, it is important to realize that, other than the possibility that there may truly be no relationship, there are several other possible reasons why there is no observed relationship between age and performance in research (McEvoy and Cascio; Rhodes; Salthouse and Maurer; Warr). First, in work organizations job performance is very important. Thus for a variety of reasons, people who are not performing well generally do not stay in a job. People may quit or find a job that they can perform better, rather than stay in a position that exceeds their capabilities. An older person who finds that he or she cannot perform the job anymore may decide to seek a different one. Also, those who cannot perform a job may be removed by the organization. They may be transferred into a different position that is more suited to their skills, or they may be terminated. The end result of either of these processes is that if older workers cannot perform well because of age-related changes in their skills, they probably will not be in the job for very long. Consequently research comparing older and younger workers in performance will not include those older workers who cannot perform and are no longer on the job. The end result will be no observed relationship between age and job performance.

A second possible reason why there is not an observed relationship between age of a worker and performance is that there may sometimes be nonequivalent responsibilities between people within the same job. That is, although the job title may be the same, the duties or responsibilities may be somewhat different across workers. If older or younger workers get different assignments (for example, easier or harder ones or assignments that rely on certain skills to different degrees), then making meaningful comparisons of the job performance of older and younger workers is difficult.

A third possible reason why there is no observed relation between job performance and age is that job performance measures often rely on supervisory ratings, which are imperfect measures of performance. To the extent that these

ratings are not accurate measures of performance, conclusions about job performance may not be accurate. Various rating biases and errors can occur in performance appraisal. For example, if a supervisor wants to be lenient or give ratings that are higher than a person deserves (a leniency bias), then the performance measure will be biased upward. To the extent that this or other types of biases influence ratings, the measure of performance may not reveal true performance differences very accurately. If there are true age-related differences in performance, they may not be reflected in the measure.

A fourth possible reason why there is no observed relation between job performance and age is that the true relationship may be curvilinear rather than linear. Most research on the age–performance issue has tested for linear relationships, meaning that as age increases, performance consistently increases or decreases. However, if the relationship is actually curvilinear, this would mean the relationship has a different form than simply higher or lower with increasing age. For example, job performance might increase up to a certain age (e.g., fifty), then level off and begin to decline at later ages (at age sixty and over), becoming increasingly lower after that. If job performance is plotted on the y axis against age on the x axis, the relationship would look somewhat like an upside-down U. (This is only a hypothetical example to illustrate curvilinearity—research has not established this trend conclusively.) If the research has been done to detect linear relationships, and the relationships are actually curvilinear, then it is possible that the linear tests will show no relationship when in fact there are curvilinear ones.

A fifth possible reason why there is no observed relation between job performance and age is that job performance is almost always multidimensional, meaning the work requires more than one important type of behavior or skill for overall success. Thus if some workers focus their efforts on one part of a job and other workers focus their efforts on other parts of a job, their overall performance may be similar, even though they reached the performance level through allocating their efforts differently. If older workers' abilities or skills decline in one aspect of work, they may focus their efforts on another aspect to achieve the same overall level of success.

A sixth and very important possible reason why research shows no relationship between job performance and age has to do with job experience. Job experience usually leads to more job knowledge (Schmidt et al.). It makes sense that someone who has been around longer will acquire more knowledge that is relevant to the task(s) at hand. Research has also shown that job knowledge is a very important predictor of job performance (Schmidt et al.). This also makes sense: those who know more about how to perform a job tend to perform it better than those with less knowledge. Thus experience leads to more knowledge, and job knowledge leads to higher performance. Age is often positively related to job experience (older workers have been around longer, on the average). This means that older workers (with more experience) may have acquired more job-relevant knowledge than younger workers (with less experience). Therefore any age-related mental or physical declines in basic abilities needed to perform the work may be offset by greater job knowledge that goes along with greater experience. As a result older workers may be able to compensate for less raw ability through the use of more job knowledge. If this occurs, then observed relationships between job performance and age may be zero because the overall performance of younger and older workers is actually equivalent, but for different reasons. That is, younger workers are relying more on their raw ability and older workers are relying more on their accumulated knowledge.

Also, Warr suggests that in many jobs declining abilities can be compensated for by other factors, such as more experience, more knowledge, taking more time to complete demanding duties, and so forth. Further, there is little evidence that the type of job in question moderates or makes a difference in the size of the job performance–age relationship (McEvoy and Cascio). Thus it is possible that in many jobs, a decline in abilities can be offset by experience and knowledge.

However, this does not address the question of whether two workers of equal experience and unequal ages will perform similarly. That is, although age may be associated with experience in many settings, it may not be in all settings. Less research has addressed the question of whether an older worker and a younger one assigned to a brand-new job at the same time will perform similarly. In fact, much of the cumulative research done on the age–job performance relationship has not controlled for differences in experience across age. Thus the effects of age on

performance by workers of equal experience but unequal age is not as well researched as the overall question of whether there is a general association between age and job performance. This is an important question because the nature of work has been changing, with an increasing number of workers being called upon to learn continuously, often changing career lines for various reasons (Hall and Mirvis). Increasingly the idea of someone working on the same job from age twenty-five through age sixty may be unlikely (Greller and Stroh). This raises the question of whether job experience can accumulate and have the same compensatory effects if workers are continuously facing changing circumstances.

To the extent that performing work successfully will increasingly involve learning and developing new skills, learning and development will be an important concern for aging workers. Some literature has noted that older workers may not participate in training and development experiences to the same extent as younger workers, and has made suggestions on how to increase motivation and participation in these activities (Maurer). However, there has not been as much research on these issues as there has been on the job performance–age issue. As rapid changes in technology and in business strategies demand new skills of workers at midlife and beyond in order to continue to perform their jobs, it is important that older workers (and younger ones) continue to be involved in learning and developing their skills at work. Further, there is potential for age discrimination in dealing with performance-relevant training and development of workers (Maurer and Rafuse). There could be a tendency to give preference to younger workers over older ones in assigning or encouraging training and development opportunities. Increasingly, as organizations manage older workers, this legal concern is a critical issue to deal with effectively for the sake of both the organizations and the workers. Some literature has suggested how to avoid these personnel and legal problems (Maurer and Rafuse).

Most research so far indicates that the age of a person, by itself, has little real meaning in explaining job performance. However, other than the possibility that there may truly be no relationship between age and performance, there are several other possible reasons why there is no observed relationship between age and performance in research. It is also important to note that age is only a number that is very loosely associated with many other more meaningful (and potentially job-relevant) changes and differences in people. Much research remains to be done on this general issue.

TODD J. MAURER
FRANCISCO G. BARBEITE

See also AGE DISCRIMINATION; EMPLOYMENT OF OLDER WORKERS.

BIBLIOGRAPHY

FULLERTON, H. N. "Labor Force Projections to 2008: Steady Growth and Changing Composition." *Monthly Labor Review* 118 (November 1995): 19–32.

GRELLER, M. M., and STROH, L. K. "Careers in Midlife and Beyond: A Fallow Field in Need of Sustenance." *Journal of Vocational Behavior* 47 (1995): 232–247.

HALL, D., and MIRVIS, P. "The New Career Contract: Developing the Whole Person at Midlife and Beyond." *Journal of Vocational Behavior* 47 (1995): 269–289.

JOHNSTON, W. B., and PACKER, A. H. *Workforce 2000.* Indianapolis, Ind.: Hudson Institute, 1987.

MAURER, T. "Career-relevant Learning and Development, Worker Age, and Beliefs about Self-Efficacy for Development." *Journal of Management* 27 (2001): 123–140.

MAURER, T., and RAFUSE, N. "Learning and Litigating: Managing Employee Development and Avoiding Claims of Age Discrimination." *Academy of Management Executive* 15, no. 4 (2001).

McEVOY, G. M., and CASCIO, W. F. "Cumulative Evidence of the Relationship Between Employee Age and Job Performance." *Journal of Applied Psychology* 74 (1989): 11–17.

RHODES, S. R. "Age-Related Differences in Work Attitudes and Behavior: A Review and Conceptual Analysis." *Psychological Bulletin* 93, no. 2 (1983): 328–367.

SALTHOUSE, T., and MAURER, T. "Aging, Job Performance and Career Development." In *Handbook of the Psychology of Aging,* 4th ed. Edited by J. Birren and K. Schaie. San Diego: Academic Press, 1996. Pages 353–364.

SCHMIDT, F. L.; HUNTER, J. E.; and OUTERBRIDGE, A. N. "Impact of job Experience and Ability on Job Knowledge, Work Sample Performance, and Supervisory Ratings of Job Performance." *Journal of Applied Psychology* 71, no. 3 (1986): 432–439.

WARR, P. B. "Age and Employment." In *Handbook of Industrial and Organizational Psychology,* vol. 4., 2d ed. Edited by H. C. Triandis and M. D. Dunnette. Palo Alto, Calif.: Consulting Psychologists Press, 1994. Pages 447–483.

K

KIDNEY, AGING

The kidneys sit, one on each side of the midline, high in the back of the abdomen—so high in fact that their top halves fall under the lower end of the rib cage. The chief roles of the kidneys are filtration of blood, reabsorption of key chemicals, excretion of fluid and waste metabolites, and the maintenance of acid/base balance, but they also have important glandular (endocrine) functions. The kidneys are particularly important in drug metabolism.

Usually, as people age, there are highly predictable changes in both the structure and the function of the kidneys, so that by age seventy-five the kidneys weigh about 15 to 20 percent less than they do at age twenty-five, due to loss of cells that make up the kidneys. Nevertheless, kidney function, in the absence of disease, remains adequate throughout life, even into extreme old age.

The cells that make up the kidney are complex, and are formed into special structures called nephrons. Blood enters the kidneys from the aorta (the major artery that leaves the heart) via the renal arteries, which branch to smaller and smaller structures known as arterioles. The blood flows into a filtration structure called a glomerulus. Filtered material passes through a complex membrane into tubules. The remainder of the blood, consisting of plasma, blood cells and certain large proteins passes into another arteriole. The tubule and arteriole are in close proximity, allowing water and other chemicals (chiefly sodium, chloride and potassium) to be reabsorbed back from the tubules into the blood in the arterioles. Reabsorption is affected both by

local factors in the kidney and by hormones. In this way, the body is able to regulate the relative proportion of water and these chemicals very precisely in response to changes in other parts of the body, and thus to changes in the environment. While all these functions are preserved in old age, the mechanisms become increasingly susceptible to even small changes. Thus, for example, in response to stress such as injury or pain, regulation of sodium reabsorption can become impaired, leading to sodium levels that are relatively too low and body water levels that are relatively too high. This, in turn, can lead to serious consequences, such as delirium.

As the filtrate (now urine) travels through the tubules, it collects in larger structures until ultimately it passes through the ureters, which emerge at the center of the kidneys. The ureter provides the piping to the bladder, where urine is stored before being excreted through the urethra.

An important consequence of impaired kidney function is a decreased ability to excrete certain commonly used drugs, which thus can accumulate and give rise to adverse drug reactions. Drug metabolism and excretion by the kidney are complex, and depend on many characteristics of the drug, including the size and solubility of its molecules, and whether other drugs are being metabolized. Also of great importance are other characteristics, such as blood flow to the kidneys. The latter can be impaired by conditions that become more common as people age (diabetes, lipid disorders, high blood pressure). In general, blood flow to the kidney decreases by about 10 percent per decade after age thirty. It must be emphasized, however, that this is the average case: when individuals are followed over time, many (up to almost one-third) do not show a significant decrease in kidney function, even in the ninth decade of life.

Decline in blood flow to the kidney, accompanied by the loss of kidney cells, means that as people age, the kidneys are less able to filter blood. The lower filtration rate needs to be taken into account when prescribing drugs that are excreted through the kidneys. A standard formula allows ready calculation of the amount by which drug doses should be adjusted in the face of lower kidney function.

For the most part, poor kidney function does not give rise to symptoms, except when it results in kidney failure. As a consequence, physicians must rely on two blood tests (of urea and creatinine) to assess kidney function. As kidneys filter less, they are less able to excrete urea and creatinine, and in consequence the level of each rises. Unfortunately, these are insensitive tests, and especially in elderly people, up to 90 percent of kidney function can be lost before these tests indicate a problem.

Kidney failure in both older and younger people is traditionally divided into three types. Failure resulting from diminished blood flow to the kidneys is called prerenal failure. As noted, many factors result in vascular disease and thus low kidney blood flow becomes more common with age. Kidney failure arising from a problem intrinsic to the kidney itself is renal failure. Many diseases can impair kidney function by direct damage to the nephrons, with various parts of the nephron being particularly susceptible to particular types of disease. For example, the complex membrane across which water and certain proteins flow to the tubules can be the site of deposition of toxic substances, including complexes that arise in autoimmune disorders. The glomeruli are particularly susceptible to diseases associated with aging. Failure that arises from blockage of the flow of urine is called postrenal failure. For example, ureters can be obstructed by strictures, by kidney stones, and, in men, by enlargement of the prostate. In consequence, urine flow backs up so that ultimately glomerular filtration is disrupted.

The kidneys are not just filters, however; but also are the sites of action of several hormones. In addition to those which respond to water handling, important hormones include erythropoietin (necessary to produce red blood cells) and vitamin D (needed for bone integrity). Vitamin D undergoes an essential step in the kidney to become metabolically active.

In general, the rise of kidney disease, and especially kidney failure, has closely paralleled the aging of the population. It is not aging in and of itself, however, but the diseases associated with aging, that is resulting in kidney problems becoming more common. How to interpret the fact that many older people have near-normal kidney function is unclear, but many scientists see in this the hope that such successful aging might be extended to more people, so as to result in less disability in late life.

KENNETH ROCKWOOD

BIBLIOGRAPHY

HAAS, M.; SPARGO, B. H.; WIT, E. J.; and MEEHAN, S. M. "Etiologies and Outcome of Acute Renal Insufficiency in Older Renal Biopsy Study of 259 Cases." *American Journal of Kidney Diseases* 35, no. 3 (2000): 544–546.
LASH, J. P., and GARDNER, C. "Effects of Aging and Drugs on Normal Renal Function." *Coronary Artery Disease* 8, no. 8–9 (1997): 489–494.
LUBRAN, M. M. "Renal Function in the Elderly." *Annuals of Clinical Laboratory Science* 25, no. 2 (1995): 122–133. (Review).
MILLER, M. "Fluid and Electrolyte Homeostatis in the Elderly: Physiological Changes of Aging and Clinical Consequences." *Baillieres Clinincal Endocrinology Metabolism* 11, no. 2 (1997): 367–387. (Review).
WOOLFSON, R. G. "Renal Failure in Atherosclerotic Renovascular Disease: Pathogenesis, Diagnosis, and Intervention." *Postgraduate Medical Journal* 77, no. 904 (2001): 68–78.

KIN

The term *kin* refers to one's relatives or one's family. The *nuclear family* consists of parents and dependent children (a structure often complicated today by divorce and remarriage). Families become more complex when children reach adulthood, marry, and have children; they then include children-in-law and parents-in-law, grandchildren and grandparents. Sisters and brothers grow up to be aunts and uncles to each others' children (i.e., their nieces and nephews). All these relatives comprise an individual's kin, or members of one's *extended family,* as opposed to one's nuclear family. In some families there are people who are not actually blood relatives, but who are considered to be so close that they are like family members. Scholars have called such people *fictive kin*. Some scholars refer to our North American kinship system as a *modified extended family* system. This term is meant to capture the fact that family relationships and obligations extend well beyond the nuclear family household, but also that the emphasis is on intergenerational ties linking parents, children, and grandchildren. The extent to which other types of ties, such as those to siblings and to aunts, uncles, and cousins, are emphasized is more open to individual choice.

In North America, our kinship system is *bilateral*; that is, both one's mother's side of the family and one's father's side of the family are considered to be equal in terms of rights and obligations. In practice, however, there is a tendency in both the United States and Canada for kinship relations to be stronger among women than men, with the mother-daughter tie being the strongest of all. As a result of this greater closeness and involvement between female kin, and especially mothers and daughters, our kinship system often tends to emphasize the mother's side of the family. Young families often have more contact with the wife's parents and siblings than they do with the husband's side of the family. As a result, grandchildren tend to see more of their maternal grandparents and to feel closer to them. This pattern is modified, however, by the nature of the relationship between fathers and their parents; when closeness and involvement are high, grandchildren have close relationships with paternal grandparents and the *matrilineal bias* decreases or disappears.

The importance of maintenance of kin ties

Despite many changes that have come with modernization, urbanization, and industrialization, the family remains a fundamental basis of social organization and a vitally important part of life for individuals of all ages. Kinship ties are important to older adults for a number of reasons. Family members are usually the first ones to whom people turn when they need help, whether this be emotional support (someone to confide in or to make you feel better when things get you down), practical help (someone to take care of you when you are ill, to help with home maintenance and repairs), or advice. At a more symbolic

level, the family provides people with a sense of belonging and a sense of personal history. Families often have special rituals that are passed down through generations (Rosenthal and Marshall). Family reunions bring widely scattered kin together.

As individuals move through adult life—as they get jobs, marry, have children, and perhaps move to a different geographic area—staying in contact with kin may prove difficult, and families may have a sense that they are drifting apart. To counter this, individuals make their own efforts to keep in touch with relatives, but, in addition, many families have someone who takes on the challenge of keeping the various family members in touch with one another. The *kinkeeper* maintains communication links with and among family members through telephoning, writing letters, visiting, and holding family gatherings (Rosenthal). Family kinkeepers are most commonly female, and are typically in late middle age.

While kin relationships are important to people at all stages of the life course, they may be especially important to older adults. Kin, especially adult children, are a major source of help for older adults, particularly those who are widowed. Ties with siblings may become more important than they were in mid-life, providing opportunities to reminisce about the distant past. Grandchildren provide a focus for enjoyment and for a sense of passing on a legacy. Older people also derive meaning and purpose from the contributions they make to the lives of their children and grandchildren. In old age, the caregiving efforts of adult children may help elderly adults in poor health remain living in the community, rather than in nursing homes.

Demographic changes affecting the supply of kin

Two demographic trends over the twentieth century, increases in life expectancy and decreases in fertility, have major implications for the number and type of relatives in individuals' kinship networks, as well as for the nature of kin relationships (Bengtson, Rosenthal, and Burton; Uhlenberg). With each successive birth cohort, a higher proportion of people survive to old age, and the duration of time spent in old age is increasing as well. As a result, middle-aged adults may have more older relatives in their kinship networks than was true in the past. As well, kin relationships extend over a longer period of time than they did in the past. For example, many grandparents now live into their grandchildren's adulthood.

Fertility is a key factor affecting the supply of kin. The number of children one has will, obviously, determine family size in later life, and whether one has many, few, or no children to whom to turn for help and emotional support. It will determine, as well, whether one has many, few, or no grandchildren. The number of children one's parents had determines whether one has many, few, or no siblings, as well as whether, in adult life, one will have siblings-in-law, nieces, and nephews. As older relatives—parents, aunts, and uncles—die, individuals with siblings will still have kin beyond their own children and grandchildren, and will thus have a larger kinship network than individuals who have no siblings. The birth rate declined considerably over the twentieth century. However, while the average number of children has declined, the key decline has been in the proportion of women having very large families (five or six children or more). There has been a corresponding increase in the proportion of women having two or three children. Peter Uhlenberg argues that, if we are concerned about the potential support to older parents, the important distinction is between having no children or only one child and having two or more. People now in old age and those who will enter old age in the near future will have two or more children, on average. This means that most middle-aged adults will have siblings as part of their kin group. In the more distant future, as baby boomers enter old age, the percentage of older people with one or no children will increase, although rates of childlessness among the old will still be lower than they were in 1990.

Other determinants of kin ties

A number of other factors, in addition to fertility and longevity, influence the availability, nature, and quality of kin ties in later life. These include gender, marital status, parent status, grandparent status, geographic proximity, sibling network, and ethnocultural background. Sexual orientation is an additional factor to consider.

Gender. In general, women have more active ties with family than do men. Women's roles as carers and nurturers in families extend over the life course—caring for children and spouses, for older parents, and for other older relatives.

Since women's life expectancy is greater than men's, women's kin ties have a longer duration than do men's and women are much more likely than men to experience widowhood and to live out a period at the end of life without a spouse. For these widowed women in particular, ties to adult children and siblings (as well as to friends) can be especially important sources of companionship and support.

Marital status. Marital status is another factor affecting kin ties. While most older adults are married, the likelihood of being married decreases with age, and gender differences in marital status are quite dramatic. Most men have wives in later life and, in the event of health declines, can depend on wives for care. As a result, men are much less likely than are women to spend time near the end of their lives in a nursing home or other long-term care facility. In contrast, the vast majority of women become widows in later life.

About 5 to 7 percent of older adults have never married. This percentage has remained relatively constant over the past several decades. Historically, and for current older adults, the never married also tend to be childless. While they lack the opportunity, therefore, to have relationships with children, they often develop close relationships with parents, siblings, or other relatives. They also may form close ties to nieces and nephews (Rubinstein). Friends may also occupy an important place in their support networks. The never married in later life tend to have smaller support networks than those who are married or widowed, but this is due to having fewer kin ties (that is, those related to having a spouse and in-laws, children, and grandchildren). Never-married older adults, particularly women, tend to be satisfied with life and to report higher life satisfaction than widowed or divorced older adults. While most never-married adults are not isolated and alone in later life, never-married women have closer ties with family and friends than do their male counterparts, and in fact never married older men are often isolated from family. Many never-married older adults have developed unique networks of family members and friends that provide them with companionship and support in their later years.

Only a small percentage of those currently in later life have experienced divorce or are currently divorced. However, with increased rates of divorce in younger age groups, the percentage of divorced older adults is expected to increase in the future. Studies of divorced older adults find them to be more socially isolated, in poorer health, and more economically disadvantaged than the married or widowed (Uhlenberg, Cooney, and Boyd), and less satisfied with life than the never married. Being divorced in later life can mean less social activity, particularly for men whose wife usually performed the kinkeeper role in the family. It can also mean more economic difficulty, particularly for women. The likelihood of remarriage after divorce for older adults is low (as it is for widowed older adults), particularly for women.

Ties to family and friends may be disrupted by divorce. Divorced older women tend to have more supportive ties to siblings, children, and friends than do divorced men. Divorced older men, even those with children, often have few ties to family members. Divorce in later life has a significant impact not only on the older couple, but also on other family members, particularly adult children. Divorce affects long-held family celebrations and rituals, such as Christmas, Thanksgiving, and birthdays. These celebrations often become sensitive and stressful events within families, creating the need for the renegotiation of family holidays and traditions.

Children and grandchildren. The majority (about 80 percent) of older adults have surviving children. Parent-child relationships are discussed in some detail elsewhere in this volume. After the marital tie, the tie to adult children is the most central for older adults. As noted earlier, the mother-daughter tie is particularly strong among North American adults. Older adults have frequent contact with children and both give and receive support, with emotional support being the most common type of help. For widowed women who experience severe health declines, help from adult children (most often daughters) may be the major factor that enables the older mother to remain living in her own home rather than having to move to a nursing home.

Almost all (90 percent) of older adults who have children also have grandchildren. With greater longevity, this tie can exist for many years. Grandparents and grandchildren provide each other with love, affection, and emotional support. Grandparents can give grandchildren a sense of history and stability in the family, while grandchildren can provide grandparents with a sense of family continuity extending into the future. There is great diversity in the role of grandparents (Kornhaber). When grandchildren are young, the relationship between grandparent and grandchild is mediated by the parent (the middle generation). With a parent's divorce, the contact between grandparent and grandchild may be significantly altered. Generally, as grandchildren become older, the amount of contact with grandparents decreases. However, close ties with grandparents endure over time for many adult grandchildren, particularly with grandmothers (Cooney and Smith).

About one-fifth of older adults do not have children or grandchildren. As adult children are a primary source of support and assistance for older people, those who are without children can be disadvantaged in some respects. However, older adults who are childless, especially those who never married, tend to have close ties with siblings and supportive friendship networks. For childless older adults who are married, the spouse tends to be the first to be called upon for support, followed by siblings, friends, and other relatives.

Geographic proximity. Geographic proximity—how close or distant kin are—is important because proximity is related to the amount of contact family members have with one another, and to the amount of practical help they are able to give one another. Several scholars have noted the decreasing proximity of older people to their kin as a result of increasing geographic mobility over time. Others, however, have argued that this pattern has been overstated and that, in fact, mobility has declined in recent decades (Uhlenberg). In North America, about three-quarters of older people who have children live within twenty-five miles of at least one of their children, a proportion that has remained remarkably stable over the past four decades. Moreover, modern technology and transportation has made it easier for kin to maintain contact than was the case in the not very distant past.

Siblings. Sibling ties are, potentially, the family tie of longest duration, often lasting into late old age. Most older adults (about 80 percent) have surviving siblings, and, typically, will not experience the death of a sibling until late in life. Therefore, siblings can share life histories and experiences over the life course. Ties between adult siblings tend to consist of fewer obligations and to be more voluntary than ties to a spouse or children. Nonetheless, for many older adults, particularly those without a spouse or children, the sibling tie is an important source of social and emotional support.

Women tend to have closer and more active ties to siblings than do men (Campbell, Connidis, and Davies), and having a sister increases contact with siblings for both men and women. Marital status also can affect the sibling tie. Older single and widowed individuals, particularly those who are childless, tend to be closer to their siblings than do married individuals. Never-married older women are more socially connected to their siblings than never-married men. Divorced and never-married men have the least contact and social connection with siblings.

In general, the quality of the relationship established earlier in life endures over the life course. Sibling ties tend to loosen during early adulthood and mid-life (often because of other competing demands, such as those related to a spouse, children, and employment). However, sibling ties tend to become closer again in later life. The essential quality of the relationship, however, remains. That is, those relationships that have been close over time remain close, while more distant ties tend to remain somewhat distant. Siblings whose relationship is close and warm can provide companionship and help each other psychologically and in other ways when major life events occur. Siblings are less likely than a spouse and children to provide practical help. However, they are often valued as a potential source of support if the need should arise. Sibling ties in later life tend to be a more egalitarian tie than other primary kin relationships, sustained by choice for mutual companionship or friendship rather than out of obligation.

Cultural variability. The structure and meaning of family, as well as the roles and responsibilities within the family, differ from one cultural group to another. Ethno-cultural differences in kin ties influence the social support available in later life. Minority families may be more likely than majority (White) families to provide social support and assistance to family members (Silverstein and Waite). This support may be the result of stronger kin ties and stronger traditions of providing help to kin (Himes, Hogan, and Eggebeen). However, while culture no doubt plays an important role in shaping family relationships and behaviors, factors such as the

needs of older parents, the availability of kin, economic assets, gender, geographic proximity, and family size also play a role.

The influence of ethnic culture within families in North America is thought to diminish over time as immigrants take on the values of mainstream culture and over successive generations. However, many people sustain their cultural beliefs and traditions, although factors such as women's increased participation in the labor force and children's geographic mobility can make it more difficult for families to meet what they see as their cultural obligations to their elders (Gelfand).

Older gays and lesbians. A definition of family often does not include lesbian and gay couples, although this is slowly changing. Older gay men and lesbians deal with similar issues and concerns as other older individuals and couples—income, health, the death of relatives and friends—but they also confront other unique difficulties (Fullmer). Like heterosexual adults, many lesbians and gay men are involved in long-term, committed relationships that provide them with love, support, and companionship. For those whose biological family is supportive of their sexual orientation, family ties are an important source of support in adulthood and later life. However, those who have not been accepted by their own family, or who have kept their sexual orientation hidden, often have a "chosen" family (consisting of friends, companions, and particular family members) that takes the place of traditional kin. Many older lesbians and gay men form strong supportive bonds with these individuals who fulfill the family role—as their "families of choice" (Fullmer).

Older adults with weak kinship ties

While most older adults are embedded in kinship networks, there is a minority who have weak ties. Those older adults who are most likely to have weak ties are those who have smaller kin networks, such as the divorced who are childless, particularly men, or the never married. Those who are older and without a spouse or children are most at risk for social isolation. Particularly vulnerable are unmarried childless women who are very old (age eighty-five and older) who have chronic illnesses or disabilities. These women are more likely than others to be institutionalized because they lack family members to provide support or assistance.

CAROLYN ROSENTHAL
LORI D. CAMPBELL

See also GAY AND LESBIAN AGING; GENDER; INTERGENERATIONAL EXCHANGES; PARENT-CHILD RELATIONSHIP.

BIBLIOGRAPHY

BENGTSON, V. L.; ROSENTHAL, C. J.; and BURTON, L. "Families and Aging: Diversity and Heterogeneity." In *Handbook of Aging and the Social Sciences*, 3d ed. Edited by Robert H. Binstock and Linda K. George. San Diego: Academic Press, 1990. Pages 263–287.

CAMPBELL, L. D.; CONNIDIS, I. A.; and DAVIES, L. "Sibling Ties in Later Life: A Social Network Analysis." *Journal of Family Issues* 20 (1999): 114–148.

COONEY, T. M., and SMITH, L. A. "Young Adults' Relations with Grandparents Following Recent Parental Divorce." *Journal of Gerontology: Social Sciences* 51B (1996): S91–S95.

FULLMER, E. M. "Challenging Biases Against Families of Older Gays and Lesbians." In *Strengthening Aging Families: Diversity in Practice and Policy*. Edited by G. S. Smith, S. S. Tobin, E. A. Robertson-Tchabo, and P. W. Power. Thousand Oaks, Calif.: Sage Publications, 1995. Pages 99–119.

GELFAND, D. E. *Aging and Ethnicity: Knowledge and Services*. New York: Springer, 1994.

HIMES, C. L.; HOGAN, D. P.; and EGGEBEEN, D. J. "Living Arrangements of Minority Elders." *Journal of Gerontology: Social Sciences* 51B (1996): S42–S48.

KORNHABER, A. *Contemporary Grandparenting*. Thousand Oaks, Calif.: Sage, 1996.

ROSENTHAL, C. J. "Kinkeeping in the Familial Division of Labor." *Journal of Marriage and the Family* 48 (1985): 965–974.

ROSENTHAL, C. J., and MARSHALL, V. W. "Generational Transmission of Family Ritual." *American Behavioral Scientist* 31 (1988): 669–684.

RUBINSTEIN, R. "Never Married as Social Type: Re-evaluating Some Images." *The Gerontologist* 27 (1987): 108–113.

SILVERSTEIN, M., and WAITE, L. J. "Are Blacks More Likely than Whites to Receive and Provide Social Support in Middle and Old Age? Yes, No, and Maybe So." *Journal of Gerontology: Social Sciences* 48 (1993): S212–S222.

UHLENBERG, P. "Demographic Change and Kin Relationships in Later Life." In *Annual Review of Gerontology and Geriatrics, Volume 13: Focus on Kinship, Aging, and Social Change*. Edited by George L. Maddox and M. Powell Lawton. New York: Springer, 1993. Pages 219–238.

UHLENBERG, P.; COONEY, T.; and BOYD, R. "Divorce for Women after Midlife." *Journal of Gerontology: Social Sciences* 45 (1990): S3–S11.

ISBN 0-02-865469-2

90000